I0418987

An artist's guide to
TAROT

Illustrating the arcana with expert artists

3dtotal Publishing

3dtotalPublishing

Correspondence: **publishing@3dtotal.com**
Website: **store.3dtotal.com**

An Artist's Guide to Tarot © 2024, 3dtotal Publishing.
All rights reserved. No part of this book can be reproduced
in any form or by any means, without the prior written
consent of the publisher. All artwork, unless stated otherwise,
is copyright of the featured artists. All artwork that is not
copyright of the featured artists is marked accordingly.

Every effort has been made to ensure the credits and contact
information listed are present and correct. In the case of
any errors that have occurred, the publisher respectfully
directs readers to **store.3dtotal.com/pages/information**
for any updated information and corrections.

First published in the United Kingdom, 2024,
by 3dtotal Publishing.

Address: 3dtotal.com Ltd, 29 Foregate Street,
Worcester, WR1 1DS, United Kingdom.

Hard cover ISBN: 978-1-912843-97-8
Printed and bound in China
by C&C Offset Printing Co., Ltd.

Visit **store.3dtotal.com** for a complete
list of available book titles.

Editor: Marisa Lewis
Designer: Matthew Lewis
Lead Editor: Samantha Rigby
Lead Designer: Joseph Cartwright
Studio Manager: Simon Morse
Managing Director: Tom Greenway

Cover artwork by Diana Naneva, based on
designs by individual artists as listed throughout
the book. Additional border decoration and
card icons by Marisa Lewis.

50%
of net profits donated
TO CHARITY

In 2022, 3dtotal Publishing became
successful enough to make a pledge to
donate **50% of its net profits to charity**.
This continues to be possible due to
the incredible support from all our
customers, employees, and partners.
At the time of printing, we have donated
over $1.62 million (USD) to charity.

We focus our giving on three charitable
areas: **environmental, humanitarian,
and animal welfare**. We use organizations
such as Effective Altruism and Founders
Pledge to guide who we help within these
causes. Some ways of doing good are over
100 times more effective than others,
so donating this way hugely increases
the impact of our contributions.

See **3dtotal.com/charity**
for full details.

MIX
Paper | Supporting
responsible forestry
FSC® C008047

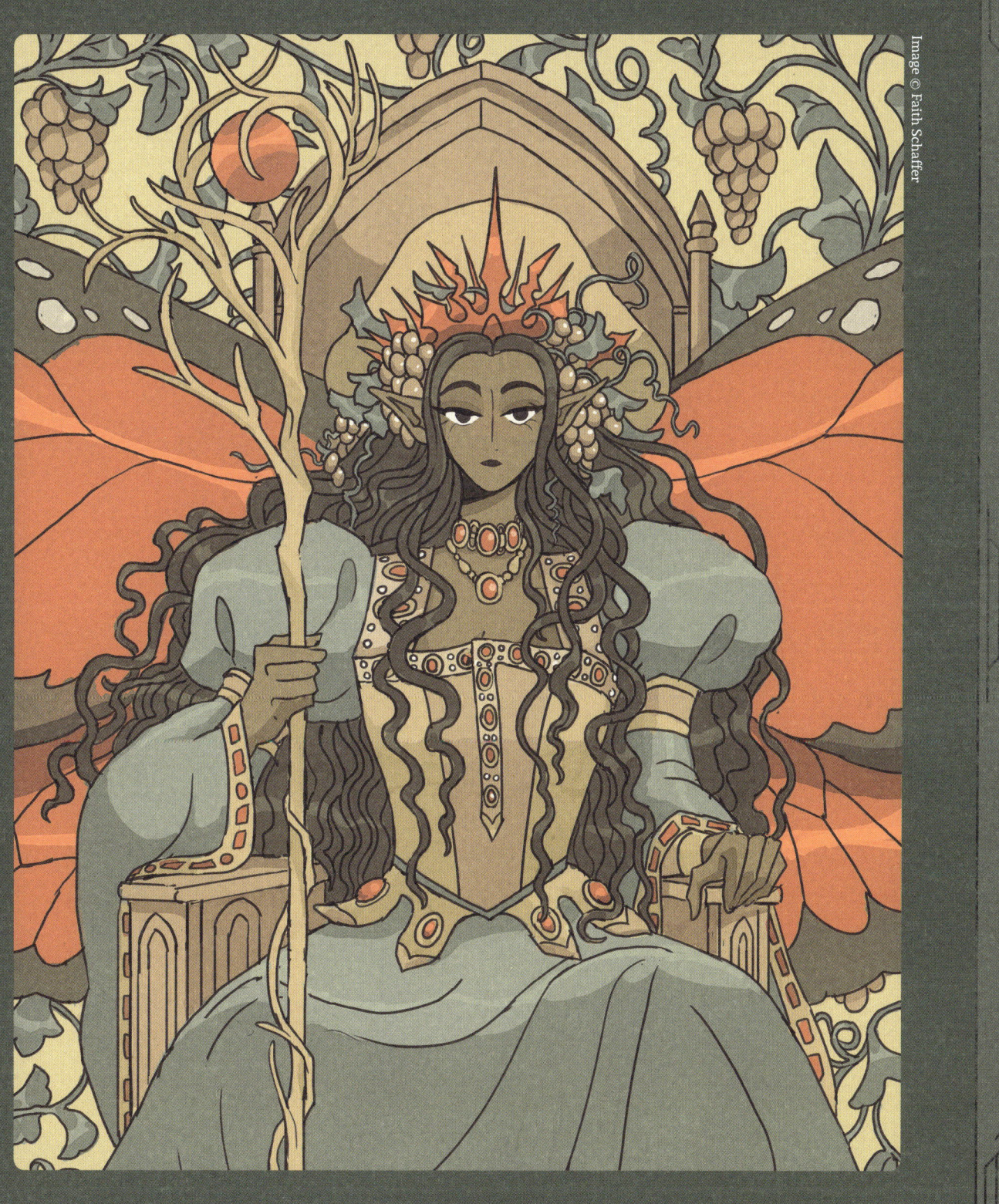

Image © Faith Schaffer

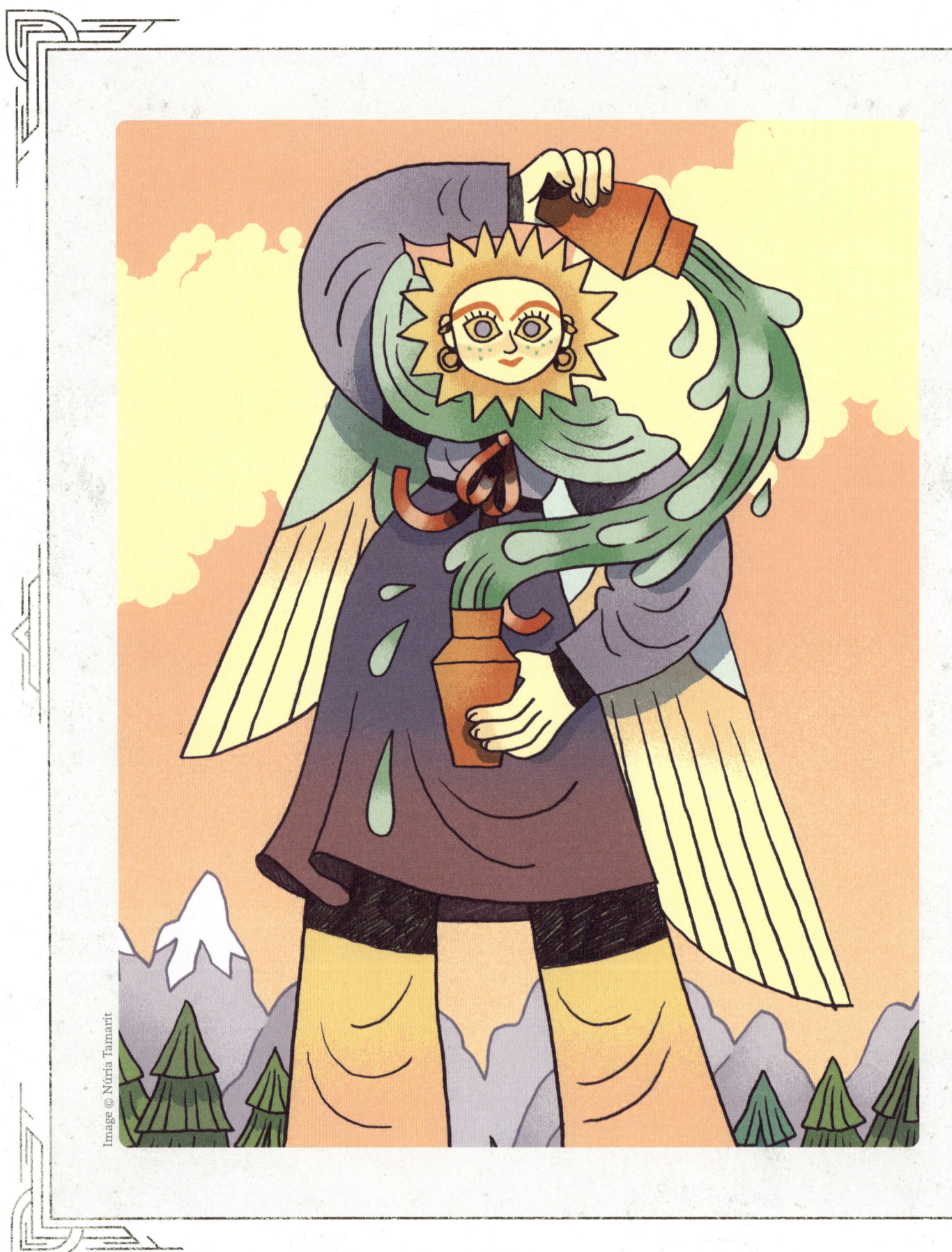

Image © Núria Tamarit

CONTENTS

WELCOME TO THE ART OF TAROT

AN INTRODUCTION BY SASHA GRAHAM

WHAT IS TAROT?

Welcome to the secret world of tarot. To crack open a pack of tarot cards is to enter a universe of fantasy, magic, and imagination. Arcane knowledge and archetypal symbols act as portals of human consciousness. The soul is revealed and the future glimpsed with every reading. You can lose yourself, find yourself, or reinvent yourself with a single flip of a card. But what is tarot? Why has it endured for centuries? Why is it so mysterious?

Tarot is a pack of seventy-eight cards similar to a standard fifty-two playing-card deck. Tarot and standard playing-card decks each have four suits with court cards. Tarot's seventy-eight cards, unlike standard playing cards, are almost always fully illustrated with scenes containing unique themes and art styles. Tarot is rarely randomly designed, but usually contained within a fully fleshed-out, connective universe.

Tarot contains a unique set of twenty-two cards called the Major Arcana, which reflect universal experiences, archetypal images, and spiritual allegories. The remaining cards in the deck are called the Minor Arcana and hold the four suits: Swords, Pentacles, Wands, and Cups, including sixteen court cards. The word 'arcane' means secret or hidden. The tarot is made up of Major and Minor 'secrets'. The nature of tarot's hidden secrets has long been a source of speculation and delight.

The skeletal structure of tarot's Major and Minor Arcana is the reason it has endured for centuries. Tarot's four Minor suits (Wands, Cups, Pentacles, and Swords) align with the four suits of standard playing cards (Spades, Hearts, Diamonds, and Clubs). The tarot suits also align with the four classical elements of Earth, Air, Fire, and Water, which are the materials and energies that make up the world around us.

Tarot's Minor Arcana reflects the everyday world; the Major Arcana displays the infinite spiritual world above, around, and inside of us. Tarot is a perfect, concise depiction of the visible and invisible worlds.

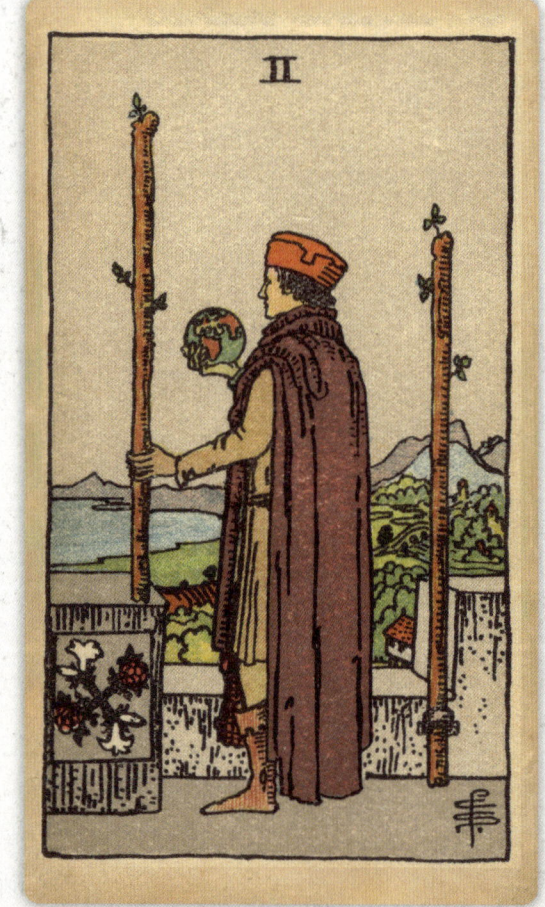

The Two of Wands, Queen of Pentacles, and Three of Cups, as illustrated by Pamela Colman Smith in the Rider–Waite–Smith tarot deck (see page 16)

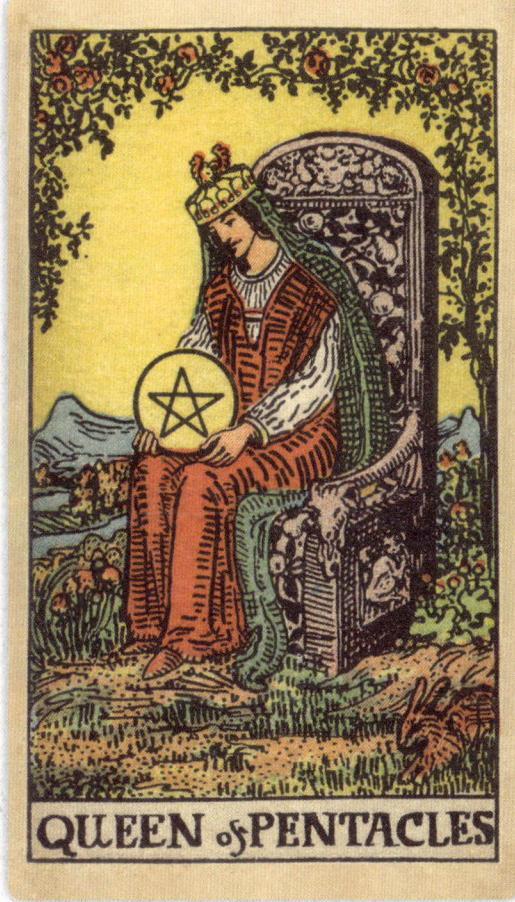

QUEEN of PENTACLES

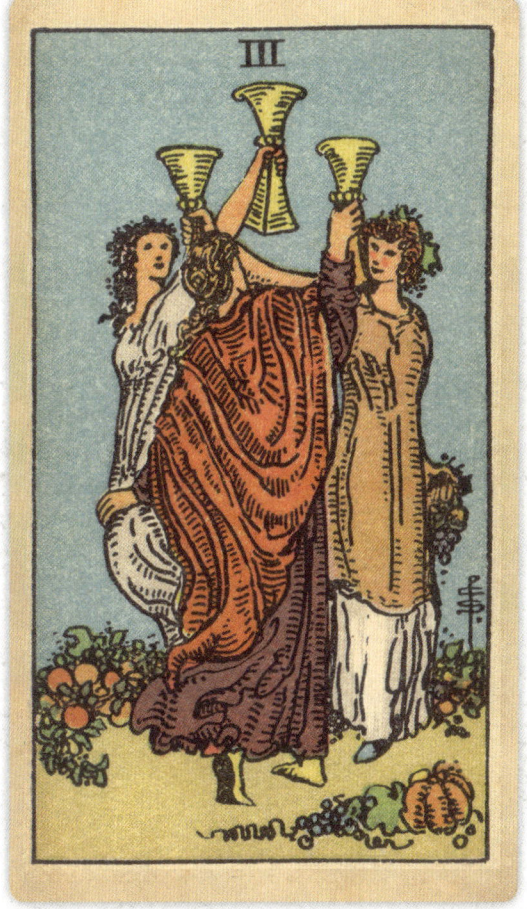

Tarot secrets exist within the symbols artists place inside the cards. The reader who is versed in symbolic language will decode tarot symbols while reading, thus becoming fluent in the language of tarot. Tarot symbols may stem from any spiritual practice and express any theme. These symbols include colours, card numbers, gendering, the graphic nature of a card, astrological signs, words and phrases, and so much more.

Tarot is an ever-changing visual book of the human condition. It may be the most important book ever written because, unlike a novel or comic with a beginning, middle, and end,

tarot is a book of constant moving parts. Like a 'choose your own adventure' book, the outcome of a tarot spread is almost always different.

Tarot is a brilliant playground for the artist to express themselves. Any artistic style, visual theme, or subject can be placed inside tarot's structure. This is why so many different styles of tarot exist. Additionally, tarot's structure aligns with arcane concepts like astrology, the Kabbalistic 'Tree of Life', ceremonial magic, numerology, and many others. This is why tarot is often utilized for fortune-telling, spiritual, and magical practices.

THE HISTORY OF TAROT ART

The oldest known tarot cards come from fifteenth-century northern Italy, although no one has been able to accurately pinpoint where and when the first tarot deck was created. Wealthy Renaissance nobility often commissioned renowned painters to create personal tarot decks the way one might commission a family portrait. Courtly tarots were painted on durable boards, meant to be collected and displayed rather than shuffled and played. The appointed cards were lushly coloured, often painted with pure gold leaf. Due to the personal nature of the commissions, the Major Arcana and court cards often included individual family members and familial symbols.

While the aristocracy enjoyed decks of fancy art, the general public used tarot for tavern games and gambling. These were played on flimsy paper. Tarot cards for the masses were printed from wood blocks wherein twenty-four cards were stamped onto sheets of paper then cut into individual cards. Few paper tarots have stood the test of time.

The Italian Renaissance and yet-to-come French Marseille style of card decks were not completely illustrated. Only the Major Arcana contained fully fleshed-out characters and scenes. The Major Arcana of early decks displayed iconography from popular culture, the church's religious

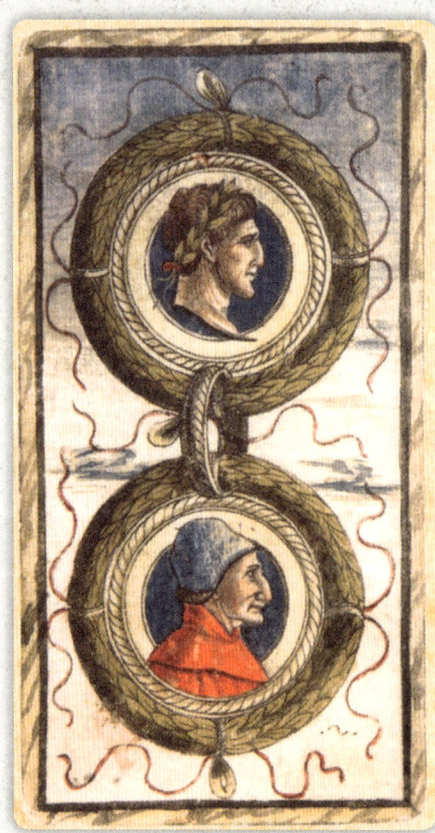

The Two and Queen of Coins from the Italian 'Sola Busca' tarot – the oldest complete 78-card deck, possibly originating in the late 1400s

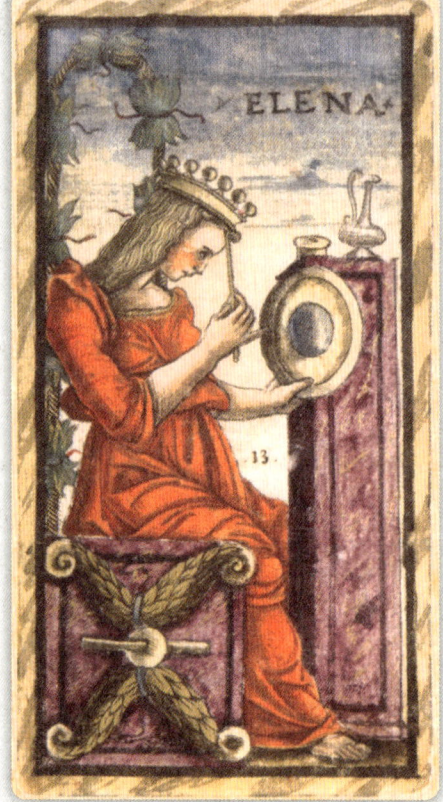

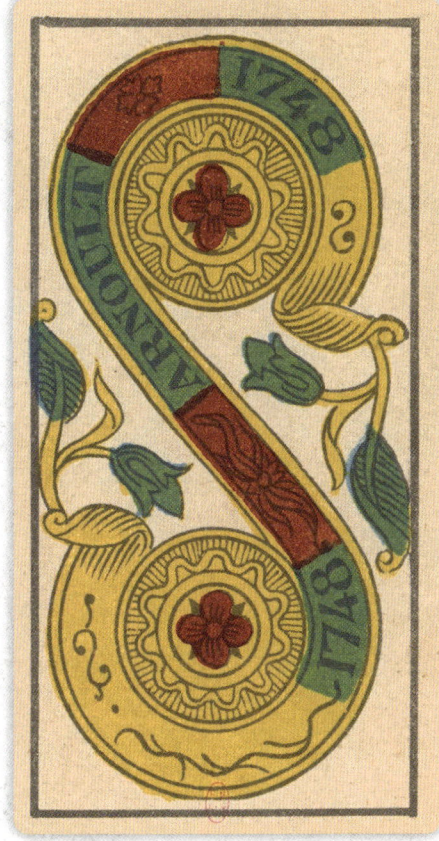

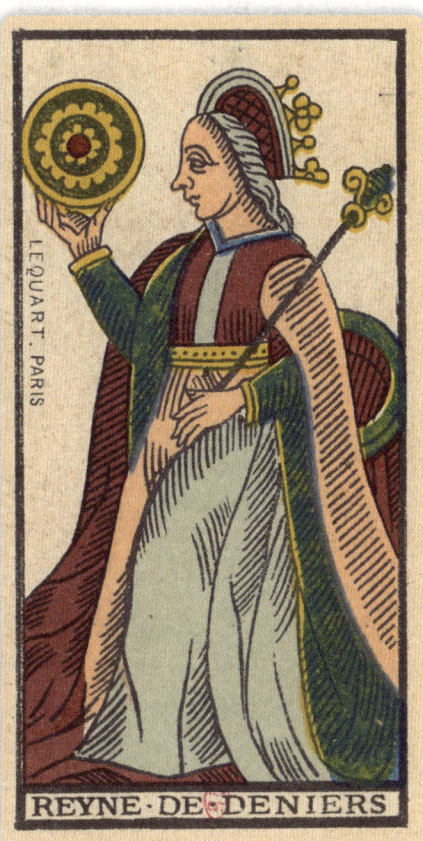

The Two and Queen of Coins from a Marseille-style tarot deck, popular in the seventeenth and eighteenth centuries

ideology, and spiritual concepts of the time. The Minor Arcana of the early European decks still looked like standard playing cards with suit symbols instead of pictures.

The Hermetic Order of the Golden Dawn, an influential, magical secret society, would change tarot's trajectory forever. Members of the group published tarot decks to suit their occult tastes. These eighteenth- and nineteenth-century magicians placed tarot at the centre of their arcane practice. Tarot was an organizing principle for the group's metaphysical work, including astral travel, scrying, and ceremonial magic.

Arthur Edward Waite commissioned fellow Golden Dawn member Pamela Colman Smith to illustrate the 'Rider–Waite–Smith' deck. Smith illustrated every single card of the Major and Minor Arcana. She crafted accessible, easy-to-read scenes for the cards while jam-packing her illustrations with esoteric and religious allegory. She enhanced the mystical symbolism of the traditional Major Arcana and thus layered more meaning and richness on top of its pre-existing history. The modern secret language of tarot was born!

The symbols and scenes of Pamela Colman Smith's deck became the gold standard of tarot cards. The deck was published with a guidebook, *The Pictorial Key to the Tarot*, by Arthur Waite. This was to become the world's most famous tarot deck, yet the author and artist would not live to see its influence or success.

MODERN TAROT AND TAROT ART TODAY

The age of modern tarot was born when an enterprising businessman named Stuart Kaplan published the Rider–Waite–Smith deck in the United States in the early 1970s. The New Age movement, born of the Age of Aquarius hippie movement, showed a profound interest in esoteric arts, astrology, and spiritual ideas. Although the Rider–Waite–Smith deck sold millions of copies, tarot was still something of a hidden practice. Newly imagined tarot decks occasionally hit the market but tarot reading was like any other niche hobby. Tarot was considered strange, even dangerous, and was widely misunderstood and even feared by the general public.

The internet and social media profoundly changed how tarot is used and shared. Individuals who were once cut off from other tarot lovers due to distance now formed groups, chats, classes, and meetups in online forums. Tarot businesses popped up online with practitioners offering tarot readings and consultations. Online marketplaces made it possible for anyone in the world to track down and purchase a tarot deck.

As tarot images, usage, and all kinds of study and experimentation spread, newly imagined tarot decks from artists and writers began flooding the market. Independent tarot-deck creators began to crowdsource funding in order to print and sell original tarot decks outside of mainstream publishing. Bookstores now stock entire sections with tarot decks containing every imaginable theme, art style, and concept. Modern tarots are available in every style: fine art, whimsical, gothic, humorous, traditional, and abstract. Artists use every imaginable tool at their disposal to create tarot images, from watercolour to digital software, photography to collage – there are no limits on how tarot can be made and illustrated.

Tarot structure, however, remains true to its Italian origins. The seventy-eight cards of any modern tarot deck are still defined as the Major and Minor Arcana. Most tarot decks are Rider–Waite–Smith 'clone decks' that borrow from and reinterpret Pamela Colman Smith's well-known scenes through fresh, original eyes. Symbols remain the heart of tarot art and are still the key to deciphering the cards, even as they are constantly reinterpreted through new cultural lenses.

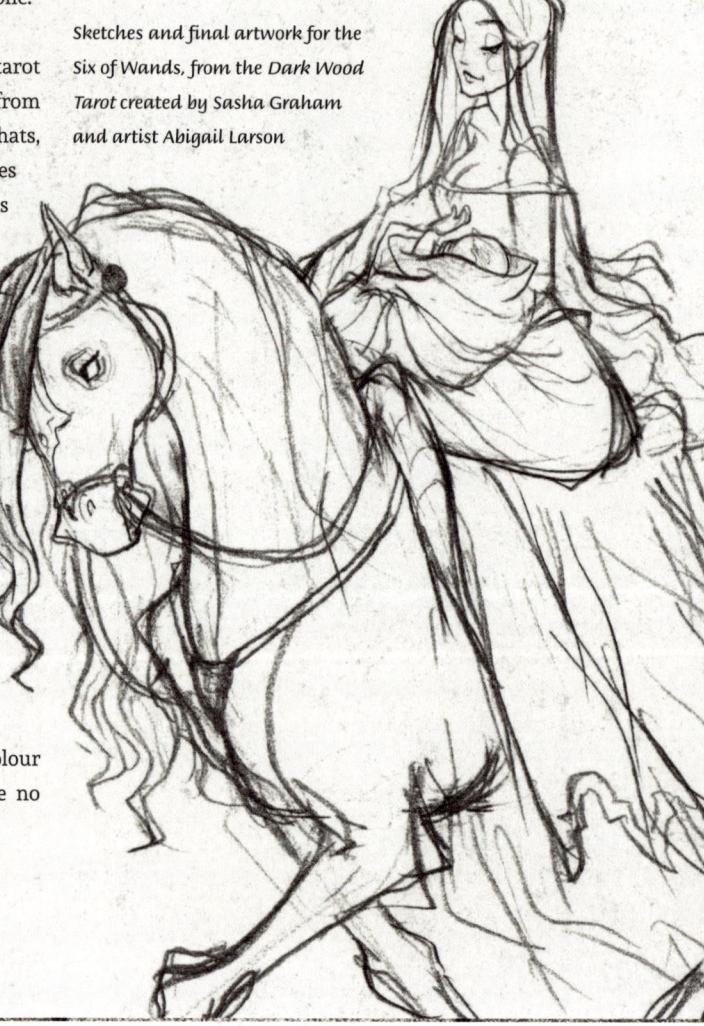

Sketches and final artwork for the Six of Wands, from the Dark Wood Tarot created by Sasha Graham and artist Abigail Larson

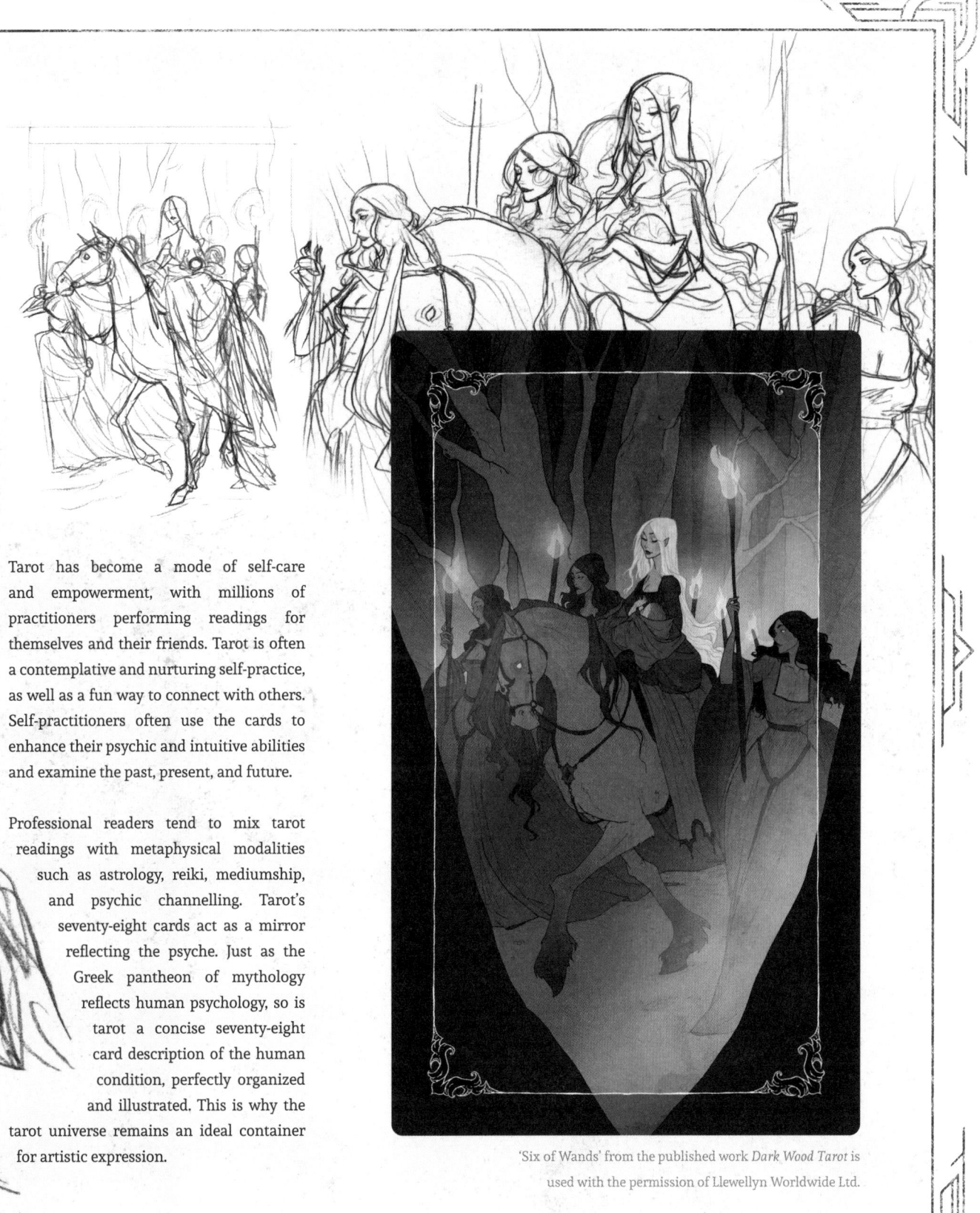

Tarot has become a mode of self-care and empowerment, with millions of practitioners performing readings for themselves and their friends. Tarot is often a contemplative and nurturing self-practice, as well as a fun way to connect with others. Self-practitioners often use the cards to enhance their psychic and intuitive abilities and examine the past, present, and future.

Professional readers tend to mix tarot readings with metaphysical modalities such as astrology, reiki, mediumship, and psychic channelling. Tarot's seventy-eight cards act as a mirror reflecting the psyche. Just as the Greek pantheon of mythology reflects human psychology, so is tarot a concise seventy-eight card description of the human condition, perfectly organized and illustrated. This is why the tarot universe remains an ideal container for artistic expression.

'Six of Wands' from the published work *Dark Wood Tarot* is used with the permission of Llewellyn Worldwide Ltd.

CREATING YOUR OWN TAROT DECK

The Major Arcana, in particular, contains important traditional symbolism. An artist must understand *why* the symbols are, before they decide if they will include or reinterpret these symbols. Always bear in mind that the symbols help to guide the reader when laying and reading the cards.

The artist will save time and energy by first creating detailed sketches of each card when constructing the Major Arcana or a complete tarot deck. The deck evolves card by card, and even meticulously planned-out tarots will change as they come to life. The artist should additionally create a written or visual outline of the entire Major Arcana before beginning the sketching phase, unless they are choosing to illustrate one or two cards.

Keep in mind that tarot is a visual 'book' – it is read like a story for those who lay the cards. Since the cards are always connecting and communicating with one another, the artist should consider their beginning sketches akin to the first draft of a book. The first draft can always be tinkered with, changed, and adapted as the world expands. Once the artist is satisfied with every card's suit and symbol, then the seventy-eight cards can be coloured and finalized.

The Ace, Seven, and Ten of Swords by Patrycja Wójcik (see page 196)

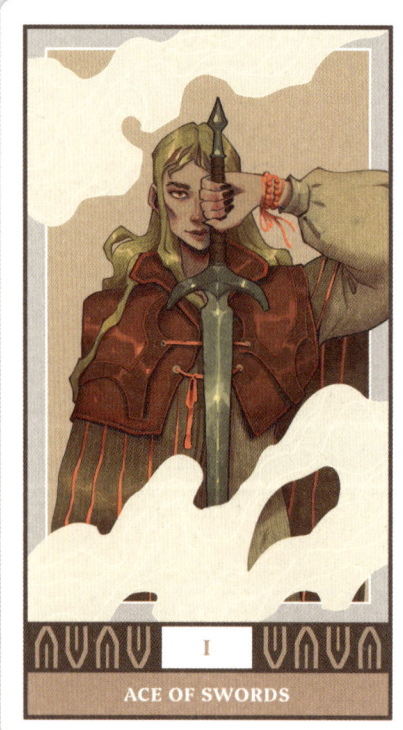

ACE OF SWORDS

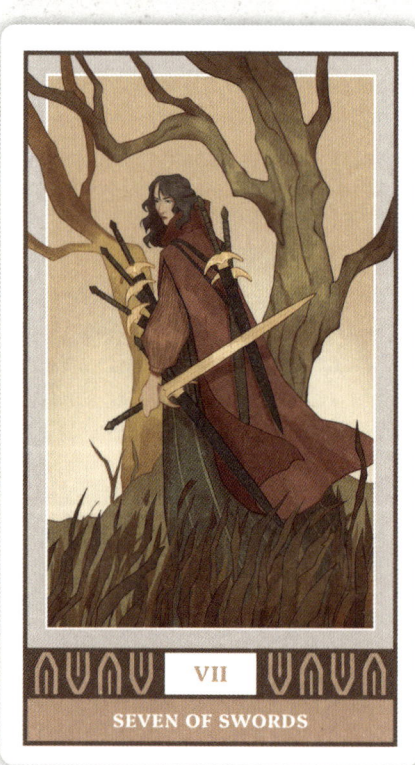

SEVEN OF SWORDS

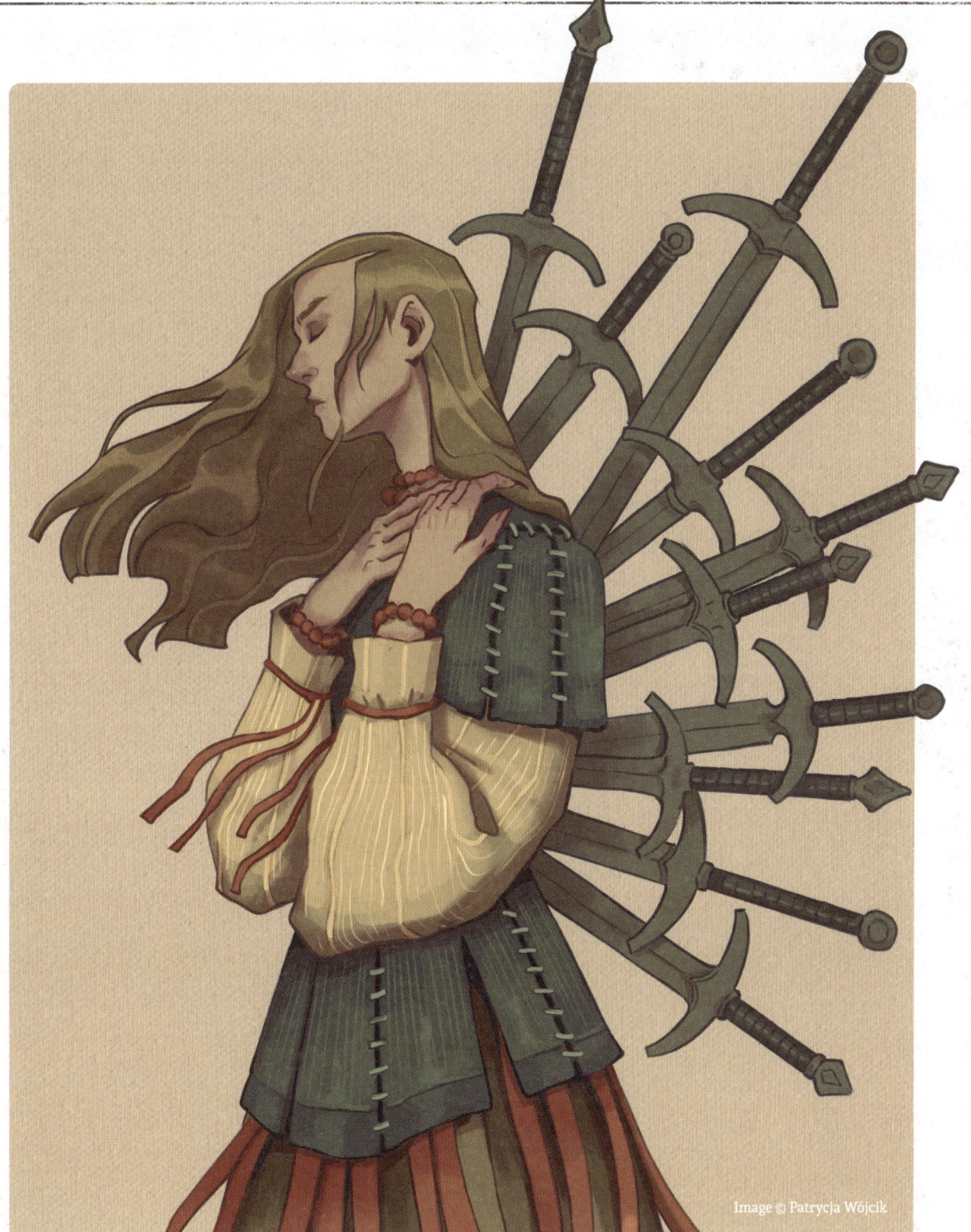

Image © Patrycja Wójcik

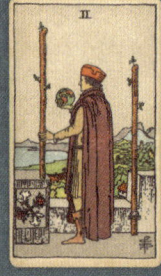
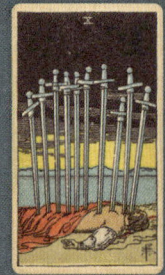
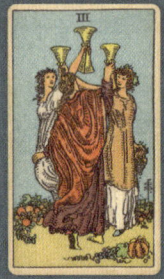
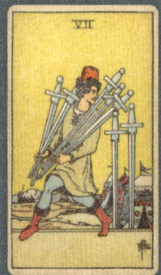
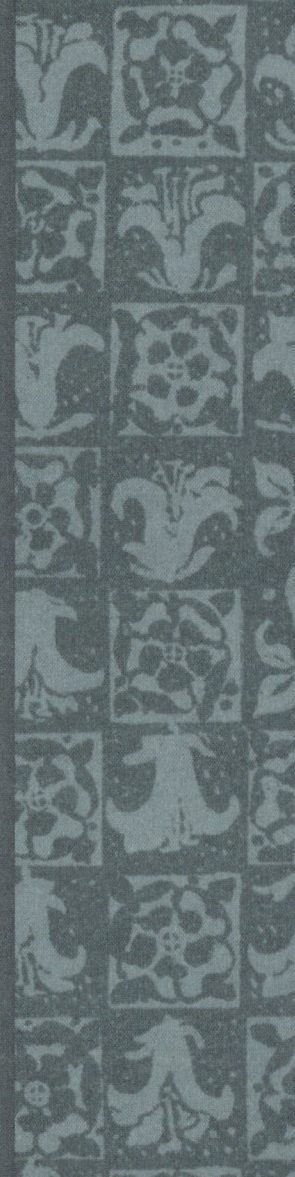

RIDER WAITE SMITH

THE 1909 *'ROSES & LILIES'* TAROT DECK

This historic deck, also known as the Rider–Waite or Waite–Smith Tarot, was devised by the mystic Arthur Edward Waite and illustrated by artist and fellow occultist Pamela Colman Smith. First published in the UK by the Rider Company in 1909, it has since become one of the most iconic and recognizable decks in tarot, inspiring countless versions and reimaginings. It is included here for reference and comparison with the new cards created in this book.

THE MAJOR ARCANA

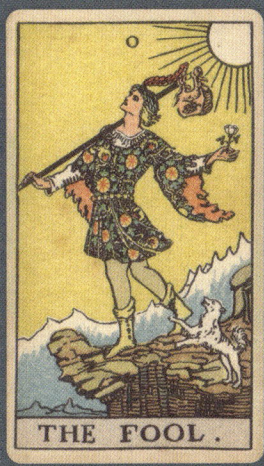

THE FOOL.

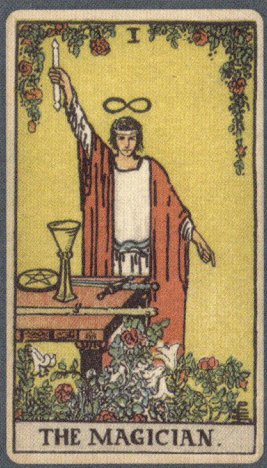

THE MAGICIAN.

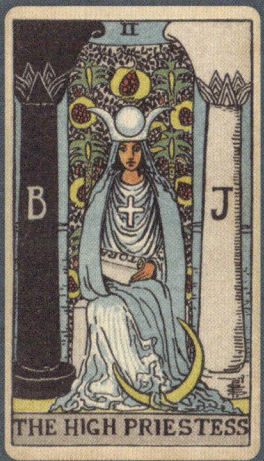

THE HIGH PRIESTESS

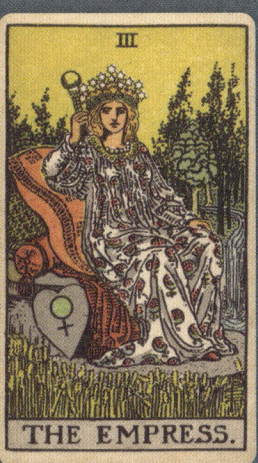

THE EMPRESS.

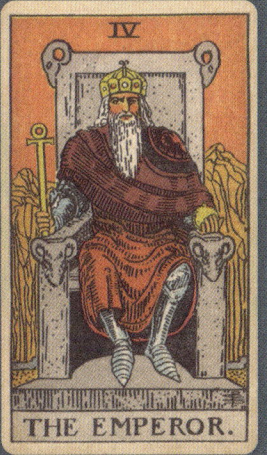

THE EMPEROR.

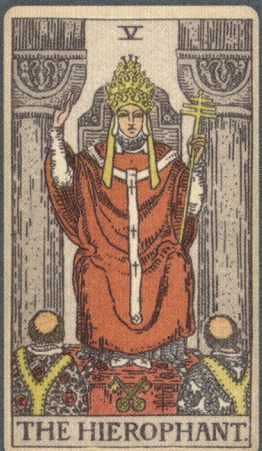

THE HIEROPHANT.

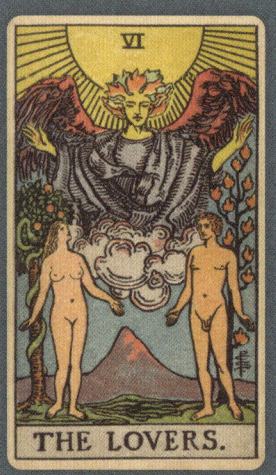

THE LOVERS.

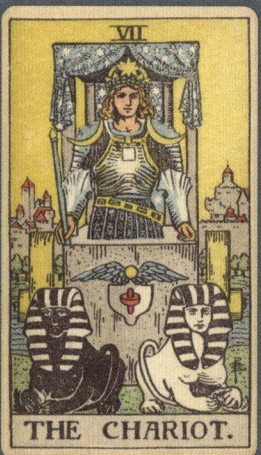

THE CHARIOT.

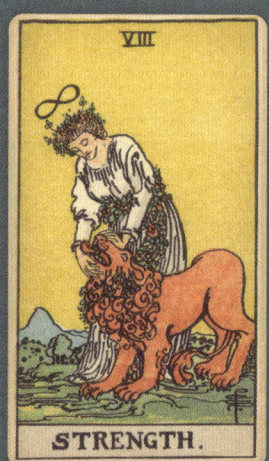

STRENGTH.

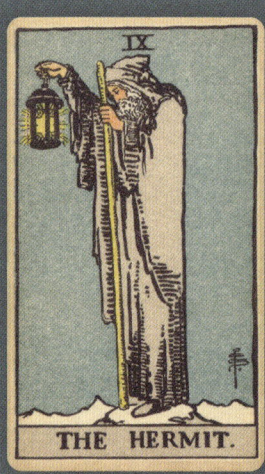

THE HERMIT.

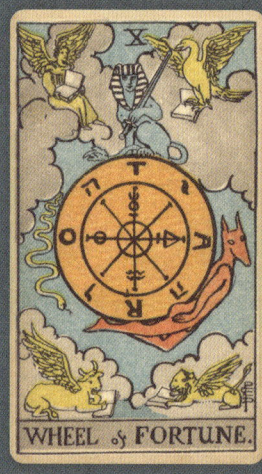

WHEEL of FORTUNE.

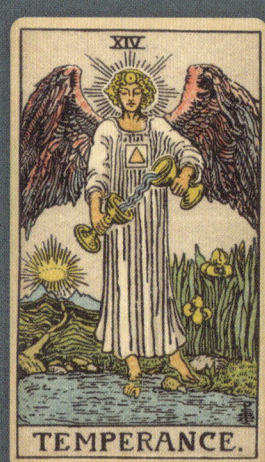

JUSTICE.

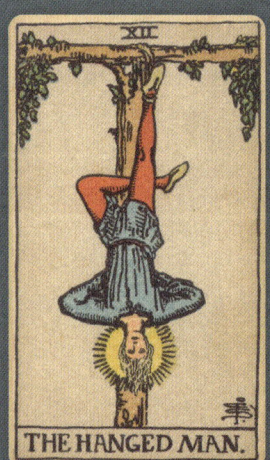

THE HANGED MAN.

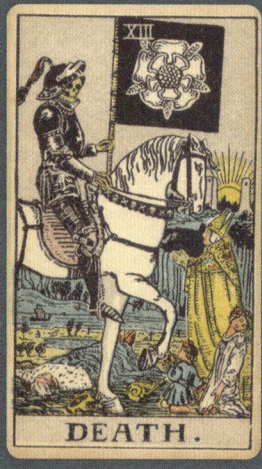

DEATH.

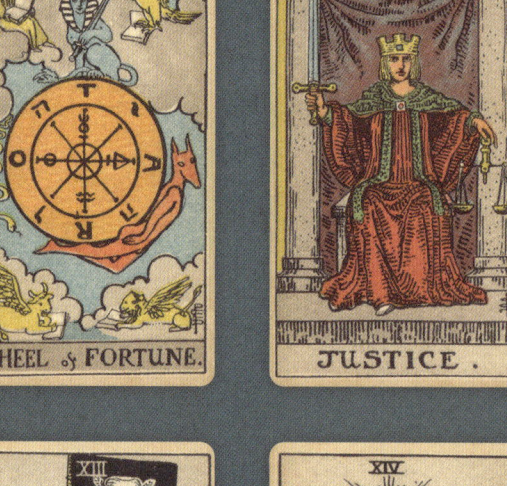

TEMPERANCE.

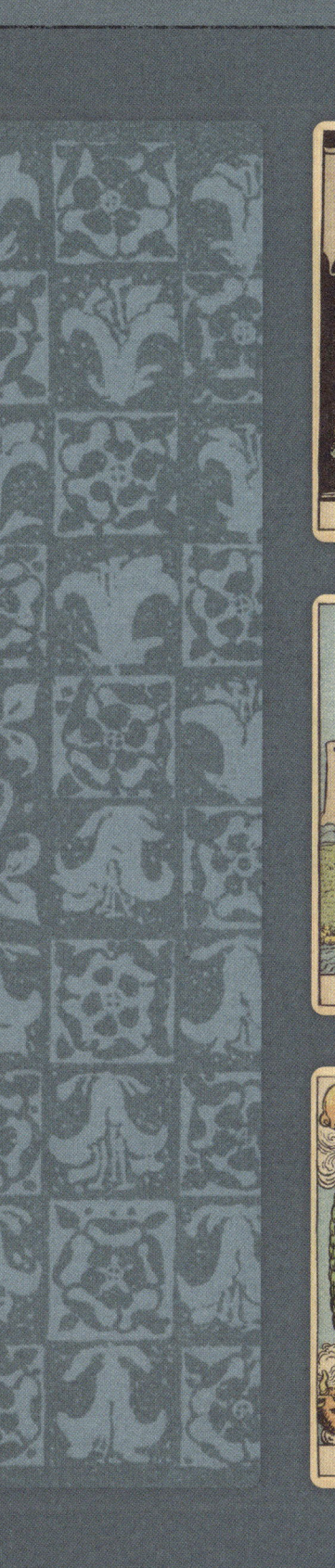

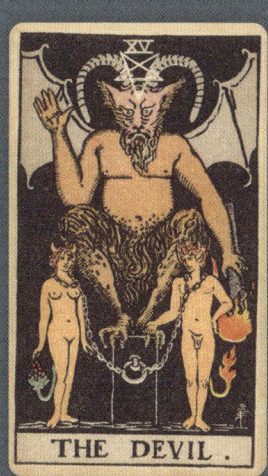

THE DEVIL.

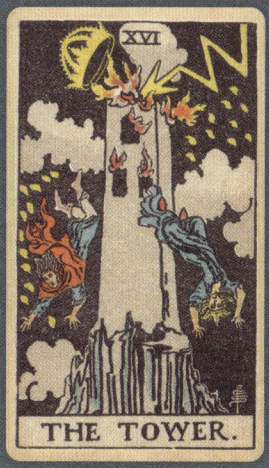

THE TOWER.

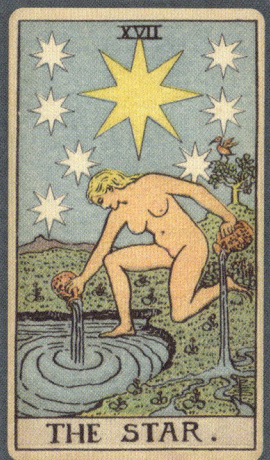

THE STAR.

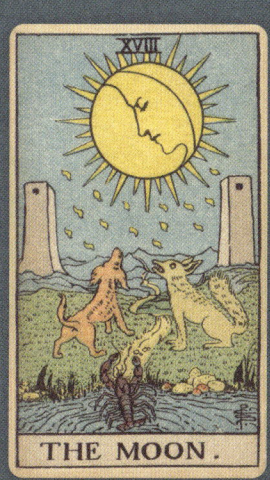

THE MOON.

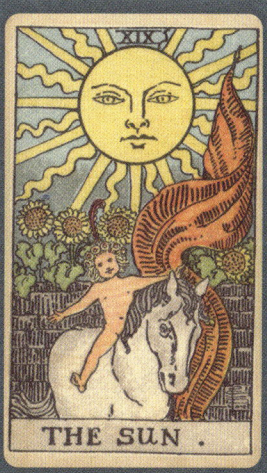

THE SUN .

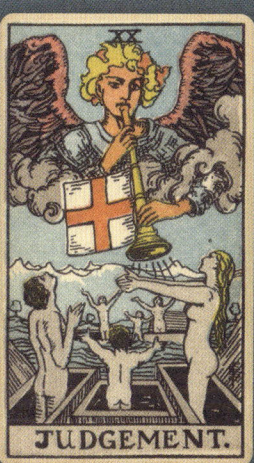

JUDGEMENT.

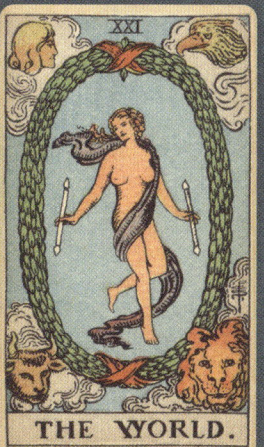

THE WORLD.

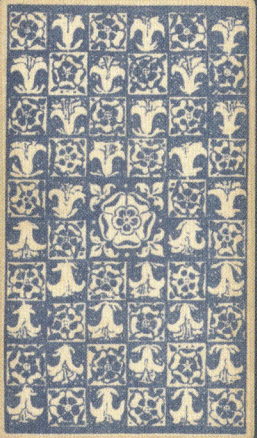

THE MINOR ARCANA

THE SUIT OF WANDS

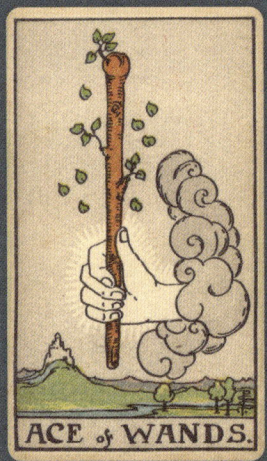

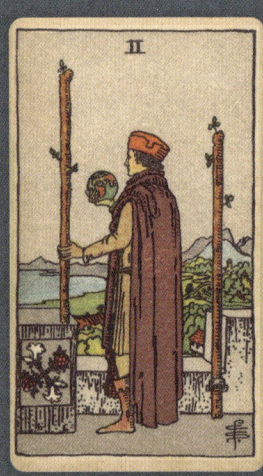

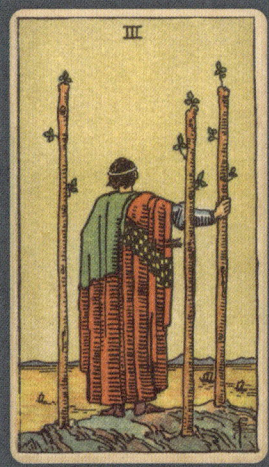

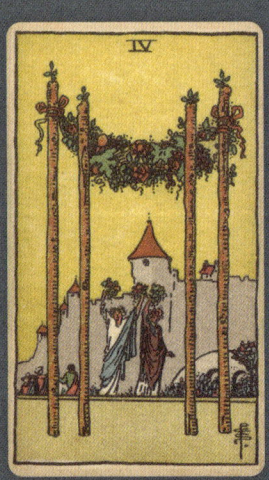

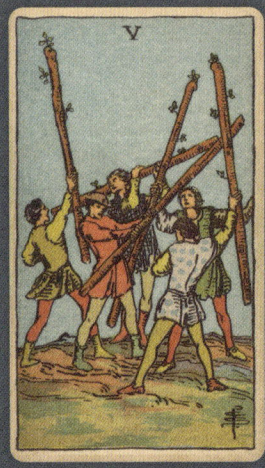

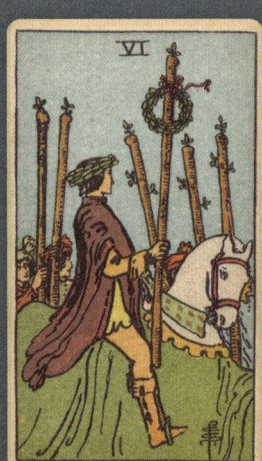

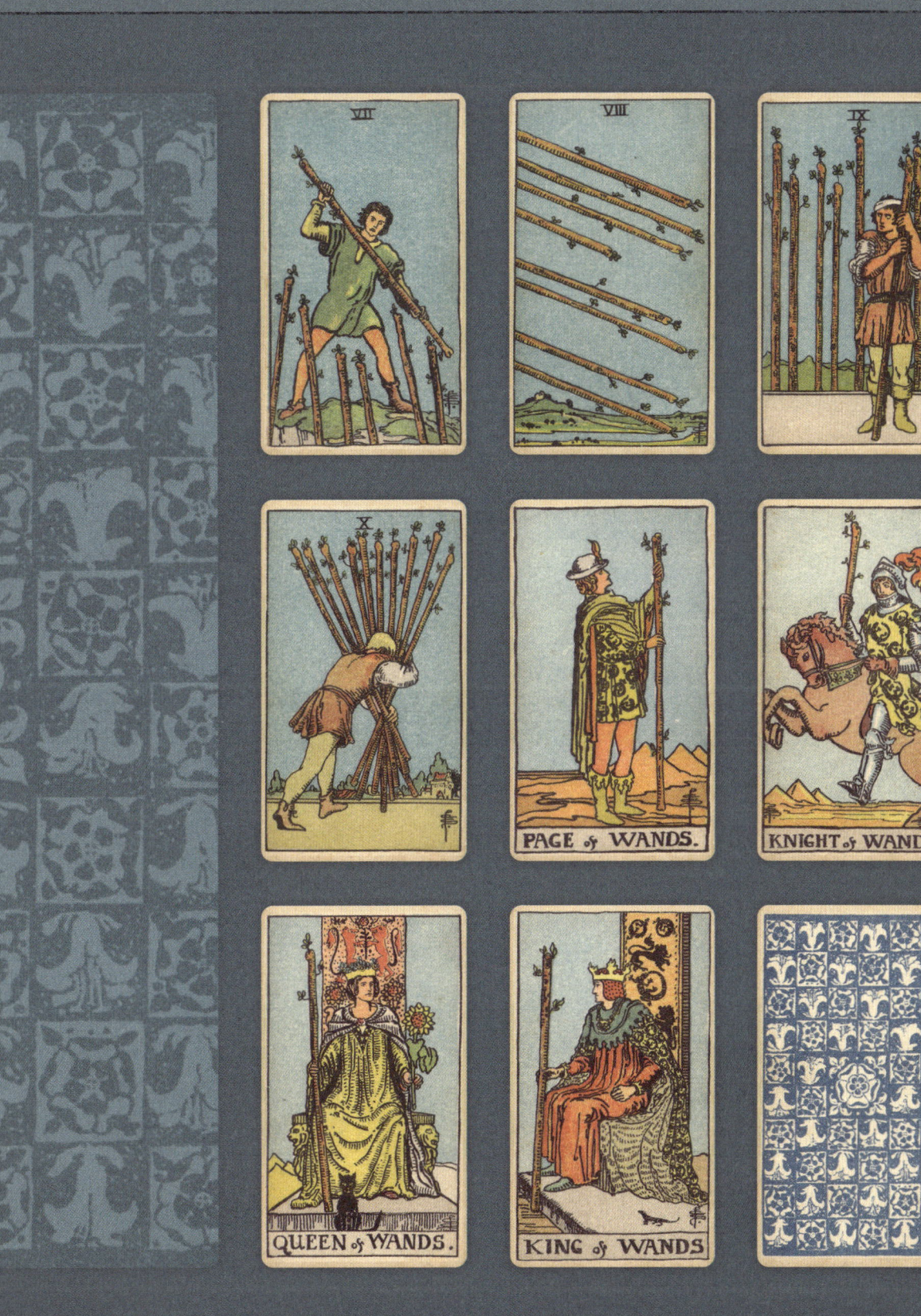

THE MINOR ARCANA

THE SUIT OF CUPS

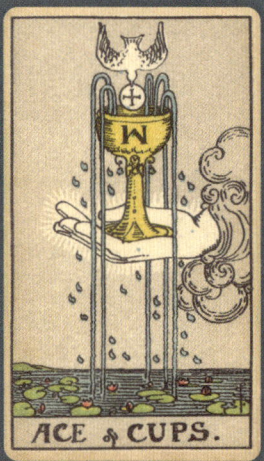
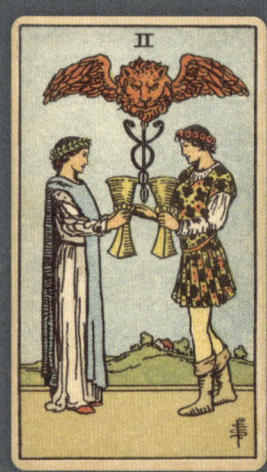
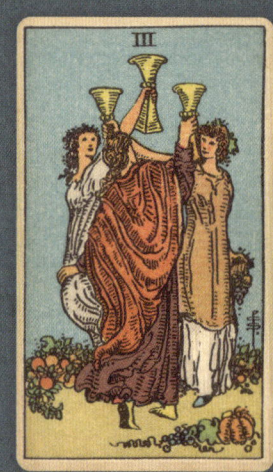
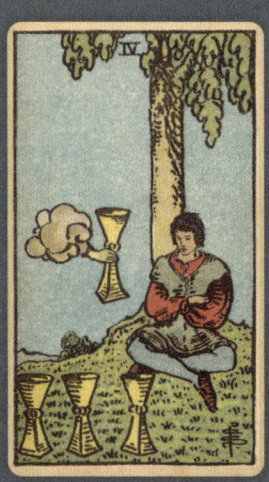
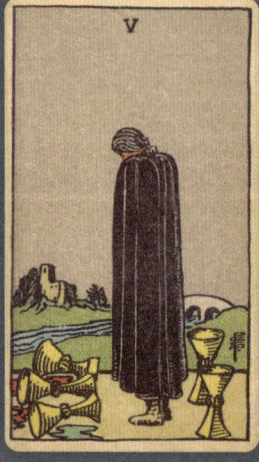
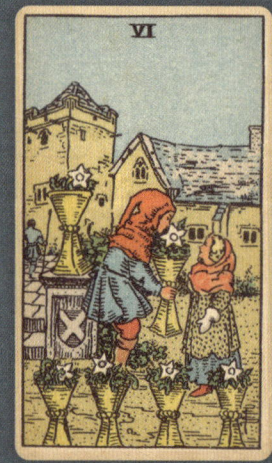

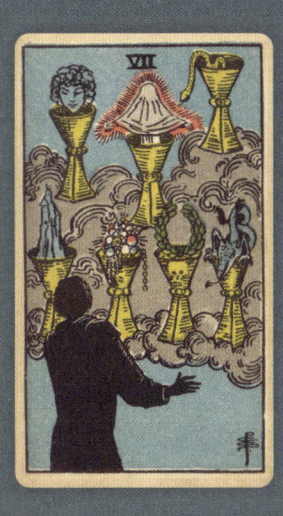

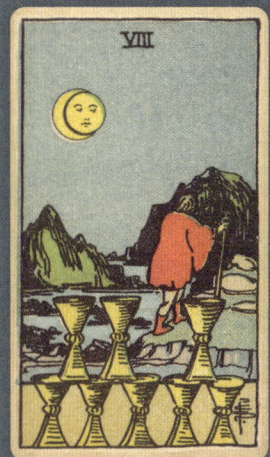

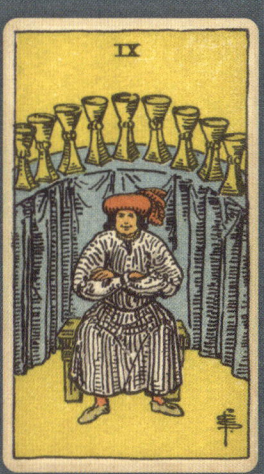

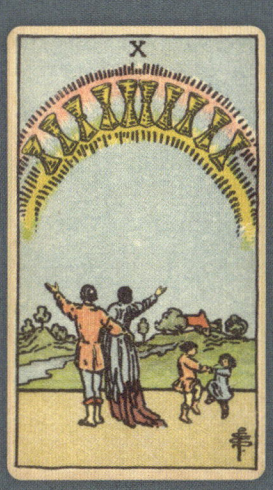

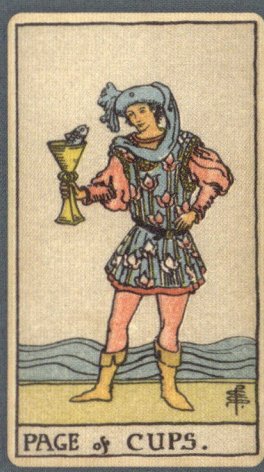

PAGE of CUPS.

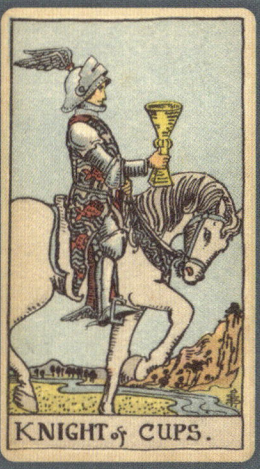

KNIGHT of CUPS.

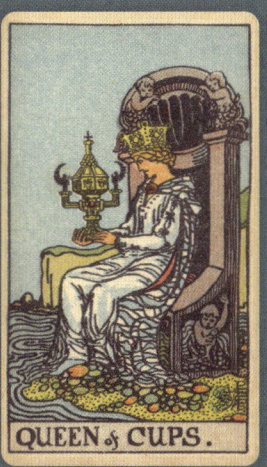

QUEEN of CUPS.

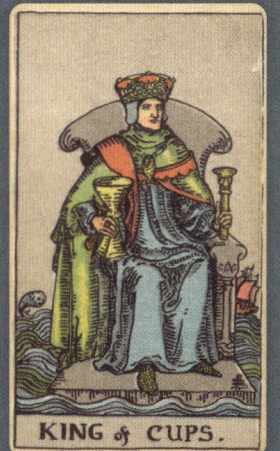

KING of CUPS.

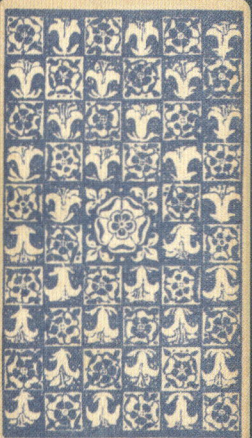

THE MINOR ARCANA

THE SUIT
OF SWORDS

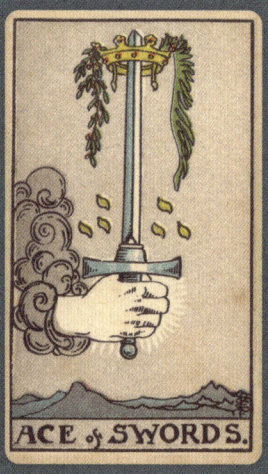

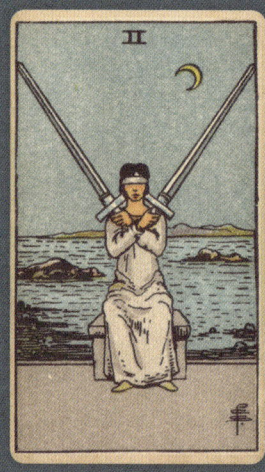

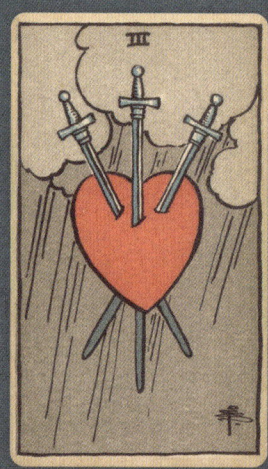

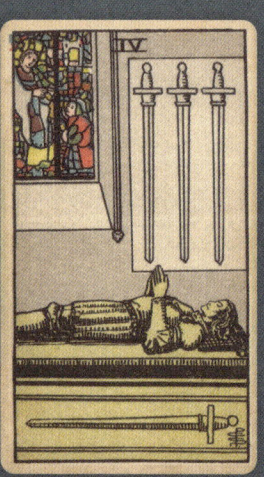

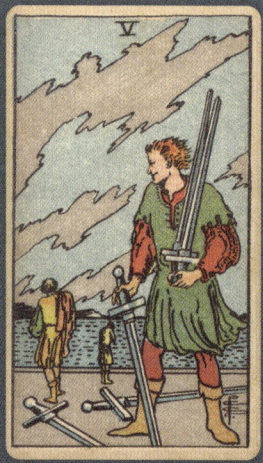

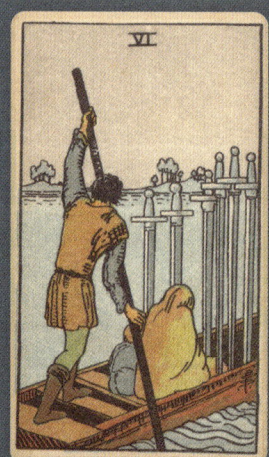

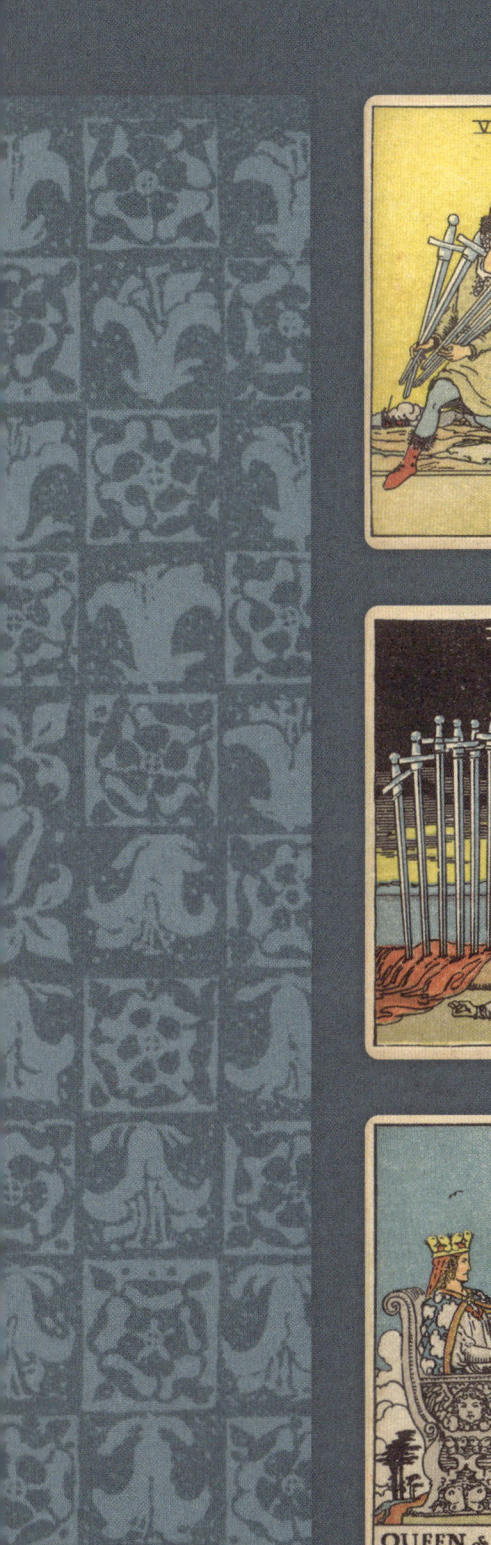

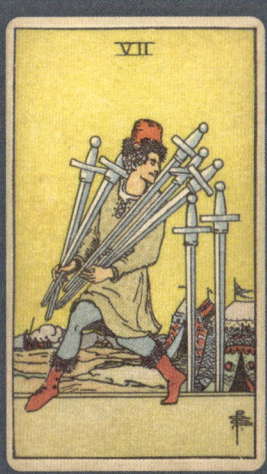

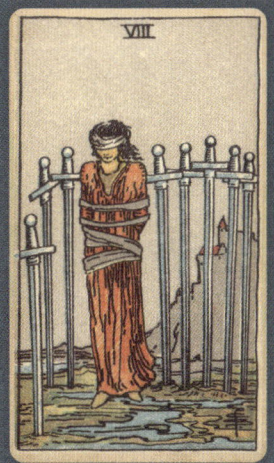

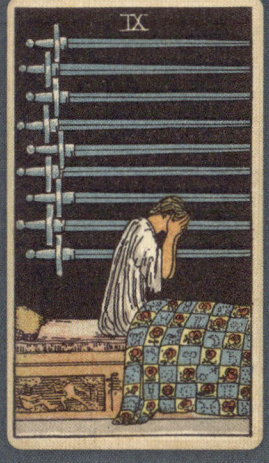

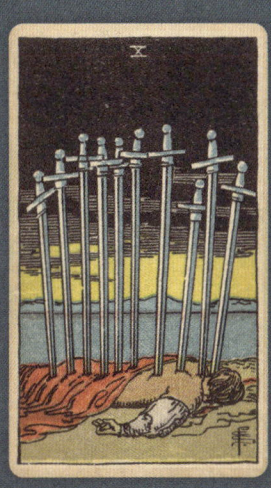

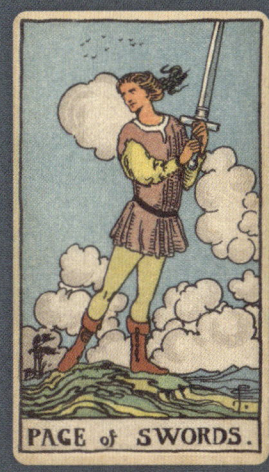

PAGE of SWORDS.

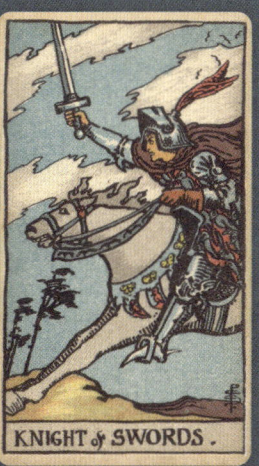

KNIGHT of SWORDS.

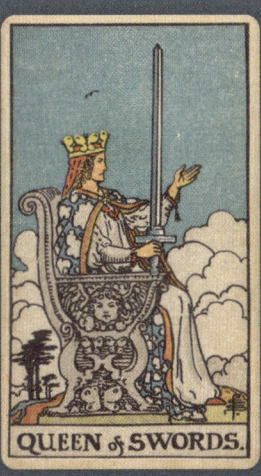

QUEEN of SWORDS.

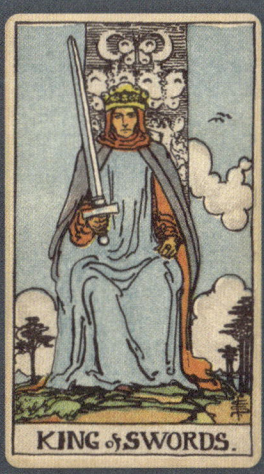

KING of SWORDS.

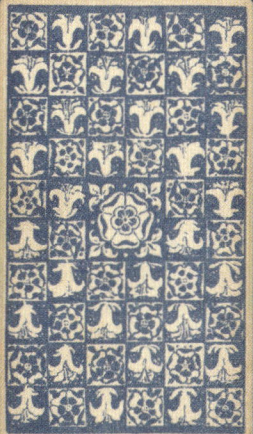

THE MINOR ARCANA

THE SUIT OF PENTACLES

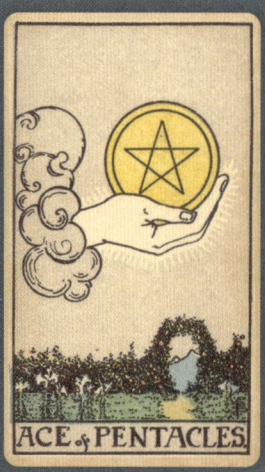

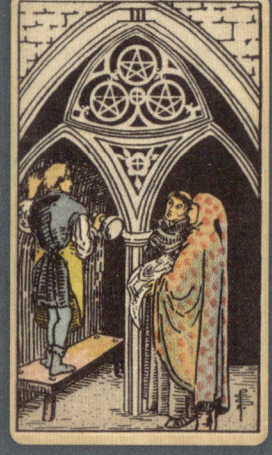
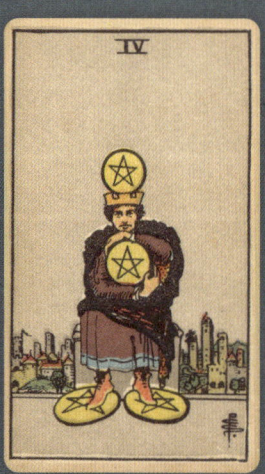
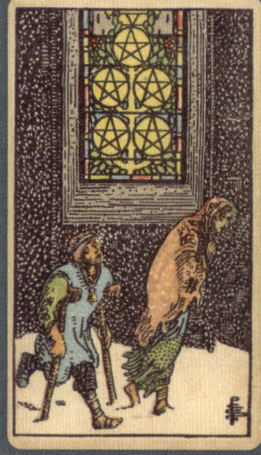
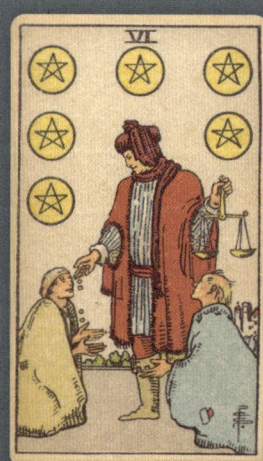
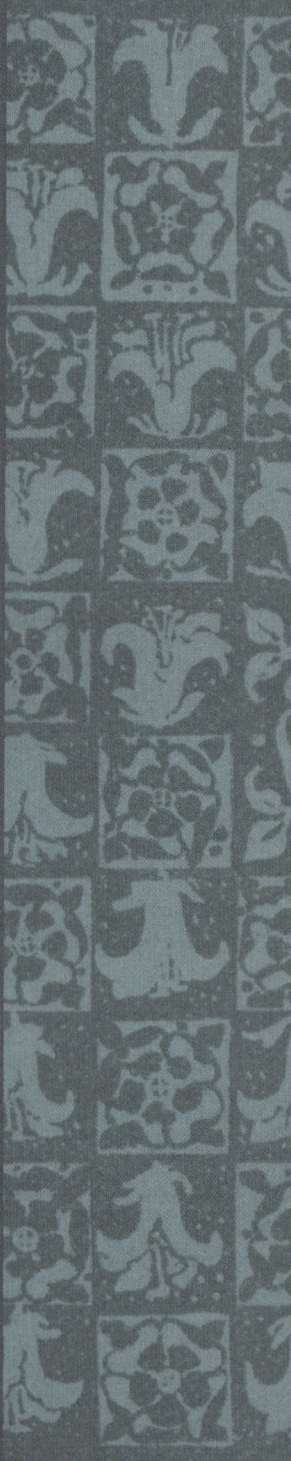

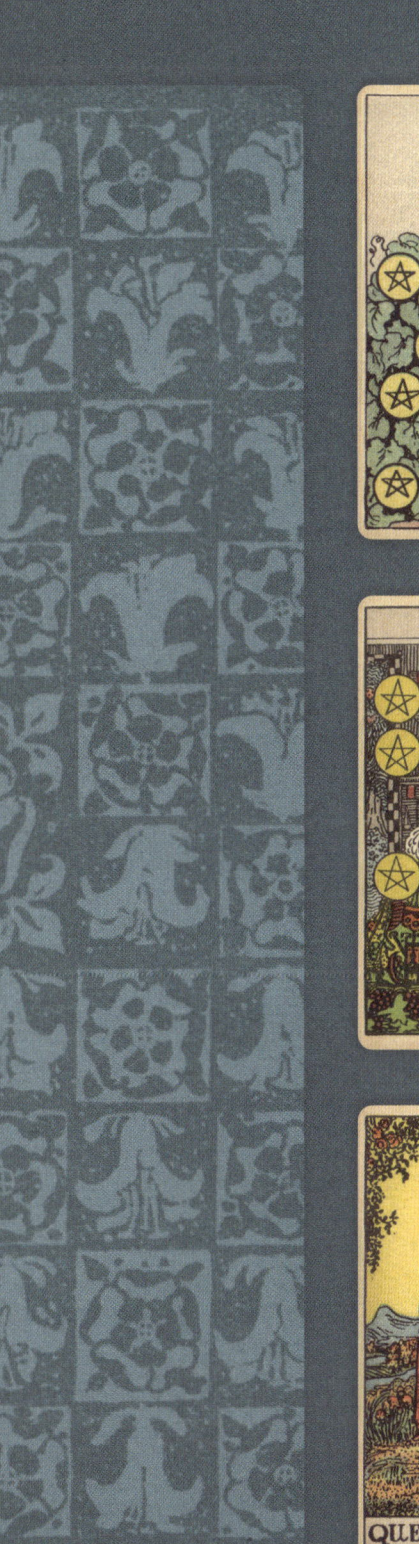

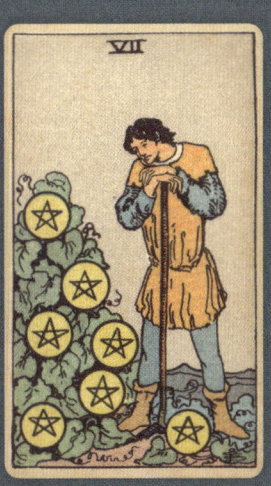

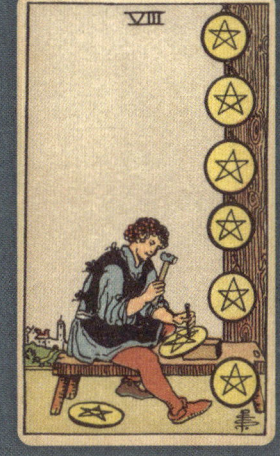

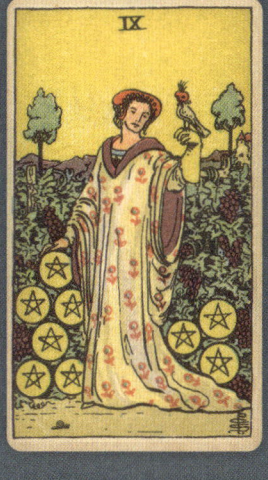

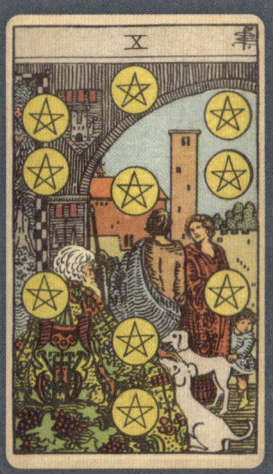

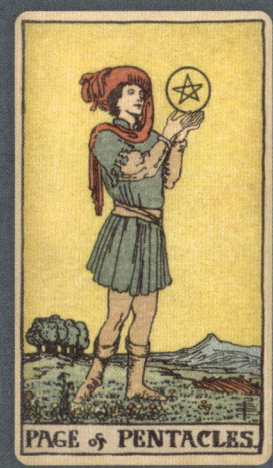

PAGE of PENTACLES.

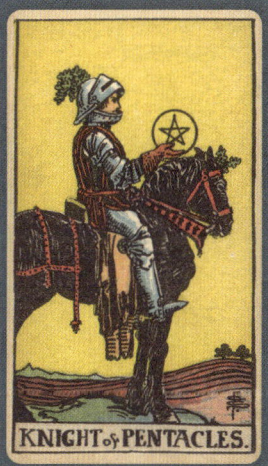

KNIGHT of PENTACLES.

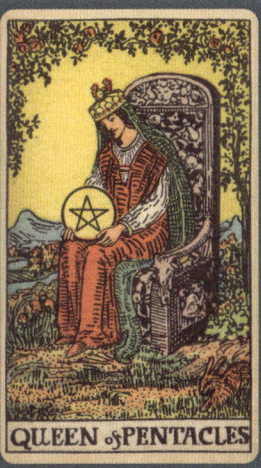

QUEEN of PENTACLES

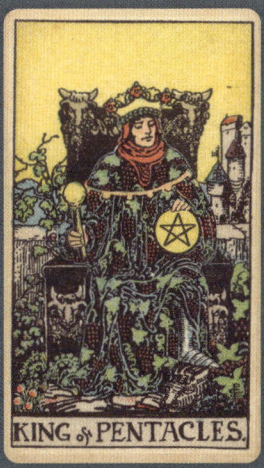

KING of PENTACLES.

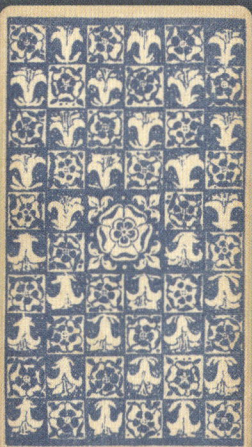

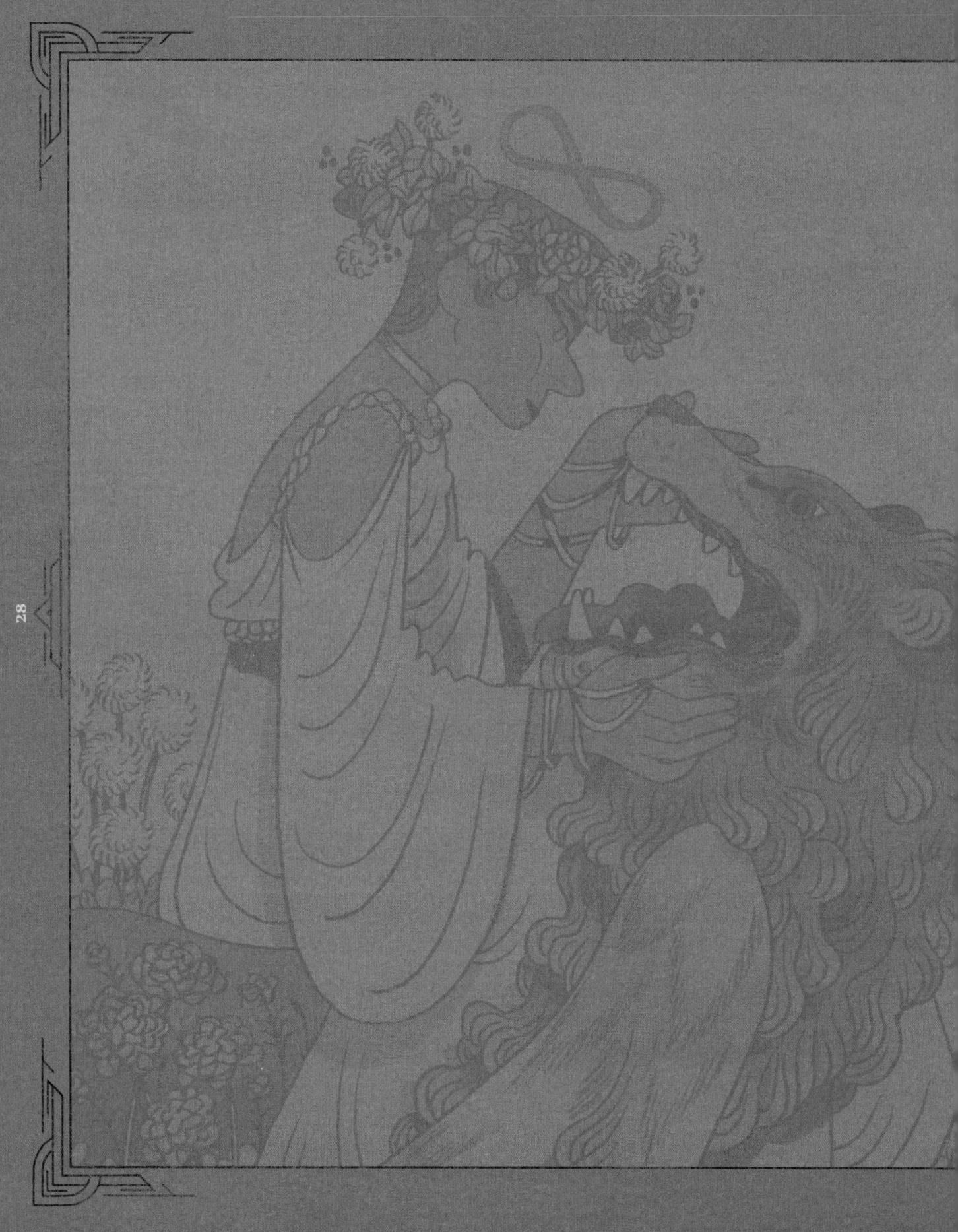

THE MAJOR
ARCANA

BY NÚRIA TAMARIT

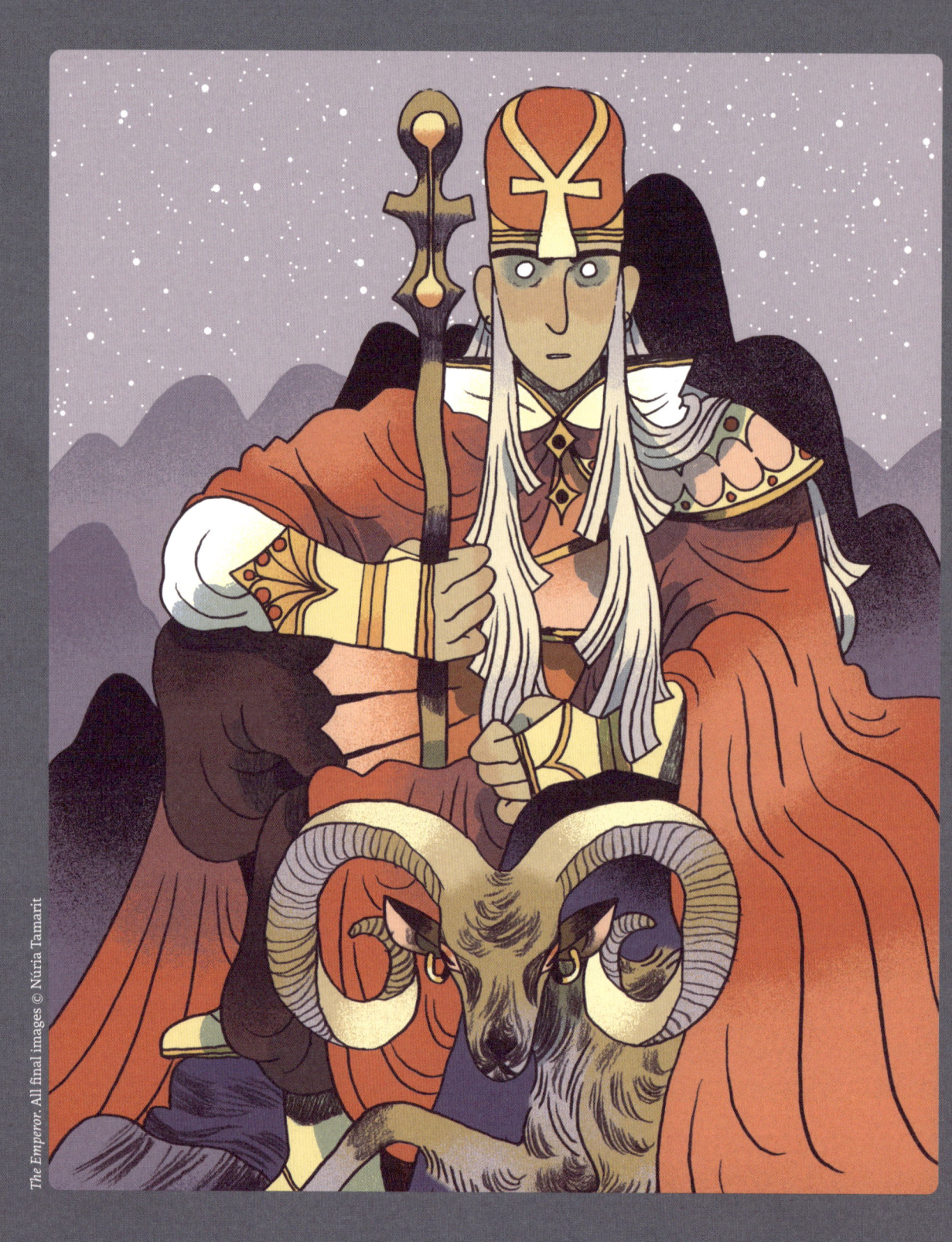

The Emperor. All final images © Núria Tamarit

THE MAJOR ARCANA

INTRODUCTION BY SASHA GRAHAM

The Major Arcana is the crown jewel of tarot, reflecting pivotal relationships and experiences in the soul's journey. These iconic figures and allegories are familiar to all people, no matter their culture or upbringing. The artist may find the Major Arcana easiest to illustrate because Major Arcana concepts are universally well known.

The Major Arcana's cards are interconnected and create an unfolding story for The Fool, who is card number zero. The Fool is like a youth who journeys through the Major Arcana, card by card. The Fool's journey is similar to the 'hero's journey', which describes a youth setting out to gain experience and accomplishment. The Major Arcana reflects a complete narrative, life cycle, and revolution. Once The Fool meets The World card, the cycle begins anew. The Fool starts at the beginning and moves through the cards again, thus echoing the cyclical nature of the universe.

The first thirteen cards of the Major Arcana (from The Fool to The Hanged Man) are larger than life. These are personality-driven archetypes leading to the formation of the psyche, with cards such as The Empress (mother), The Emperor (father), The Chariot (explorer), The Hermit (sage), and so forth.

The second half of the Major Arcana (from Death to The World) are experiential archetypes, which carve the personality and provide life experience, like The Devil (shadow), The Moon (dream state), The Sun (waking life), Judgement (evolution of consciousness), and The World (nirvana).

NÚRIA TAMARIT

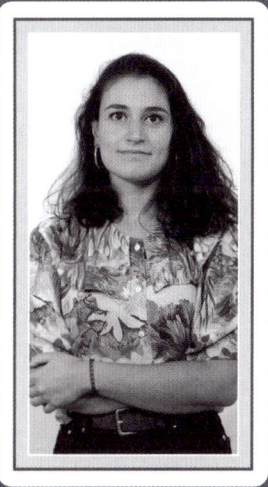

ARTIST'S INSIGHT

What fascinates me most about tarot is that it is the only fictional story that truly adapts to the person who reads it. Regardless of what is anchored or not to reality, throwing tarot cards serves as an excuse to take a break from frantic life, pause for a moment, and reflect; to analyse what is happening in your life, take action, and redirect its course towards what you are looking for.

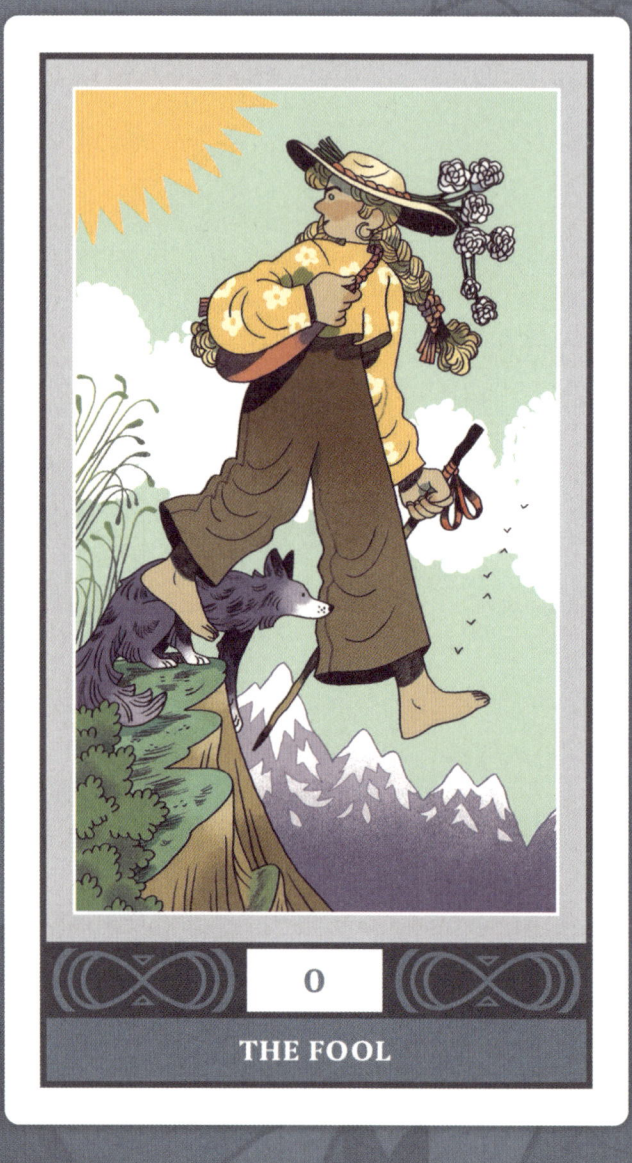

0

THE FOOL

THE FOOL

JOURNEY, BIRTH, DESCENT

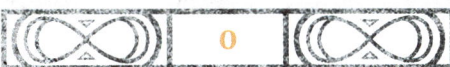

0

I like the traditional depiction of a figure that walks diagonally across the card, since it will give the image more sense of direction and movement. The character is carefree and also determined to continue the journey. I draw the dog as her companion and guide; it looks closely at her steps, ready to jump up and help. I draw a huge sun as the symbol of great new beginnings.

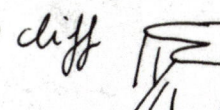

* mountains

* cliff

* white rose

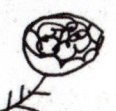

* stick.

hat with
white rose

* add a raincoat (?)
* add a notebook (?)
* guide dog
OR FOX
freedom of expression.

flip
horizontal
more dinamism

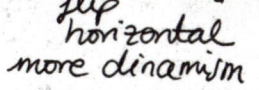

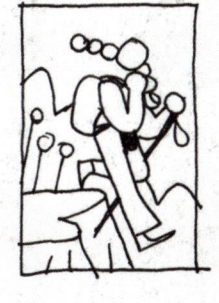

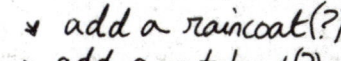
on top of mountains
going down.

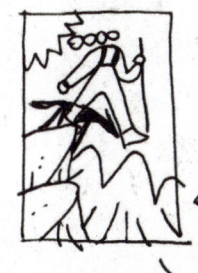

looks like
close but
on the background.

 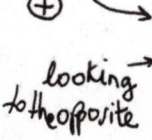
looking
to the opposite

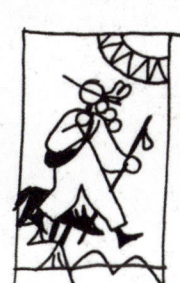

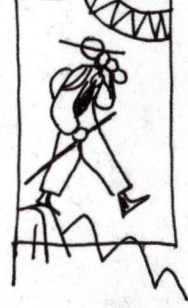

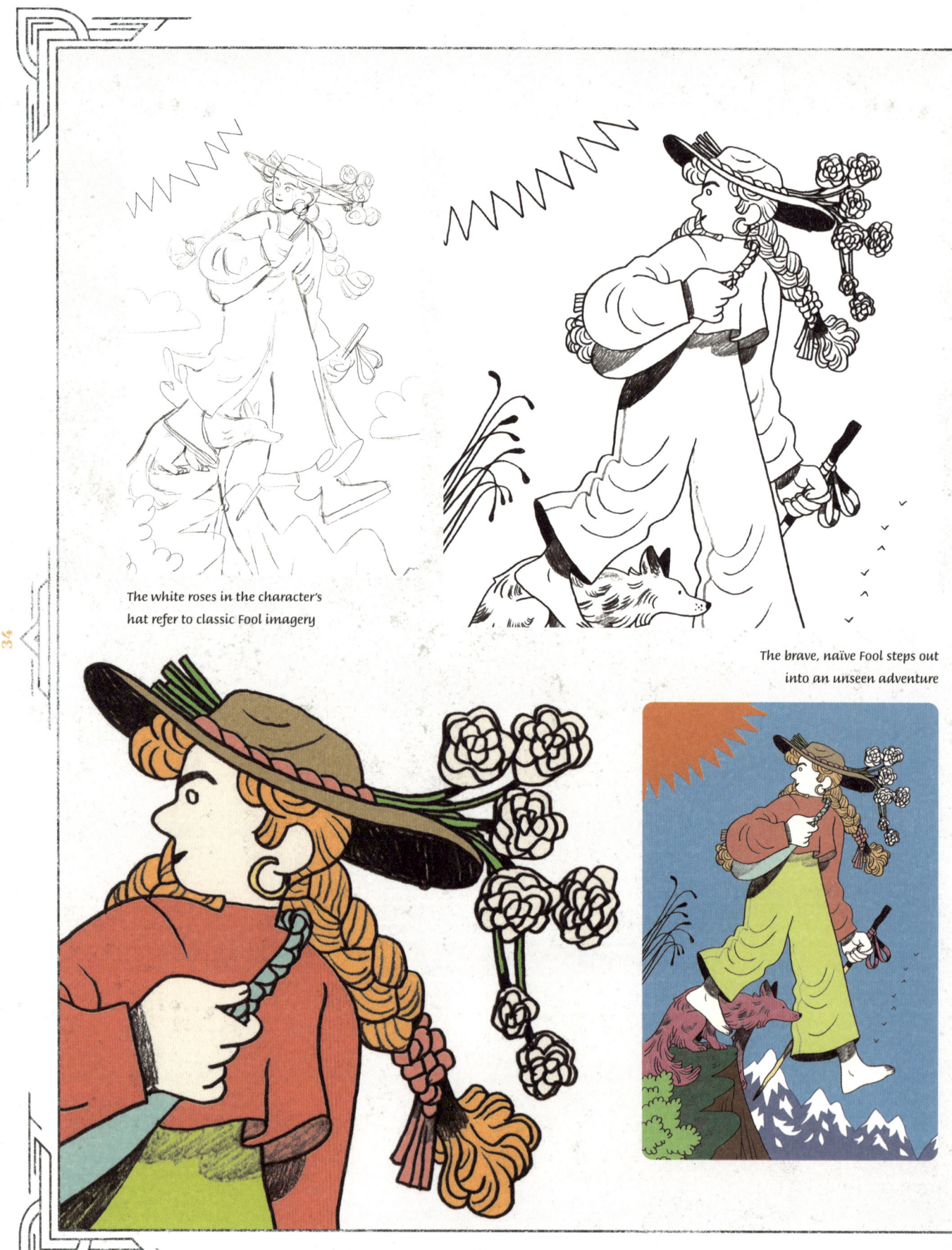

The white roses in the character's hat refer to classic Fool imagery

The brave, naïve Fool steps out into an unseen adventure

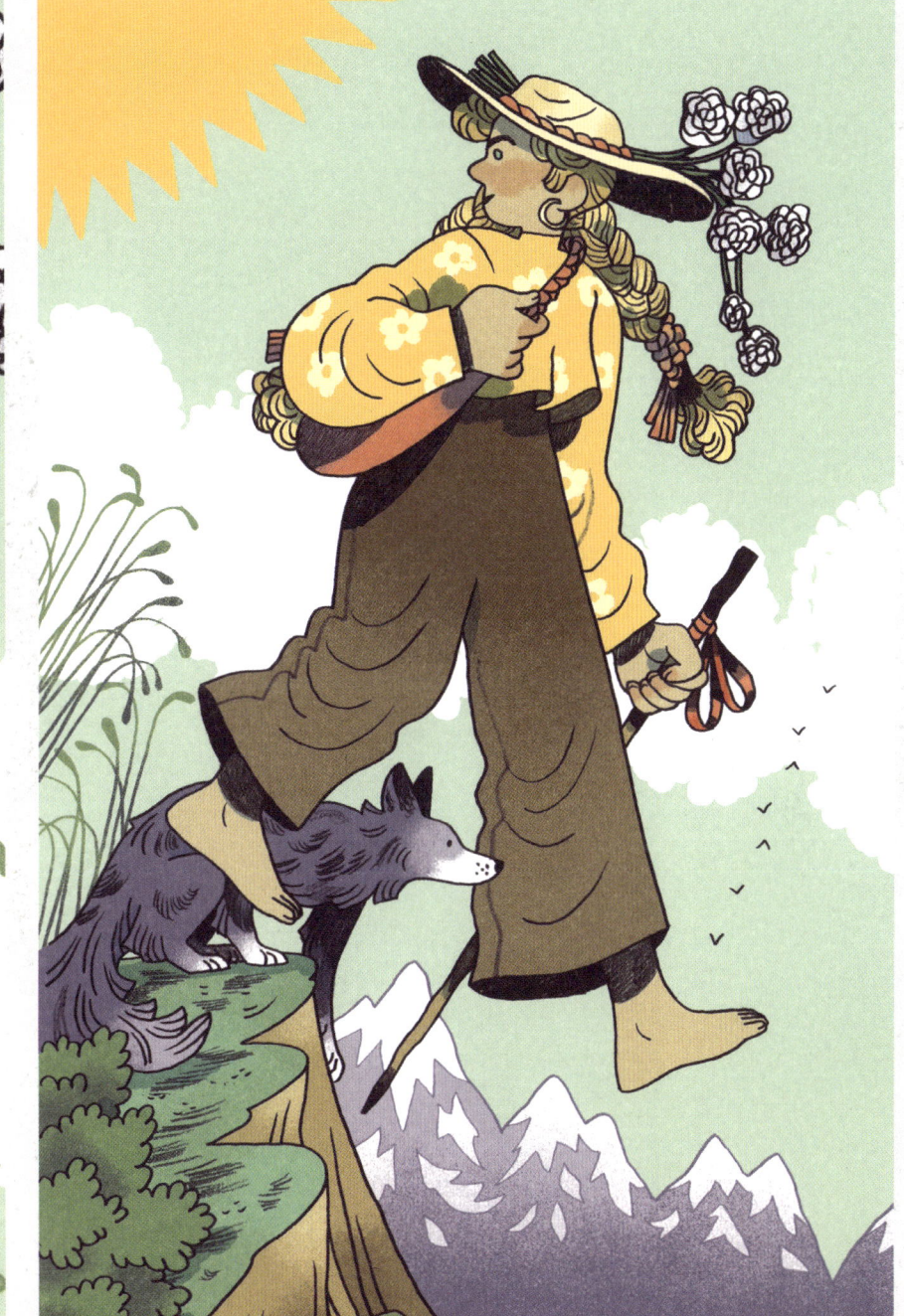

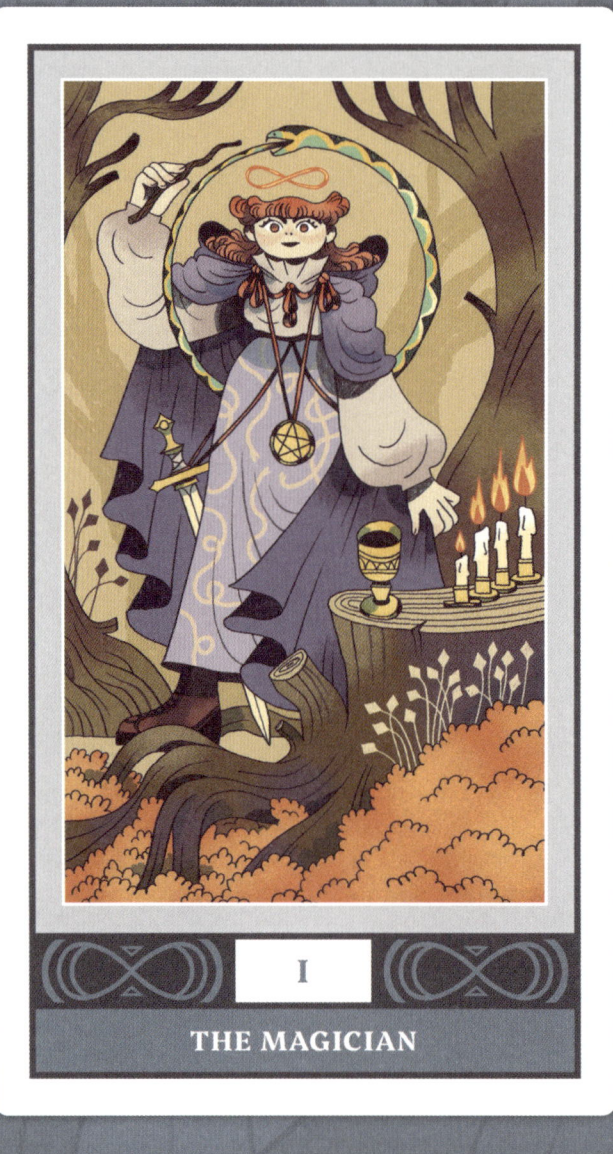

I

THE MAGICIAN

THE MAGICIAN

CHARM, SHOWMANSHIP, ILLUSION

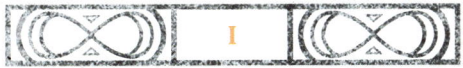

Here I end up with a more fantastic figure, some distance from the traditional representation of The Magician standing at a table of items. She is in the woods – nature will be present in all of my cards. She stands determined, in a more present way, and she's in the middle of a ritual, referring to all the energies that the card talks about. The Ouroboros – a snake eating its own tail – is a protagonist too, since I feel it's important to point to the concept of regeneration.

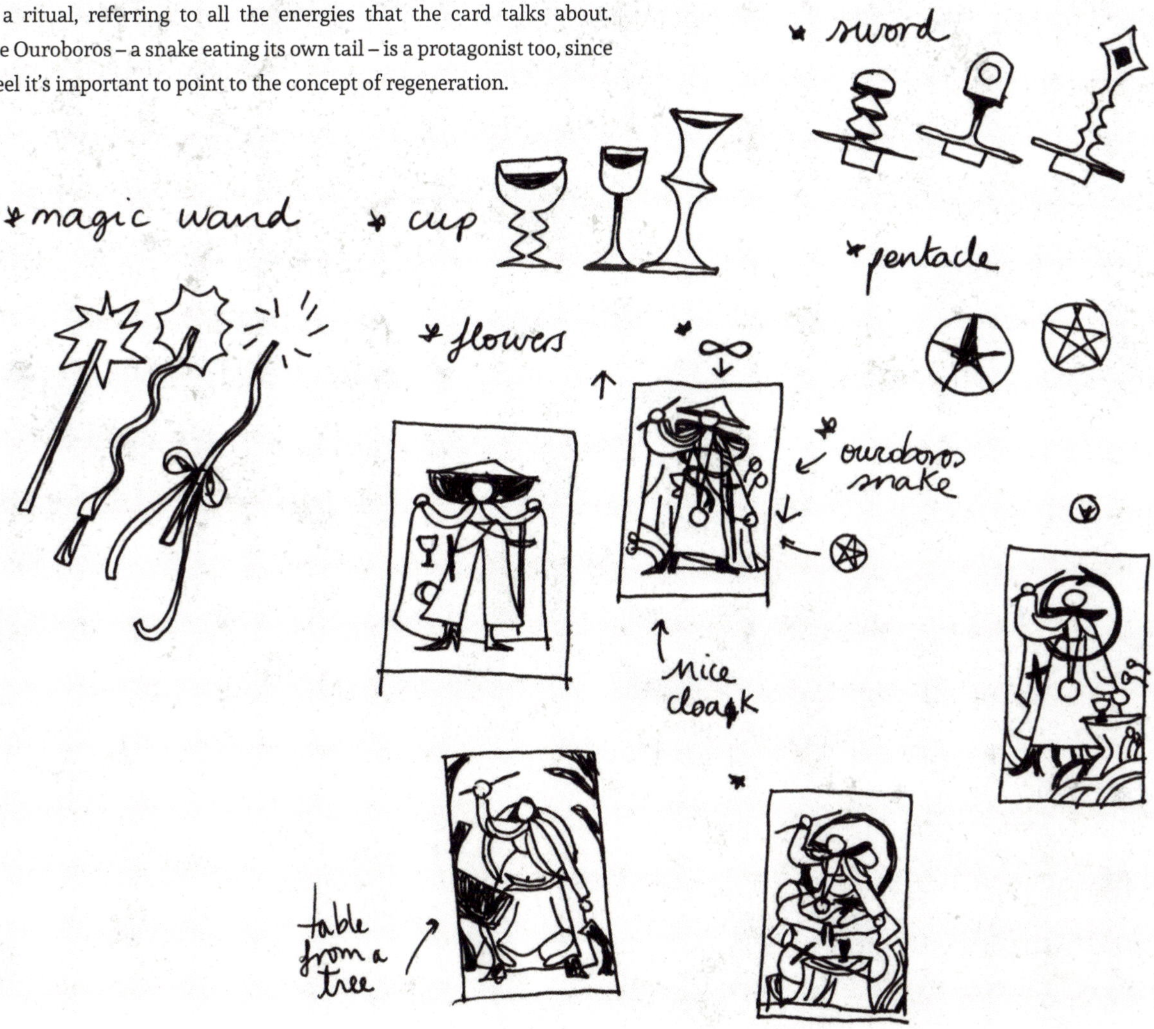

★ sword

★ magic wand   ★ cup   ★ pentacle

★ flowers   ∞   ★ ouroboros snake

nice cloak

table from a tree

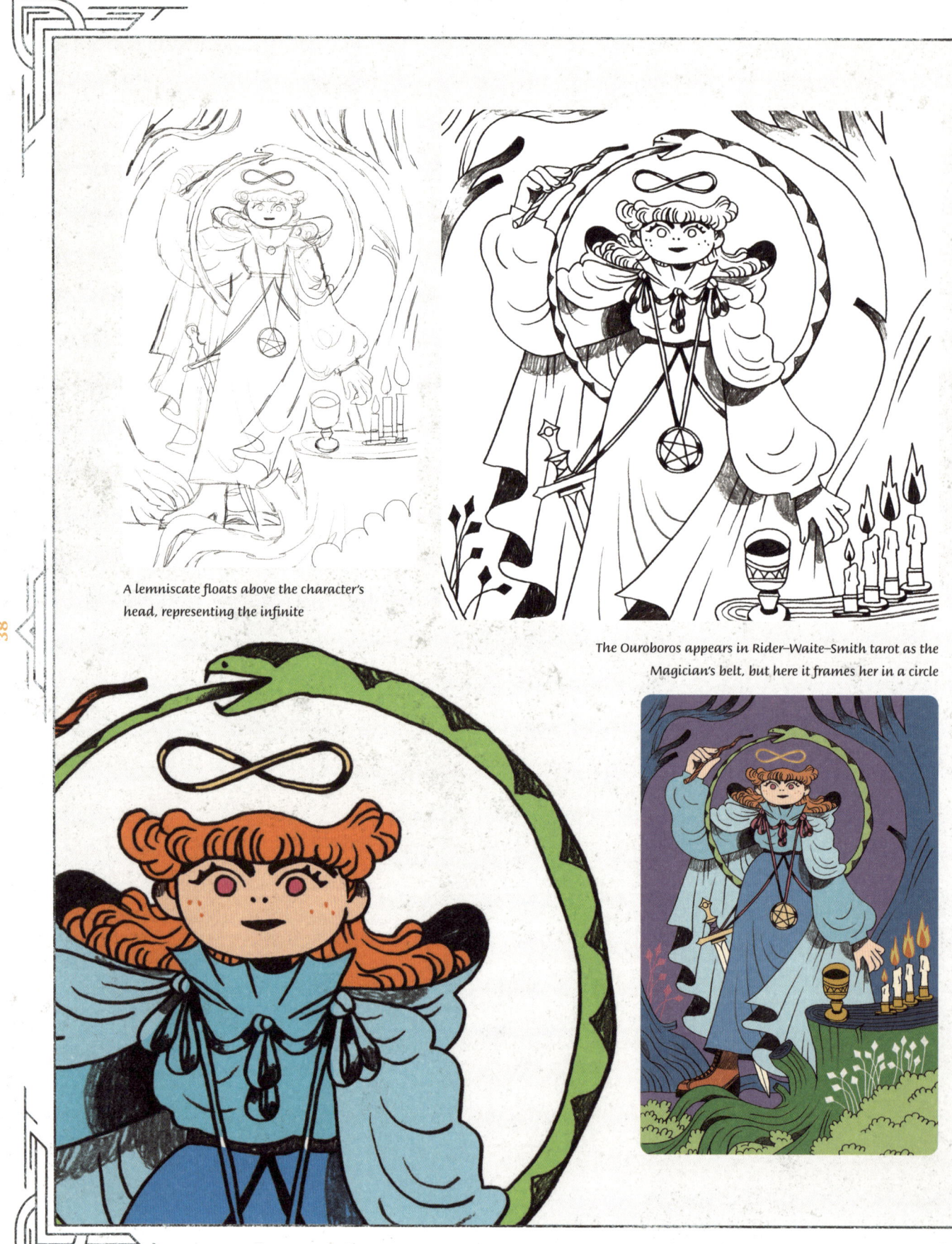

A lemniscate floats above the character's head, representing the infinite

The Ouroboros appears in Rider–Waite–Smith tarot as the Magician's belt, but here it frames her in a circle

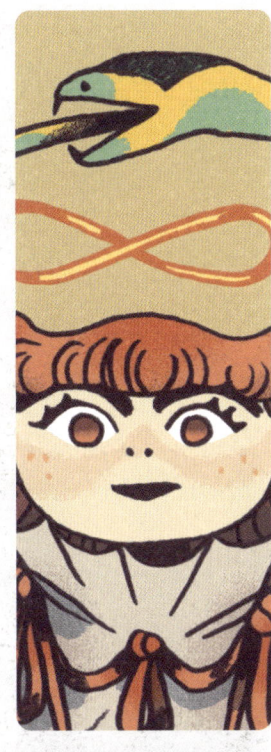

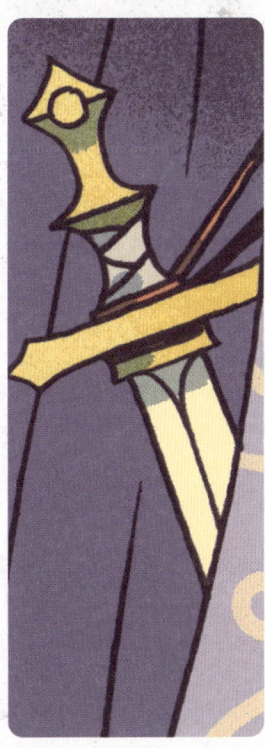

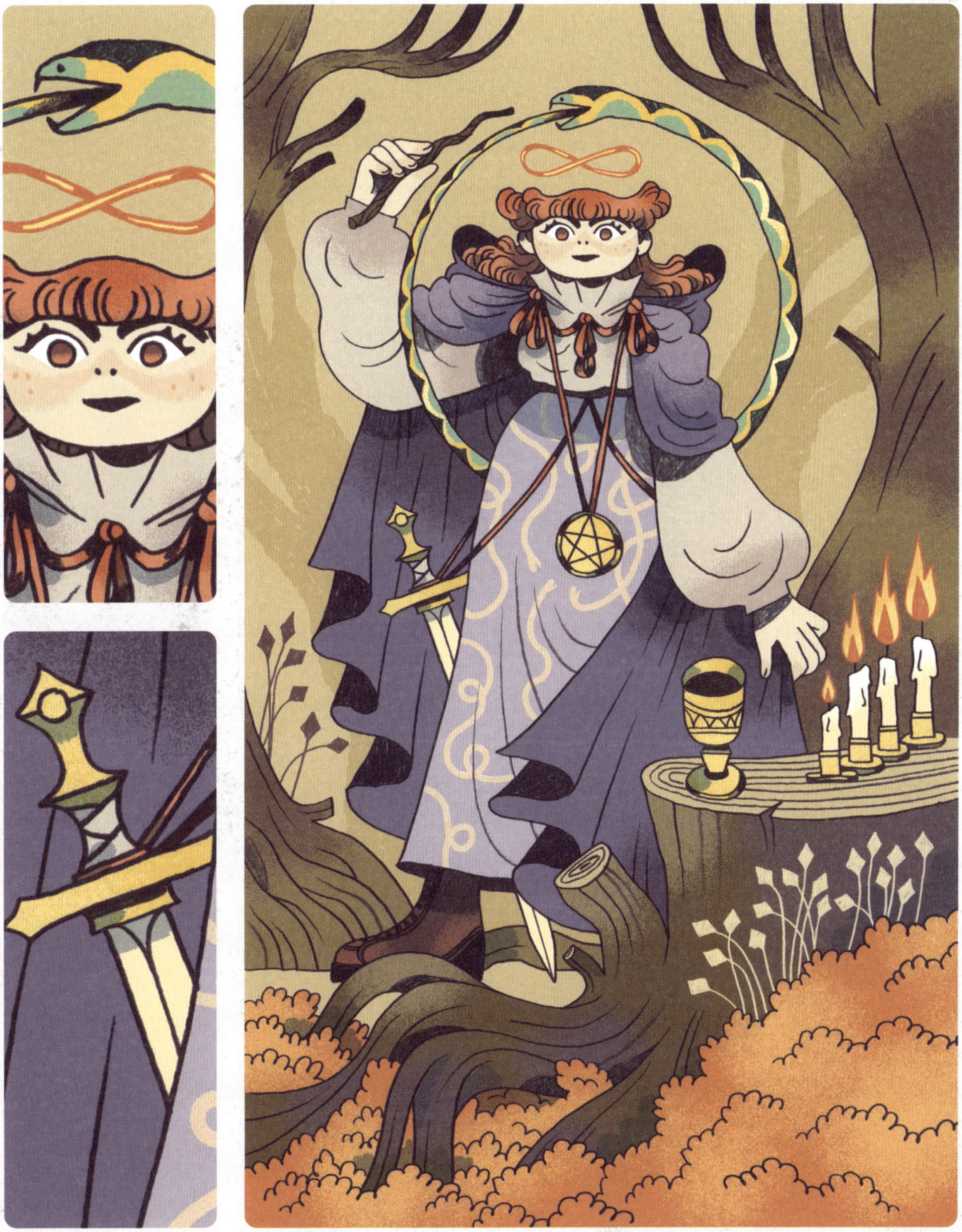

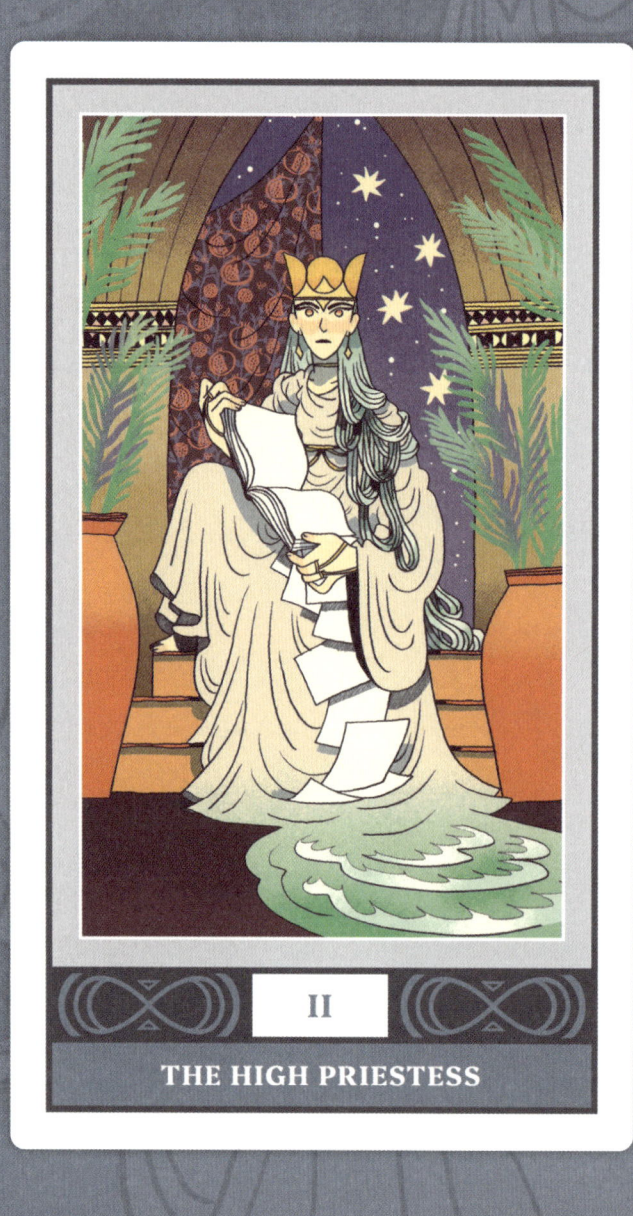

II

THE HIGH PRIESTESS

THE HIGH PRIESTESS

INTUITION, SILENCE, PRESENCE

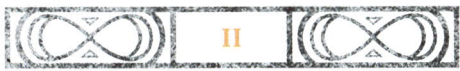

II

I keep all the traditional imagery in this one. I draw a figure that sits firmly; we can see that The High Priestess has just stopped reading to stare powerfully at us. The two columns are usually one black and one white, representing the masculine and feminine, but I unify their colours as I'd like to erase the division of the two genders. Her cloak transforms into water, and she's surrounded by palms, all symbols of nature and fertility.

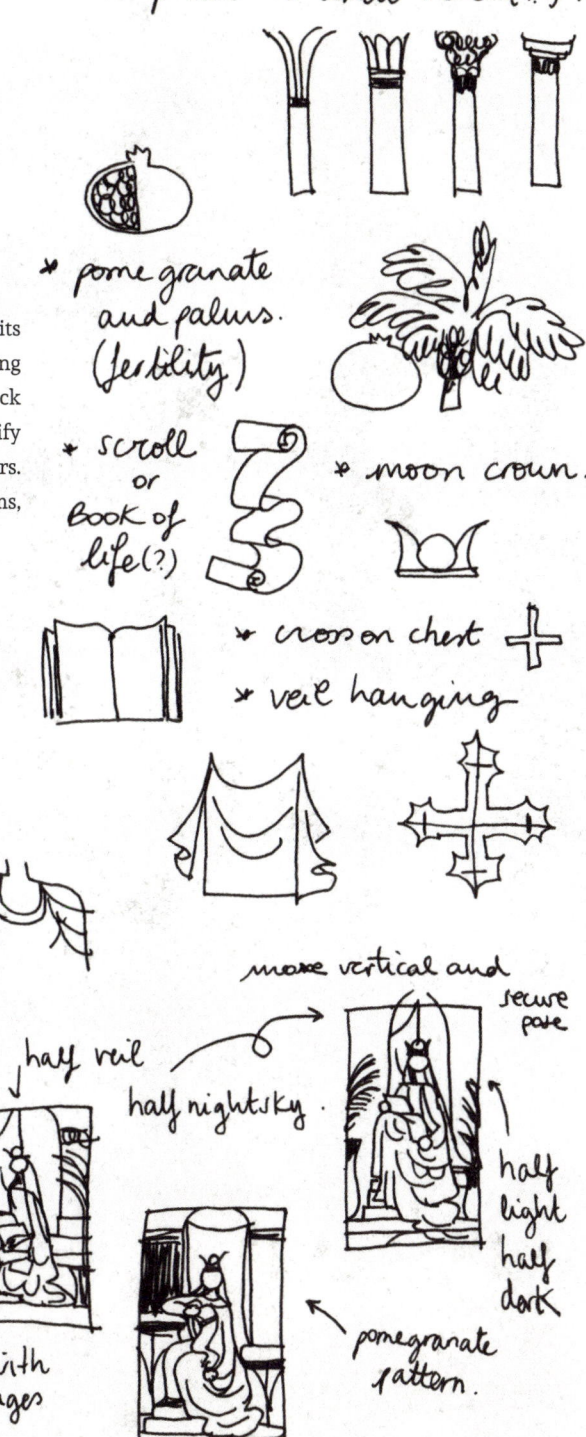

* pilars → what kind (?).

* pomegranate and palms. (fertility)

* scroll or Book of life (?)

* moon crown.

* cross on chest
* veil hanging

* water → robe as waves

gothic columns
constellations.
moon necklace
half veil
half nightsky.
more vertical and secure pose
half light half dark
pomegranate pattern.
palms
bouquet with pomegranates
book with fallen pages

41

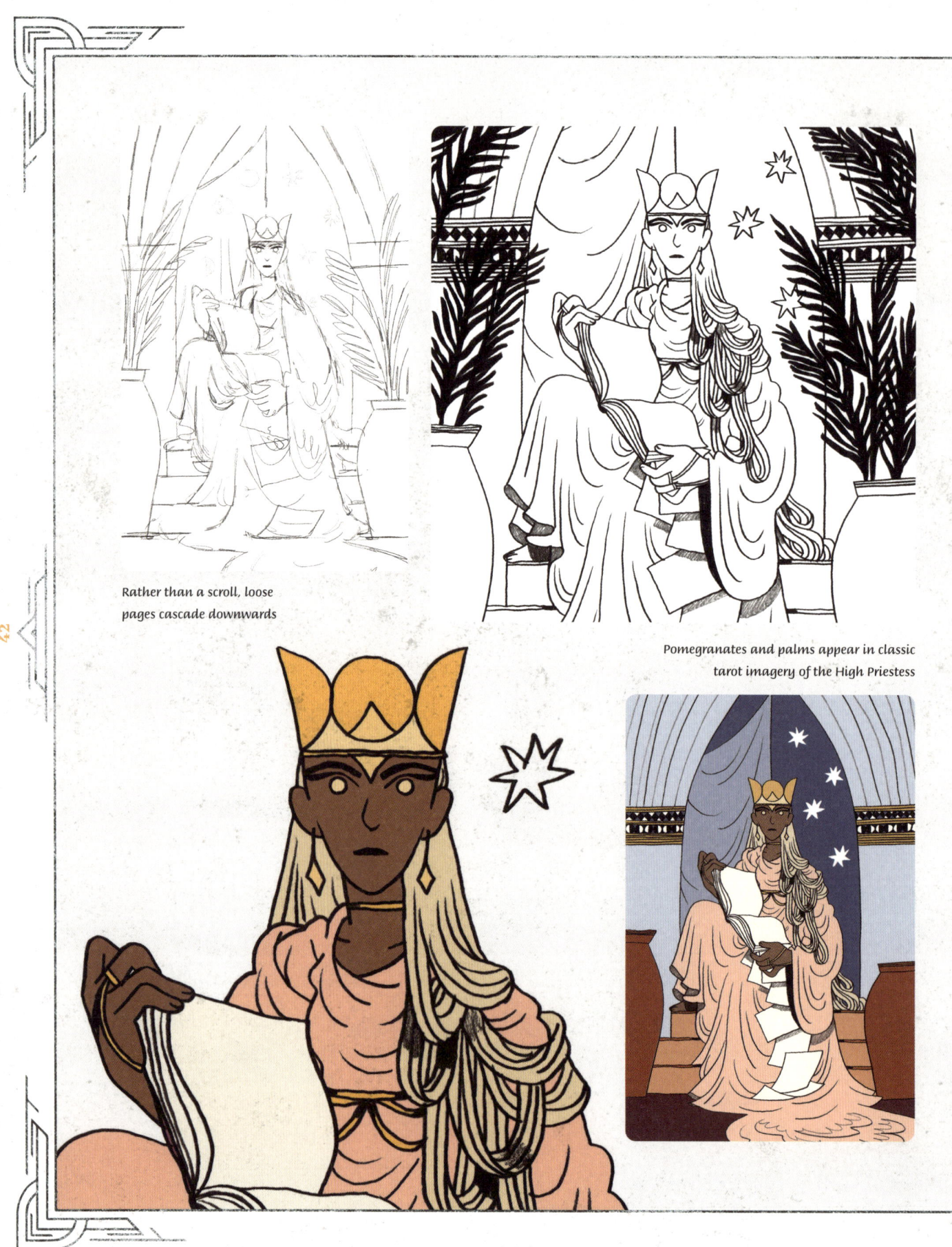

Rather than a scroll, loose
pages cascade downwards

Pomegranates and palms appear in classic
tarot imagery of the High Priestess

42

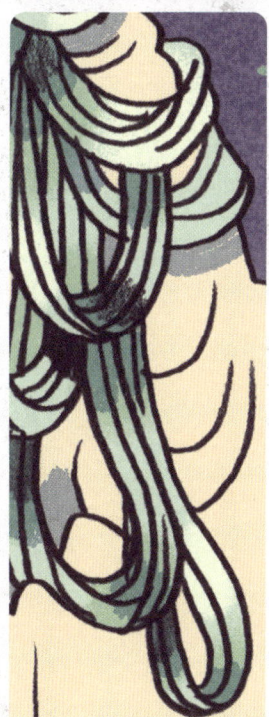

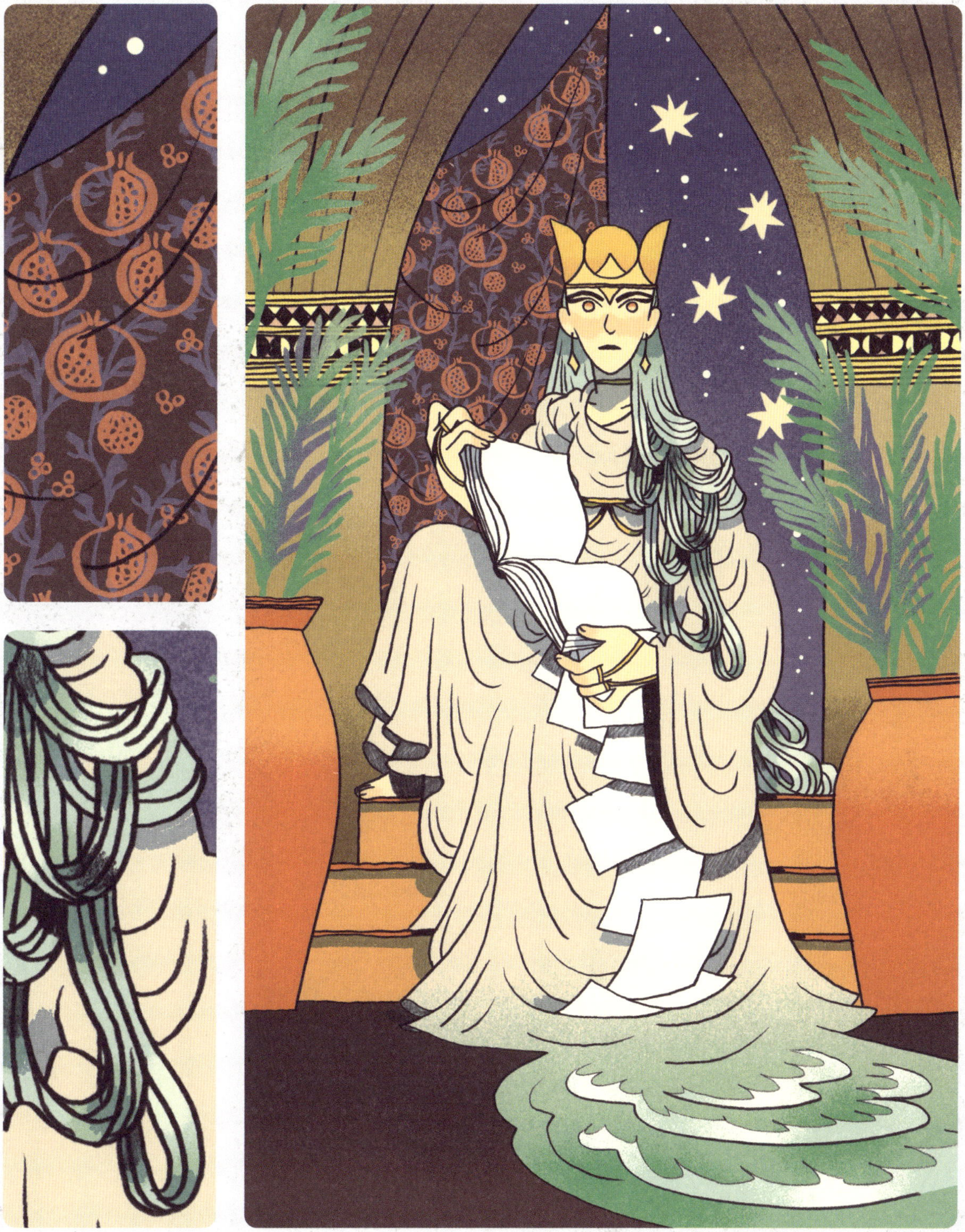

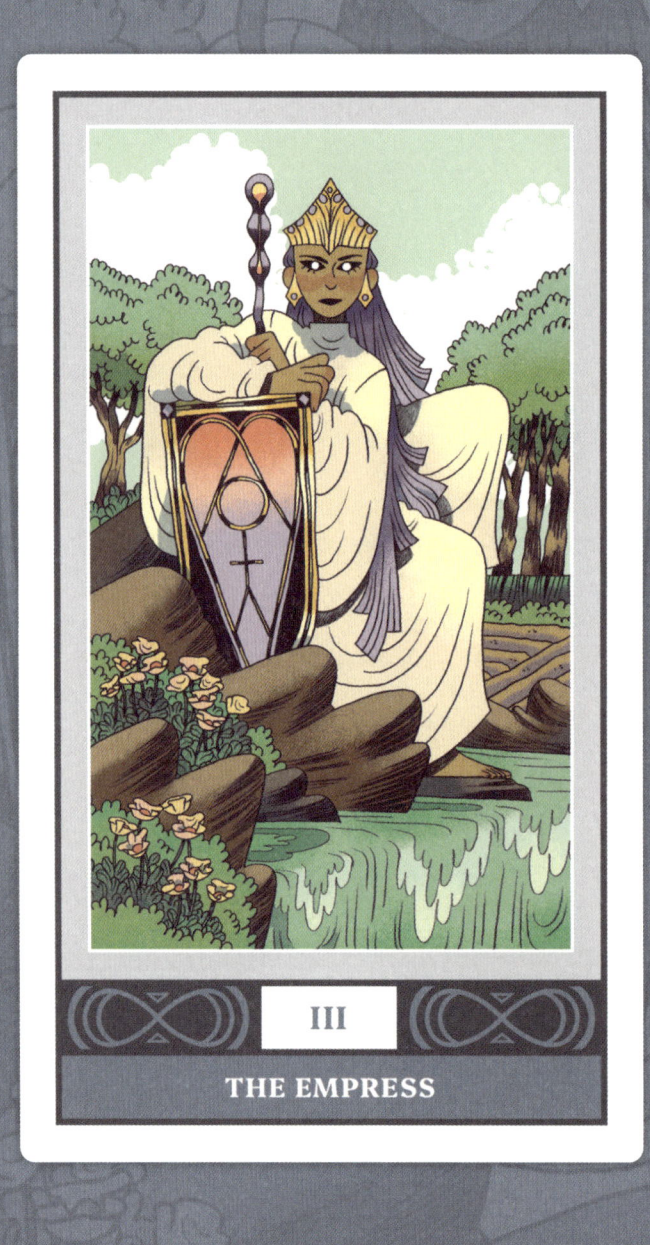

III

THE EMPRESS

THE EMPRESS

FERTILITY, MOTHERHOOD, LOVE

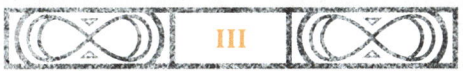

III

This card is linked with The Emperor, so I want to use a similar composition for both. The characters will both be seated on their thrones of stone, all parts of nature. Here The Empress is confident and powerful. She's surrounded by water, symbolizing flow, and fields, flowers, and trees, symbolizing fertility and abundance. She firmly holds a shield bearing the symbol of love.

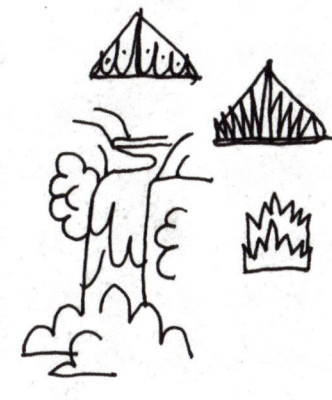

* venus symbol
* heart shield
* pregnancy
* crown with 12 jewels.
* waterfall
* field meeting forest
* Sceptre

venus and heart a bit a less obvious (?)

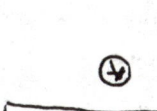

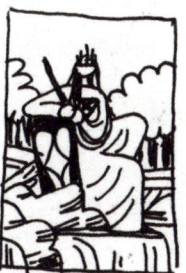

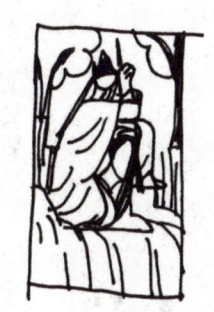

forest

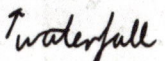
waterfall

crops

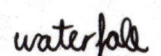

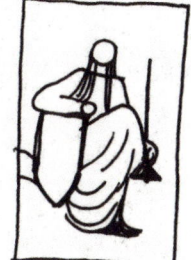

waterfall

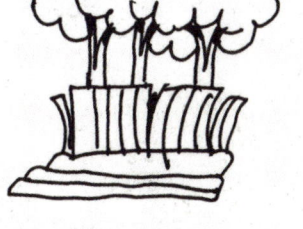

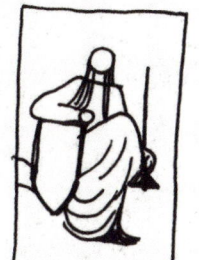

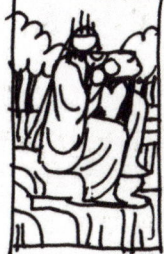

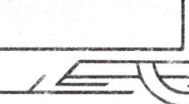

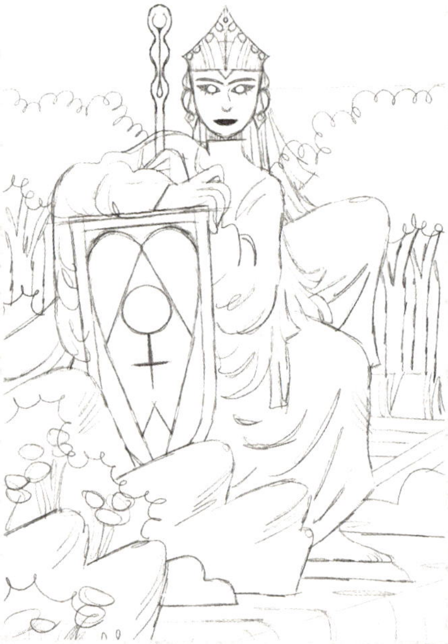

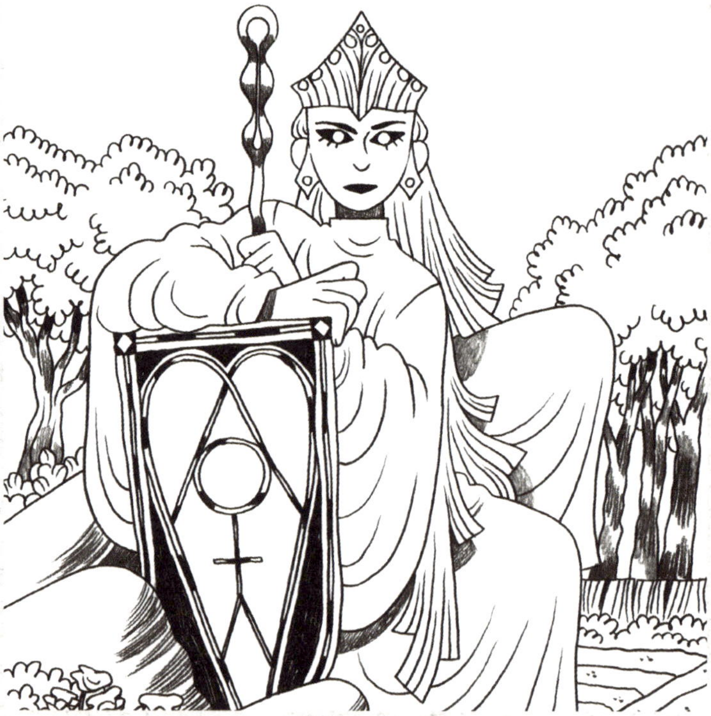

The character is surrounded by
nature, full of energy and water

The Empress's classic heart-shaped shield
is prominent in the composition

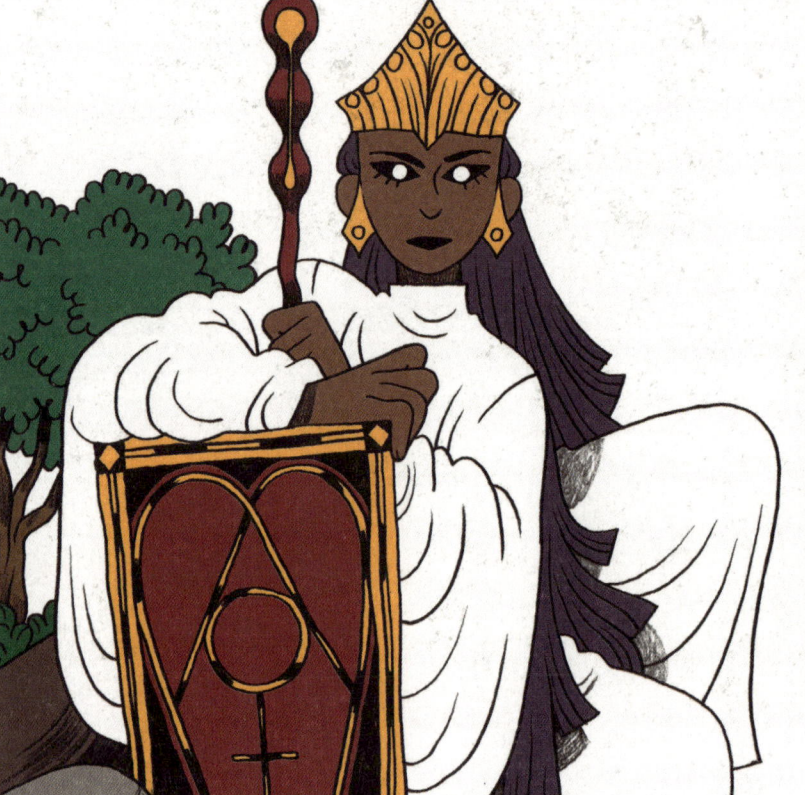

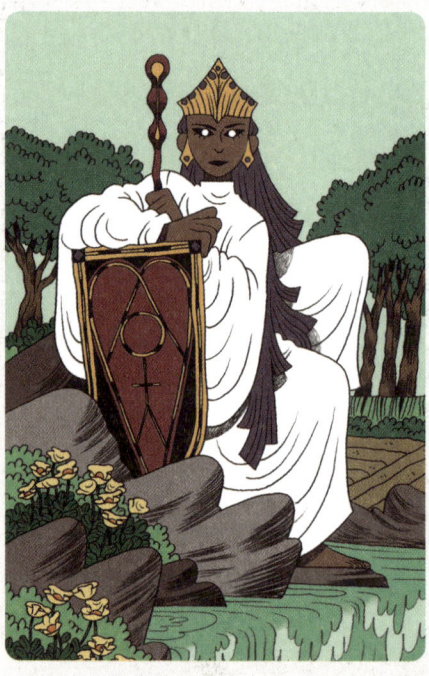

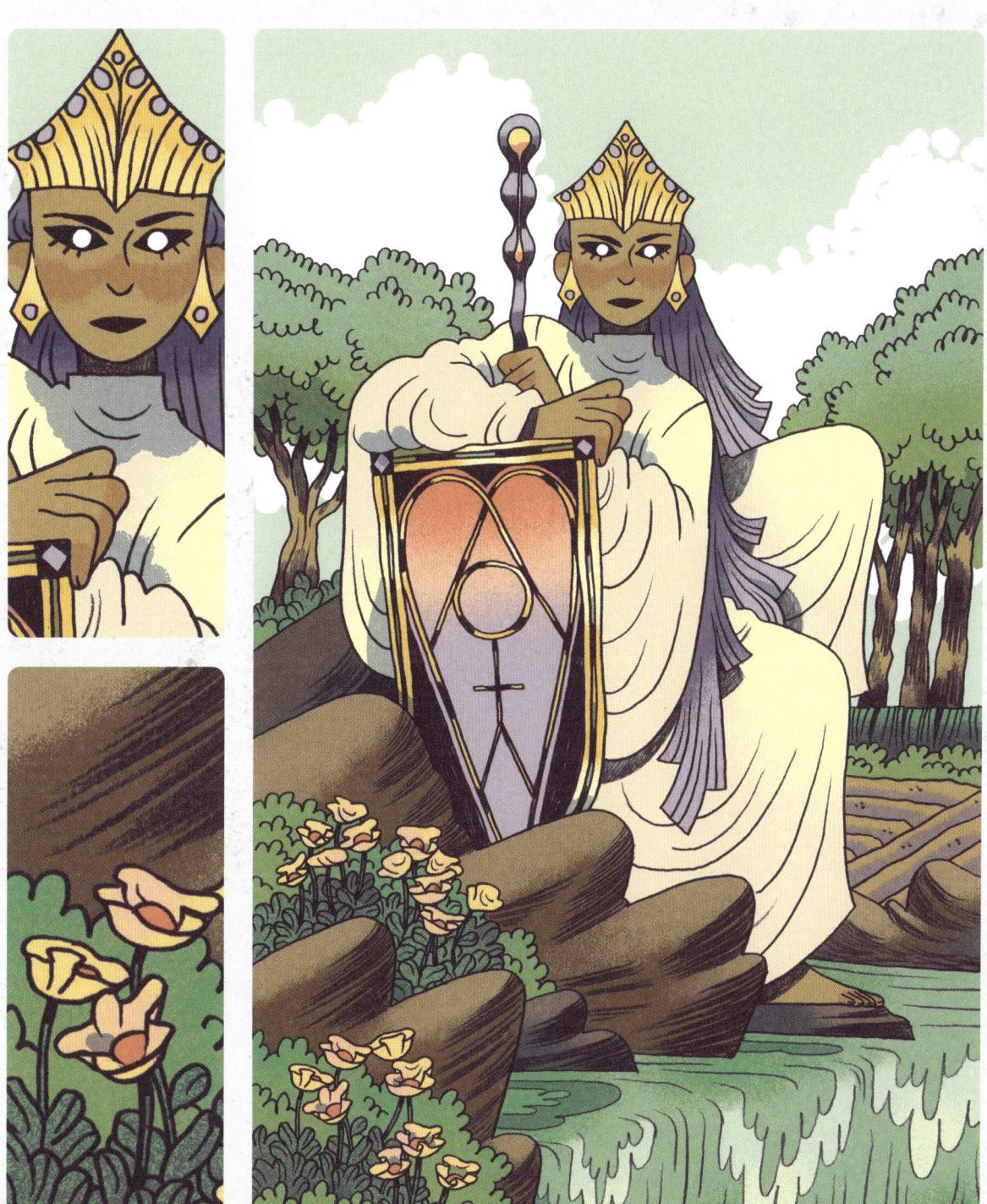

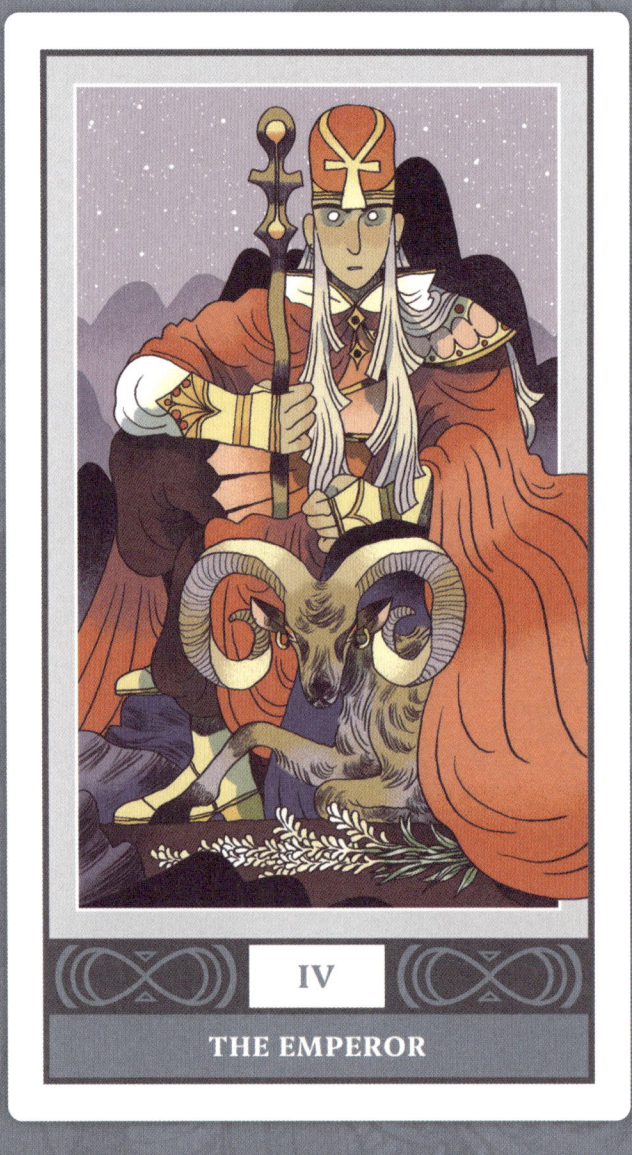

IV

THE EMPEROR

48

THE EMPEROR

DOMINEER, CONTROL, LIMITS

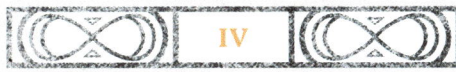

I decide to draw the character younger than in the traditional imagery, since I believe one can achieve control at a younger state. I decide to add the ram as a character rather than a decoration, giving the image more of a sense of domination. The ram appears from under The Emperor's cloak, referring to the idea of protecting oneself and others. The throne is integrated into the mountains, showing that we are all a part of nature and no one should dominate over her.

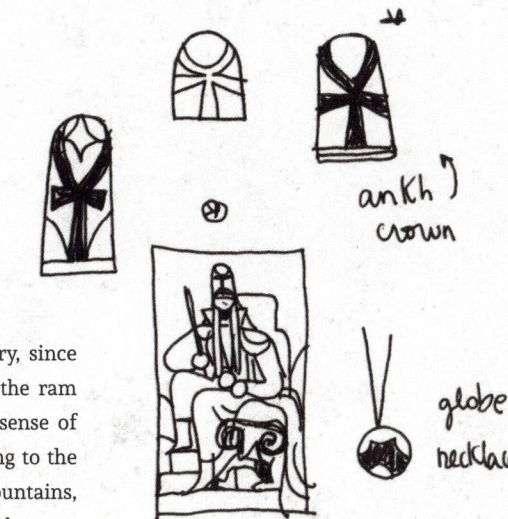

ankh
crown

globe
necklace

ram
companion

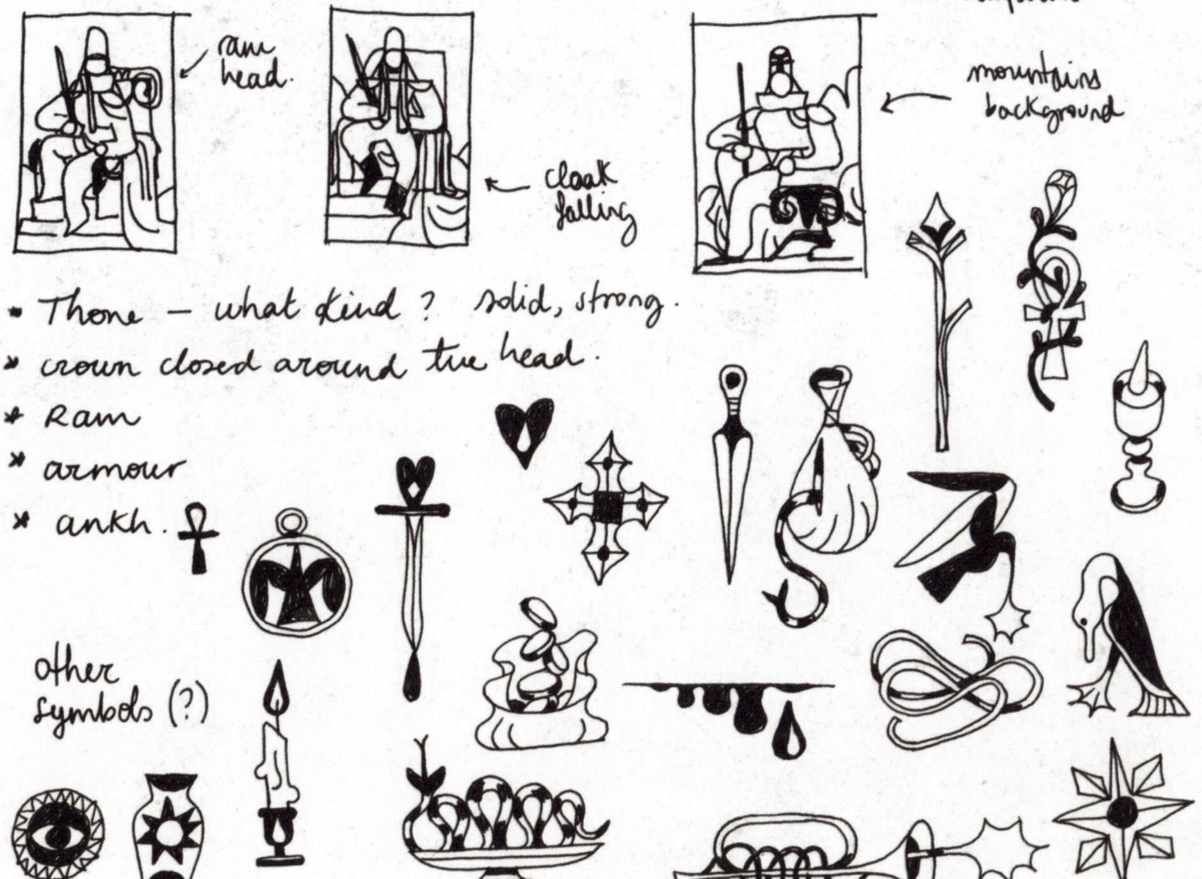

← ram
head.

← cloak
falling

mountains
background

* Throne — what kind? solid, strong.
* crown closed around the head.
* Ram
* armour
* ankh.

other
symbols (?)

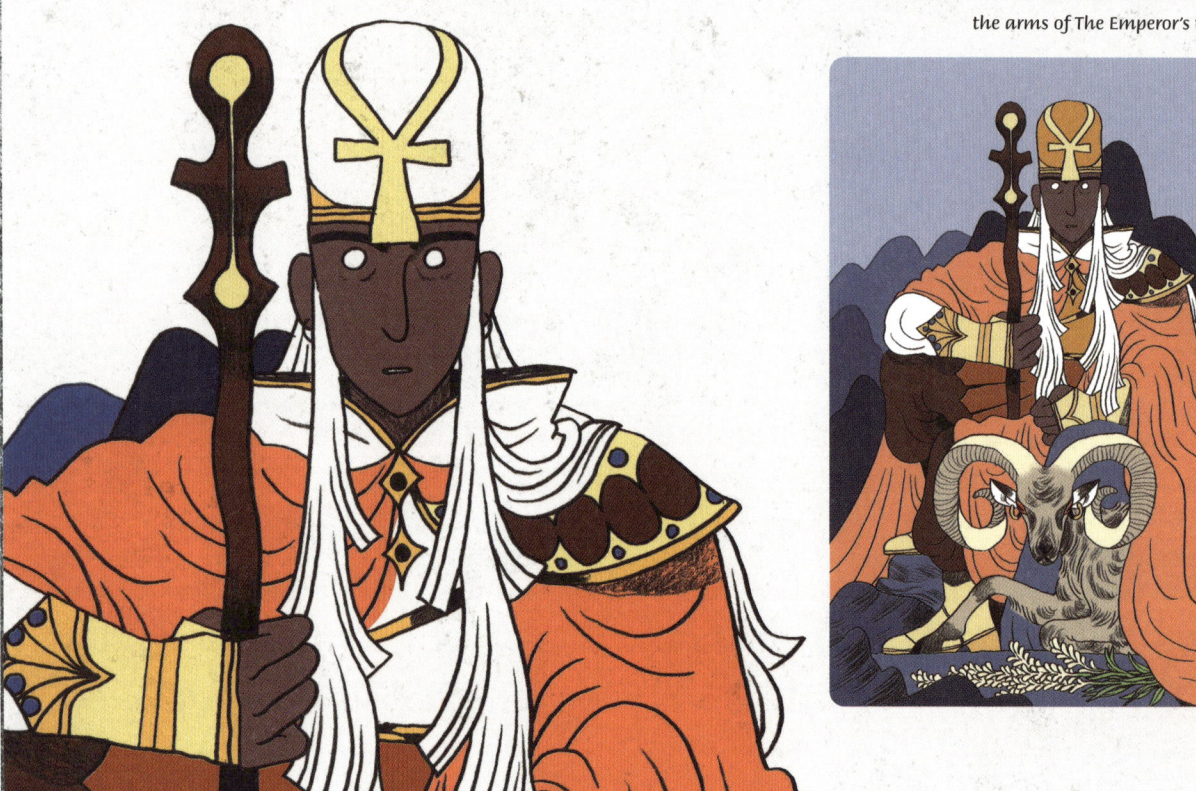

Like The Empress, The Emperor is seated among stones rather than on a typical throne

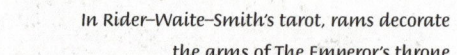

In Rider–Waite–Smith's tarot, rams decorate the arms of The Emperor's throne

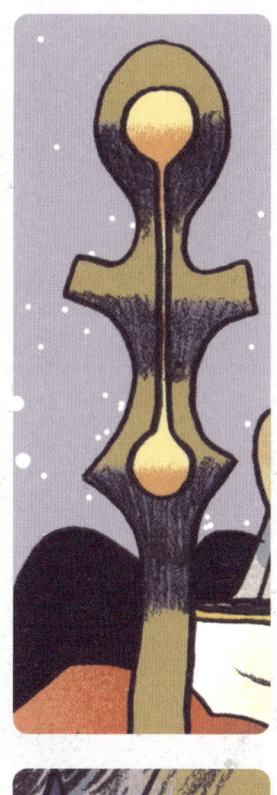

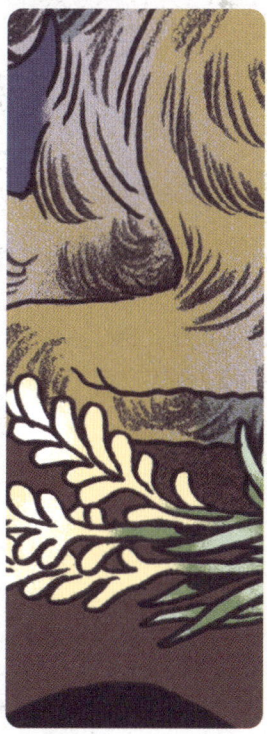

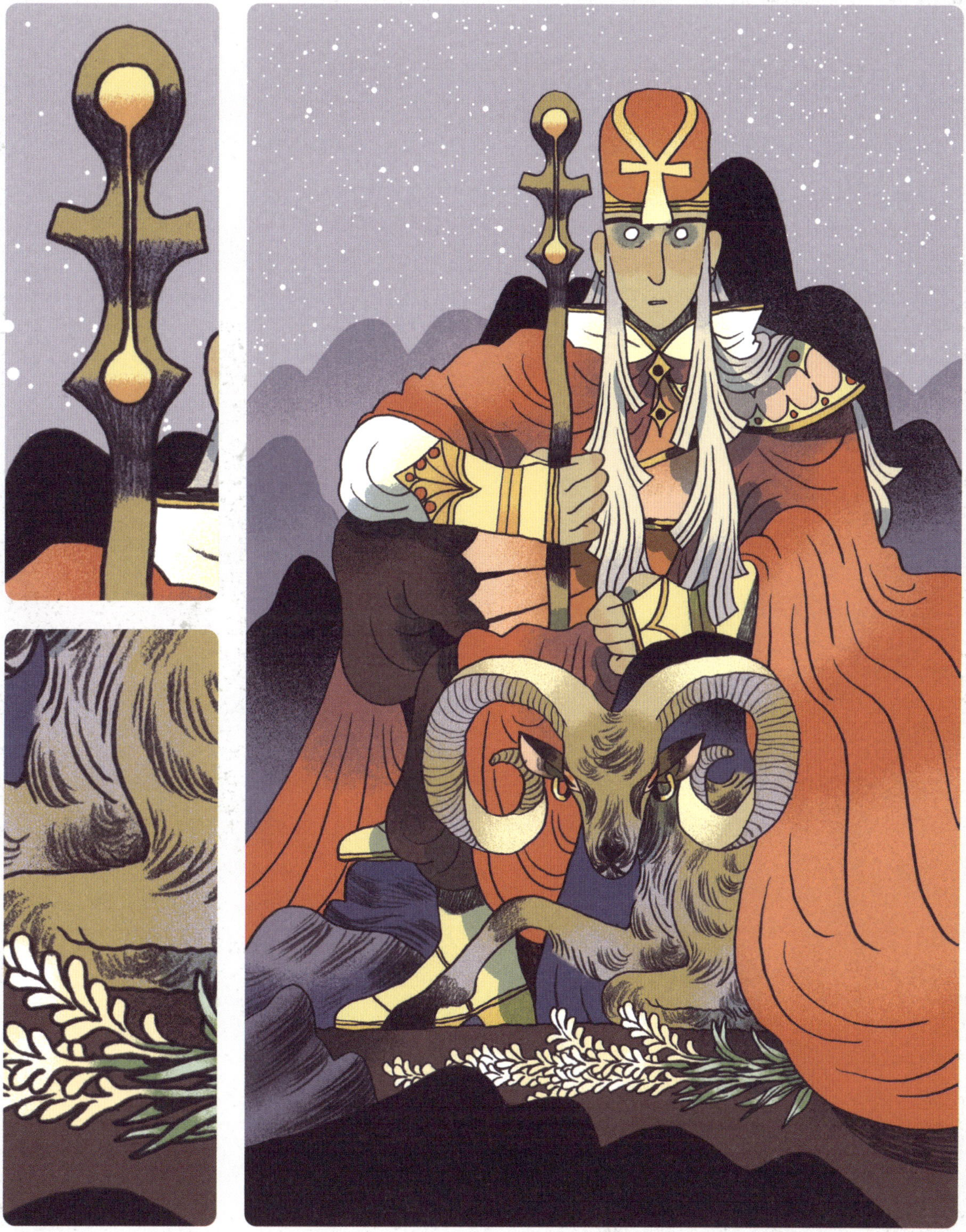

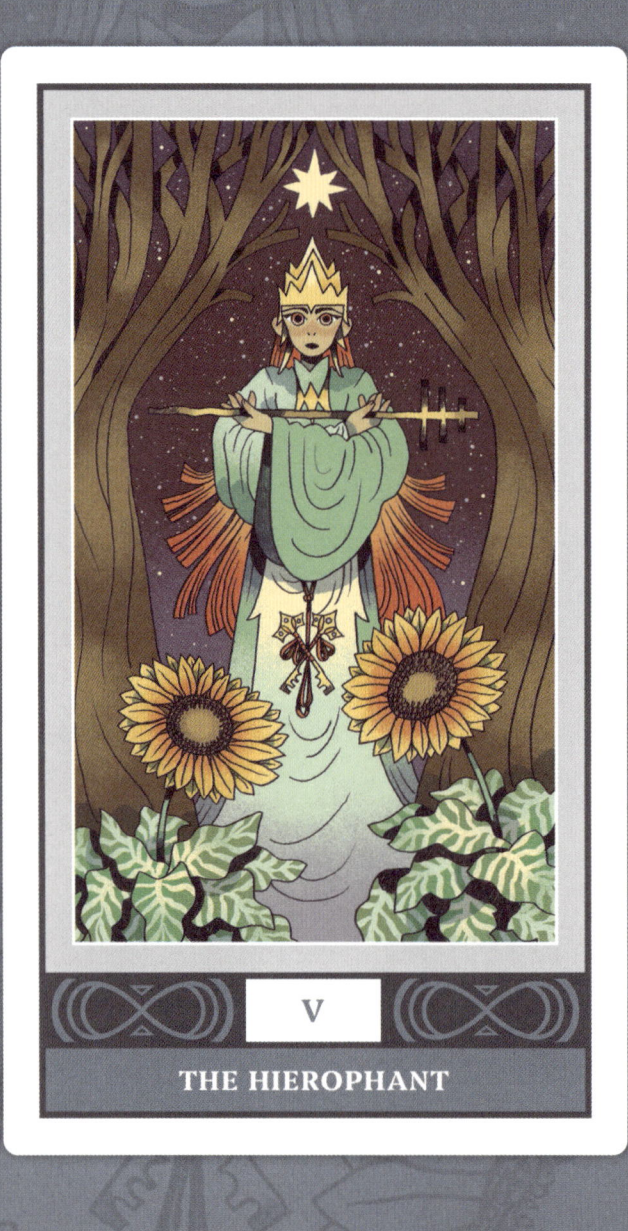

V

THE HIEROPHANT

THE HIEROPHANT

DOGMA, CEREMONY, SECRETS

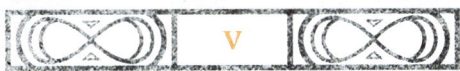

V

I change the gender of this figure, as I want to break the cliché of wisdom, dogma, or education always being linked to manhood. Since the teacher is usually the centre of the class and the students follow, I decide to replace the two lower figures with sunflowers, as they follow the sun. I also replace the two pillars with trees, creating a link between this card and Justice.

* Pillars , could be a tree?

central figure

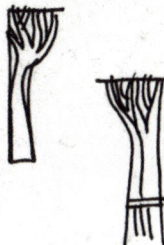

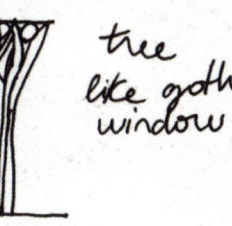

tree like gothic window?

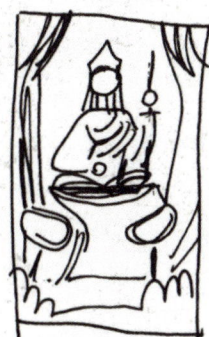

* triple staff

Book?

* triple crown

made of flowers (?)

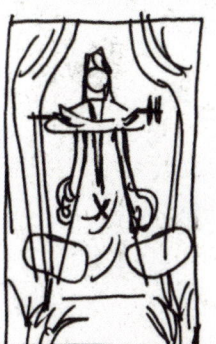

↑ tree table?

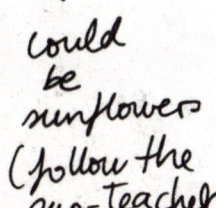

* two students

↓

could be sprouts (?)

↓

could be sunflowers (follow the sun-teacher)

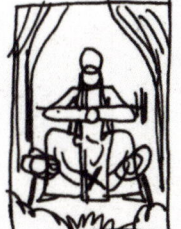

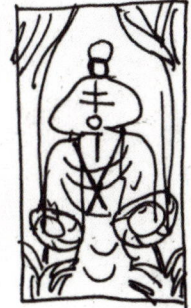

* crossed keys

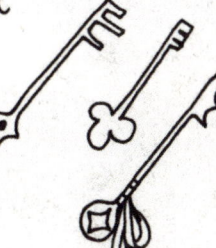

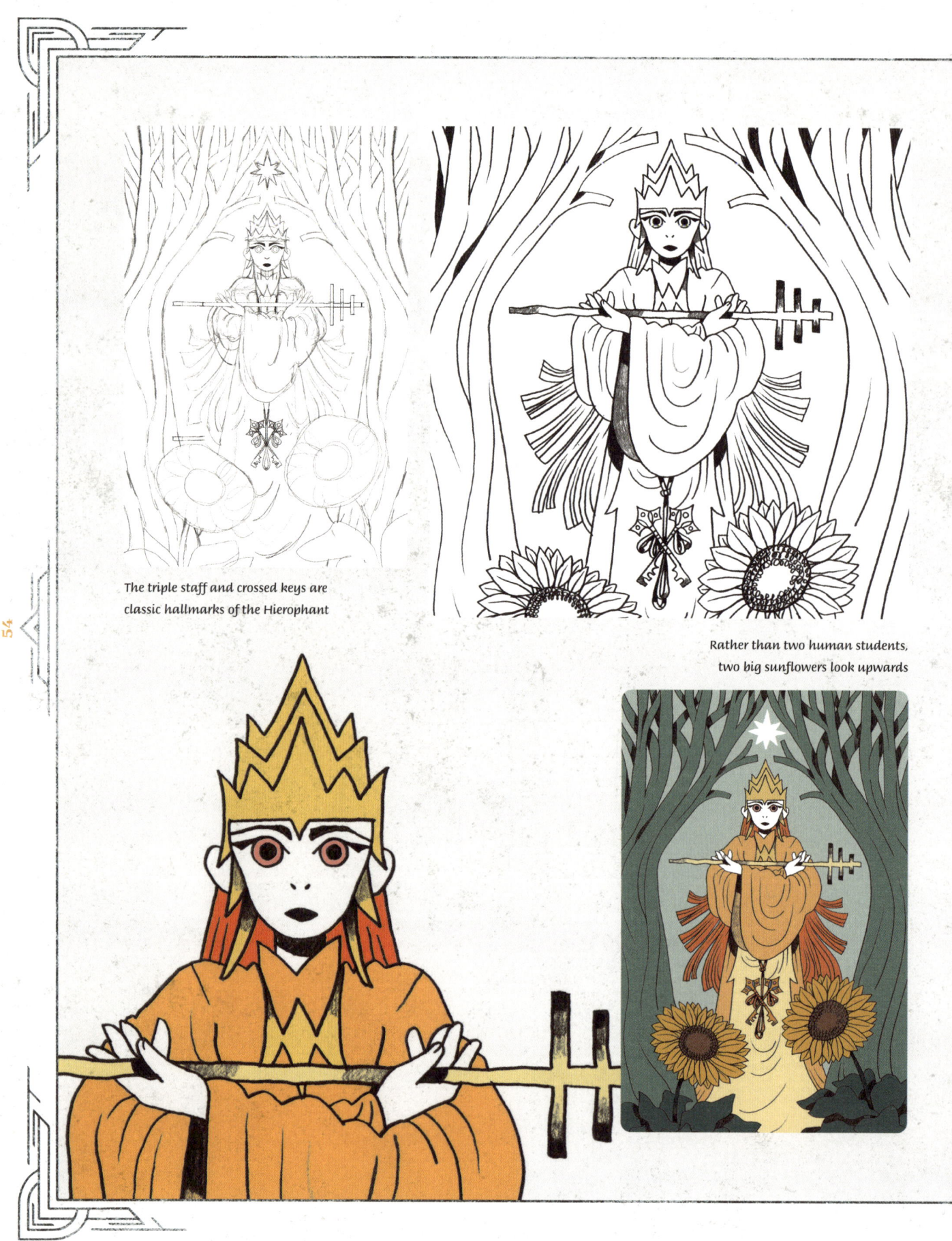

The triple staff and crossed keys are classic hallmarks of the Hierophant

Rather than two human students, two big sunflowers look upwards

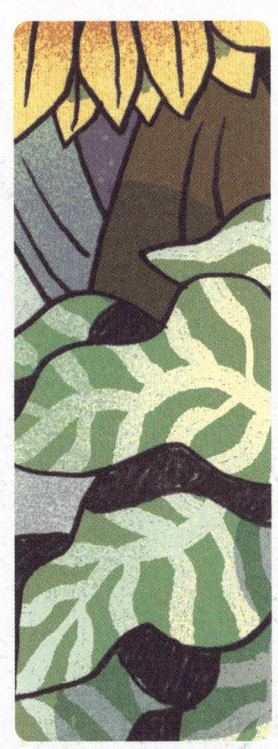

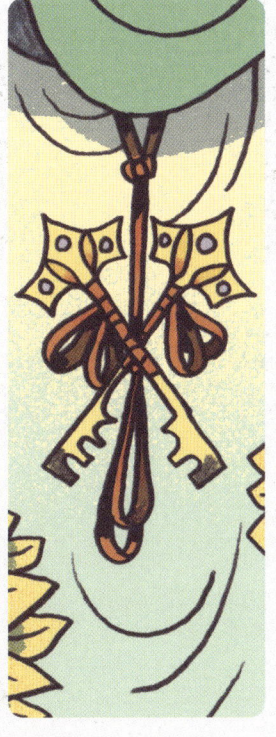

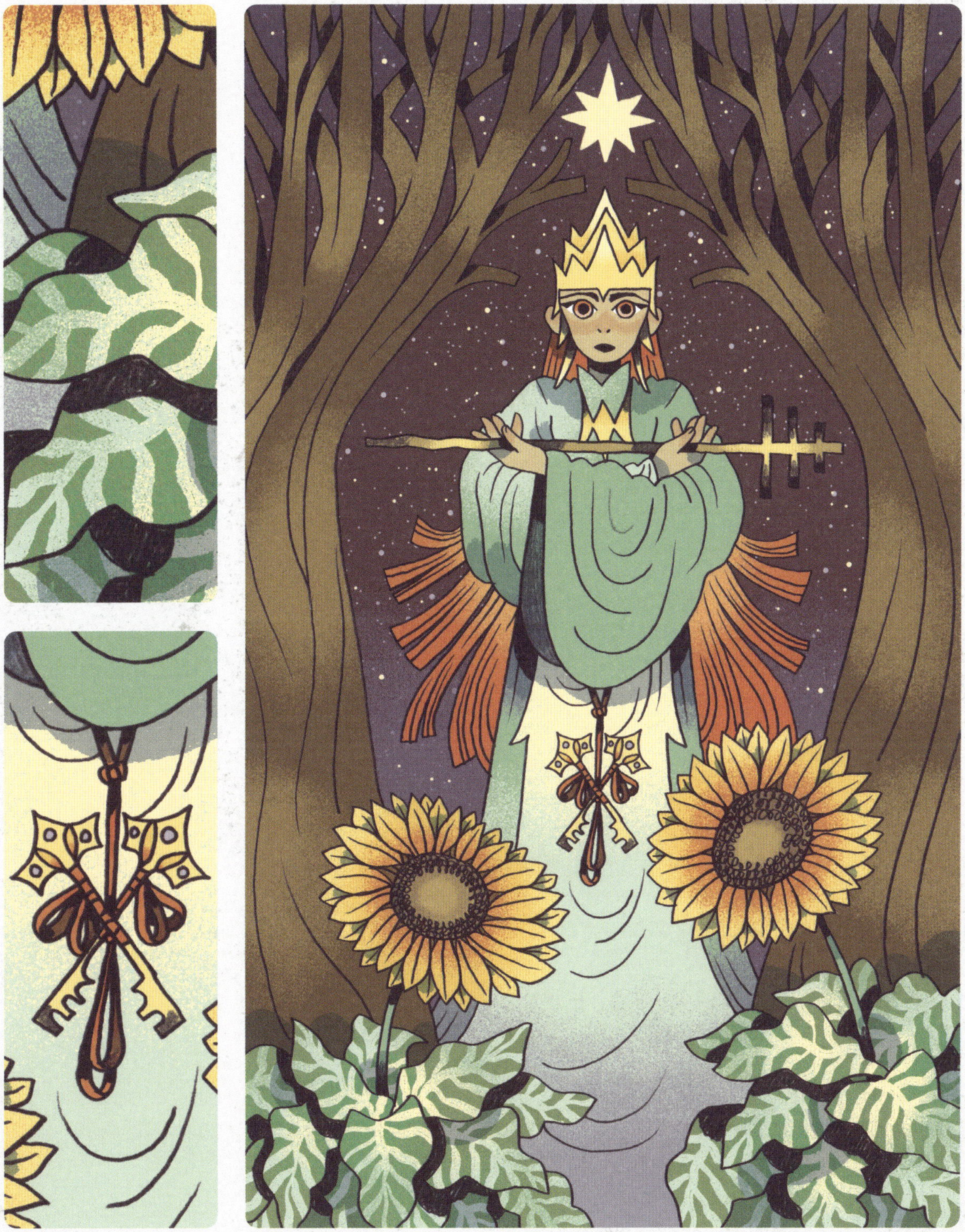

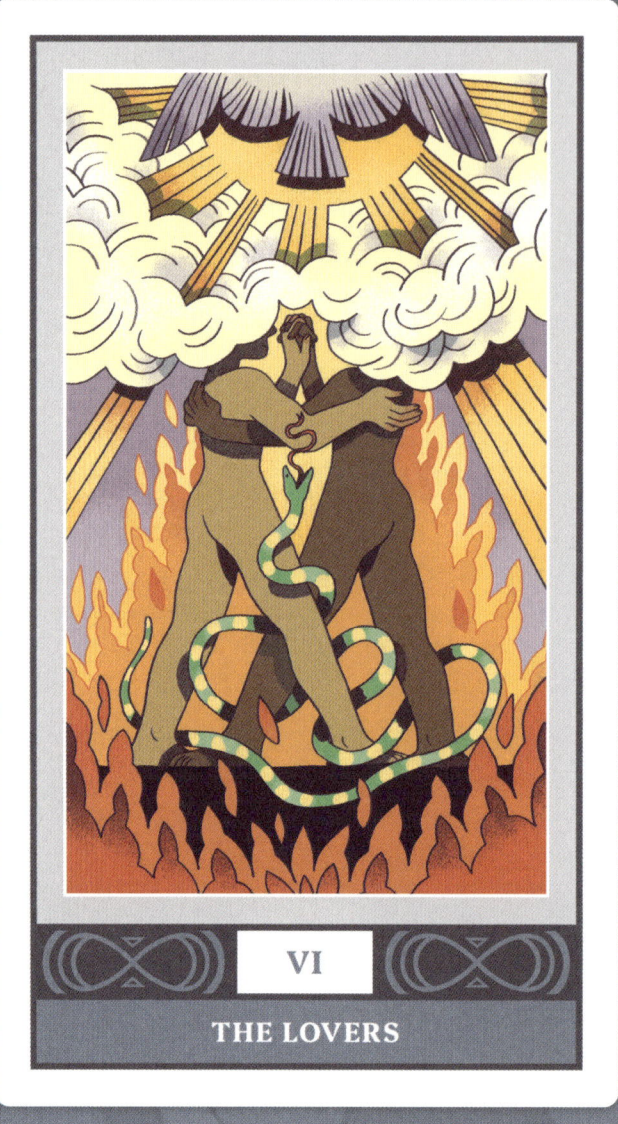

VI

THE LOVERS

THE LOVERS

EROTIC ATTRACTION, CHOICE, ROMANCE

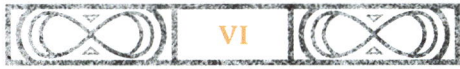

VI

I dramatically change this card from its traditional imagery. I want to move away from the traditional representation of a woman and man, and the temptation of Eve. I draw two figures in a position where we cannot see their sexes. I keep the symbol of the snake as something you should be careful about. I add lots of fire, referring to the heat of erotic attraction and romance. I replace the angel with a bird, which is more neutral, while also referring to the divinity of nature.

abstract
sun (?)

* nudity
* relationship
* divine intervention
* cloud
* sun
* snake
* fire

non catholic symbols (?)

Bird (angel)

show no sex

inclusive

clouds cover their faces

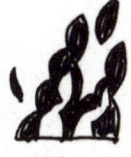
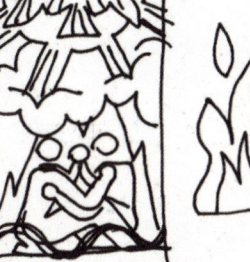
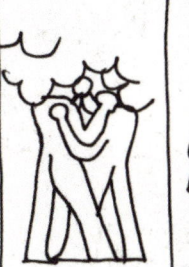

fire background.

more than one snake (?).

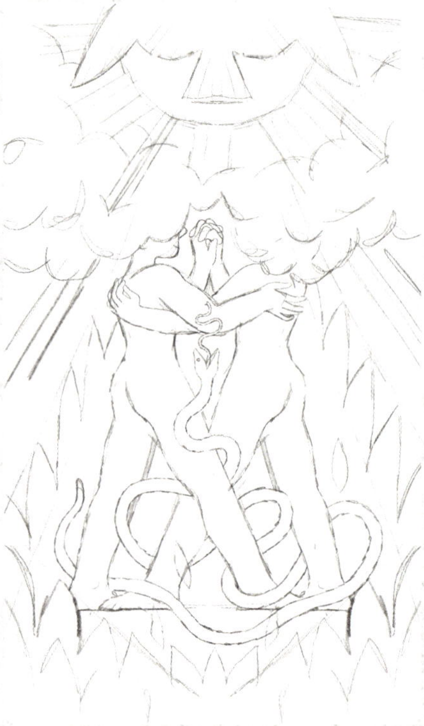

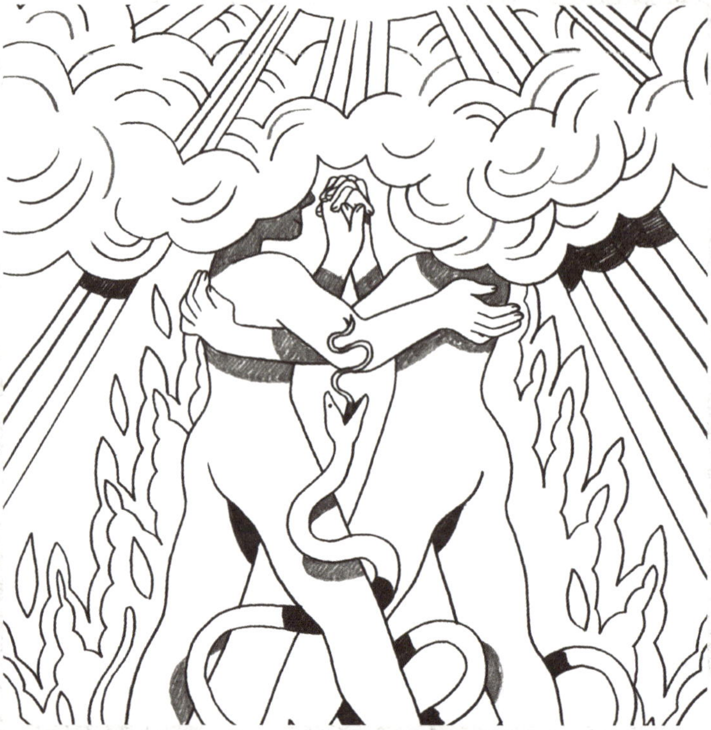

The two somewhat obscured Lovers could be of any gender

The angel and the two figures form a triadic composition that is typical of the Lovers card

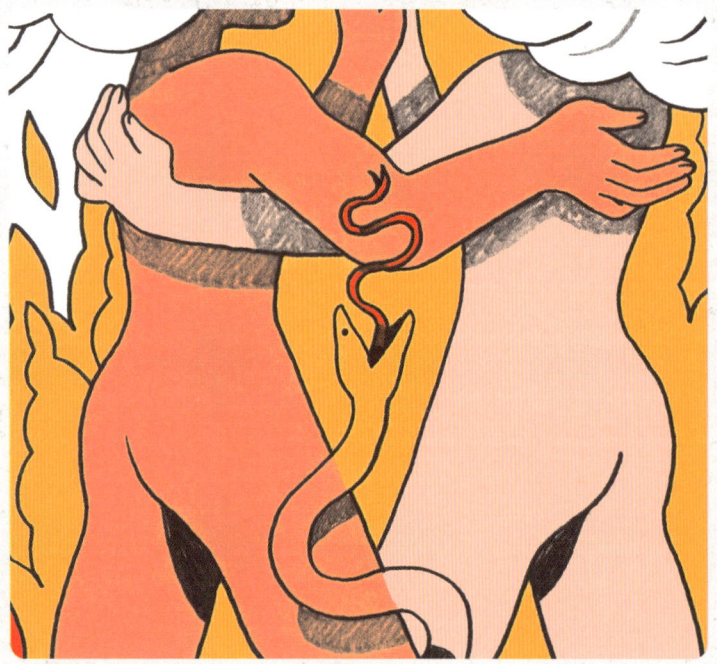

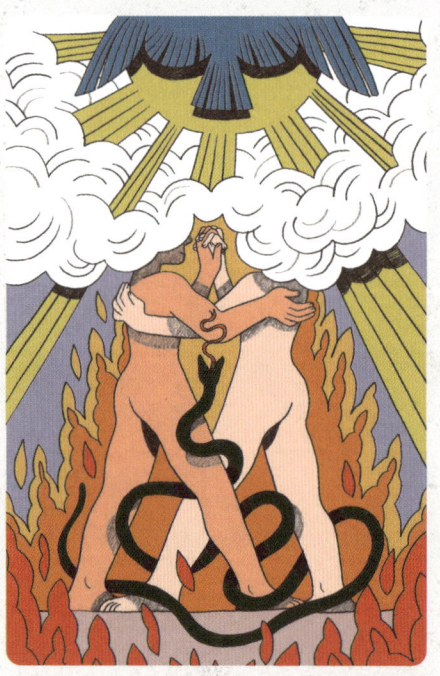

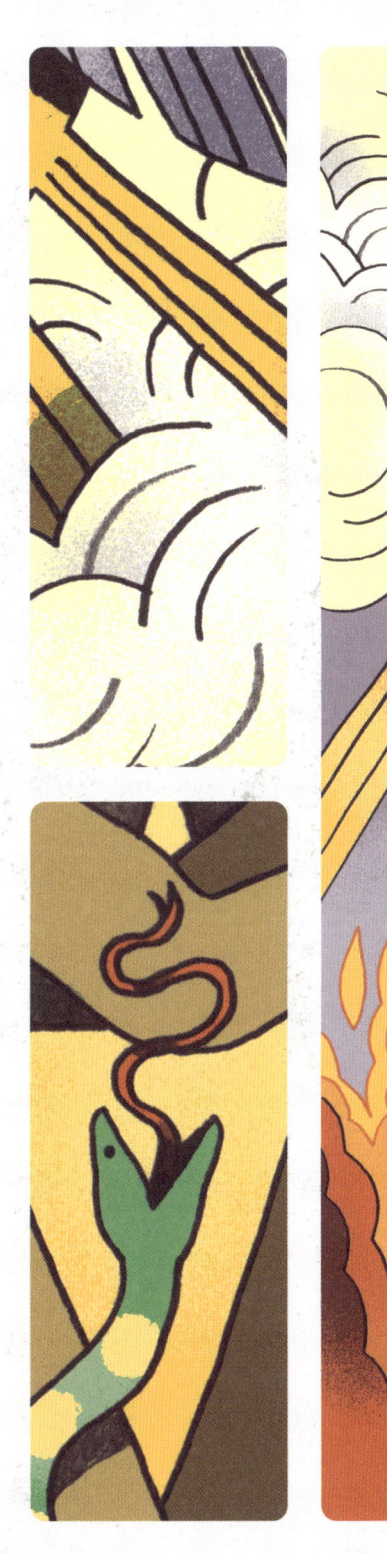

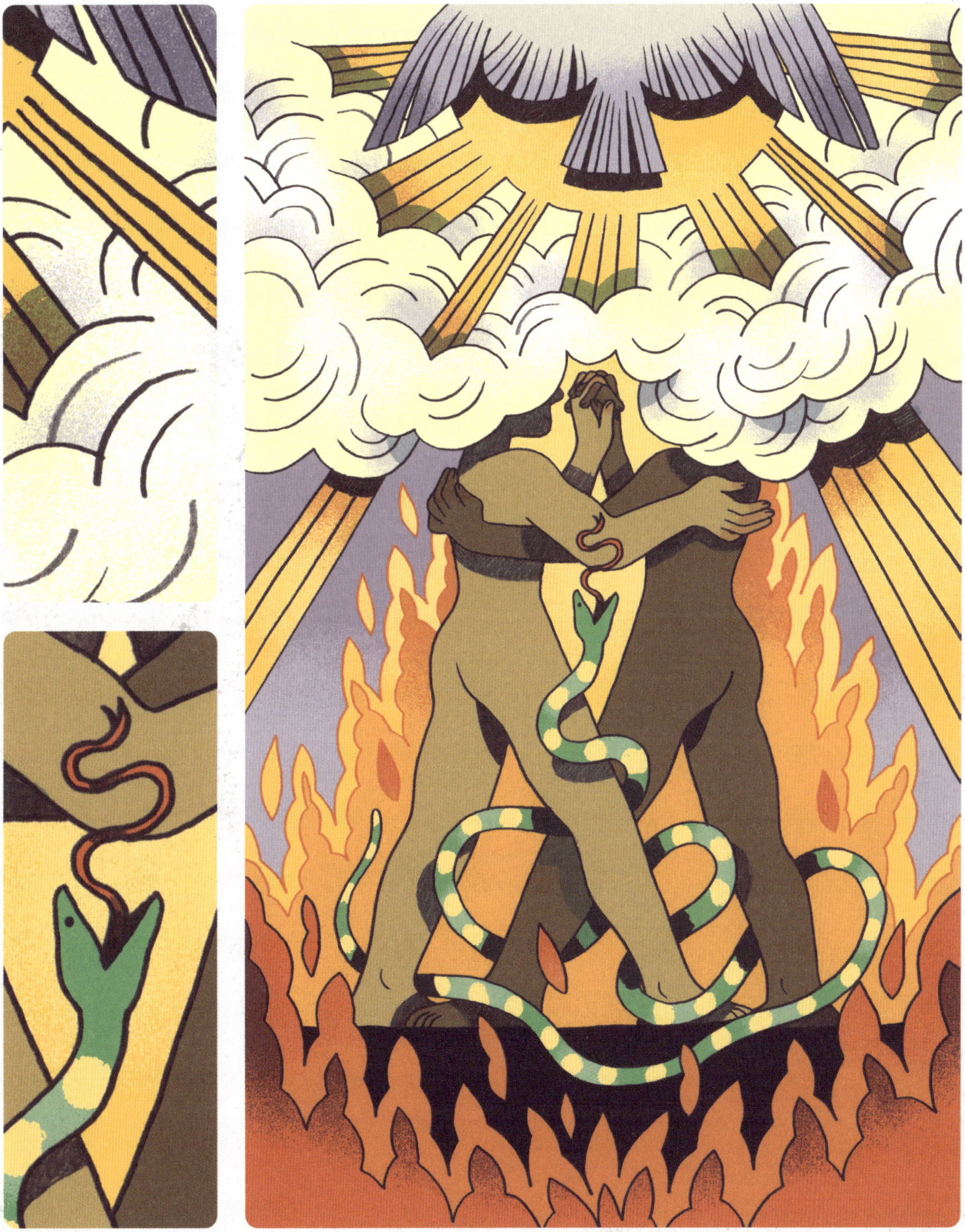

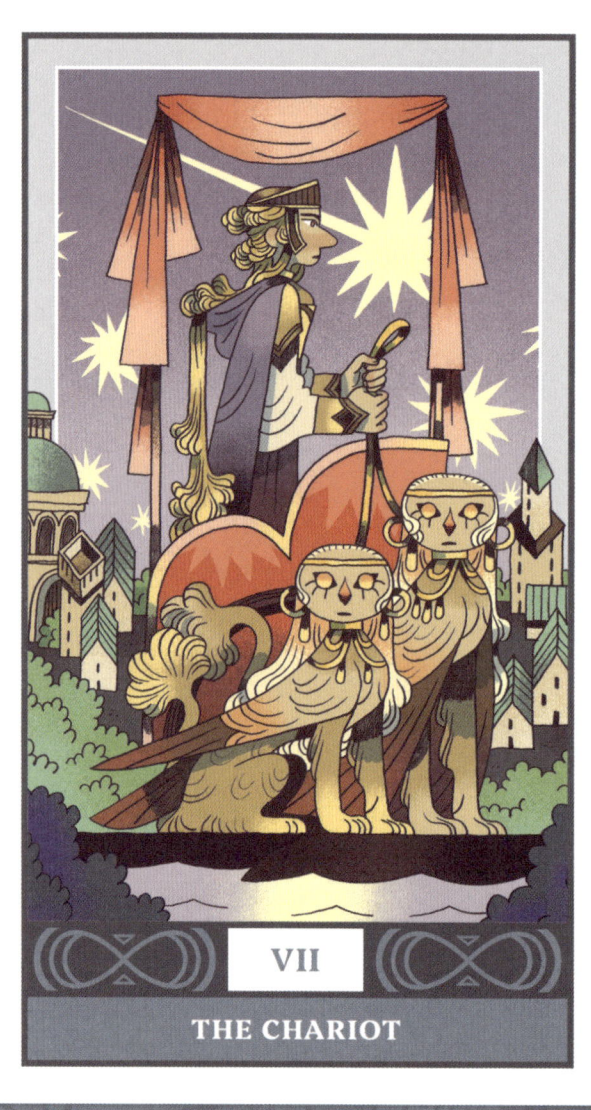

VII

THE CHARIOT

THE CHARIOT

SPEED, MOMENTUM, TRIUMPH

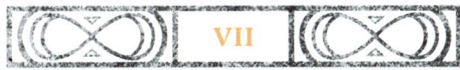

VII

I keep most of the traditional imagery for this card. I make the chariot a bit less heavy than it might normally appear, since the card talks about transport and movement. I review the design of the horses or sphinxes, and create these fantastic beasts that appear to be friendly yet mysterious and powerful. I want the animals to have the feeling of obedience and confidence, and to put the charioteer at the centre of power in this card.

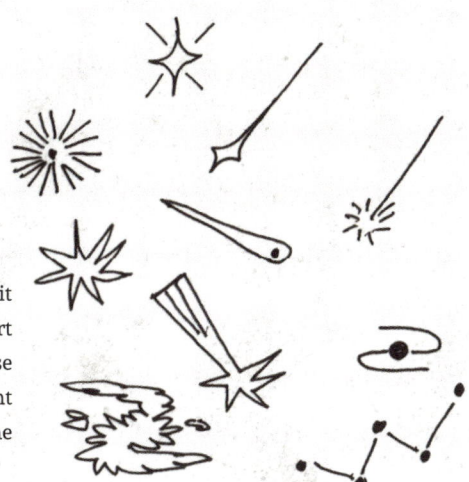

* Chariot (or mode of transport)
* Beyond the city limits
* moon, stars (the universe)

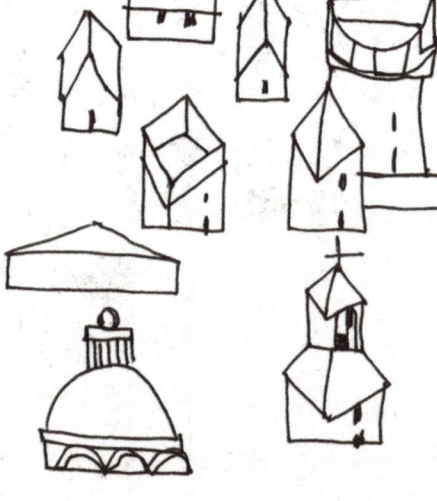

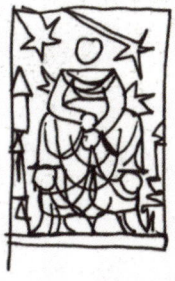

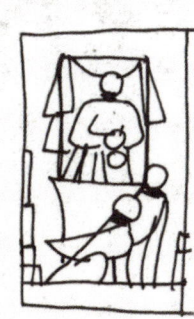

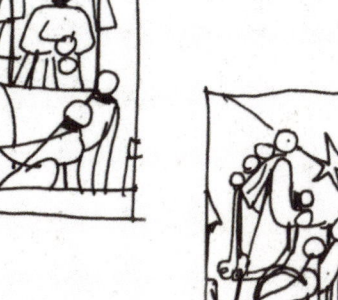

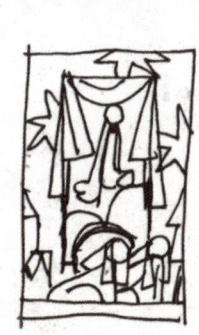

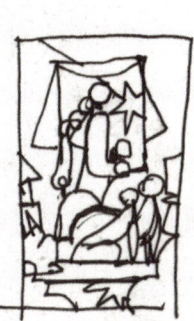

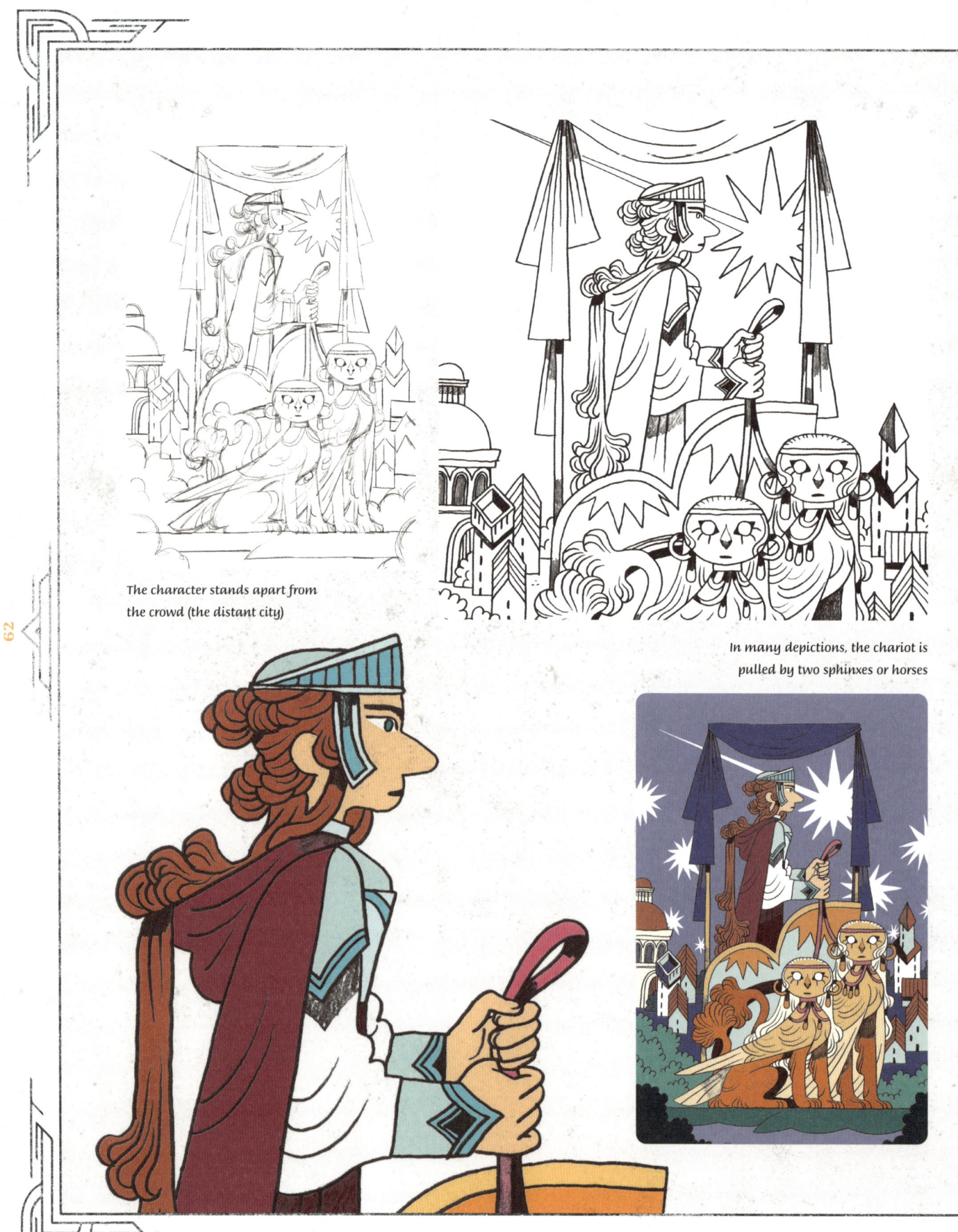

The character stands apart from
the crowd (the distant city)

In many depictions, the chariot is
pulled by two sphinxes or horses

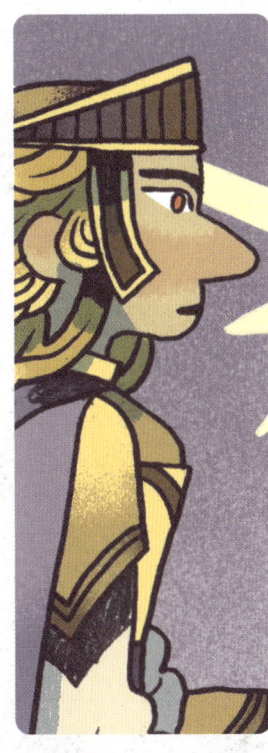

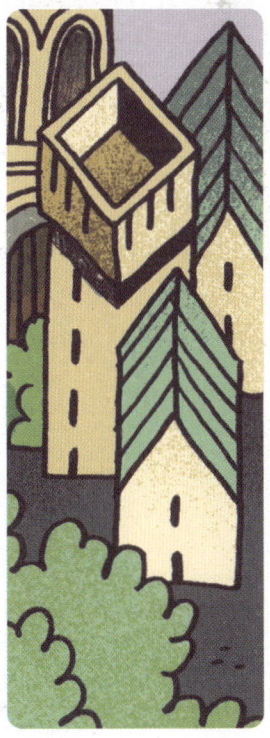

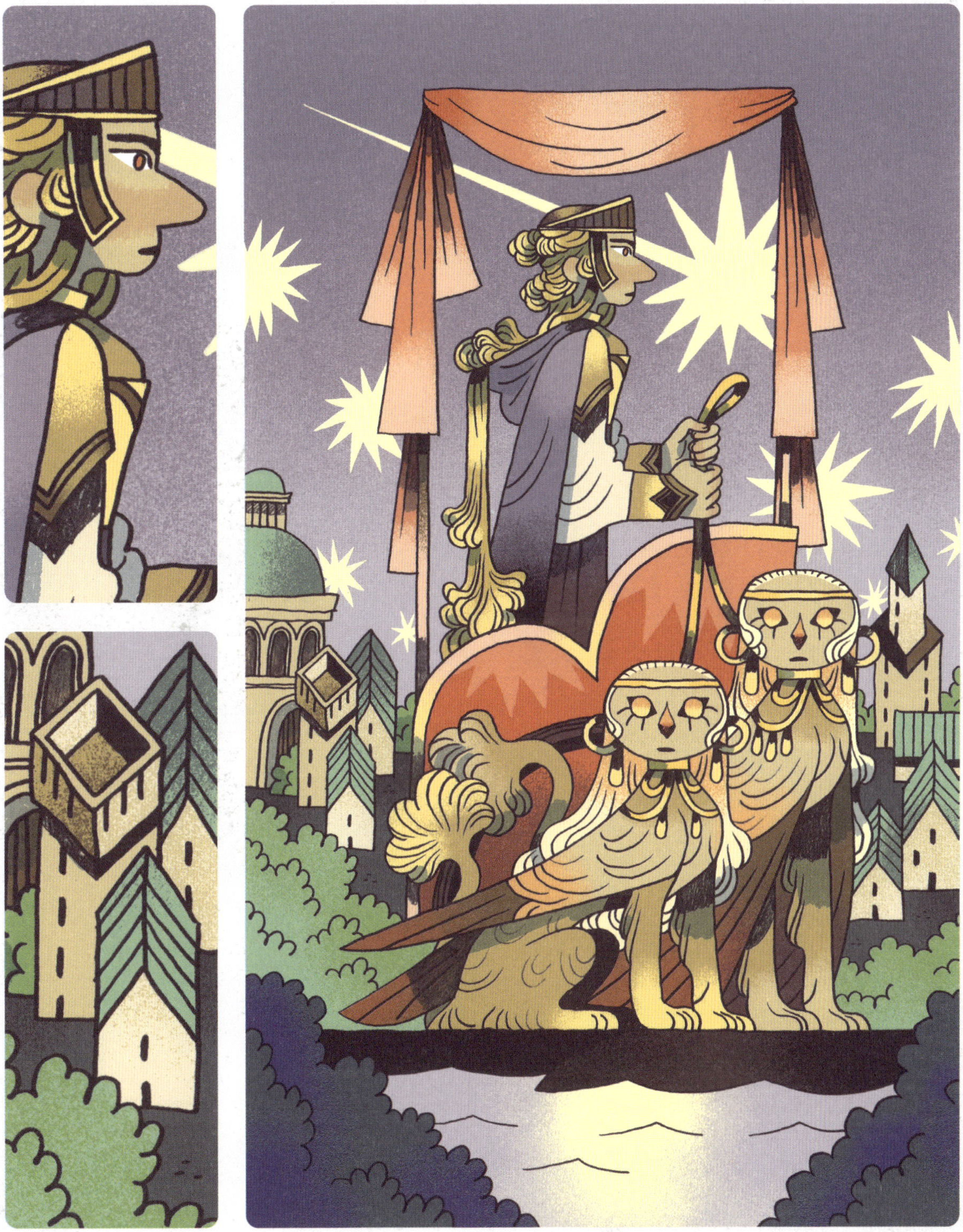

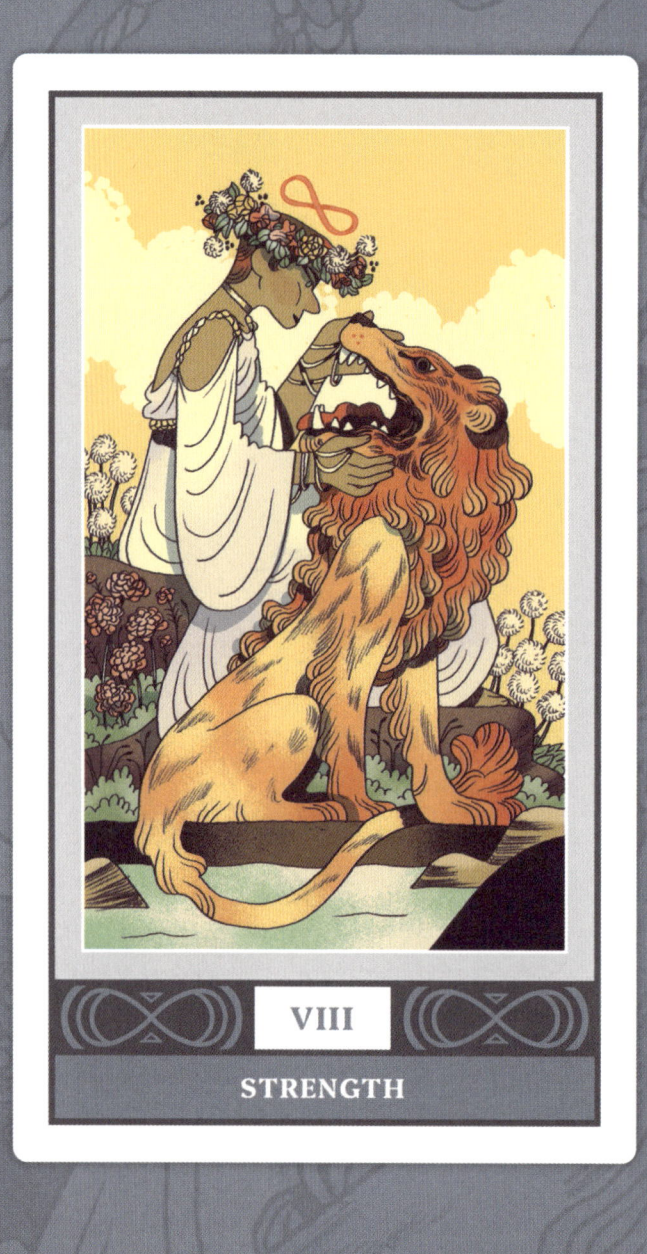

VIII

STRENGTH

STRENGTH

GENTLE FORCE, VALIANT
WINNER, CONTROL OF SELF

 VIII

I want this design to feel a bit gentler than the traditional card. The card talks about force and control of the self, so I decide to draw a calm scene. The figure is relaxed, surrounded by nature, and she is kind to the lion. The flowers have a dual meaning, referring both to the strength of nature and to its infinite energy.

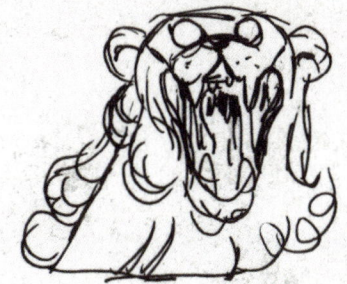

* strong figure
* lion
* lemniscate ∞
* opening lion's mouth

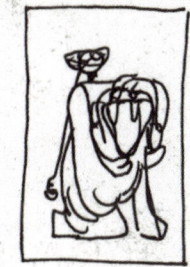
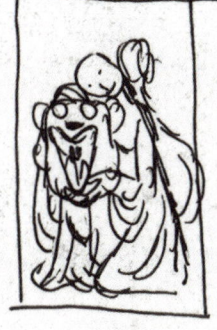

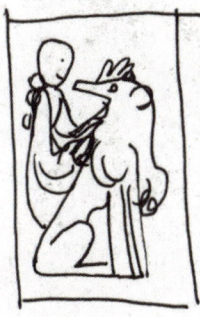
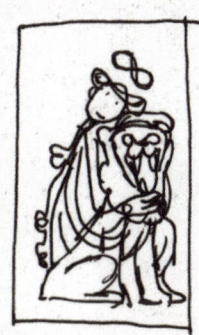
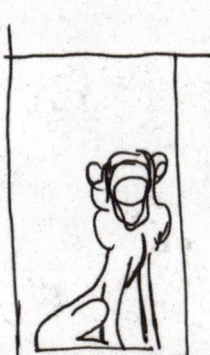
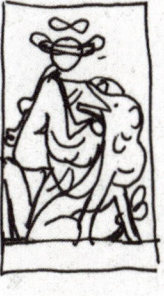

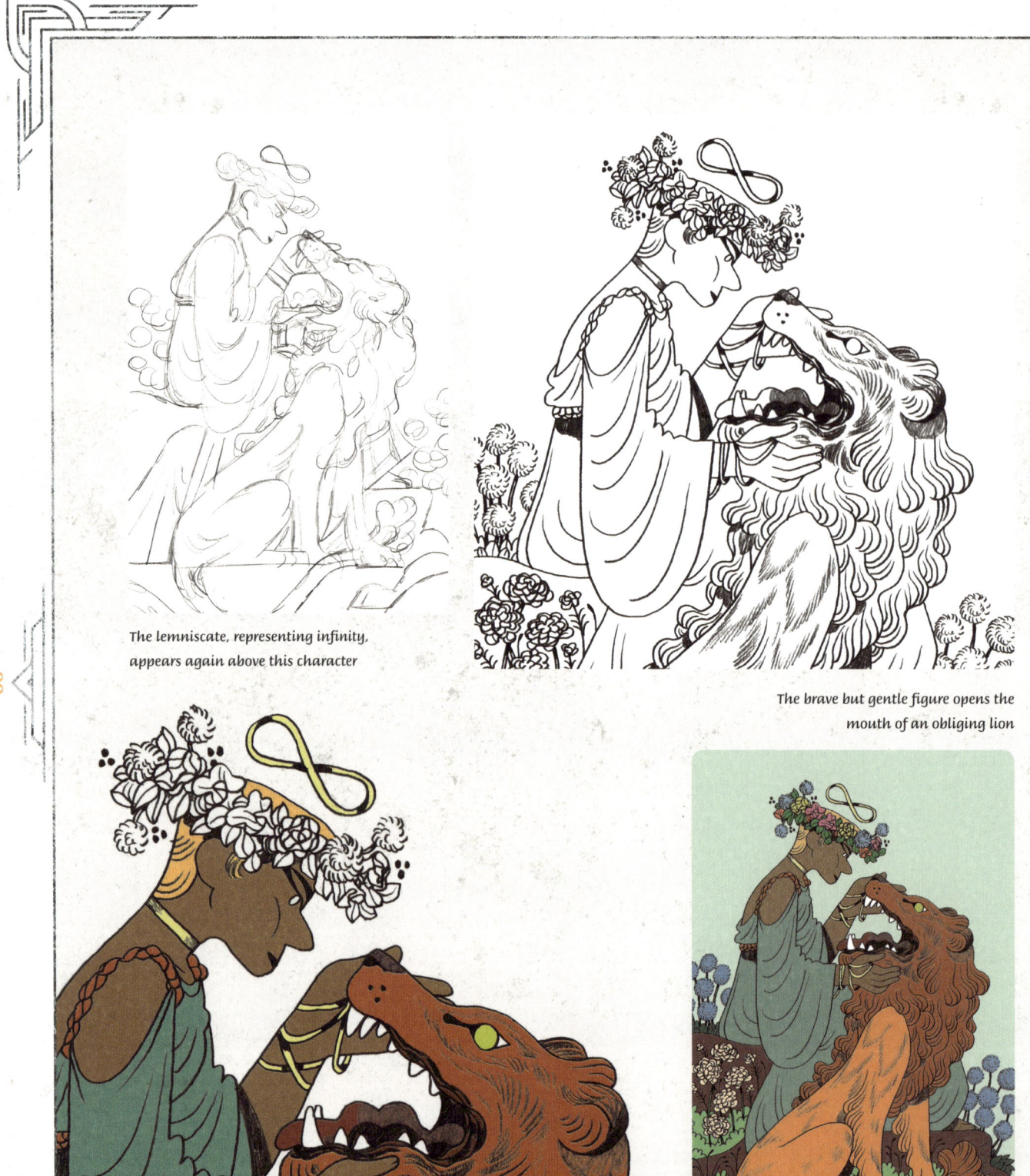

The lemniscate, representing infinity,
appears again above this character

The brave but gentle figure opens the
mouth of an obliging lion

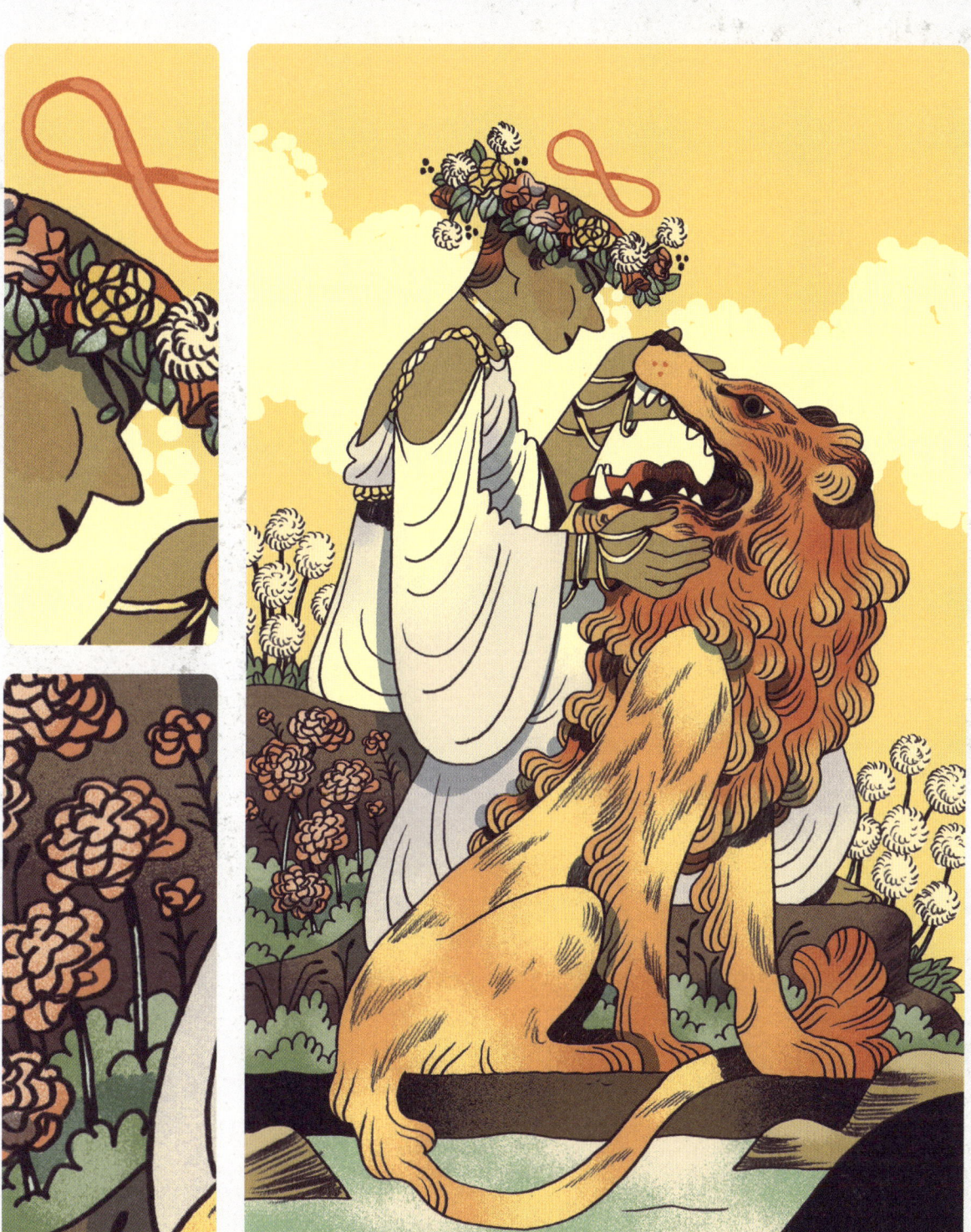

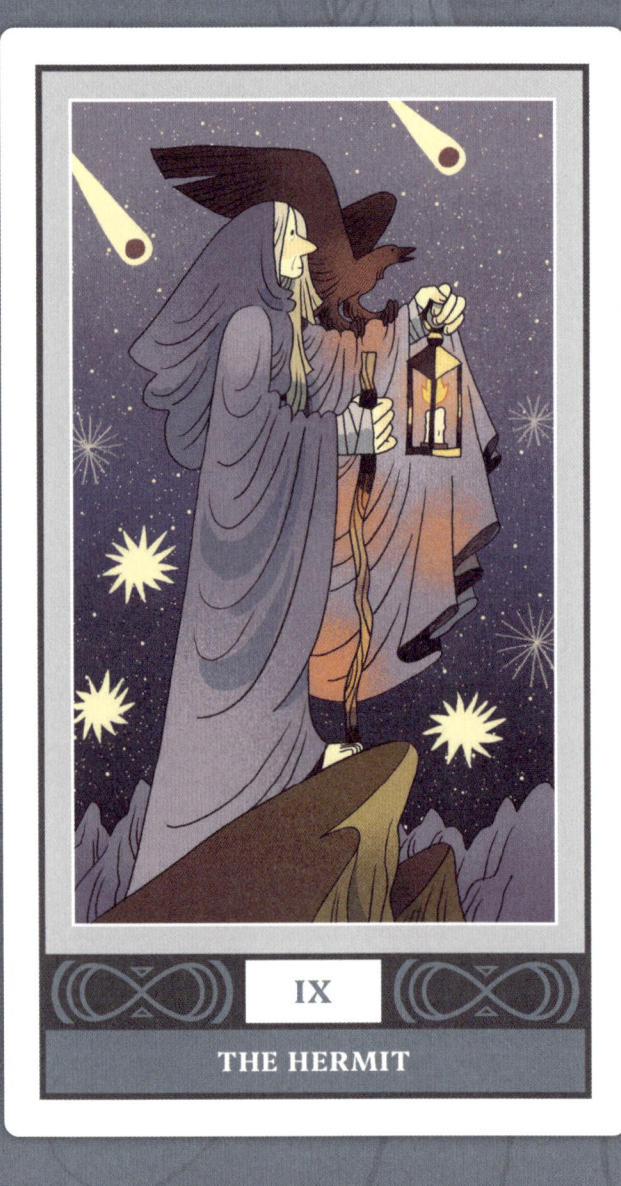

IX

THE HERMIT

THE HERMIT

SOLITUDE, REMOVAL, PHILOSOPHER

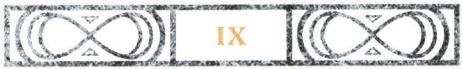

IX

I would like to break away from the stereotype of the 'wise man' for this card, so we can't really tell if this character is a woman or a man. I also add a crow, one of the most common symbols for wisdom. Since this card talks about solitude, thoughts, and guidance, I think it would also be useful for the character to have a faithful bird companion to rely on and ask for help.

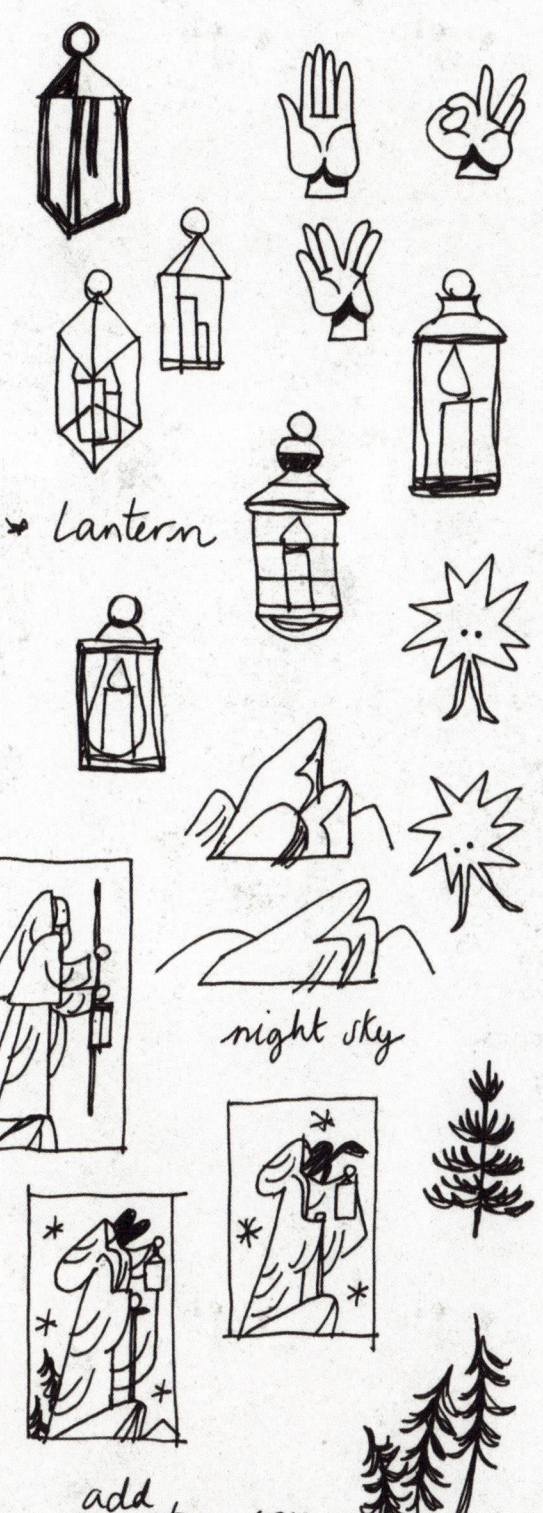

Lantern

* cloak - hood

* staff
* mountaintop
* grey hair

wisdom > raven too (?)

night sky

Raven

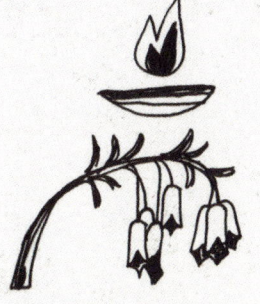

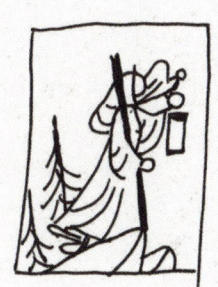

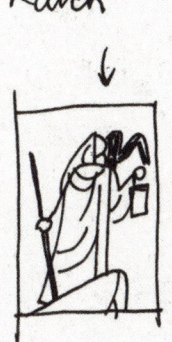

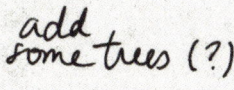

add some trees (?)

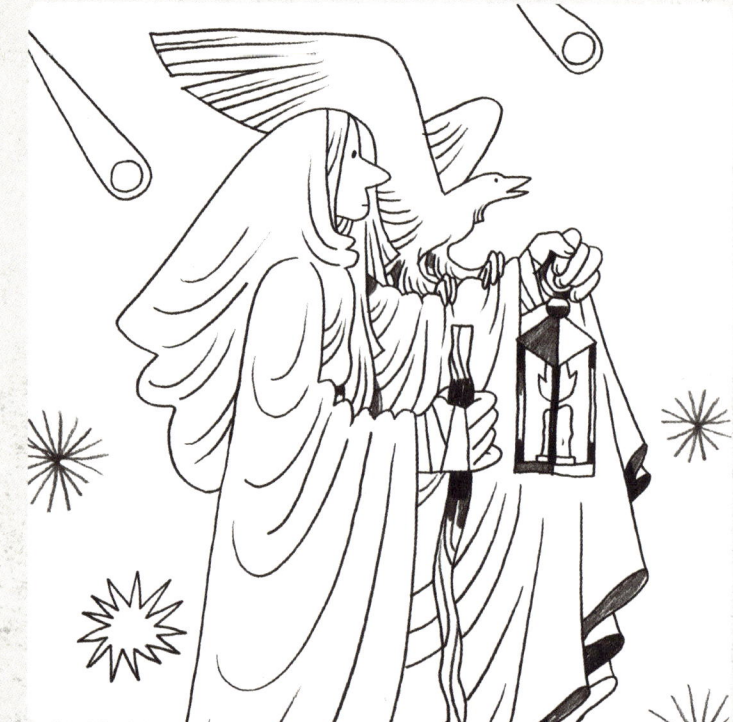

Like in classic tarot imagery, my Hermit stands isolated on a high mountain

The wise Hermit's lantern shines a guiding light in the darkness

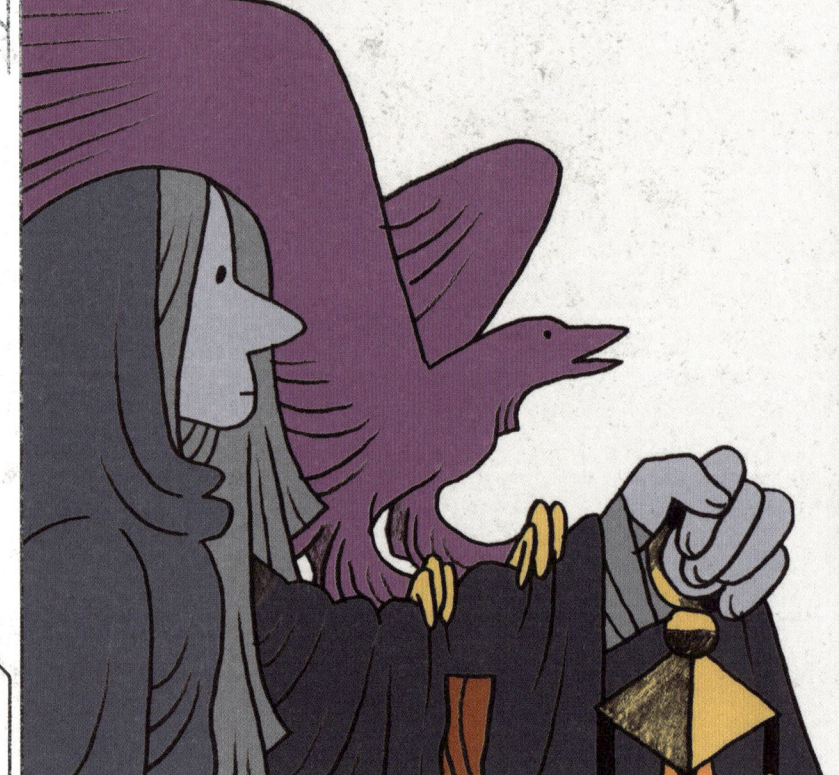

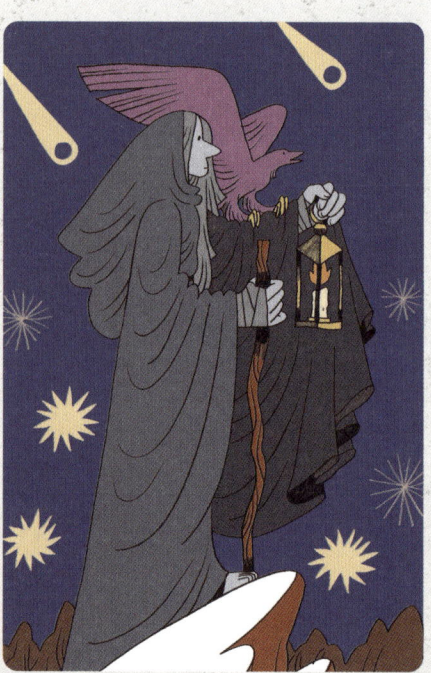

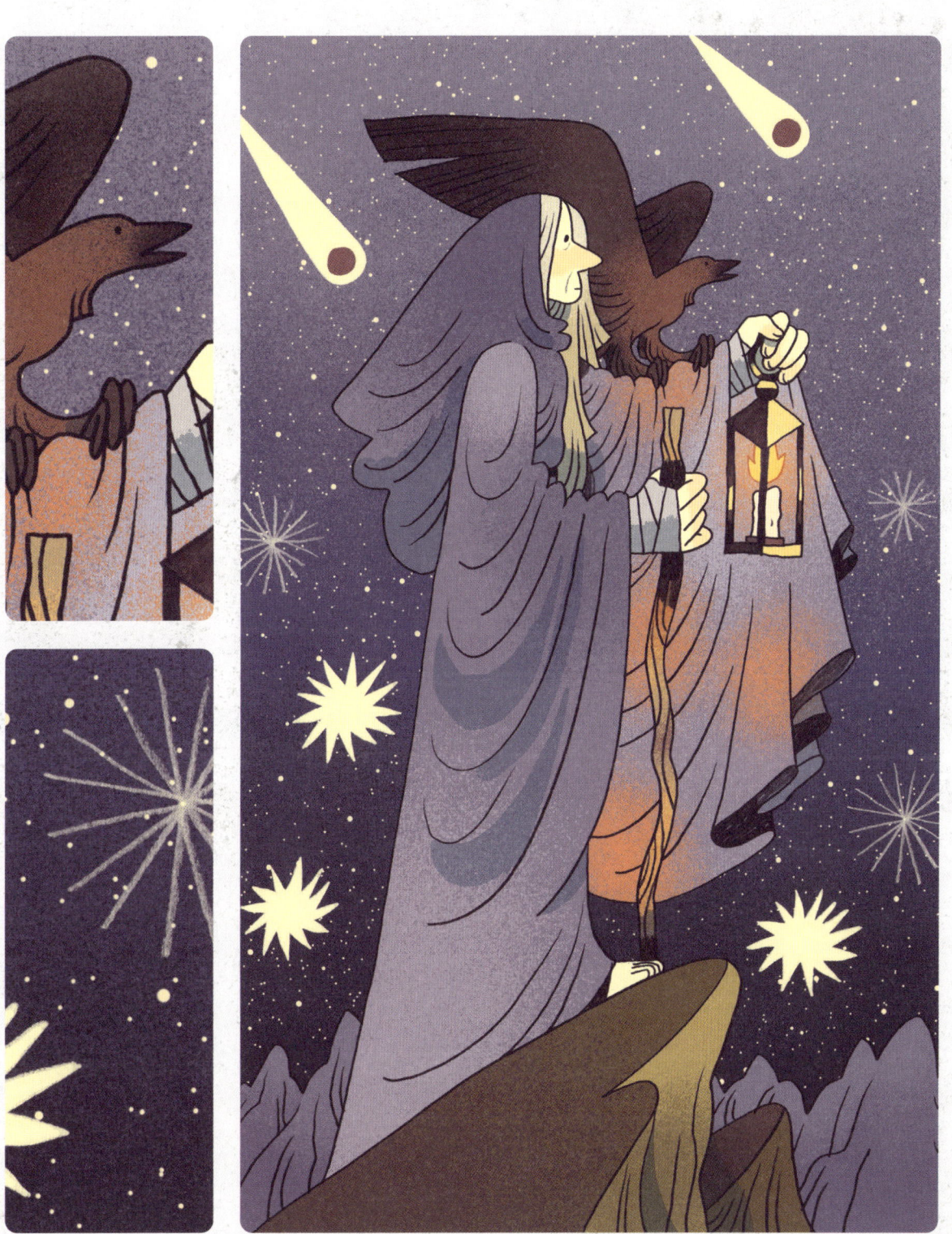

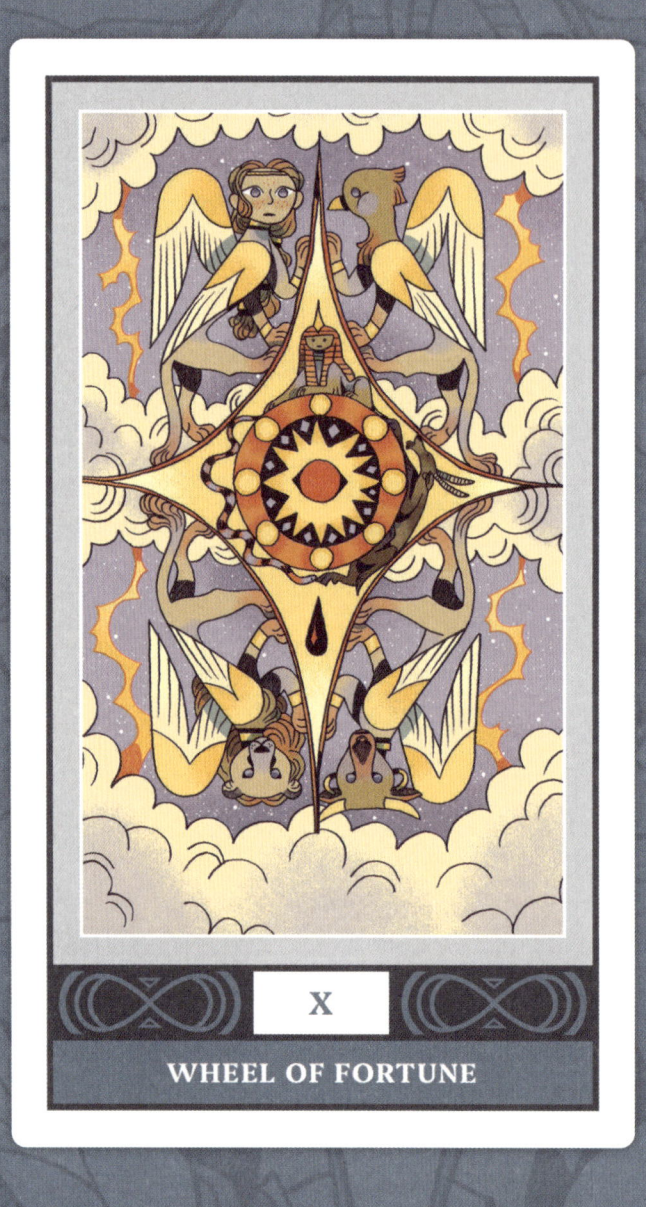

X

WHEEL OF FORTUNE

WHEEL OF FORTUNE

CHANGE, FORTUNE, DESTINY, REVOLUTION

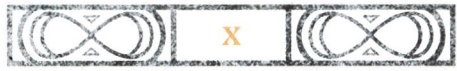

X

I keep almost all the traditional imagery with this card. I really enjoy the classic Rider–Waite–Smith composition with the four corner creatures, so I make my own version here. The lightning signifies power, change, electricity, and movement. I also add an eye at the centre of the card to point to the idea of the visible and invisible worlds.

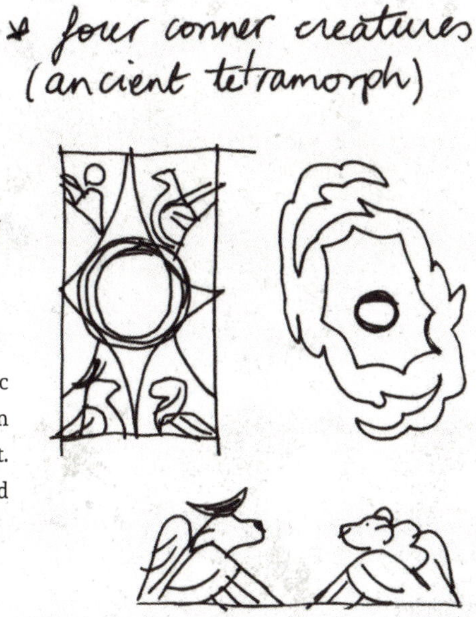

✳ four corner creatures
(ancient tetramorph)

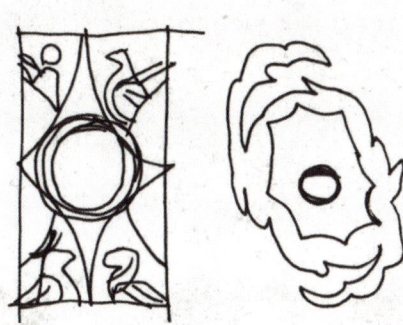

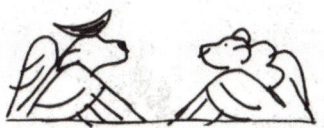

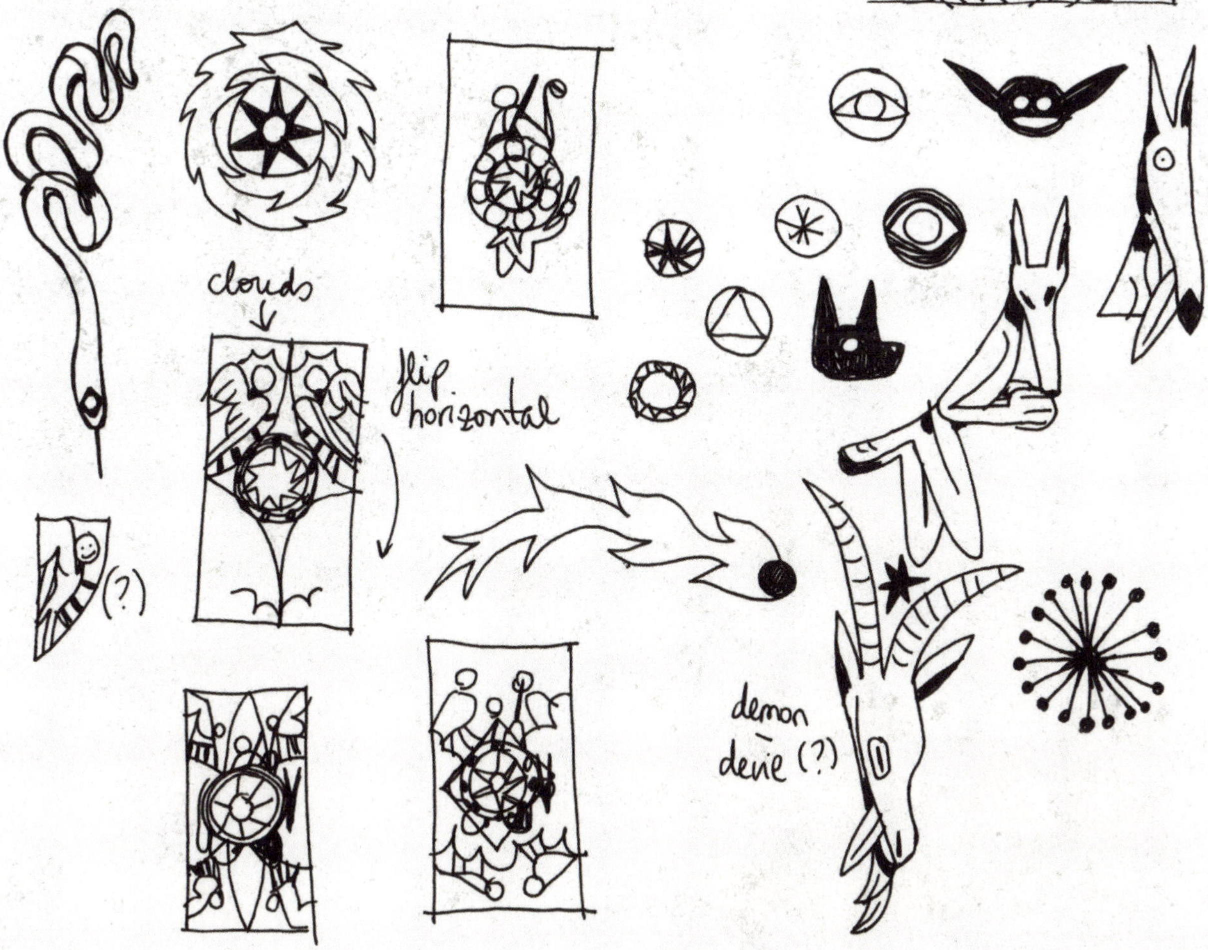

clouds

flip
horizontal

(?)

demon
deve (?)

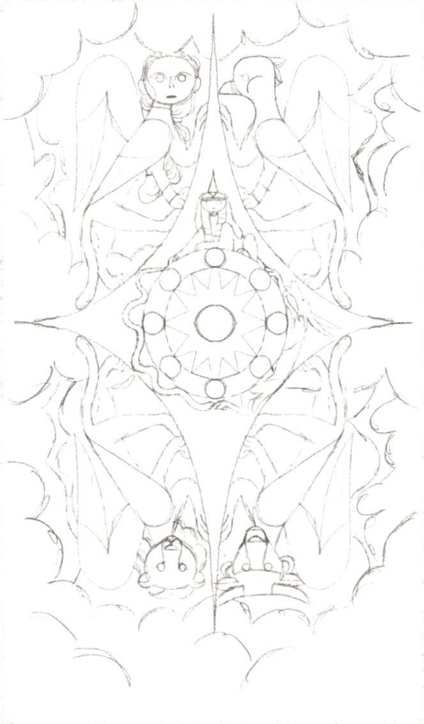

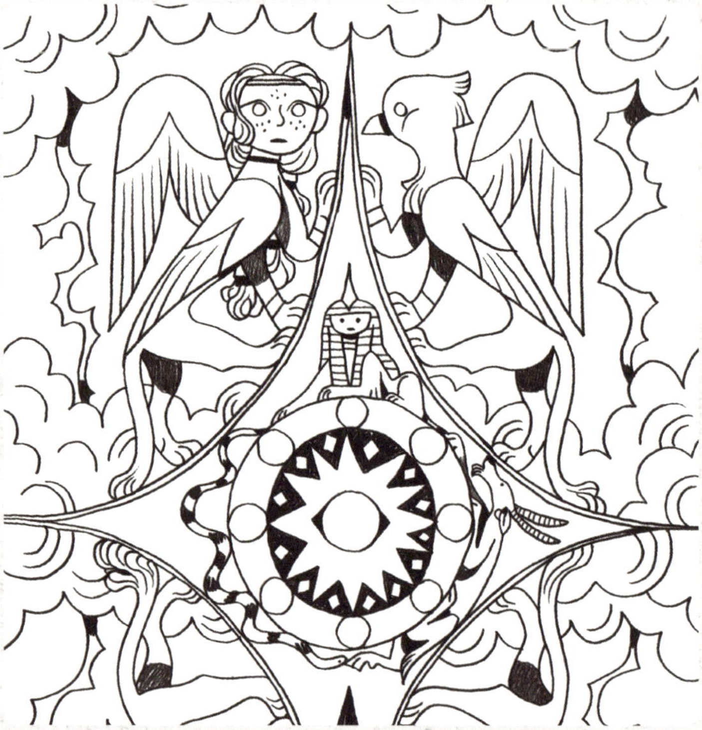

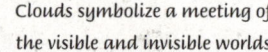

The sphinx, snake, and winged guardians
draw upon classic Wheel of Fortune imagery

Clouds symbolize a meeting of
the visible and invisible worlds

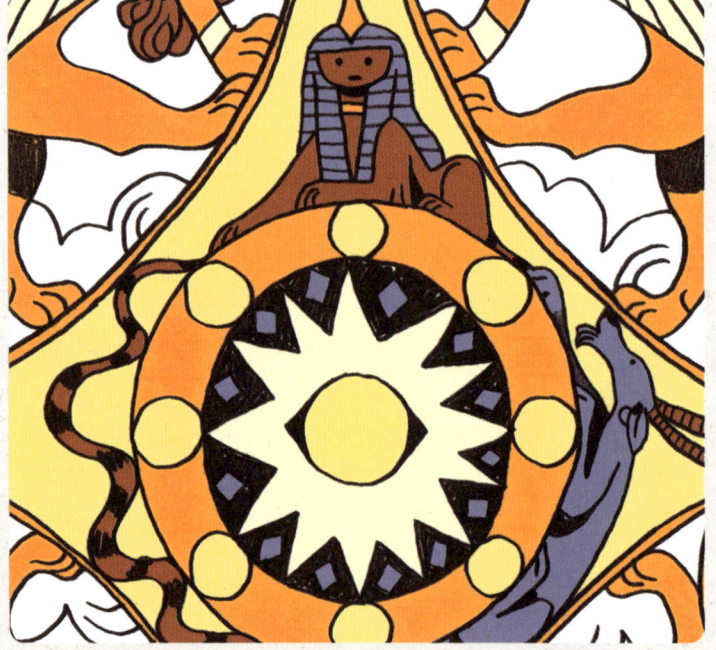

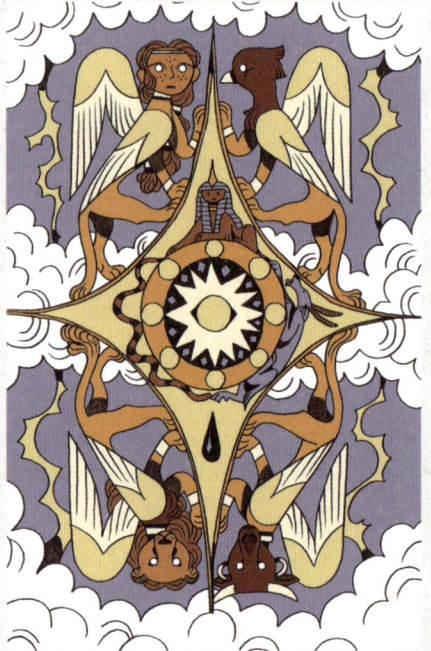

74

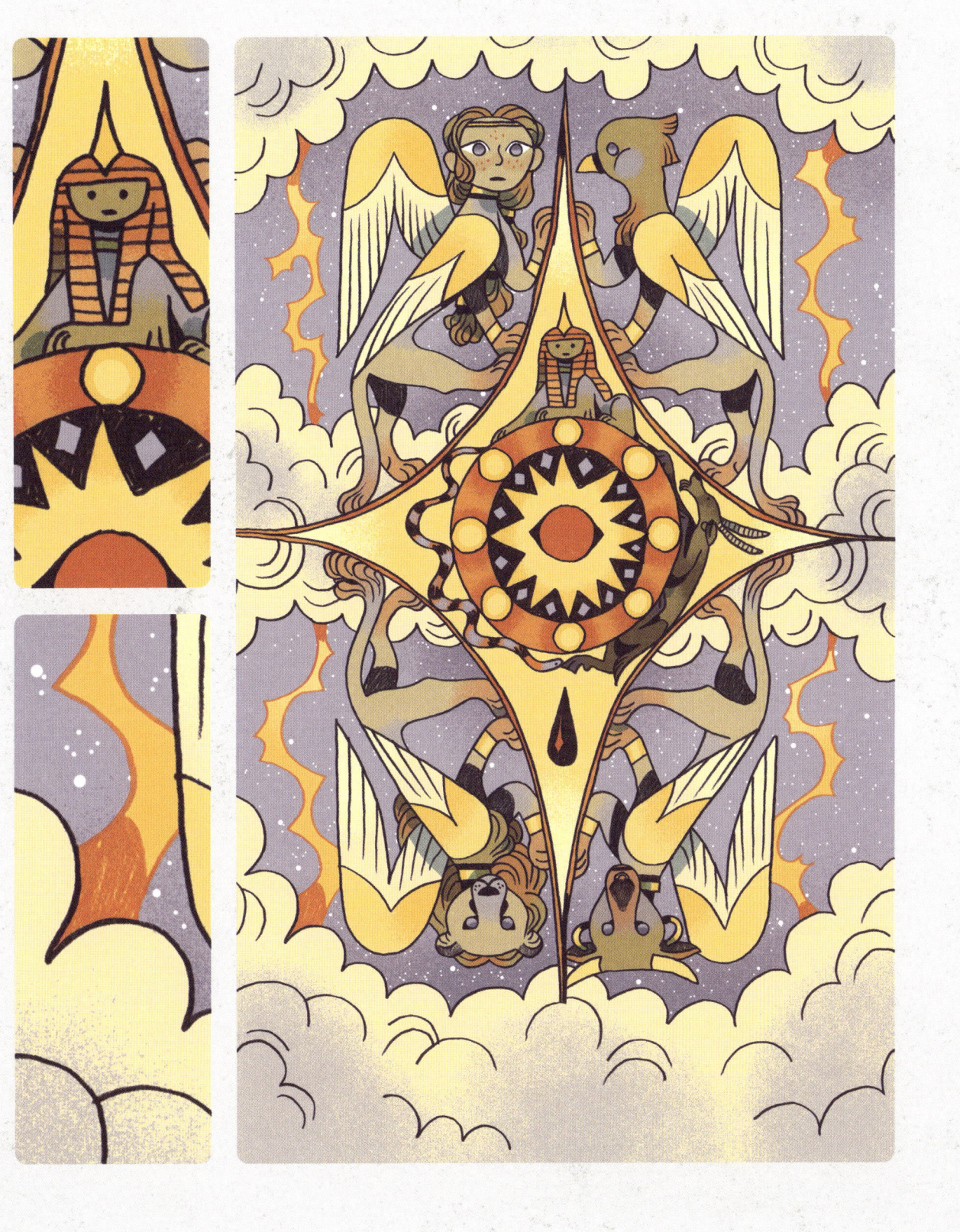

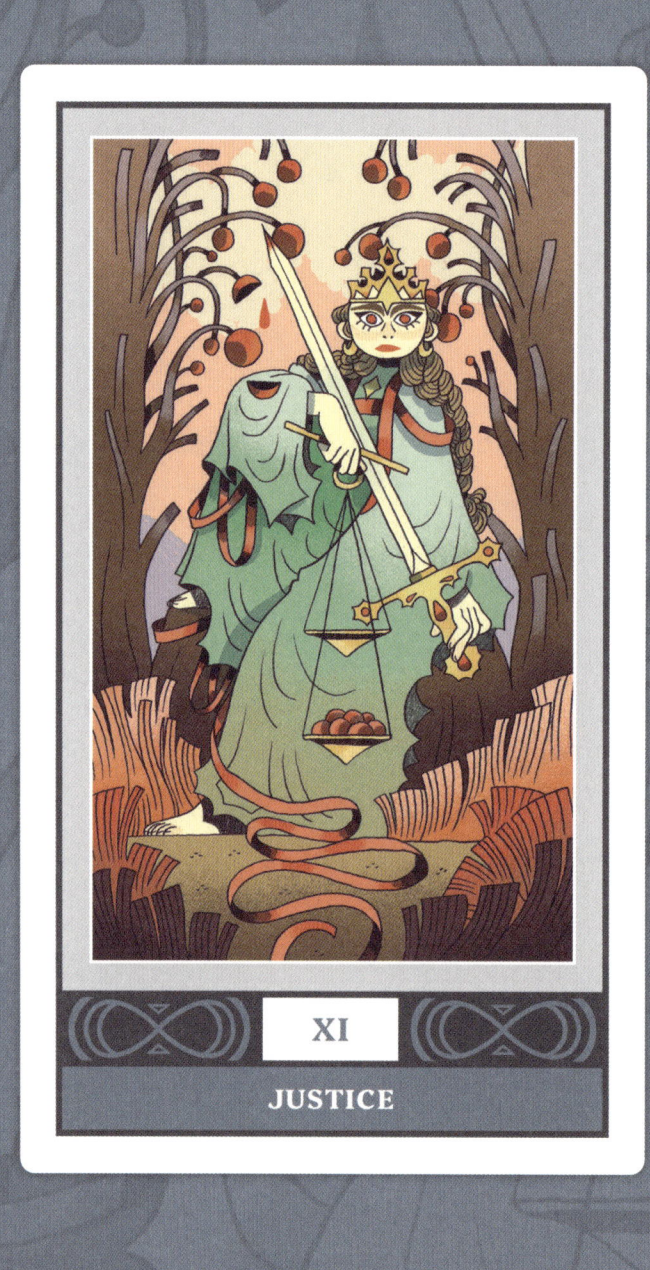

XI

JUSTICE

JUSTICE

KARMA, DECISIONS, LEGAL

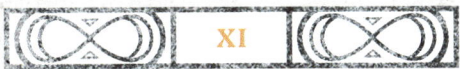

I decide to make this card a little more unconventional. I keep the central figure but replace the two pillars with two trees, as I just love the idea of having Justice among trees. I draw her totally determined but also reflective. Her sword cuts a nearby fruit in half, referring to her power and sovereignty. At the same time, she's holding weighing scales laden with fruit.

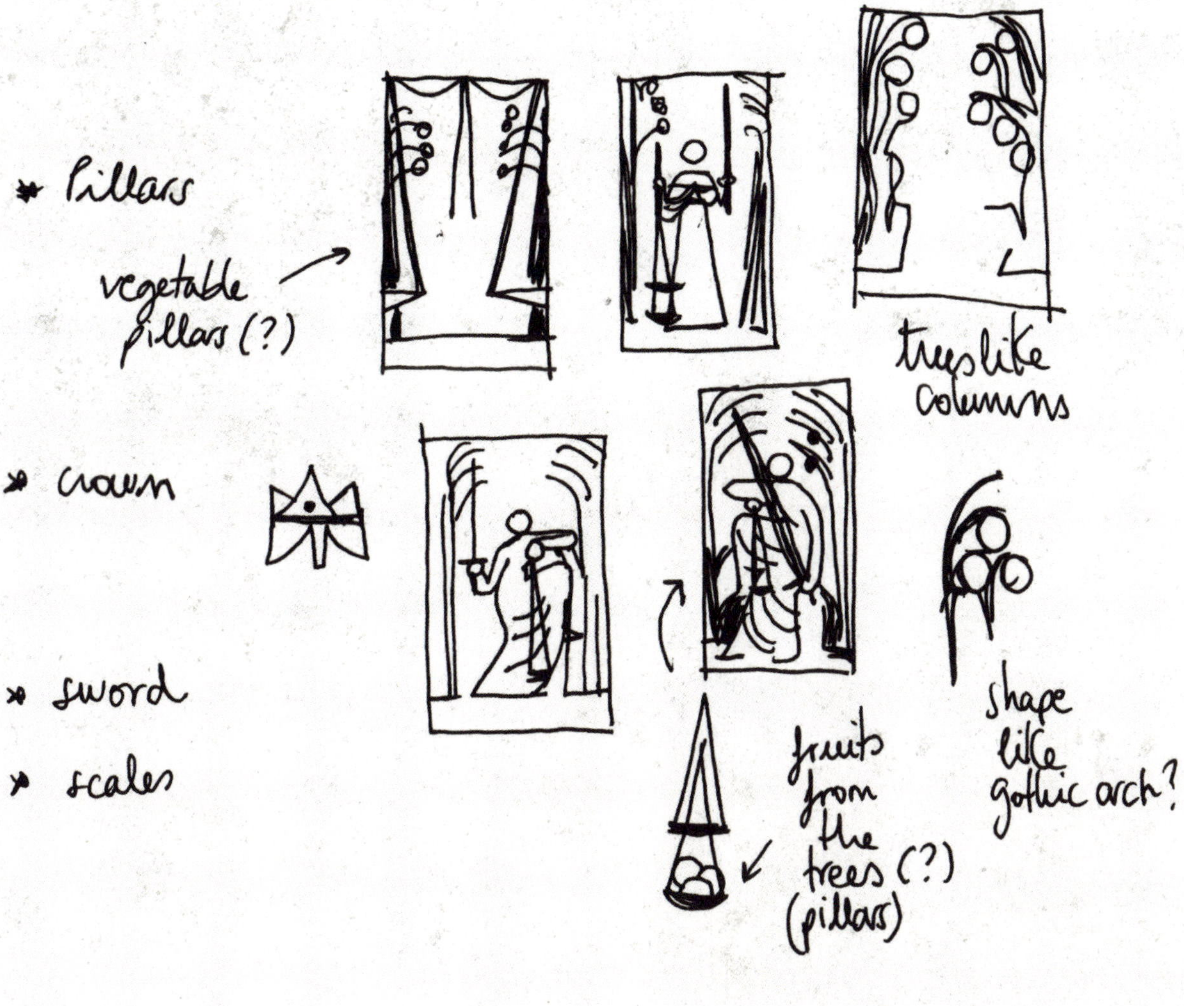

* Pillars

vegetable pillars (?)

* crown

* sword

* scales

trees like columns

fruits from the trees (?) (pillars)

shape like gothic arch?

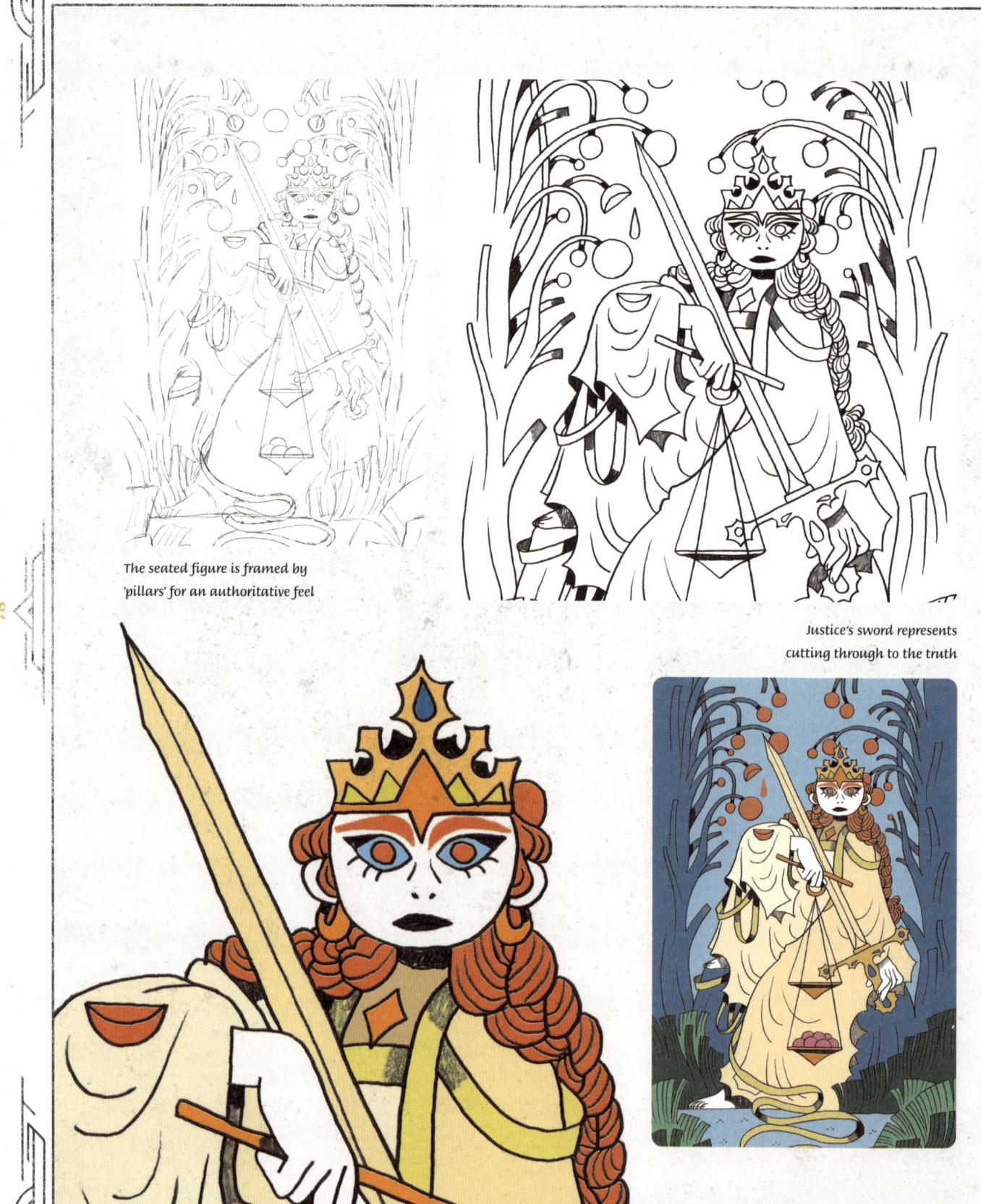

The seated figure is framed by
'pillars' for an authoritative feel

Justice's sword represents
cutting through to the truth

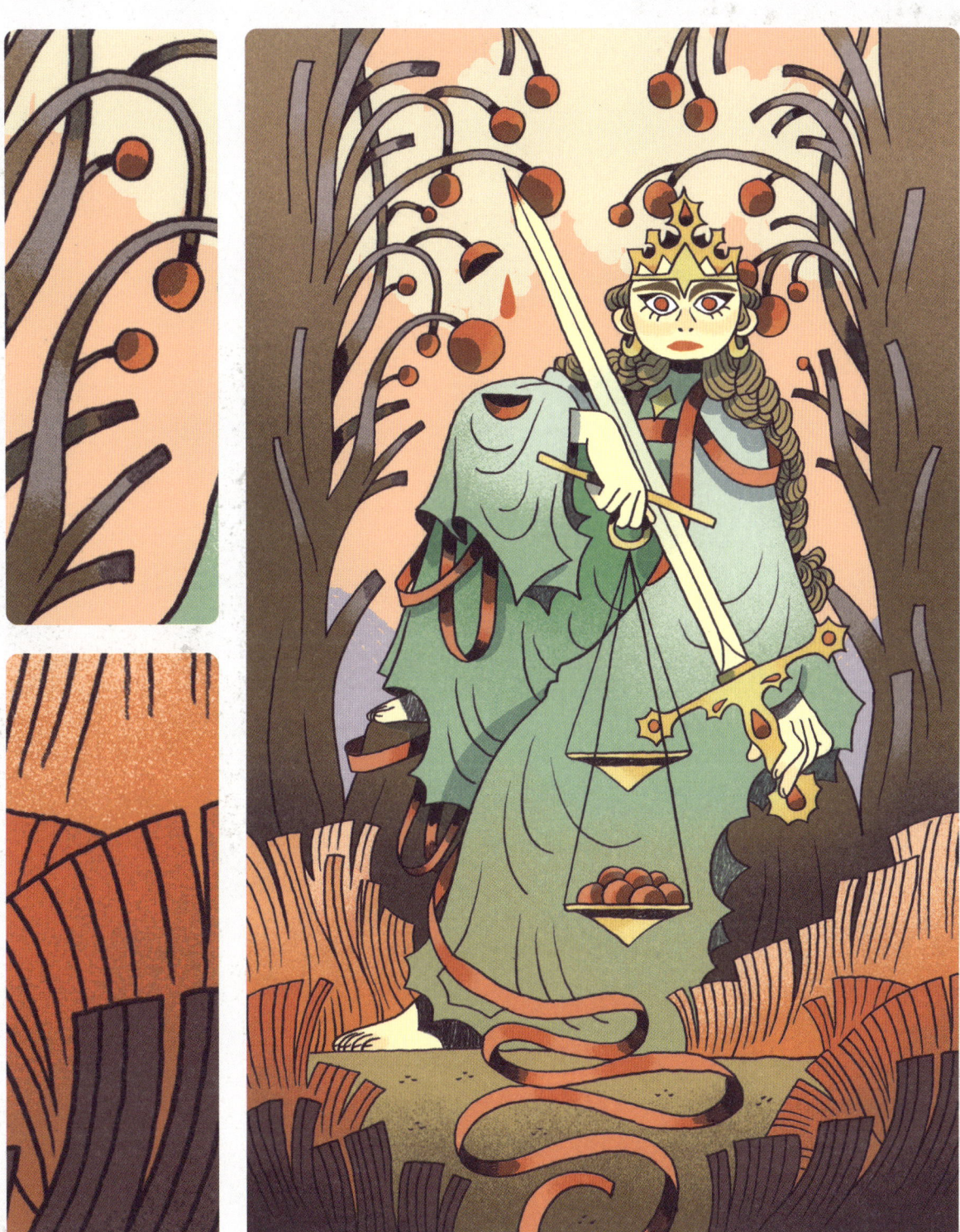

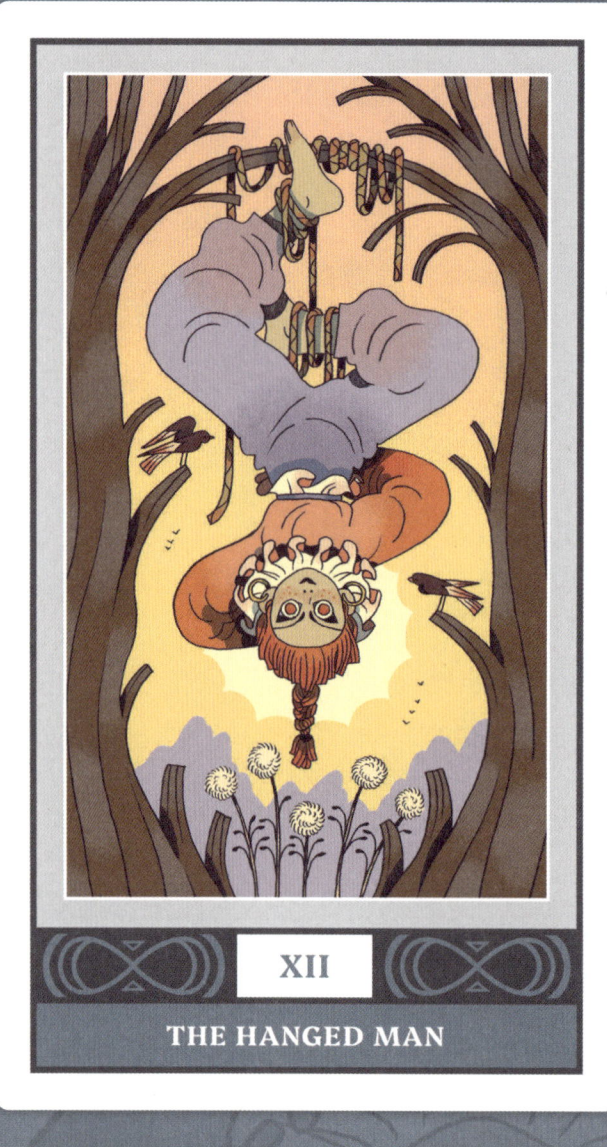

XII

THE HANGED MAN

THE HANGED MAN

SACRIFICE, PERSPECTIVE, EMERGING CONSCIOUSNESS

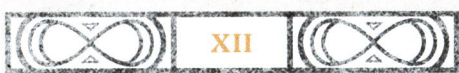

XII

I want to keep this card classical but in a revised way. I place the sun exactly behind the character's head, so it creates a sense of spiritual illumination. The character is upside down but in a comfortable manner. The rope is slightly untied, meaning it's your choice to change perspective whenever you like. I also add flowers, referring to the idea of growth, as the card talks about one's emerging consciousness.

* upside down figure
  ↓
  new point of view

* hands and foot behind body

* head illumination

trees like window.

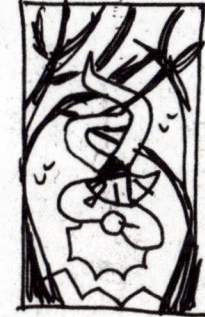

less static
or symetric

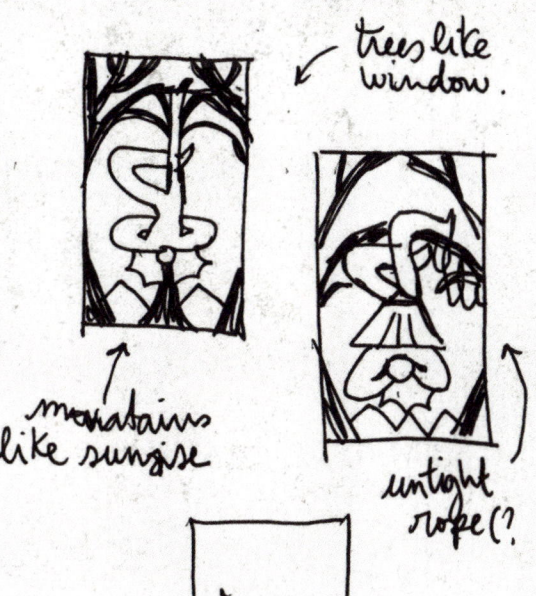

mountains like sunrise

untight rope (?

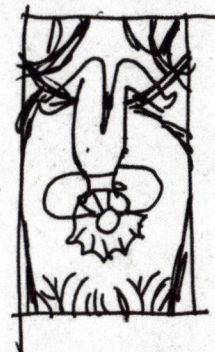

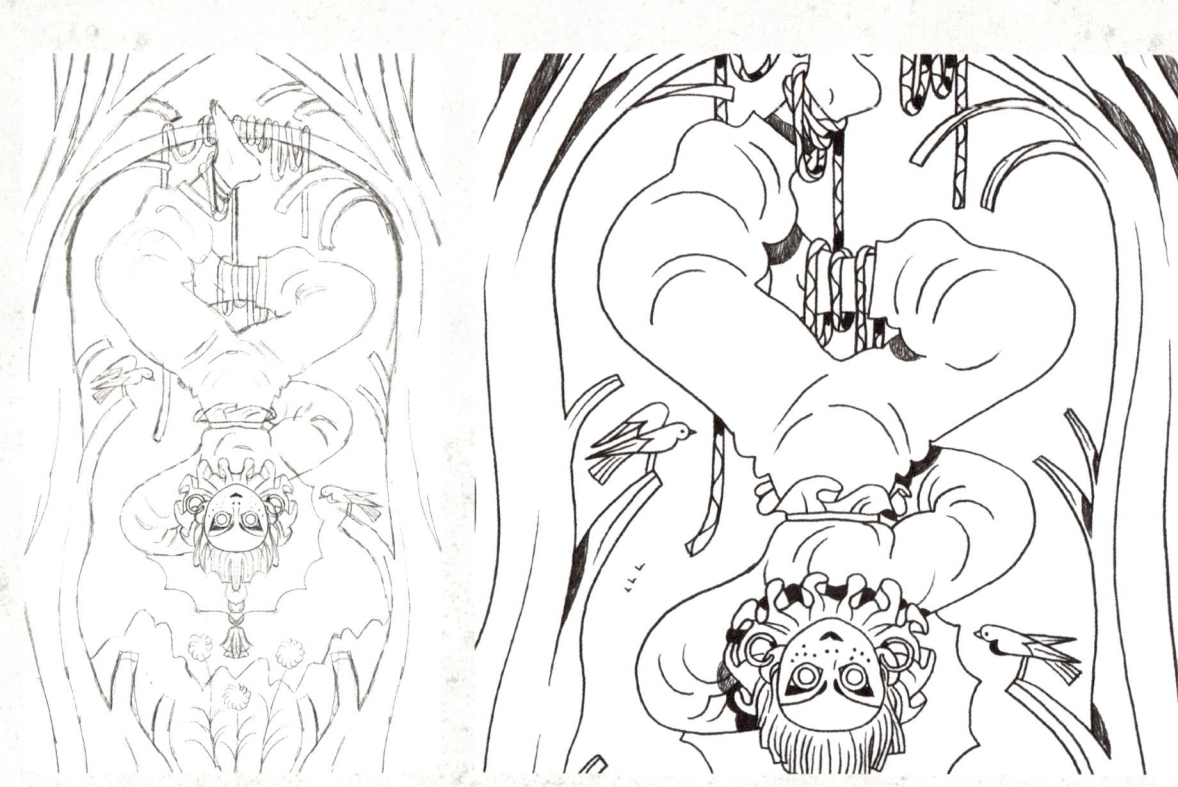

The upside-down character can see
things from a new perspective

The glow of newly gained insight
surrounds the figure's head

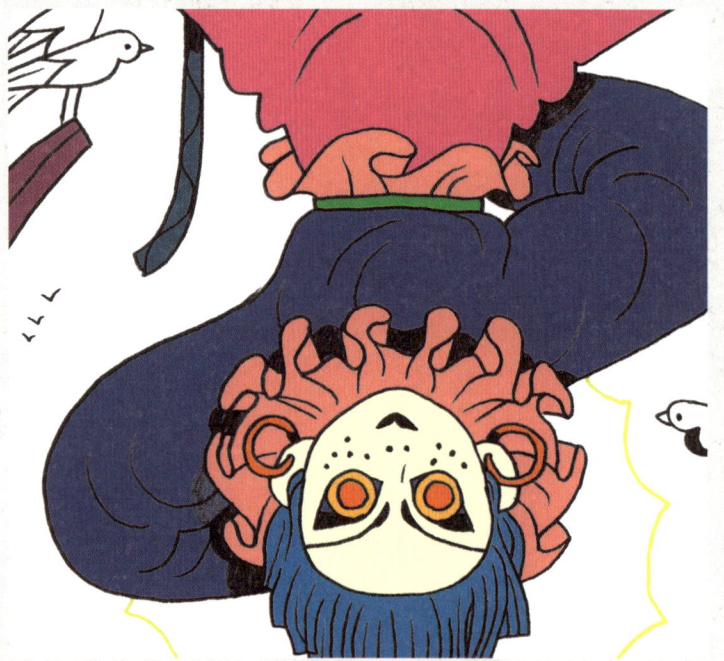

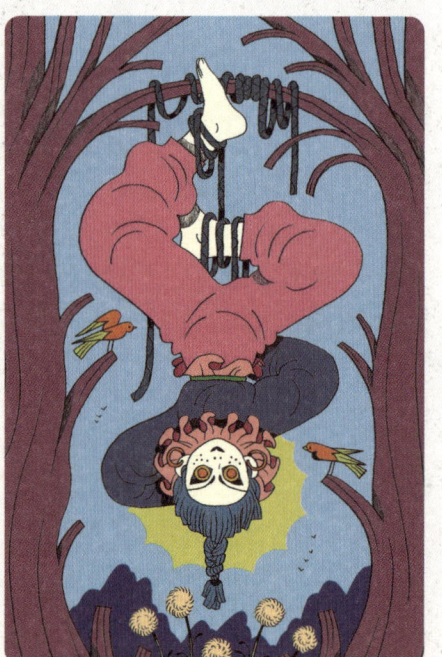

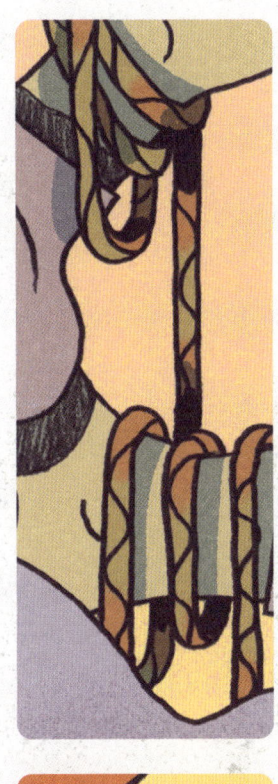

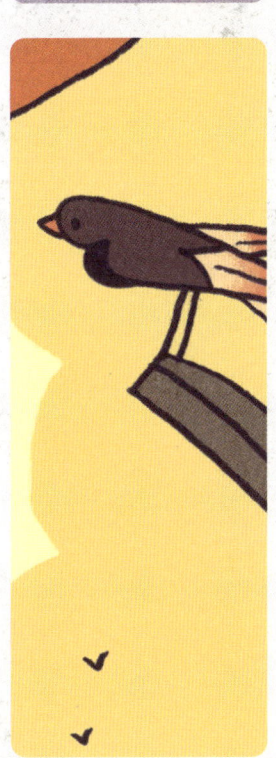

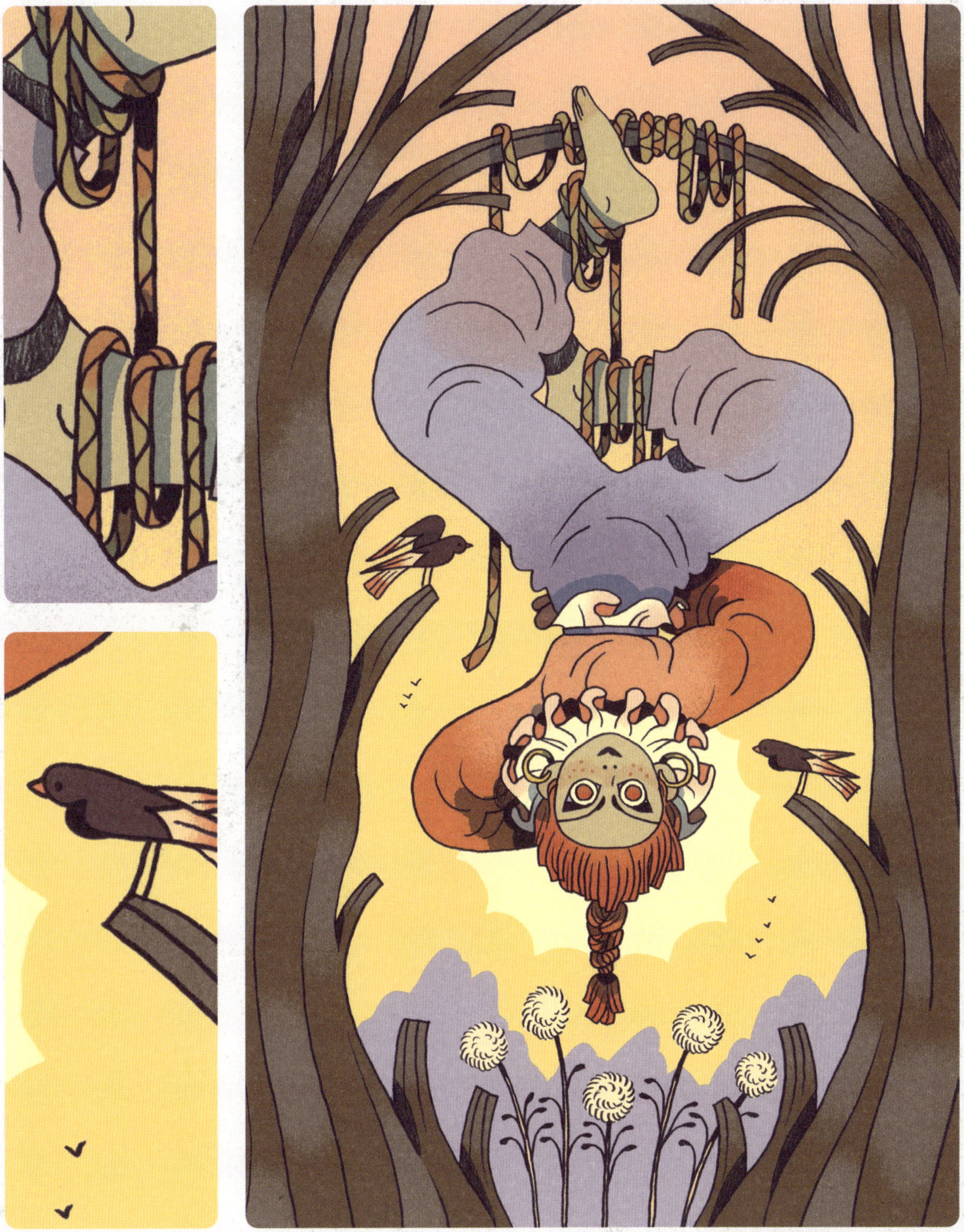

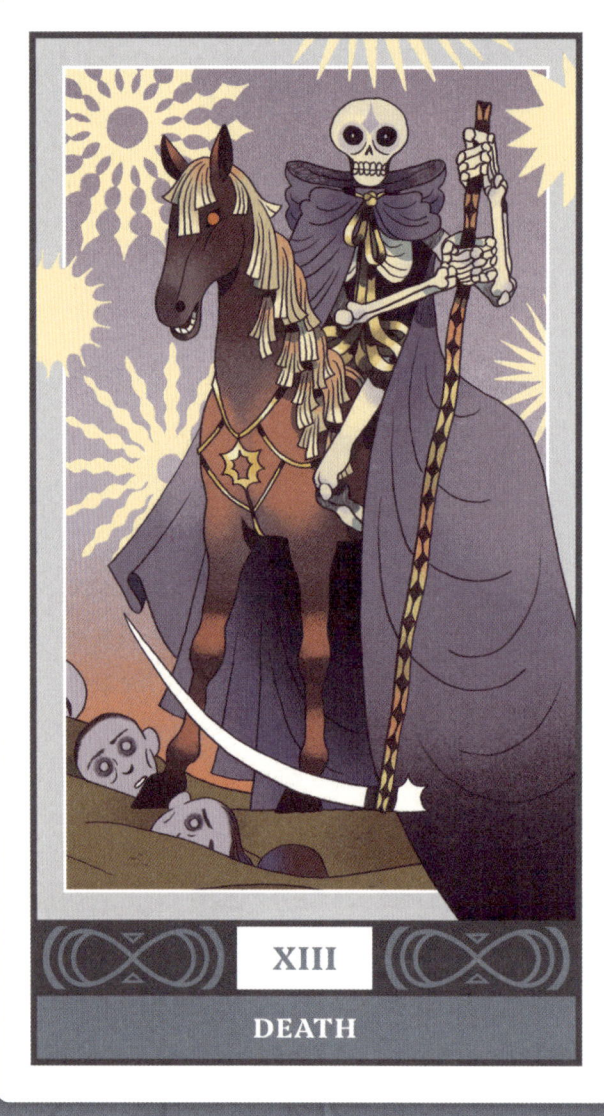

XIII

DEATH

DEATH

ENTROPY, CHANGE, REBORN

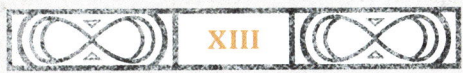

| XIII |

I especially like this card, since it is positive despite appearing morbid. I draw the skeleton with a long cloak. I like to imagine that Death contains the whole universe in it, so I also add lots of strange stars. I feel the cloak and stars add some movement and brightness, as I want to convey the idea that Death is something we should embrace and not fear. I add some heads to represent the lives that Death has come to collect.

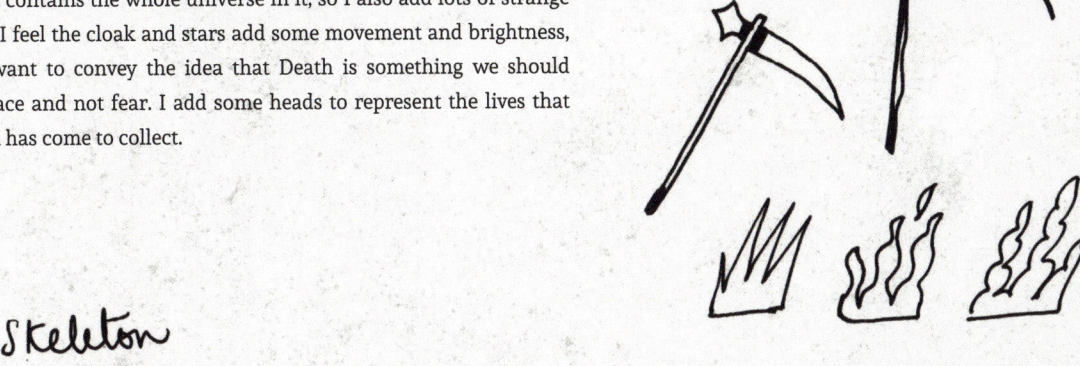

* skeleton
* scythe
* rising sun
* people dying and fearful

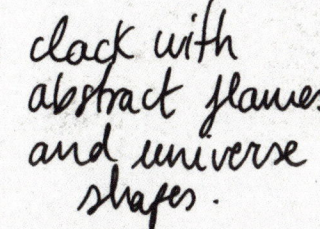

cloak with abstract flames and universe shapes.

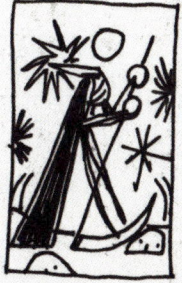
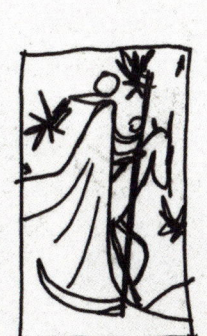
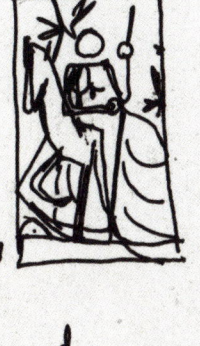

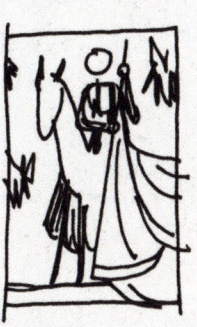
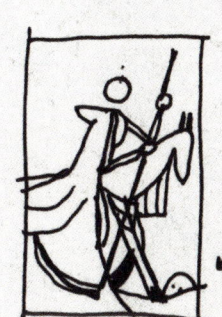

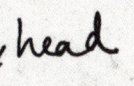
head

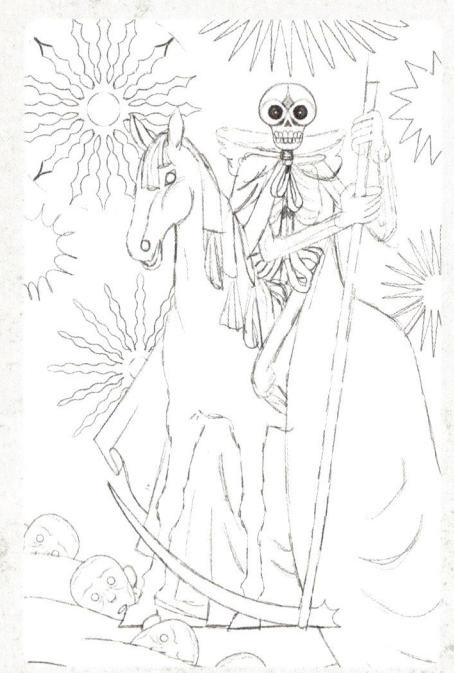

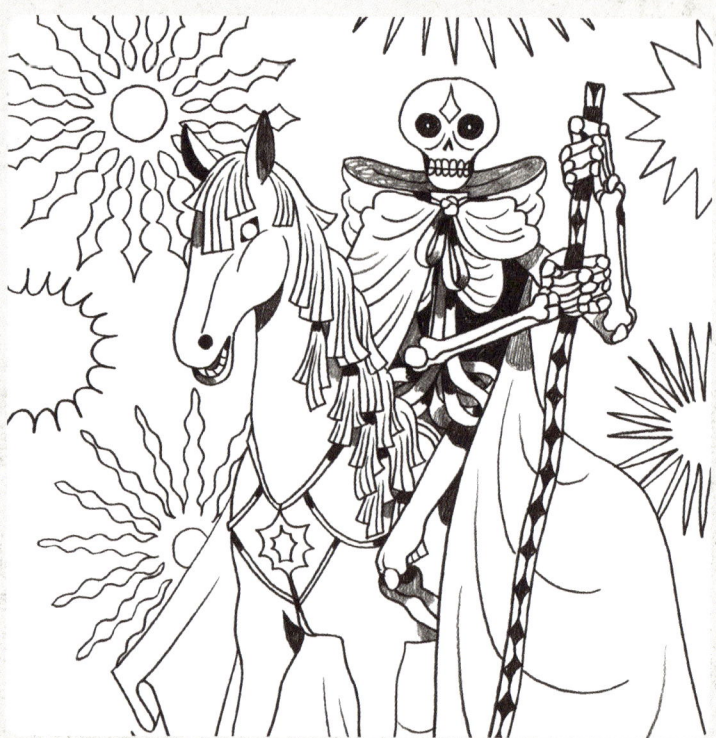

Like the archetypal Reaper, my
depiction of Death carries a scythe

Fallen figures lie in the path
of Death and its horse

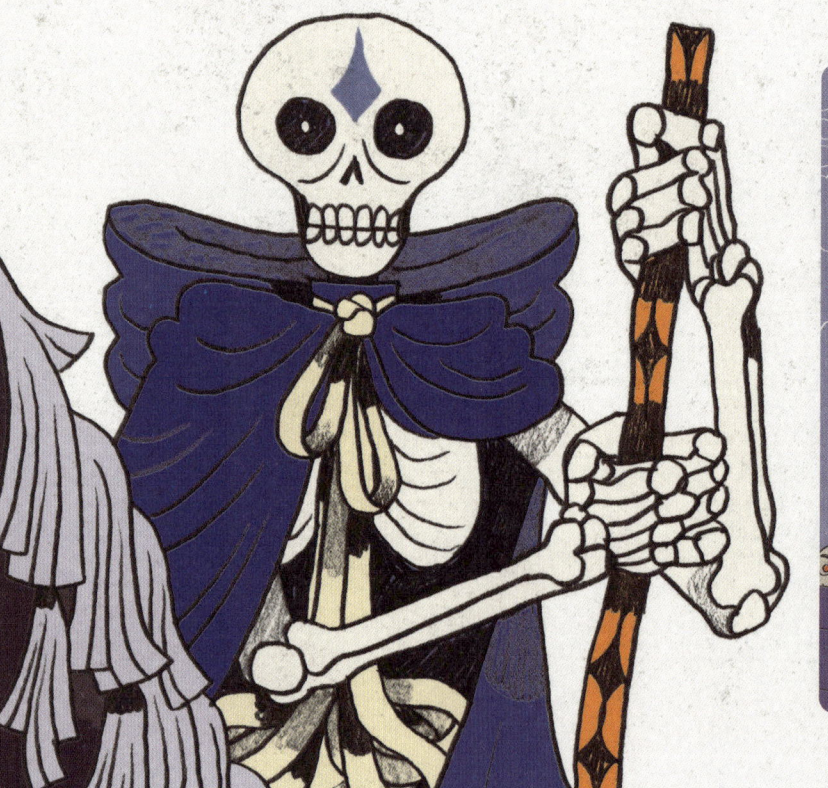

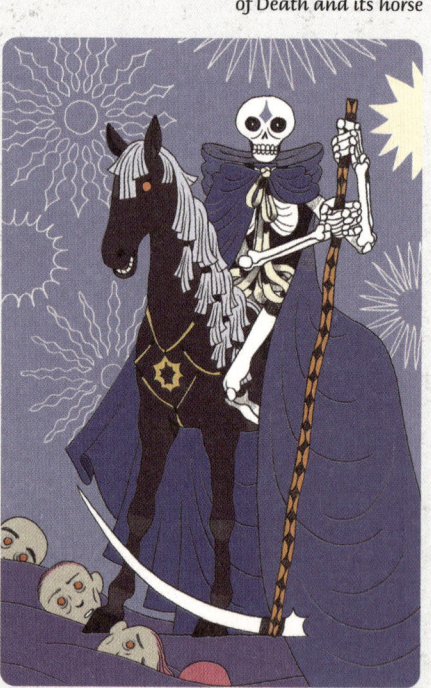

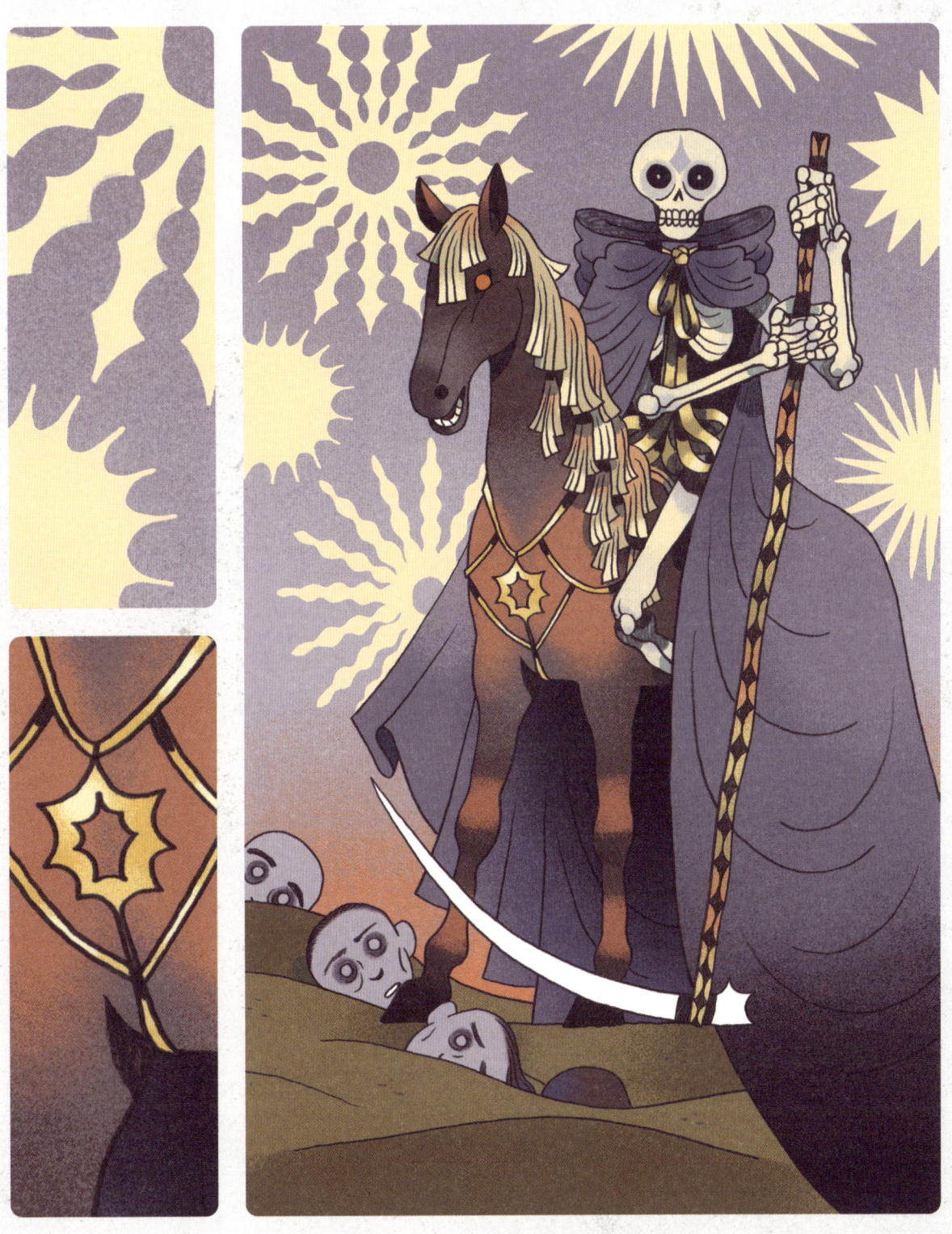

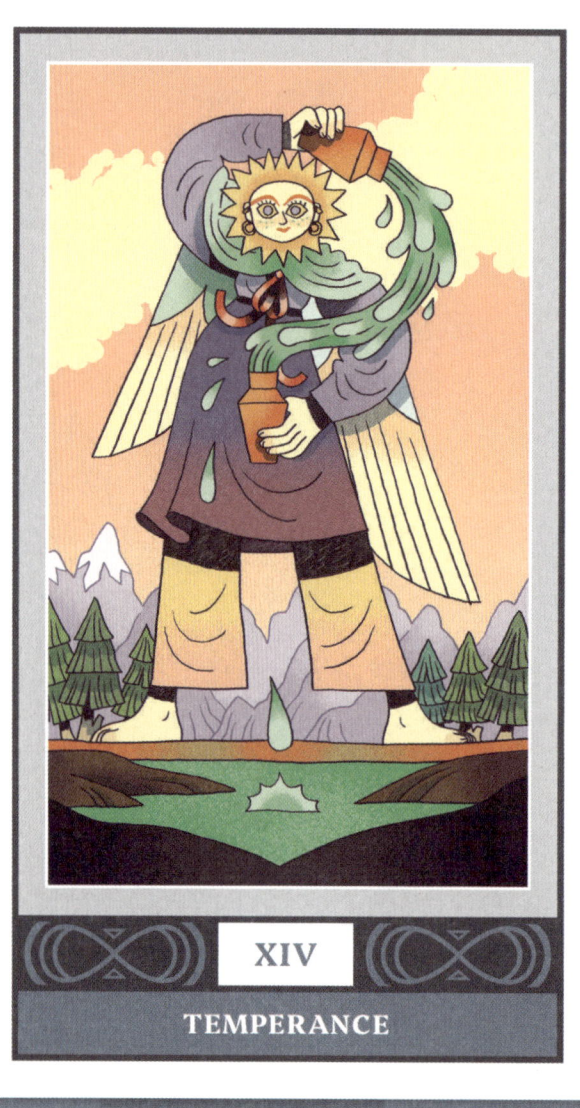

XIV

TEMPERANCE

TEMPERANCE

HONING SKILLS, BALANCE, NATURAL HARMONY

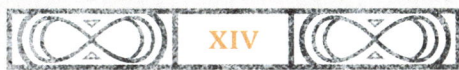

For this card, I decide to represent the angel in a non-religious way, instead creating this fantasy figure of a sun or star, showing the divine power of nature and the universe. I focus on representing the idea of balance, peace, and reflection. A drop falls out of the vessel – a reminder that no matter where we travel or what we are, we're all part of the ecosystem.

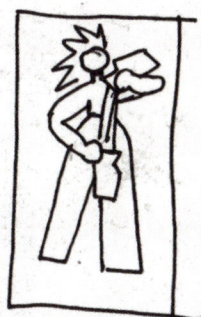

* angel with wings (divinity)
* mixing two cups (holding two things)
* pond (ecosystem)
* mountains
* path (journey)
* glowing crown
* head illumination
* ~~triangle in square~~

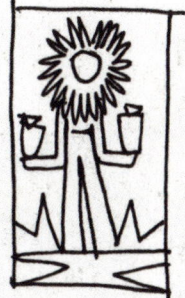

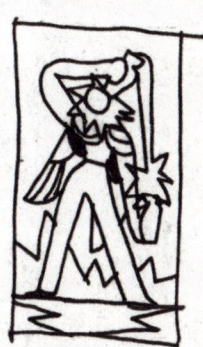

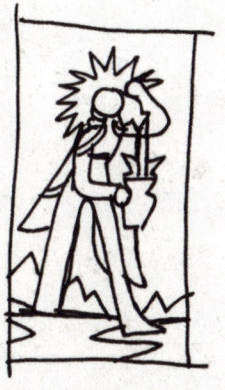

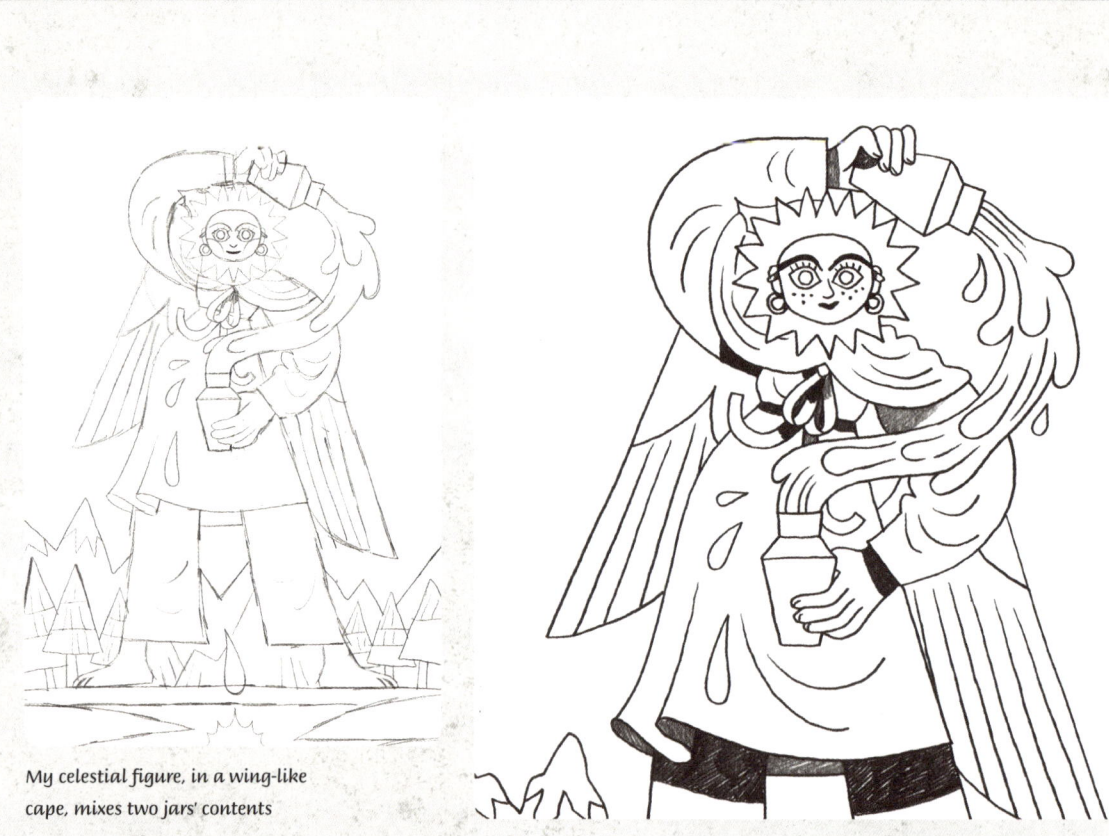

My celestial figure, in a wing-like
cape, mixes two jars' contents

The character's head is illuminated,
representing spiritual insight

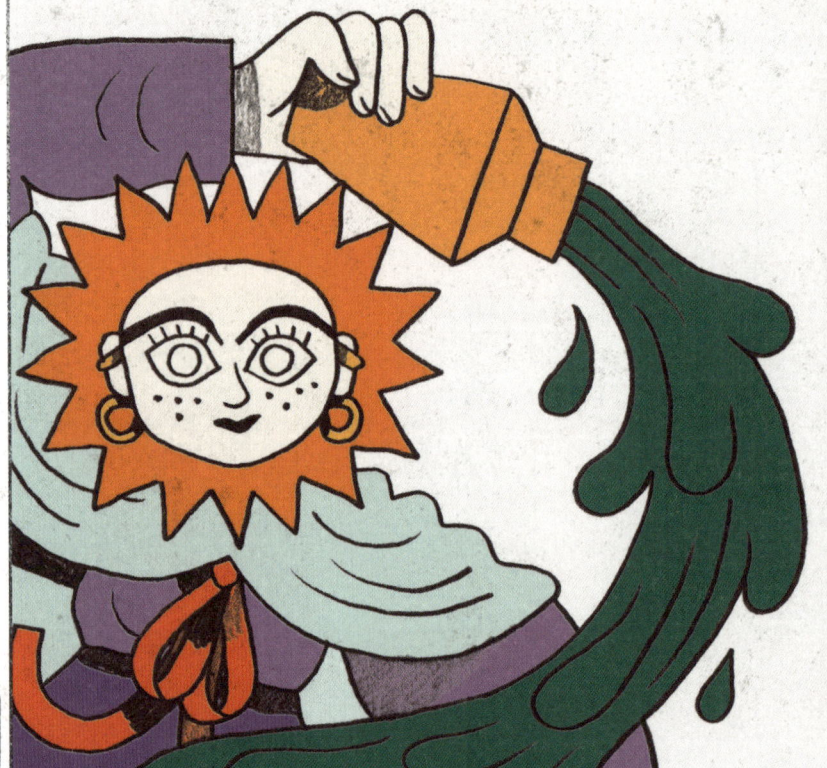

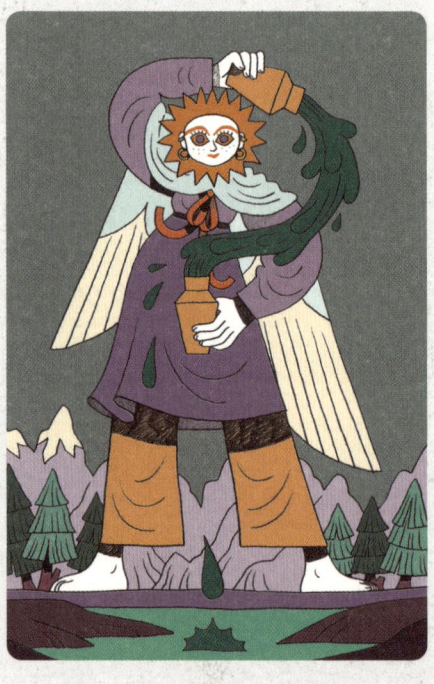

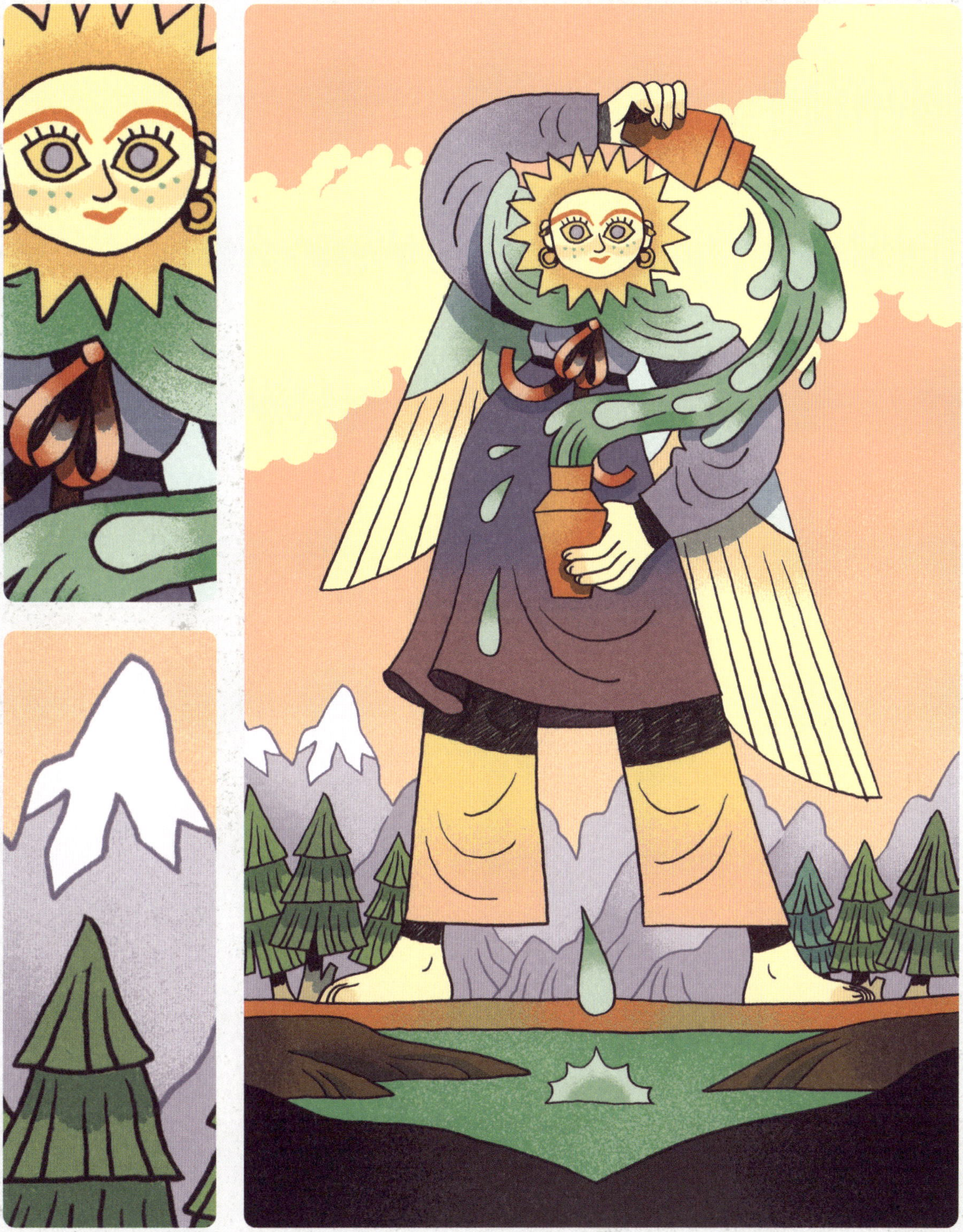

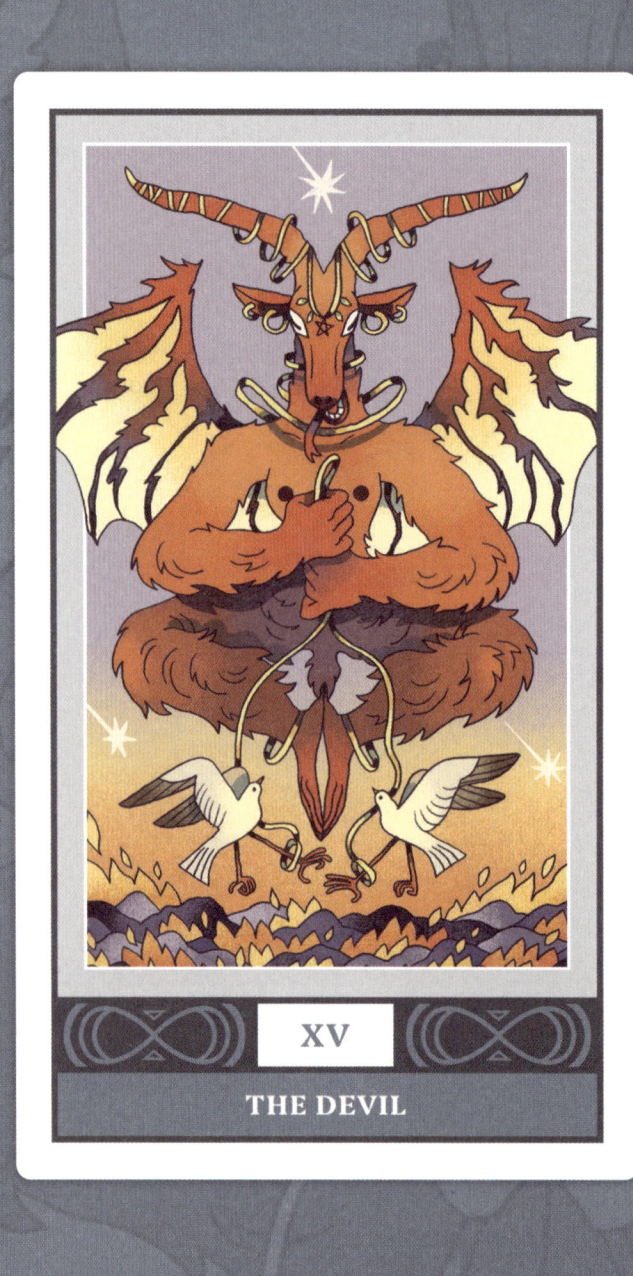

XV

THE DEVIL

THE DEVIL

ILLUSION, ABUSE, HATRED

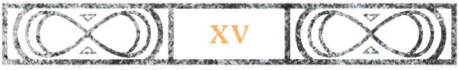

XV

For this card I want to keep the figure of the traditional Devil with a goat's head and bat's wings. I feel this card can actually be positive, so I decide to remove the people and change them for a couple of birds, since they are linked to what is earthly and yet they can set themselves free. I also add a land of fire and ashes, linked to the idea of illusion and the place you leave behind when it fits you no longer.

* devil figure
* two figures
* nudity
* removable chains

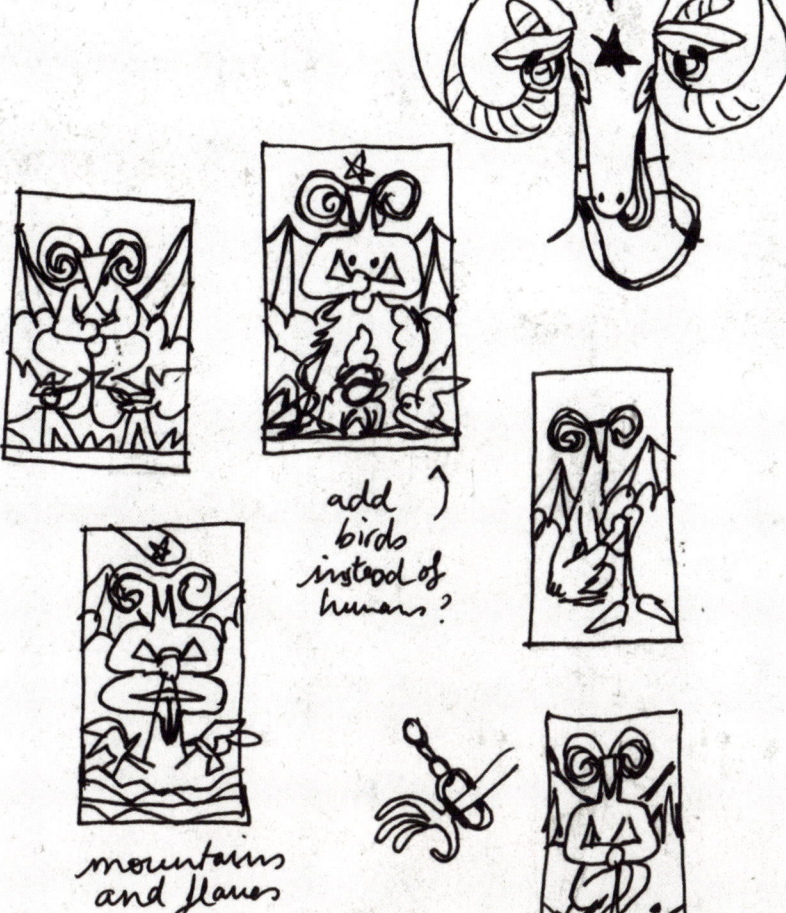

add birds instead of humans?

mountains and flames

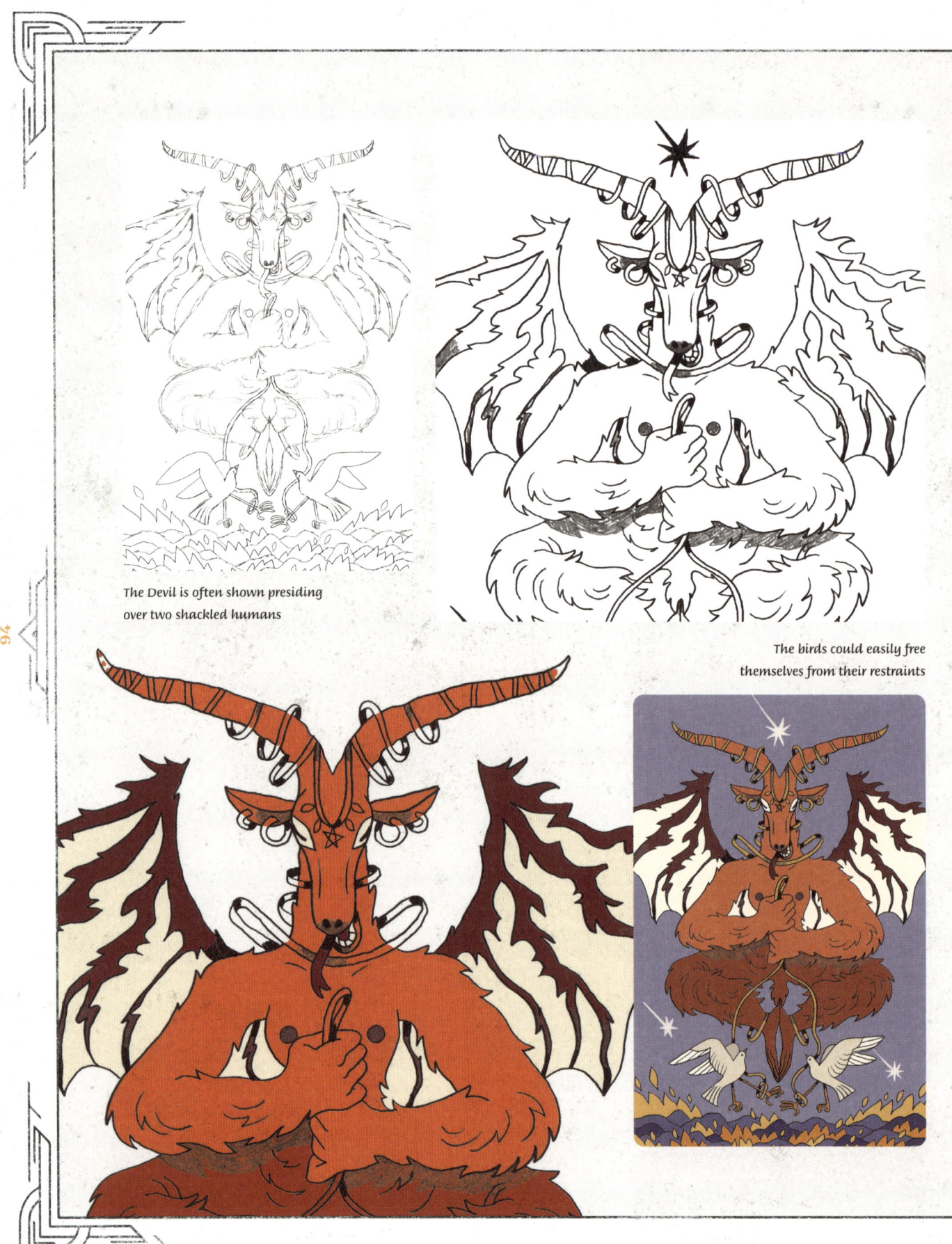

The Devil is often shown presiding
over two shackled humans

The birds could easily free
themselves from their restraints

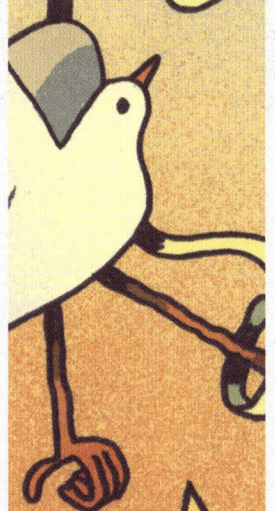

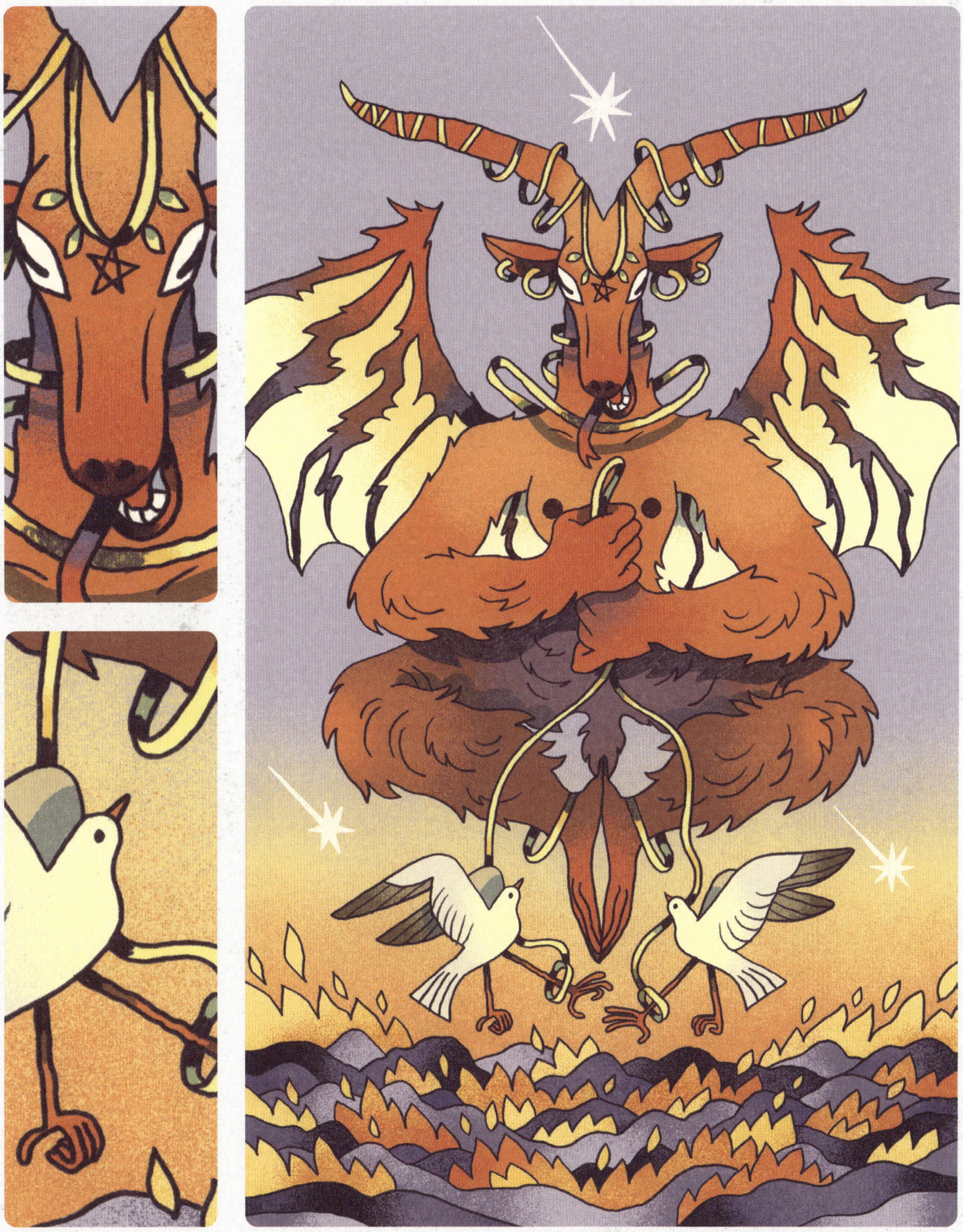

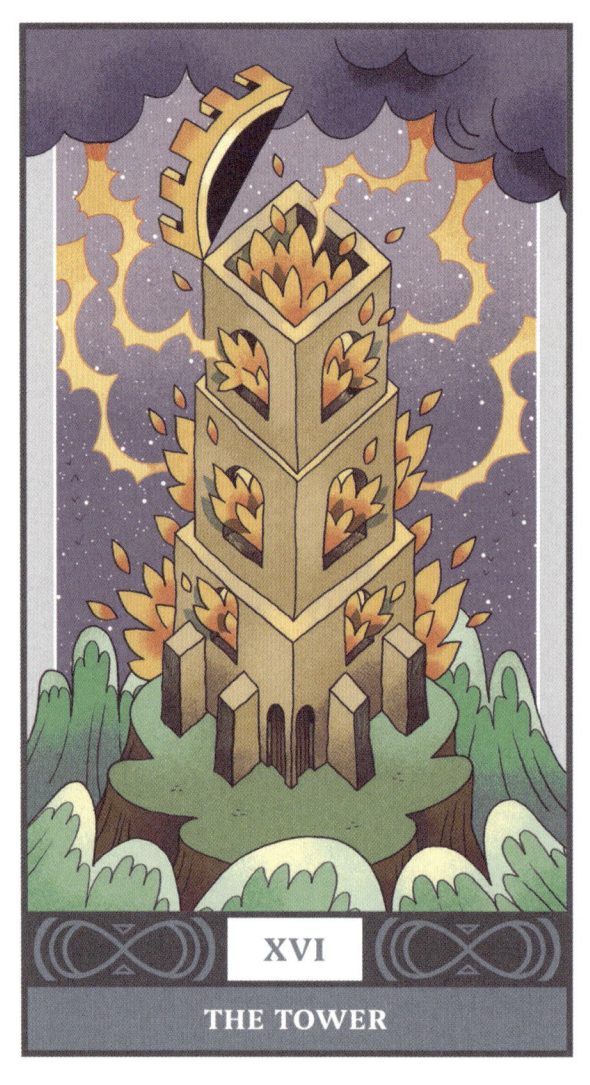

XVI

THE TOWER

THE TOWER

ILLUSION SHATTERED, SHOCK, CHAOS

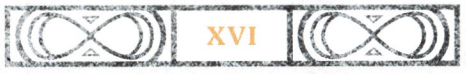 XVI

This card is especially difficult, since a tower is not really attractive for me to draw!
I decide to draw it in an unusual perspective, referring to the 'illusion' aspect in a
way. I use traditional symbols such as the crown and lightning. I want the scene
to look really chaotic and shocking, having so much fire coming from inside The
Tower. I remove the people falling from The Tower, usually represented in this
card, and instead add huge waves to refer to both destruction and the divine.

✴ lightning bolt (divine intervention)

✴ Tower (what had been created)

✴ Fire

✴ circle crown
  and square tower

✴ Figures falling

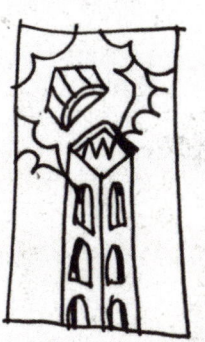
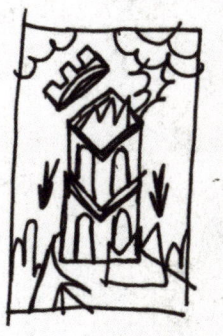
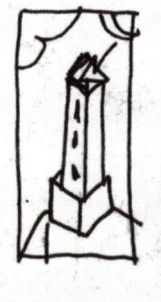
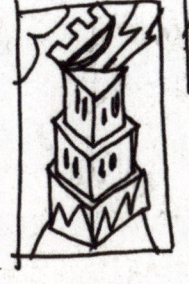
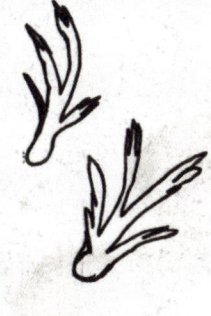
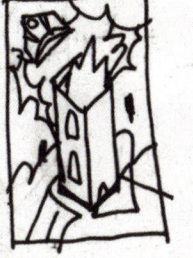

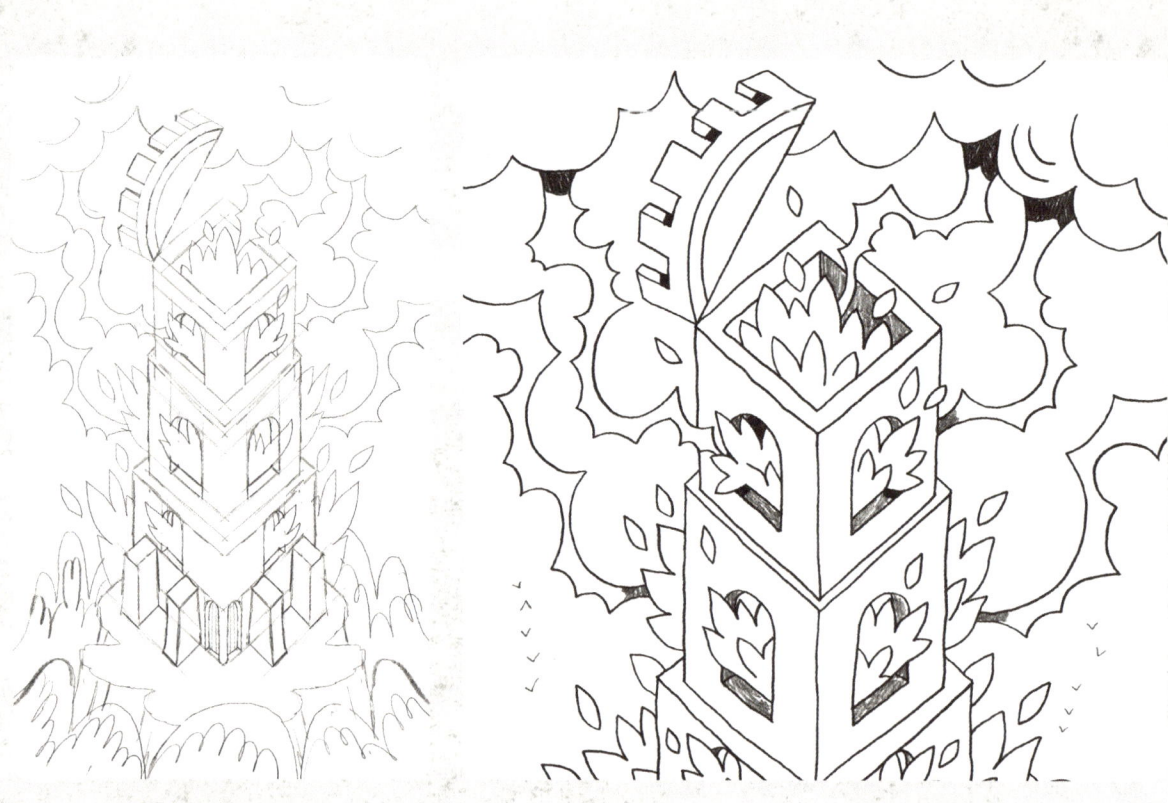

The circular crown topples from
the top of the square Tower

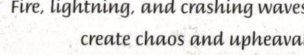

Fire, lightning, and crashing waves
create chaos and upheaval

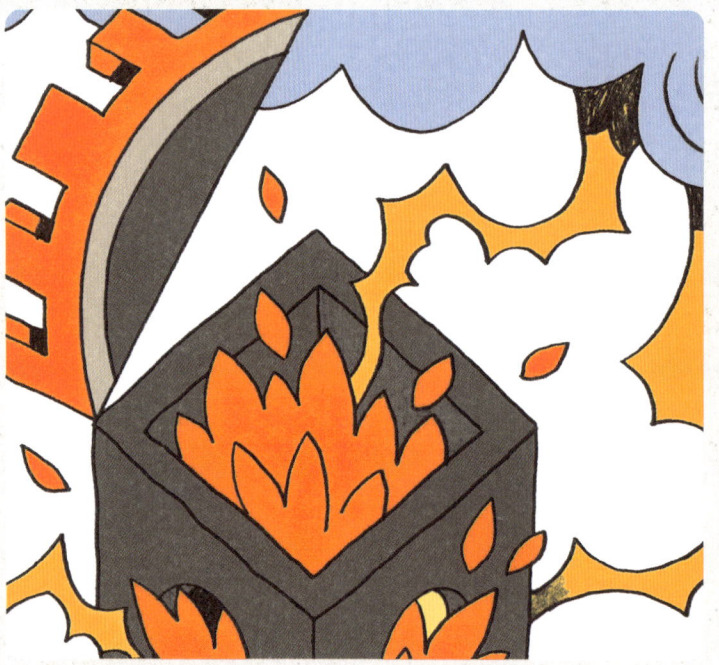
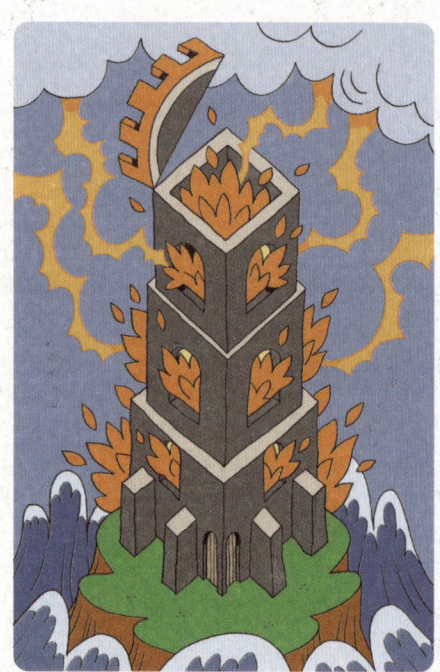

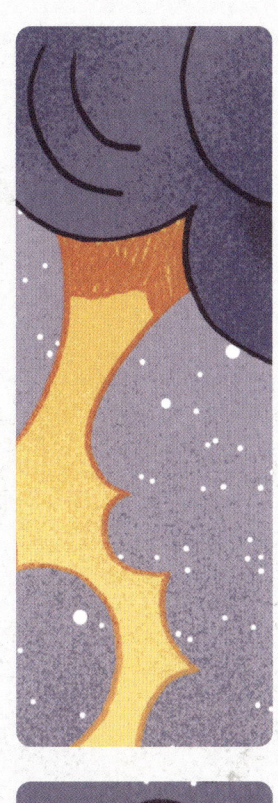

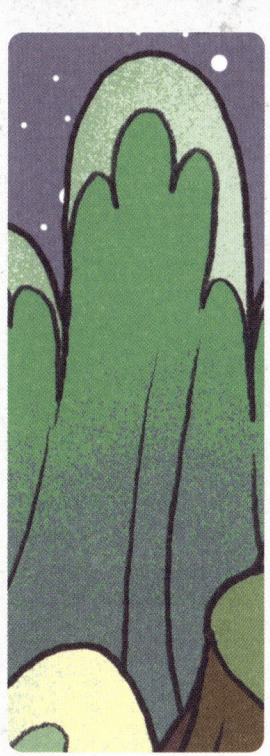

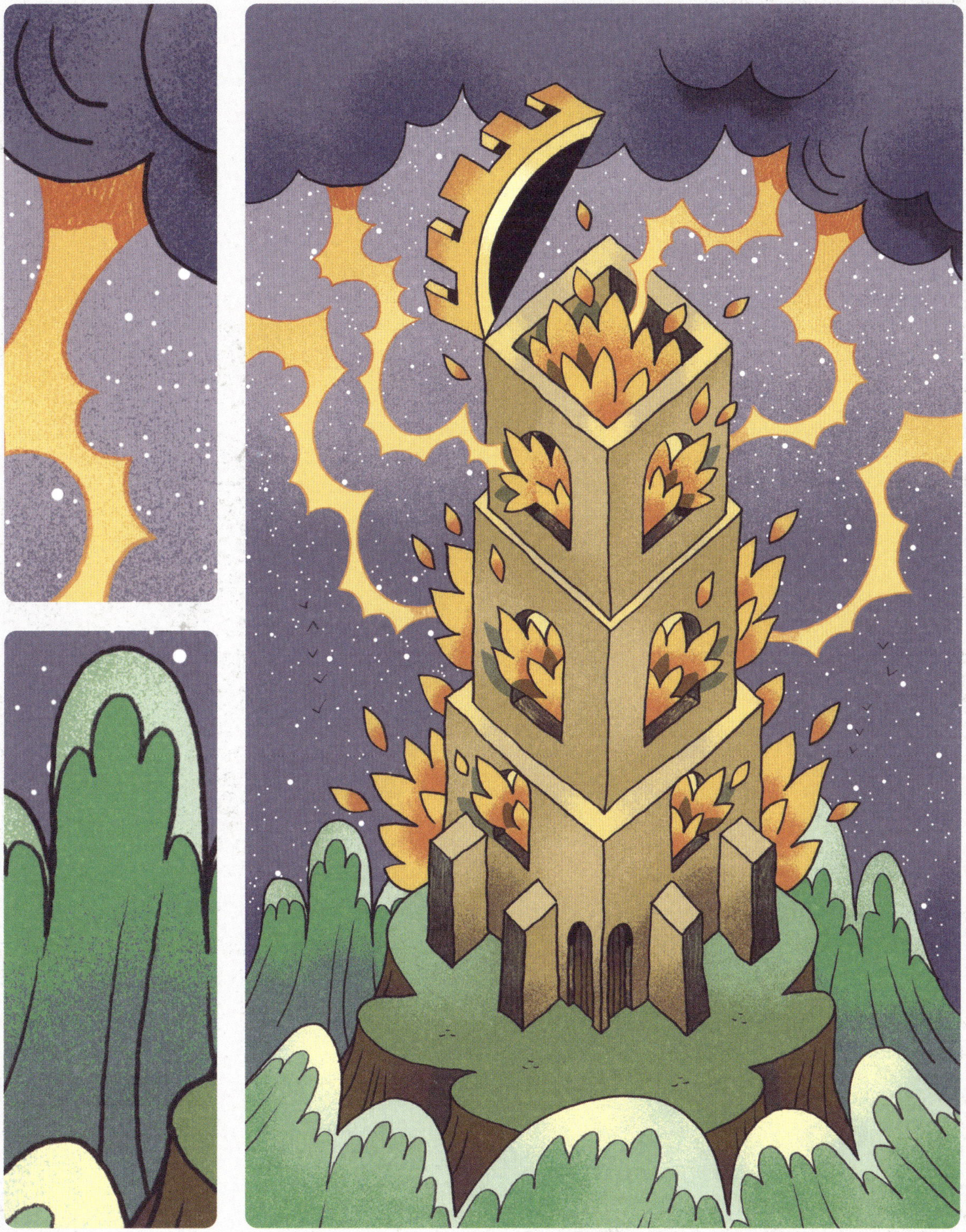

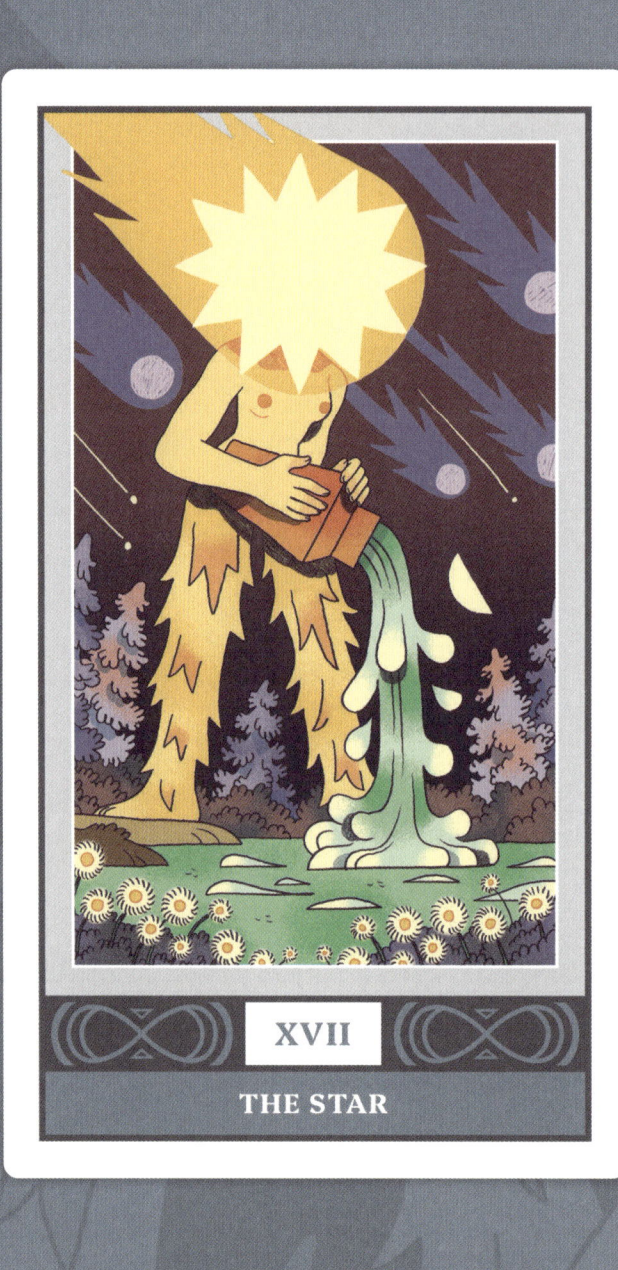

XVII

THE STAR

THE STAR

MUSE, RENEWAL, INSPIRATION

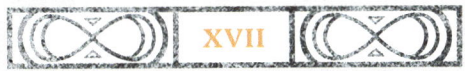

XVII

For this card I adapt the traditional figure of a naked woman to create this fantasy character of The Star. I like to think she fell suddenly from the sky, which is sometimes how true inspiration feels! The figure is pouring water with determination, ready to fly again. Around and above her is dark and silent nature. I want this scene to feel like a link and a pause between those two worlds – the visible and invisible – that the card talks about.

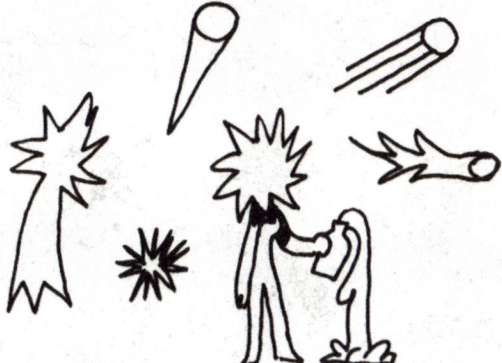

* star
* nude woman pouring liquids
* one foot over water, the other on land
* nudity.

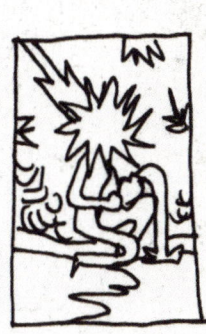
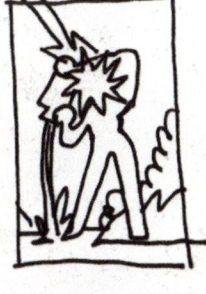
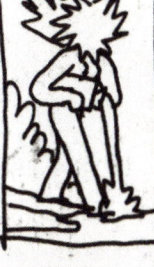
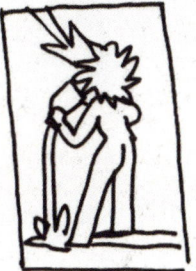
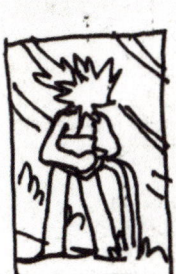

character with star as face, linked to the sun and the moon cards (?)

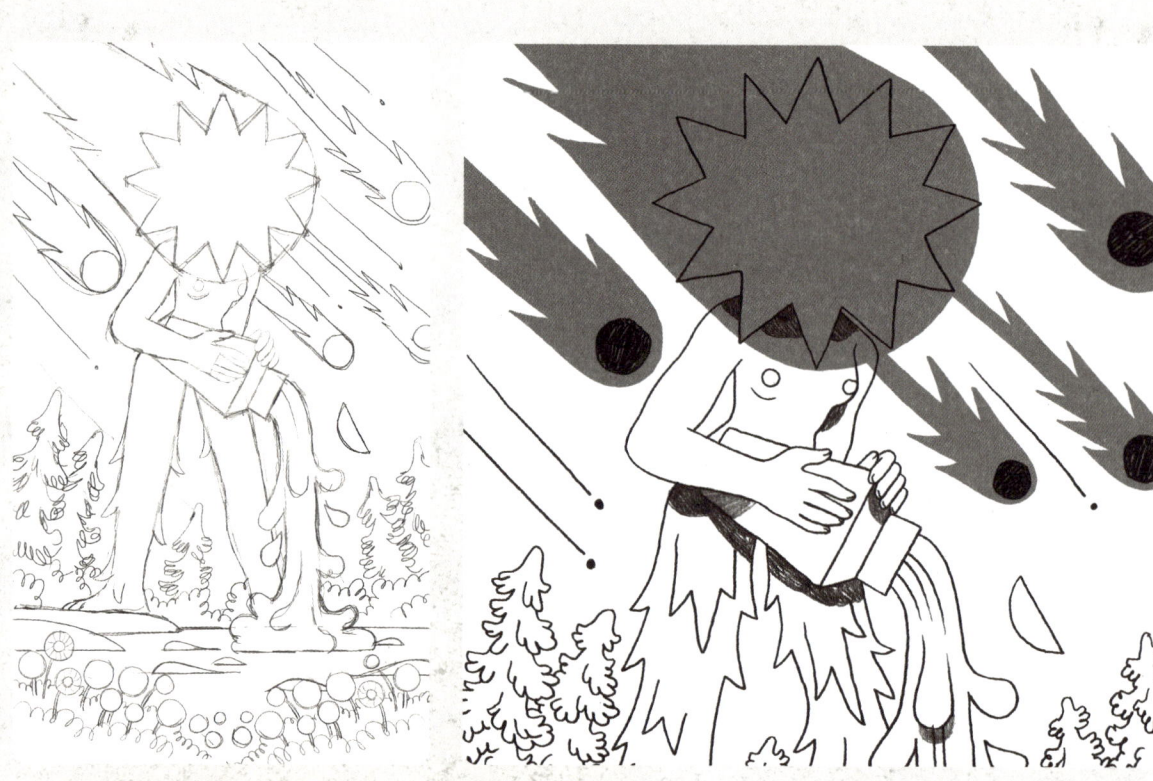

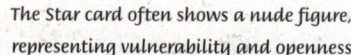

The figure steps between land and water – two different worlds

The Star card often shows a nude figure, representing vulnerability and openness

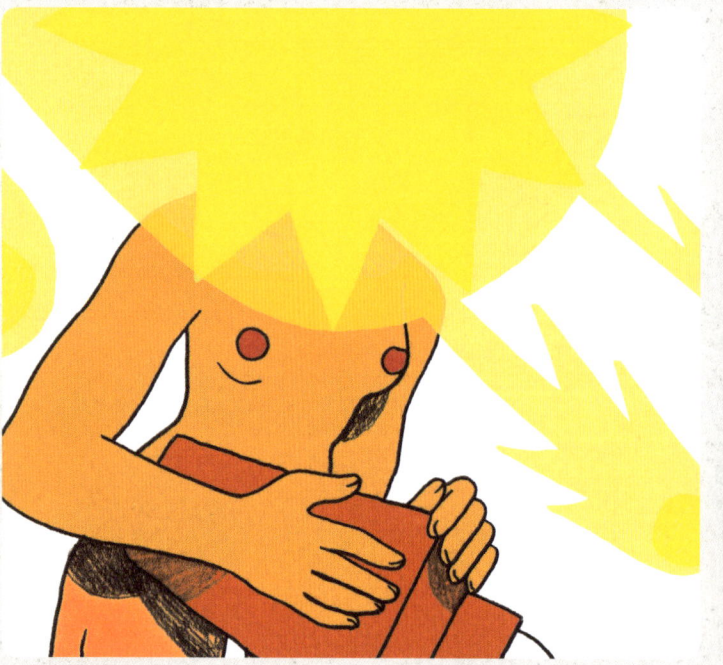

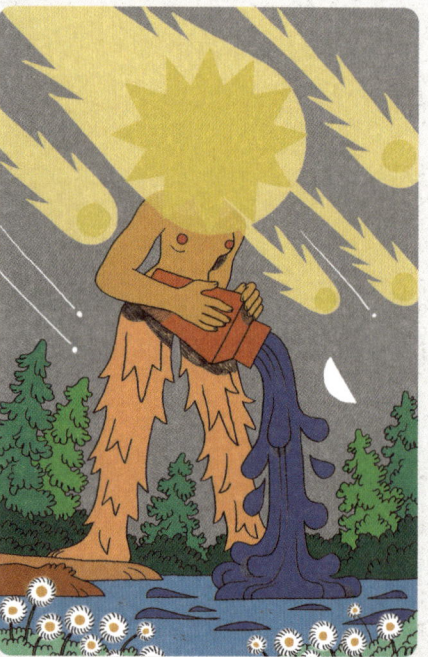

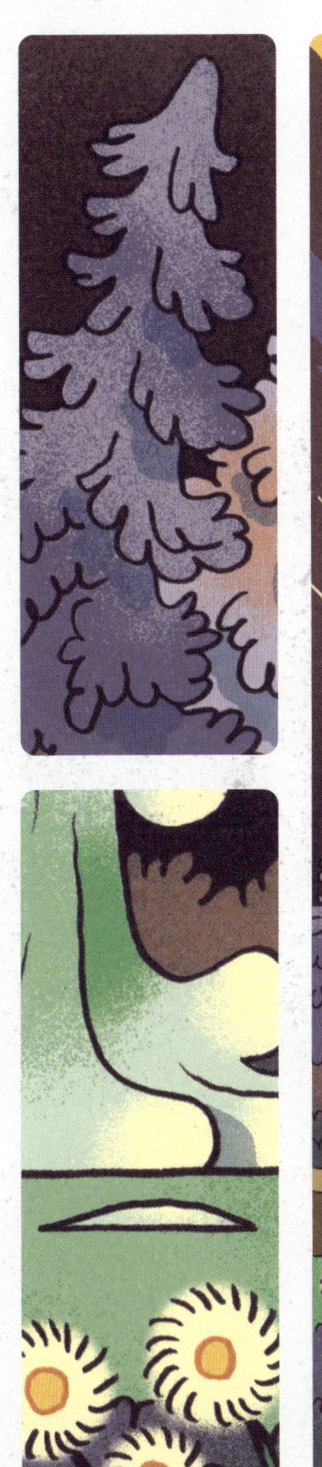

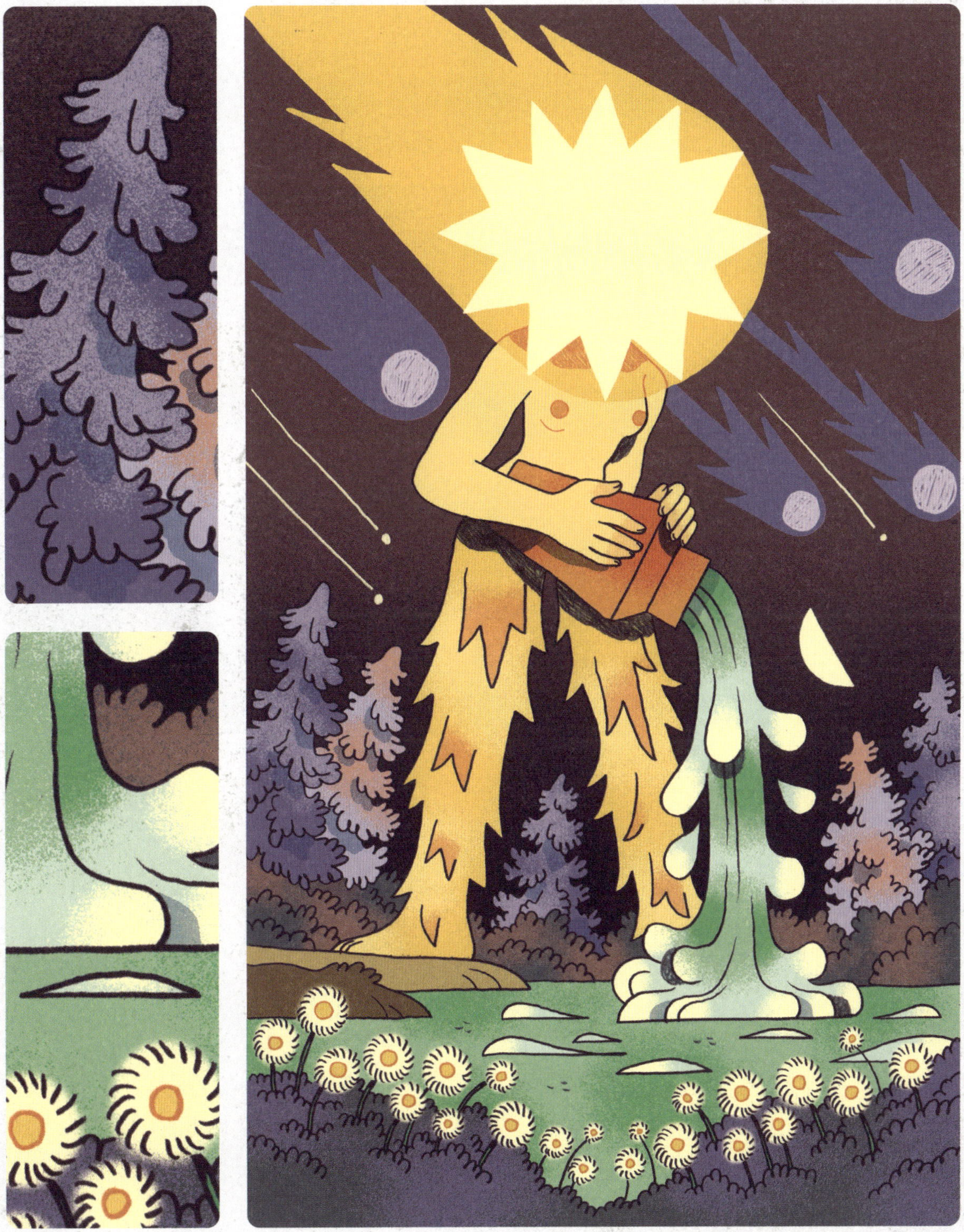

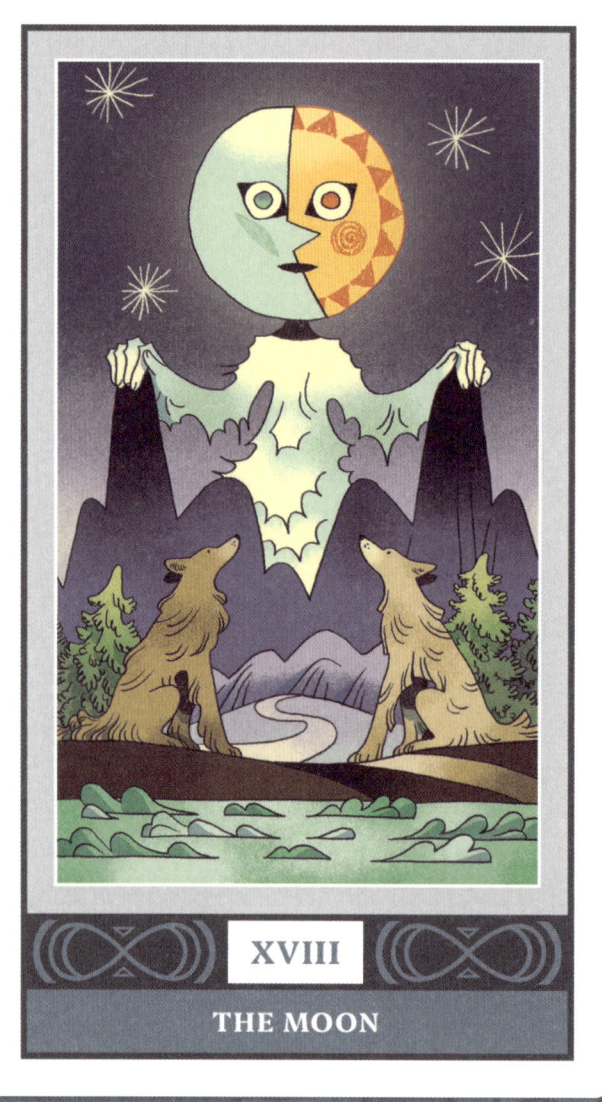

XVIII

THE MOON

THE MOON

MADNESS, DREAMS, ILLUSION, PROPHETIC POWER

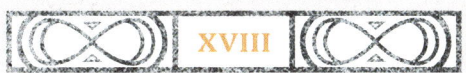

XVIII

Since this card speaks of the subconscious and dreams, I draw this fantasy figure that emerges from behind two mountains that act as the traditional two towers. The Moon has The Sun integrated into its design, since moonlight is reflected sunlight. I remove the traditional crawfish because I prefer the idea of the reader being the one that begins the trip up a path to the mountains. The two dogs (or wolves) stare at The Moon, listening to it and its prophetic power.

* Pool
* crawfish
* path up to mountain
* two beasts, dog and wolf
* two towers
* sun inside the moon

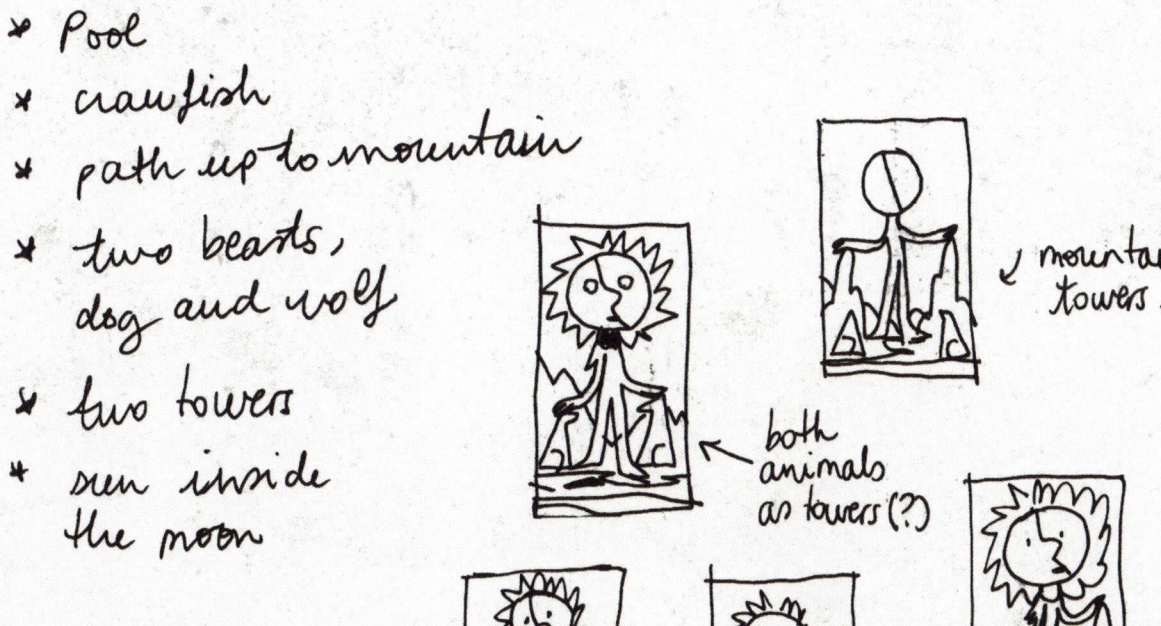

mountain towers.

← both animals as towers (?)

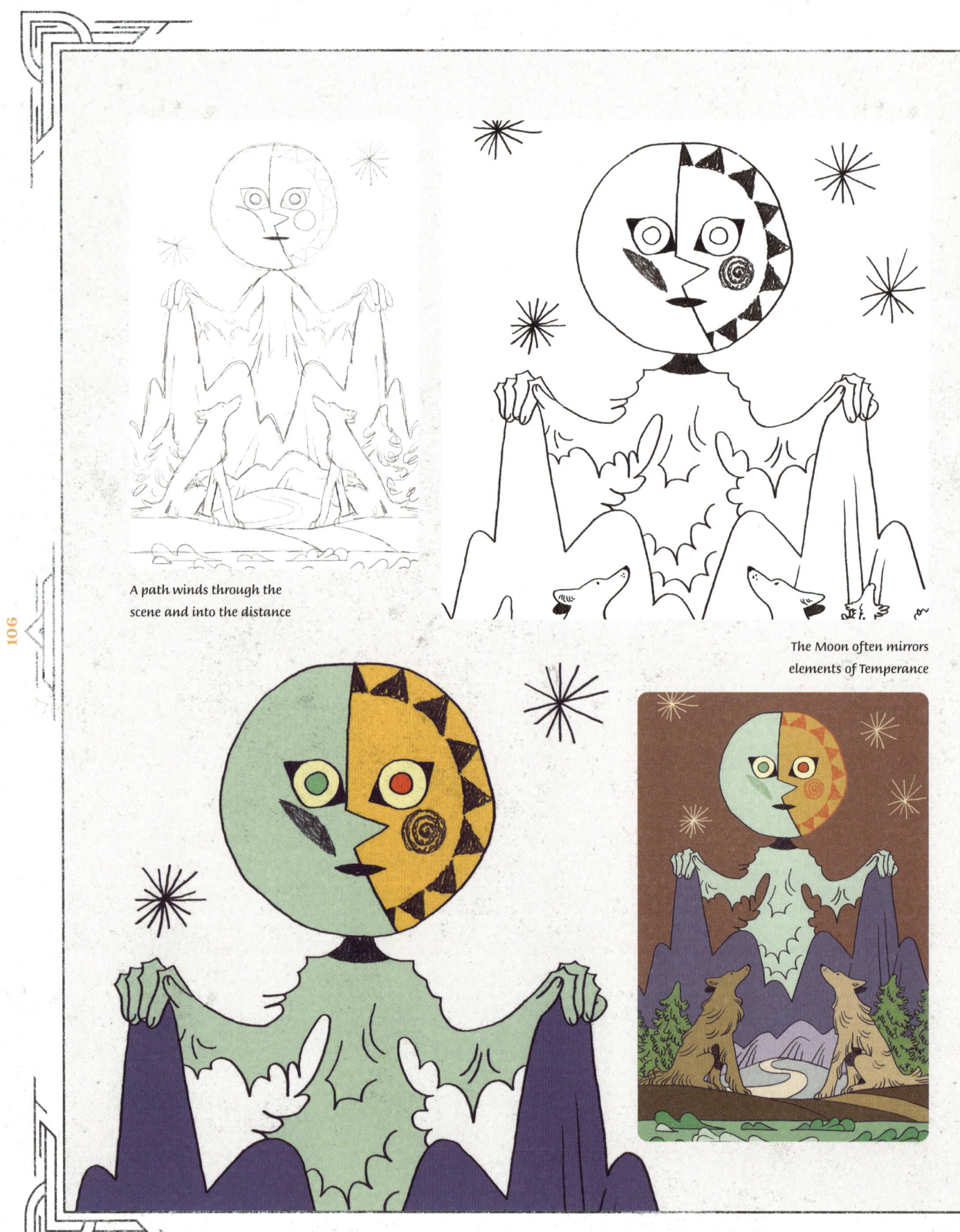

A path winds through the
scene and into the distance

The Moon often mirrors
elements of Temperance

106

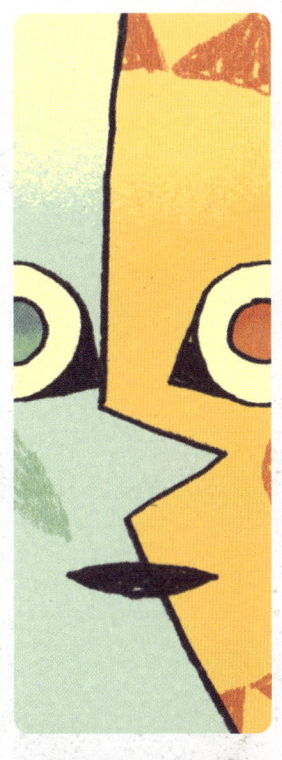

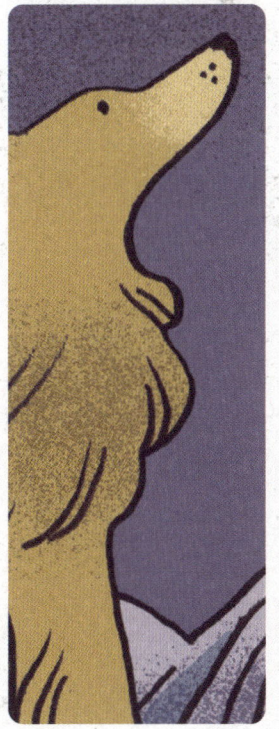

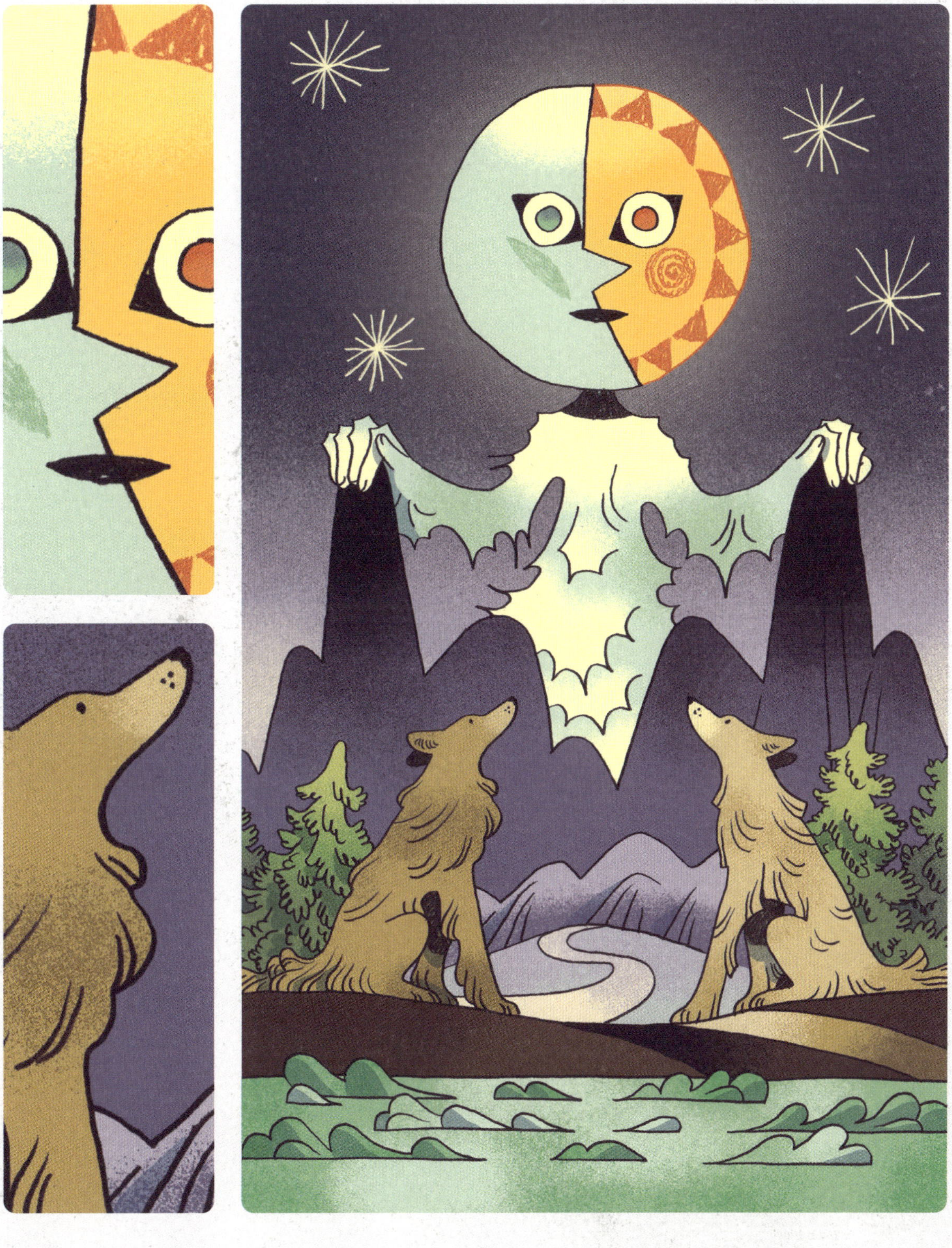

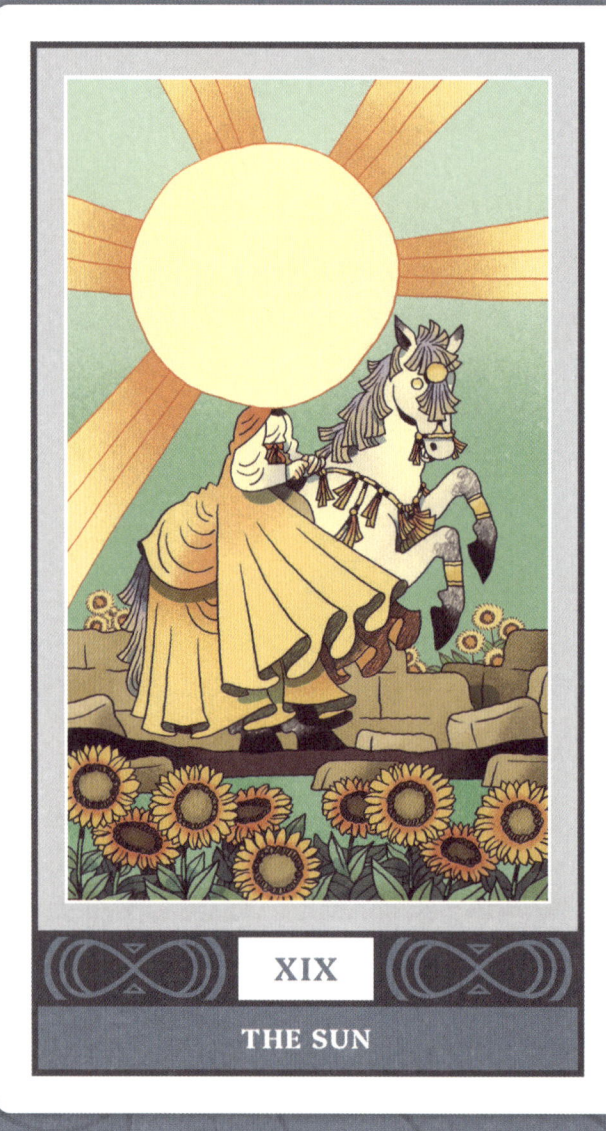

XIX

THE SUN

THE SUN

HEALTH, EXPANSION, ATTENTION

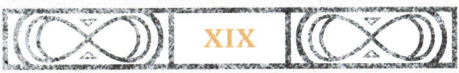

I love the idea of the child riding a horse and, since this card is The Sun, I want the figure to be huge and powerful and bright and indomitable. And the horse, too! The Sun itself expands through the card and shines on the sunflowers. The wall is thick but also not that tall, so it's not impossible to climb. I remove the traditional banner, since I want to concentrate attention on The Sun, and add some water to bathe the plants and all the life on Earth.

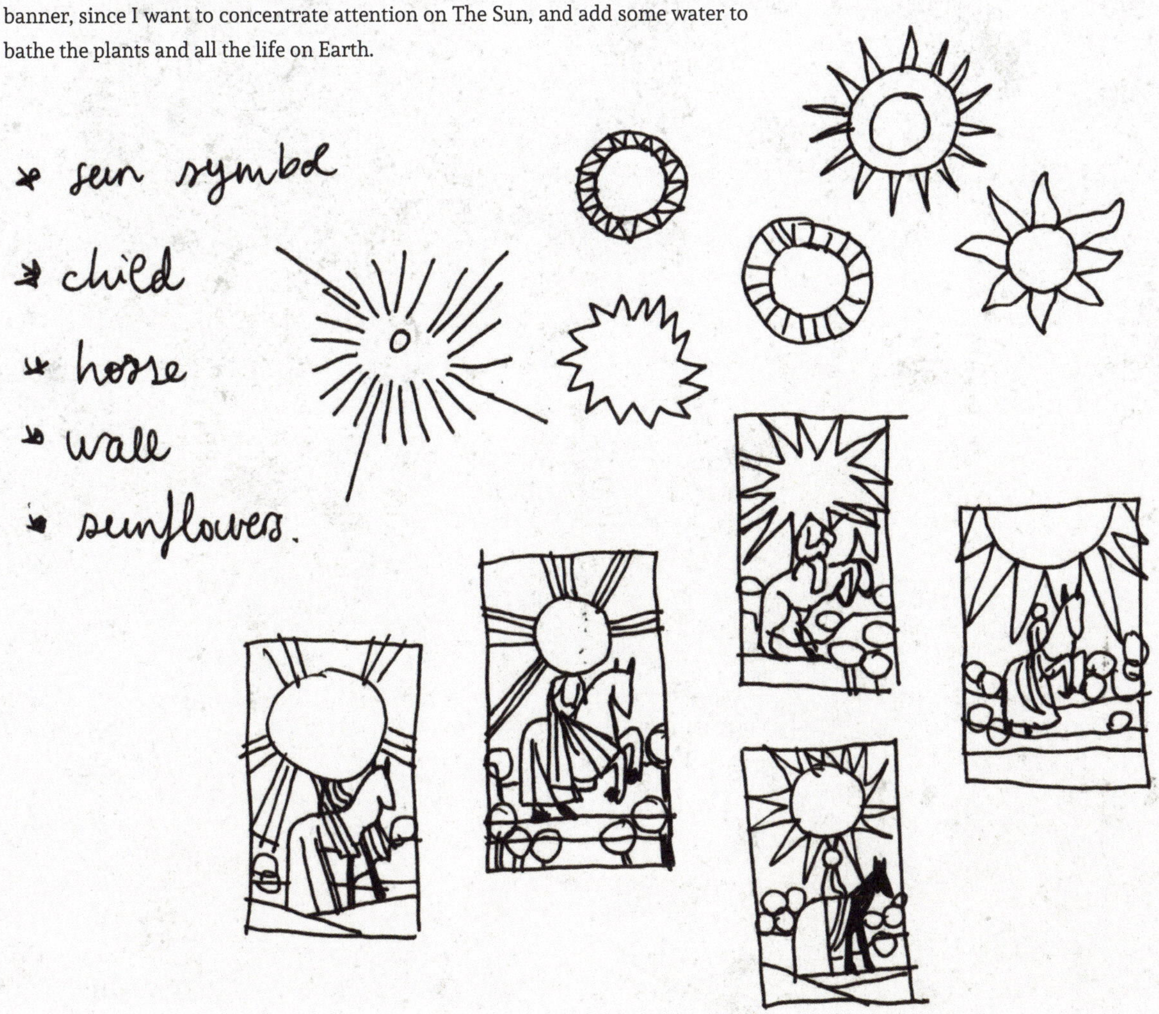

* sun symbol
* child
* horse
* wall
* sunflowers.

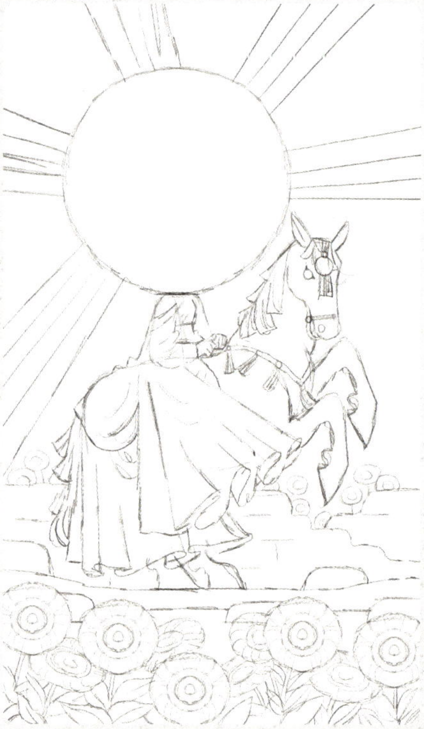

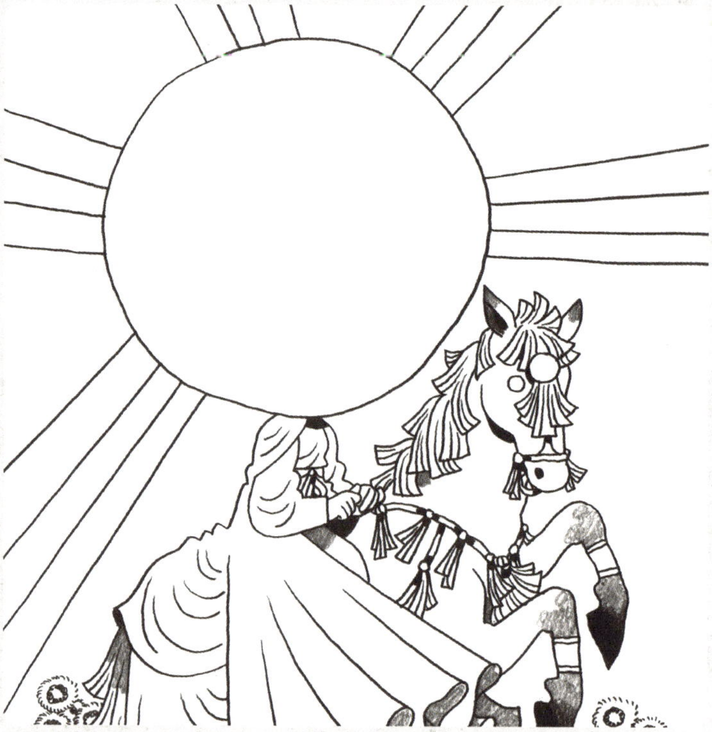

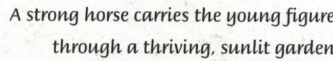

Sunflowers appear on the classic Sun card, as well as elsewhere in my designs

A strong horse carries the young figure through a thriving, sunlit garden

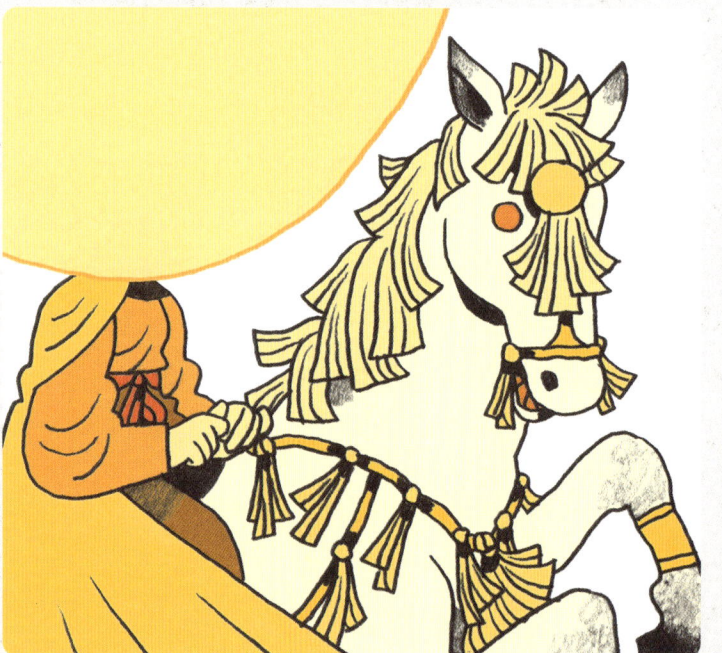

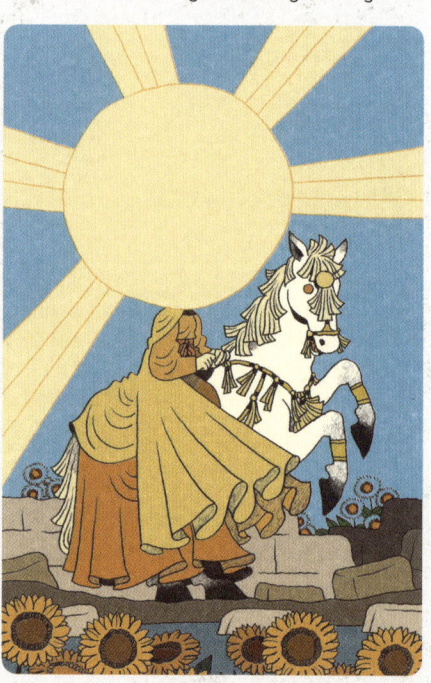

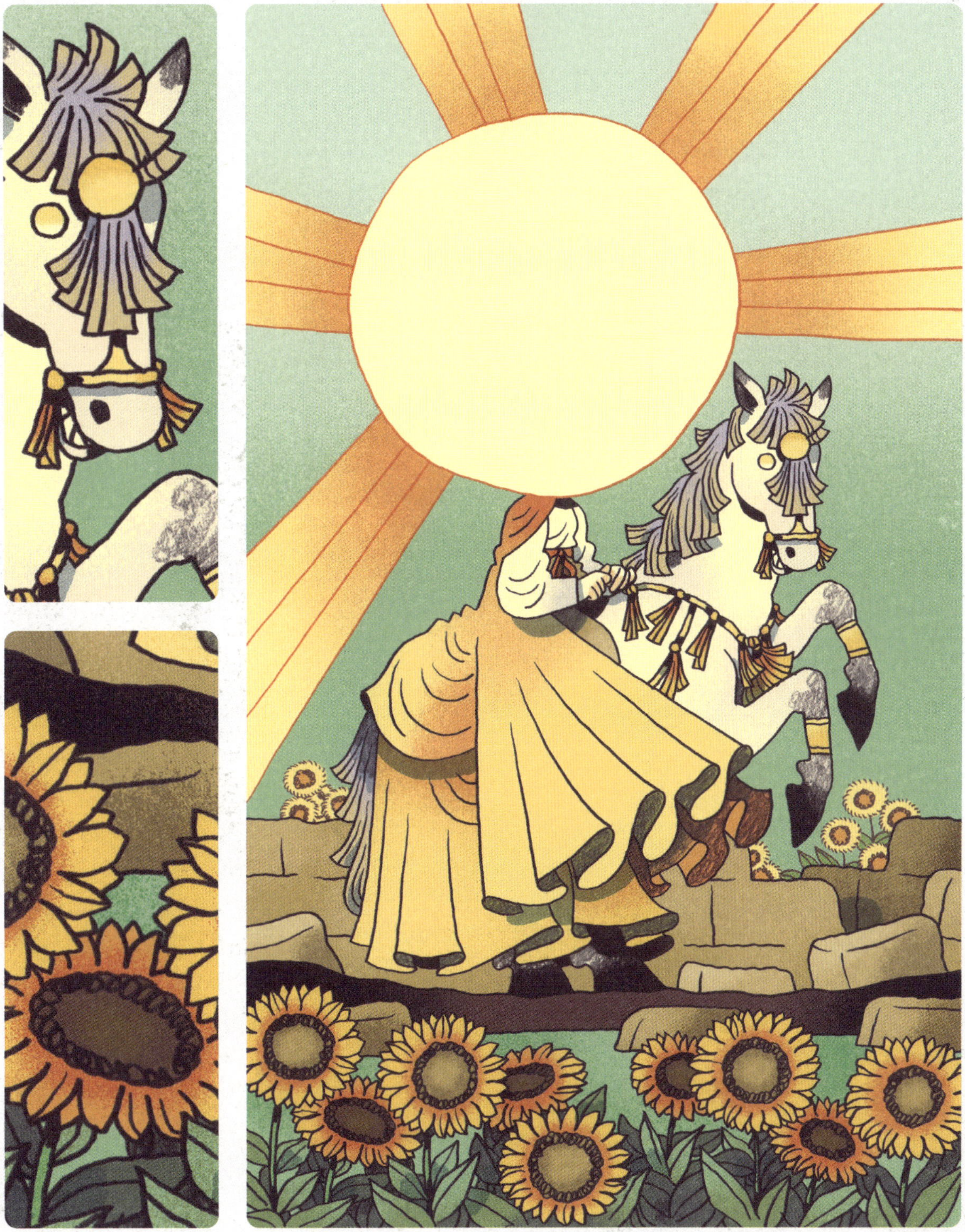

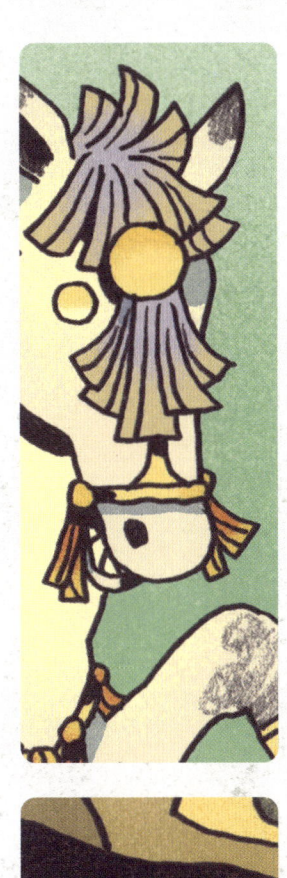
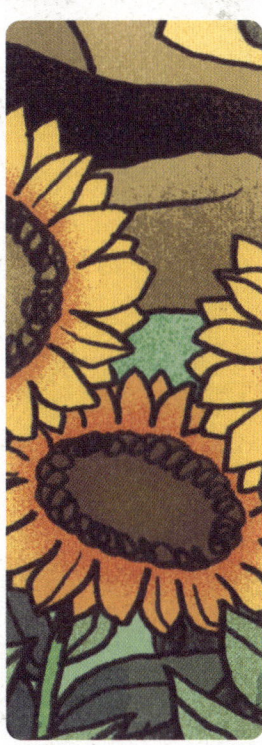

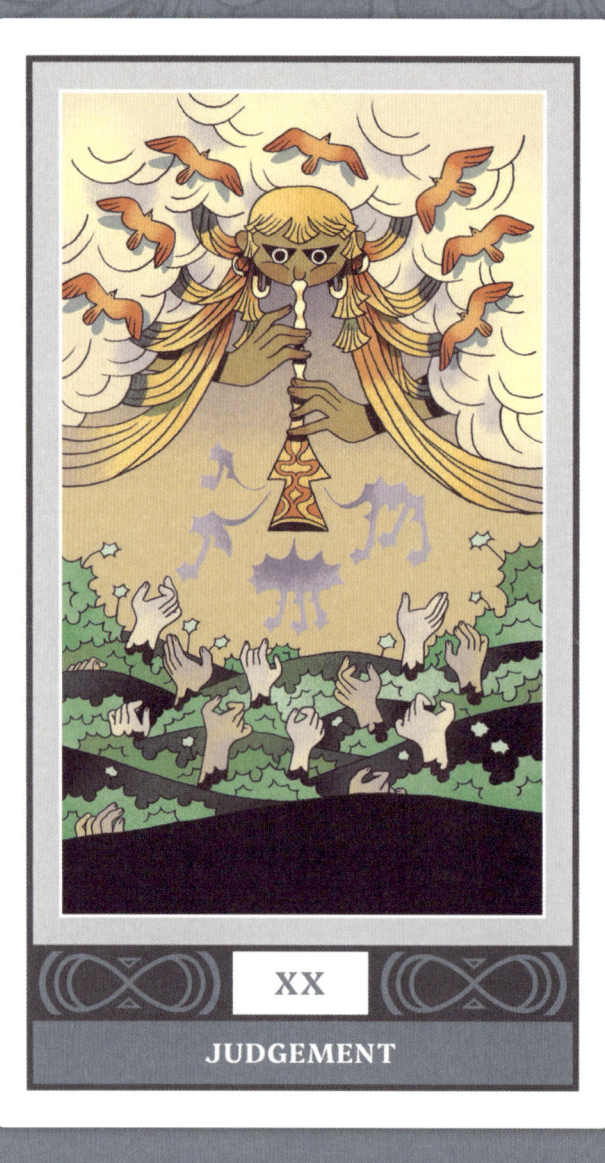

XX

JUDGEMENT

JUDGEMENT

RESURRECTION, RISE, REVOLUTION

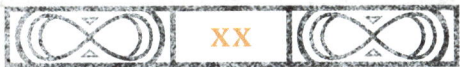

XX

In this card, I again try to represent the angel in a neutral way – I want it to be a strong and powerful figure, capable of raising the dead. I add some red birds to refer to the themes of revolution and resurrection, linked through colour with the figure of the phoenix and the flames. I decide not to show the bodies of the dead, and just suggest them by their rising hands, since the fist is also a symbol of revolution. I want the trumpet to be cool and fun, and try to imagine and draw the music that might come out of it!

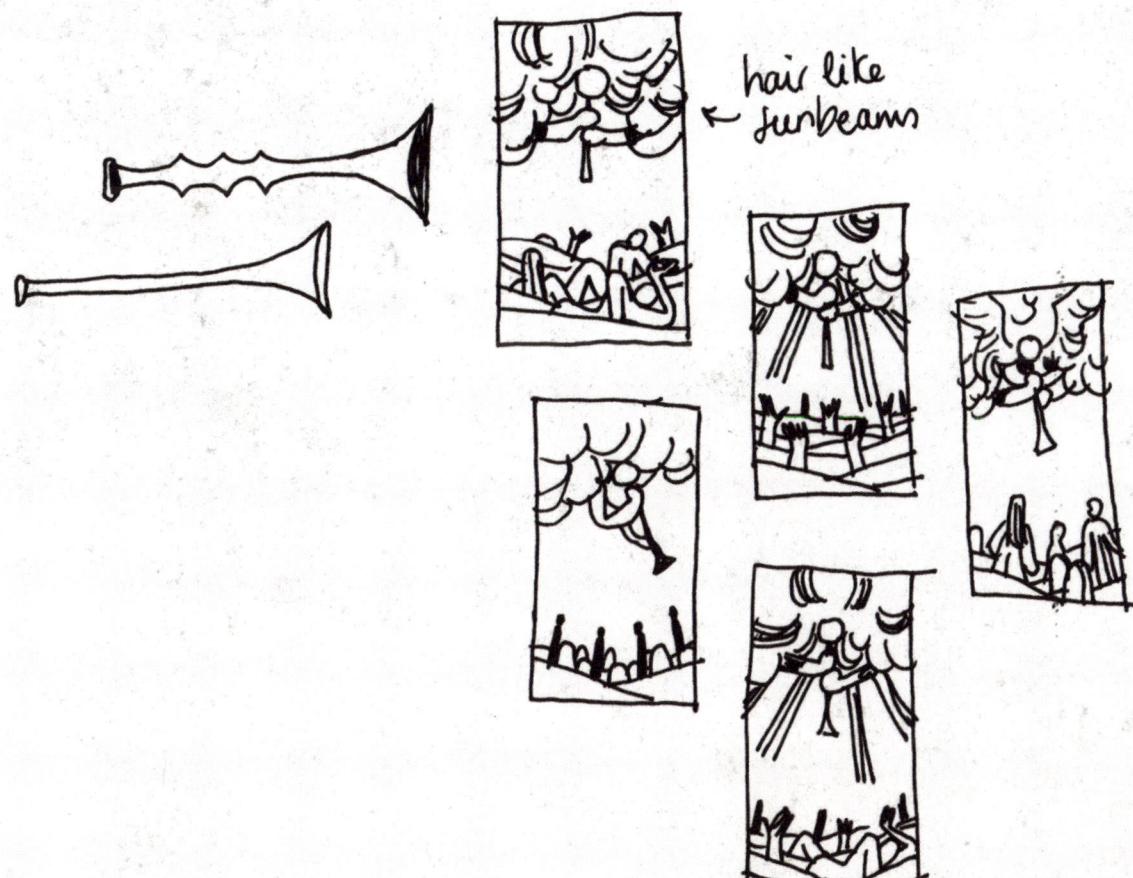

hair like sunbeams

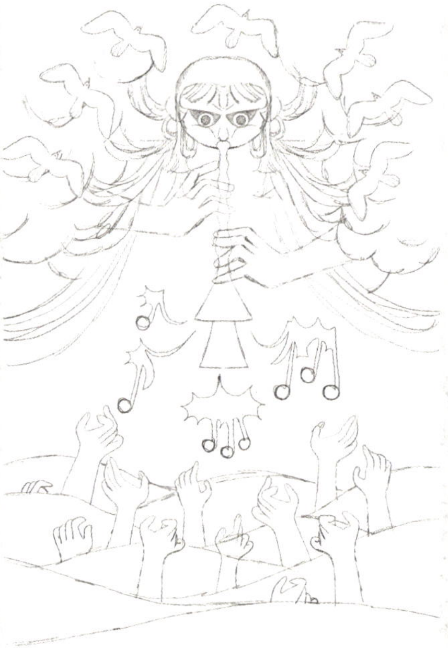

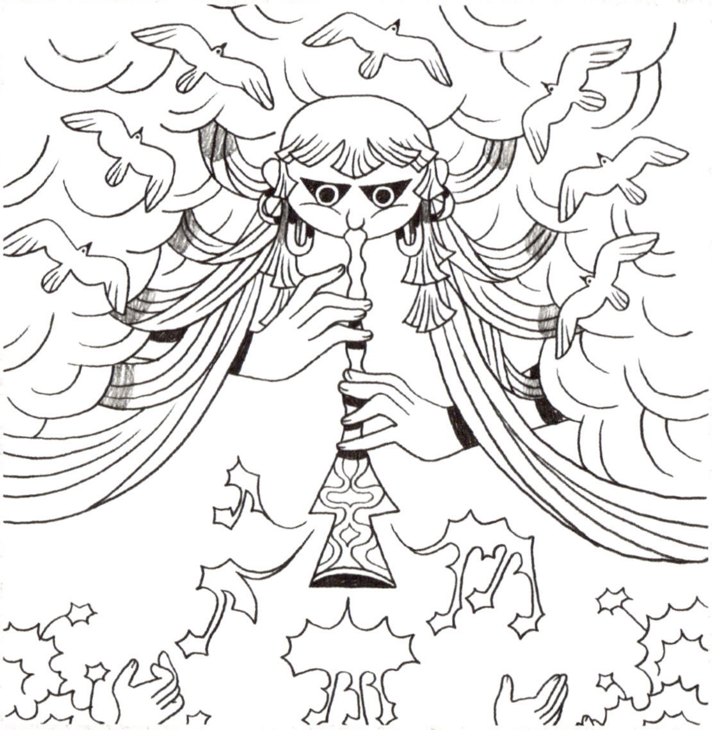

The dead are woken by the
call of the angel's trumpet

The angel's golden hair
almost resembles sunbeams

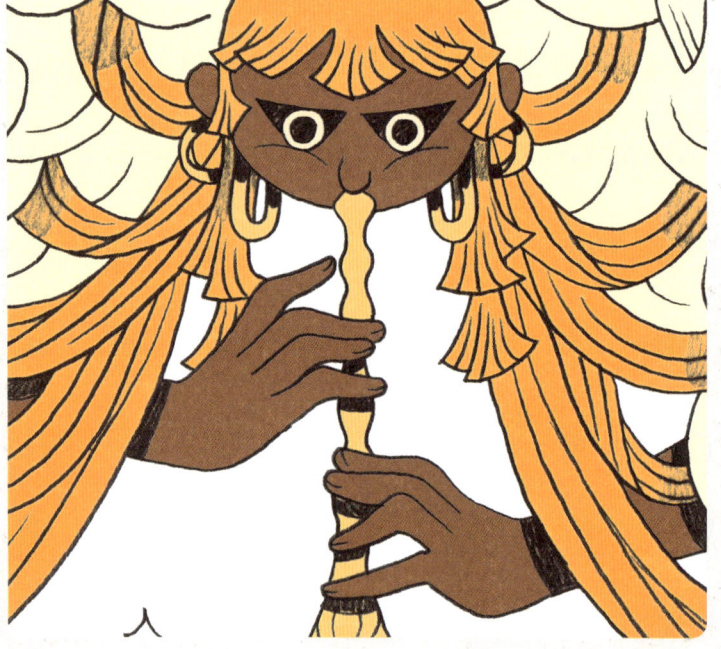

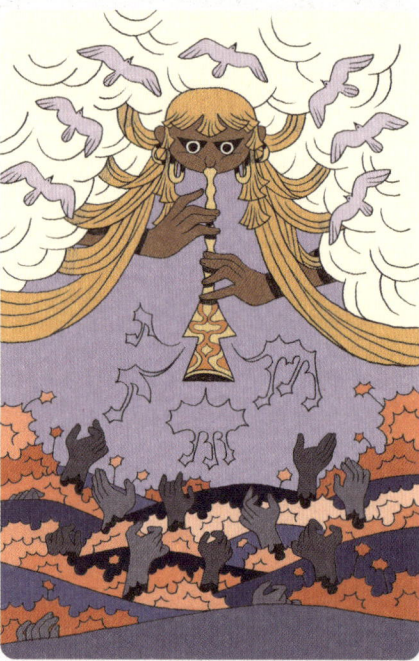

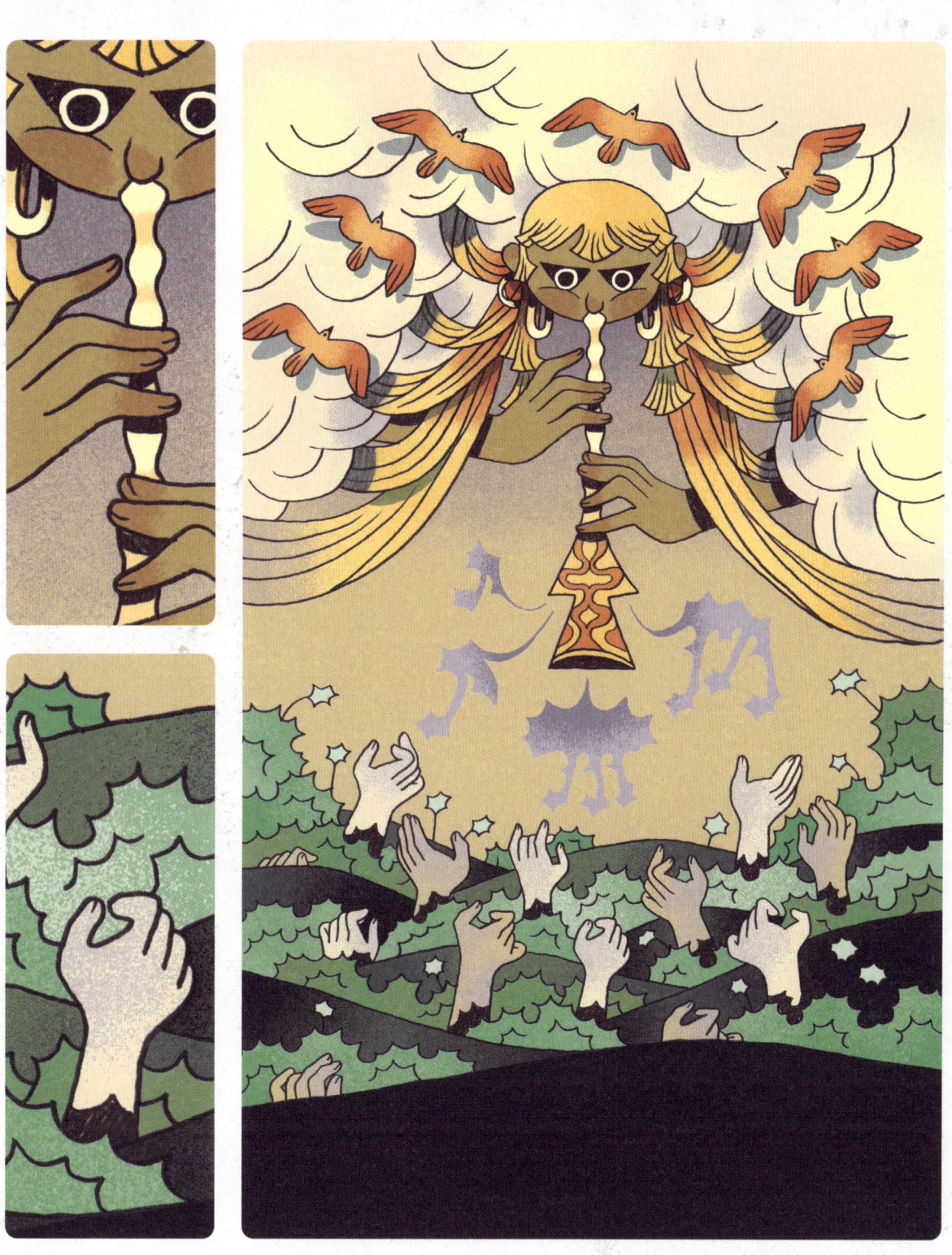

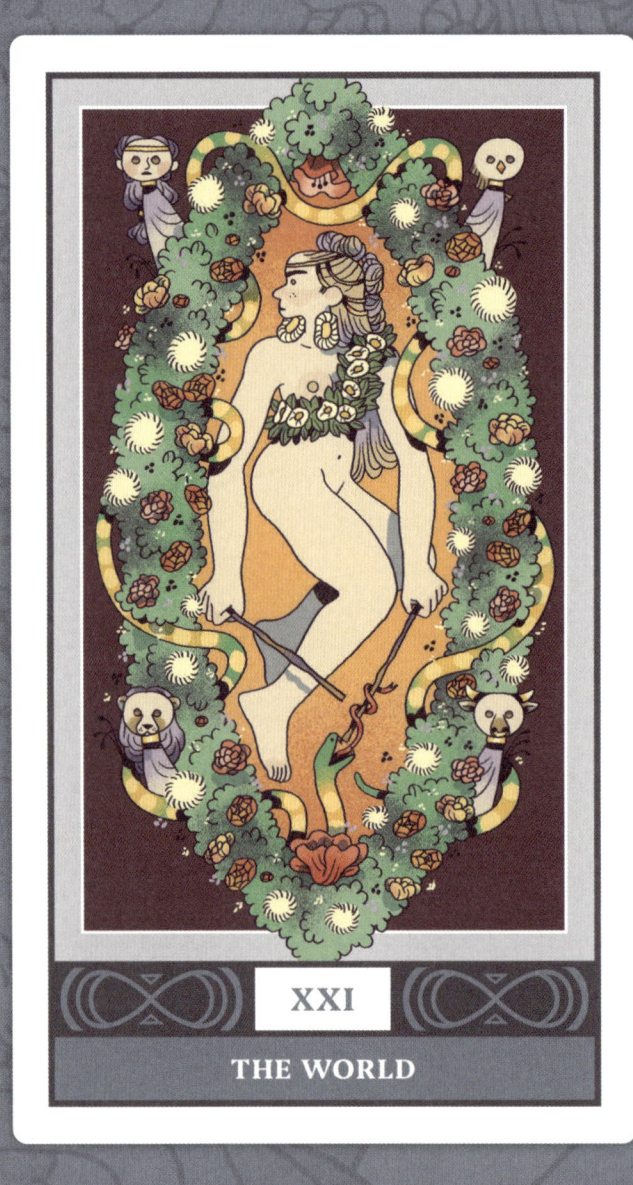

XXI

THE WORLD

THE WORLD

SUCCESS, NIRVANA, INTEGRATION

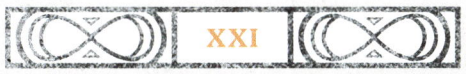

XXI

I initially want to show strength and determination, as this is a card that is linked to success and freedom. I like the idea of representing the wreath with a suggestive, vulva-like shape, in reference to the birth canal as well as pleasure. In my card, the main figure stands firm and relaxed. She wears another wreath of flowers and is surrounded by the four figures of the ancient tetramorph, which accompany her almost as familiars.

* Dancing figure
* nudity
* two magic wands
* wreath
* four corner creatures
  (ancient tetramorph)

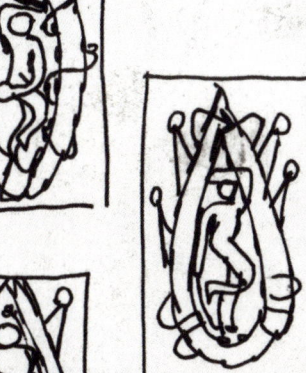

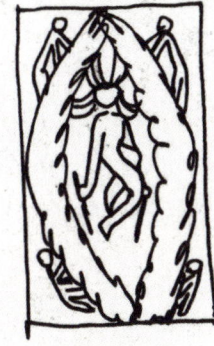

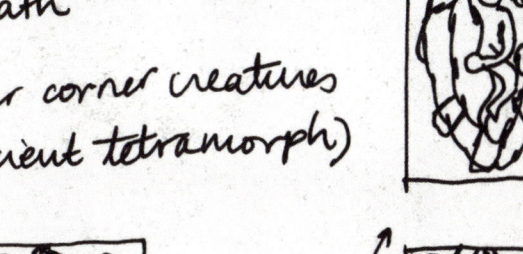

snake

wands
with flowers.

more of
a seed
shape (?)

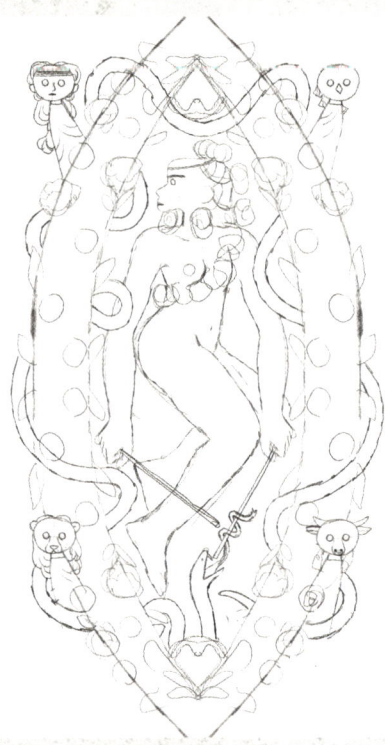

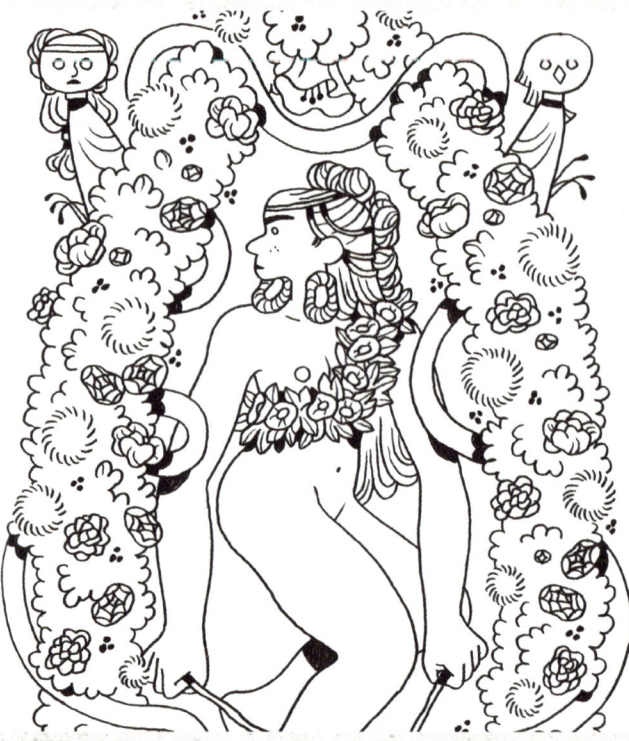

My design leans into the traditional idea of the wreath representing birthing

The figure holds two wands representing the flow of magical energy

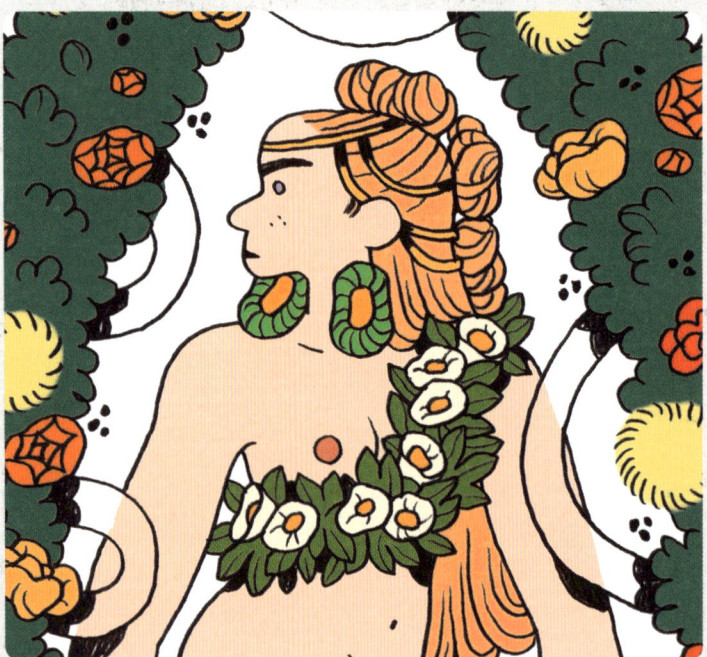

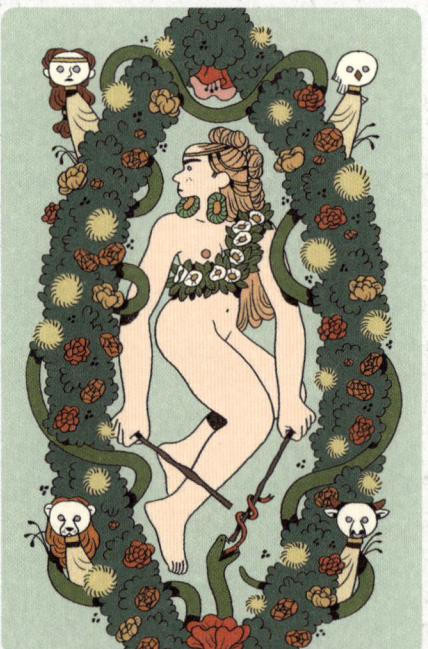

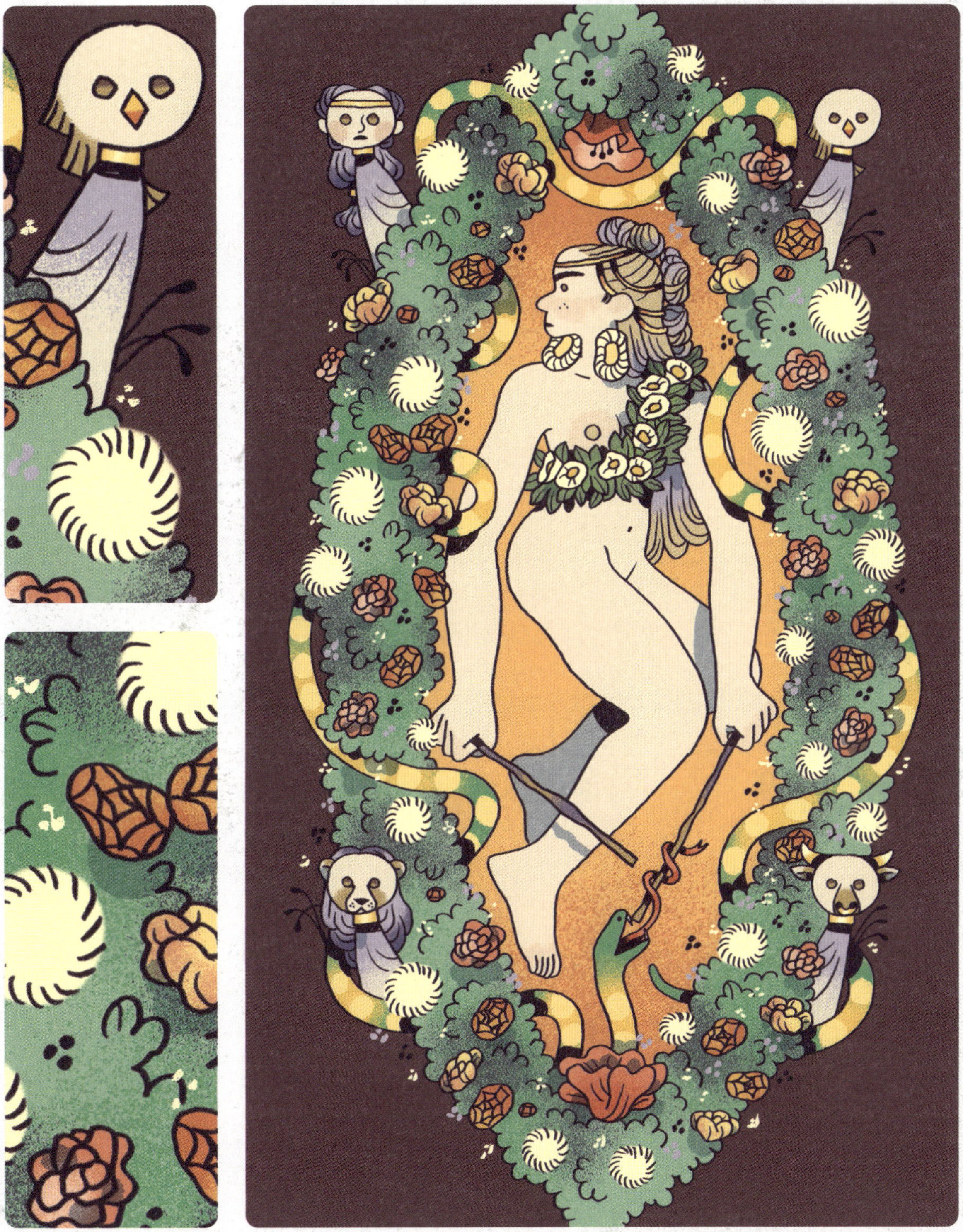

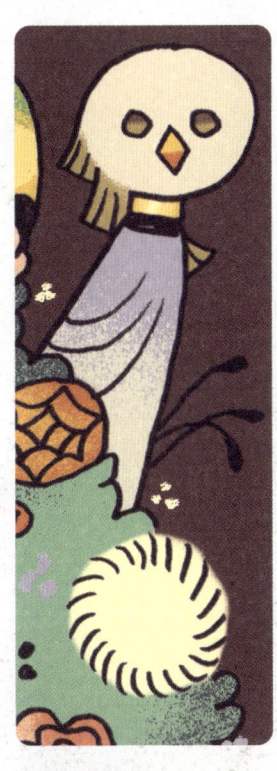

ARTIST'S CONCLUSION

In this project, I dived into the imaginative world of tarot like I never had before, which made this adventure totally enjoyable! Paying attention to all the details and creating a unified yet diverse universe for the Major Arcana was a great challenge. When looking at the final illustrations, I'd like the reader to pay special attention to the forms that are repeated, and let themselves be carried away by the focused and mysterious looks of the characters.

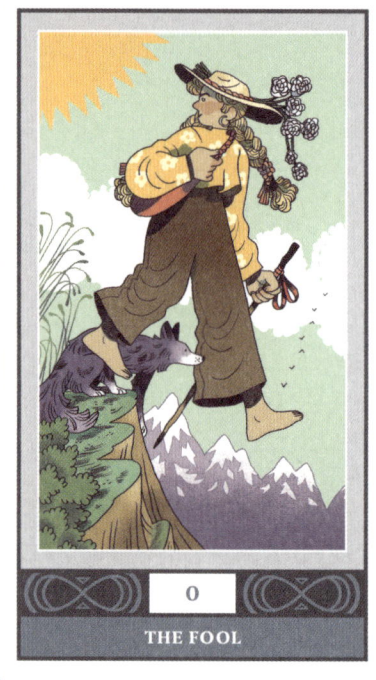

THE FOOL

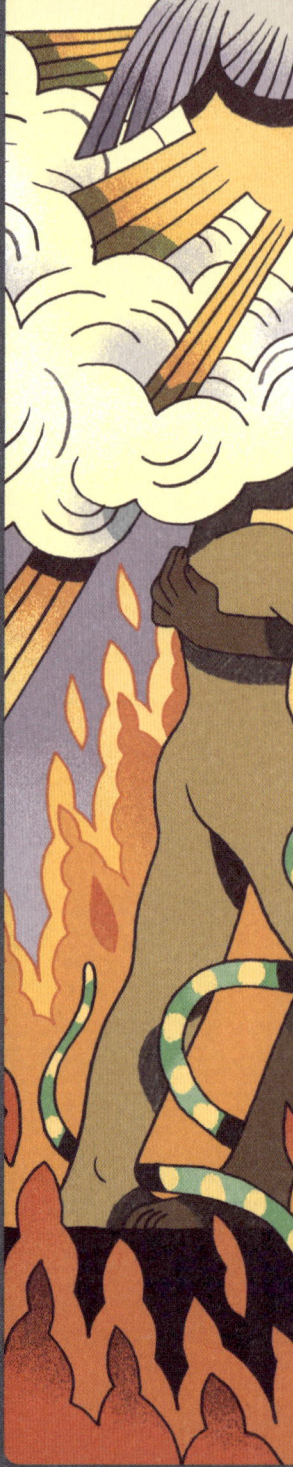

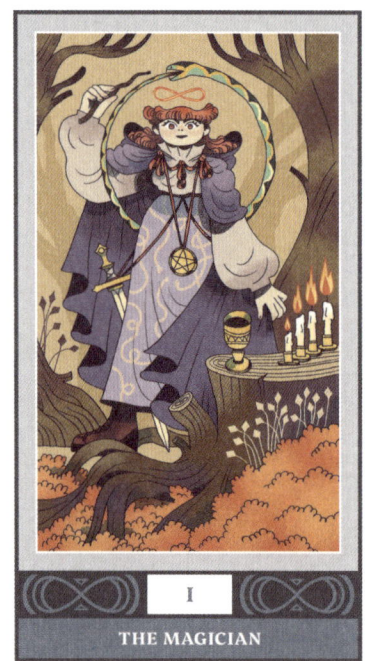

THE MAGICIAN

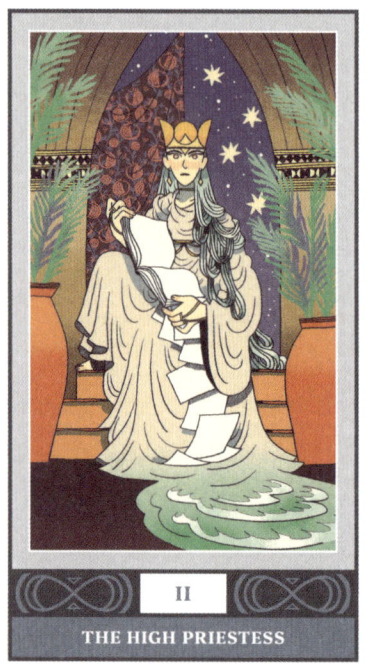

THE HIGH PRIESTESS

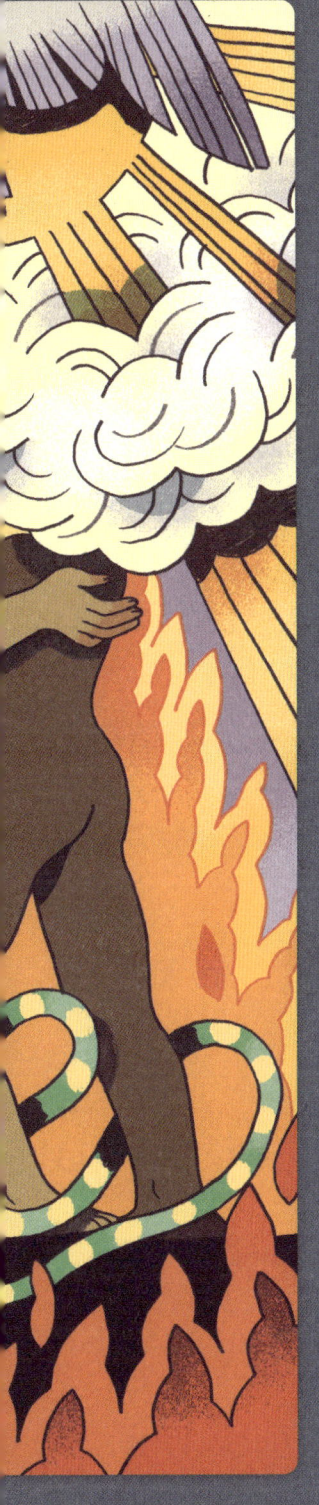

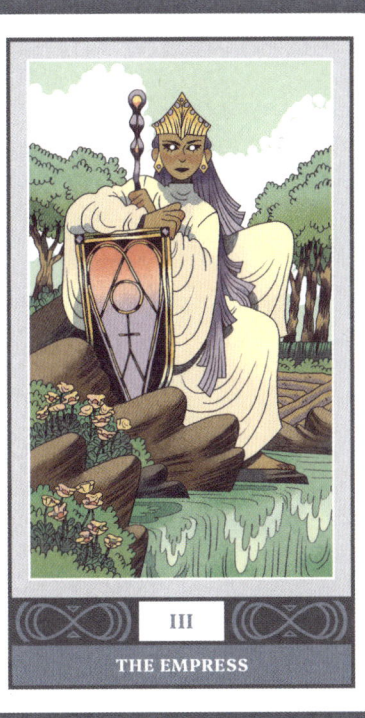

III

THE EMPRESS

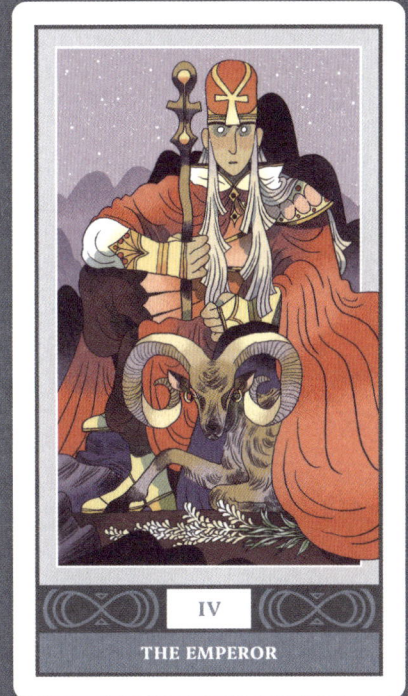

IV

THE EMPEROR

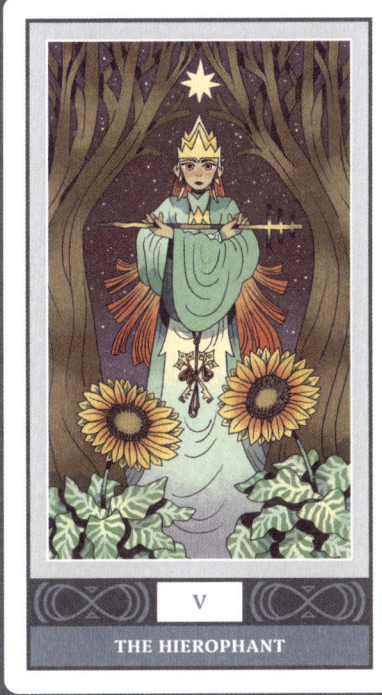

V

THE HIEROPHANT

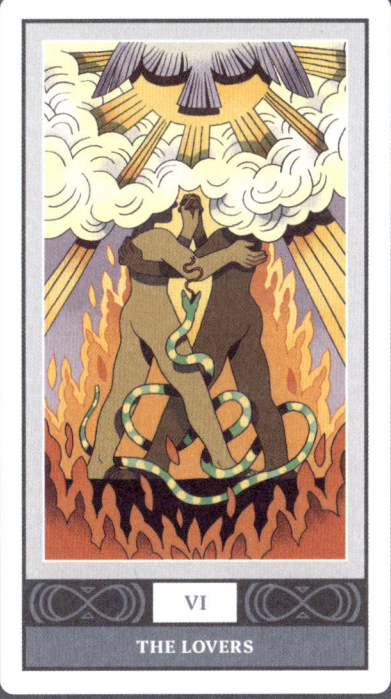

VI

THE LOVERS

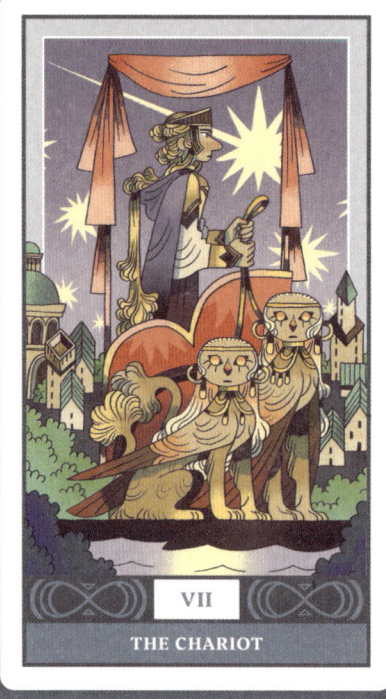

VII

THE CHARIOT

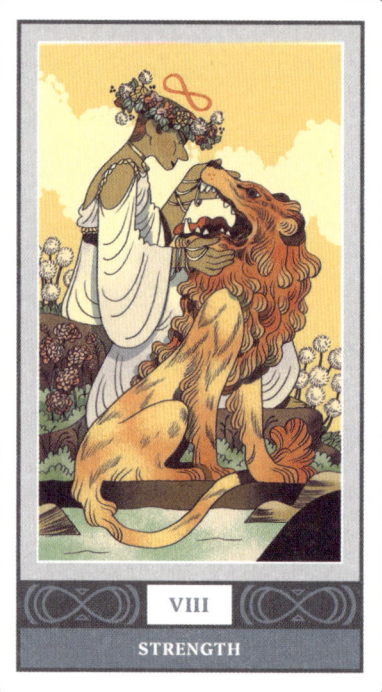

VIII

STRENGTH

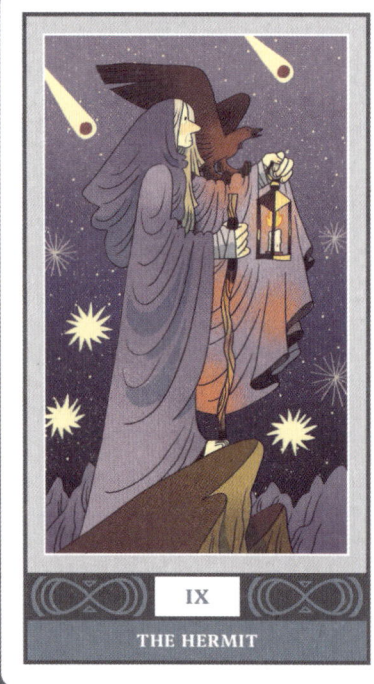

IX

THE HERMIT

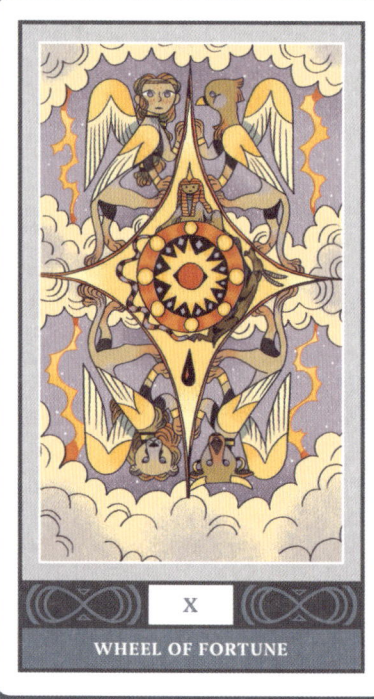

X

WHEEL OF FORTUNE

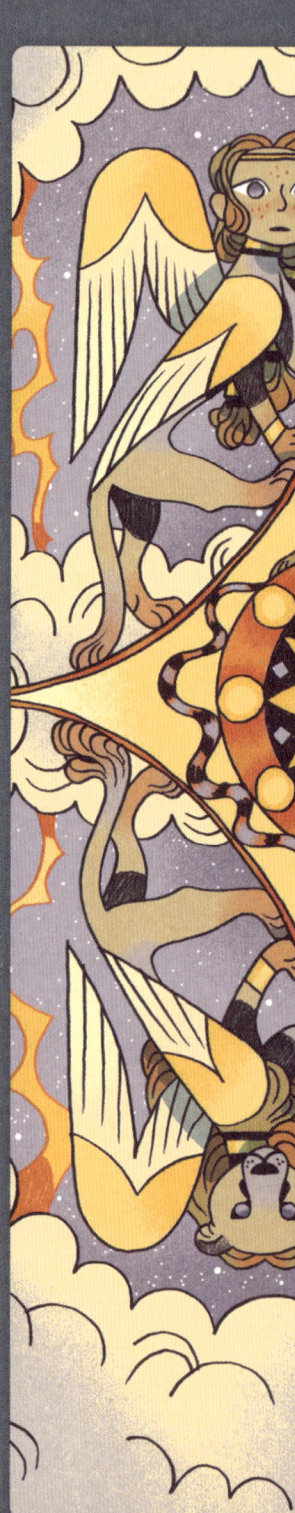

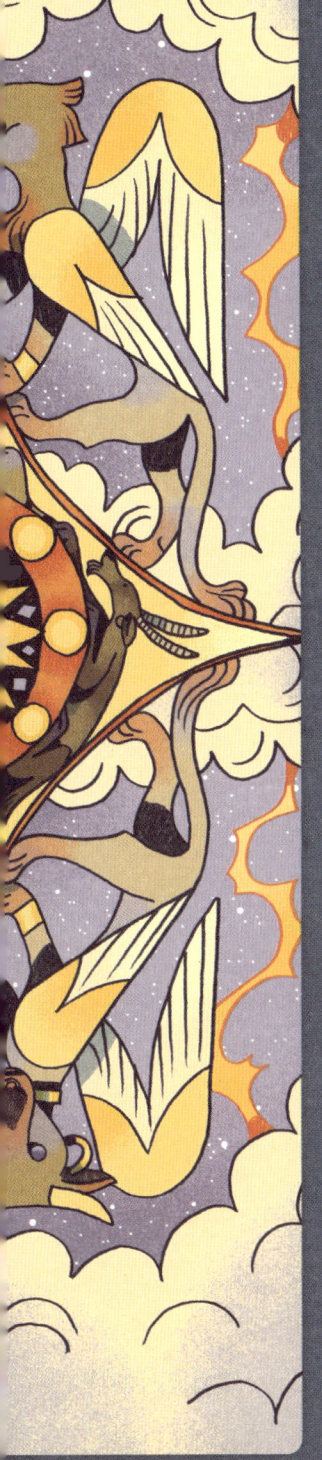

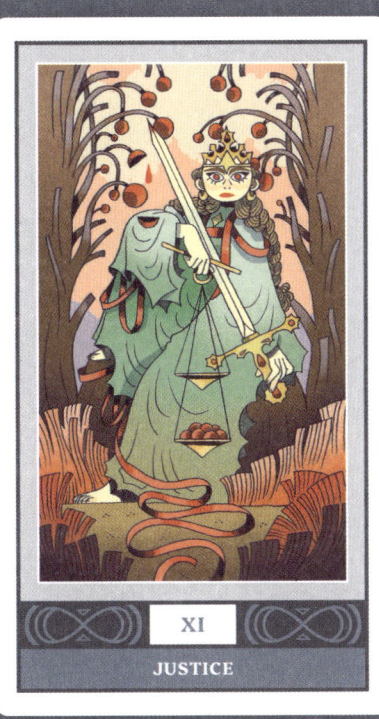

XI

JUSTICE

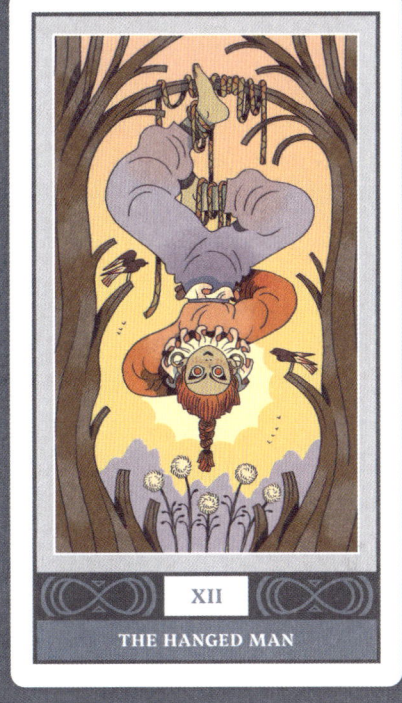

XII

THE HANGED MAN

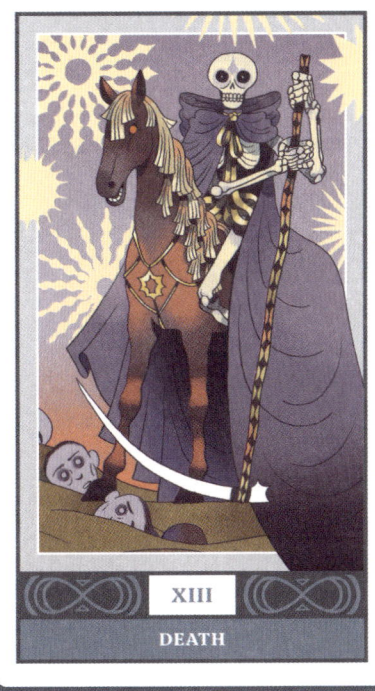

XIII

DEATH

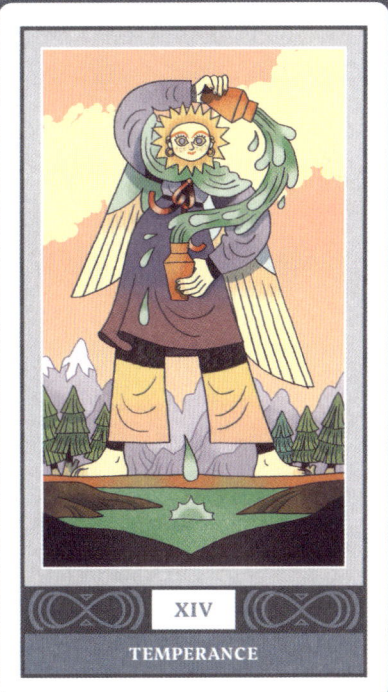

XIV

TEMPERANCE

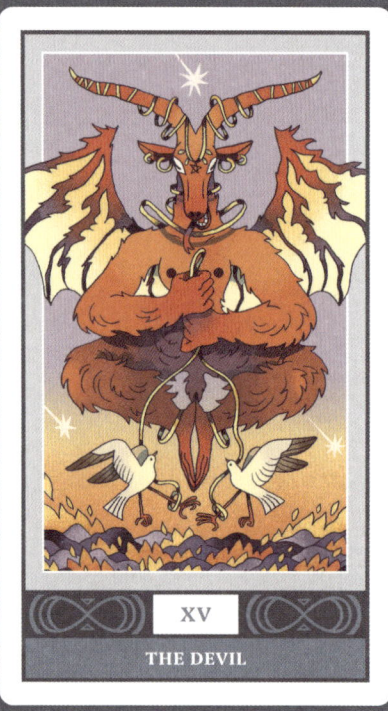

XV

THE DEVIL

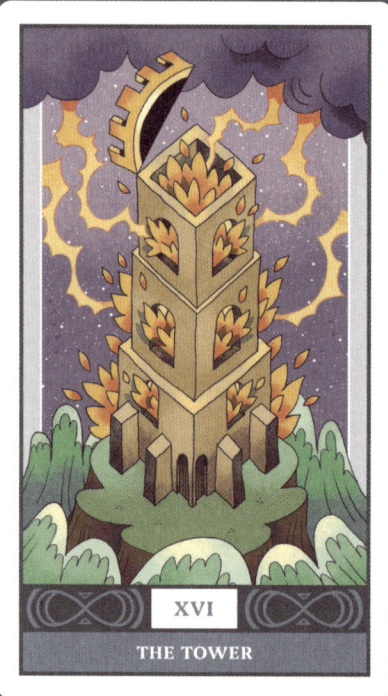

XVI

THE TOWER

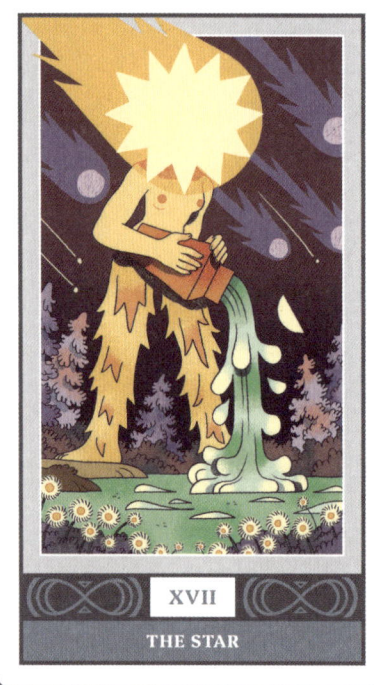

XVII

THE STAR

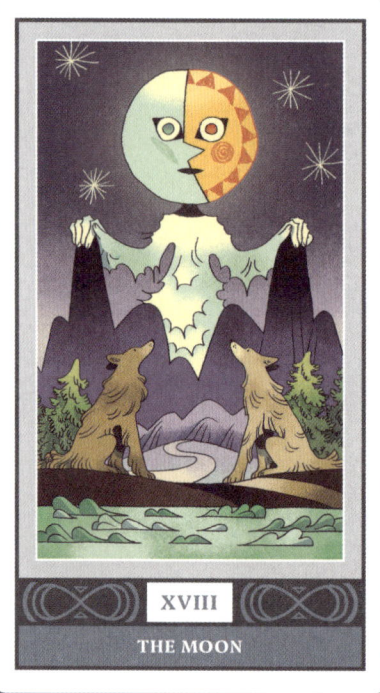

XVIII

THE MOON

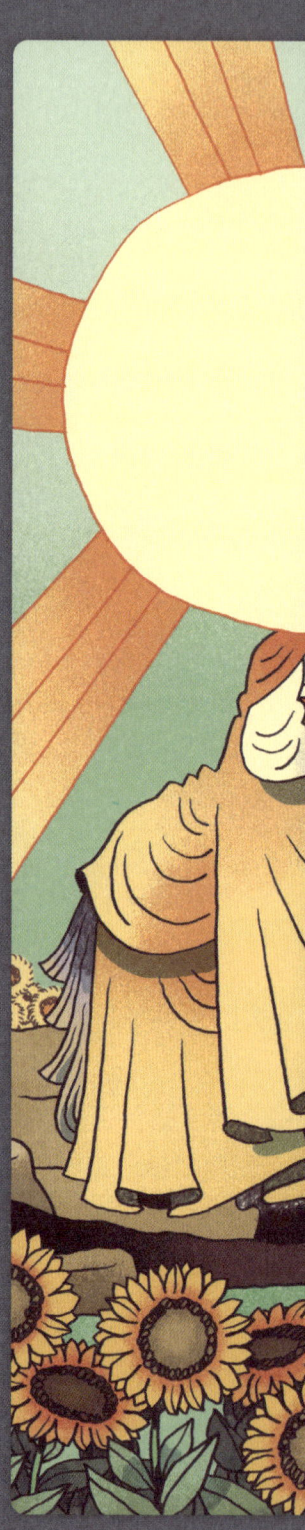

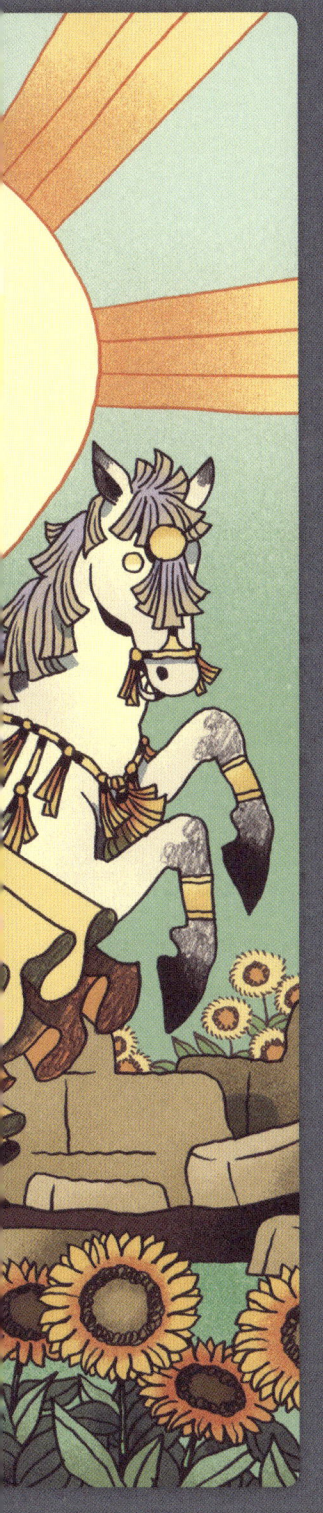

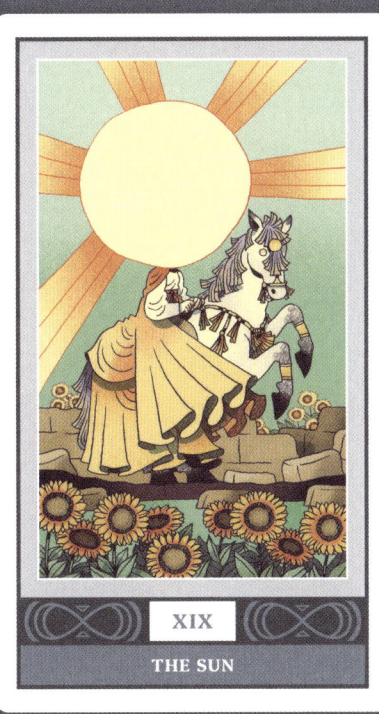

XIX

THE SUN

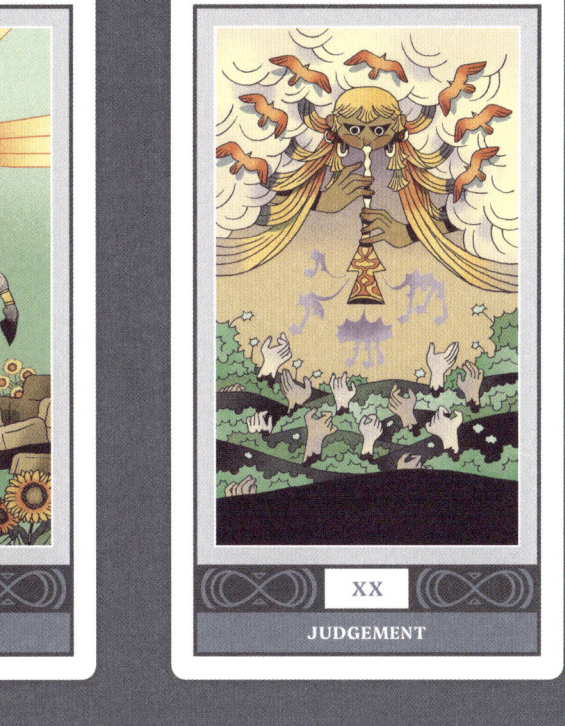

XX

JUDGEMENT

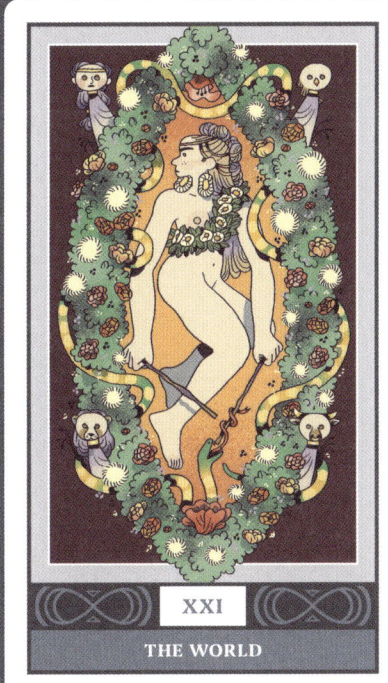

XXI

THE WORLD

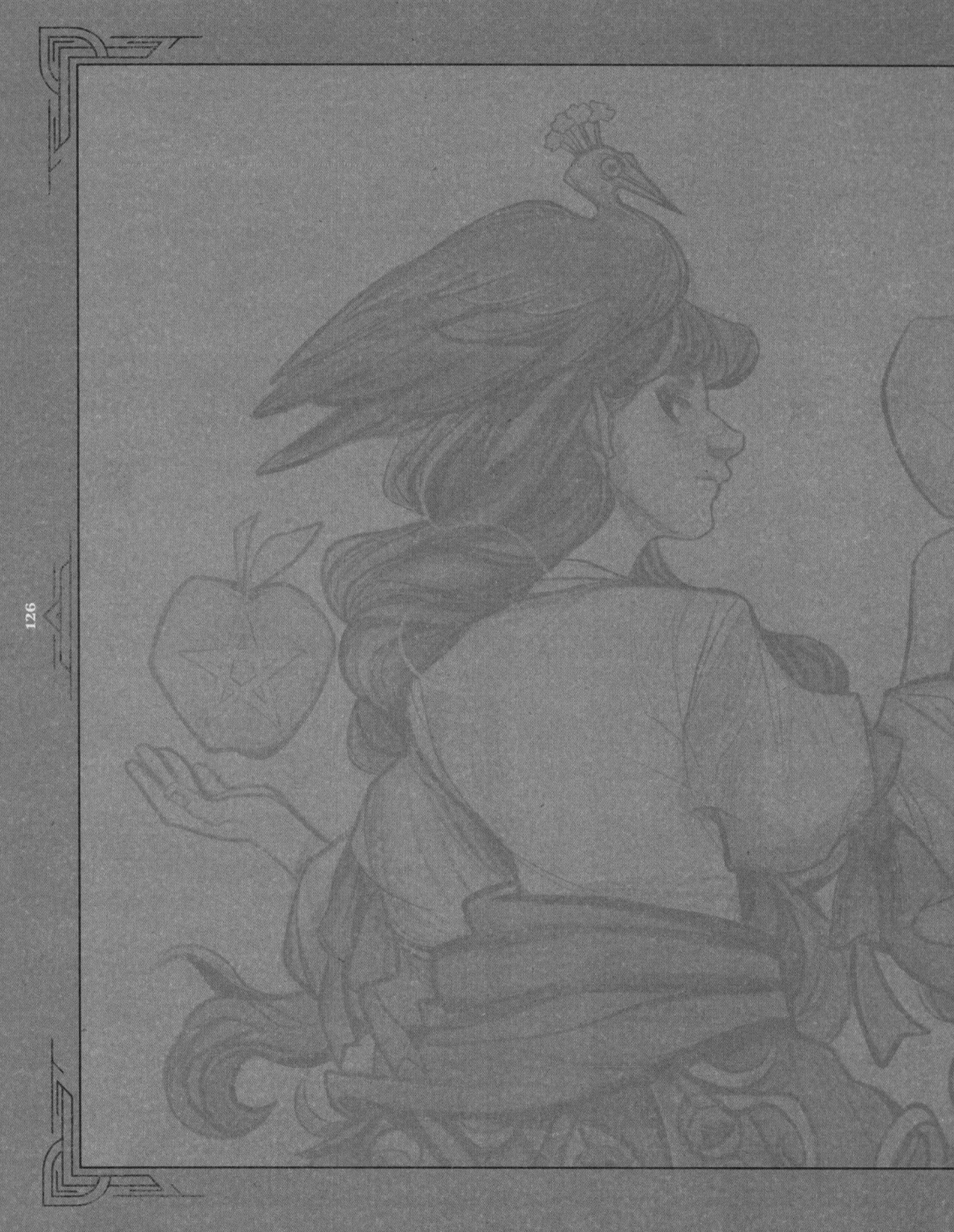

THE MINOR
ARCANA

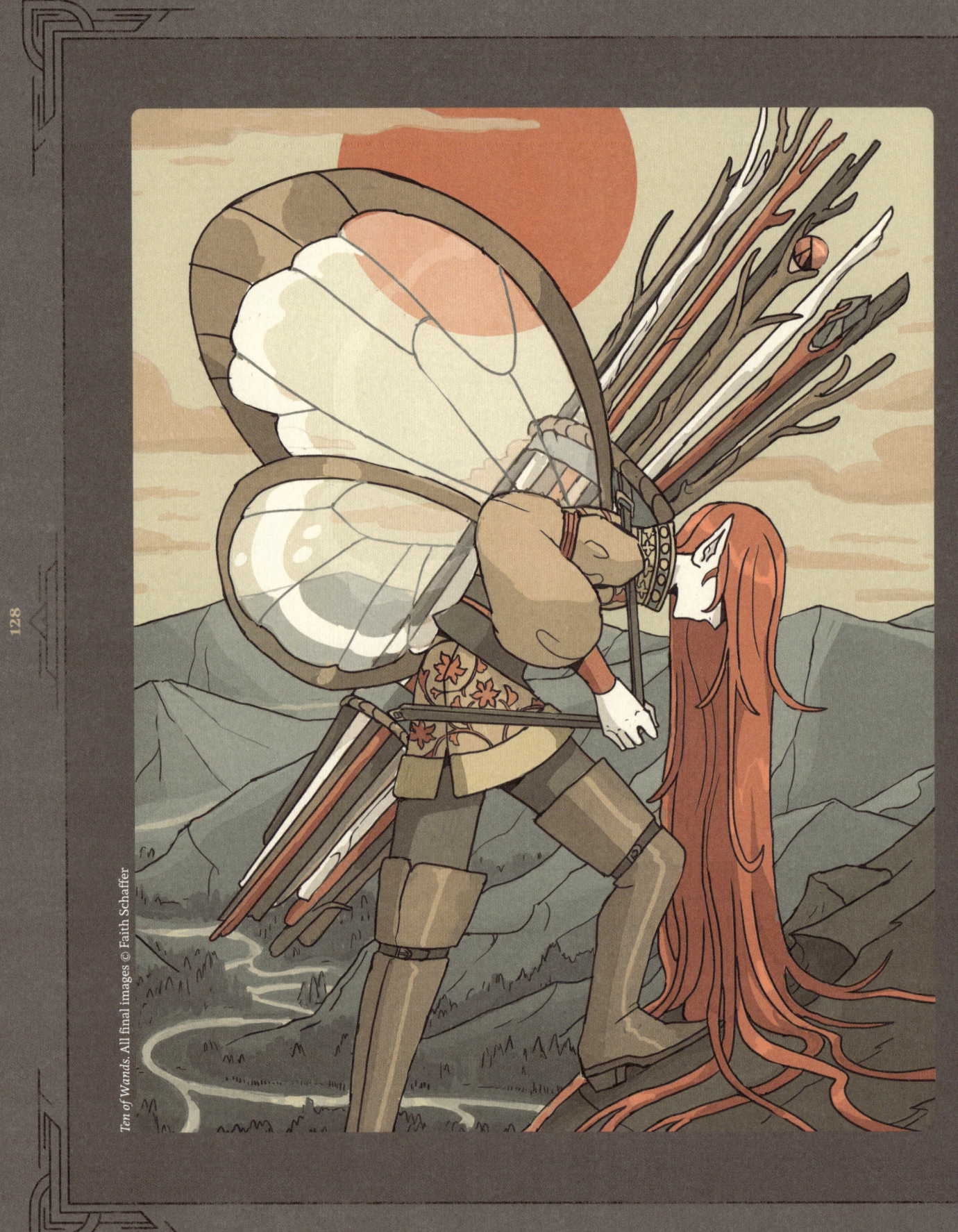

Ten of Wands. All final images © Faith Schaffer

THE SUIT OF
WANDS

INTRODUCTION BY SASHA GRAHAM

Wands reflect the world of elemental Fire. Wands and Fire represent all energetic human qualities: passion, inspiration, spirituality, virility, and enthusiasm. Wands are molten desires racing through the veins, pumping the fluttering heart, and waking us up in the morning. Wands and Fire energy drive us out of bed and into our day. Elemental Fire inspires crowds to action. Wands drum up collective energy. They also direct energy. Consider how, in popular culture and our imaginations, all magicians, witches, and magical folk point their magic wands to direct their intentions.

How will the symbol of Wands (also called batons, rods, staves, sticks, torches, or clubs) appear through the suit? Will the characters hold and collect wands as the suit progresses? Will they wield wands, using them as tools of magic, or simply use them as torches that light the way for the characters to move about the world?

The Ace of Wands is like a spark of fire in darkness. It spreads through the suit, gaining strength until reaching the blazing Ten of Wands. How will the landscape of Wands and elemental Fire appear? Is it molten lava or dark forests with glowing firelight? Is it populated by the passion and energy of the characters? Are there salamanders, snakes, dragons, and demons, or unique fire creations? What objects and symbols will populate the world of elemental Fire? How would it feel to move through this universe? Would the body pulse with excitement upon entering a Wands card? How might a reader use these cards for a magic spell?

The Wands court cards are the King, Queen, Knight, and Page of Fire. How can the human embodiment of Fire be visually expressed? Consider what the King of Fire might look and feel like. Is the King of Fire a rock star like Jim Morrison or a preacher in a pulpit? Is the Queen of Fire an actress with the charisma to mesmerize millions, or a goddess of sensuality, or both?

FAITH SCHAFFER

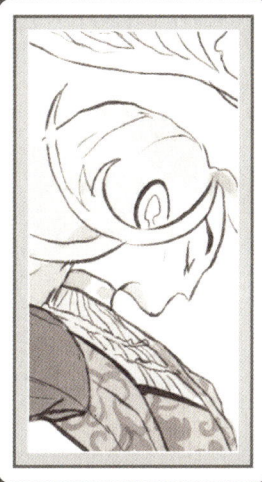

ARTIST'S INSIGHT

To me, tarot is the purest form of illustration: a collection of art loaded with symbols to be mused on and interpreted. I was drawn to the suit of Wands because the wands are such a fun and varied compositional element. They can add strong diagonals or stark verticals to a piece, which I intend to explore fully in my version of the suit.

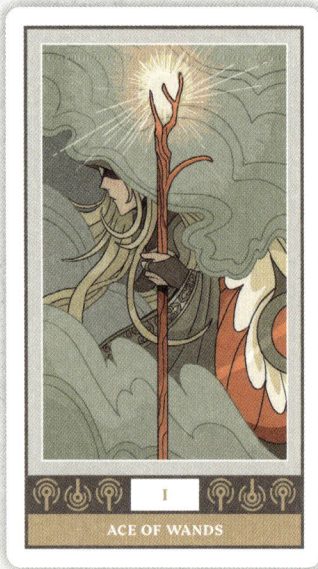

ACE OF WANDS

ACE OF WANDS

DESIRE, INTENTION, INSPIRATION

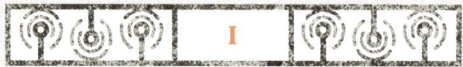

The key symbols here, other than the wand itself, are the clouds and a hand. I interpret the clouds as mist to add some dynamic movement to the piece. This also adds a feeling of mysticism and mystery. Obscuring the wand-bearer's face makes their hand the most interesting part of them that we can see, so the hand still reads cleanly as an important symbol. The wand glows with a magical light that illuminates the mist.

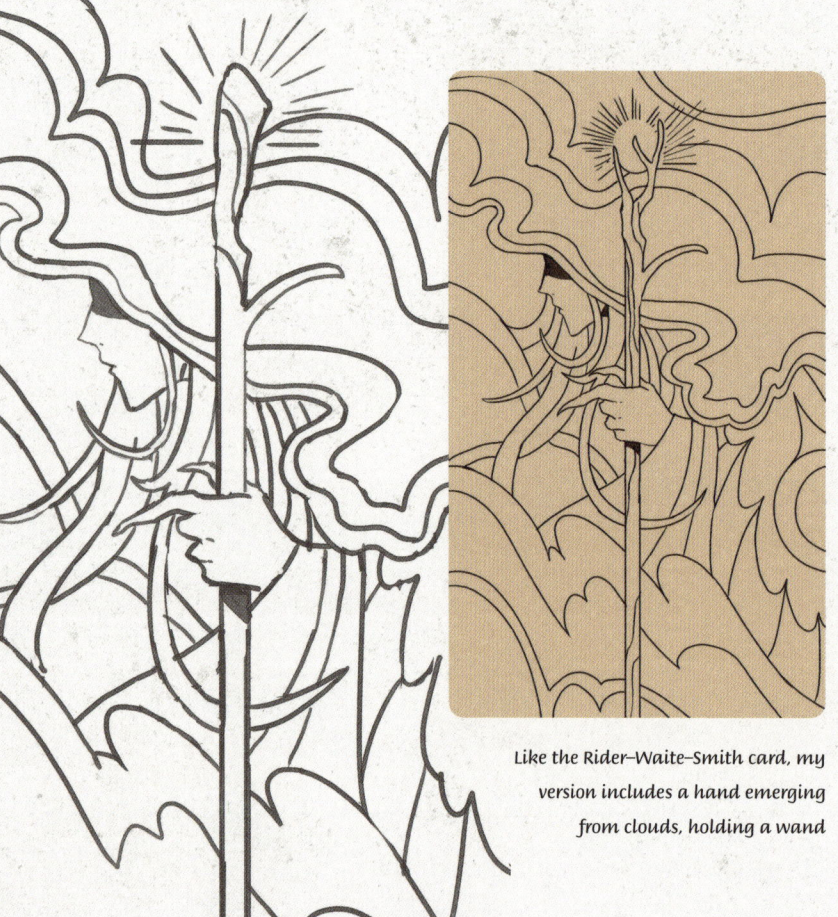

Like the Rider–Waite–Smith card, my version includes a hand emerging from clouds, holding a wand

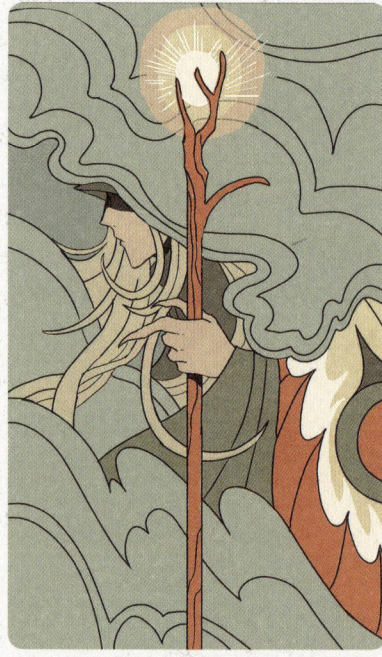

The character is cloaked in mist, making the wand the focal point

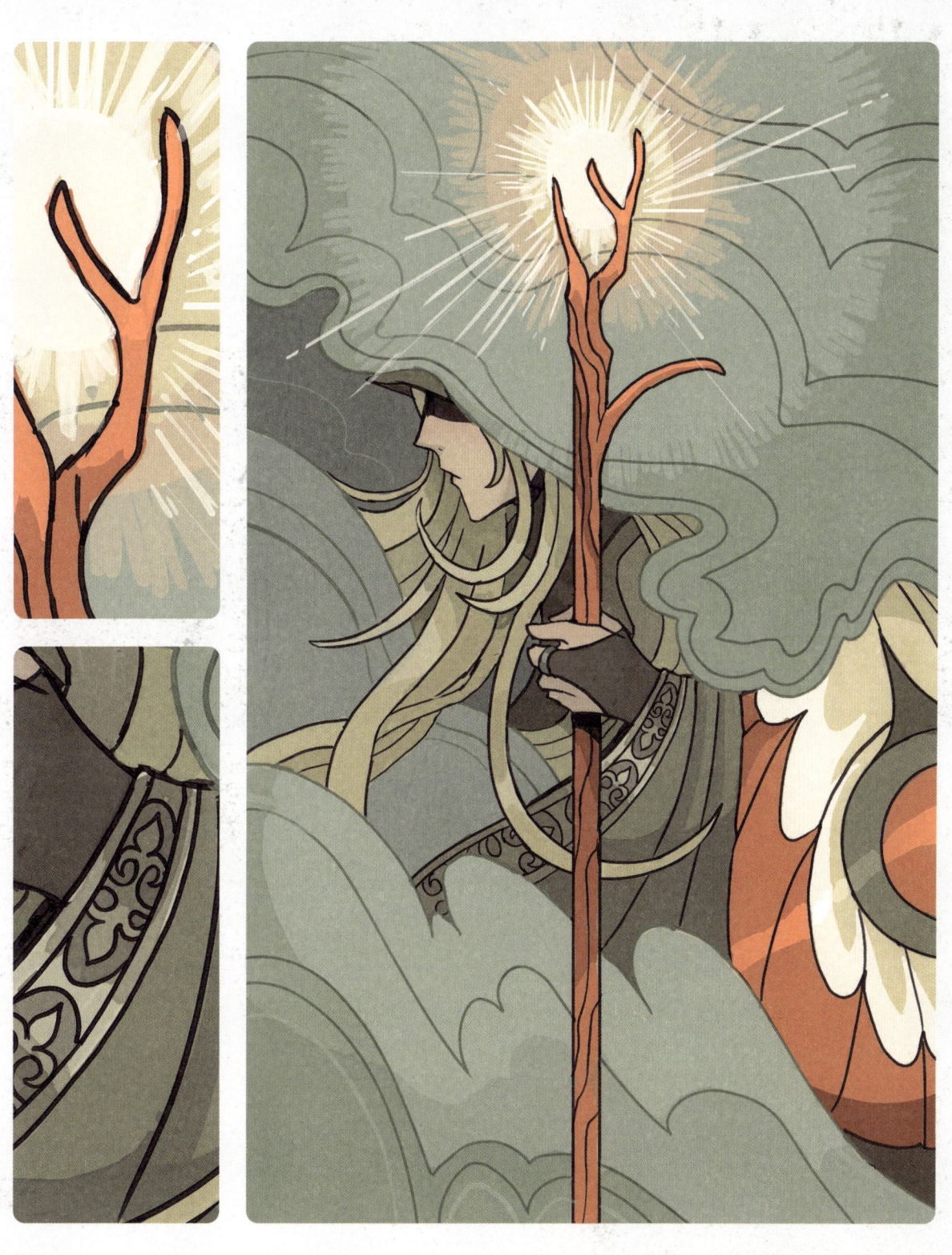

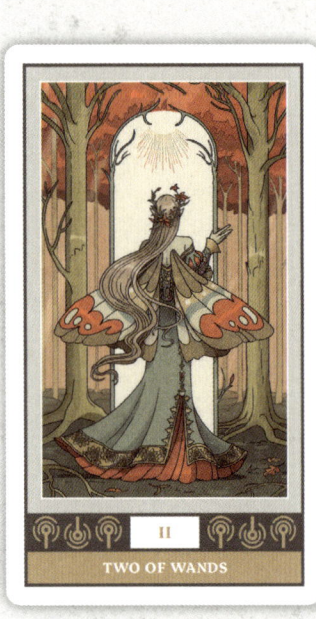

TWO OF WANDS

TWO OF WANDS

ENTERPRISE, PLANNING, GATHERING

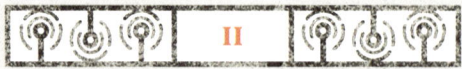

The wands on this card form a gateway and a figure ponders at the threshold, hesitating to enter. The composition for this image comes to me almost immediately in the planning stage. While it's fairly simple and straightforward, it will create a strong parallel with the Nine of Wands, which symbolizes stepping over the threshold. Here the figure has their back to us; in the Nine of Wands, they will be facing the viewer.

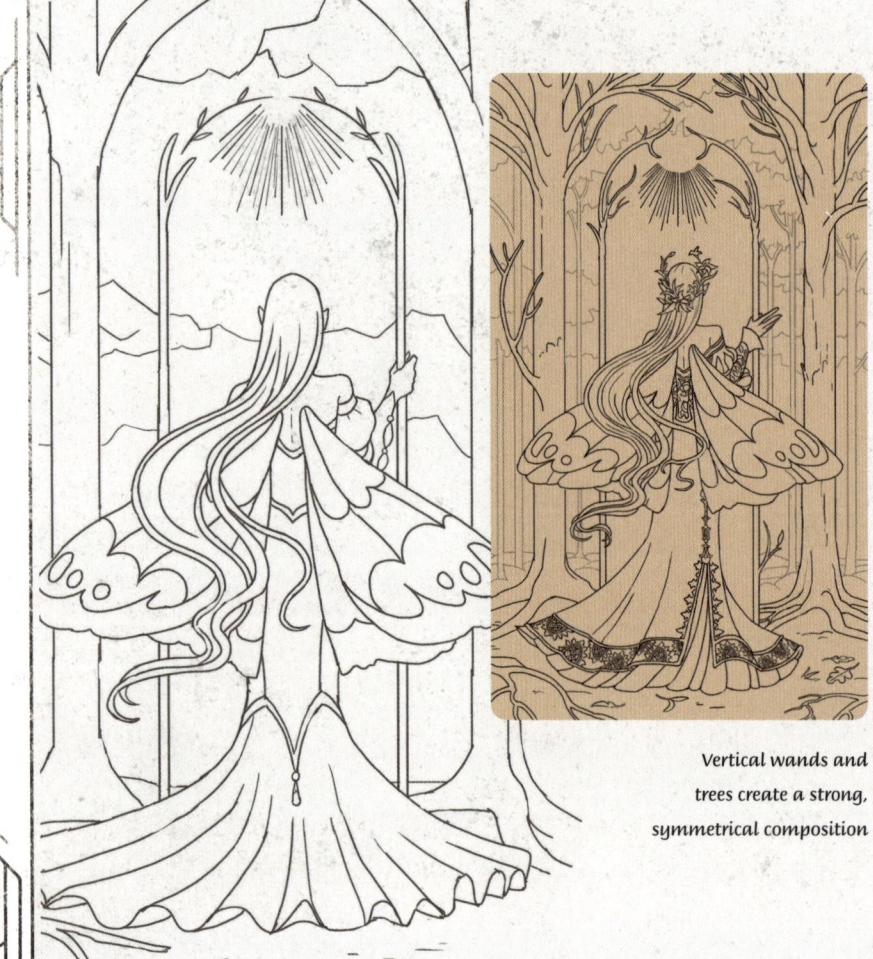

Vertical wands and
trees create a strong,
symmetrical composition

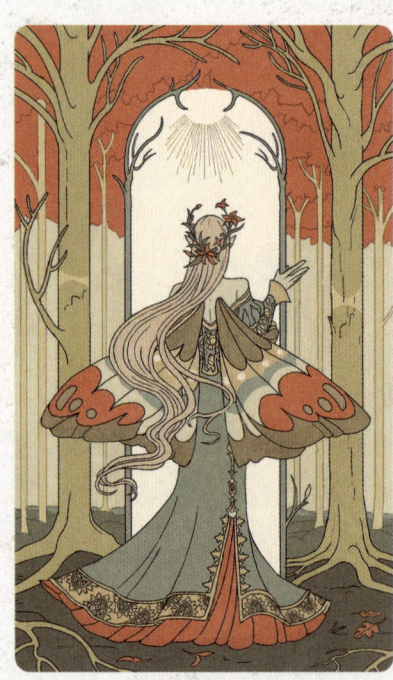

The open portal is mysterious
and inviting. Will the character
dare to step through?

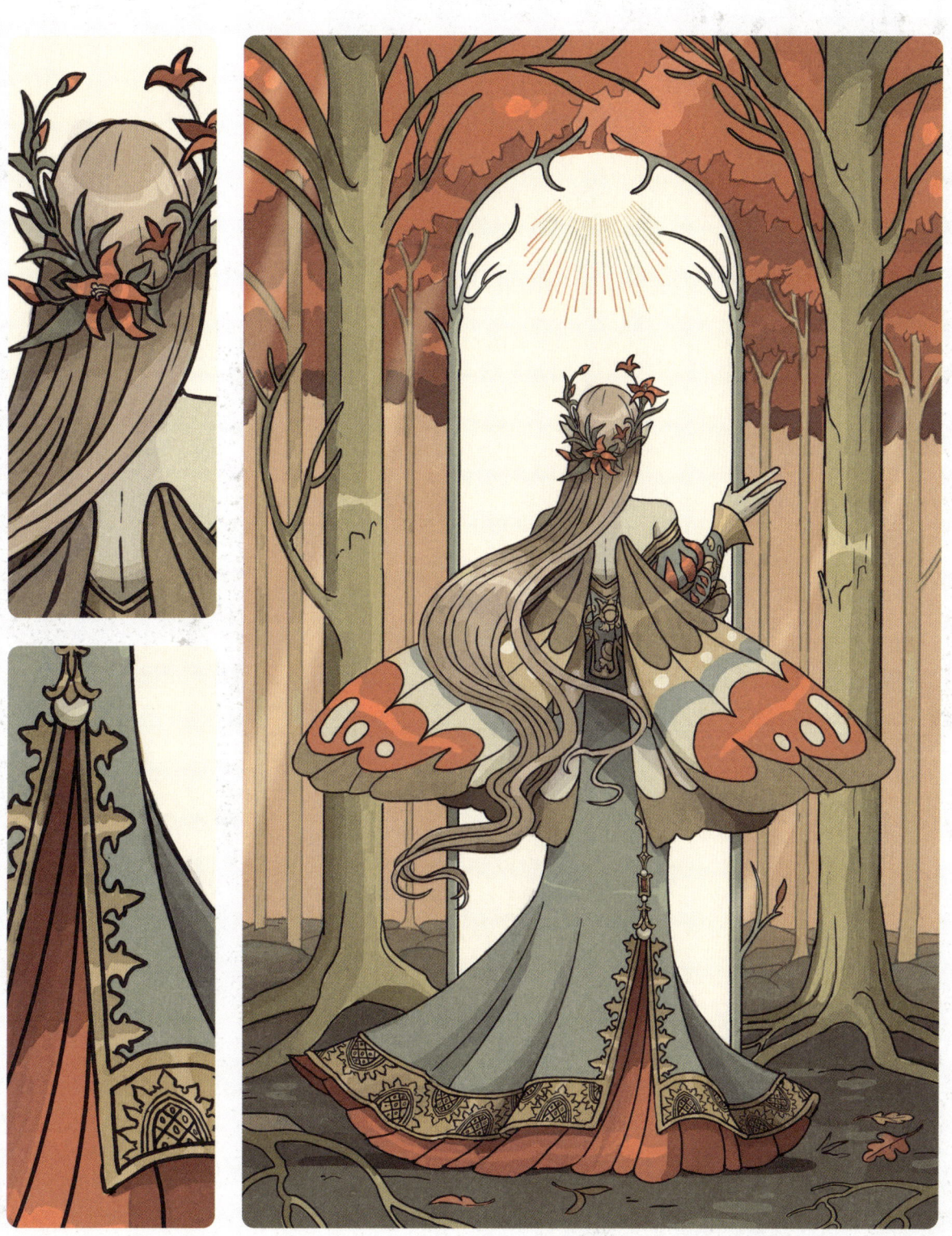

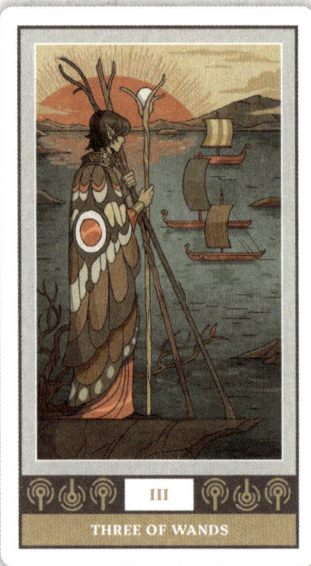

THREE OF WANDS

134

THREE OF WANDS

COLLABORATION, BUSINESS PARTNERSHIPS, MOVING FORWARD

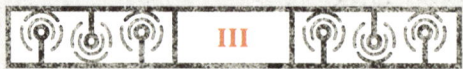

The Three of Wands shows a figure watching ships as they depart. This piece is where I really decide on my more graphic style for this suit – the image flattens perspective for the sake of an easy visual read of all the components. Here the wands add a diagonal element to a composition that would otherwise be static and boring. The round orange sun creates contrast with the straight lines elsewhere.

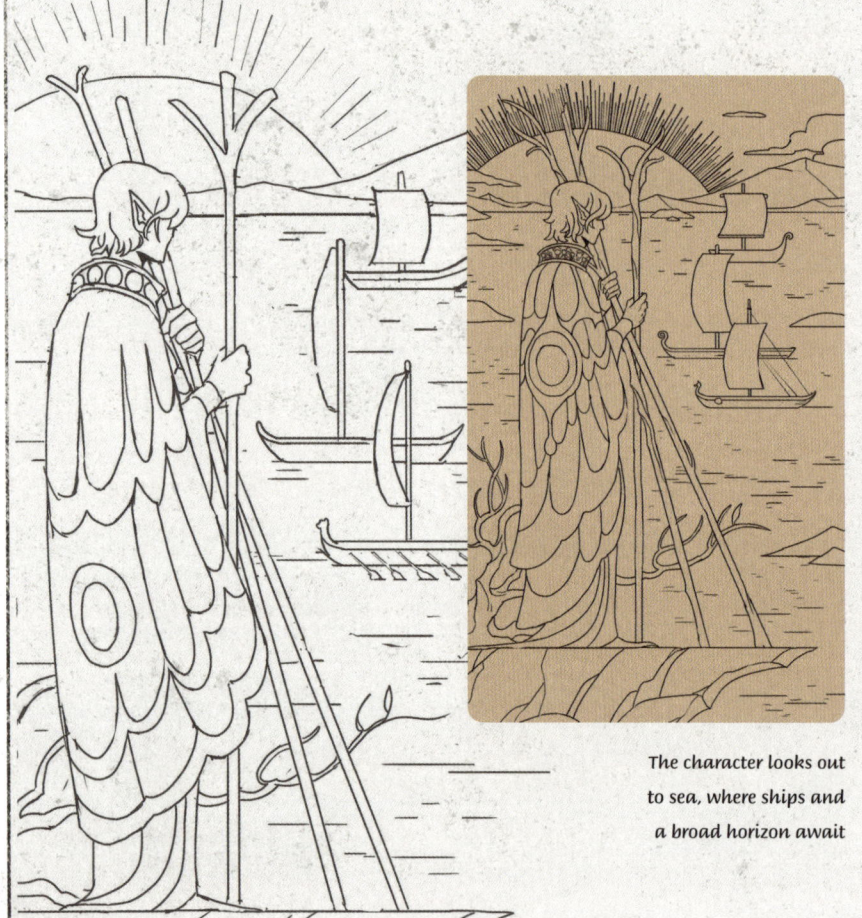

The character looks out to sea, where ships and a broad horizon await

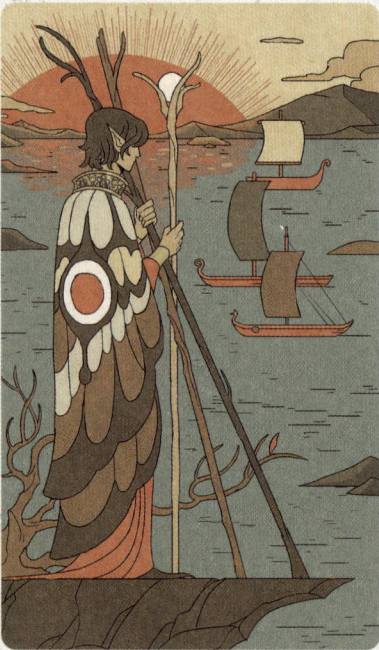

The palette is reminiscent of Rider–Waite–Smith's (page 20), with red robes and a yellow sky

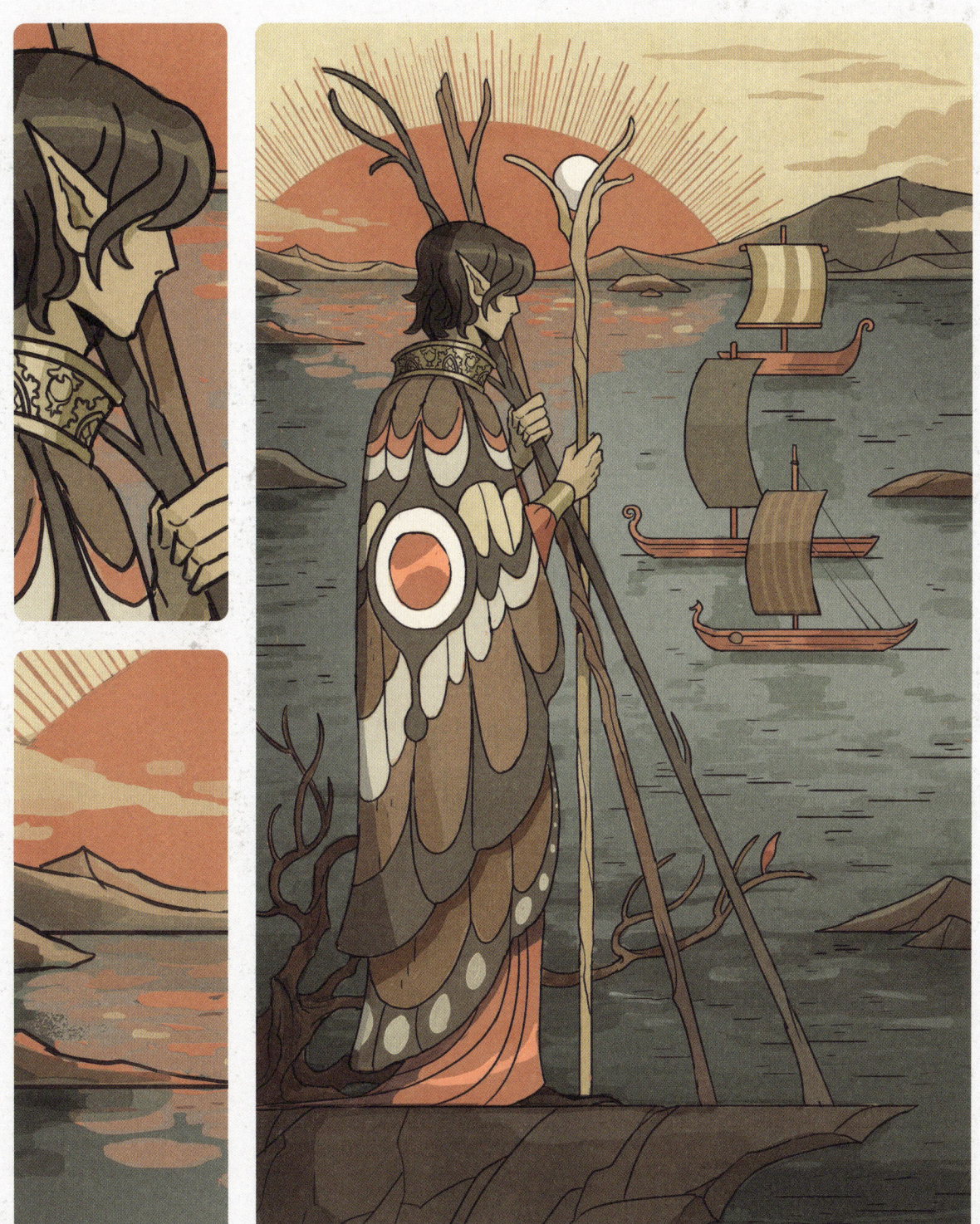

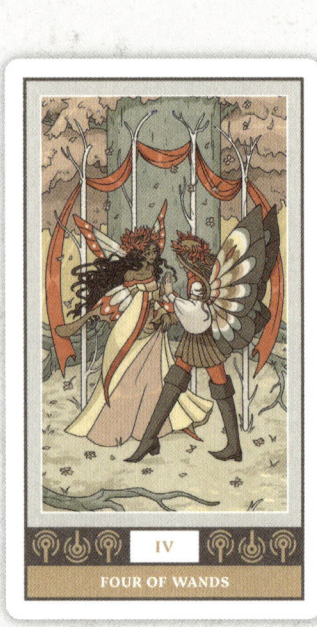

FOUR OF WANDS

CELEBRATION, PLEASURE, FESTIVALS

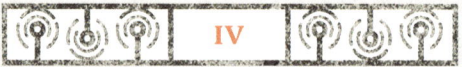

IV

The Four of Wands represents celebration, and here I follow tradition, drawing the wands as decoration for a festive scene. Since they are visually smaller in this piece, not interacting with the dancing figures, I make them stand out with colour. On the topic of colour, I will base the suit's palette around earthy yellow and brown tones, complemented by my interpretation of the primary colours: desaturated greyish blue and orange-red that recalls the theme of fire.

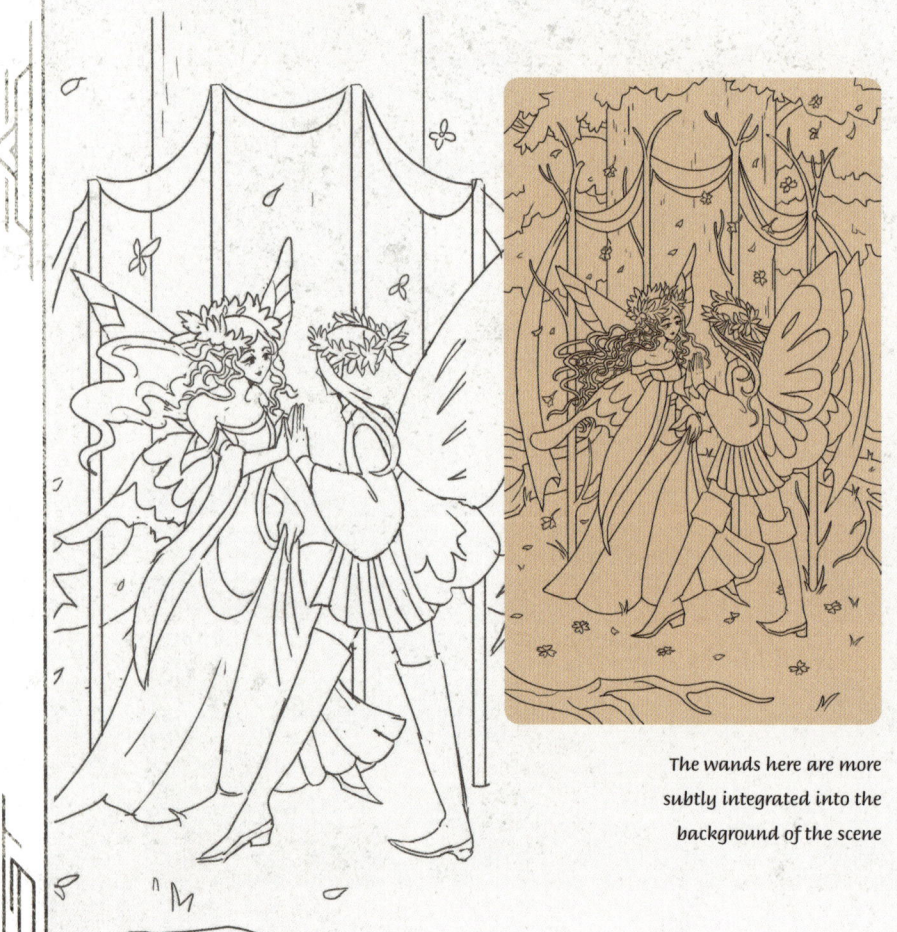

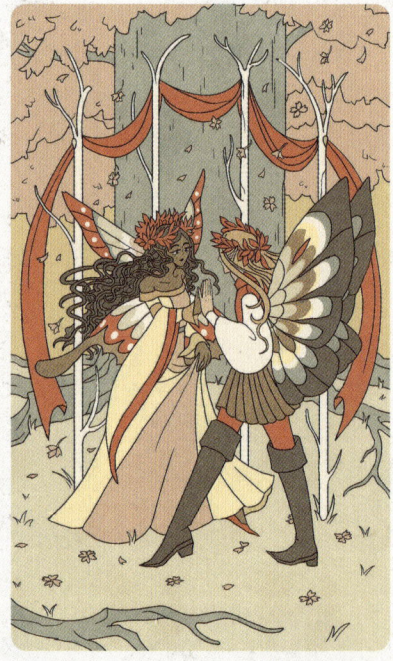

The wands here are more subtly integrated into the background of the scene

I use orange-red shapes to allude to the element of fire, balanced by grey-blue and earthy yellow

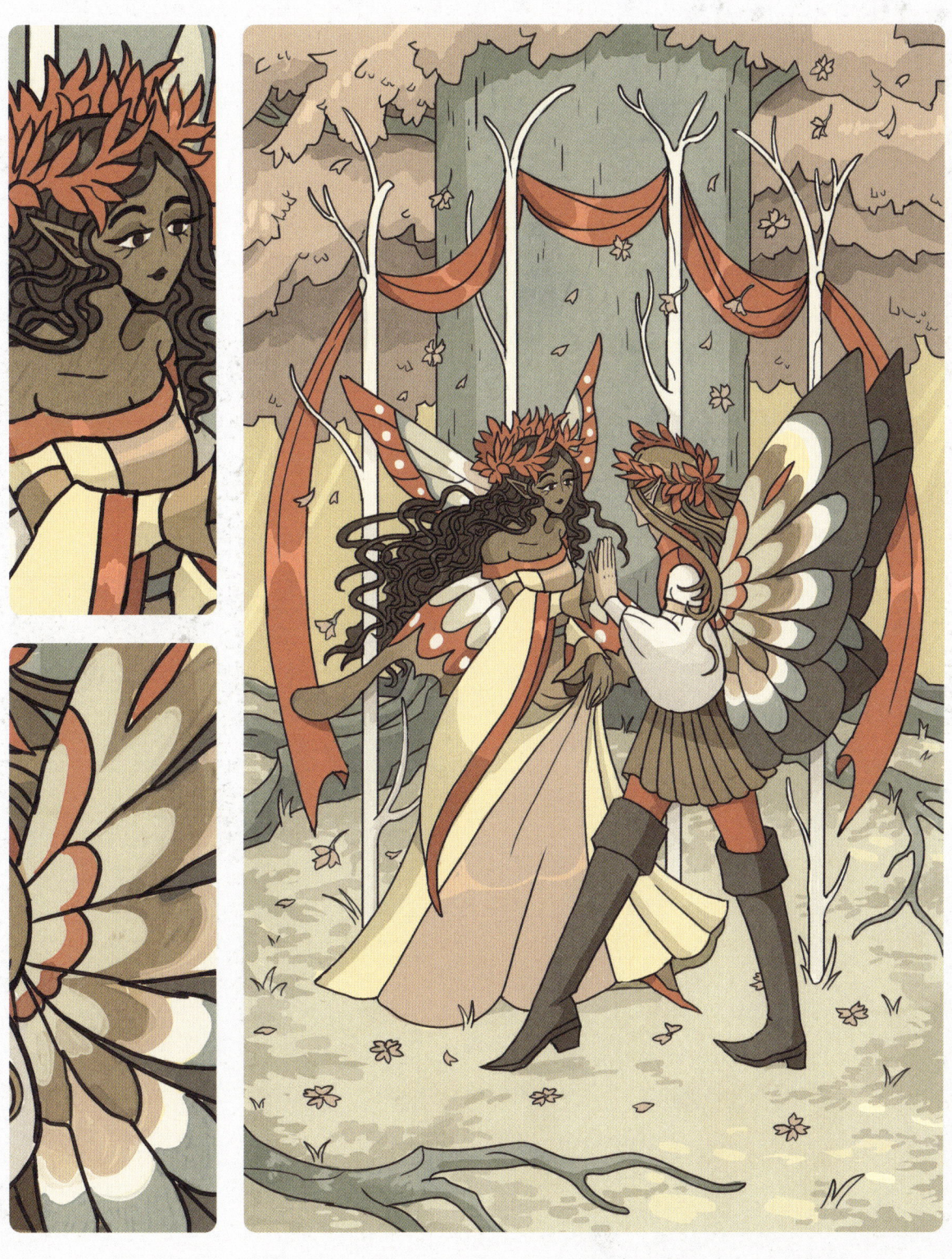

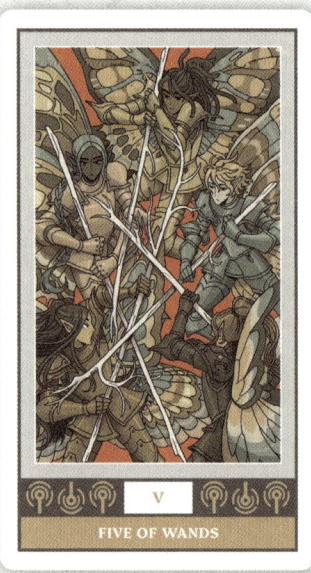

FIVE OF WANDS

FIVE OF WANDS

DRAMA, ENERGY, ACTION

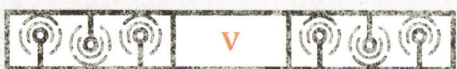

This card features five figures skirmishing with wands. I already know I'm making a fairy-themed suit, but when I get to this card and start thinking about adding big wings to the piece, I start to sweat about how clearly the image will read! I achieve clean visuals in the end, aided by the warm red background that helps the figures pop forward, and by making the wands all the same light colour.

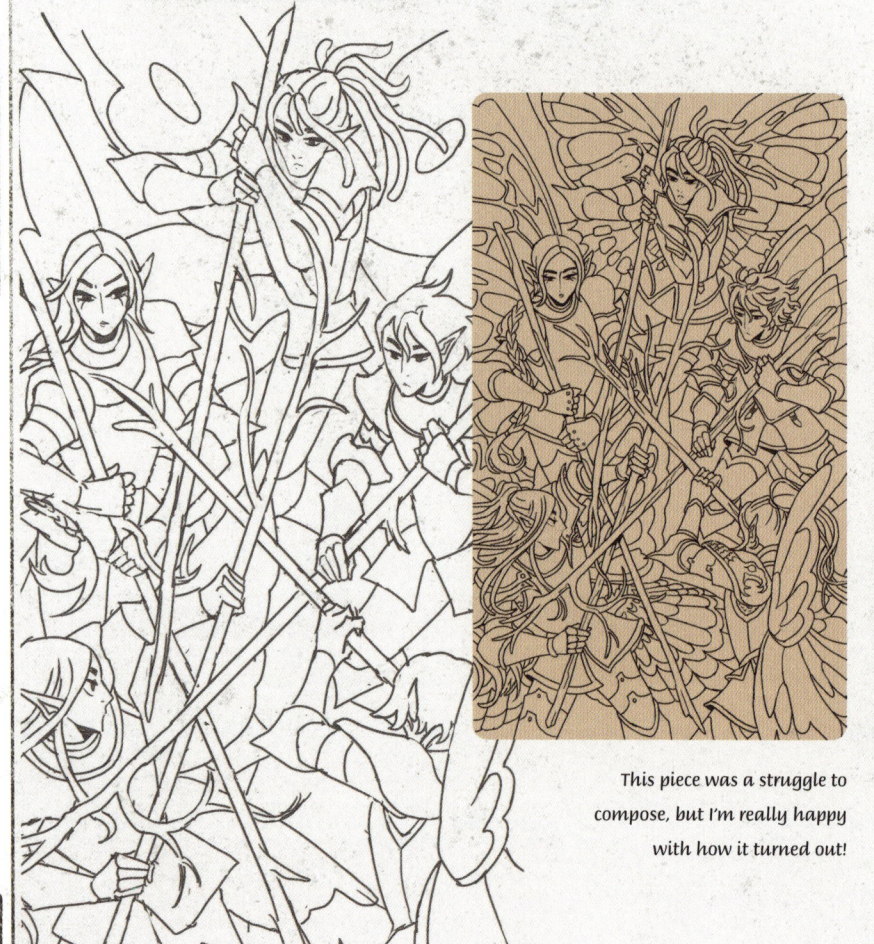

This piece was a struggle to compose, but I'm really happy with how it turned out!

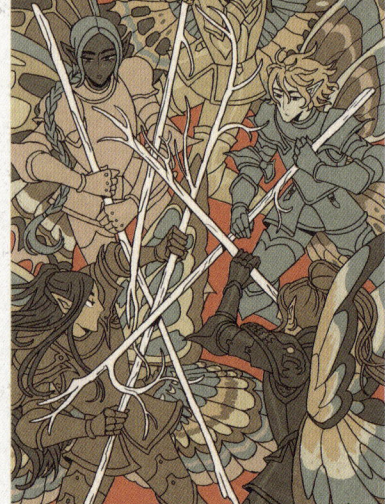

The plain orange-red backdrop pops through, giving energy and intensity to the combat scene

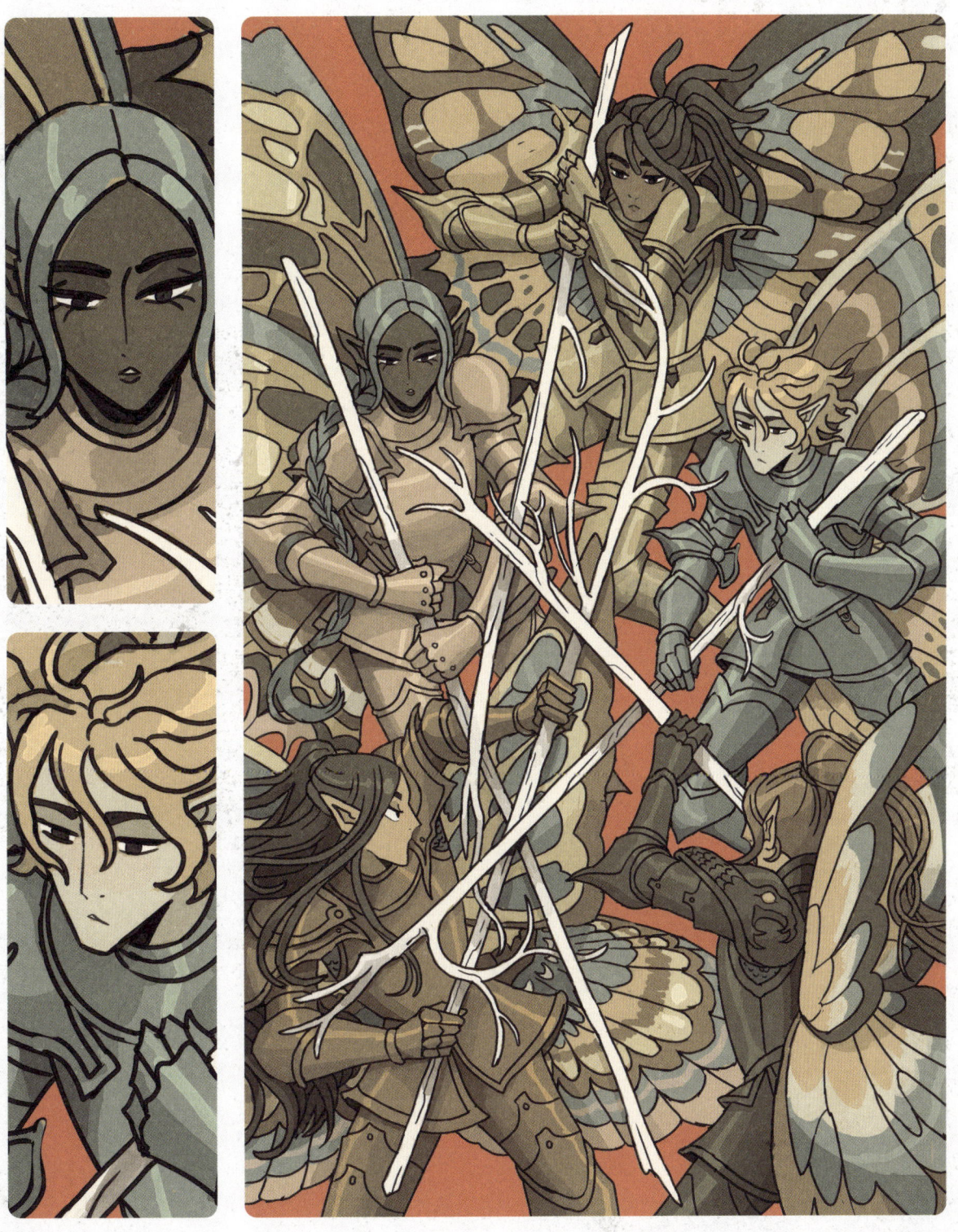

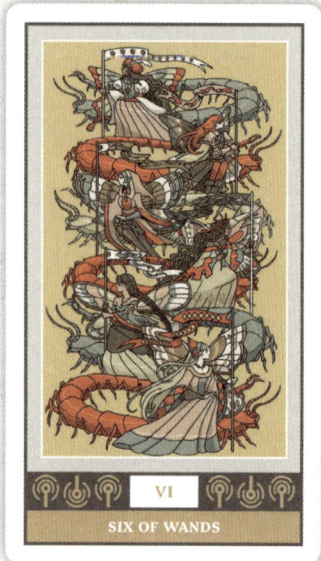

SIX OF WANDS

SIX OF WANDS

TRIUMPH, GOOD NEWS, ADULATION

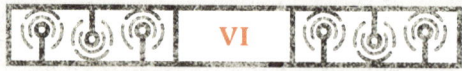

The Six of Wands is traditionally represented by a parade, and for this one I want to use the format of the card to make a more graphic design. In most cards the parade is on horseback, but because I am working with insect-themed fairies as my subject, I switch the horses to centipedes. This actually gives me a much better composition, adding more organic movement to a piece that could otherwise be a little stiff.

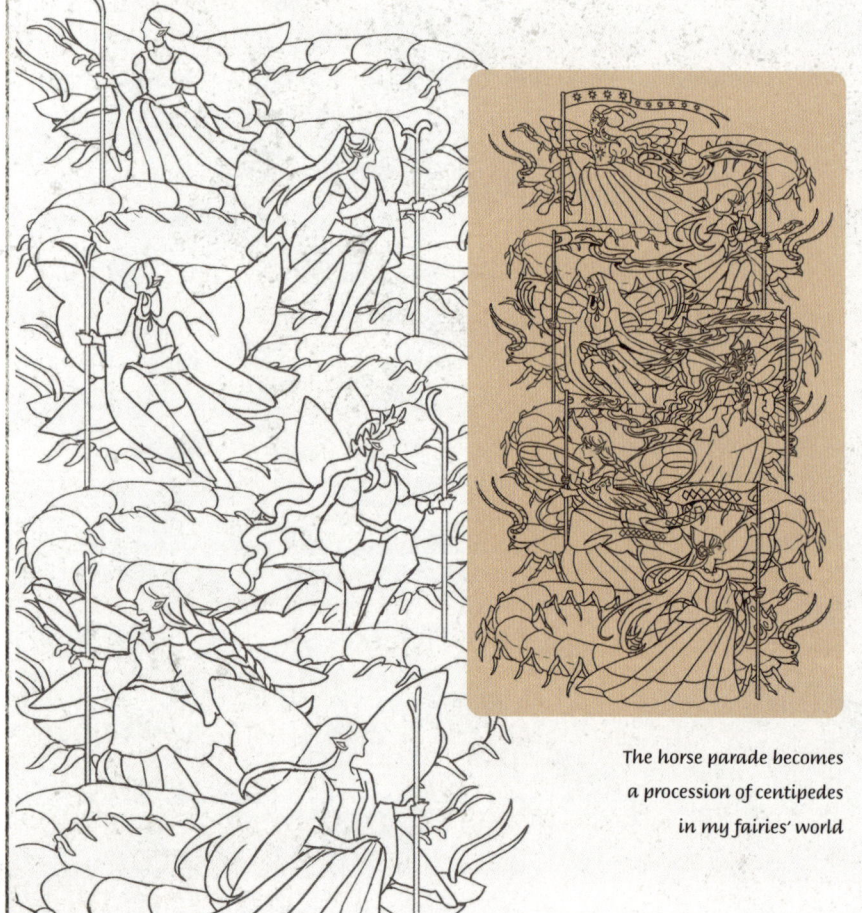

The horse parade becomes a procession of centipedes in my fairies' world

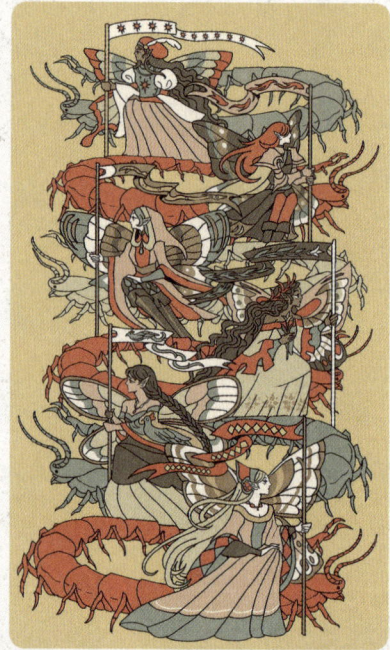

I use a flat background, like the previous cards, to balance out the detailed figures

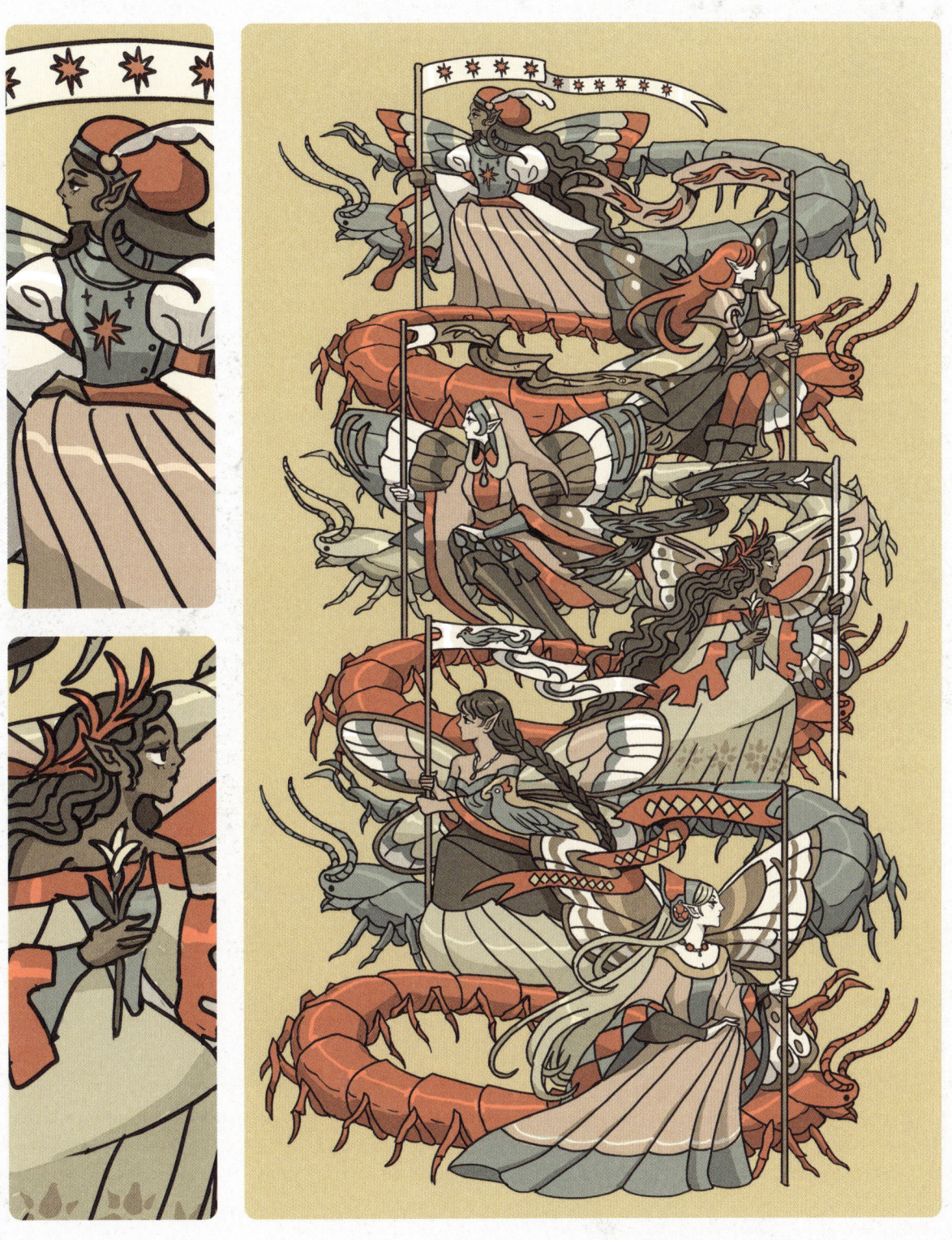

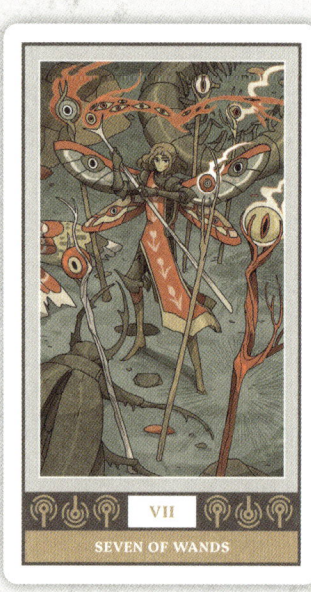

SEVEN OF WANDS

SEVEN OF WANDS

DEFENCE, PROTECTING, HIGHER GROUND

The Seven of Wands is all about defence and protection. This theme gives me a lot of room to play with. I want to help the symbolism of the card by having it set on a battlefield, but I don't want to show anything gruesome. In the end I choose to add some large insects on the ground, which ties in perfectly with other cards in this set and creates visual interest. The flaming wands add elements of dramatic movement to the scene.

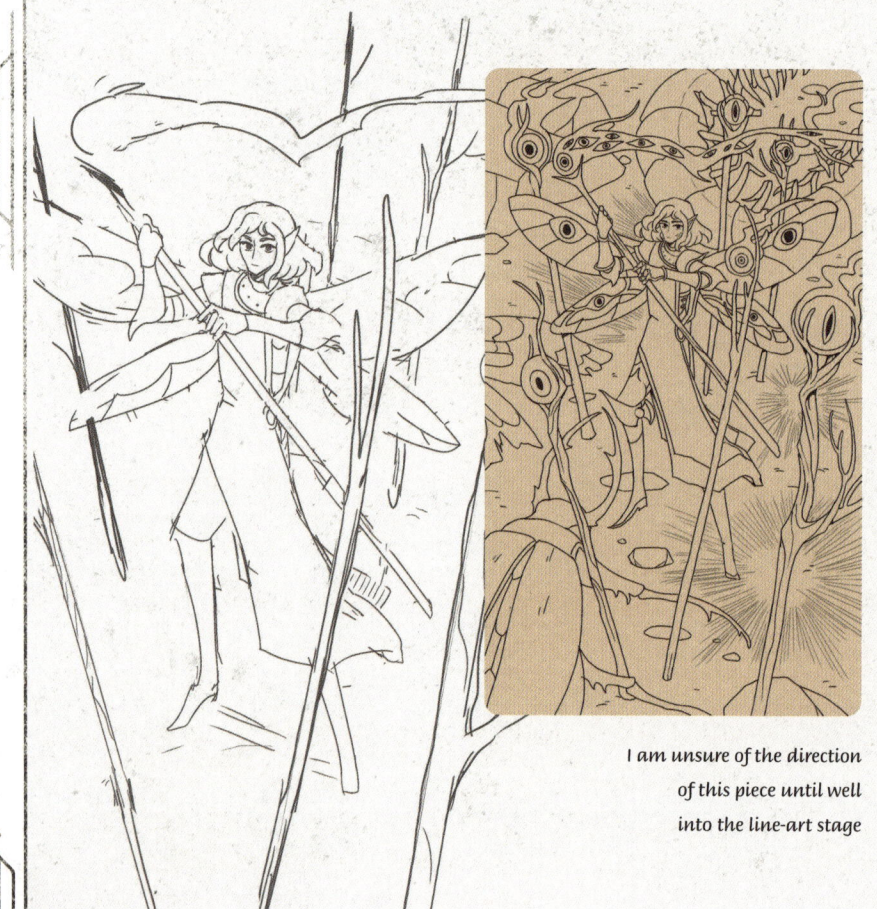

I am unsure of the direction of this piece until well into the line-art stage

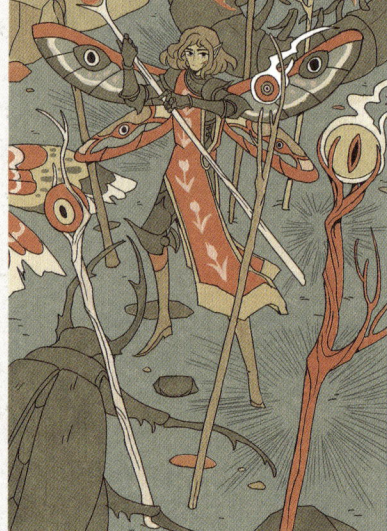

Fallen insects transform the vague sketch idea into a battle scene

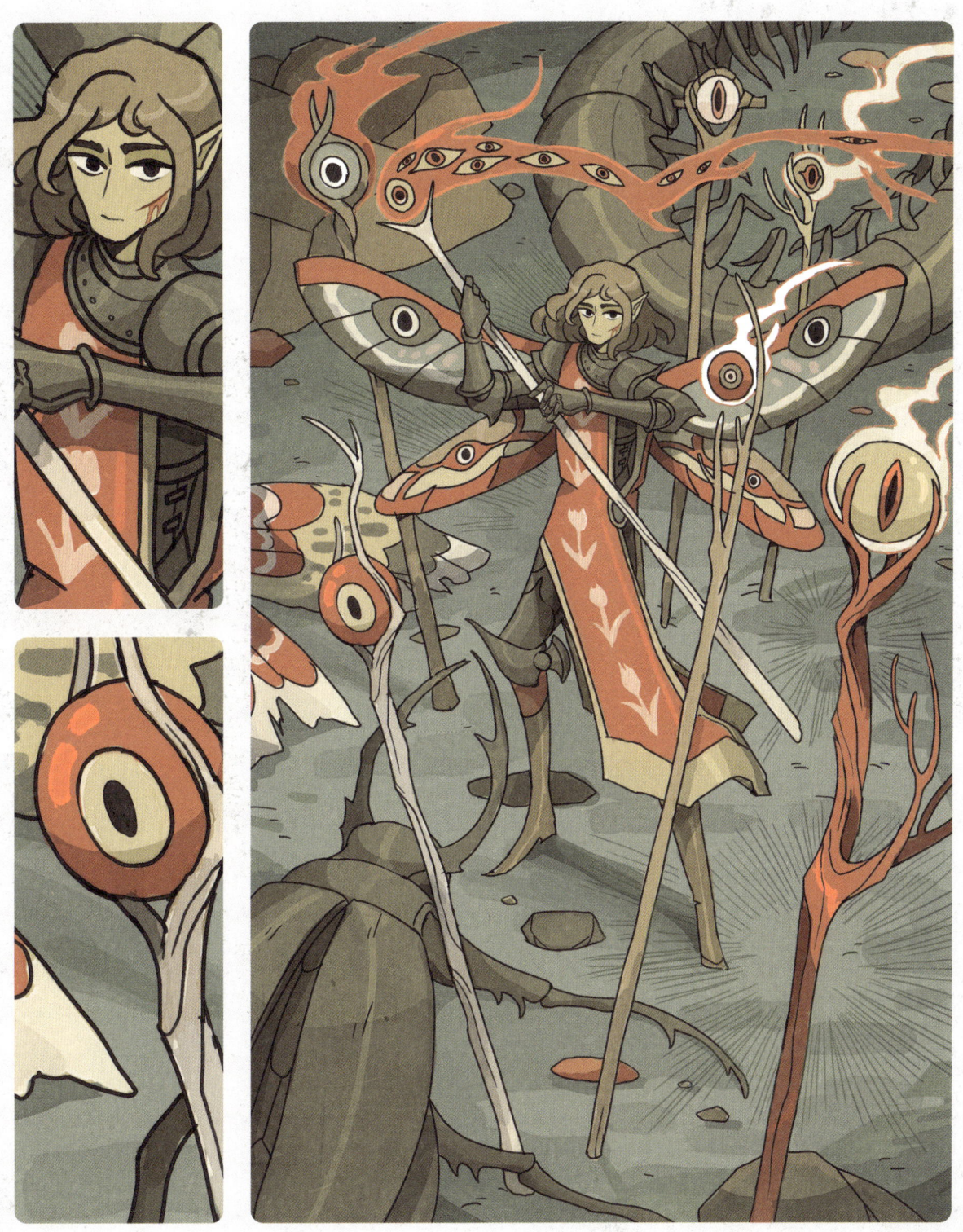

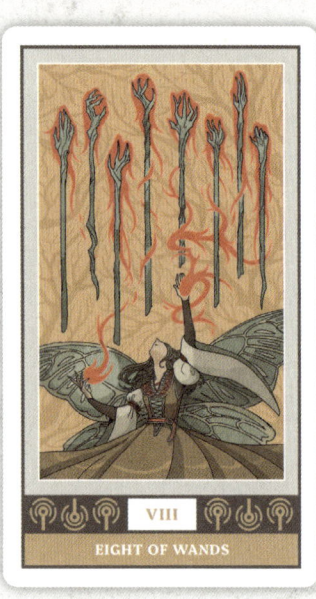

EIGHT OF WANDS

INTENTIONS, RAMIFICATIONS, ACTION

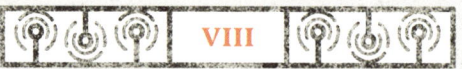

The Eight of Wands is a card full of energy, showing wands launched through the air. For this card I lean into wands' association with magic, setting them alight with mystic fire. I also make the wands look more dynamic by shaping them like outstretched hands. As the card's still a little visually static, I add subtle branches behind the wands to help the eye move around, continuing my suit's nature motif.

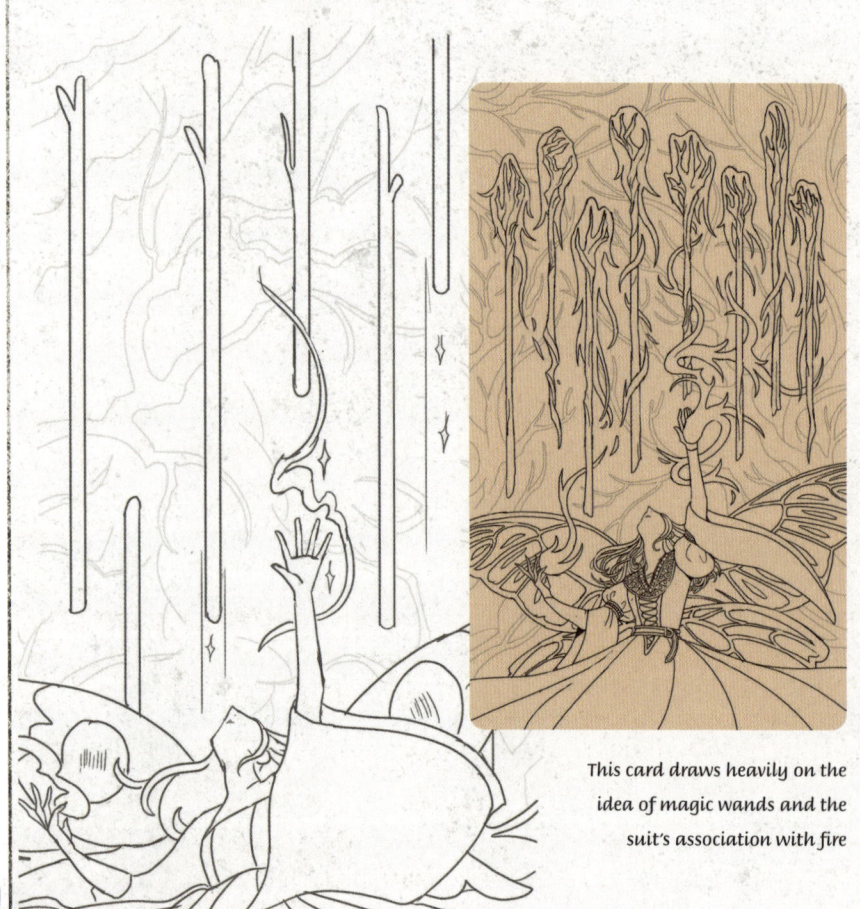

This card draws heavily on the idea of magic wands and the suit's association with fire

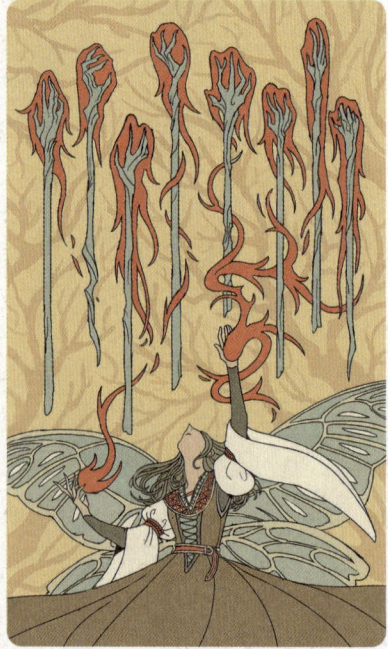

The fiery wands echo the character's pose, reaching upwards like arms

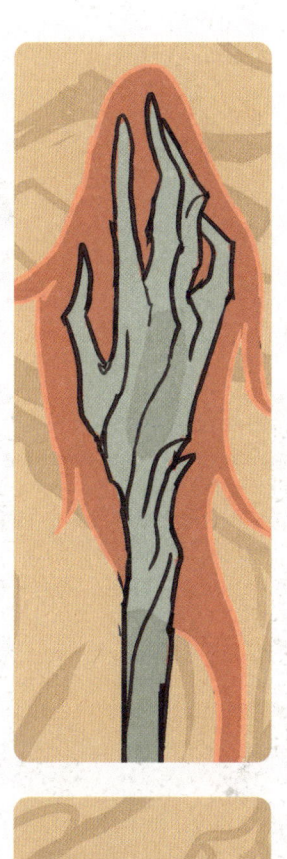

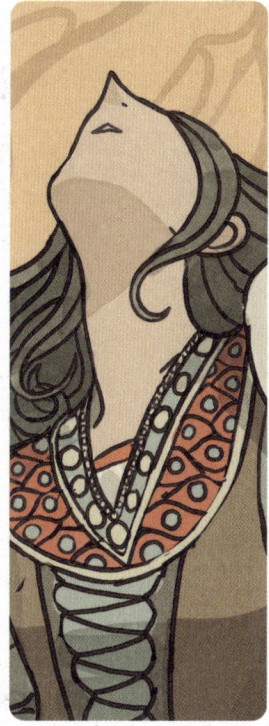

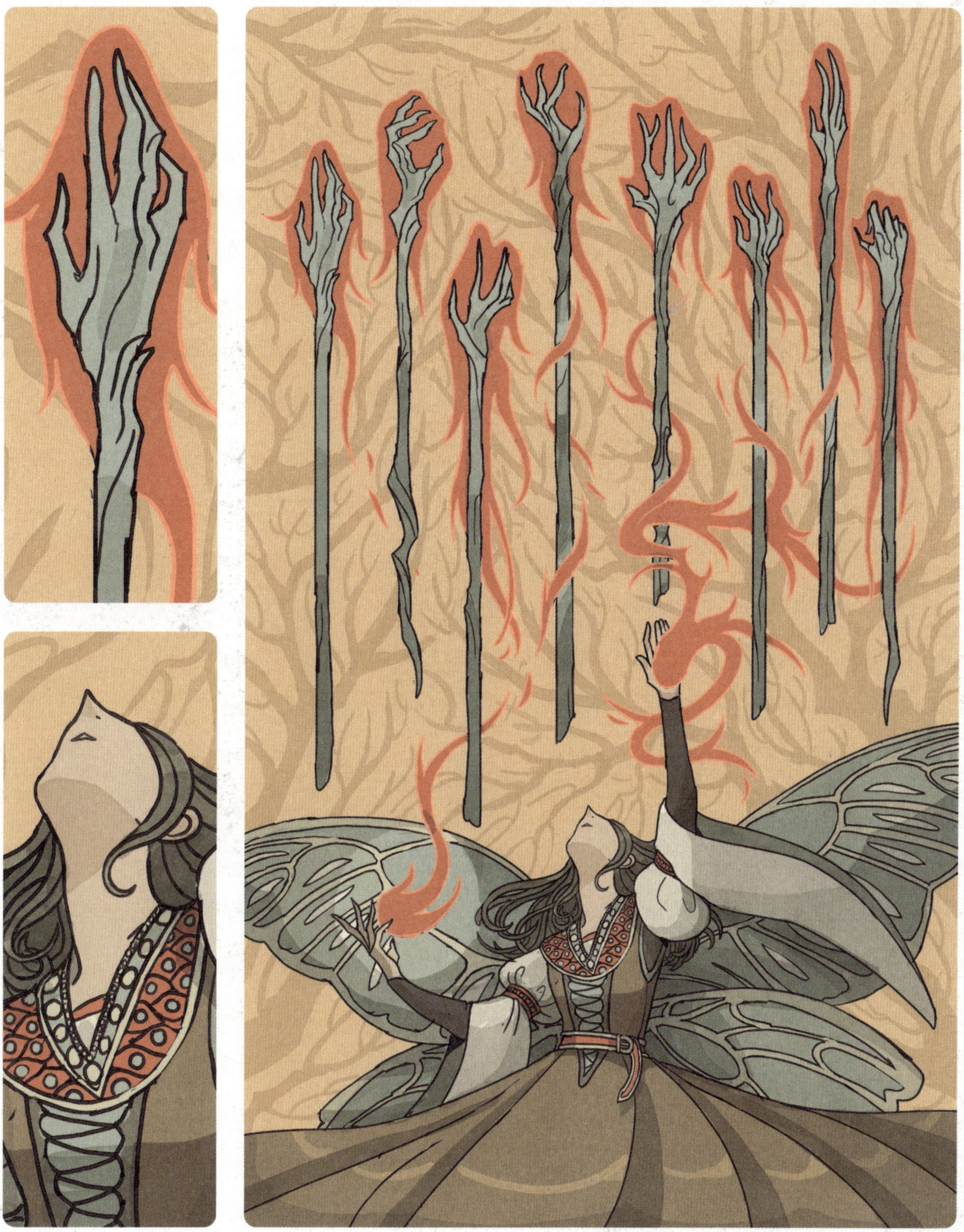

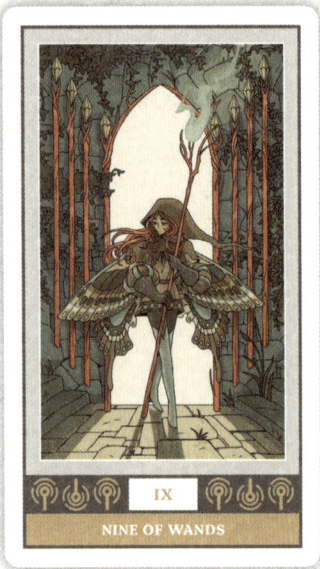

NINE OF WANDS

NINE OF
WANDS

BREAKING BARRIERS,
UNKNOWN TERRITORY, BRAVERY

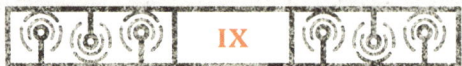

This is the companion piece to the Two of Wands. While that piece shows a figure at the threshold, this one shows a figure stepping through. I like the implication of more wands waiting for the figure after passing through a difficult threshold, growing more powerful from their progress. Initially I wanted this card to be mostly black, but it wouldn't go with the other pieces visually. Instead I make the background a ruin with ivy climbing the walls to add much-needed organic shapes.

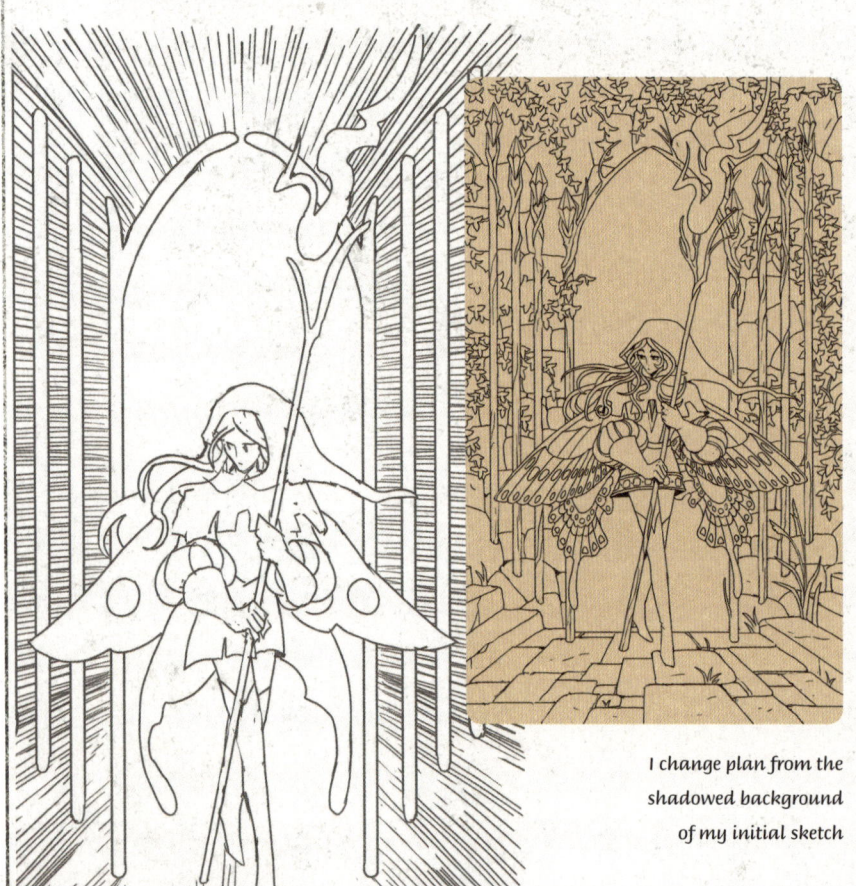

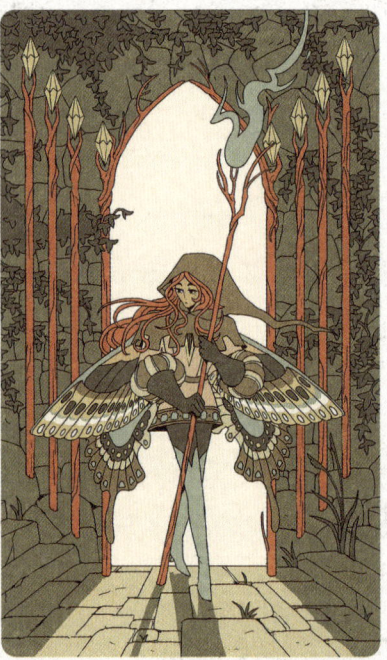

I change plan from the
shadowed background
of my initial sketch

The wands' colours stand
out against the relative
plainness of the wall

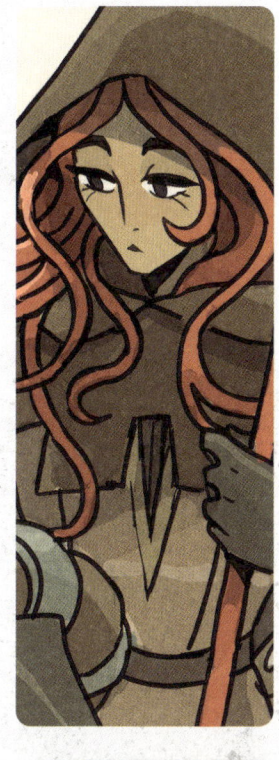

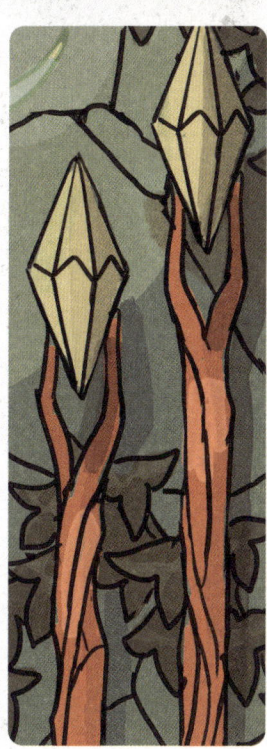

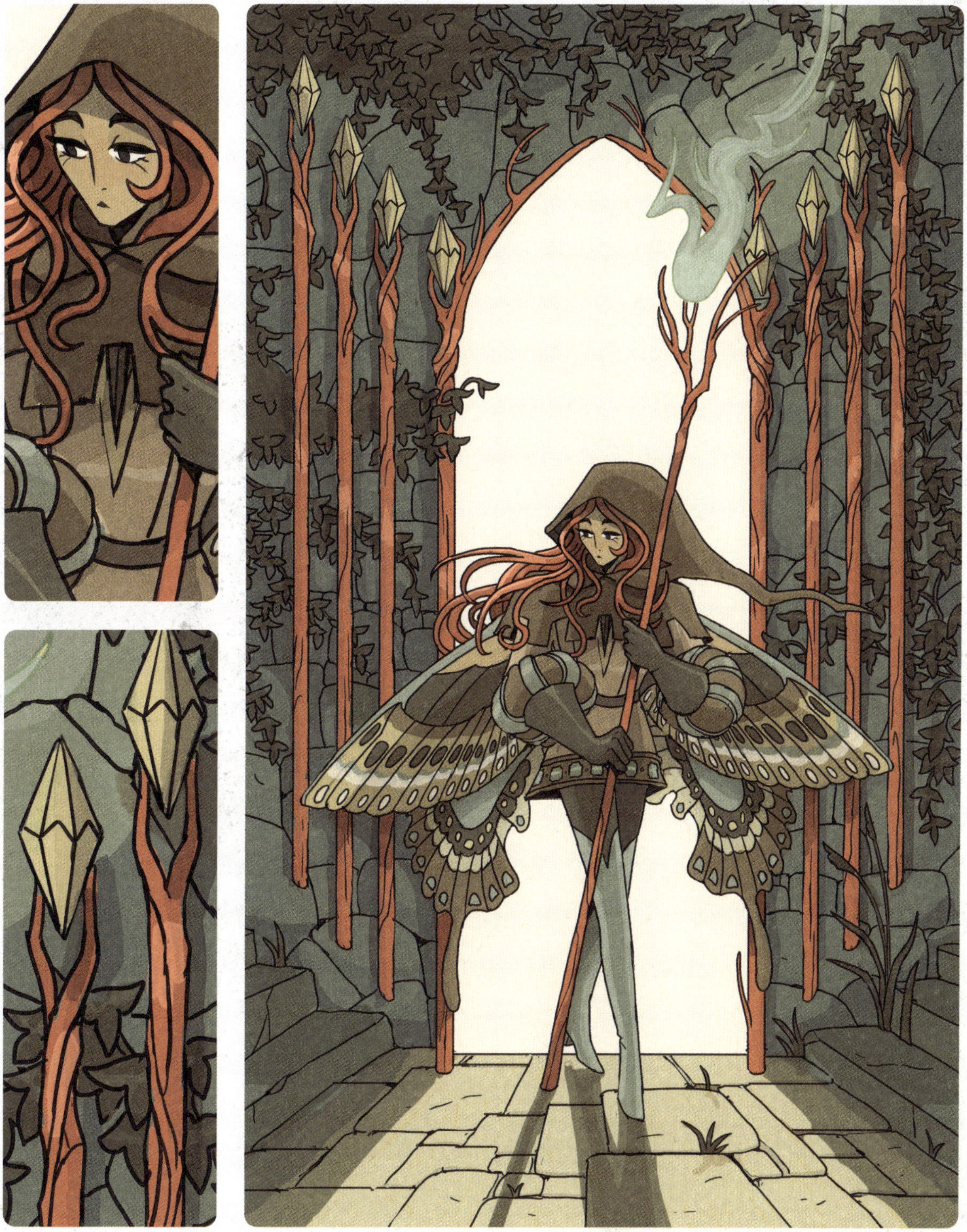

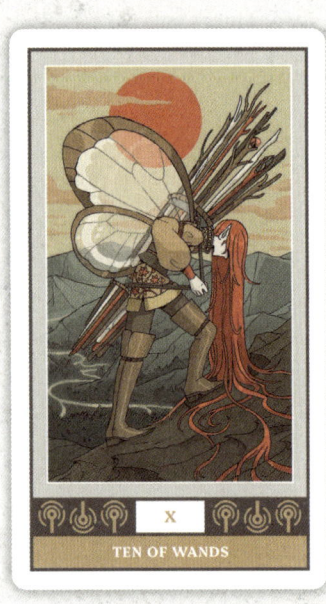

TEN OF WANDS

TEN OF WANDS

FATIGUE, ENDING, REST

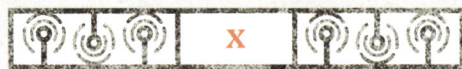

The key image of this card is a figure carrying ten wands, exhausted and near the end of a journey. The wings on this fairy prove tricky to compose around (and I actually forget about them in my rough pass). I eventually settle on a transparent wing and I'm happy with that solution. Not only can the viewer see all ten wands clearly, but the faded, ghostly wings help drive home the symbolic fatigue.

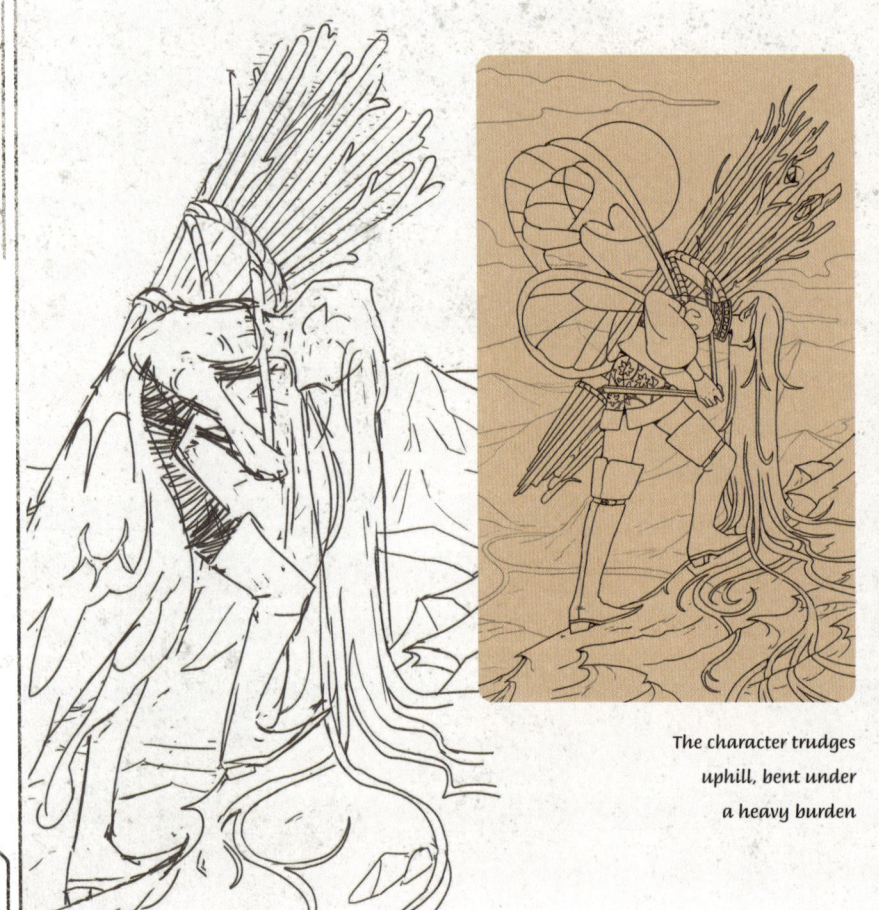

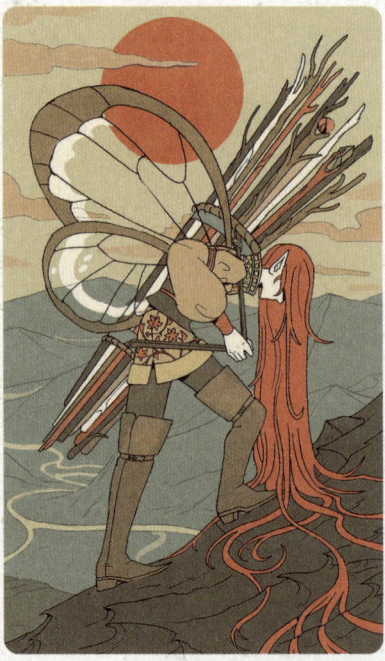

The character trudges
uphill, bent under
a heavy burden

Long red hair flows down over
the rocks, like molten lava
at the character's feet

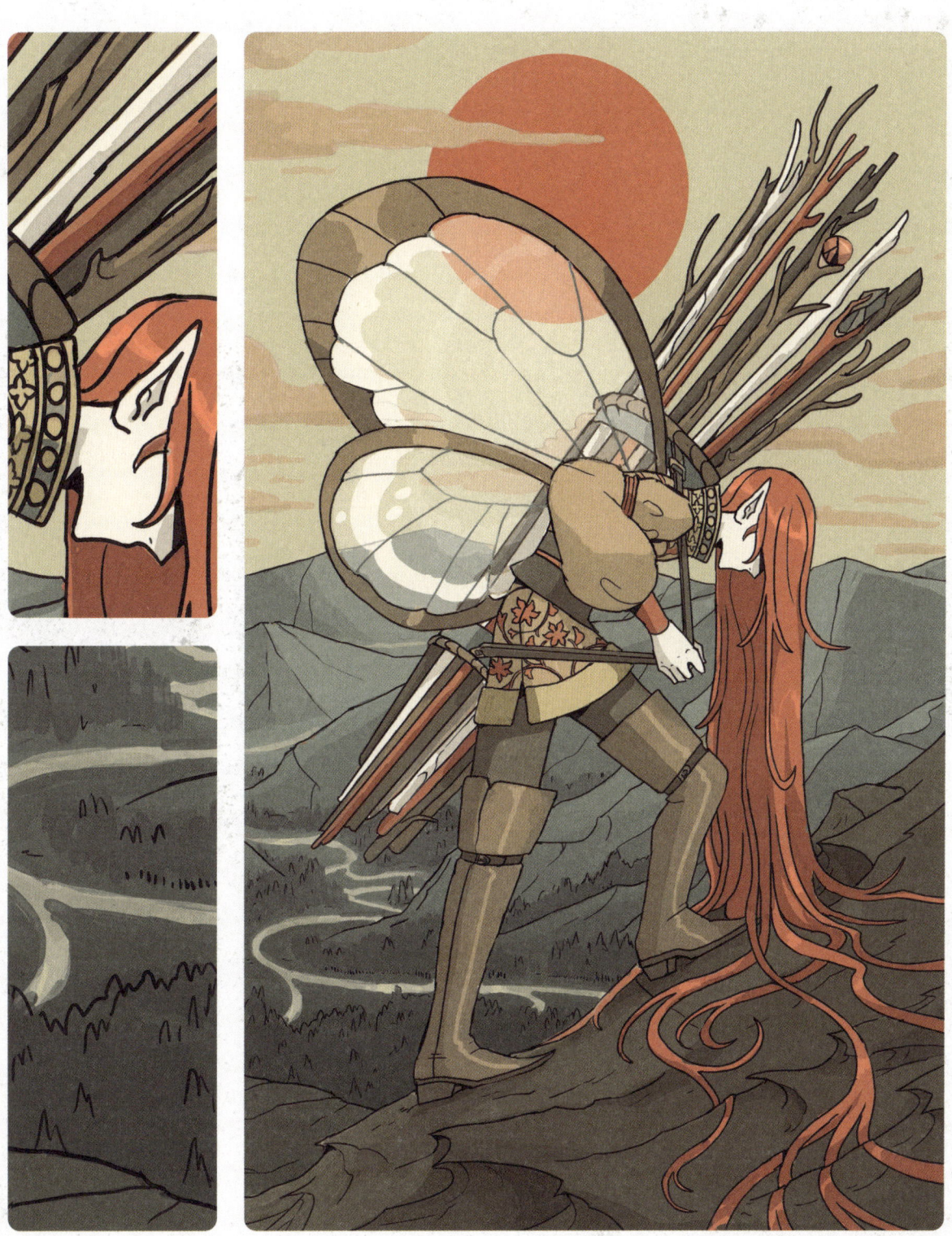

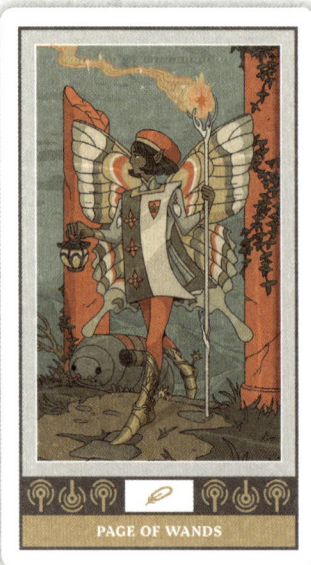

PAGE OF WANDS

ADVENTURER, TRAVELLER, CURIOSITY

While the Ten of Wands shows the fatigued end of a journey, the Page shows the buoyant start of a new one. My initial pass has a character that feels very whimsical, looking around in wonder. However, this looks too animated compared to the rest of the deck. Instead I decide on a character with a more fanciful and impractical outfit for his journey, showing the romance and naivety of a first real adventure.

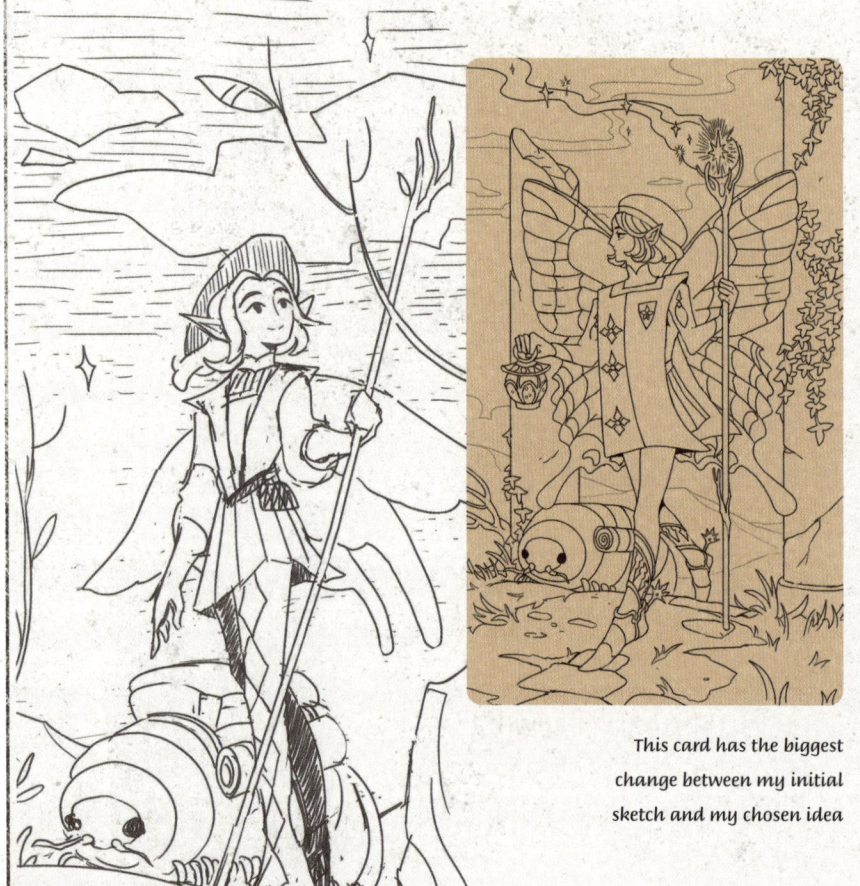

This card has the biggest change between my initial sketch and my chosen idea

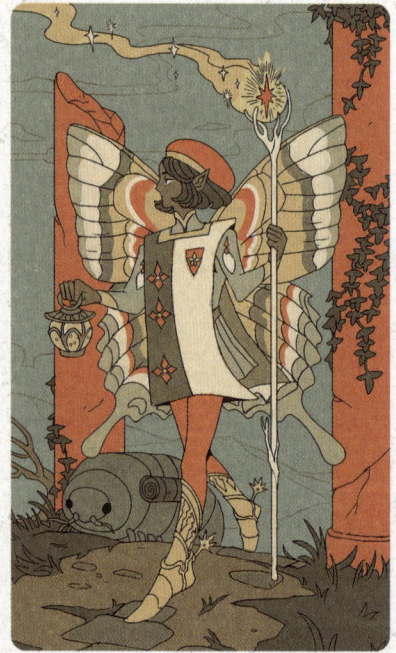

The Page's ornate, courtly appearance suggests an inexperienced adventurer

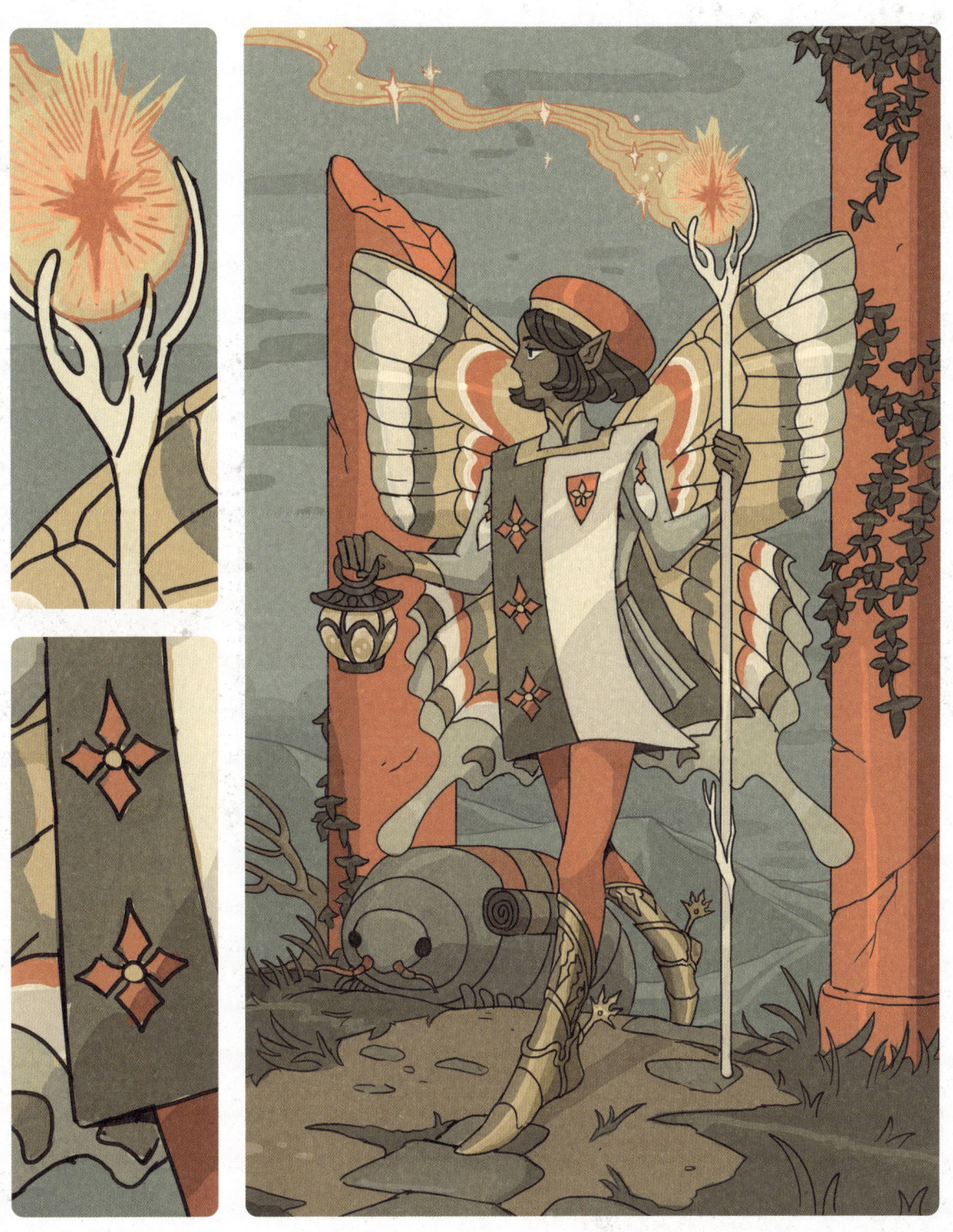

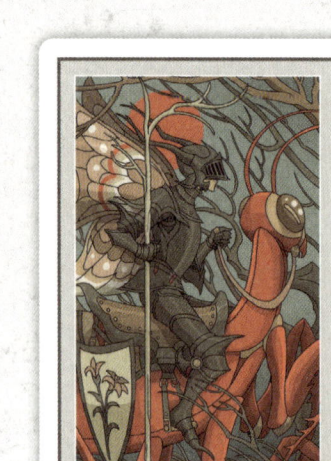

KNIGHT OF WANDS

KNIGHT OF WANDS

BRASH, PASSIONATE, IMPULSIVE

This might be my favourite piece. It's easy to make a knight read as a knight – just add armour – so I just have fun with the rest of it. To keep the insect theme, I have the knight ride a mantis, as a centipede wouldn't be dynamic enough in the composition. The knight's helmet mimics both a beetle's pincers and the shapes of the branches and trees he is riding through. The tangled terrain and night sky create the narrative of a more seasoned adventurer, braving stranger paths than the Page might.

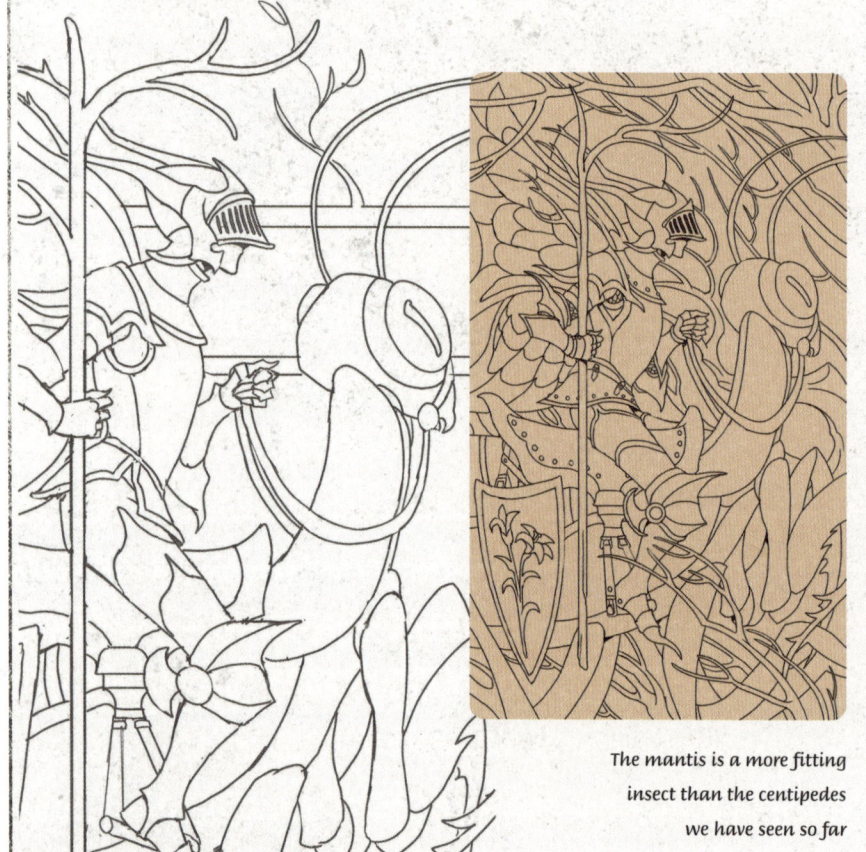

The mantis is a more fitting insect than the centipedes we have seen so far

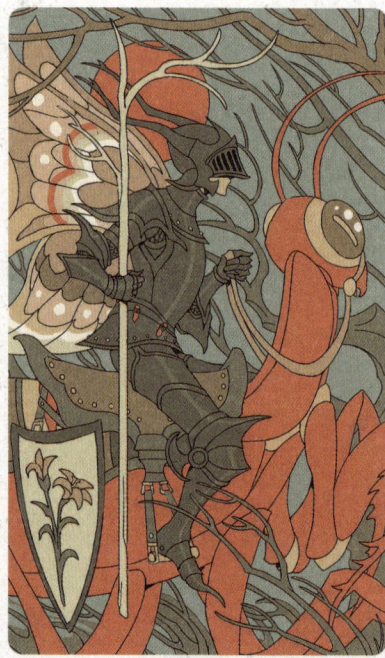

The knight, heavily armoured, rides boldly through a dark, dense forest

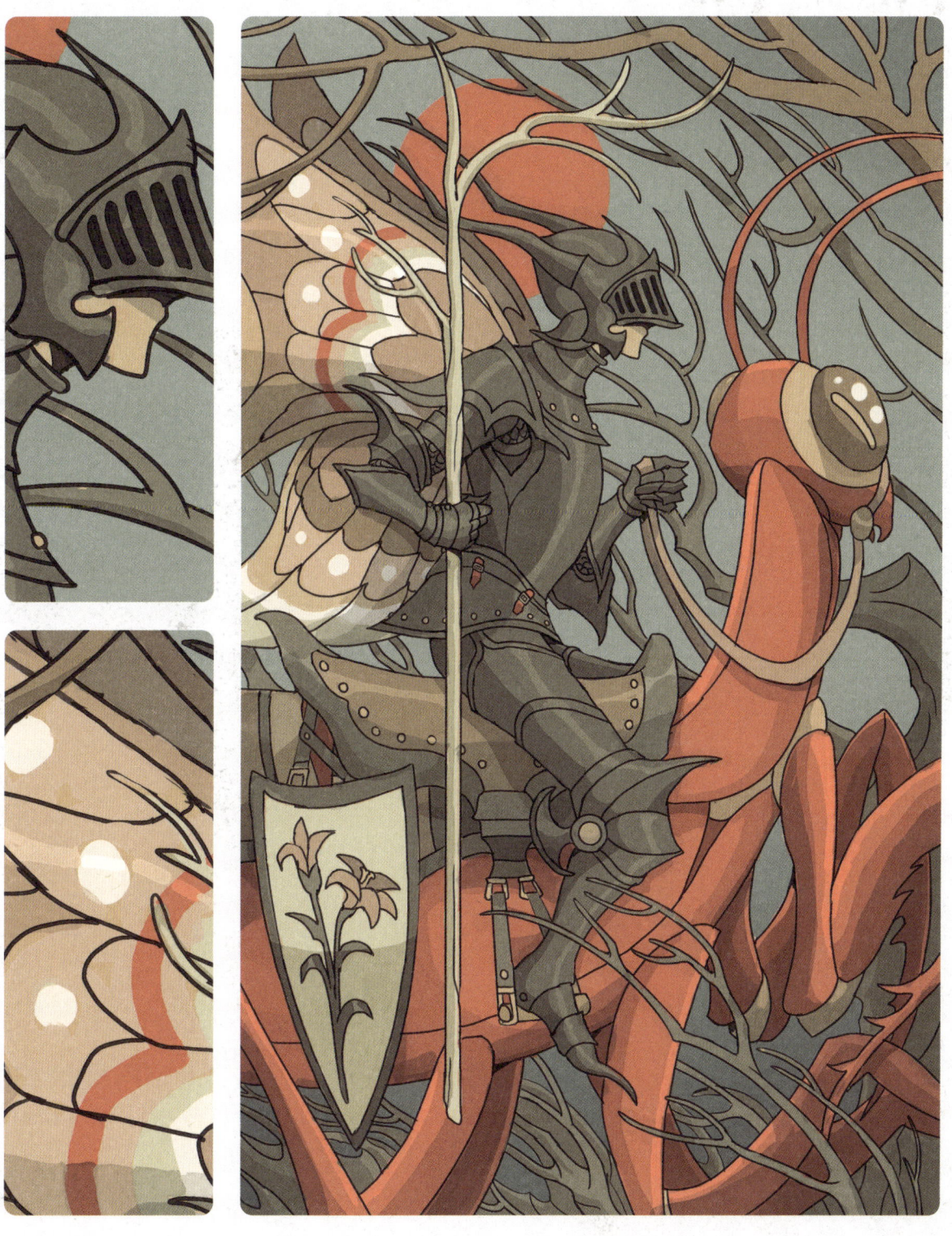

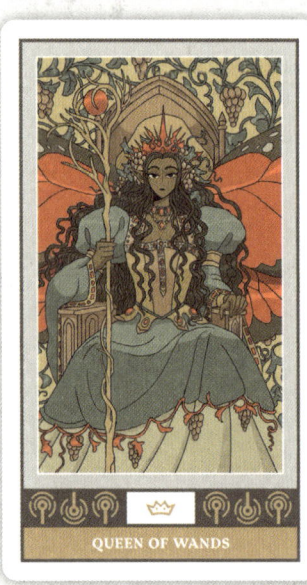

QUEEN OF WANDS

QUEEN OF WANDS

MESMERIZING, POWERFUL, KNOWLEDGE

I want to keep the King and Queen cards fairly straightforward; they are a pair and I want them to look like it. Instead of insects, I follow the motif of trees and branches in a different direction, surrounding the Queen with lavish fruit. These add a great rhythm in the background of this formal piece, which might otherwise feel stiff. Adding vines and branches gets more organic, flowing lines into the scene. The Queen holds an ornate wand as she regards us with cool, knowing dignity.

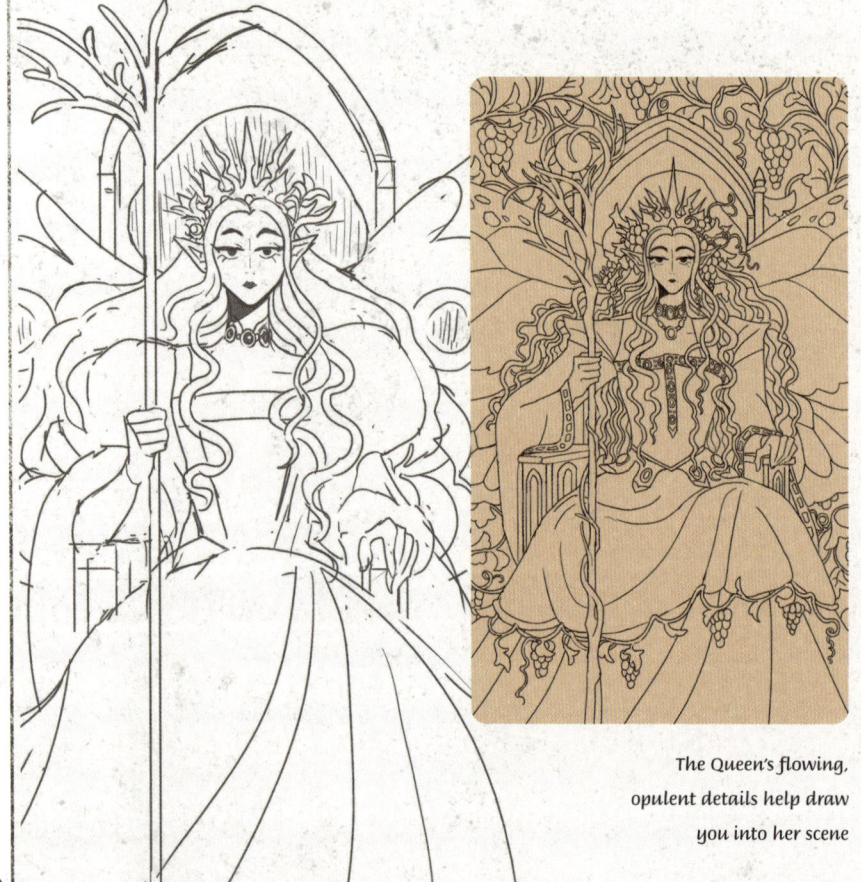

The Queen's flowing, opulent details help draw you into her scene

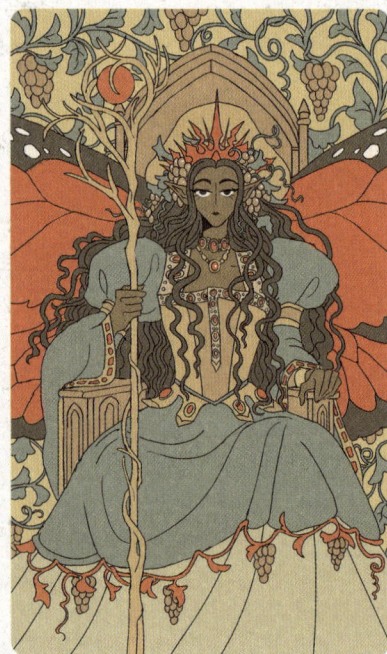

A central, front-on pose makes the character feel magnetic and imposing

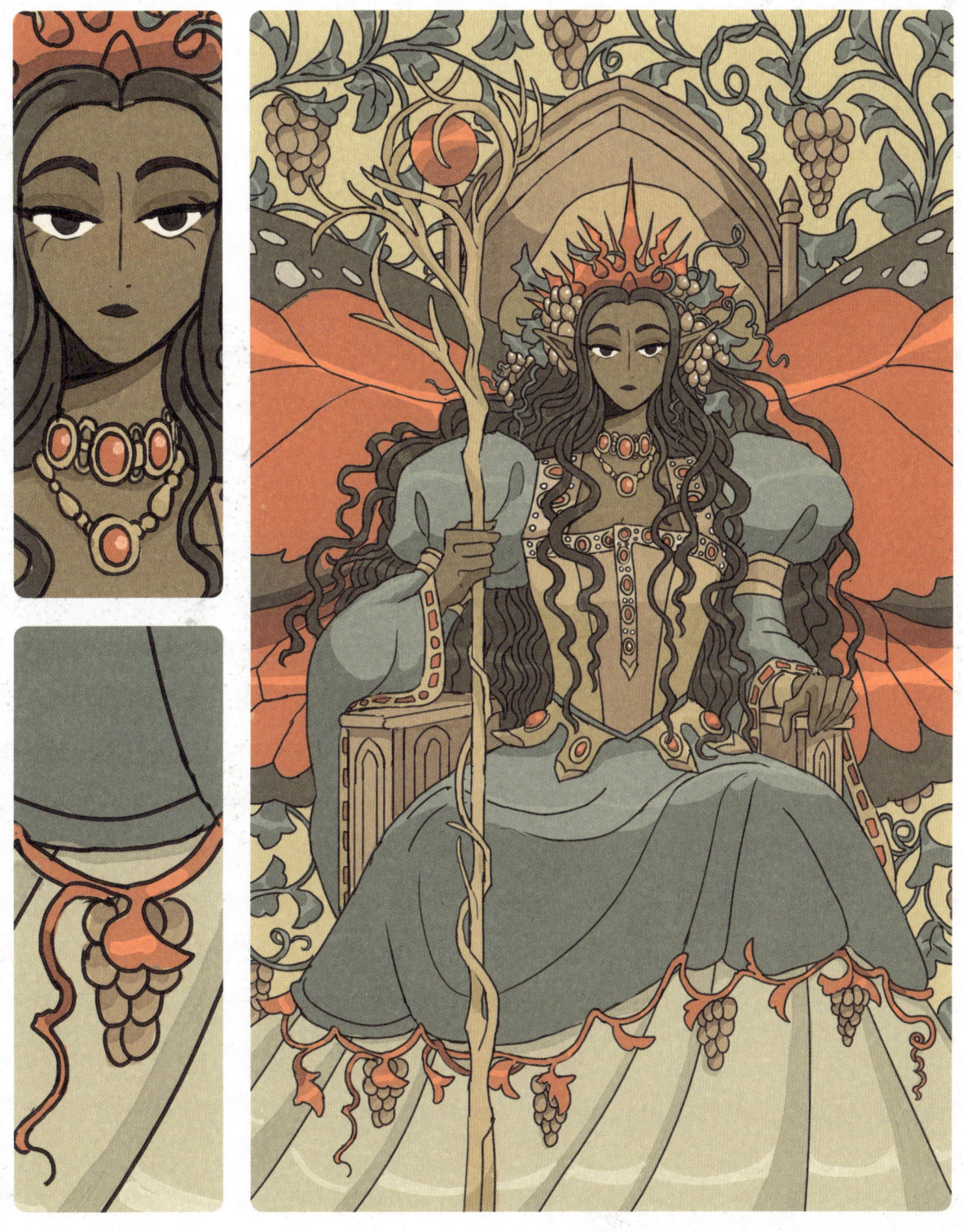

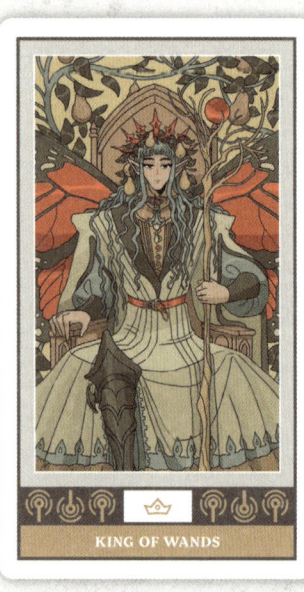

KING OF WANDS

KING OF WANDS

EXPANSIVE, RULING, COMMANDING

The King card complements the Queen, mirroring her composition and signalling they are a matched pair. Here again we see the branches and fruits in the background, which add a lot of energy and an enticing quality to the image. If those weren't there, the King and Queen would be too static and less appealing. A static composition isn't necessarily a bad thing, but with the branches these designs also go better with the rest of the deck's nature motifs.

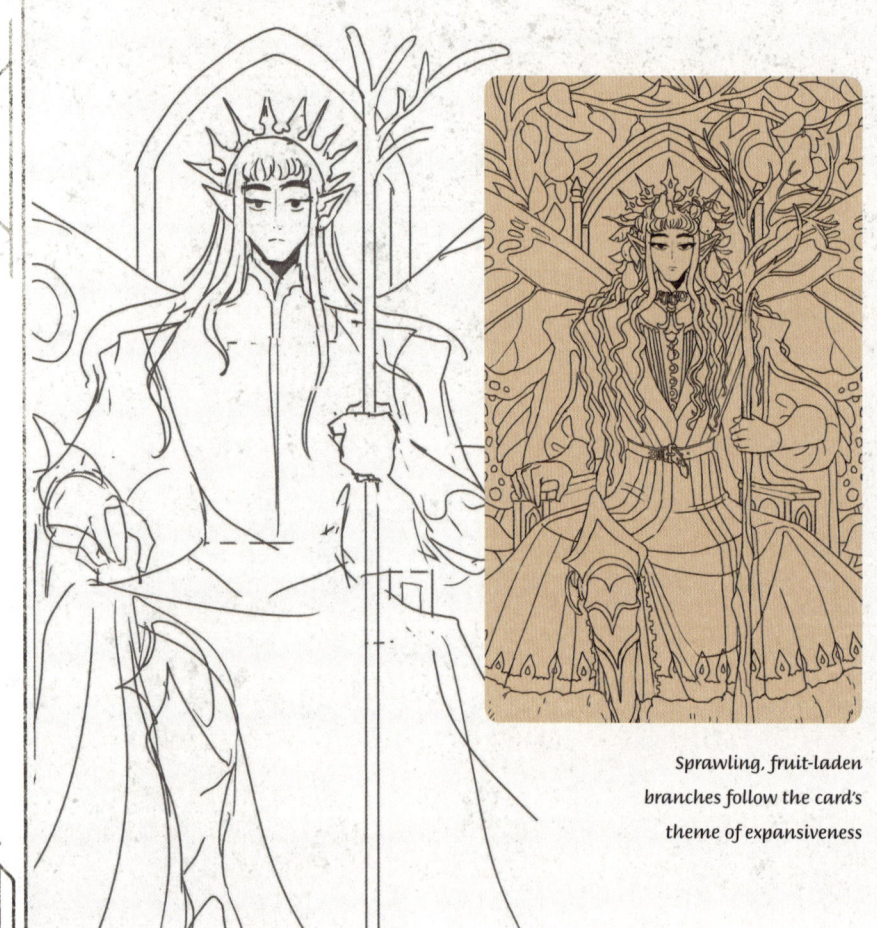

Sprawling, fruit-laden branches follow the card's theme of expansiveness

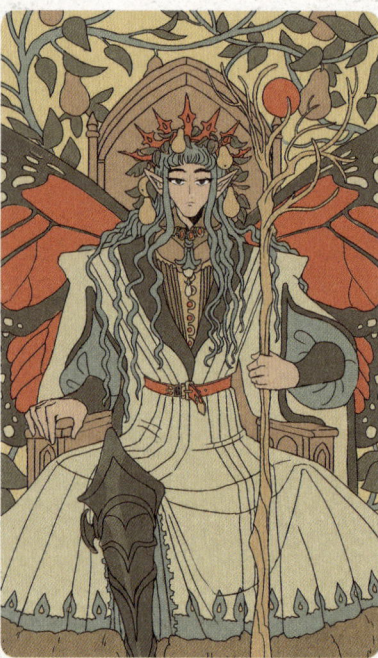

Like the Queen card, the even composition creates a feeling of strength and authority

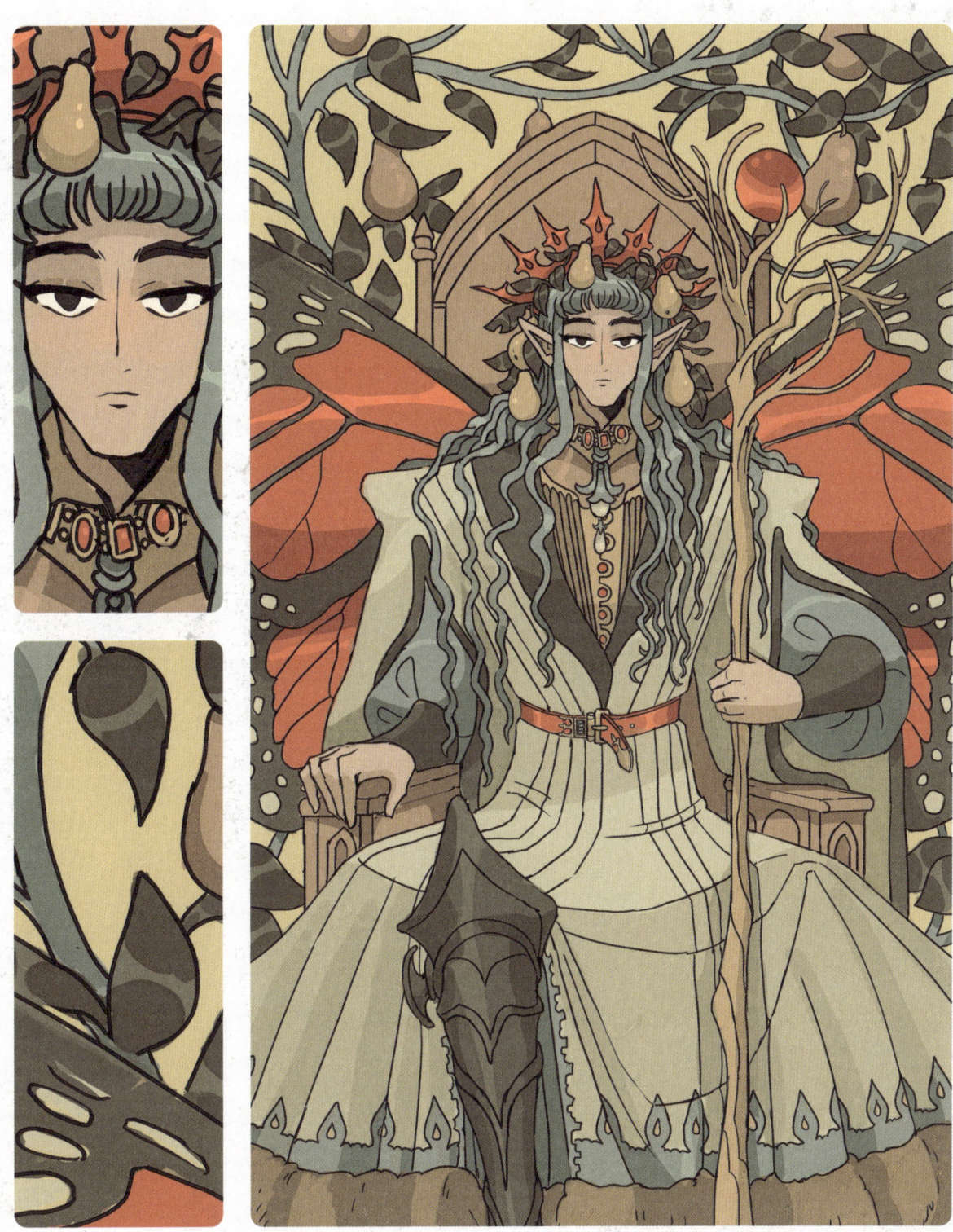

ARTIST'S CONCLUSION

I really enjoyed working on this suit. When I have a project, I like to give myself an additional theme; in this case, I chose fairies and explored the world that they and the wands might inhabit. Between the colour palette, subject matter, and linear art style, the final suit is very cohesive and lends itself to the magic inherent in wands.

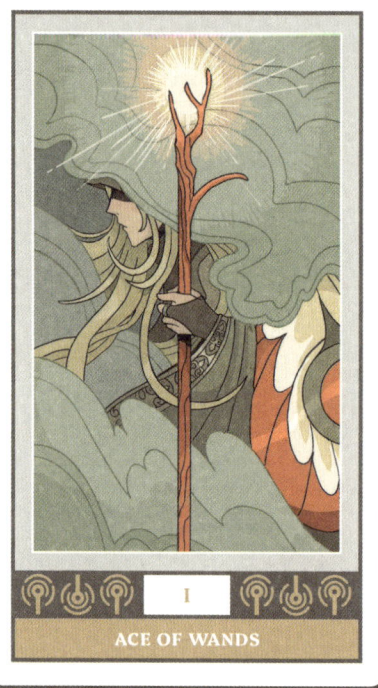

ACE OF WANDS

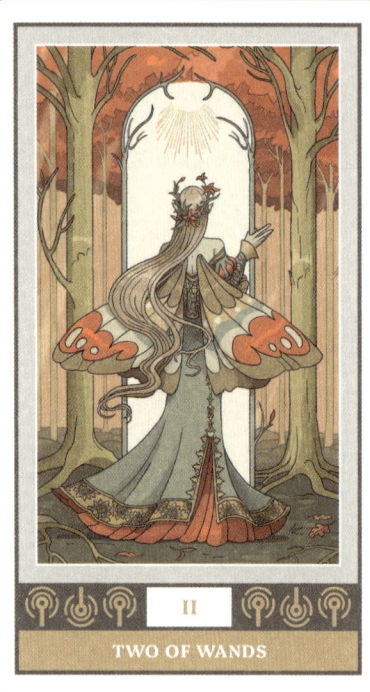

TWO OF WANDS

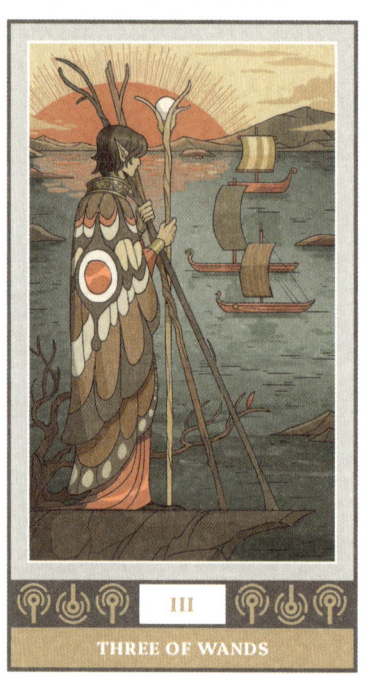

THREE OF WANDS

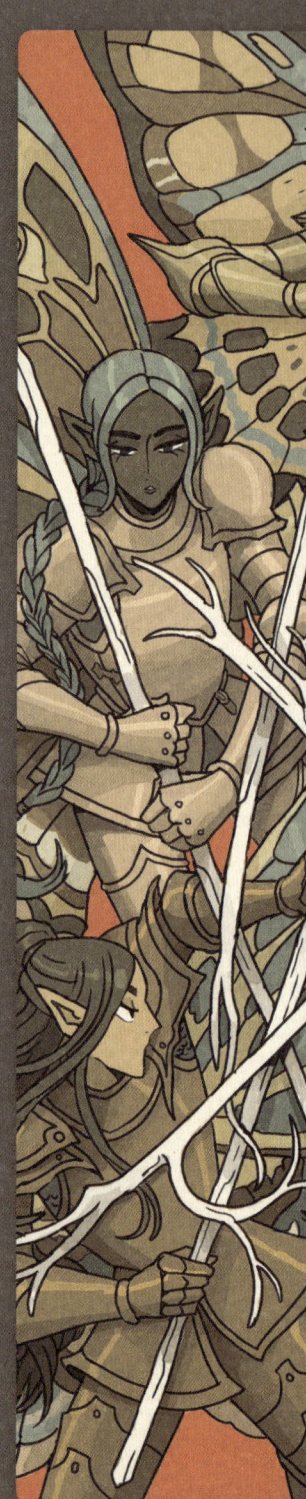

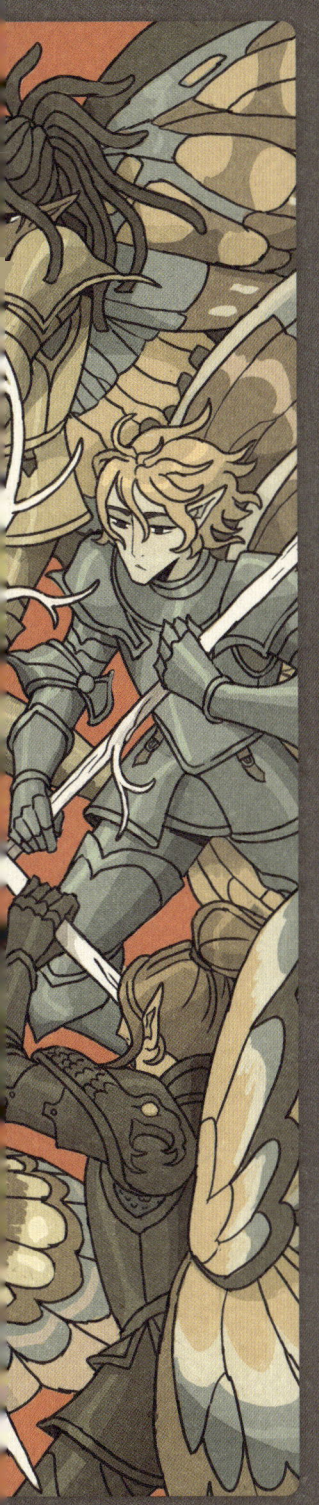

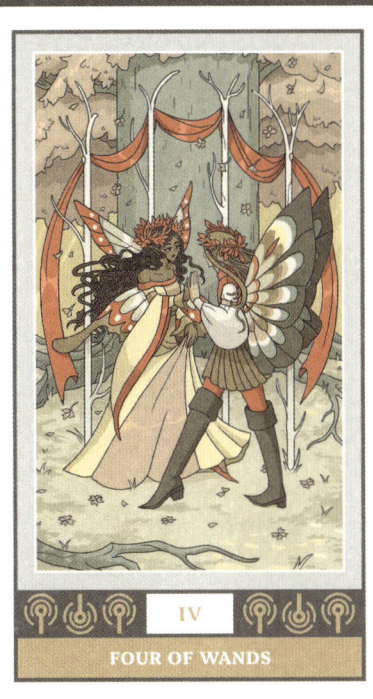

IV

FOUR OF WANDS

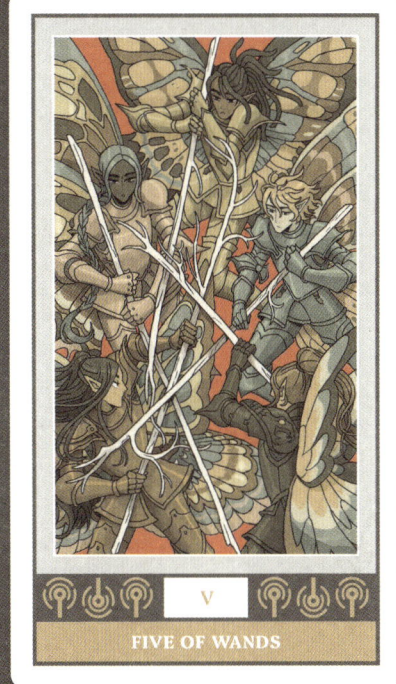

V

FIVE OF WANDS

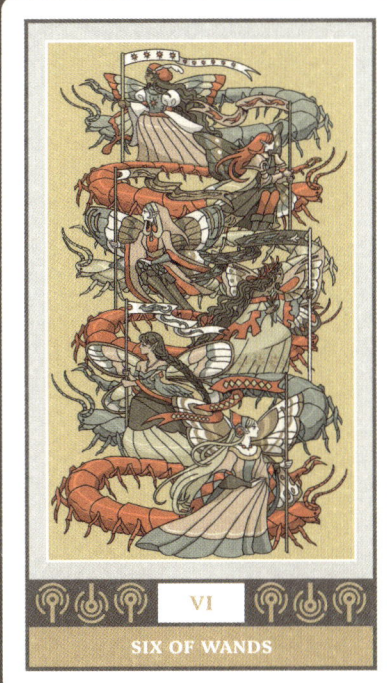

VI

SIX OF WANDS

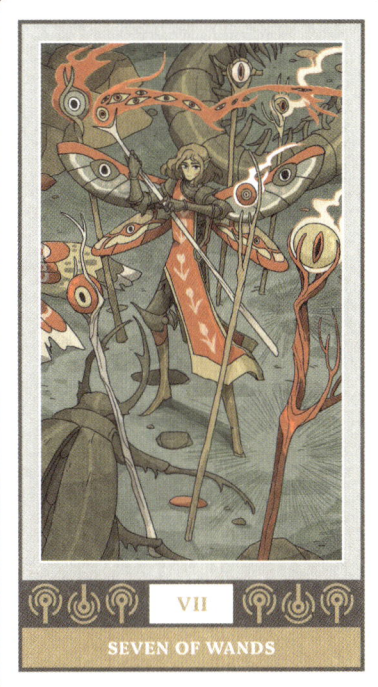

VII

SEVEN OF WANDS

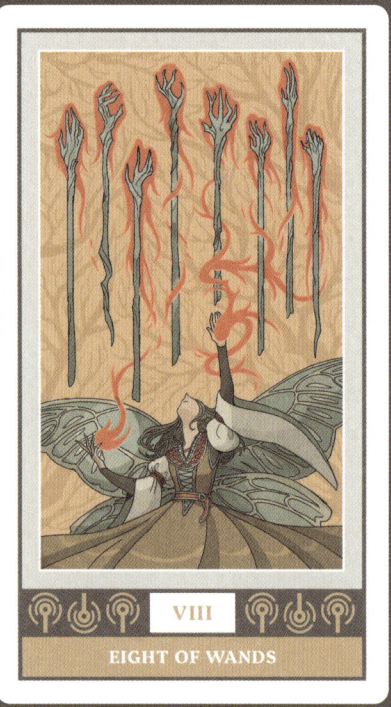

VIII

EIGHT OF WANDS

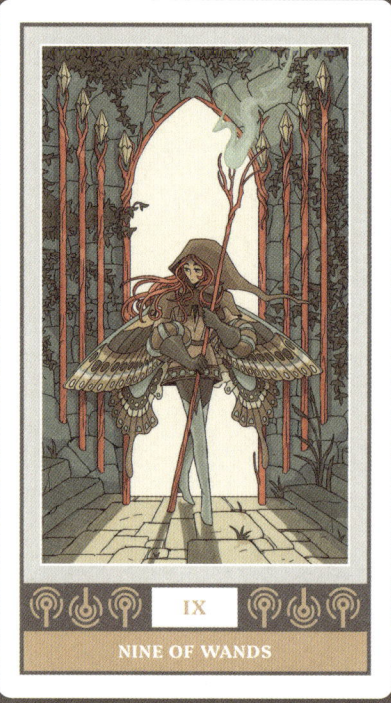

IX

NINE OF WANDS

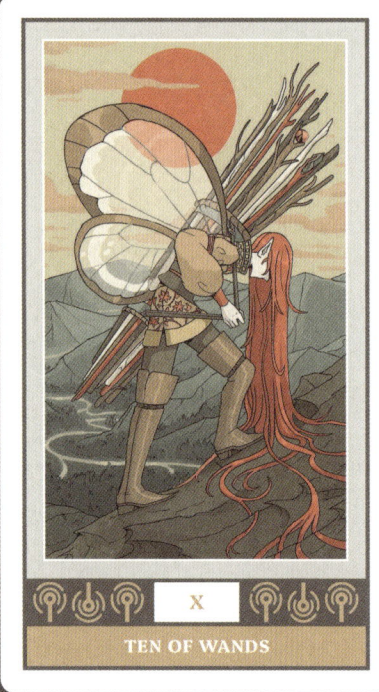

X

TEN OF WANDS

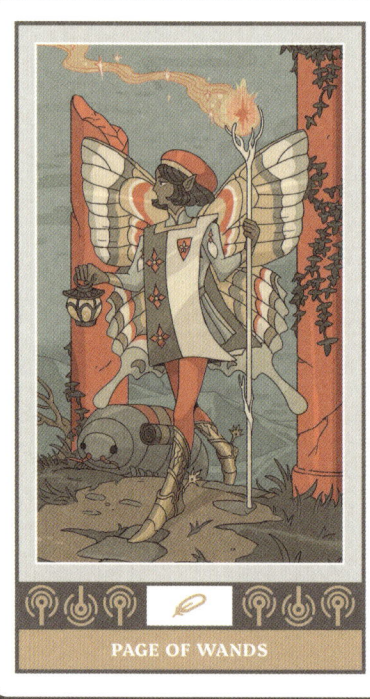

PAGE OF WANDS

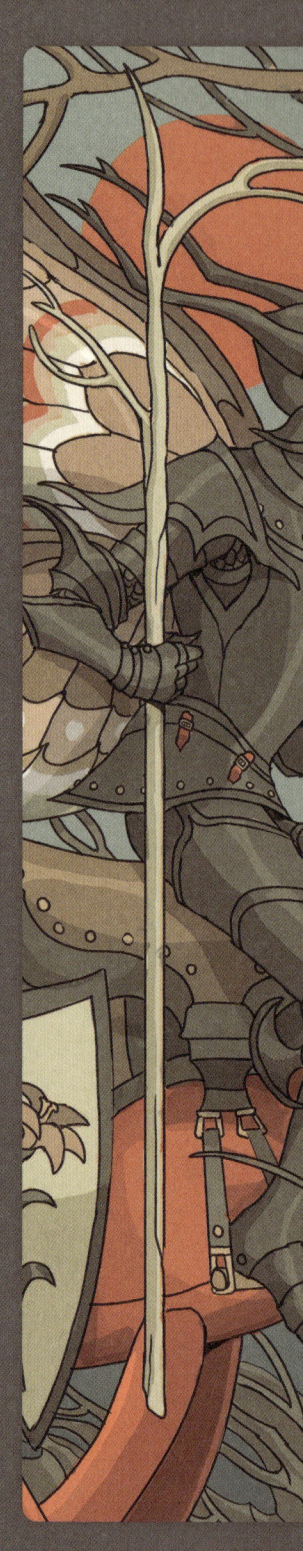

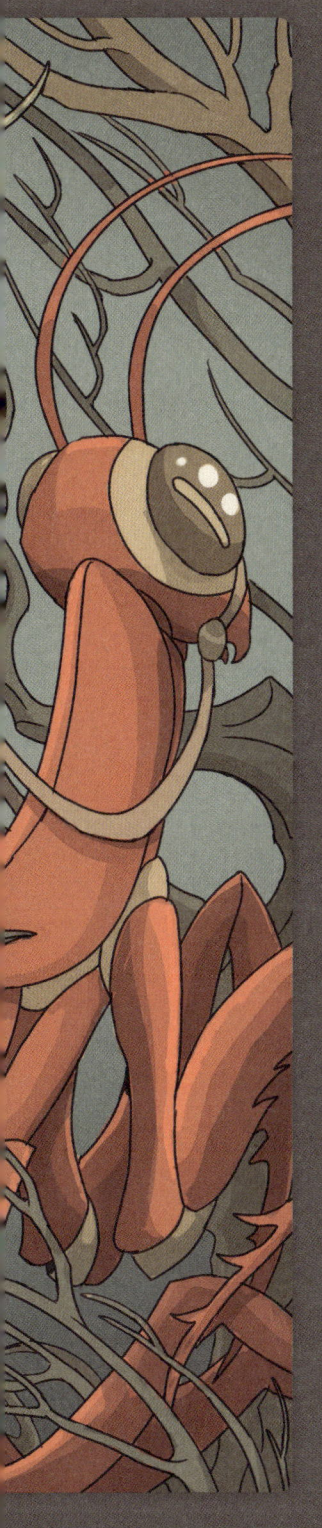

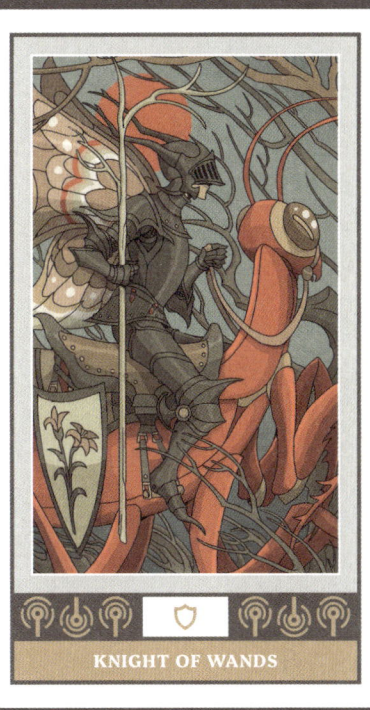

KNIGHT OF WANDS

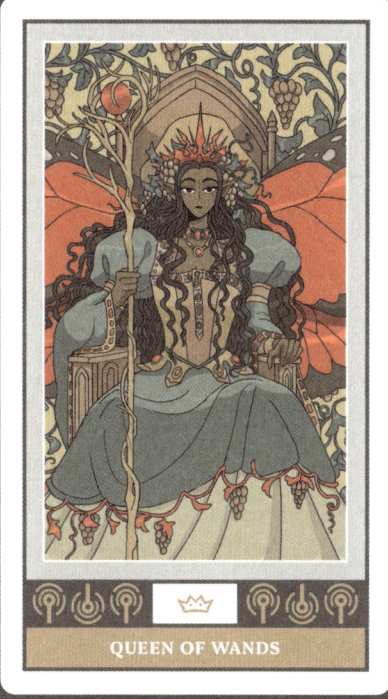

QUEEN OF WANDS

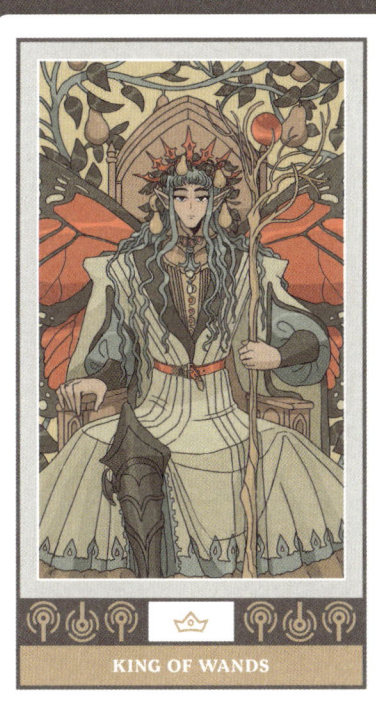

KING OF WANDS

Ten of Cups. All final images © Anaïs Flogny

THE SUIT OF
CUPS

INTRODUCTION BY SASHA GRAHAM

Cups reflect the entire world of elemental Water. Cups and Water represent all emotional human qualities, such as feelings, creativity, dreams, love, and imagination. Just as the Major Arcana is a progression beginning with The Fool who travels to The World card, so does the Ace of Cups (the font or flow of elemental Water) pour into the suit of Cups and flow through each card until reaching fullness in the Ten of Cups. The cycle thus begins afresh in the Ace.

When illustrating this suit, it's important to decide how the symbol of Cups (also called goblets, chalices, bowls, or vessels) will appear through the suit. Will it be the same style of cup or different cups? Placing the number of cups in a card to reflect the card's number makes it easy for the reader to identify and interpret which card they are looking at. For instance, the Seven of Cups usually includes seven cup symbols, the Eight of Cups has eight cups, and so forth.

Consider not only how the landscape of Cups will appear, but what distinctive qualities, animals, symbols, clothing, characters, and appearance the suit of Cups will have. Will the watery suit of Cups be expressed as an aquatic world populated by nymphs, naiads, mermaids, fish, scales, and sea ships, or will it simply be a landscape in which characters are using cups and acting with strong emotions, loving drama or artistic expressions?

The Cup court cards are the ruling noble family of the suit: a mother (Queen), father (King), son (Knight), and daughter (Page). Each court card embodies emotional water qualities according to their age, station, and life experience. Will your court cards wear courtly, luxurious clothing with crowns and thrones, or will they be imagined differently? If different, what sets the court cards apart from the 'regular' characters inhabiting the suit? There is no right or wrong as long as your worlds are well thought out and intentional.

ANAÏS FLOGNY

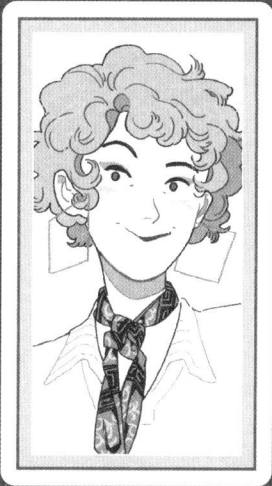

ARTIST'S INSIGHT

Tarot's unique imagery is what makes it fascinating to me. I have never played with or received a tarot reading myself, but the cards themselves have always struck me – they are the richest canvas any illustrator could hope for. I like the idea that, as with astrology, we can connect with the cards' meanings on a deep, personal level. And what better way to illustrate the Cups suit, associated with emotion, than with one of the most expressive human attributes, the hands?

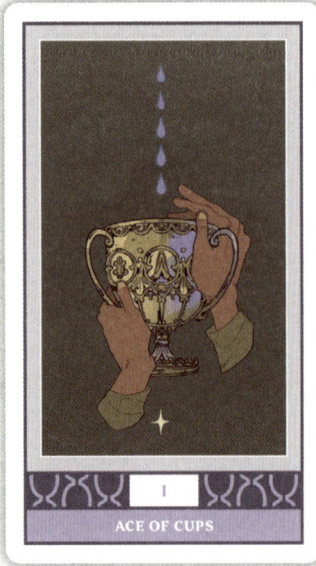

ACE OF CUPS

ACE OF CUPS

NOURISHMENT, JOY, OPENING

I

The Ace is the opening card of the series, so I want it to tease what's to come. It's important to show the cup, the hands, and the droplets, as the Cup suit is associated with the element of Water. This card is also about nourishment: a huge cup is slowly being filled with small droplets, as waiting hands are holding it. The Ace is also a card that is half numeral, half figure – I decide to have a central 'character' and cup rich with flourishes and details, but coloured with a palette similar to how I will begin the number cards.

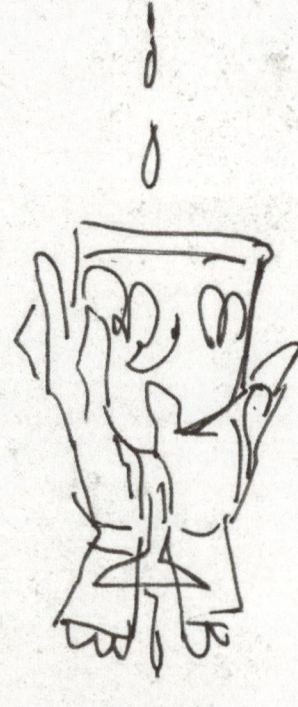

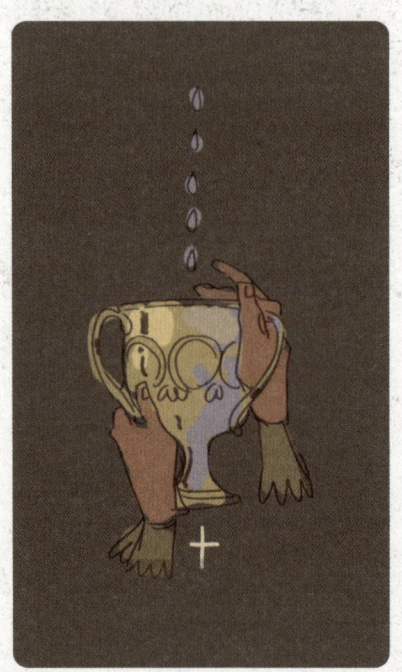

My rough sketches explore
the idea of two hands
catching water in a cup

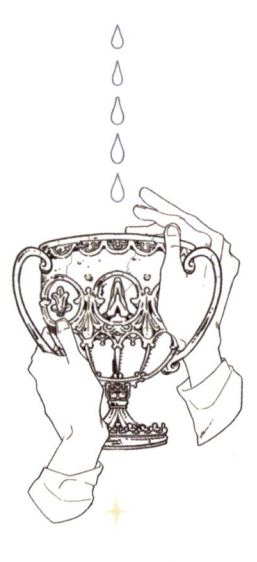

The single, focal cup is large
and detailed, like the court
cards' cups will be

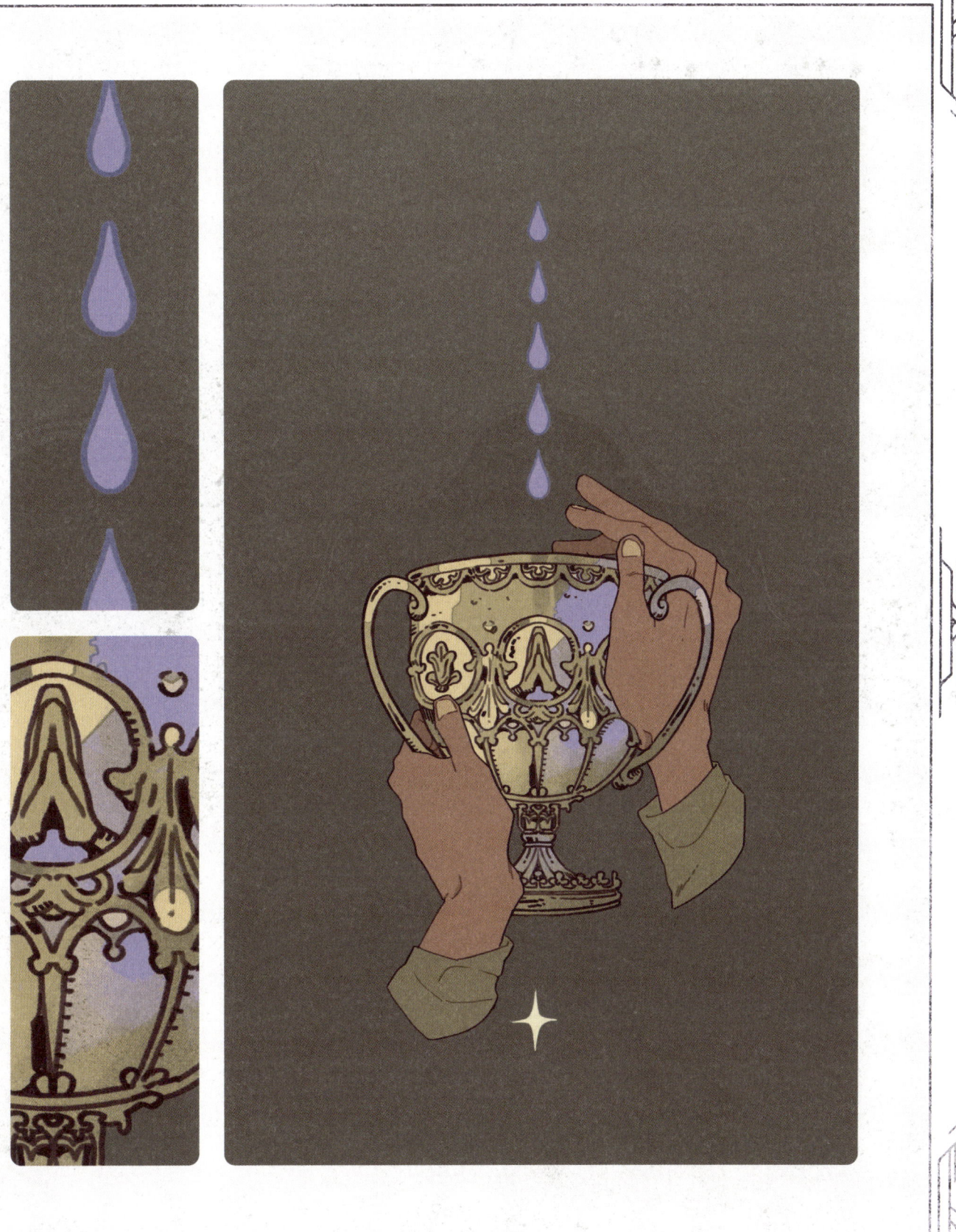

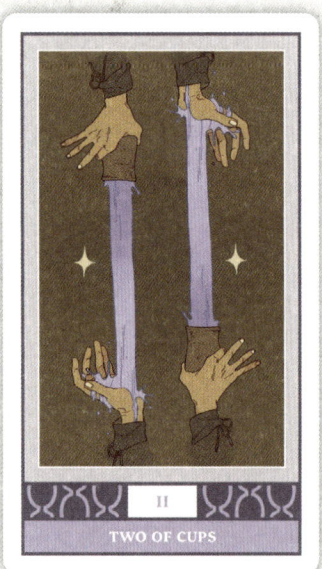

TWO OF CUPS

FRIENDSHIP, ADORATION, MIRROR

The Two of Cups is often associated with the idea of duality, be that in gender, age, or life and death. I want to play around with this idea, with two sets of hands mirroring each other. We don't know their gender, but even upside down, with water flowing up and down both ways, they are the same.

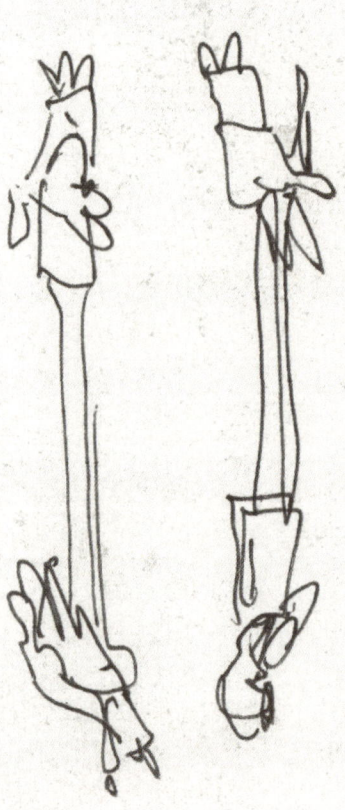

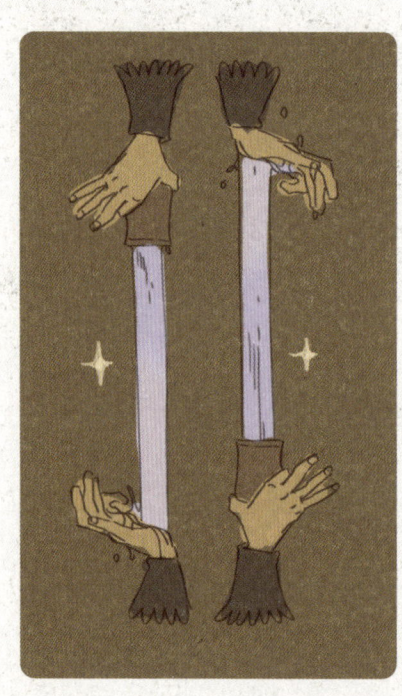

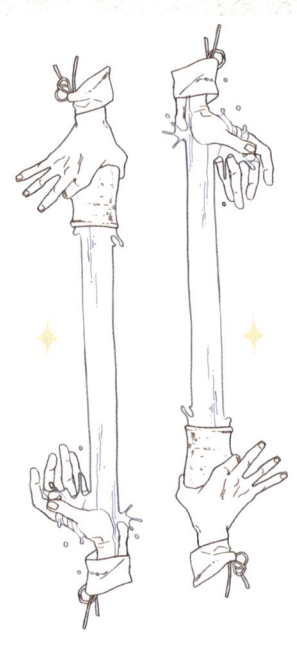

The two pairs of hands reflect each other like twins, friends, or partners

I want the suit's colour palette to progress from dark to light

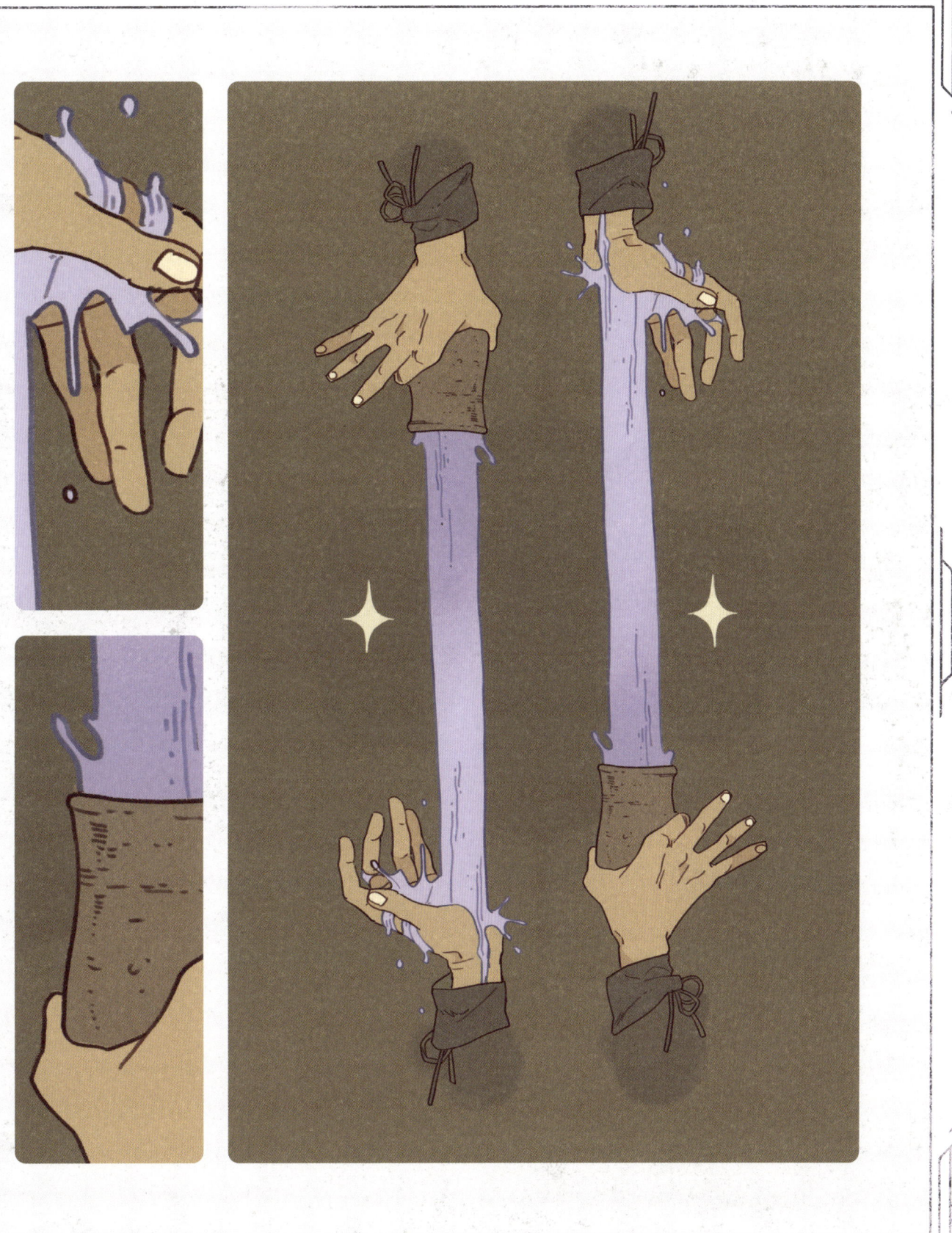

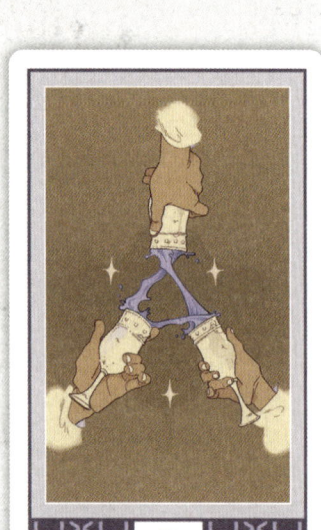

THREE OF CUPS

FRIENDSHIP, BONDING, SUPPORT

III

The Three of Cups showcases three hands playfully clinking their glasses, water jumping from each cup in an infinite three-branched cycle. This third card is linked to the idea of bonding, friendship, and support. The triangle is the strongest shape in nature, one that can support so much pressure and weight. I want to show Water, the element of emotion, being the testimony of these characters' solid bond.

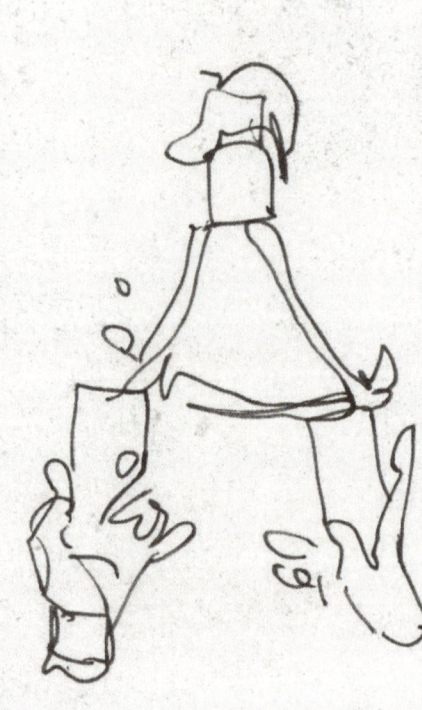

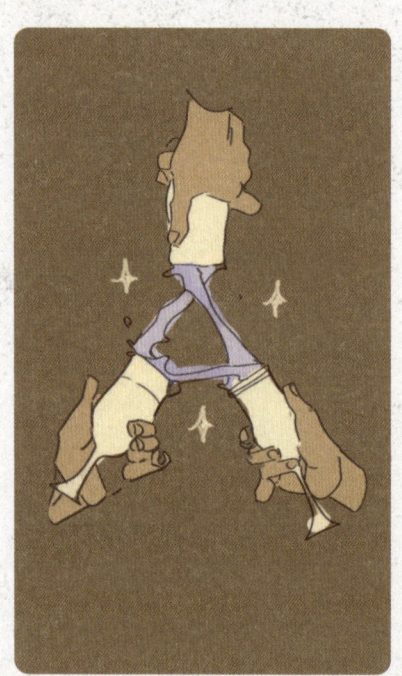

Water passes between three companions in a strong, triumphant shape

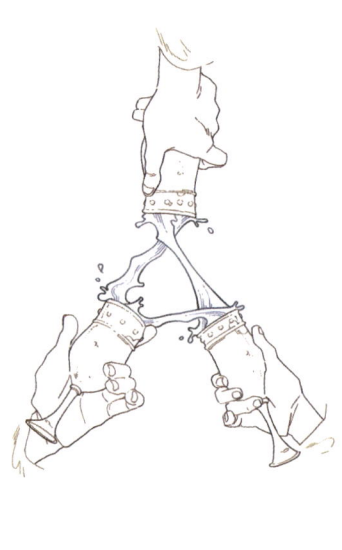

This card's colour palette is brighter to help represent its theme

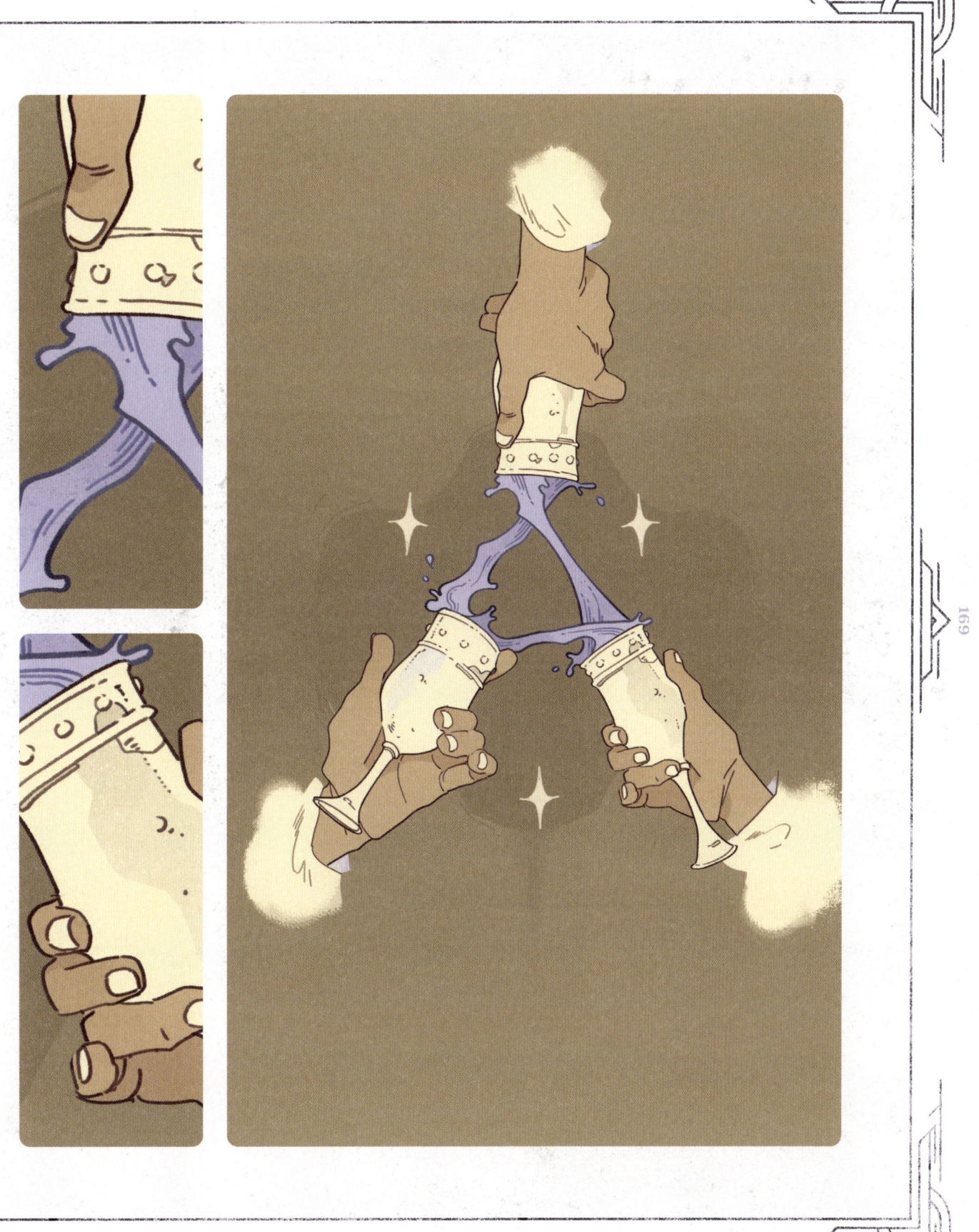

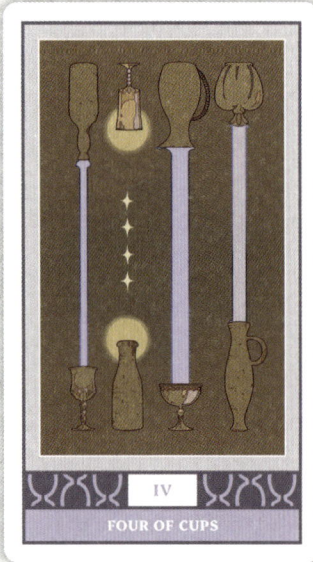

FOUR OF CUPS

FOUR OF CUPS

BOREDOM, PAUSE, DAYDREAM

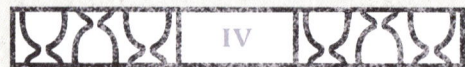

The Four of Cups presents two distinct ideas: the idea of stability, as a binary number, but also the symbolism of a pause and boredom. In this piece, we see four sets of cups and their respective bottles, with water flowing between them, except for one of the sets. They seem to be set apart, but the stars (used to number the cards) remind us of the cards' meanings: stability and imagination. Even without the water flowing, they are still connected.

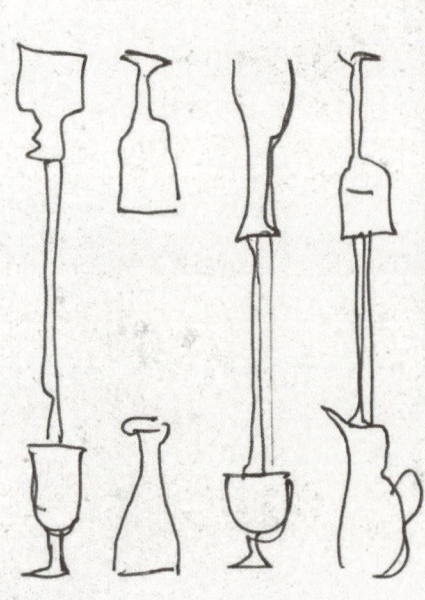

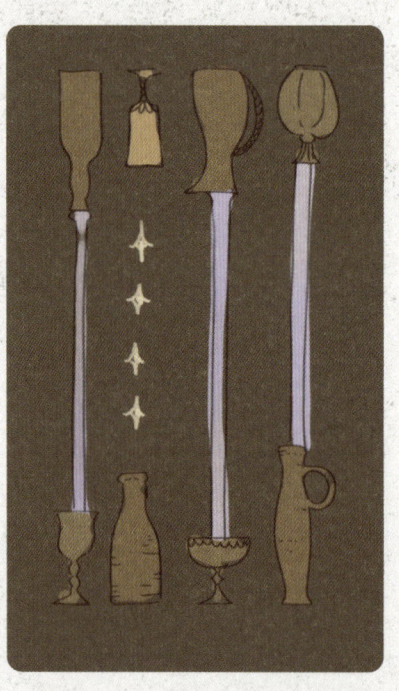

The pouring water forms straight, stable shapes, almost like pillars

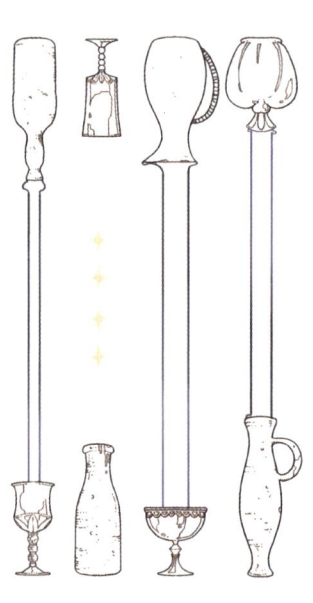

The waterless pair represents the Four of Cups' quality of pause or stasis

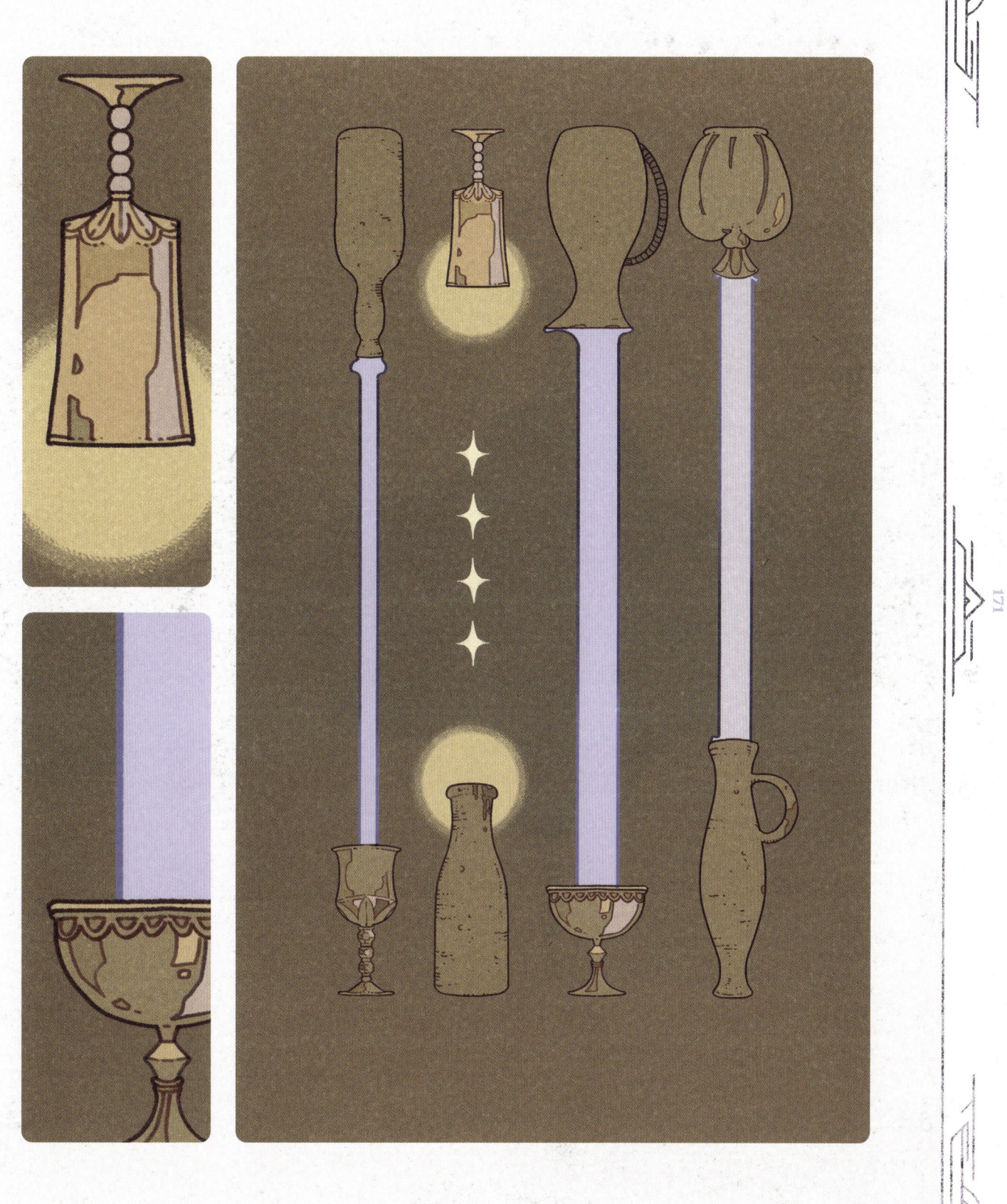

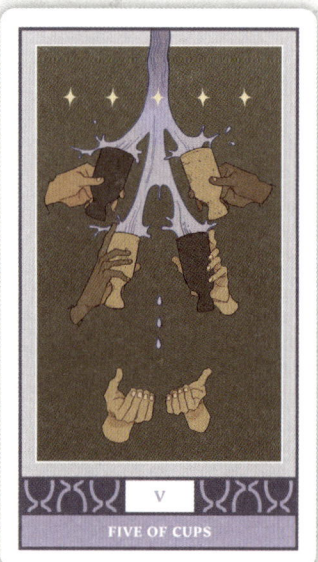

FIVE OF CUPS

LOSS, DEPRESSION, ADDICTION

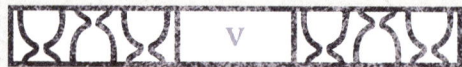

The Five of Cups is the card of loss and addiction. Four cheerful hands celebrate as water flows with creative motions into their cups. A fifth pair of hands tries to catch a few droplets falling from the party up above. This character doesn't hold a cup, and has to use their own hands as such. It can be seen as an act of addiction, despair, and wanting to be part of whatever is going on without them.

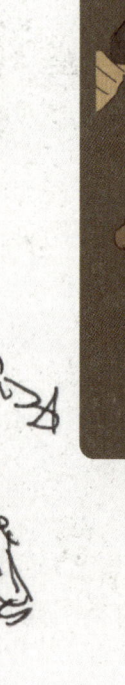

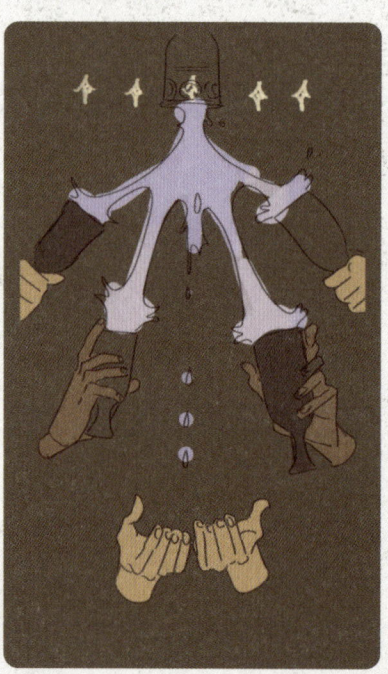

Four hands cheers their cups as water pours down from above

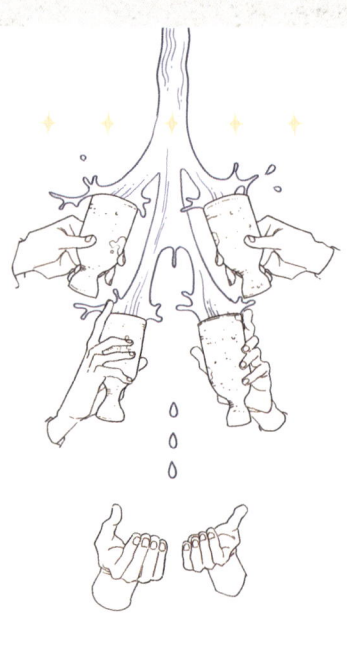

The fifth pair of hands is desperate for water, or perhaps lonely and isolated

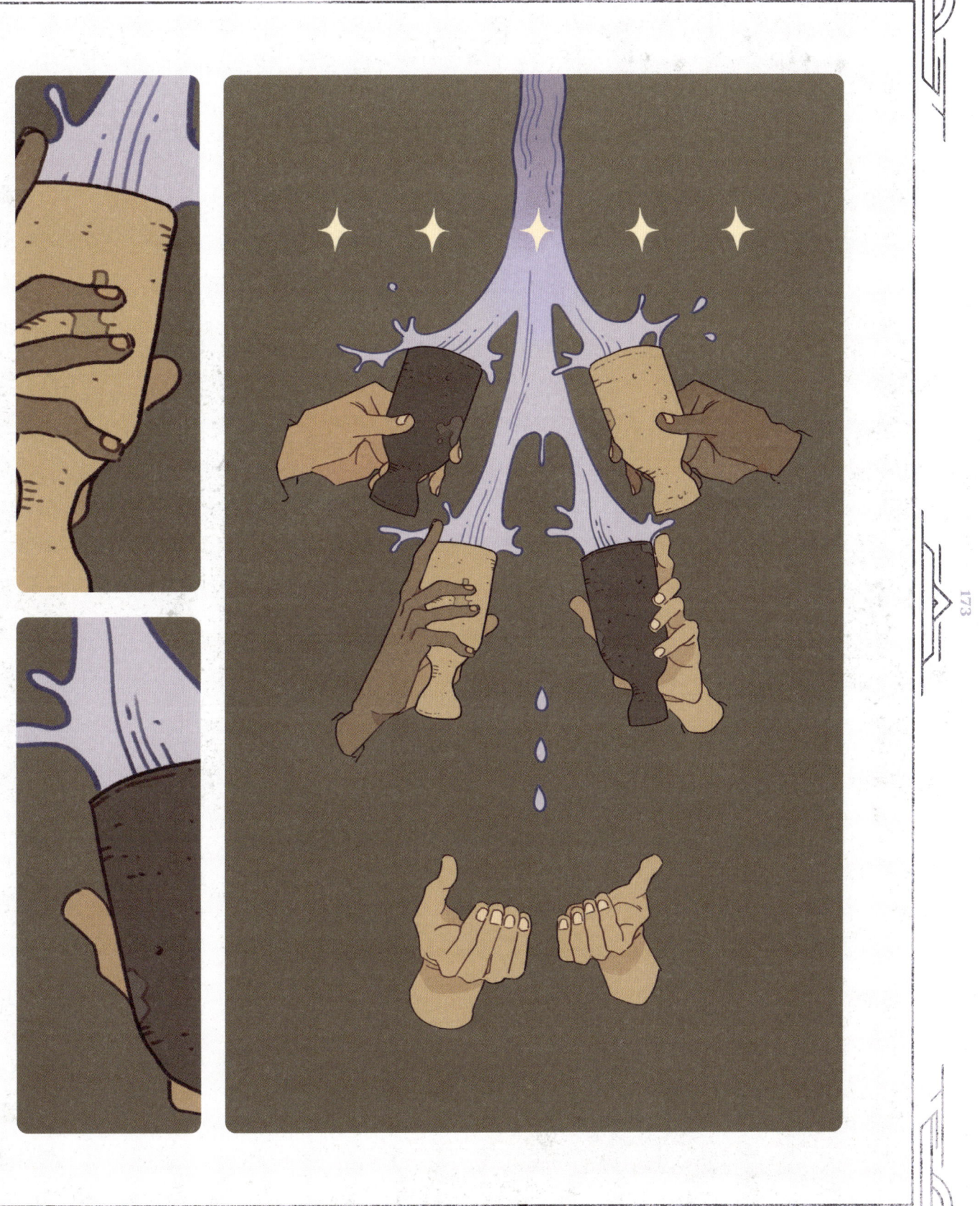

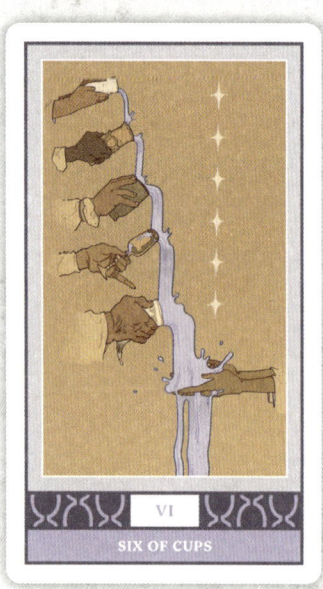

SIX OF CUPS

NOSTALGIA, GIFTS, KINDNESS

VI

The Six of Cups showcases five hands gently pouring the water from their cups into the ones below, creating a waterfall. The sixth pair of hands gathers the overflowing water. I design this card in opposition to the fifth one, with the last pair of hands receiving plentiful water instead of a few droplets. The Six of Cups is associated with nostalgia and kindness, which I want to emphasize with a vertical composition, with hands of every age gently sharing their cups with the others.

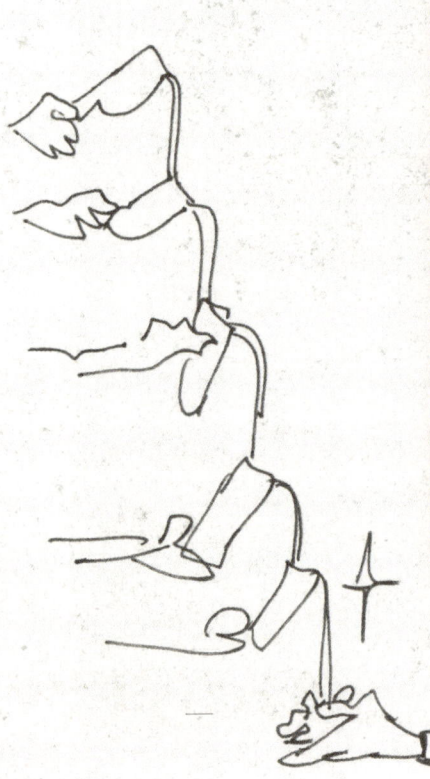

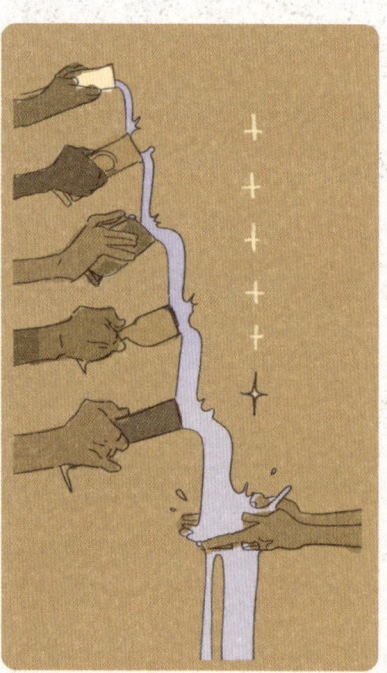

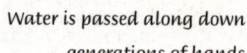

Water is passed along down generations of hands

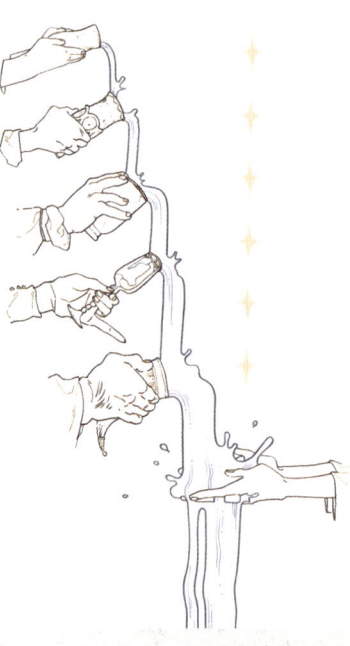

The colour palette is lighter than the Five of Cups

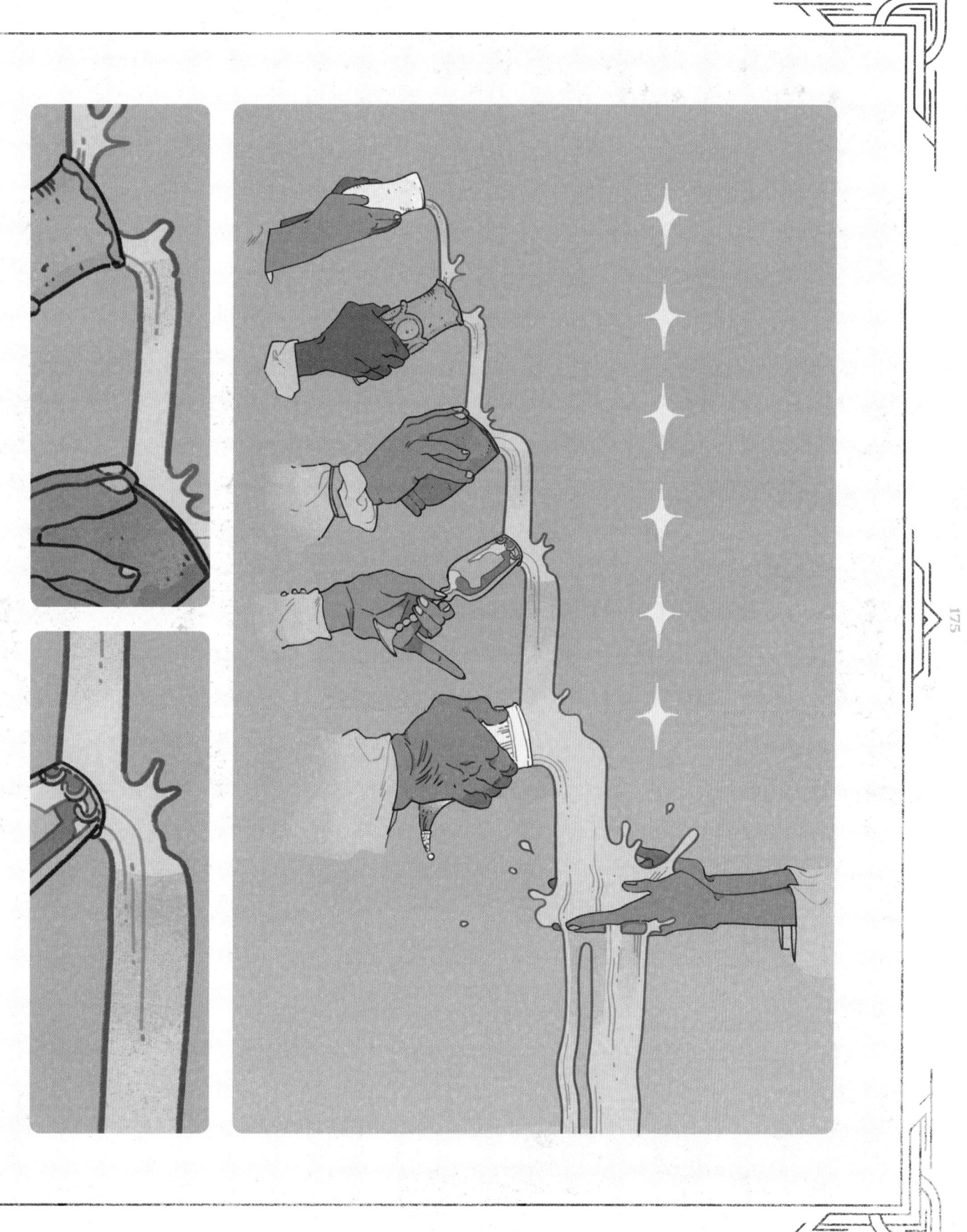

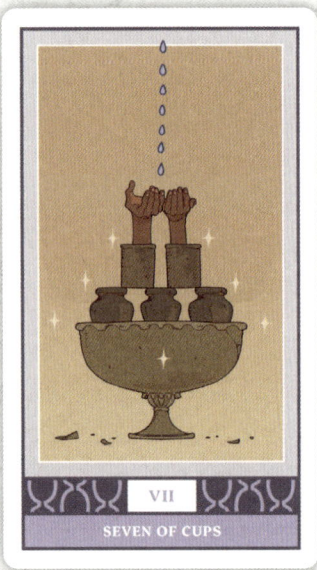

SEVEN OF CUPS

EDITING, MOVING, HATCHING

VII

The Seven of Cups is associated with magic and empathy, and holds a lot of other significances, like luck or wisdom. In the Rider–Waite–Smith version (see page 23), we can see a figure running away as a symbol of a plan that may not work. I want to explore this idea but twist it a little: instead of running away, two hands reach out of a pyramid of goblets, trying to catch seven droplets of water. Maybe, if they try hard enough, they can fill themselves and fulfil all the cups below.

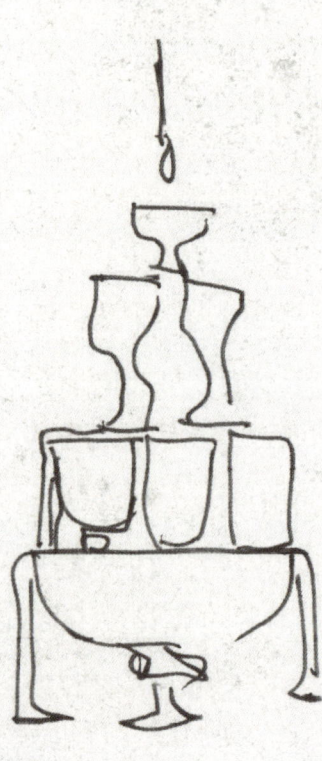

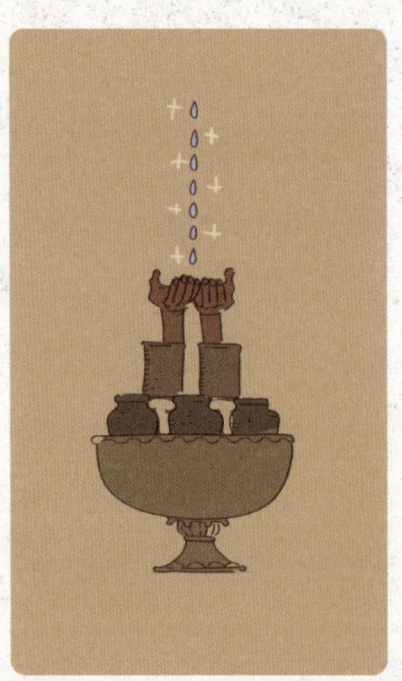

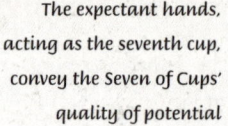

The expectant hands, acting as the seventh cup, convey the Seven of Cups' quality of potential

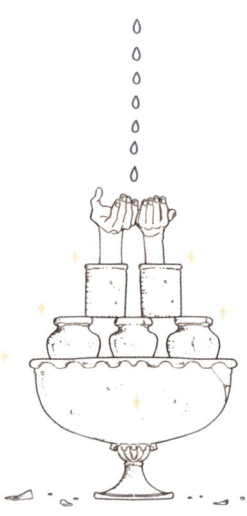

Seven droplets of water are ready to be caught by the hands and cups below

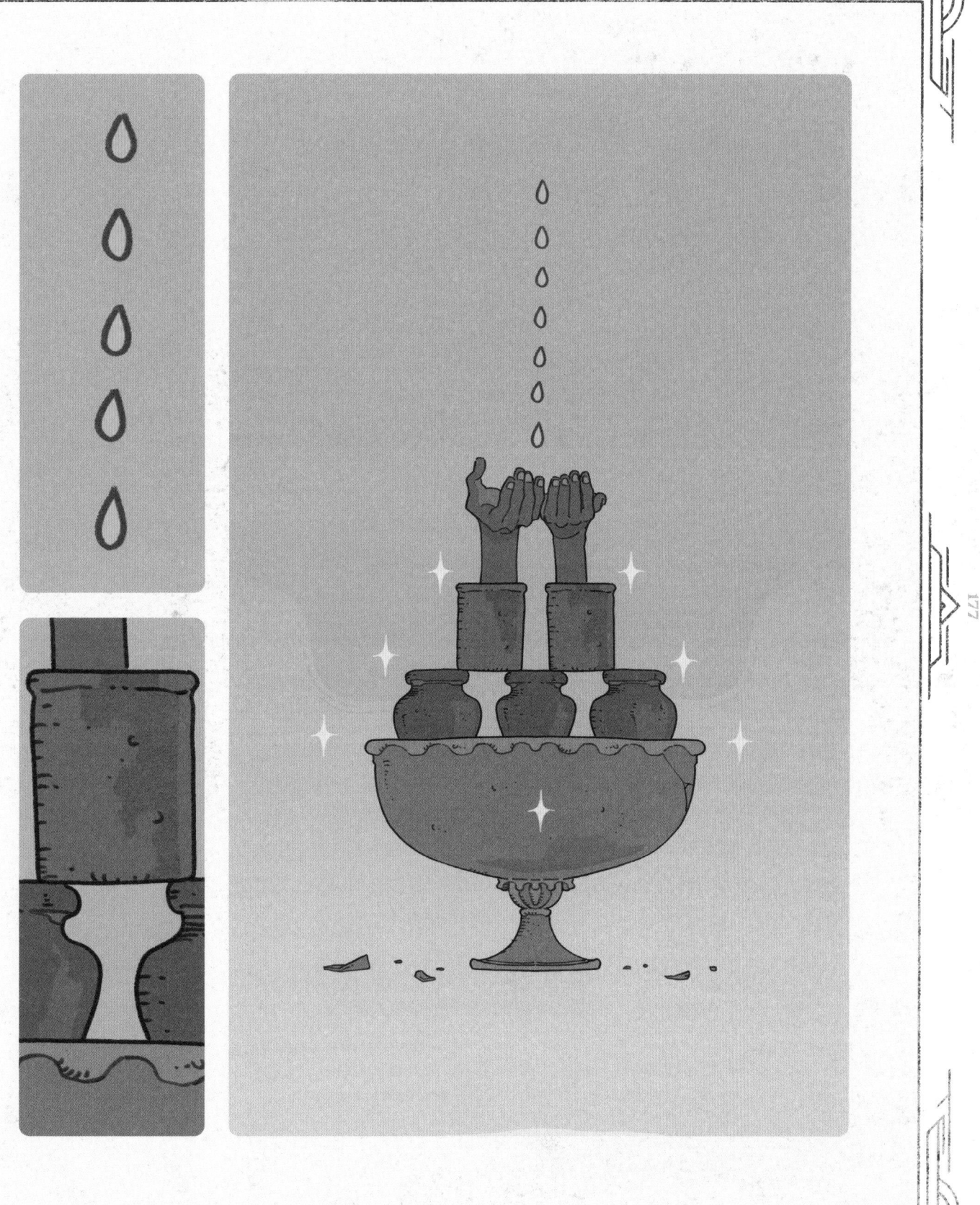

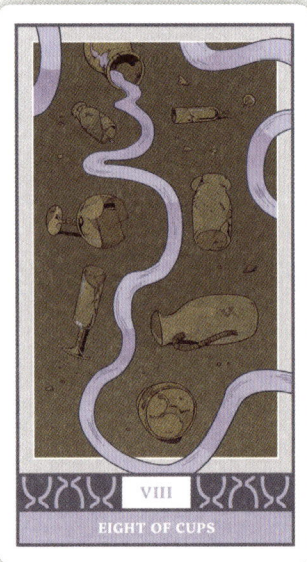

EIGHT OF CUPS

DEPARTURE, ABANDONING, ASCENT

The Eight of Cups is about abandonment. Water flows from a lonely pot, the only source of water in the scene. Broken cups of different shapes and materials lie beside the pitcher, but the water seems to avoid them, as its natural flow circles around them. I associate the purple tint with the element of water, and add some to the highlight of the cups, as a reminder of what was once full. The colour scheme evolves throughout the suit, growing darker for cards with heavier meaning.

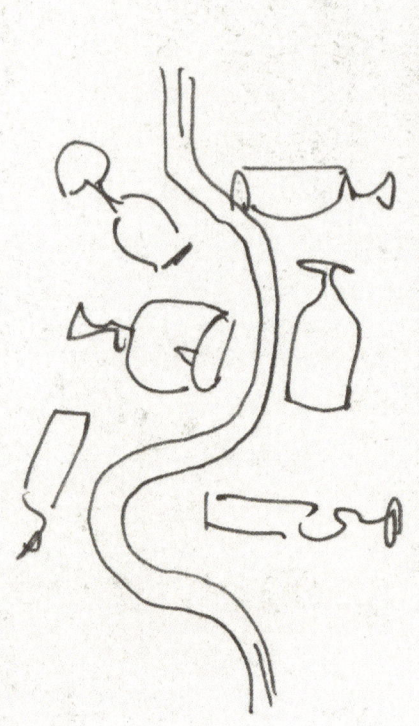

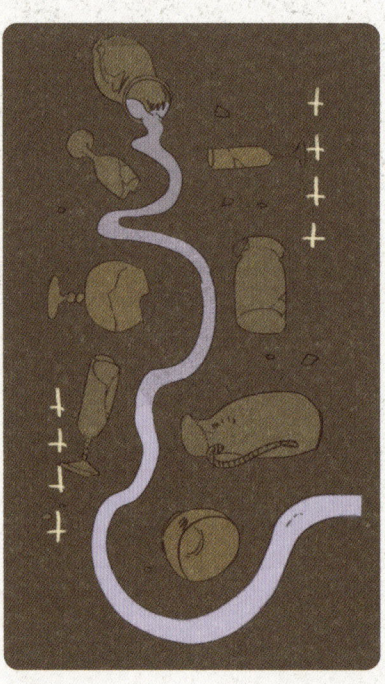

The colour palette darkens again to reflect the card's themes

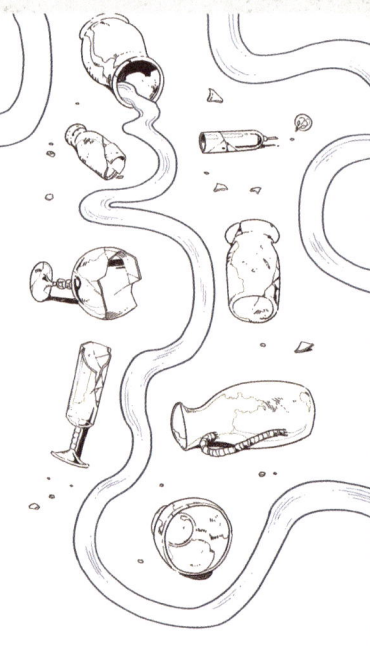

The stream of water curves around the shattered cups as if to steer clear of them

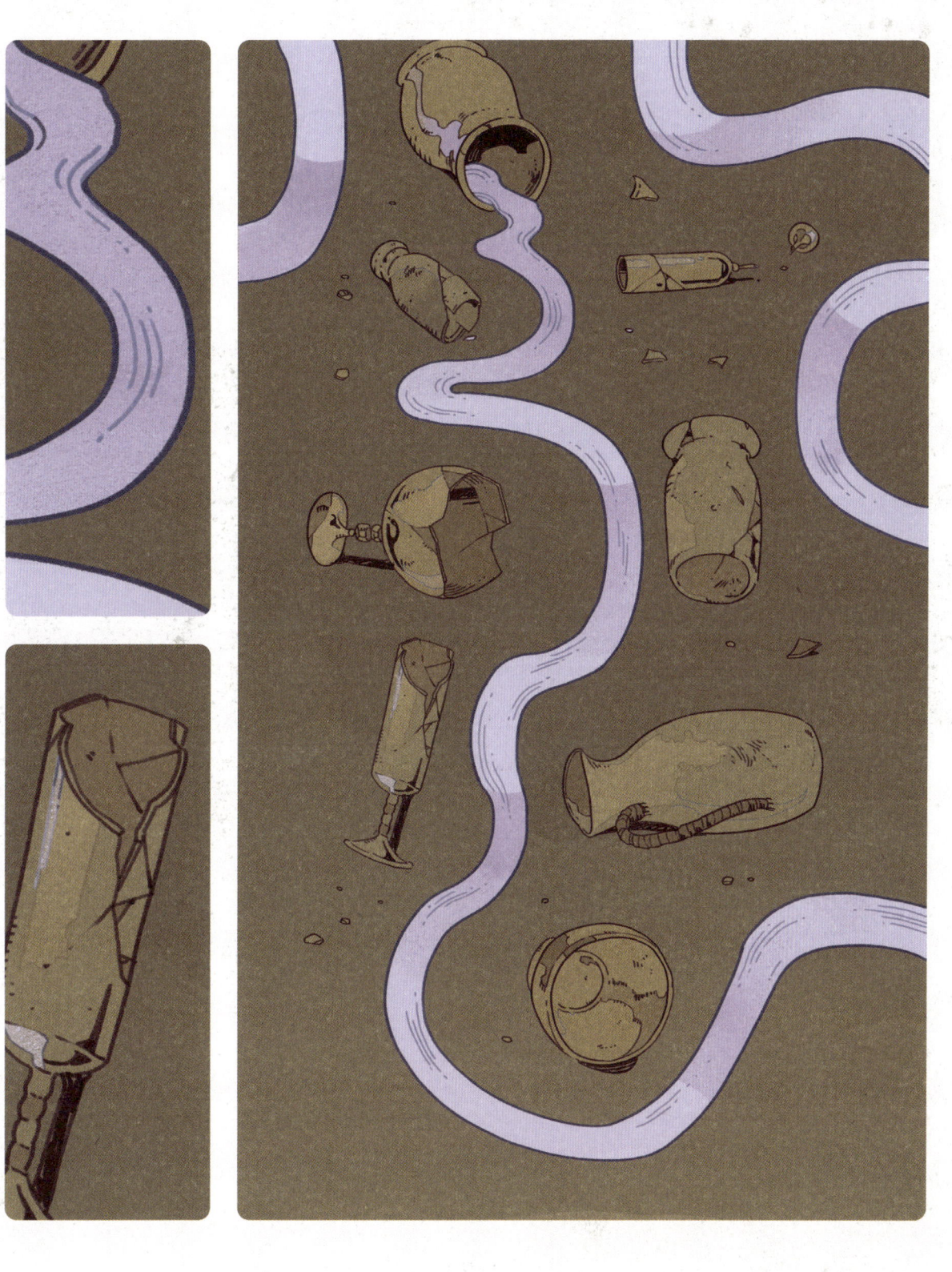

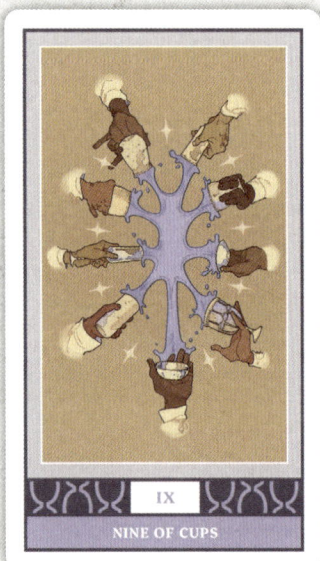

NINE OF CUPS

NINE
OF CUPS

RESULTS, WISHES COME TRUE, RECEIVING

IX

The colour scheme suddenly shifts for the Nine of Cups. This speaks of wishes fulfilled, the idea of receiving, and the result of an effort. Nine hands of all backgrounds and origins share their water in cups of varying sizes and shapes. I want this card to contrast with the previous card, almost like its opposite: a very light colour scheme, bright cups, and water colliding in a central focal point. Perspective and gravity don't matter in this suit: the emotions are the most important, as the suit is driven by feelings, not logic.

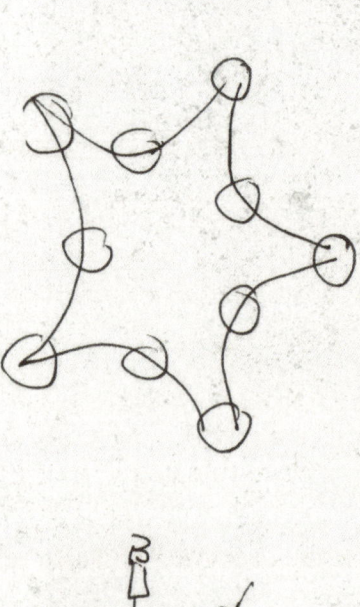

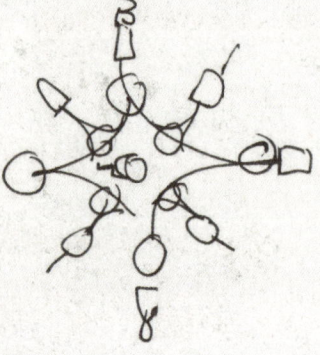

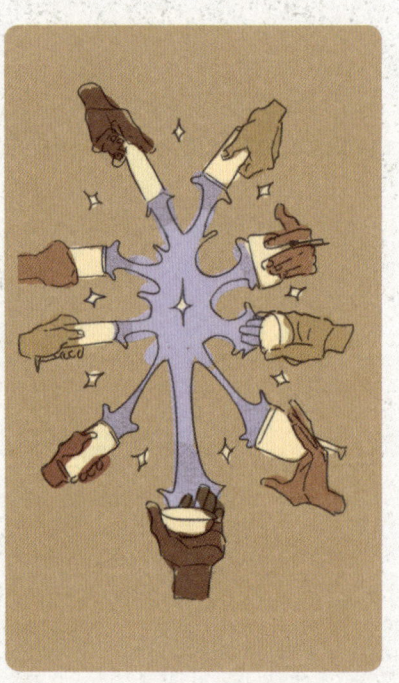

*The palette brightens again
compared to the previous card*

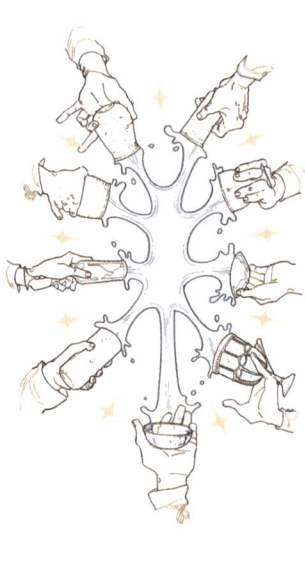

*Water from the nine cups
meets in one generous,
celebratory splash*

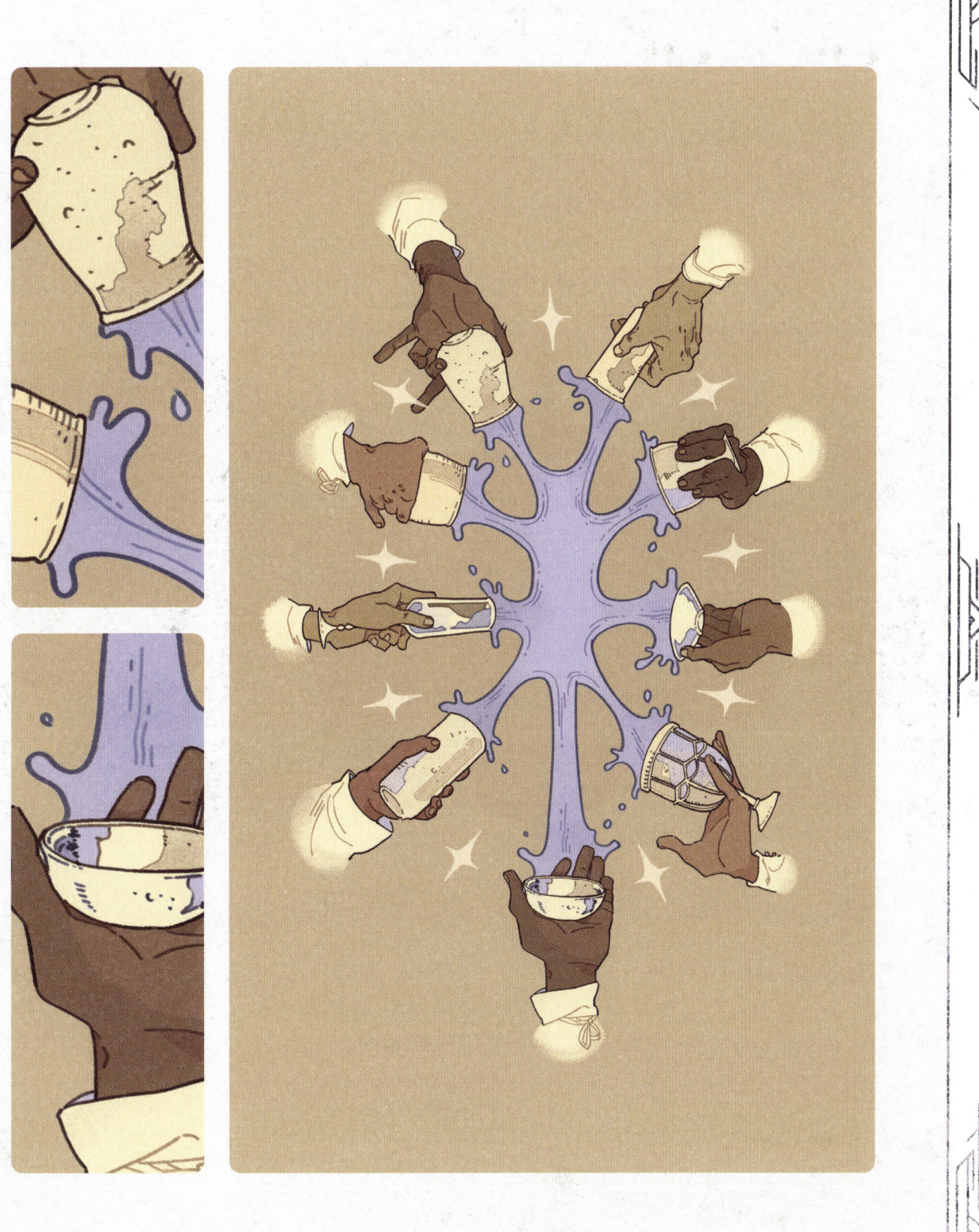

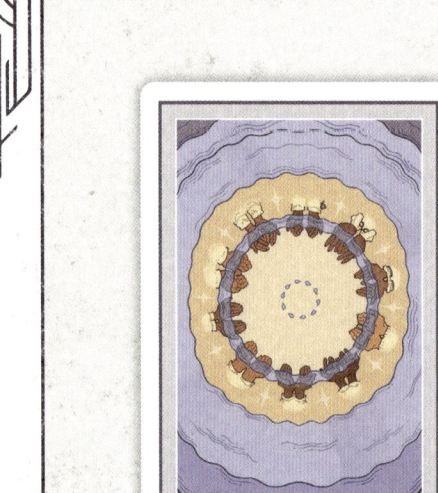

TEN OF CUPS

HAPPILY EVER AFTER, FAMILY, CONTENTMENT

The Ten of Cups is the culmination of the numeral part of the suit. It shows ten pairs of hands, united as water flows in a circle through their palms. The hands act as cups, but the water feels natural, not forced as in the fifth card, or overflowing as in the sixth. Balance has been reached and the hands are all connected. The colour palette is one of the lightest in the suit, dominated by the purple hues of the water.

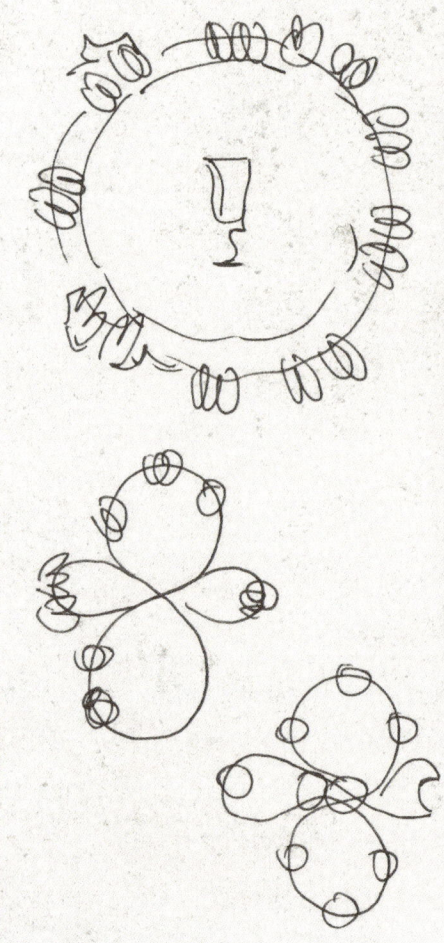

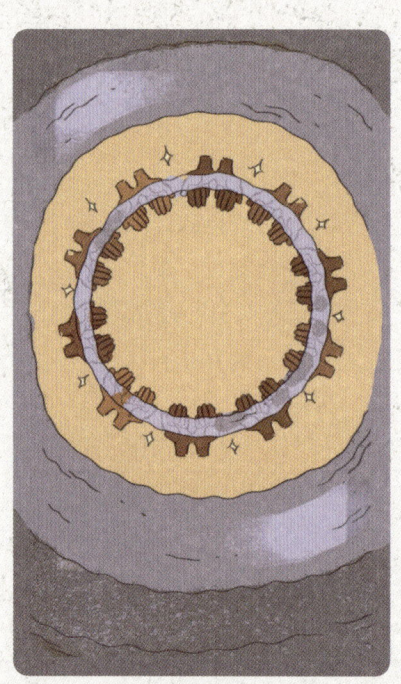

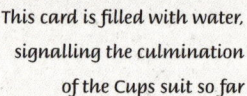

This card is filled with water, signalling the culmination of the Cups suit so far

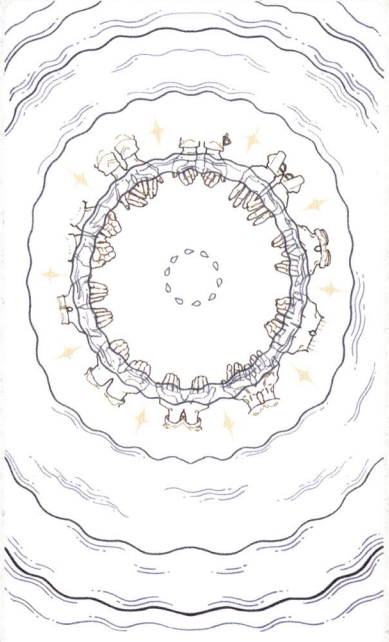

The water flows directly between ten pairs of hands in a perfect circle of sharing

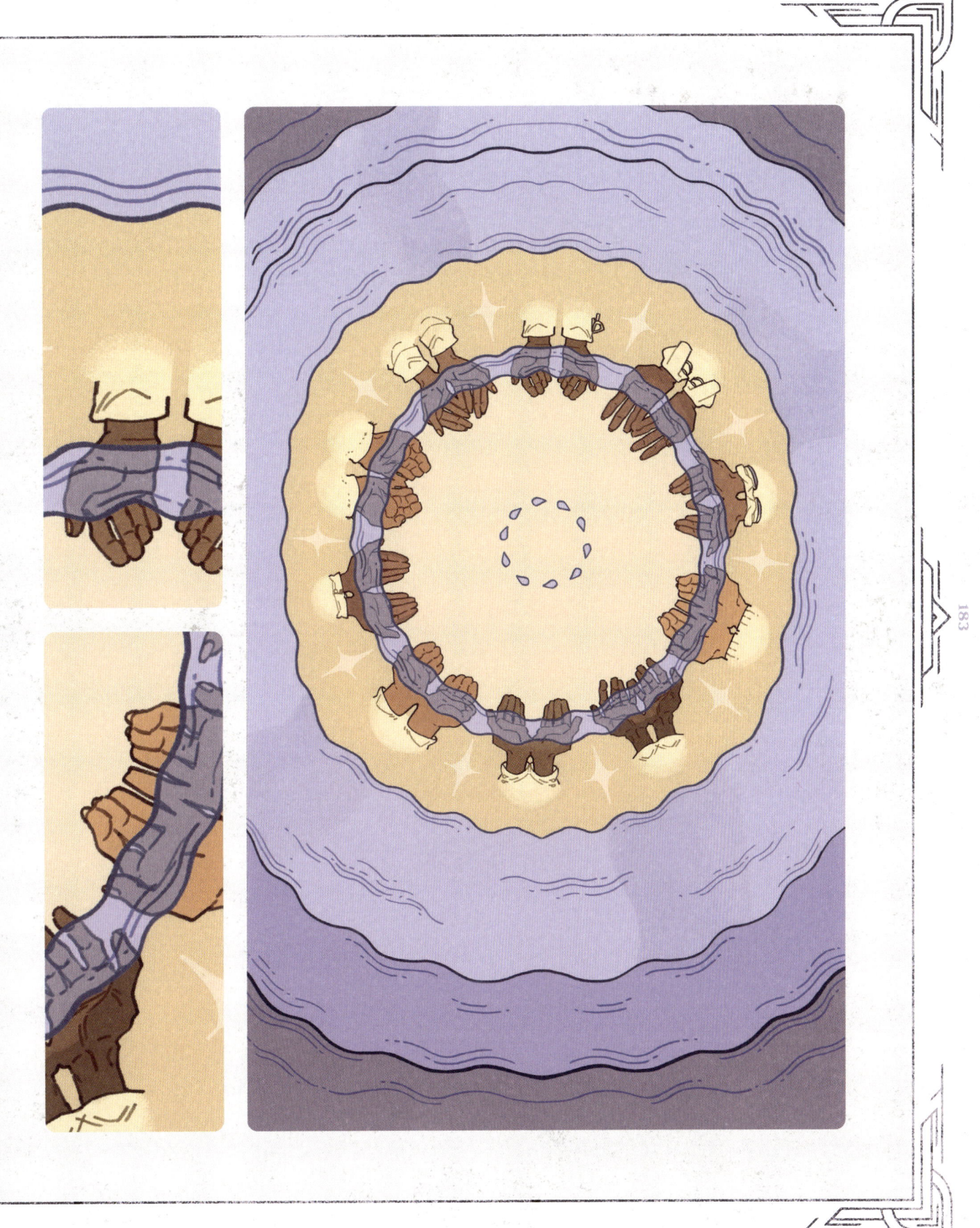

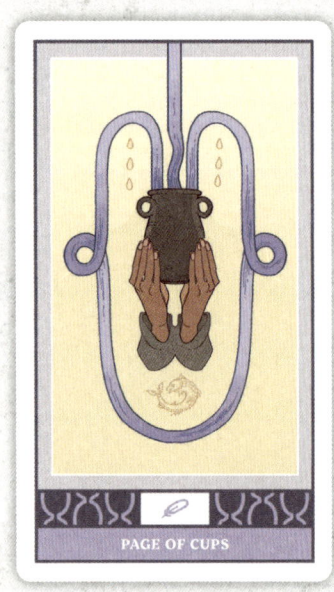

PAGE
OF CUPS

IMAGINATION, PSYCHIC ABILITY, DREAMING

The Page of Cups is associated with childhood and creativity. My Page shows two young hands holding a cup, water flowing from it in unnatural, beautiful, symmetrical shapes. The character holds his cup with both hands, showing a connection to his feelings and reality, but the water's arabesques showcase his imagination. There are visual symbols associated to the court cards, and I decide to add one here, in the style of a medieval engraving. The fish out of water relates to the Page's imagination and intuition.

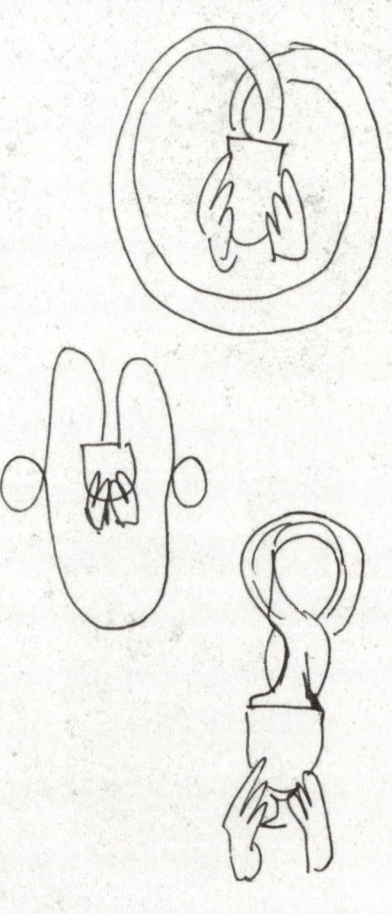

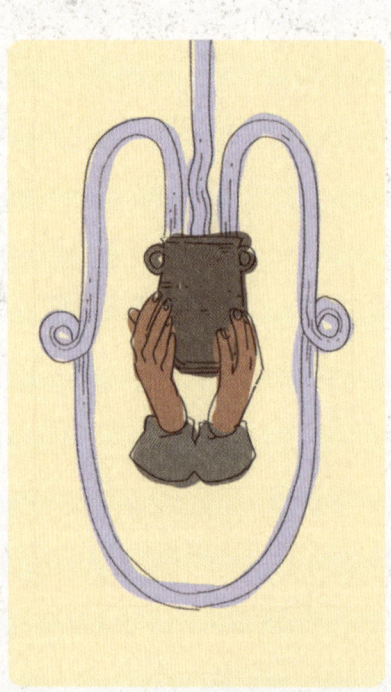

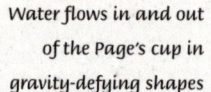

Water flows in and out of the Page's cup in gravity-defying shapes

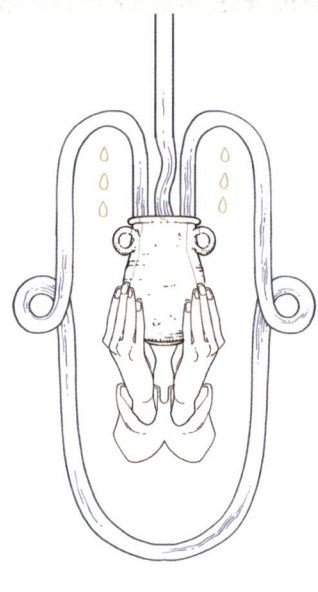

I leave space below the hands to fit a fish, in reference to the classic depiction of the Page's cup

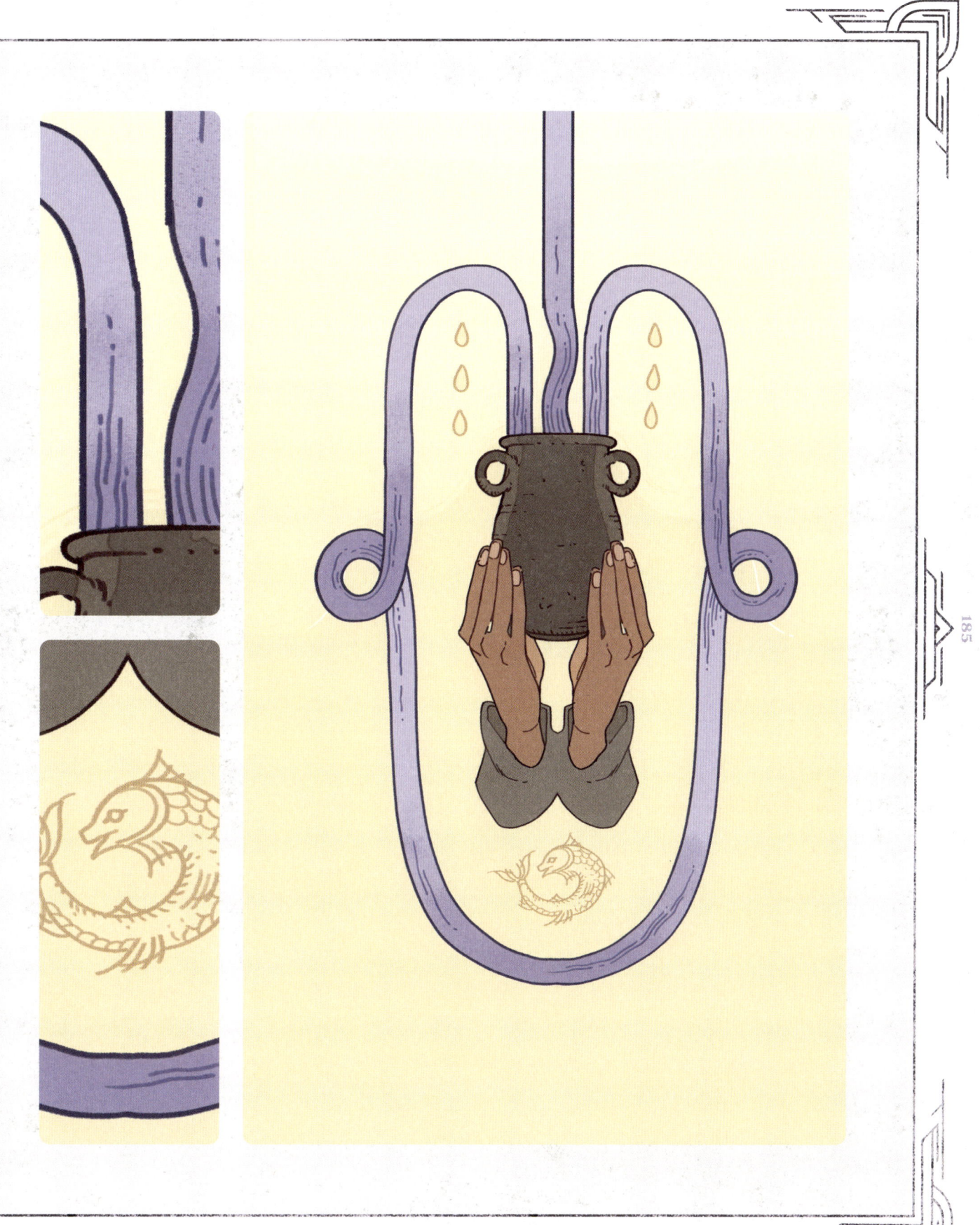

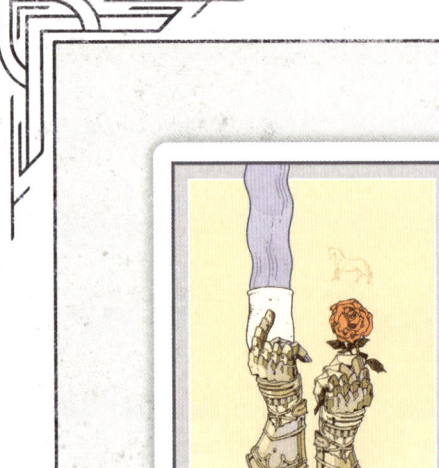

KNIGHT OF CUPS

KNIGHT OF CUPS

FLATTERY, POETRY, ROMANCE

The Knight of Cups is a being of pure emotions, associated with the feeling of romance and flattery. This is symbolized by the water flowing up and down, almost forming a river: one goes out of the cup, the other pours directly from the armour. Knights are driven by desire, devotion, and passion. The purple tint of the water even reflects on the gauntlets. The rose is there to remind us of poetry and beauty, a symbol of romance. The horse, about to step forward, is a symbol of deliberation.

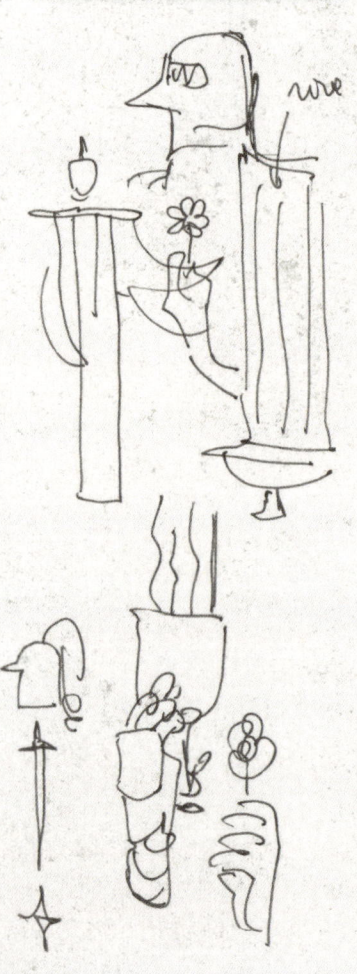

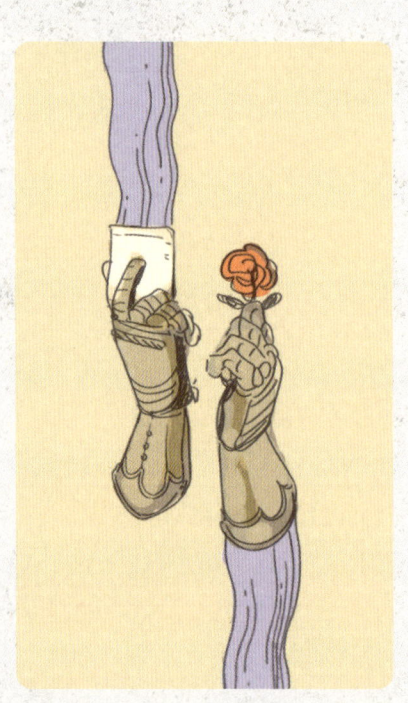

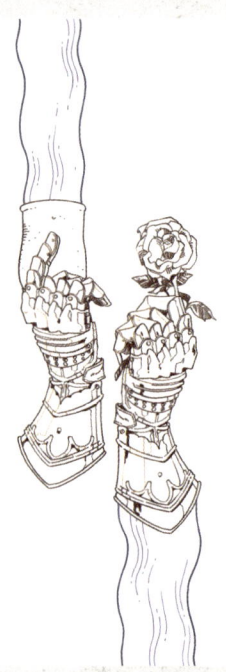

Strong rivers of water
flow directly in and out
of the Knight of Cups

The metal gauntlets contrast with
the flowing water and delicate rose

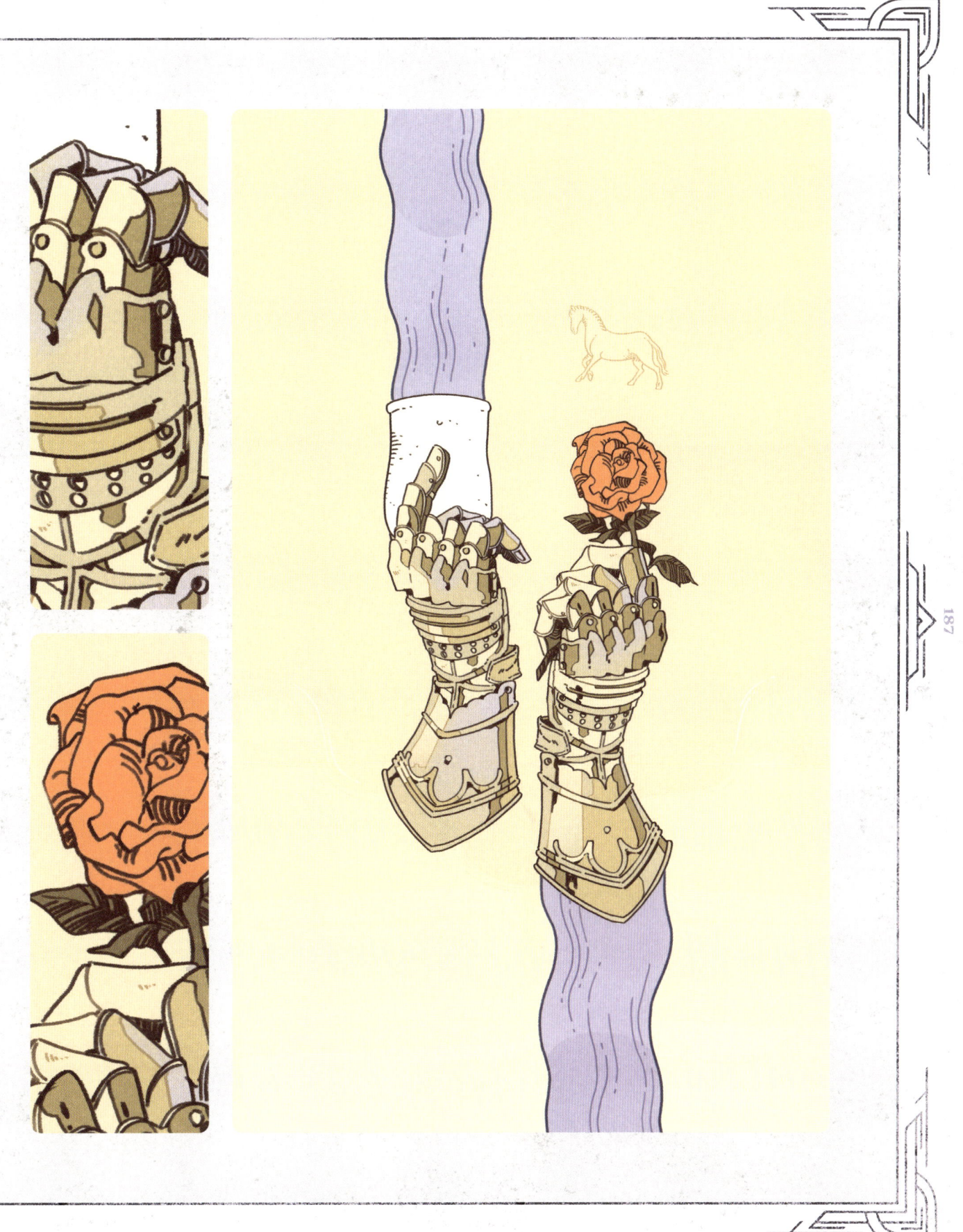

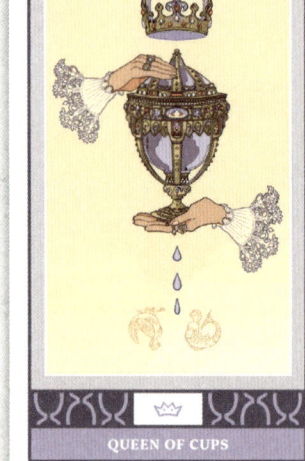

QUEEN OF CUPS

QUEEN OF CUPS

EMPATHETIC, COMFORTING, UNDERSTANDING

The Queen is my favourite card of the set. She holds a beautifully detailed cup with both hands: one on the bottom, the other on the lid. A pair of eyes stares directly at us on the cup. The scene is solemn, but some droplets of water seem to have escaped the chalice. We expect women to be comforting and empathic, but a closed cup could refer to contained emotions. Maybe the Queen has more to say than we think. Are her hands about to open the cup, like Pandora's box? The medieval engravings represent mermaids, a symbol for change and growth.

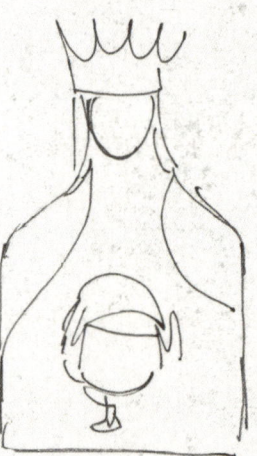

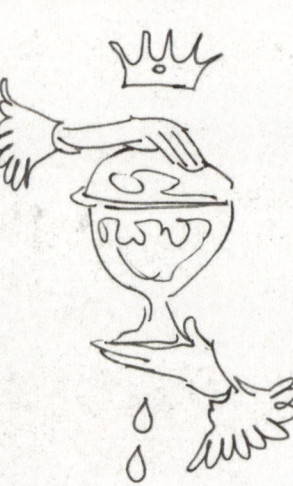

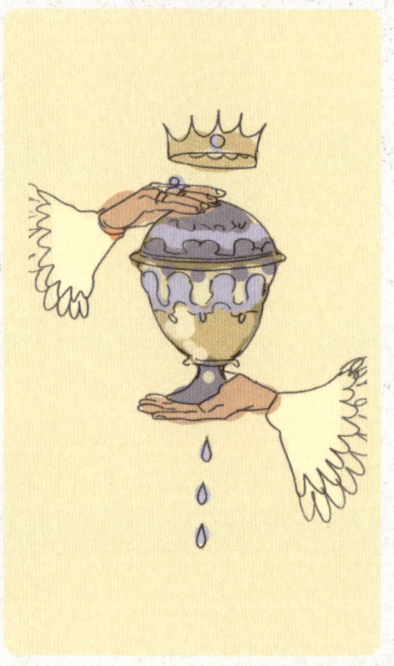

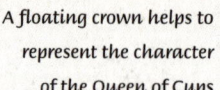

A floating crown helps to represent the character of the Queen of Cups

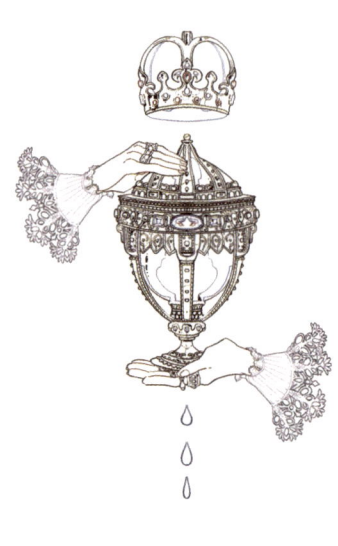

The cup is now an ornate chalice in which the water is carefully contained

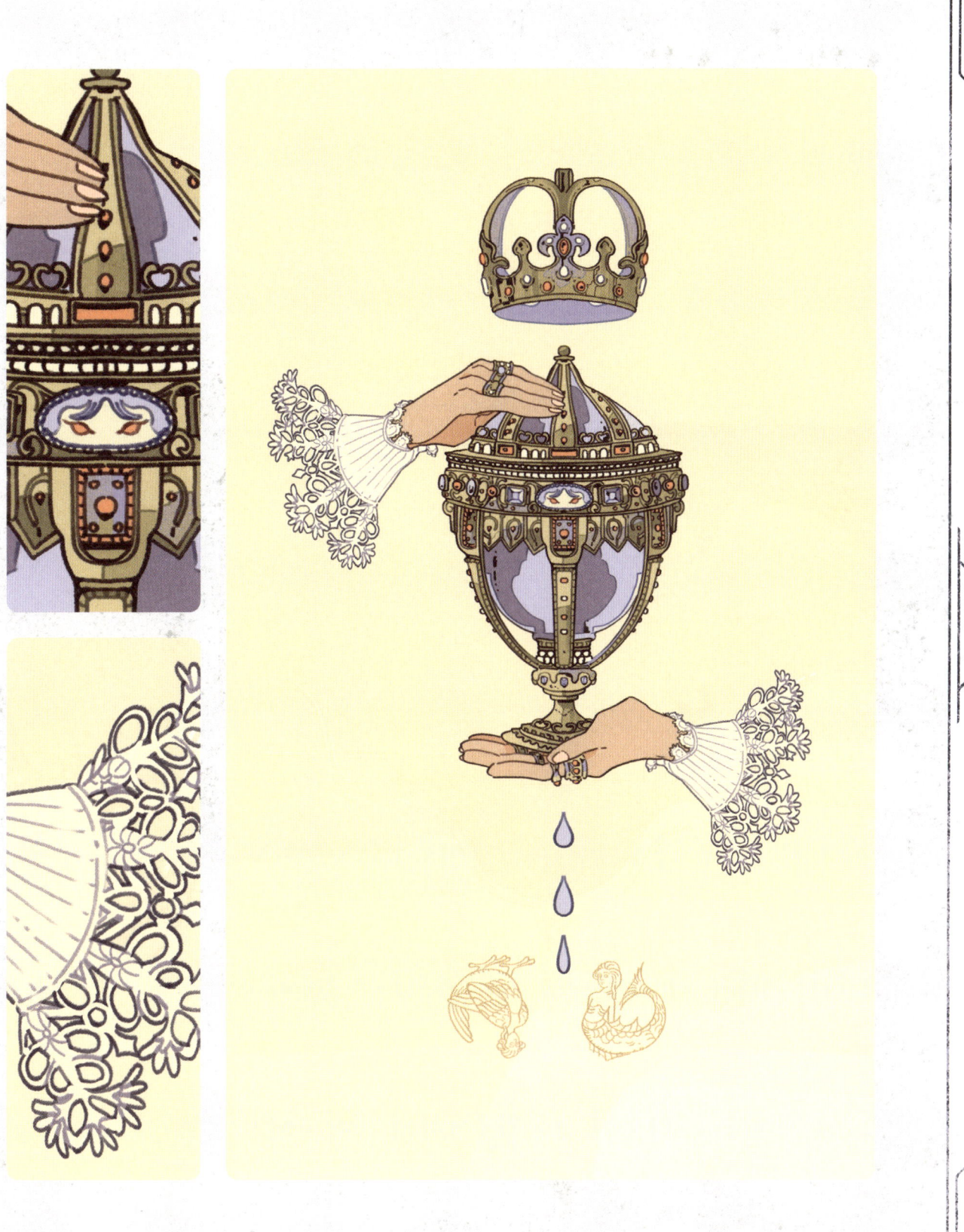

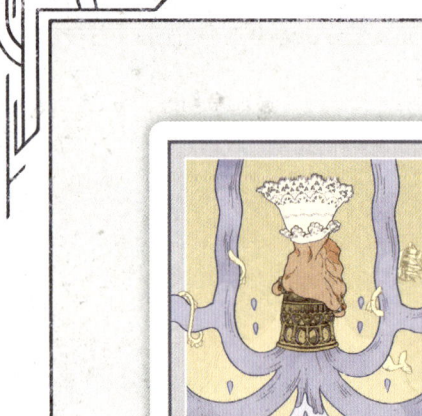

KING OF CUPS

KING OF CUPS

ARTISTIC, EMOTIONAL, PHILOSOPHICAL

The King is the last figure and final card of the suit, a culmination of every narrative that has unfolded within the Cups family. A King is not only someone mature and thoughtful, he is also emotional, understanding, compassionate, and philosophical – everything the Cups suit is about. As the King's firm hand grasps his cup, the medieval engravings flow freely on the water. The ships representing opportunity and the creatures representing fears are all under his control. Even if the waves make his cup overflow, they are always symmetrical and under control.

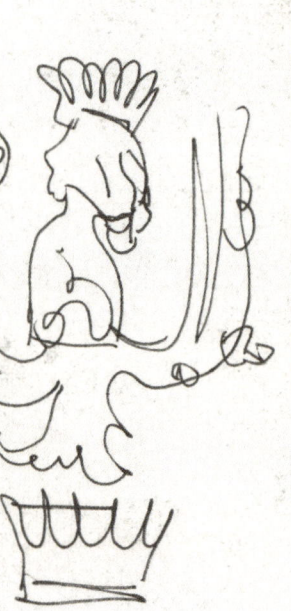

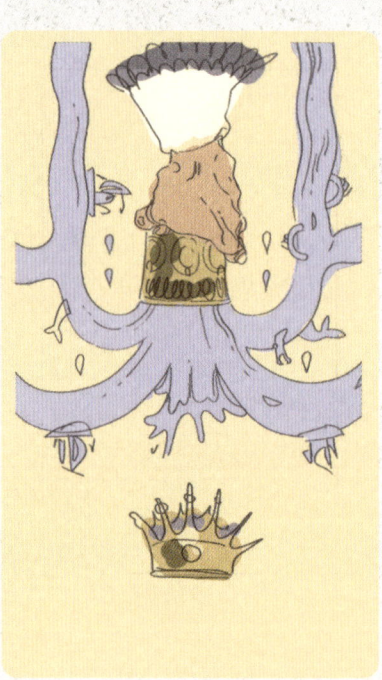

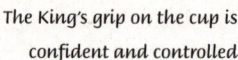

The King's grip on the cup is confident and controlled

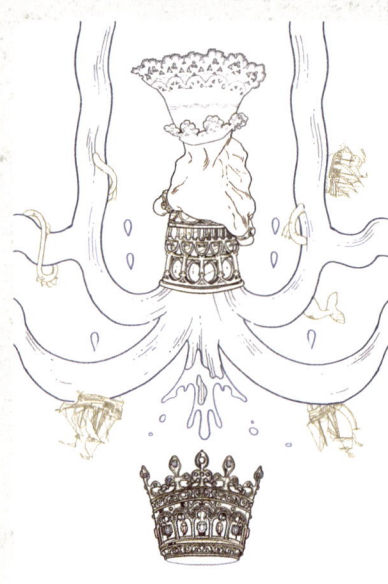

Symbols such as ships and sea serpents spill from his overflowing cup

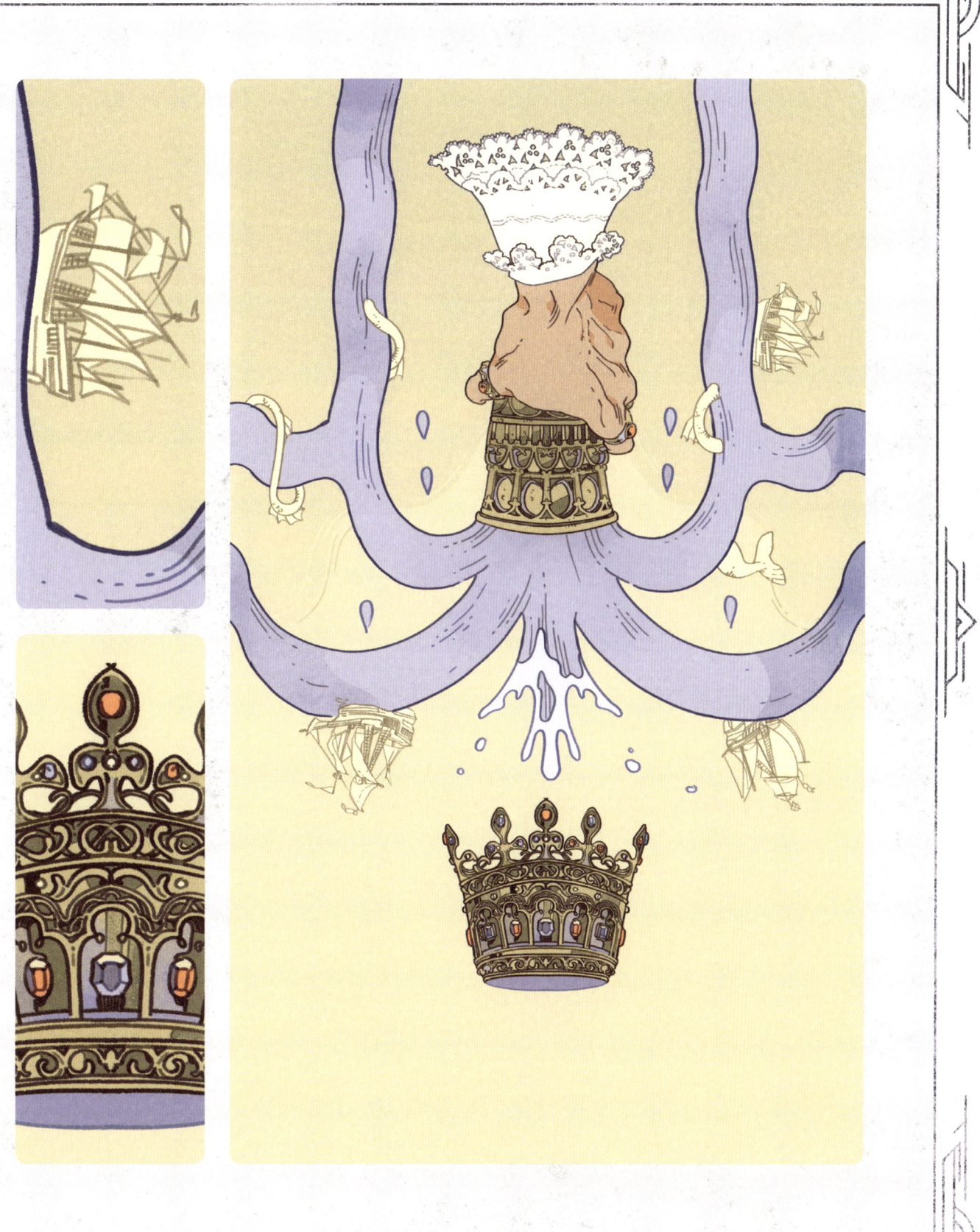

ARTIST'S CONCLUSION

Every tarot family is interesting, as narratives unfold before our eyes: each suit has a beginning and an end. The Cups suit is all about maturity and balance. I loved playing around with shapes, with physics that would not make sense in real life, and with showing emotions only through hands. I would love for you, the reader, to feel the cards and what the characters go through, making sense of them with your emotions and not your logic. Every card is somewhat tied to the others, and I hope you will enjoy tying and untying each narrative.

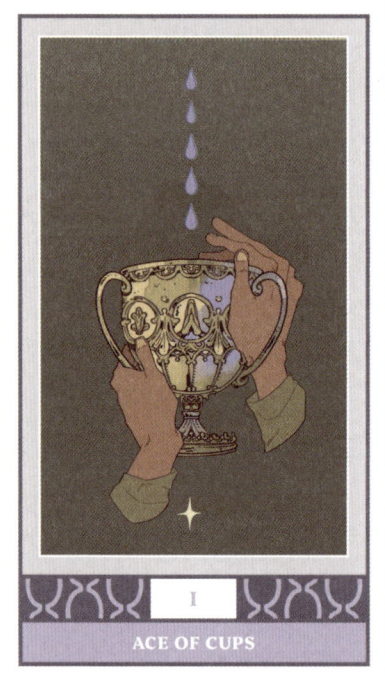

I

ACE OF CUPS

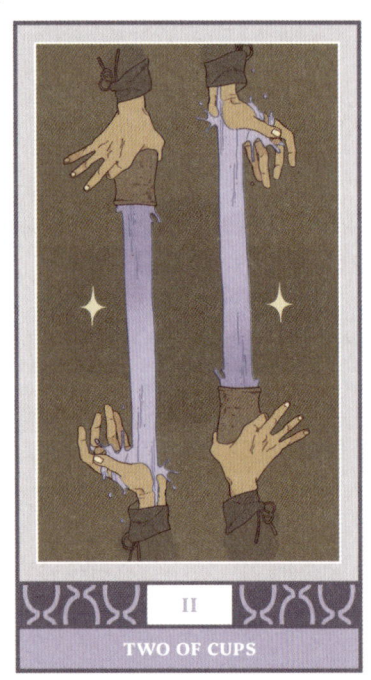

II

TWO OF CUPS

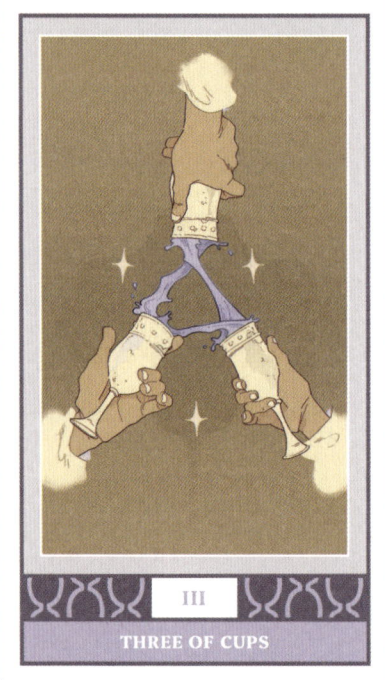

III

THREE OF CUPS

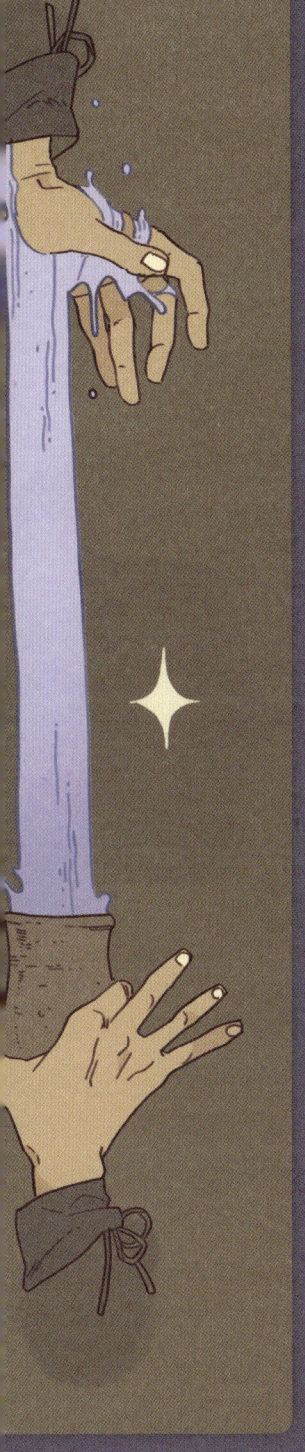

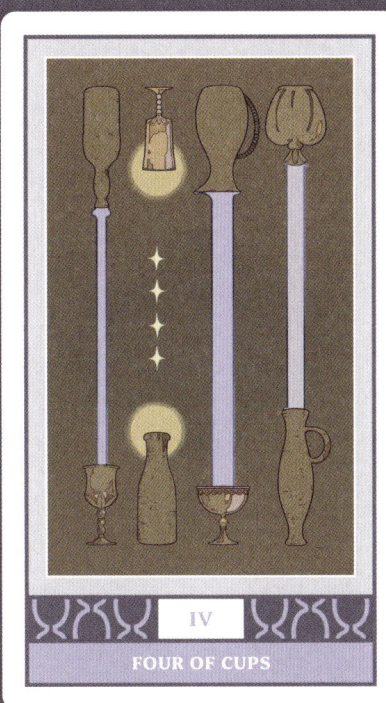

FOUR OF CUPS

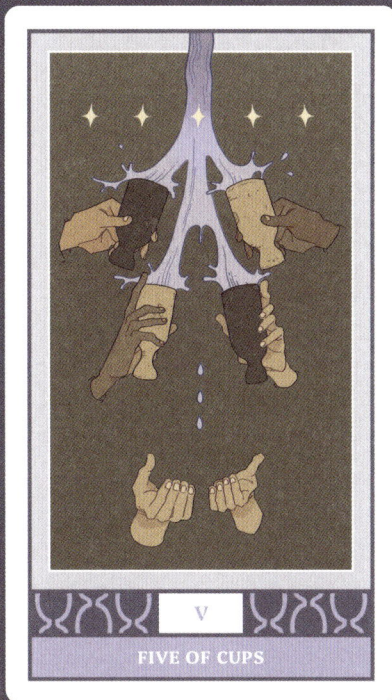

FIVE OF CUPS

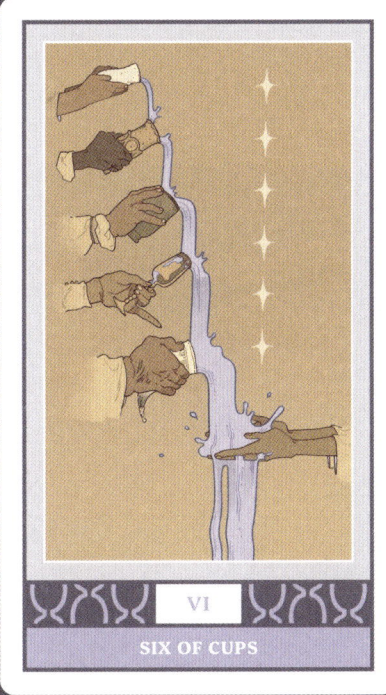

SIX OF CUPS

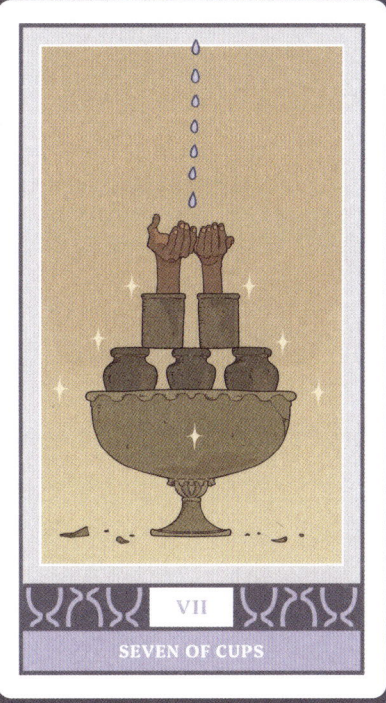

SEVEN OF CUPS

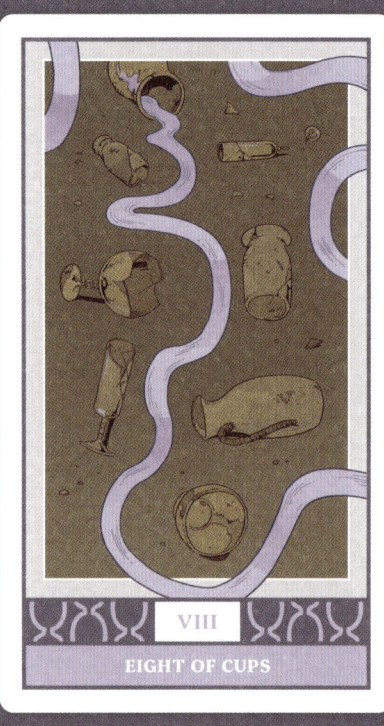

VIII

EIGHT OF CUPS

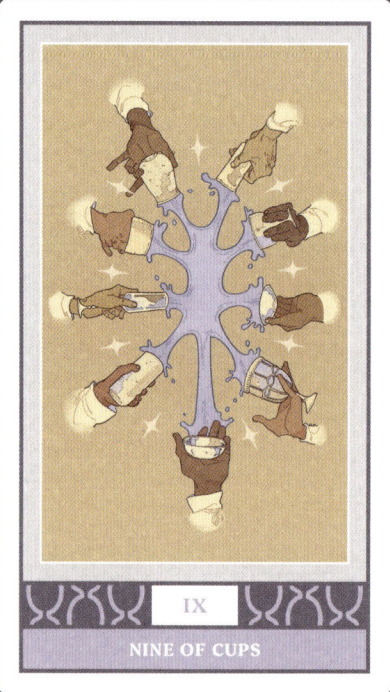

IX

NINE OF CUPS

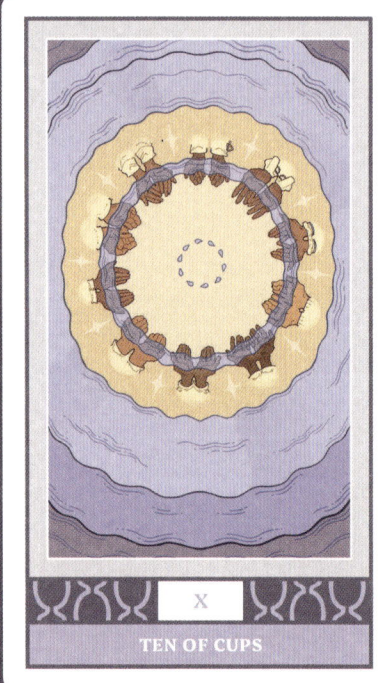

X

TEN OF CUPS

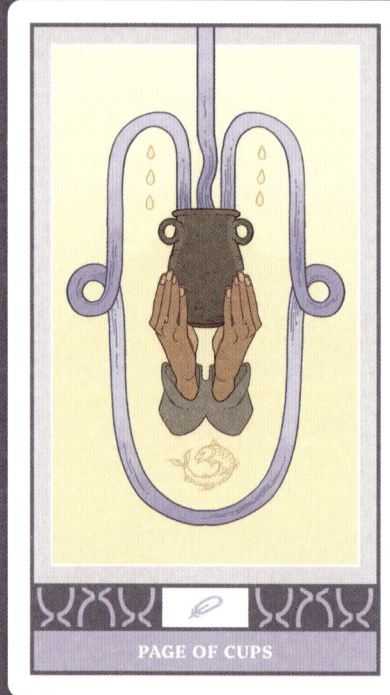

PAGE OF CUPS

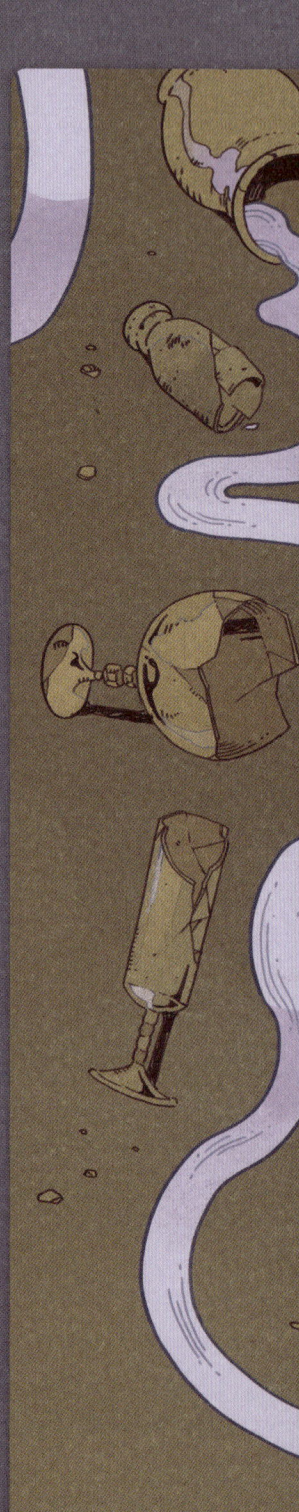

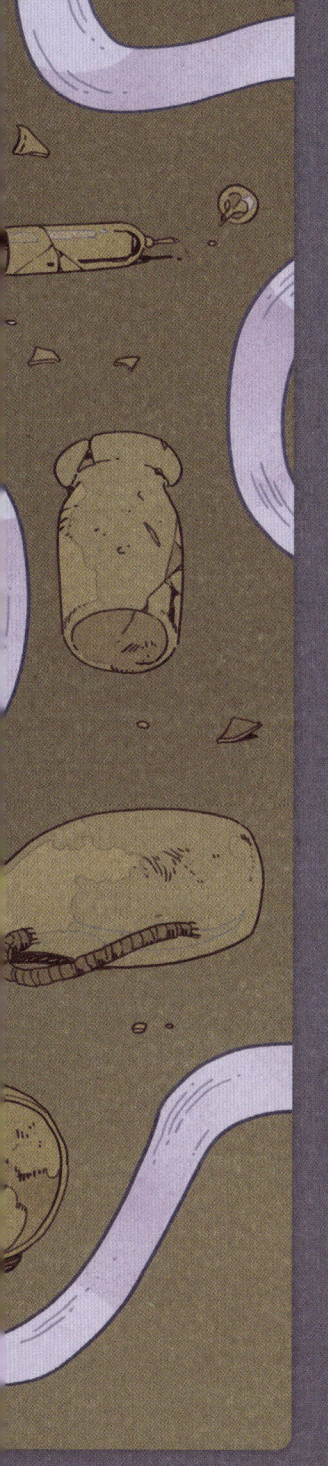

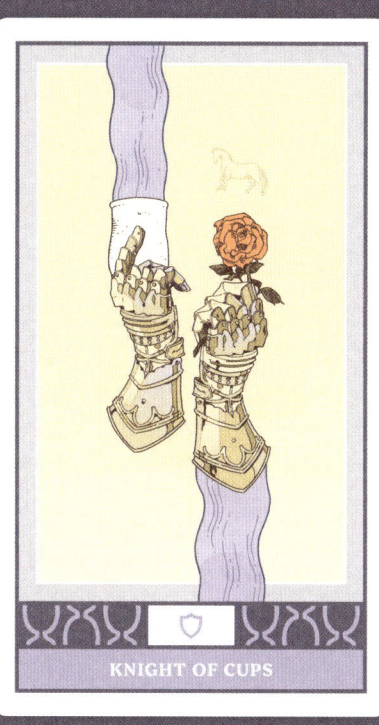

KNIGHT OF CUPS

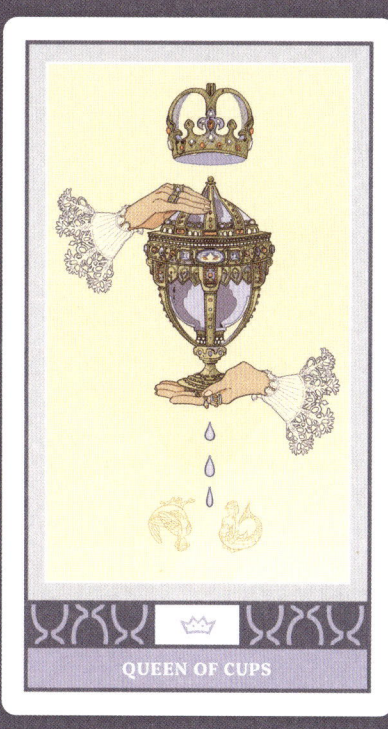

QUEEN OF CUPS

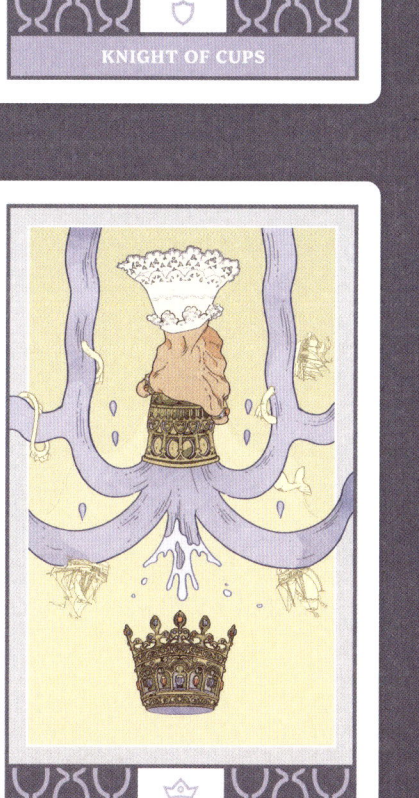

KING OF CUPS

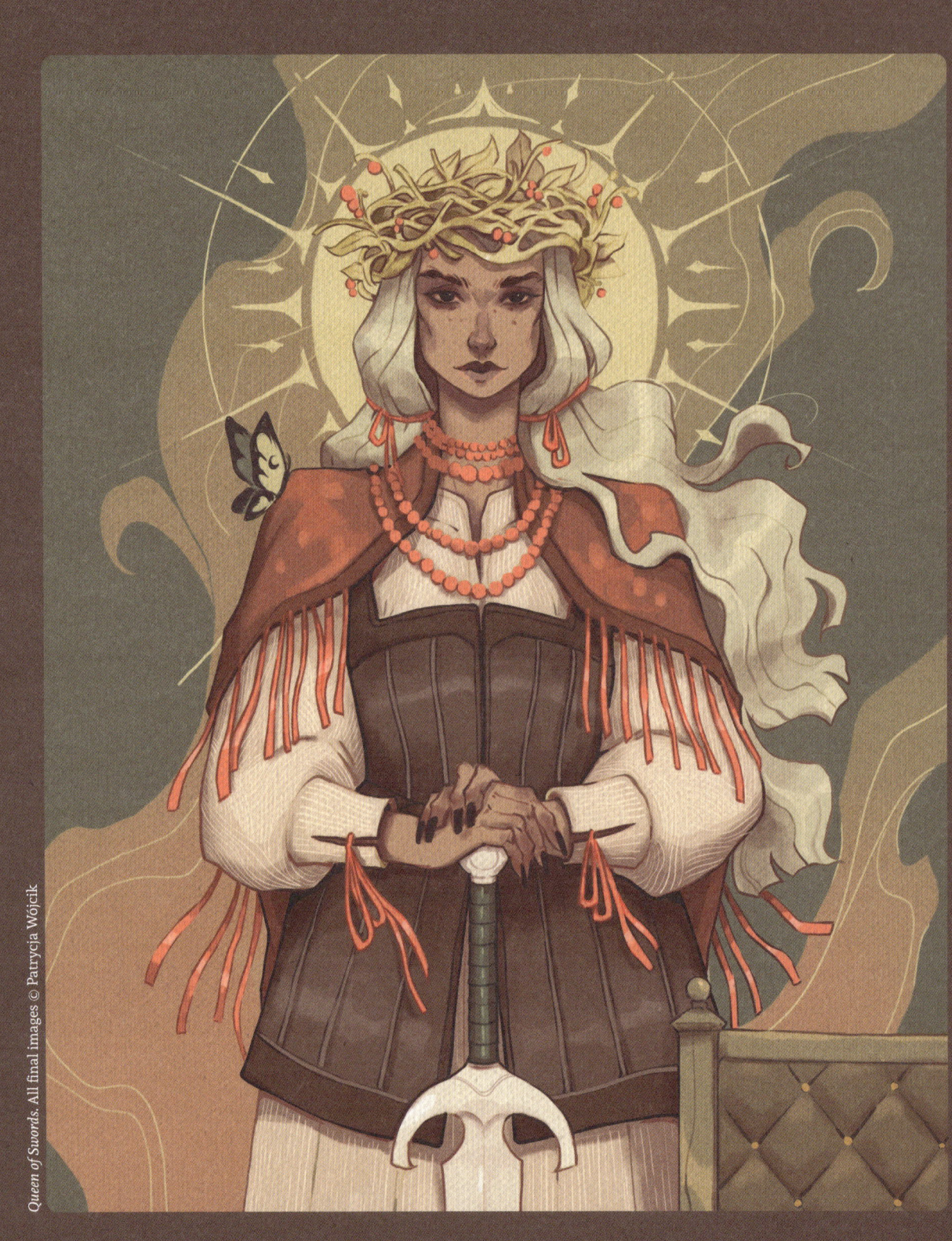

Queen of Swords. All final images © Patrycja Wójcik

THE SUIT OF
SWORDS

INTRODUCTION BY SASHA GRAHAM

The suit of Swords reflects elemental Air. Swords and Air represent mental abilities such as thinking, decision-making, and storytelling. Swords reflect interpersonal narratives, calculation, and speaking. Swords are inner and outer monologues. They reflect the way people communicate with each other. Swords are often the most frightening suit because of the internal voices inside our heads. Nothing is more hurtful than the voice of self-criticism and negative or anxiety-ridden self-talk and thoughts. Air reflects intellectual aspects because it is quick, speedy, and invisible, like thoughts and words.

Decide how the symbol of Swords (also called knives, daggers, guns, arrows, athames, or spades) will appear throughout your suit. The Sword can be used for protection but also used to impale and kill. A tarot figure holding a sword pointed towards the sky marks the channelling of information from the spiritual world. The sword acts as a conduit for the mind and clear thinking.

What distinctive qualities, animals, symbols, and clothing will appear in the suit of Swords? Is the landscape a dry, airy climate amid alpine mountains, full of sharp details and jagged rocks? Will there be sylphs, fairies, birds, butterflies, bats, crows, and air creatures decorating the cards? Are Sword characters warriors who wield swords for keeping the peace or for waging war? Perhaps the characters are regular folk who pick up the sword only when necessary.

The King, Queen, Knight, and Page rule with the powers of the mind. They are full of genius, articulation, and thought. How can this be visually displayed? If they sit on thrones, what symbols would be engraved upon them? Is the Knight of Swords charging into battle on a winged horse or is he a demon flying through the sky? Does the Page of Swords sit in an infinite library surrounded by beloved books or is she slipping undetected through a forest on an epic intellectual quest?

PATRYCJA WÓJCIK

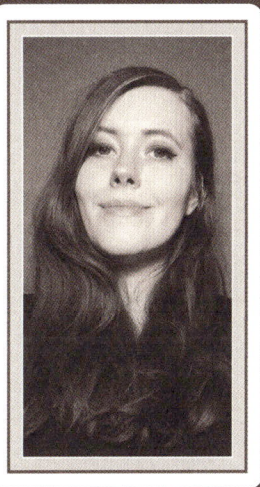

ARTIST'S INSIGHT

I personally associate tarot cards with the mystical – I think this is due to the common belief that reading tarot is the domain of sorceresses or witches. In my interpretation of the suit of Swords, my goal will be to feature characters that reflect different aspects of witches and femininity, putting a twist on this weapon that has always been the domain of men.

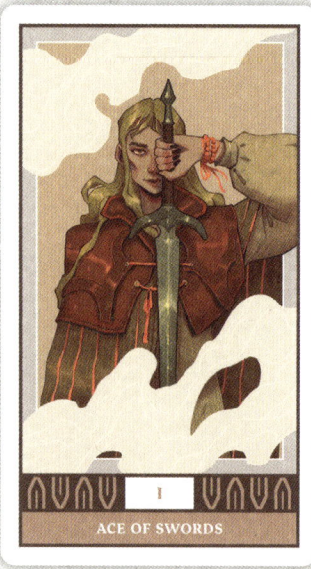

ACE OF SWORDS

ACE OF SWORDS

INSIGHT, GENIUS, VICTORY

The Ace of Swords is the first card in the suit, so I want to create the feeling that this composition is 'opening' for the rest of the cards' illustrations. The figure is grabbing the sword with obvious pride on her face – she may just have defeated someone in a fight, or is just about to start a duel. In both cases, her character is victorious.

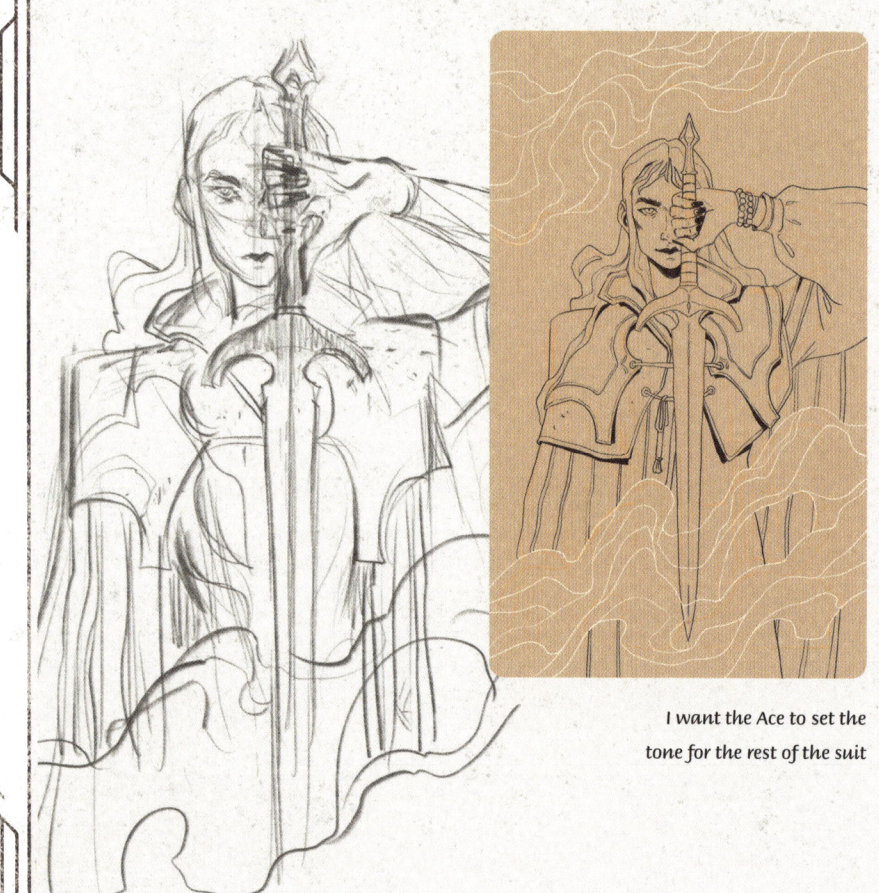

I want the Ace to set the tone for the rest of the suit

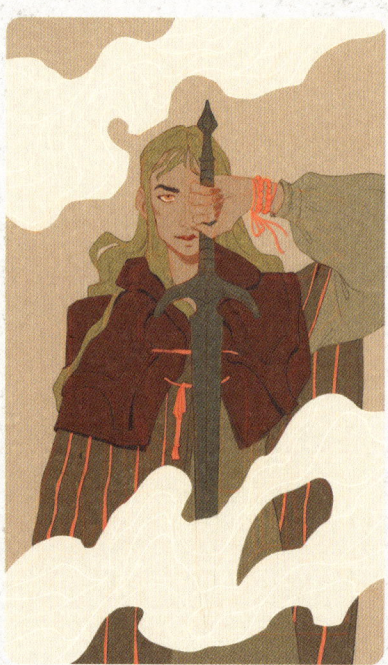

The character looks bold, knowing, and assured as she raises her weapon

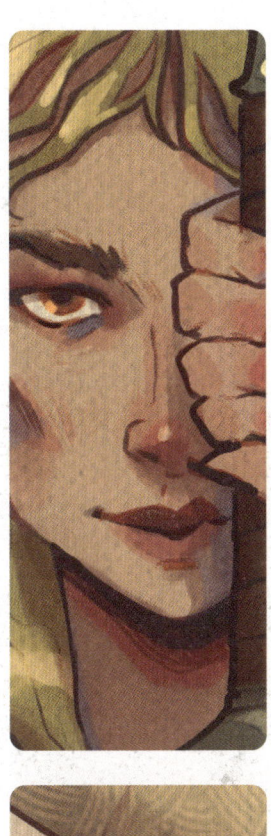

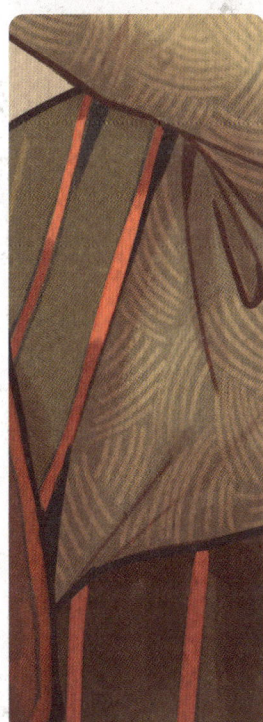

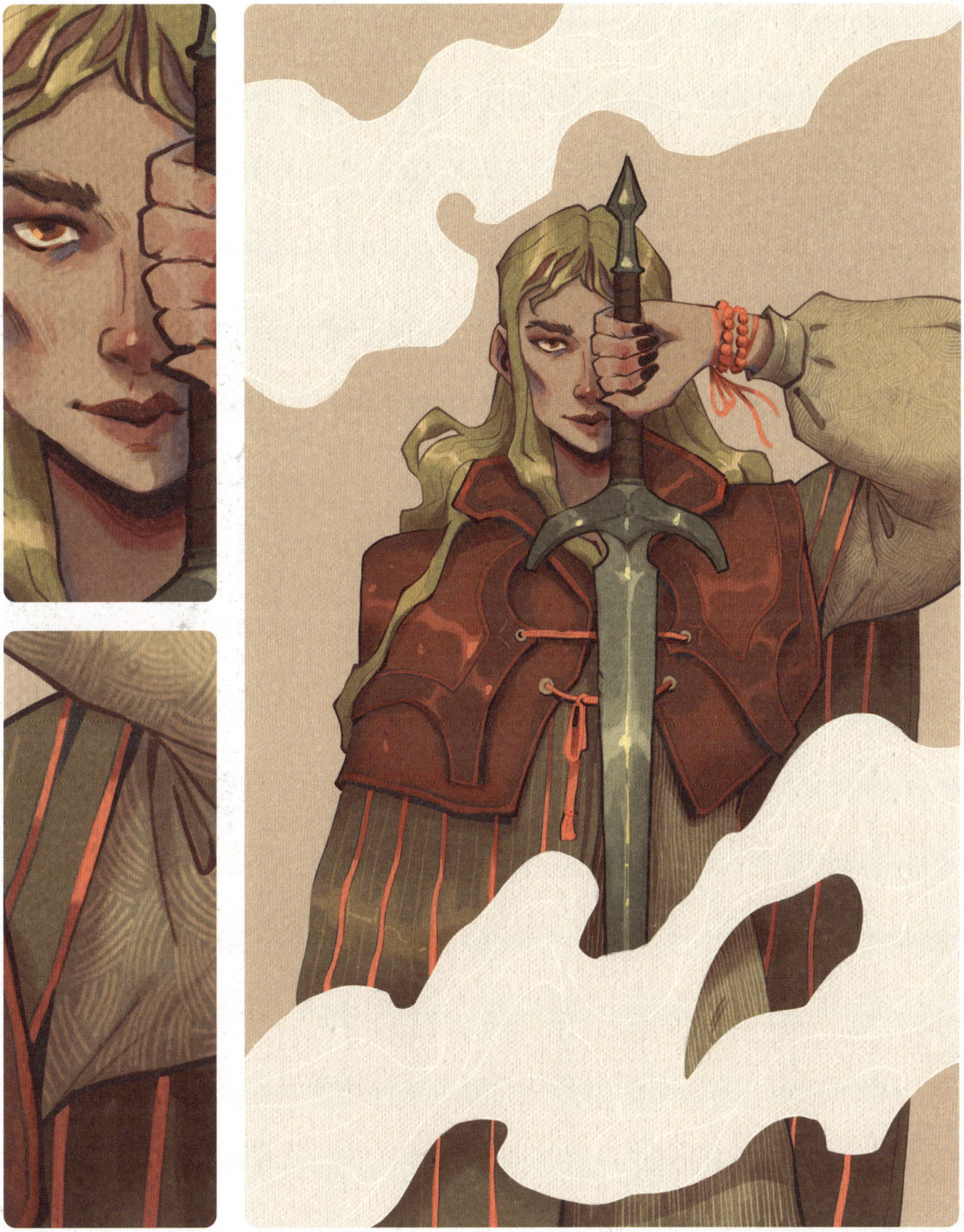

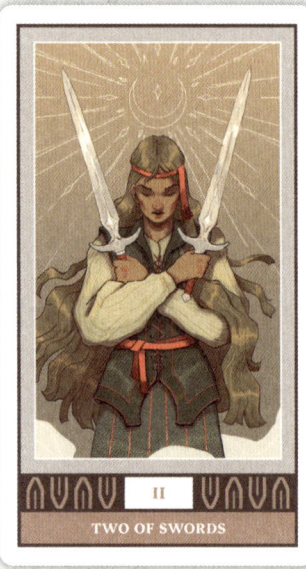

TWO OF SWORDS

TWO OF SWORDS

REFLECTION, PAUSE, OBSERVATION

I associate playing cards such as tarot with very symmetrical compositions, so I also want to compose my illustrations in such frames. This female figure is holding swords, seemingly at rest, or perhaps preparing for battle. In any case, there is concentration in her pose. In the traditional Rider–Waite–Smith deck (see page 24), this character is blindfolded, but I decide to symbolize focus by closing her eyes.

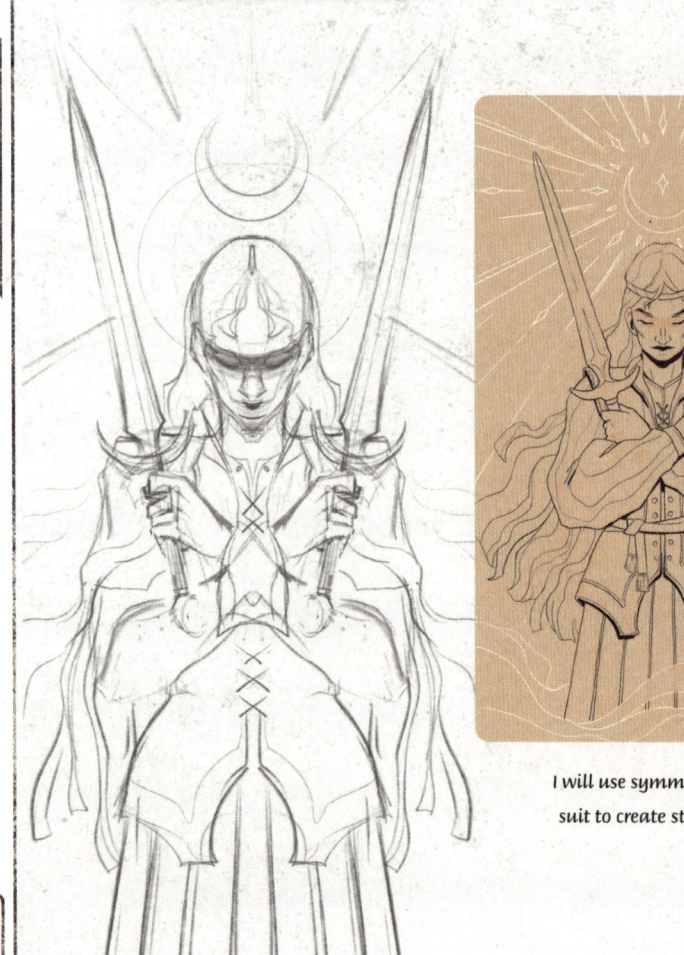

I will use symmetry throughout the suit to create striking compositions

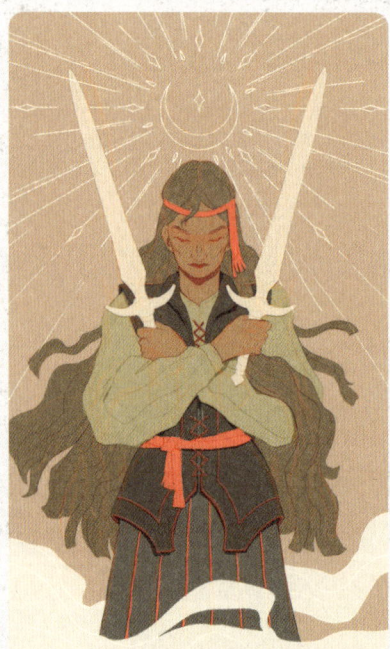

The character's closed eyes and slightly lowered head give her a still, meditative look

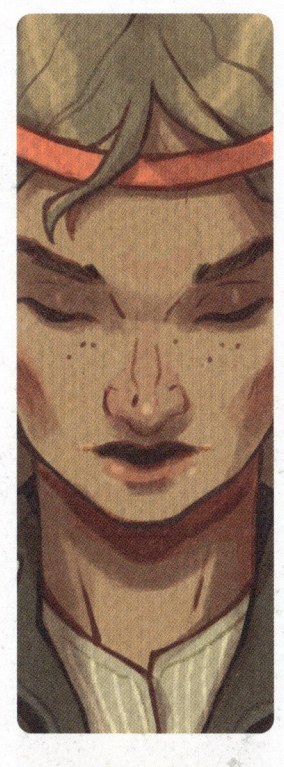

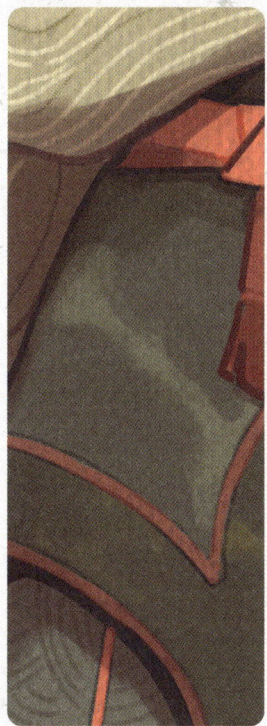

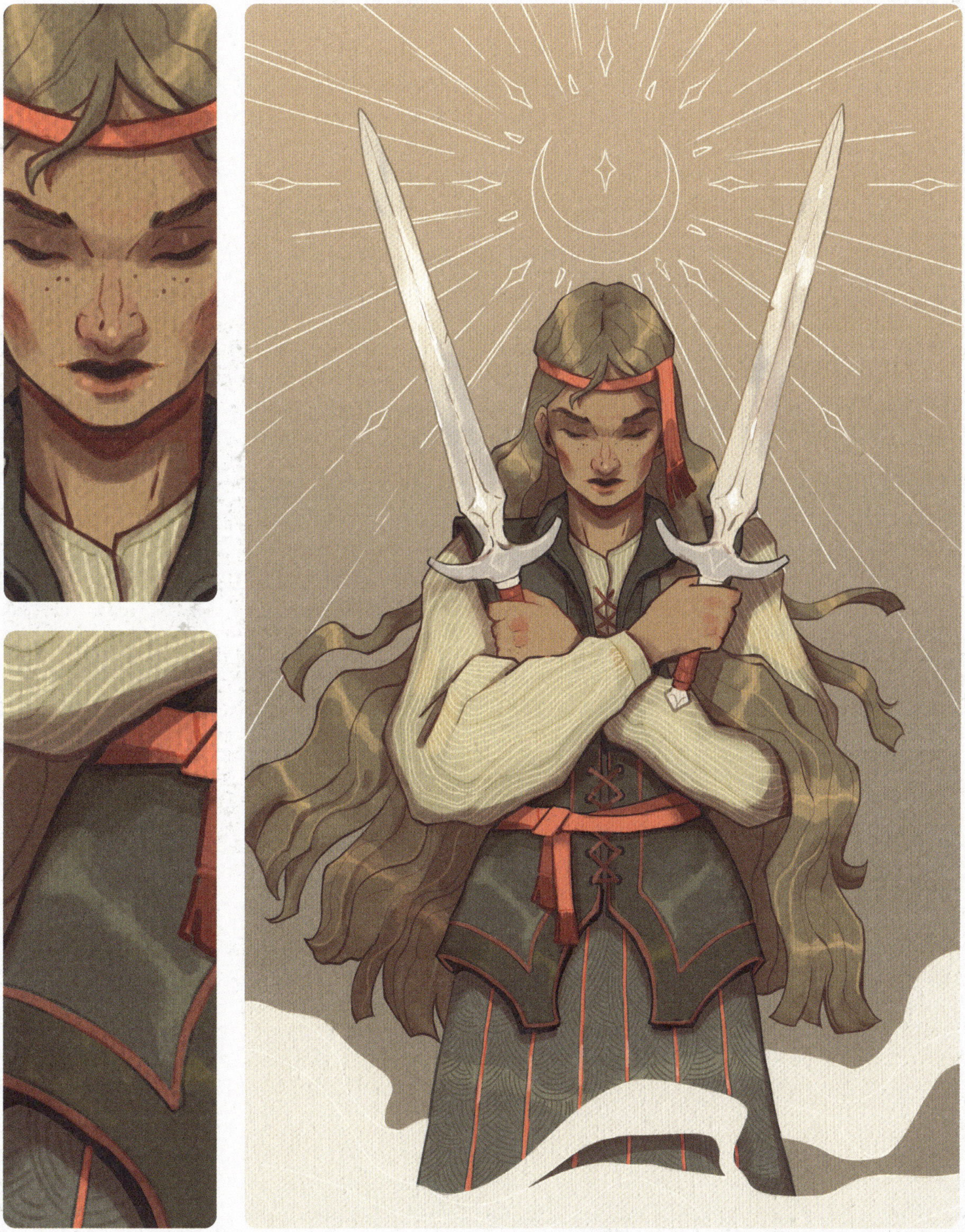

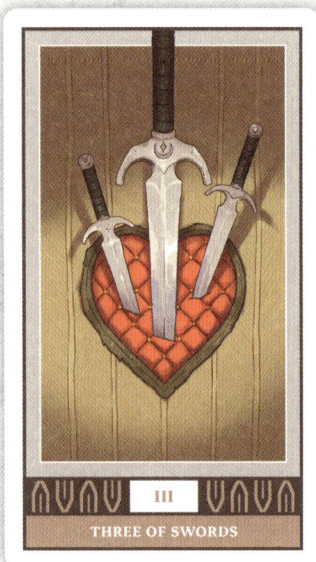

THREE OF SWORDS

THREE OF SWORDS

HEARTBREAK, DISTRESS, BETRAYAL

III

Some of my main inspirations for this suit are Slavic folklore and folk art, where hearts often appear as a motif. I represent the Three of Swords' heart as sewn from several materials, while retaining the traditional imagery of something pierced with three swords. The middle sword marks a symmetrical line in the composition and the sewn heart its centre. The previous card's moon-and-star motif reappears here as a small detail.

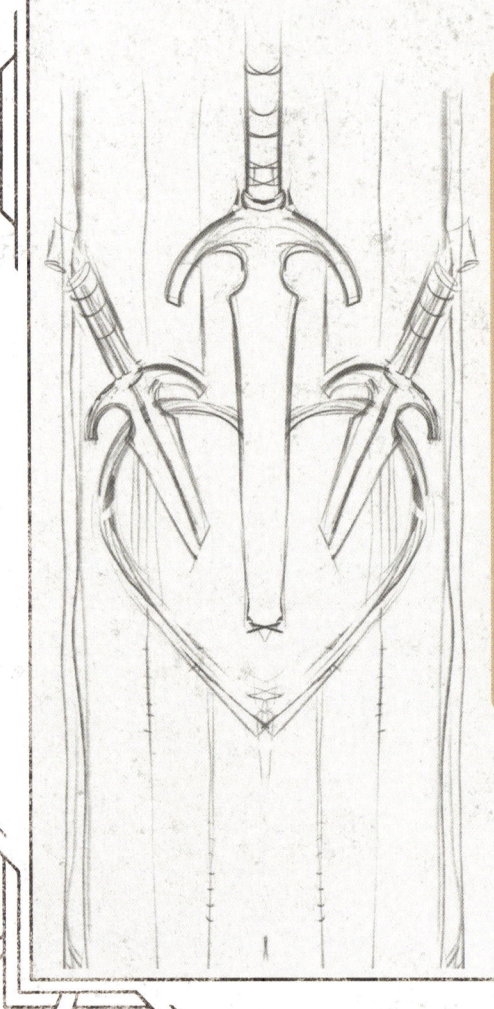

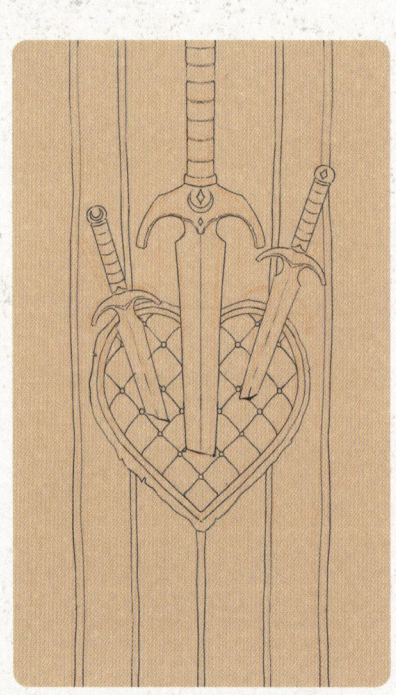

I put a Slavic folk-inspired twist on the classic image of an impaled heart

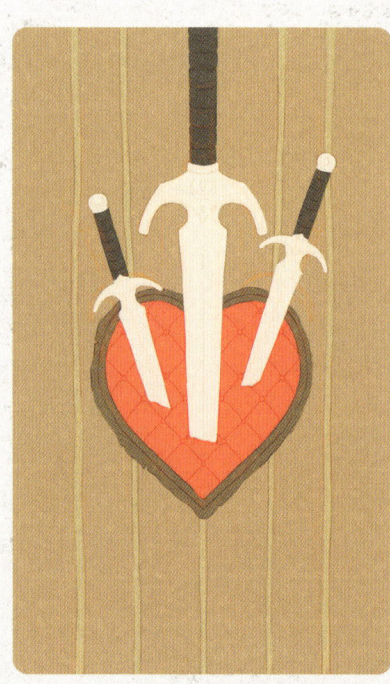

The piercing swords create a stark contrast with the heart's soft fabric

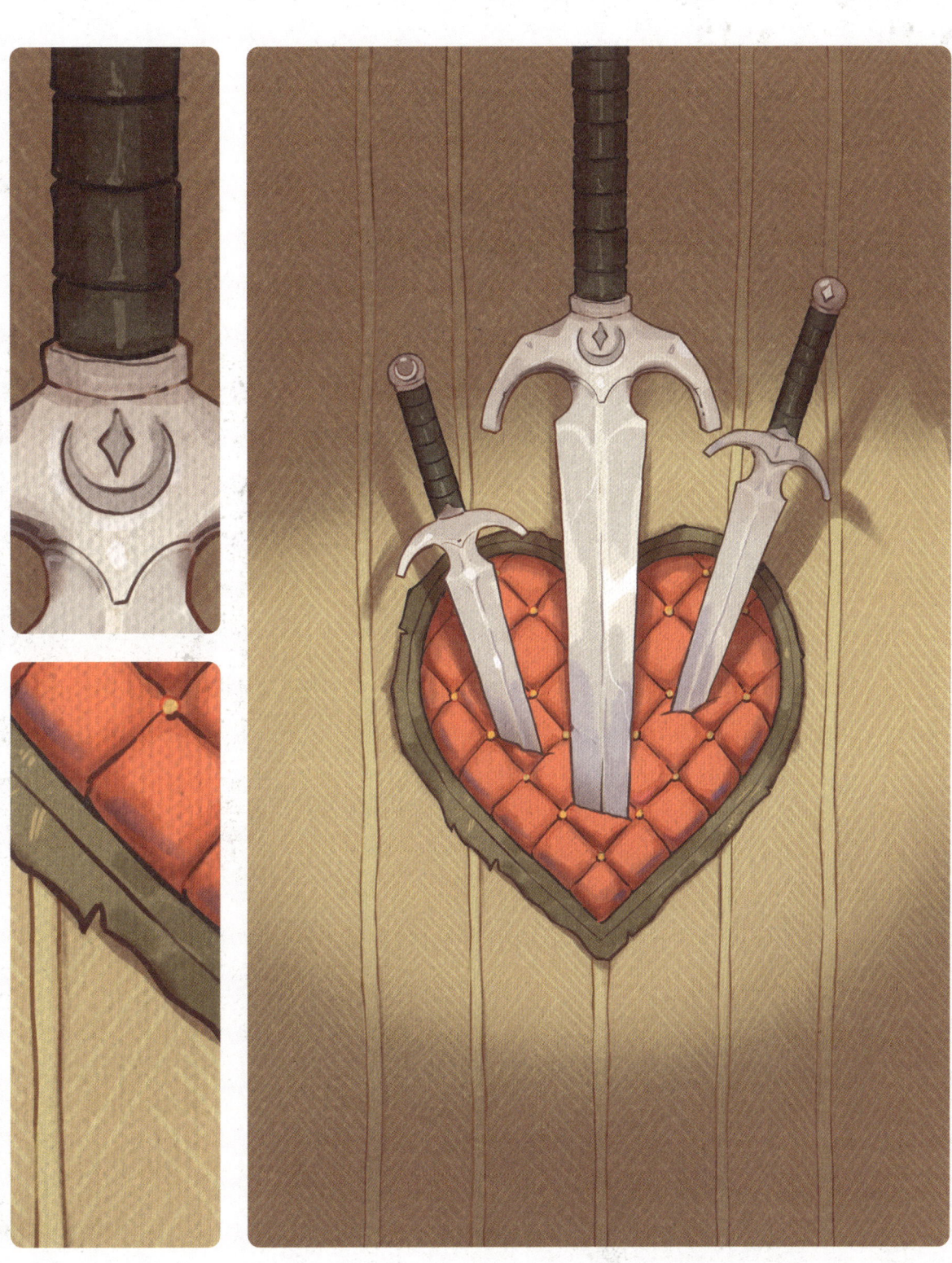

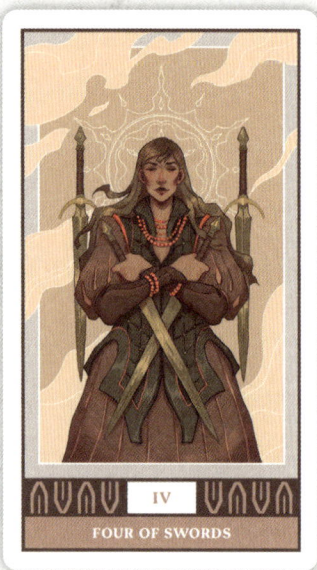

FOUR OF SWORDS

FOUR OF SWORDS

REST, RESTORATION, PEACEABLE

IV

The Four of Swords is meant to represent peace and rest. I decide to convey this with the character's tranquil face and balanced pose. Gently moving clouds in the background break the symmetrical composition of the figure and the swords surrounding her, adding a soft, organic element to the illustration. An ethereal sun-like pattern seems to emanate from her.

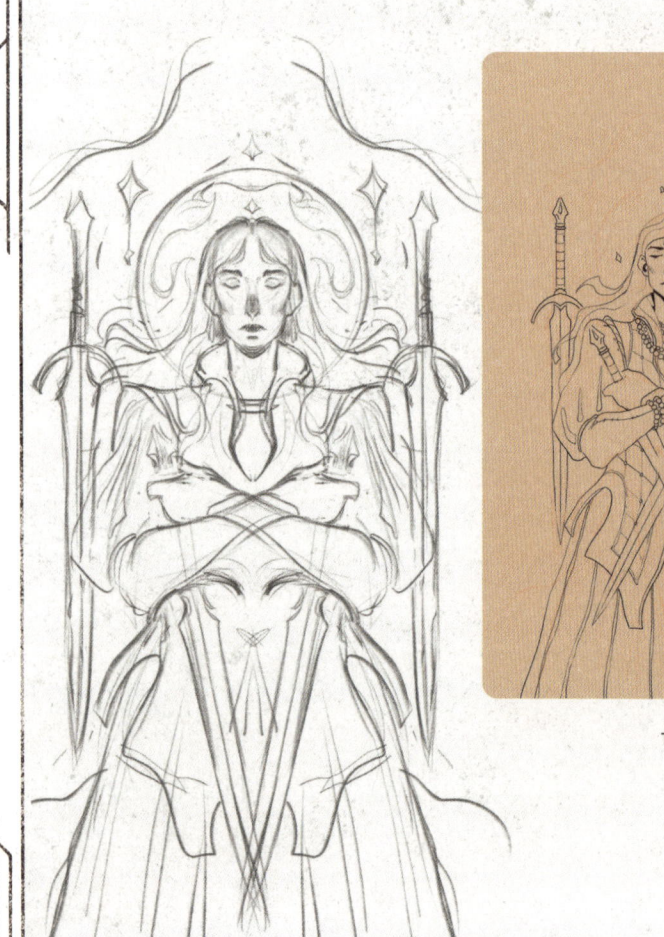

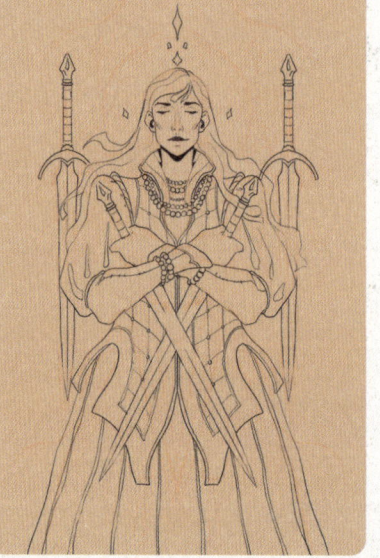

The character's eyes are closed and her face is relaxed and peaceful

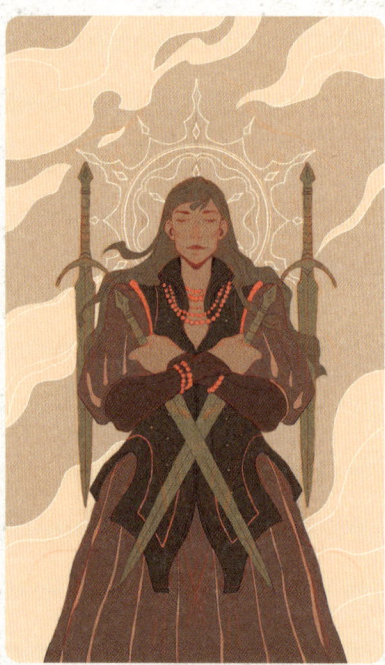

The flowing, delicate clouds will be a recurring motif throughout this suit

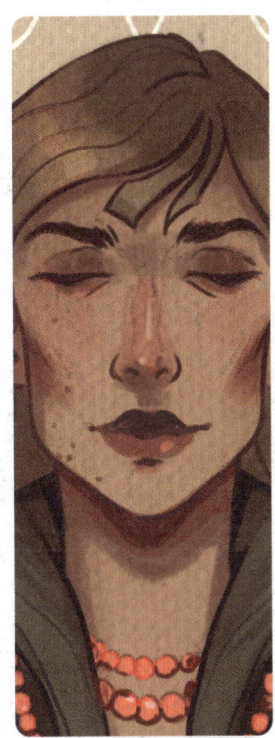

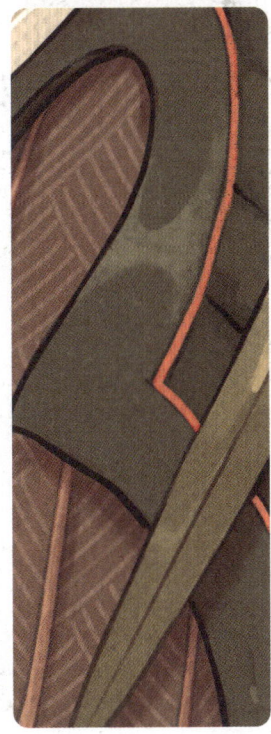

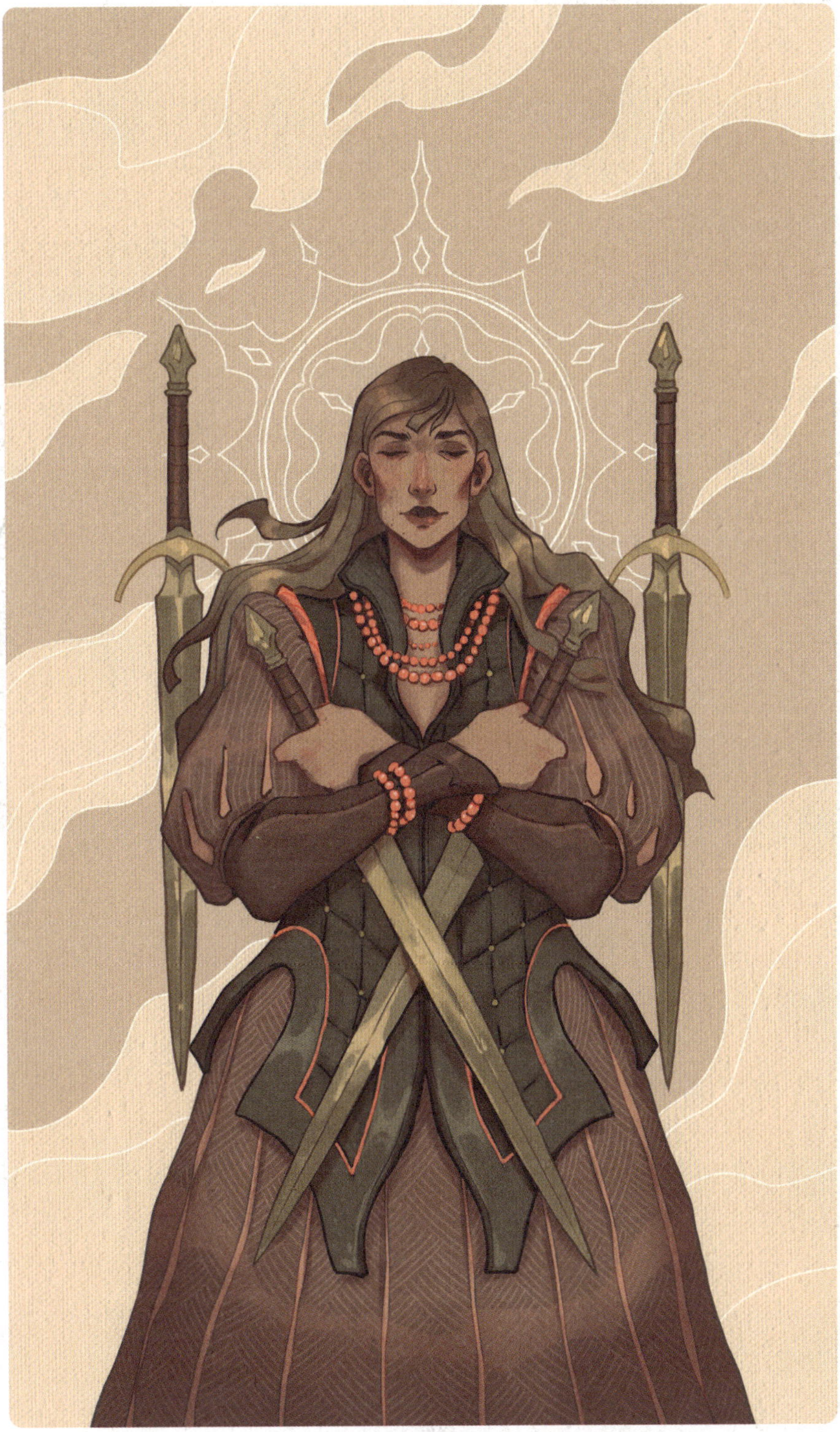

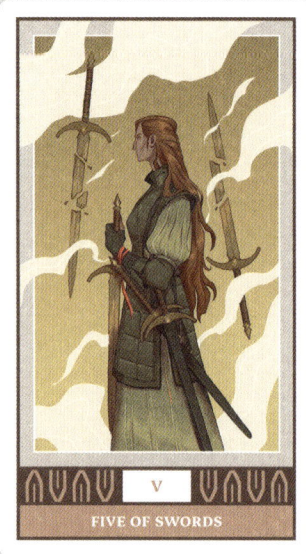

FIVE OF SWORDS

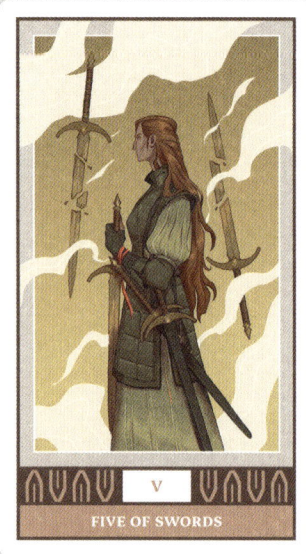

FIVE OF SWORDS

FIVE OF SWORDS

CRUELTY, CHEATING, BULLY

The Five of Swords is supposed to contain the symbolism of cruelty, torment, and cheating. I want to show a character who is seemingly presented as a winner, without obviously showing the losers beside her. Instead, the cracked swords around the figure symbolize the opponents who were defeated in battle. The drifting clouds are thin and ragged, more like smoke.

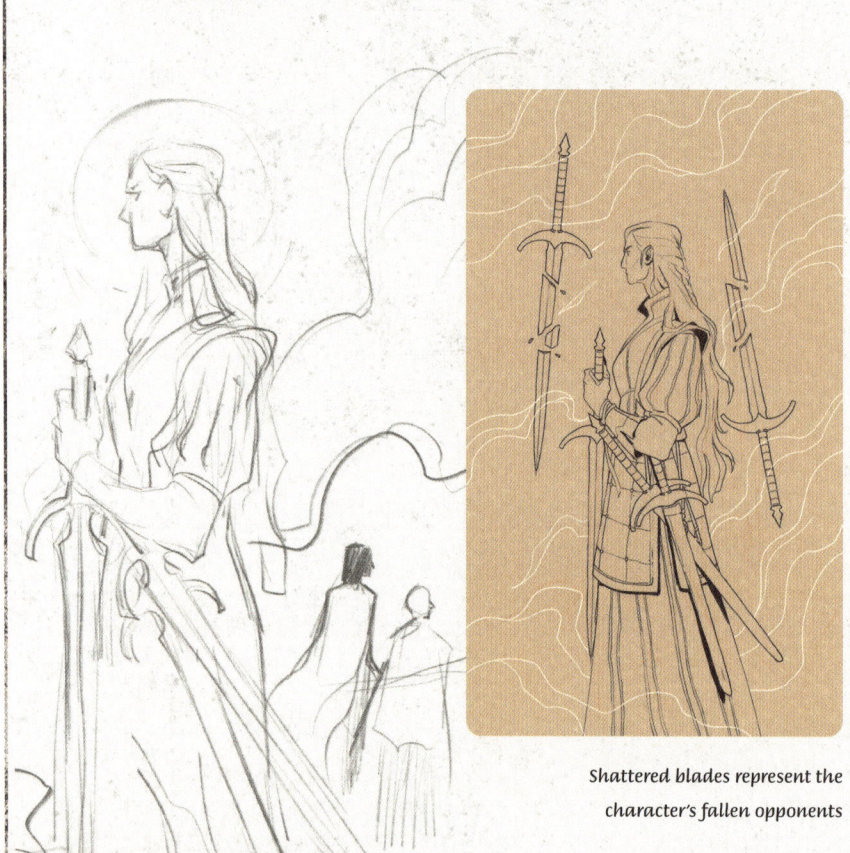

Shattered blades represent the character's fallen opponents

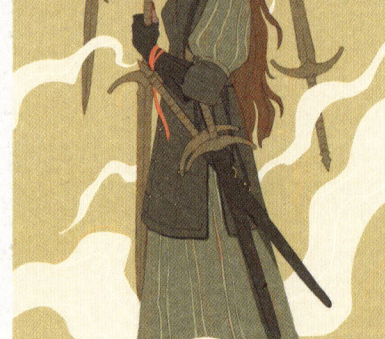

The victor's pose and expression are cold and aloof, almost facing away from us

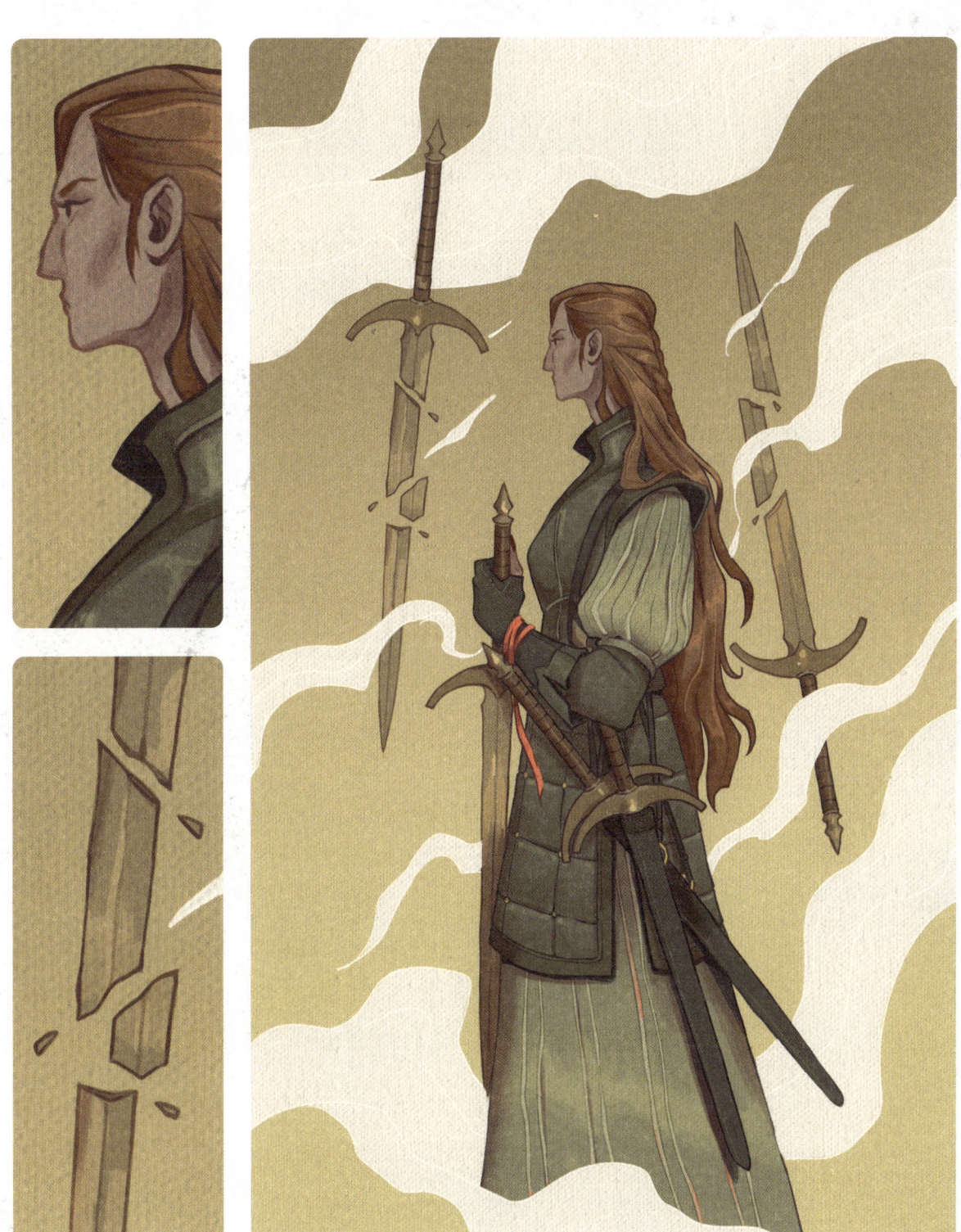

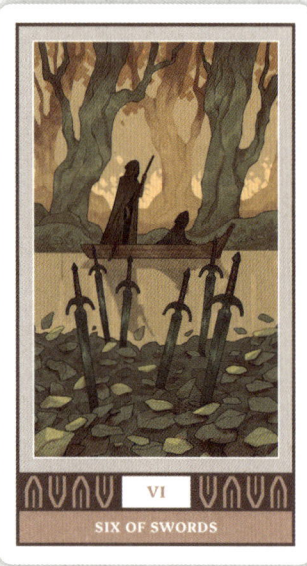

SIX OF SWORDS

JOURNEY, PASSAGE, MOVEMENT

This card is meant to represent a journey – a transition to another, better world. I decide to compose this illustration in such a way that the surroundings resemble a graveyard. In the foreground there are swords left in the ground, surrounded by fallen leaves, stuck like relics of the past. In the background, the characters on the boat traverse this somewhat nostalgic landscape.

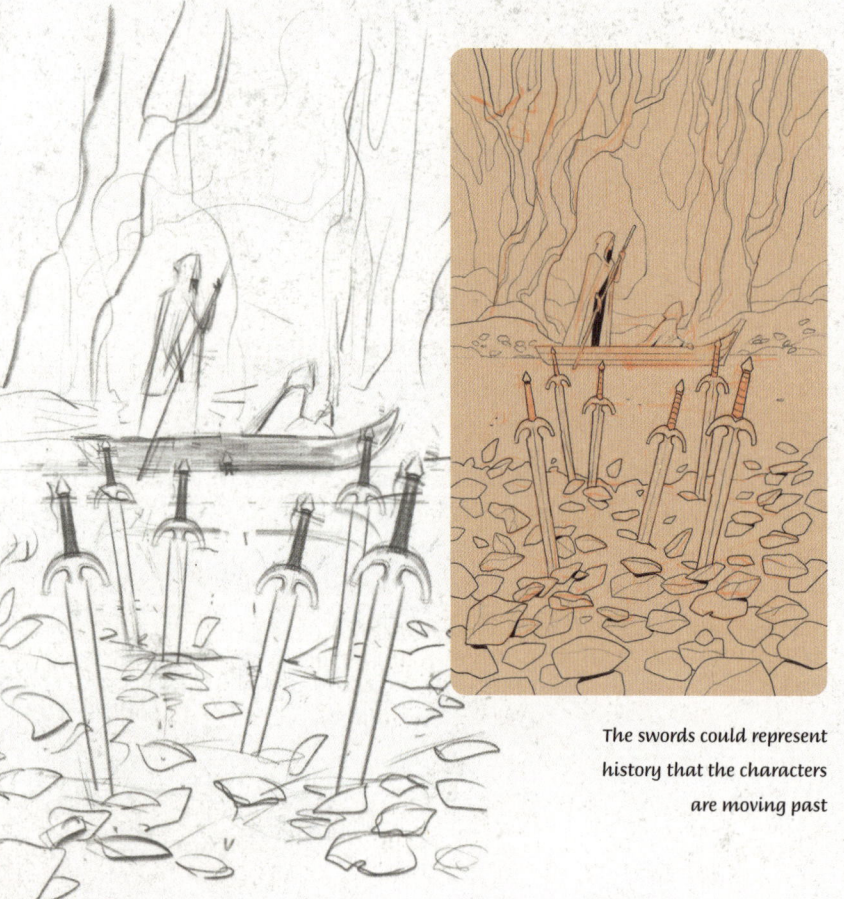

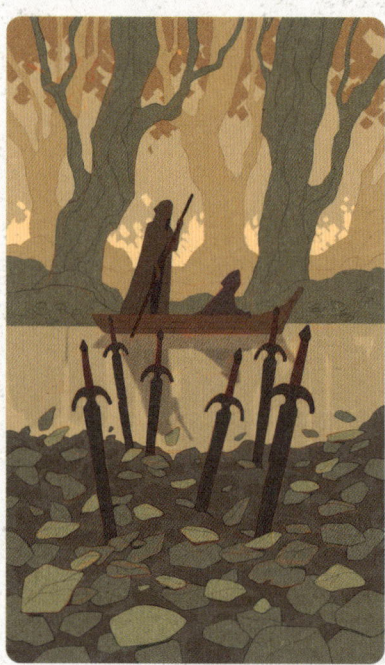

The swords could represent history that the characters are moving past

The characters sail through an enclosed forest, perhaps towards the open air

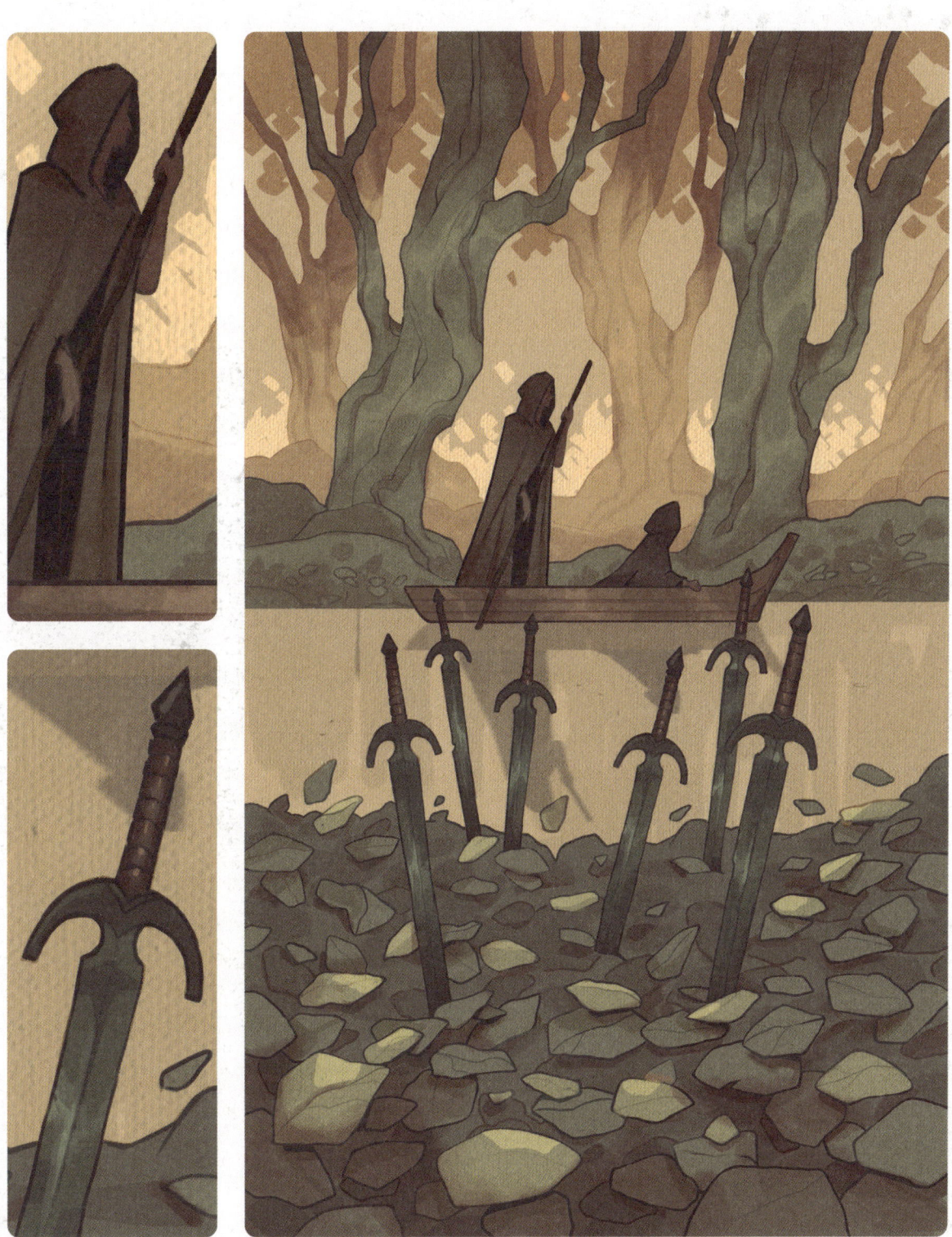

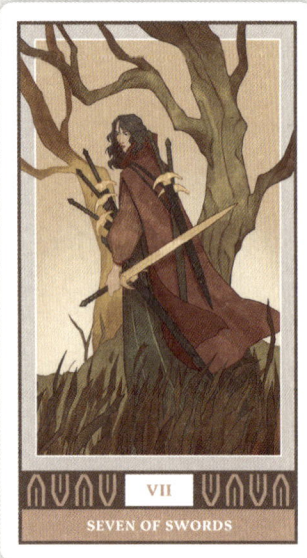

SEVEN OF SWORDS

VII

SEVEN OF SWORDS

EDITING, MOVING, HATCHING

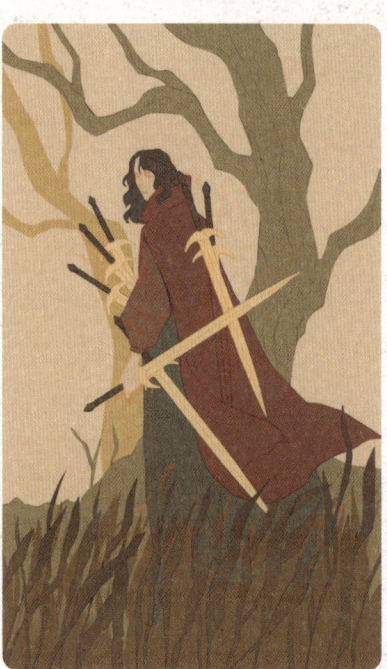

VII

The Seven of Swords is represented by a figure holding all seven swords. I want to show this character holding the swords close to her, as if she's planning to run away with them. She is slightly turned, as if she's looking behind her at the road that she has already travelled. The wind pulls at her coat and the tall spikes of grass, expressing movement. The irregular shapes of the trees are also intended to reflect this.

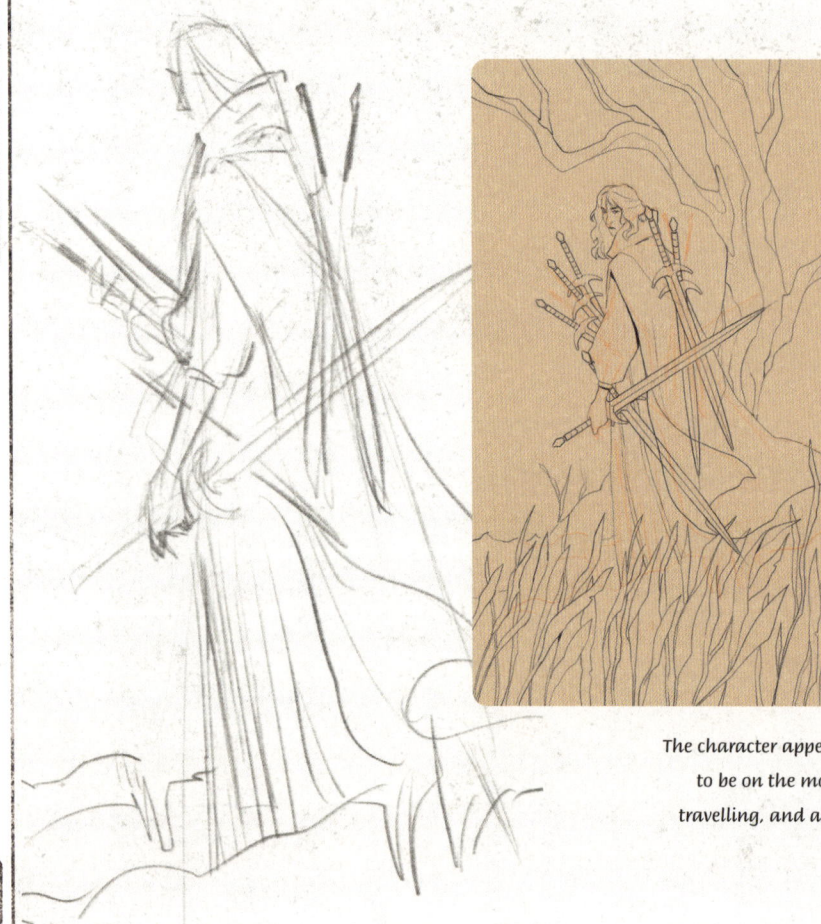

The character appears to be on the move, travelling, and alert

Where is she going with those swords? Where did she get them?

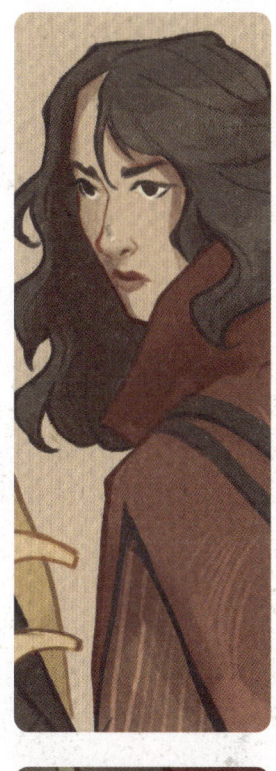
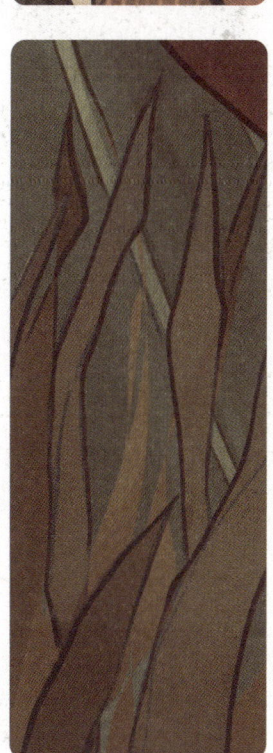

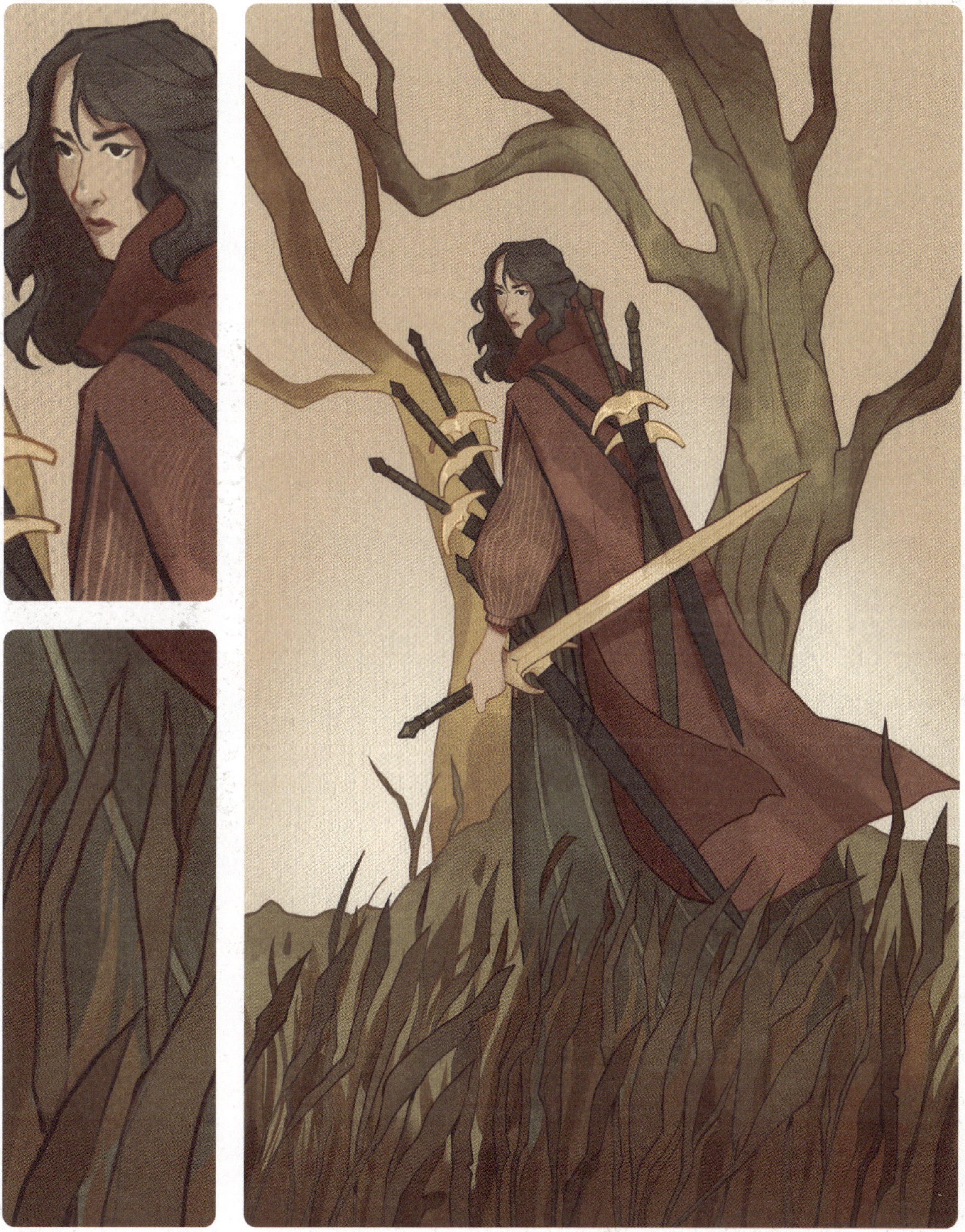

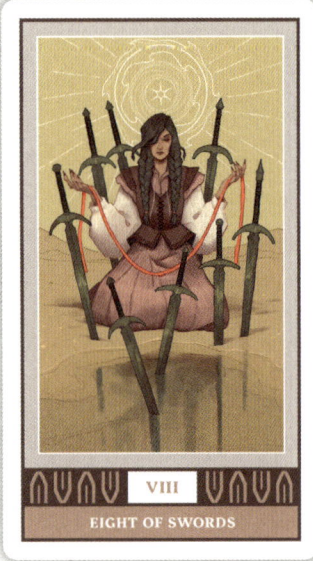

EIGHT OF SWORDS
VIII

EIGHT OF SWORDS

INVITATION, COCOON, RESTRICTION

VIII

Surrounded by eight swords, the figure is in a state of concentration, kneeling on the sand. The beach setting with pooling water is a reference to the original Rider–Waite–Smith setting (see page 25). Keeping other traditional symbols in mind, I decide to show her without a blindfold, but closing her eyes to show her focus. She is not restrained with rope, but she holds a ribbon in her hands. Above her is a star that is almost a whirlpool.

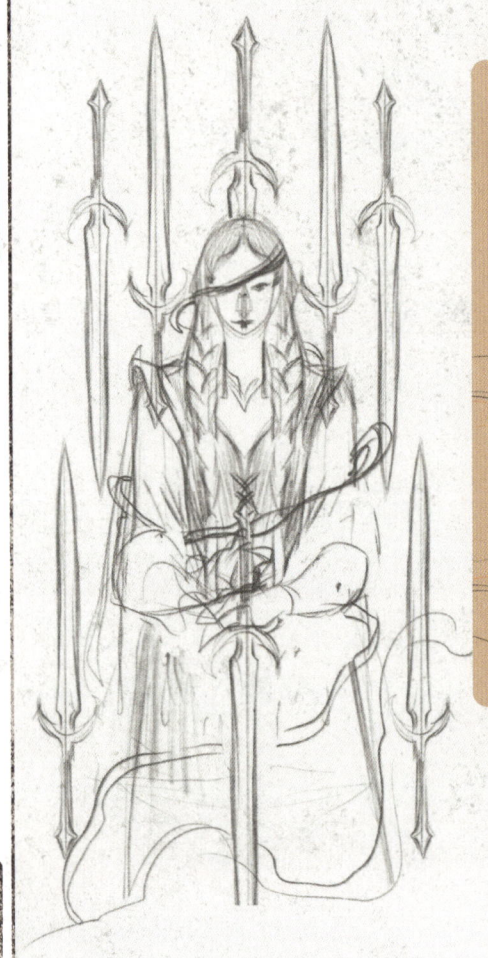

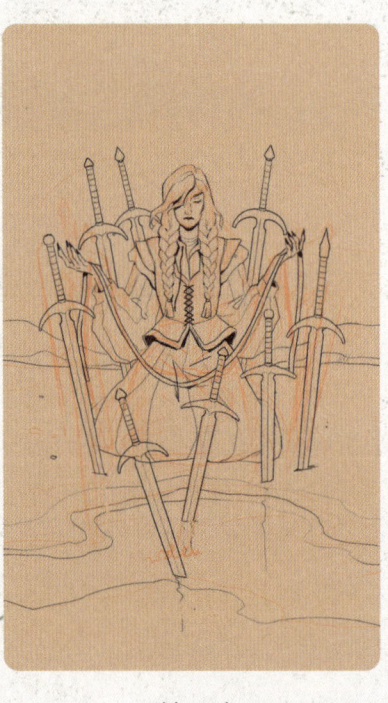

This card returns to a more symmetrical composition for this still, meditative character

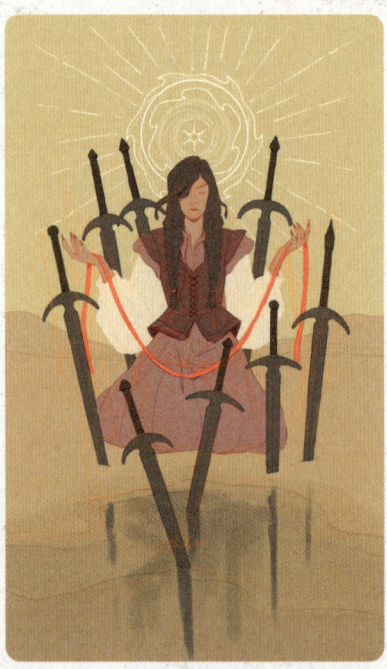

I put my own twist on the traditional image of a restrained and blindfolded figure

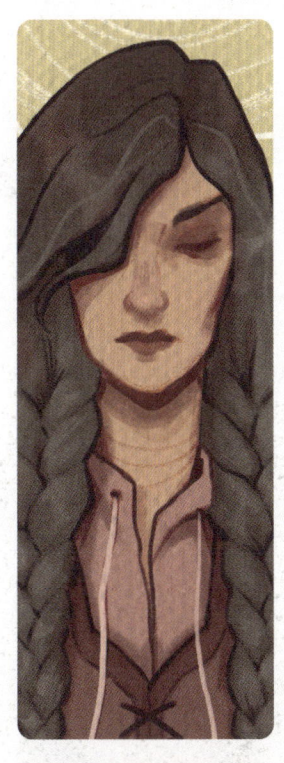

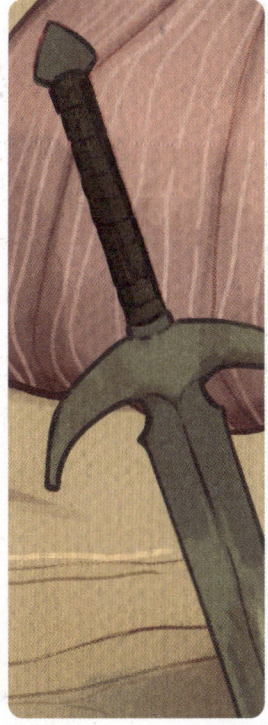

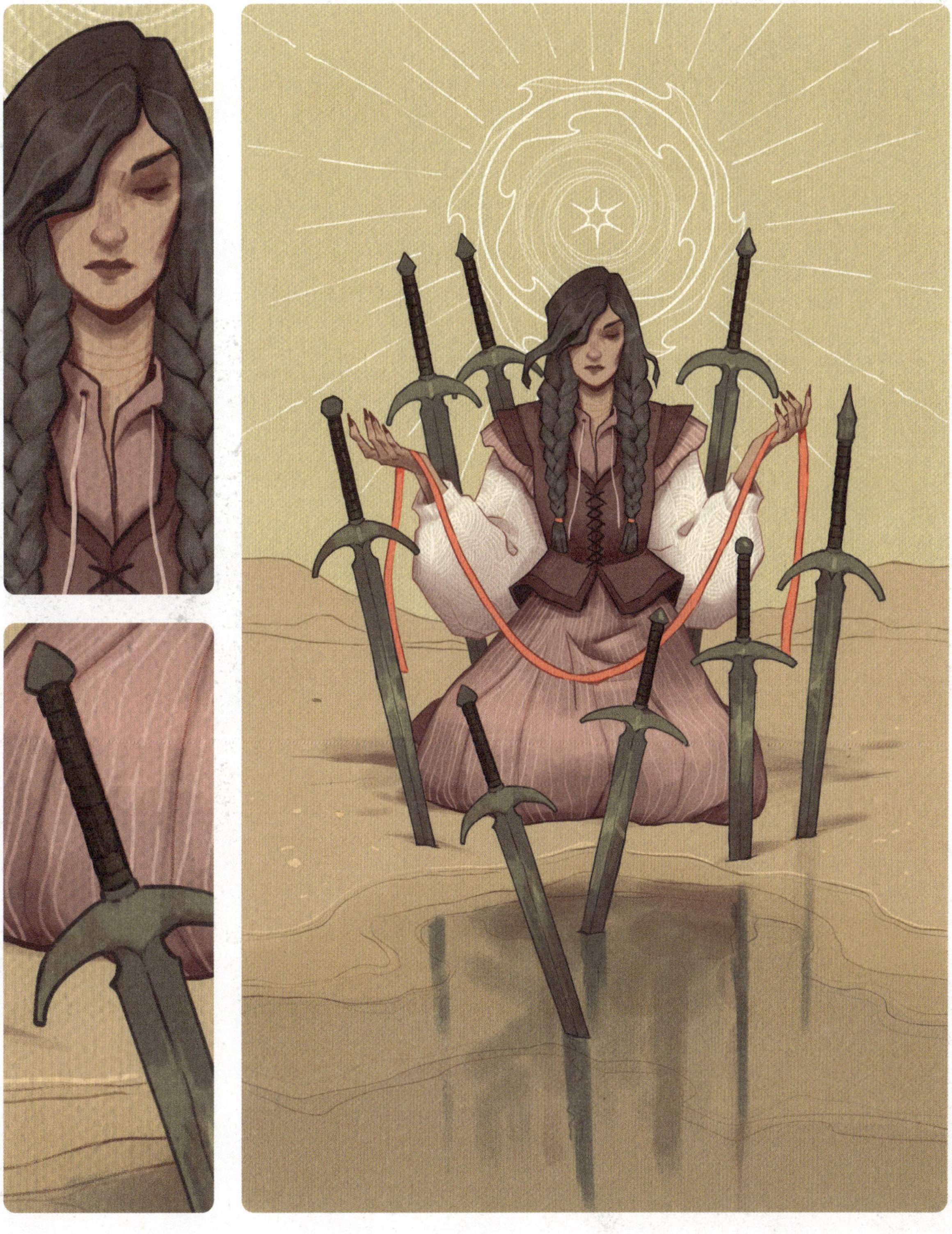

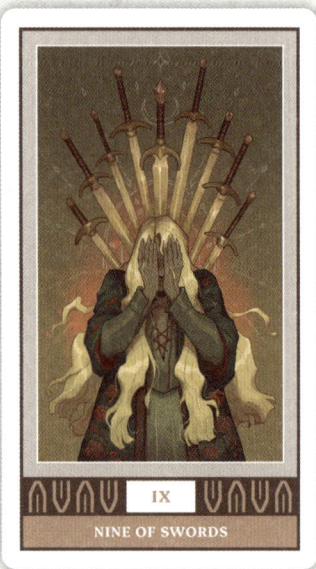

NINE OF SWORDS

NINE OF SWORDS

HORROR, DISTRESS, AGONY

IX

Suffering a nightmare, torn from sleep, the Nine of Swords depicts a woman with her hands covering her face and her hair flowing, intended to represent the character in the moment of awakening. A symmetrical arrangement of swords behind her back suggests that they were the ones she was seeing in her nightmare.

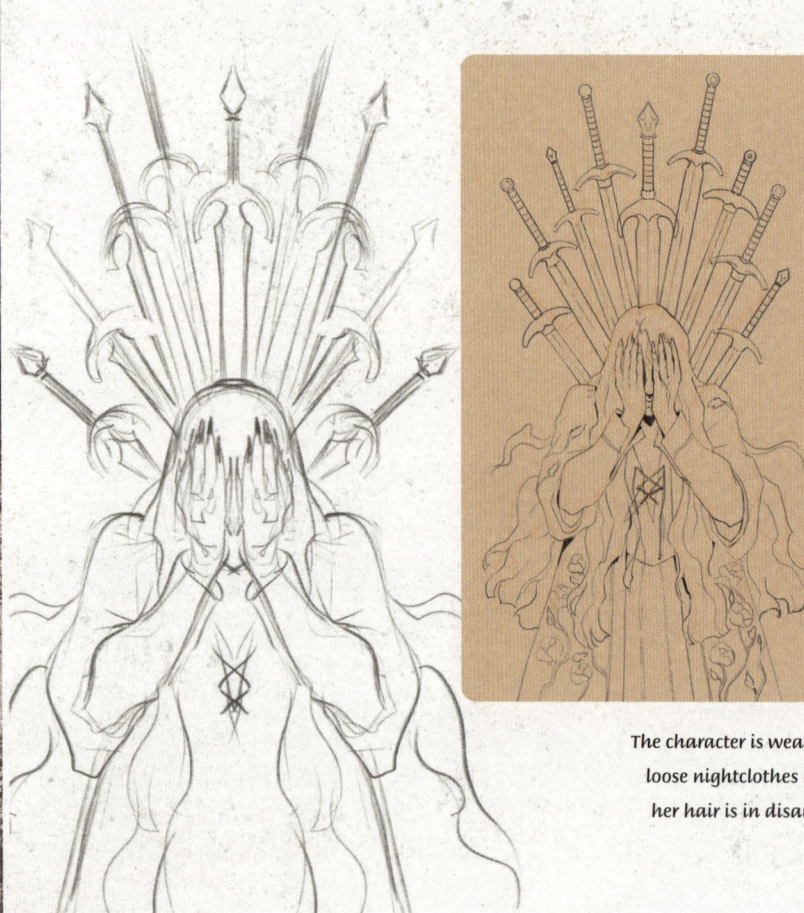

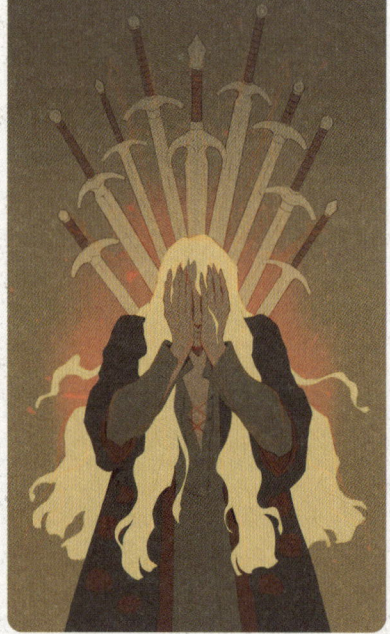

The character is wearing loose nightclothes and her hair is in disarray

The swords stab down at her to represent her tormented dreams

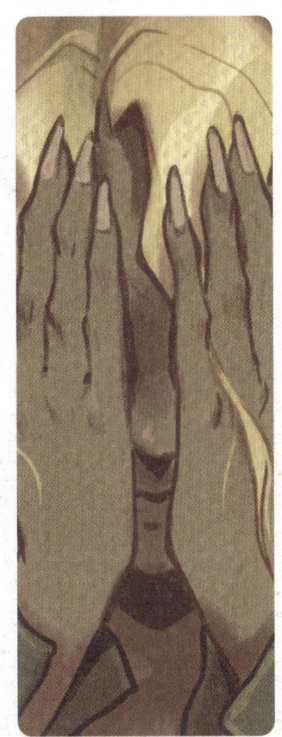

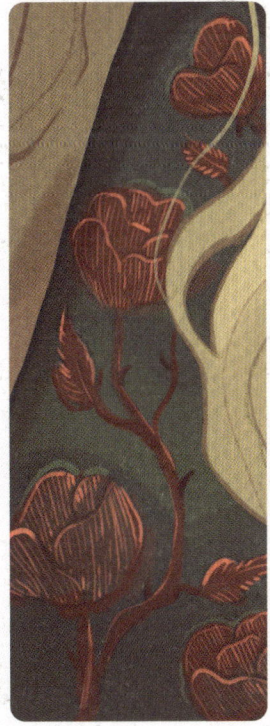

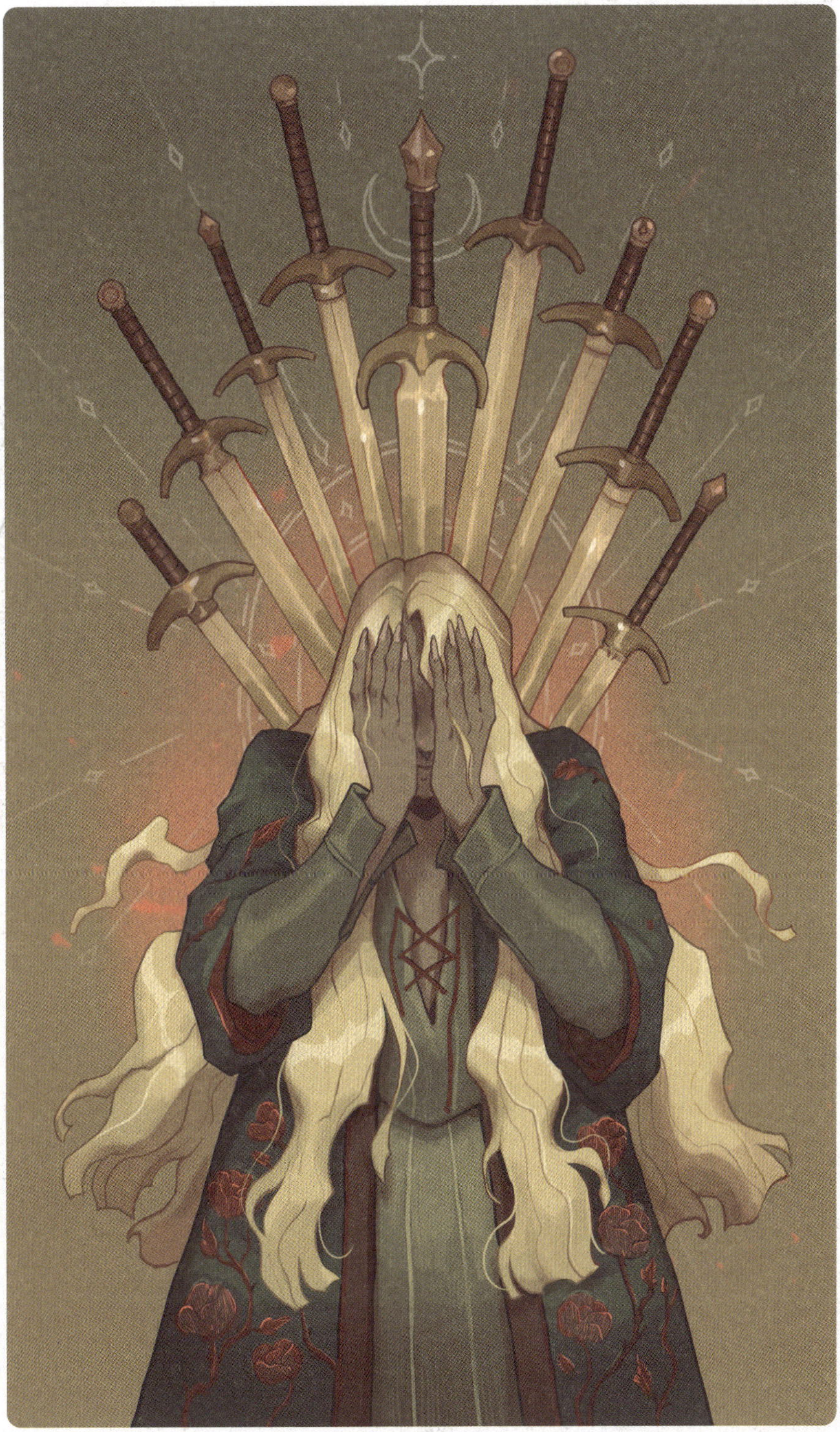

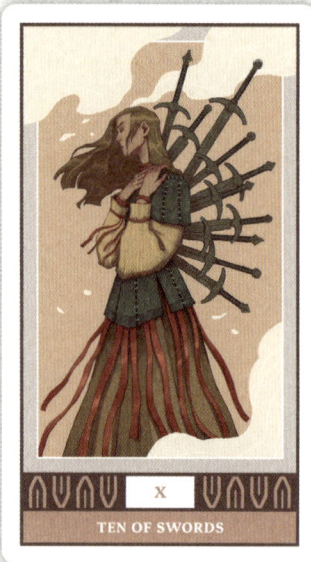

TEN OF SWORDS

FINALE, ENDING, OVER

This card represents ending and reconciliation. However, I do not want to show the death of this character, but rather to illustrate the rejection of the ego. The swords placed along the line of her spine do not cut it – they are only a symbol. The character's face shows peace and relief, conveying the end of her journey and struggles.

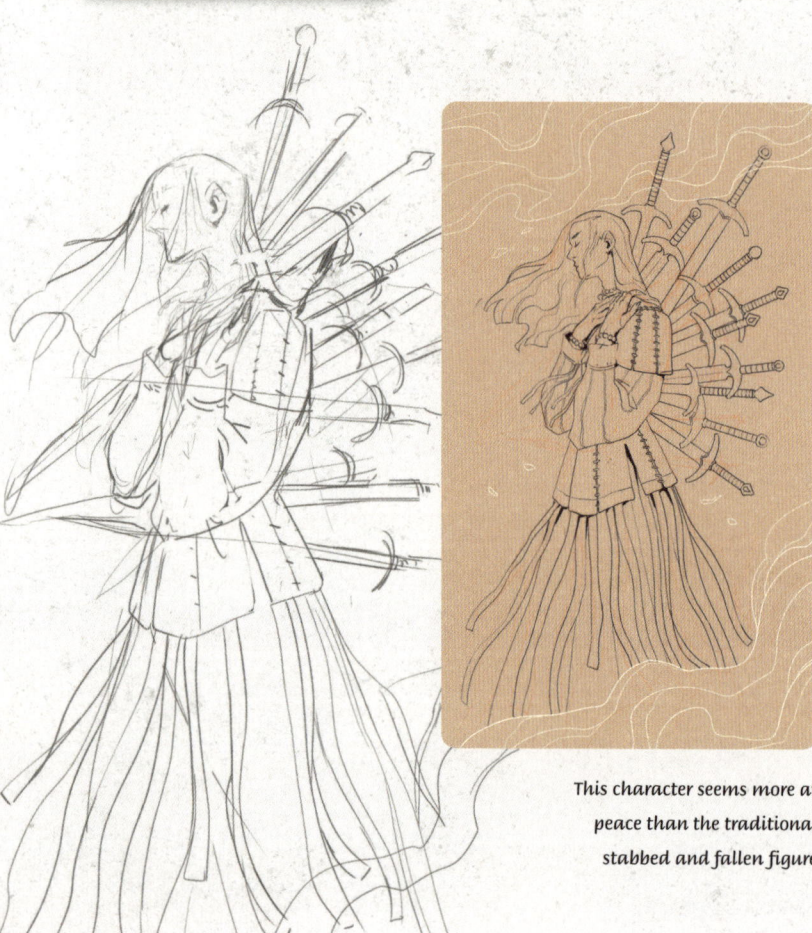

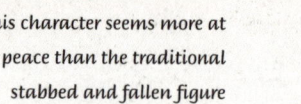

This character seems more at peace than the traditional stabbed and fallen figure

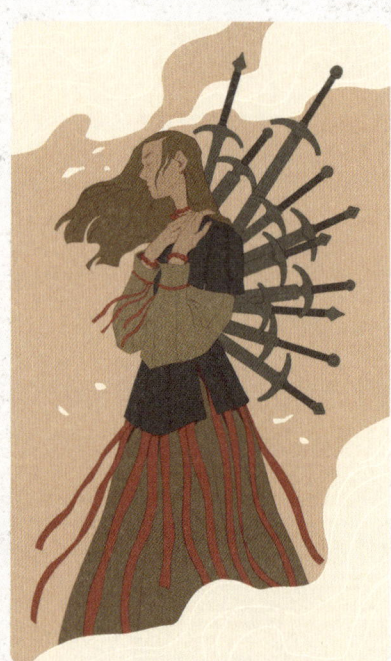

The light, flowing clouds make a return in this card

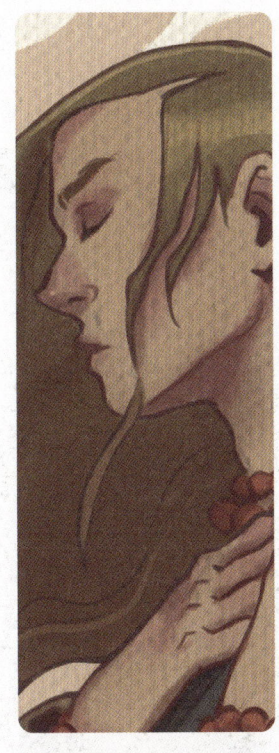
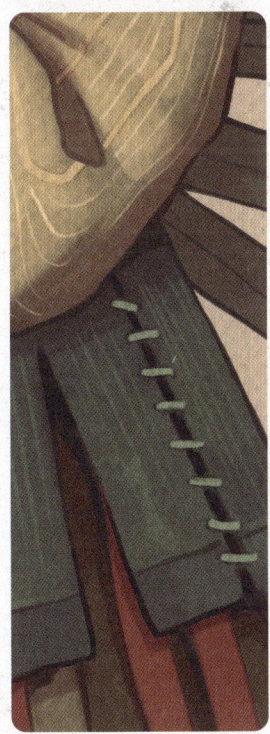

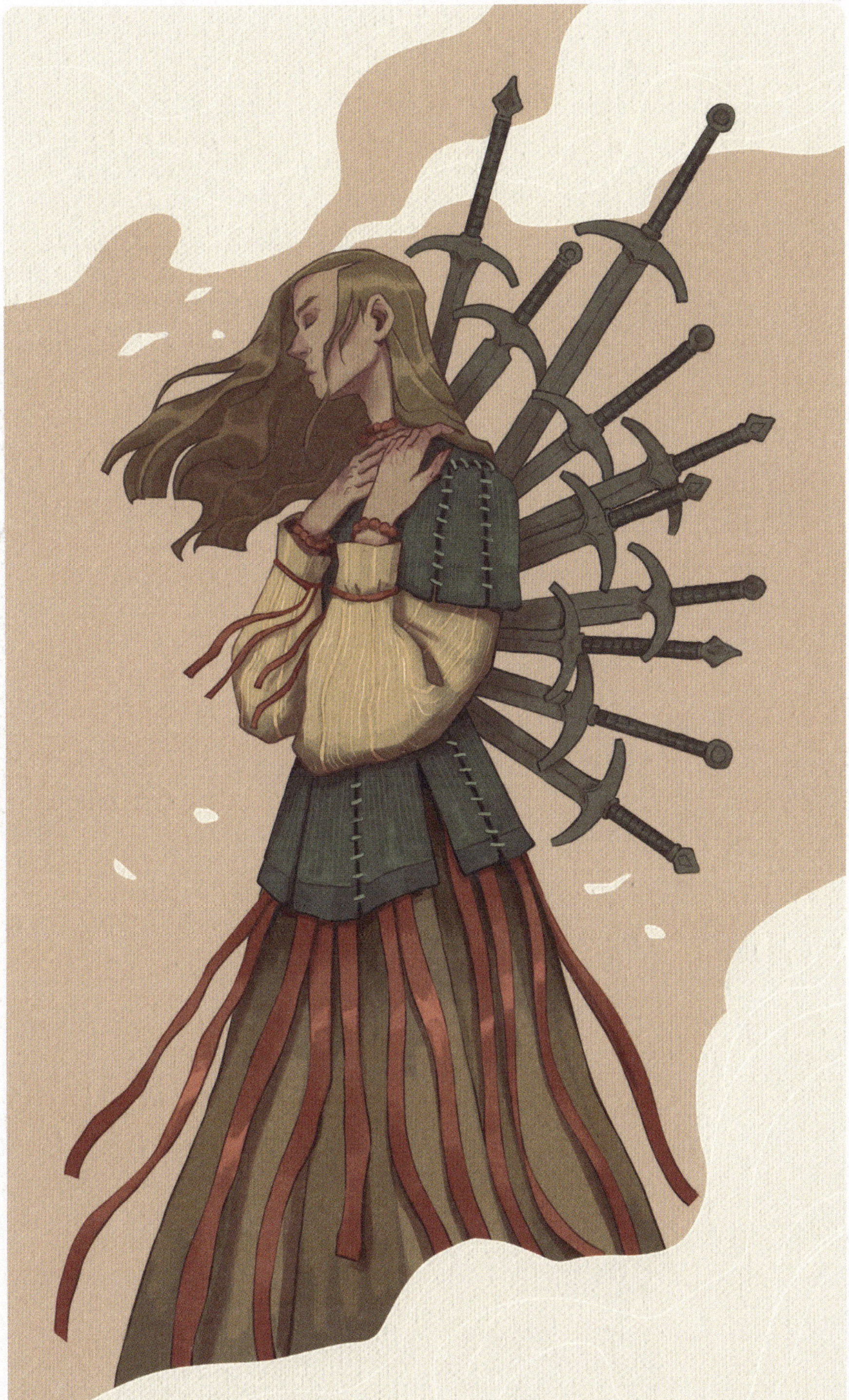

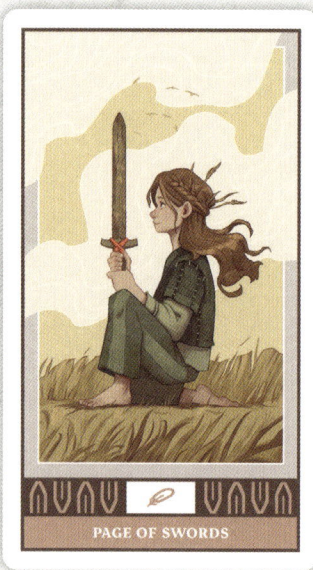

PAGE OF SWORDS

PAGE OF SWORDS

DETECTIVE, CLEVER, QUICK

Creating this illustration gives me a lot of joy. Since the main characters of the suit I am illustrating are women, I decide that the Page of Swords – the 'child' of the suit – will depict a young girl holding a wooden sword. Her hair and the grass around her are moving in the wind, and she is focused on the toy sword in her hands.

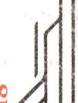

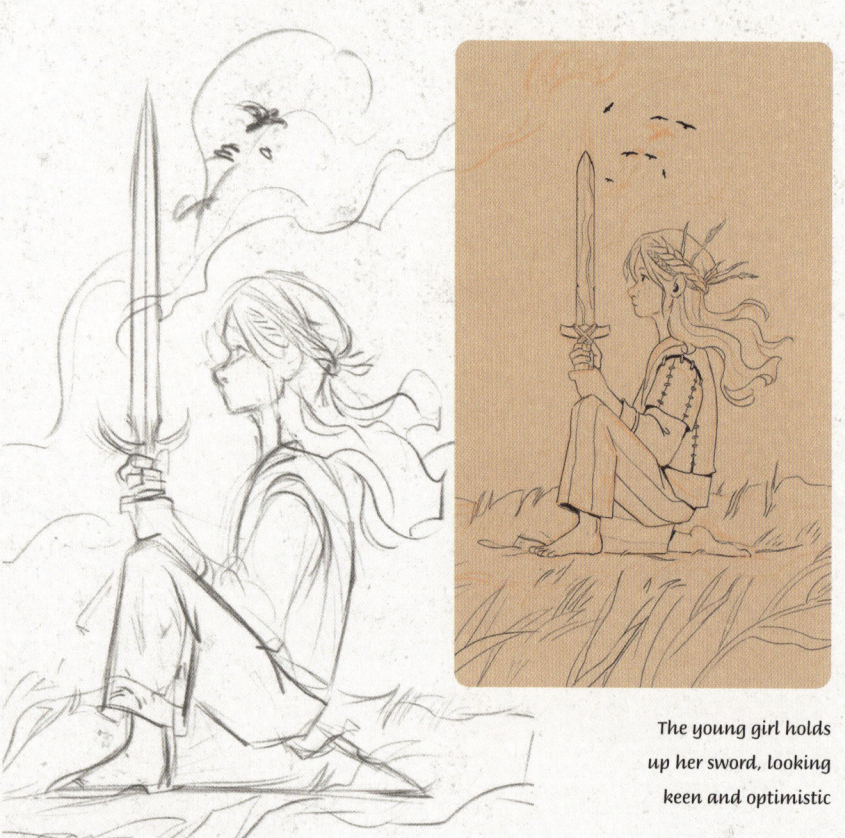

The young girl holds up her sword, looking keen and optimistic

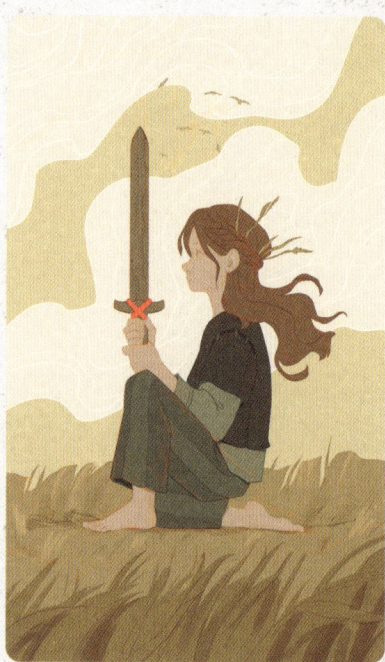

A flock of distant birds is a direct reference to the Rider–Waite–Smith Page card

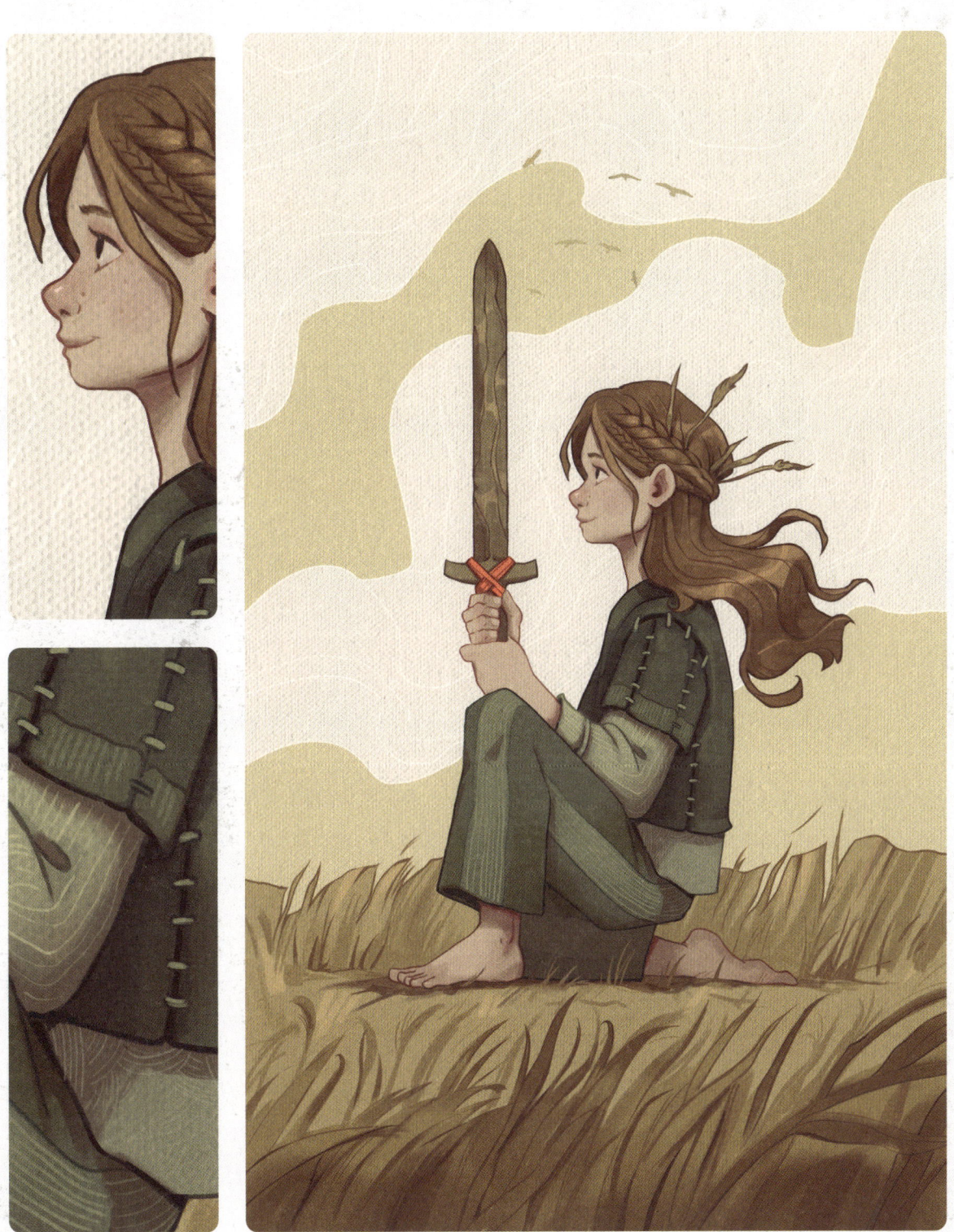

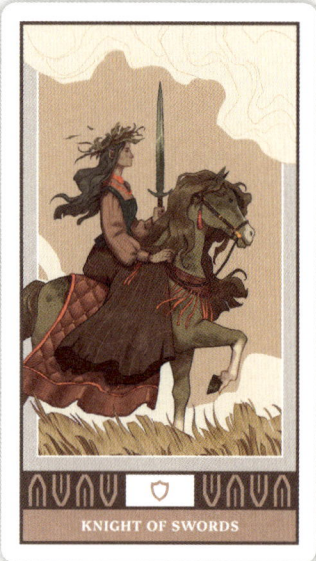

KNIGHT OF SWORDS

KNIGHT OF SWORDS

SPEED, HASTE, RUSHING

The proud silhouette of a young woman appears on the Knight of Swords card. At first I think of her as a knight, but she changes to reflect the main theme I have chosen – women who look like Slavic witches, in worn dresses decorated with embroidered weaves. She is holding her sword raised, her straight pose conveying her determination and self-confidence.

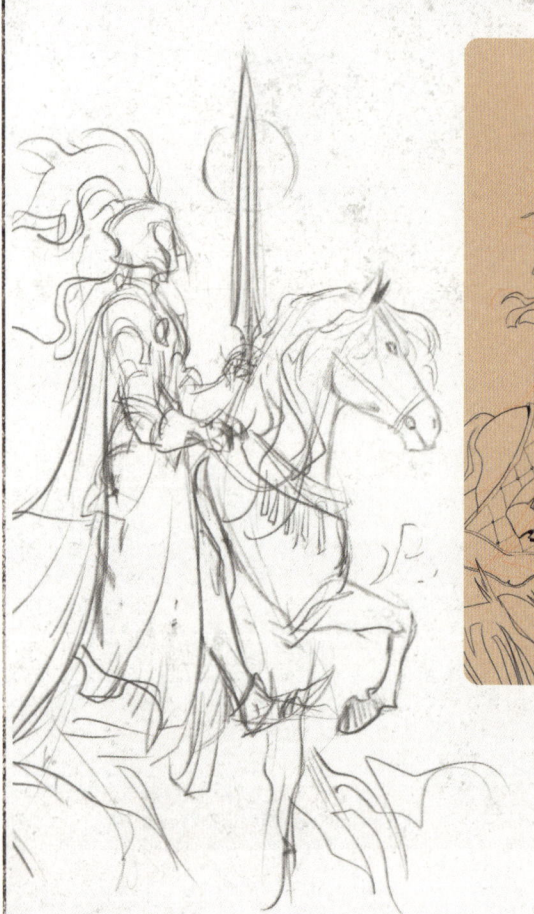

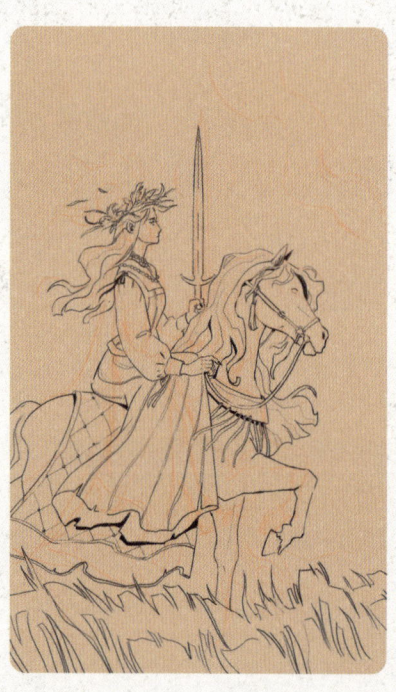

The young woman's face and posture look proud and determined

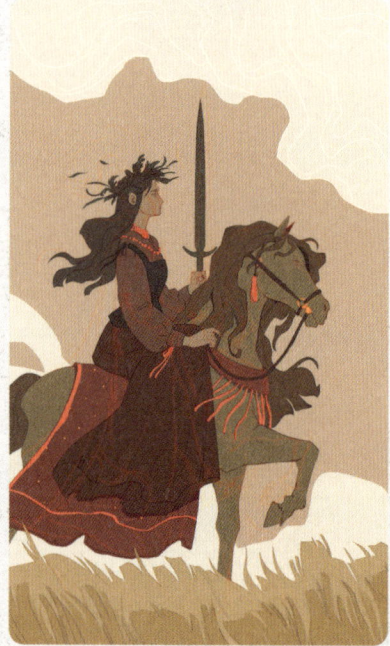

Wind blows through the character's hair and clothes, and through the long grass

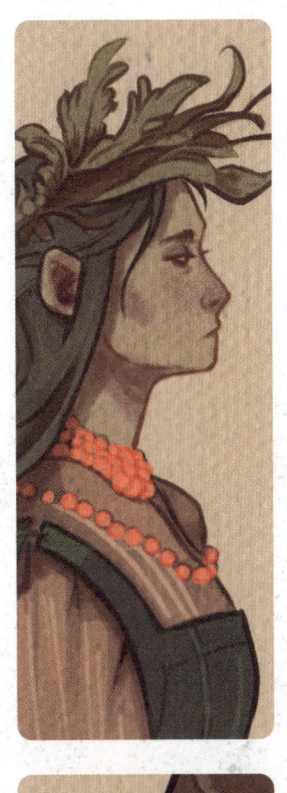

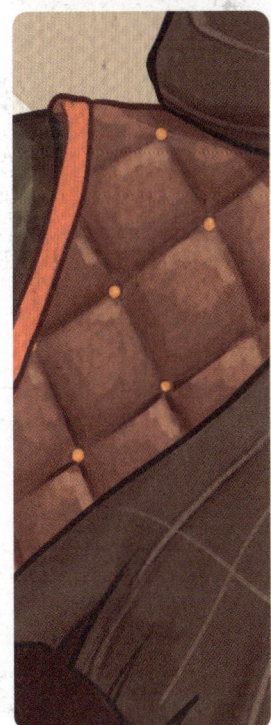

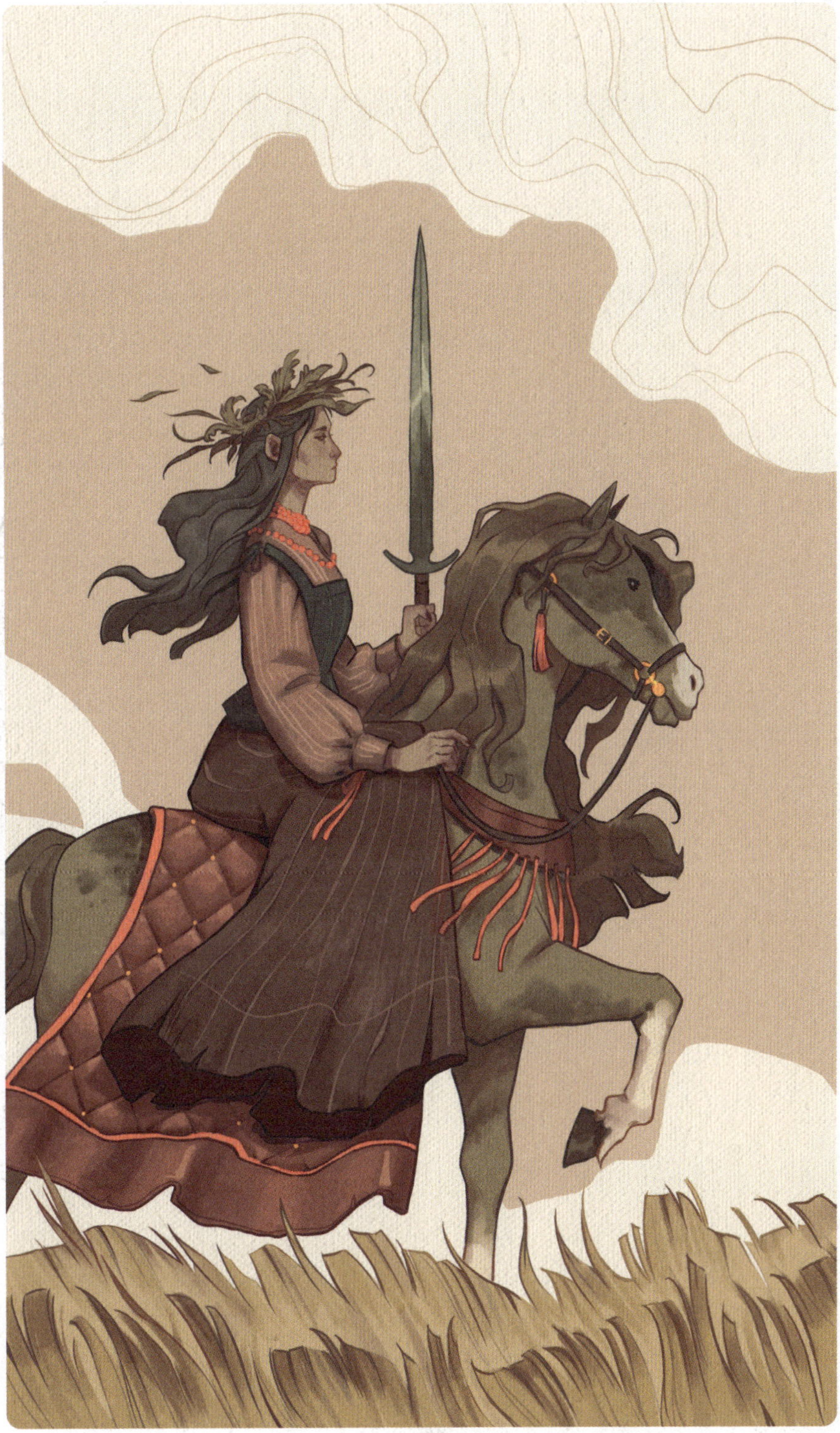

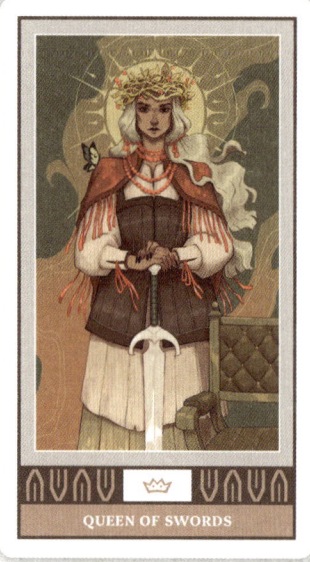

QUEEN OF SWORDS

QUEEN OF SWORDS

ARTICULATE, PRECISE, KNOWLEDGE

A woman with a crown of twigs and grass stands next to a chair that symbolizes a throne. She is the last female character in the suit. She holds the sword and proudly looks straight ahead, a slight smile suggesting that she knows something. This card forms a diptych with the King of Swords because I want these two illustrations to be connected symbolically and directly.

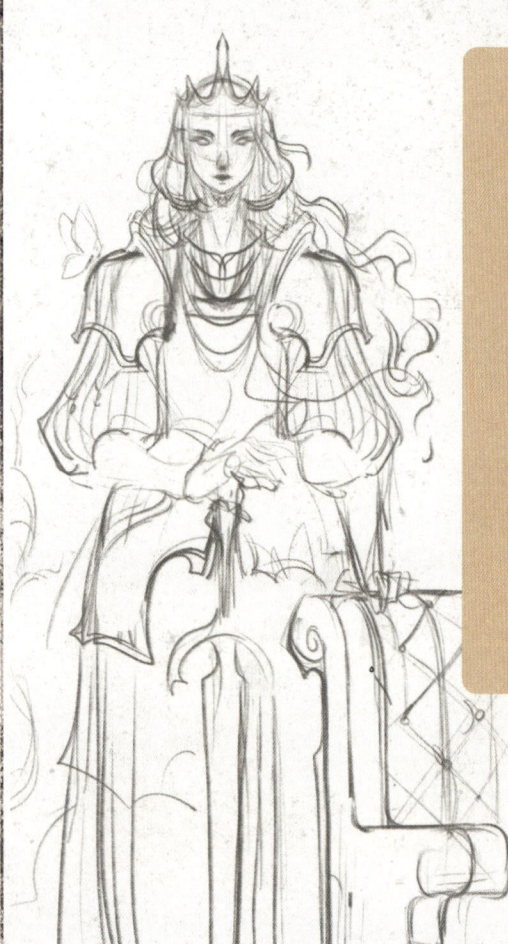

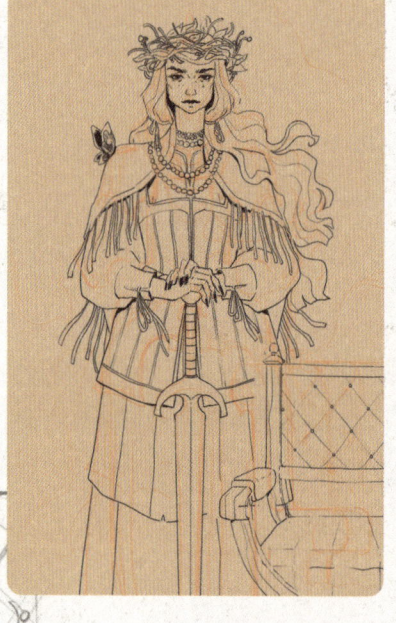

The Queen of Swords is poised and knowing; her long grey hair makes her age ambiguous

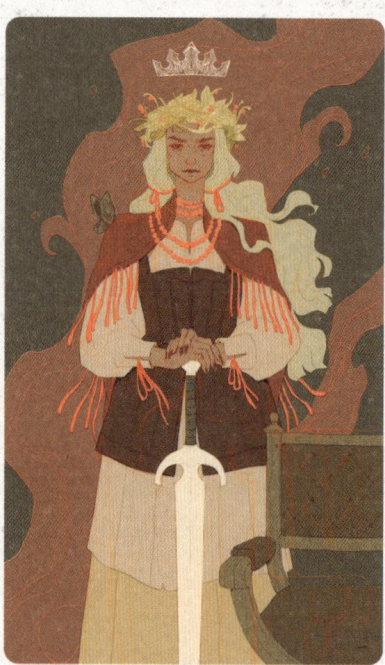

The traditional motif of a butterfly, an Air creature, appears on her shoulder

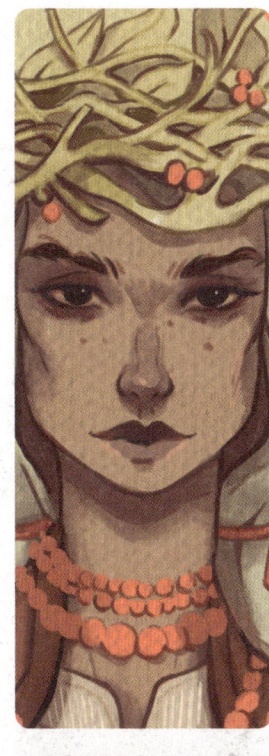

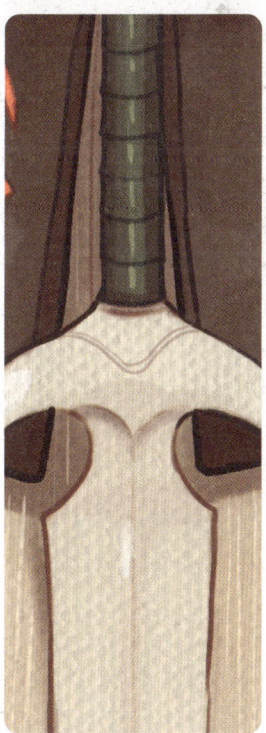

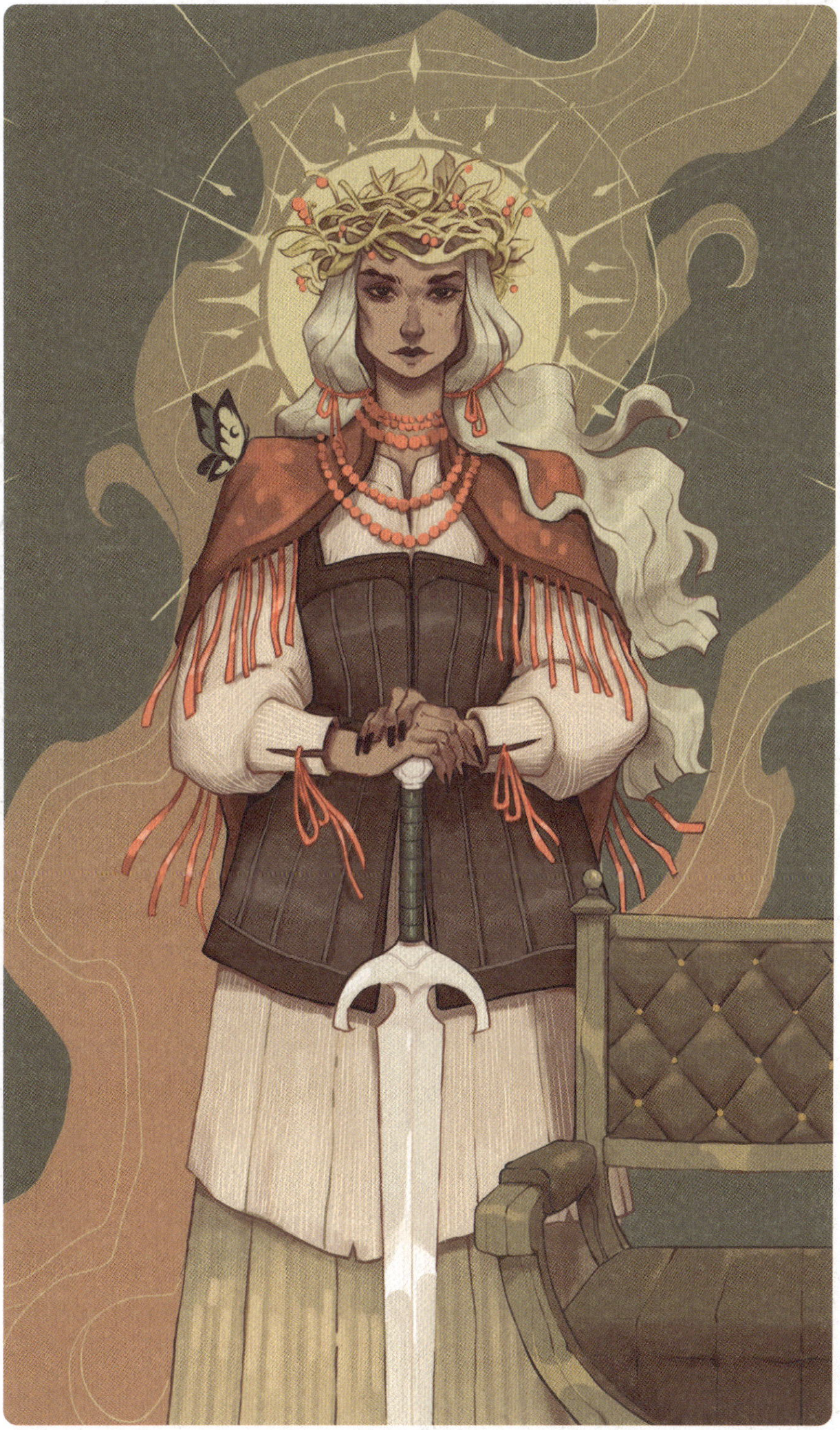

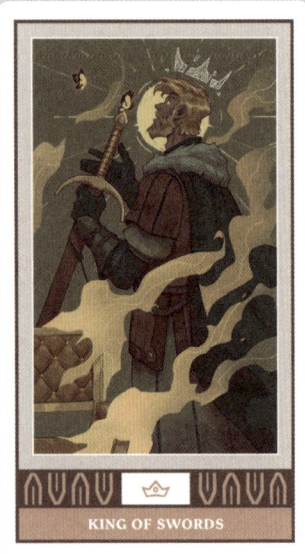

KING OF SWORDS

COMMANDING, COMMANDEERING, ORATOR

The King is the only male character in this suit. This card is the second part of a diptych with the Queen of Swords. It features the same chair as the Queen card, symbolizing the throne. Not wanting to present a typical king sitting on the throne, I show him as part of an unfolding story – he is reaching for his sword, but does not have time to protect himself from the spell of the Queen of Swords.

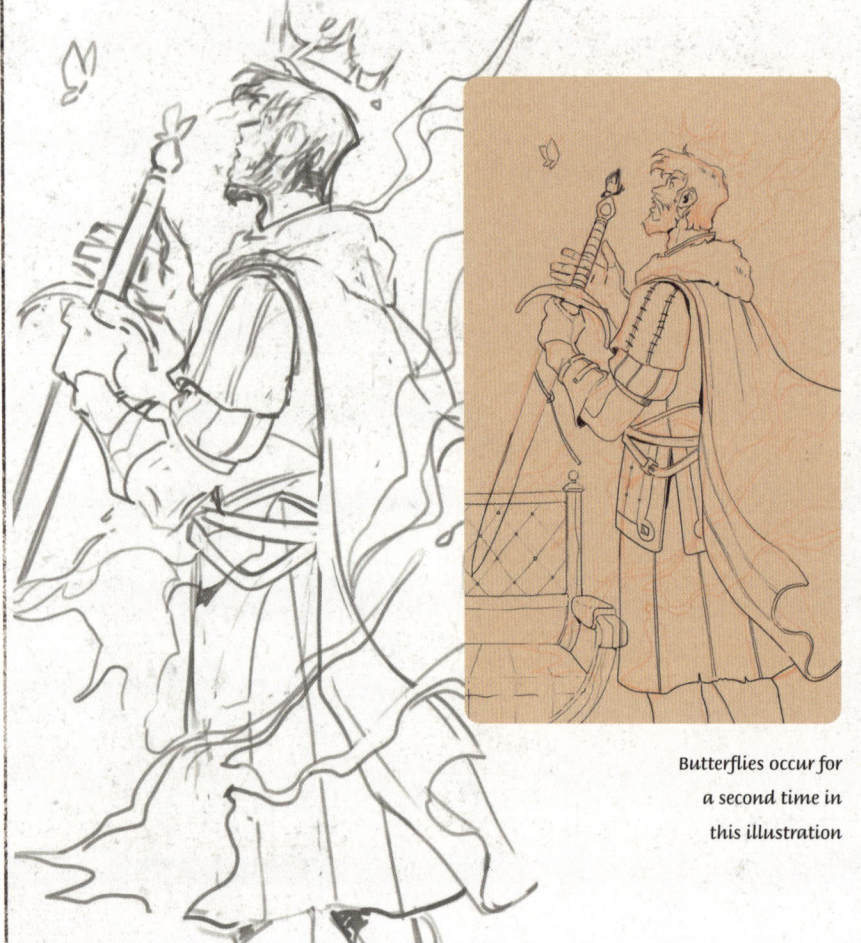

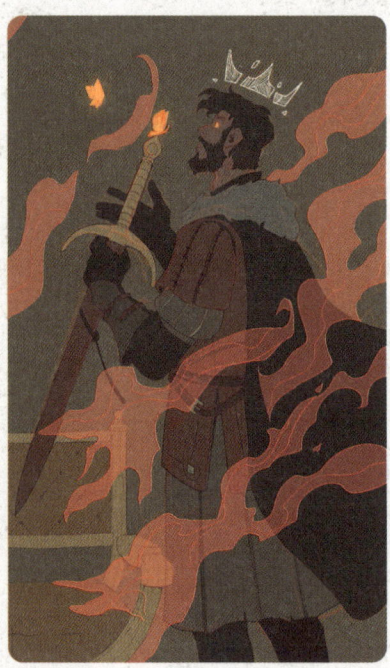

Butterflies occur for a second time in this illustration

The king's attire is simple and pragmatic, giving him a serious appearance

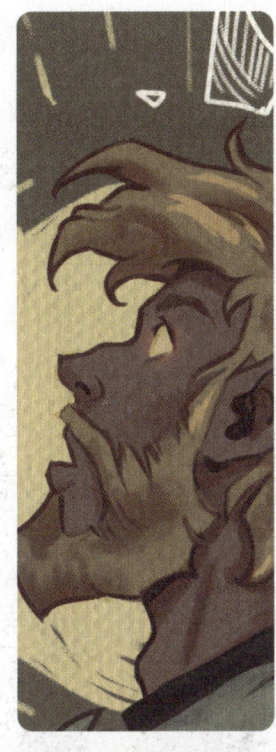

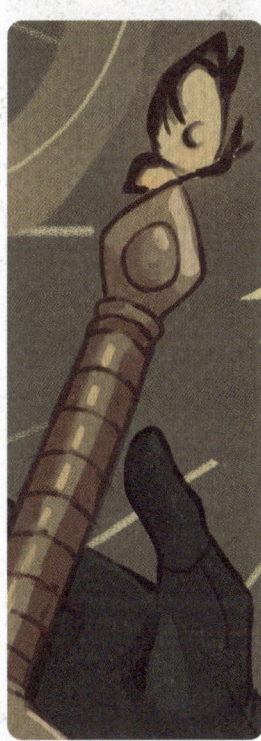

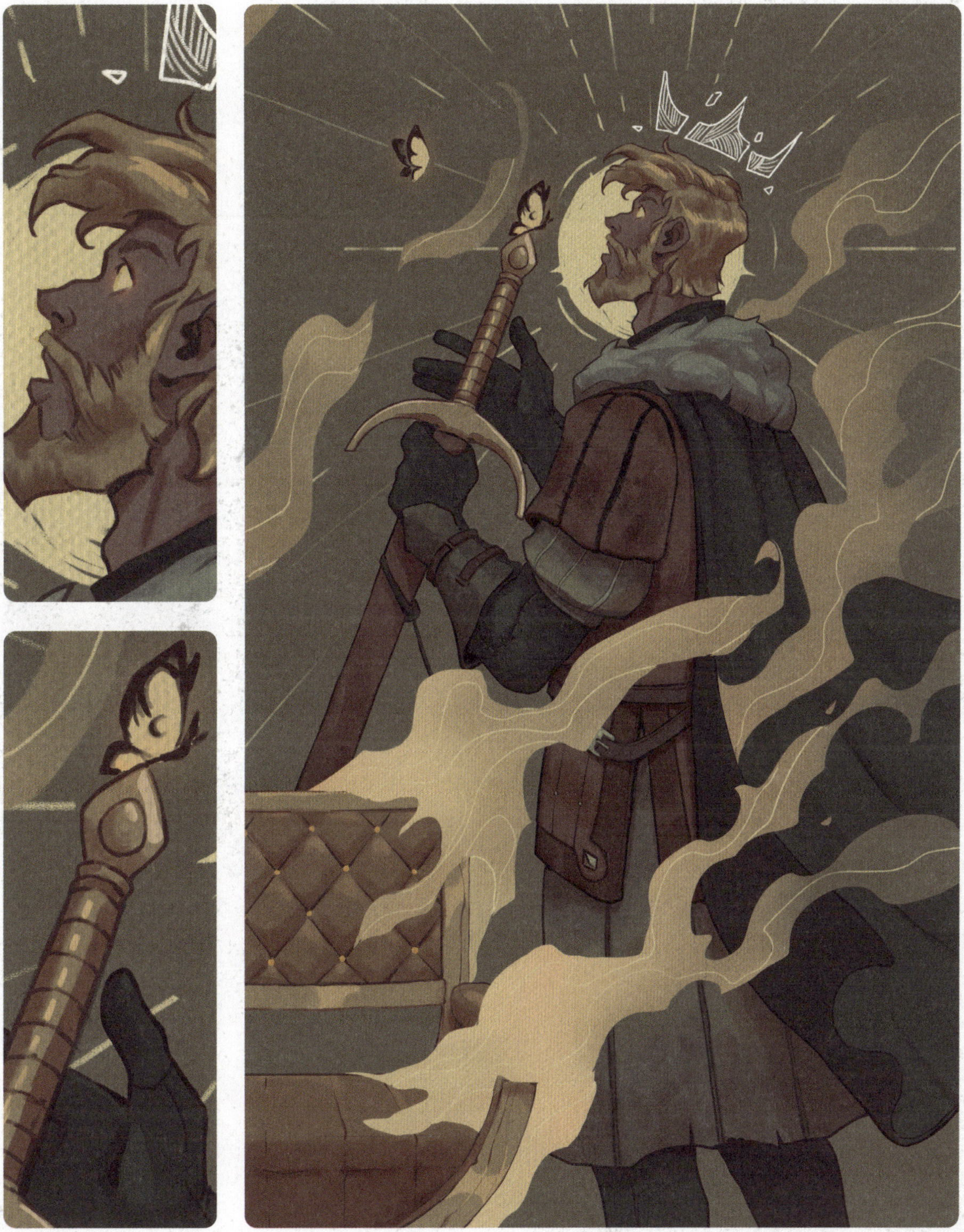

ARTIST'S CONCLUSION

I am very pleased with how the illustrated suit of Swords looks as a whole, and with the fact that it creates one story. The Slavic motifs interwoven into almost every card create a folkloric look, which fits well with the theme of swords and their wielders. Gusts of wind or clouds, which are intended to emphasize the Air element of the suit, connect all the illustrations into one whole.

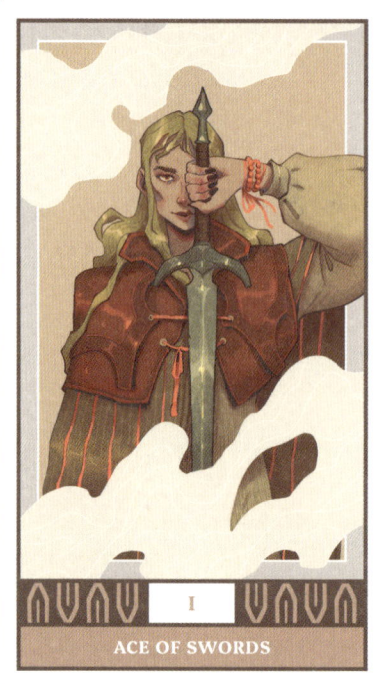

ACE OF SWORDS

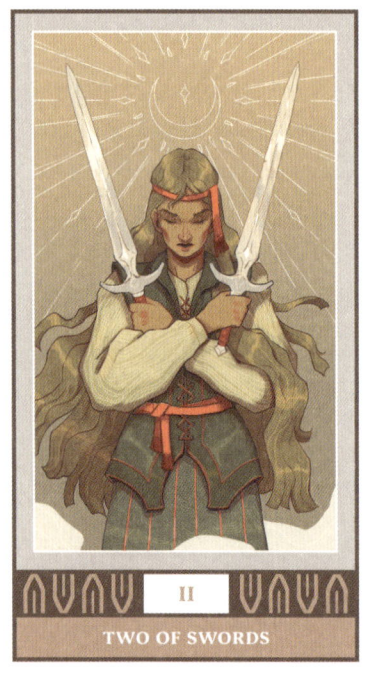

TWO OF SWORDS

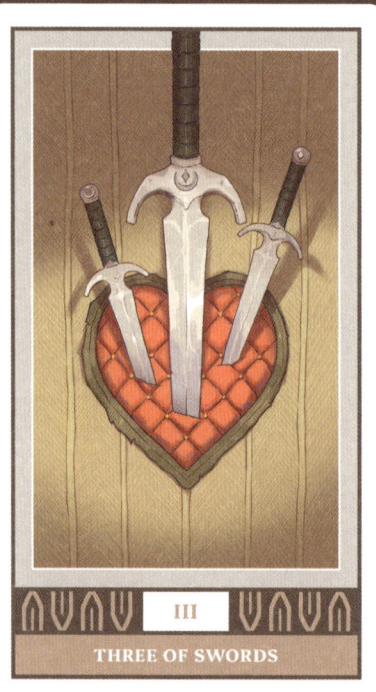

THREE OF SWORDS

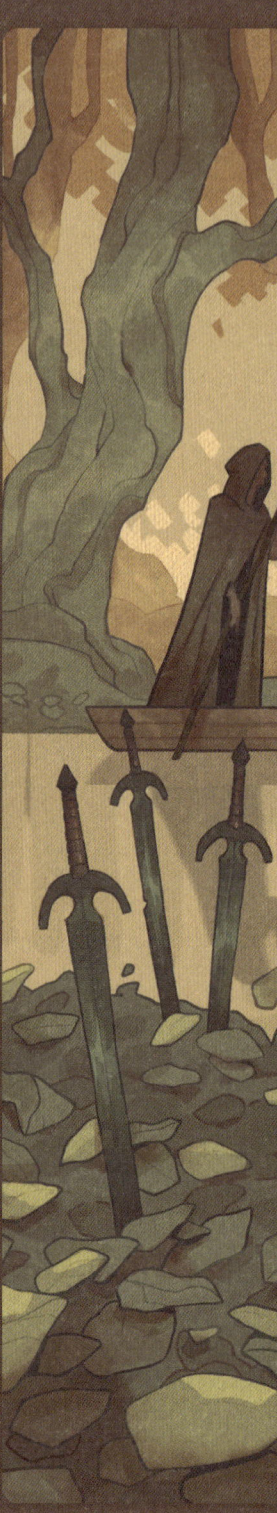

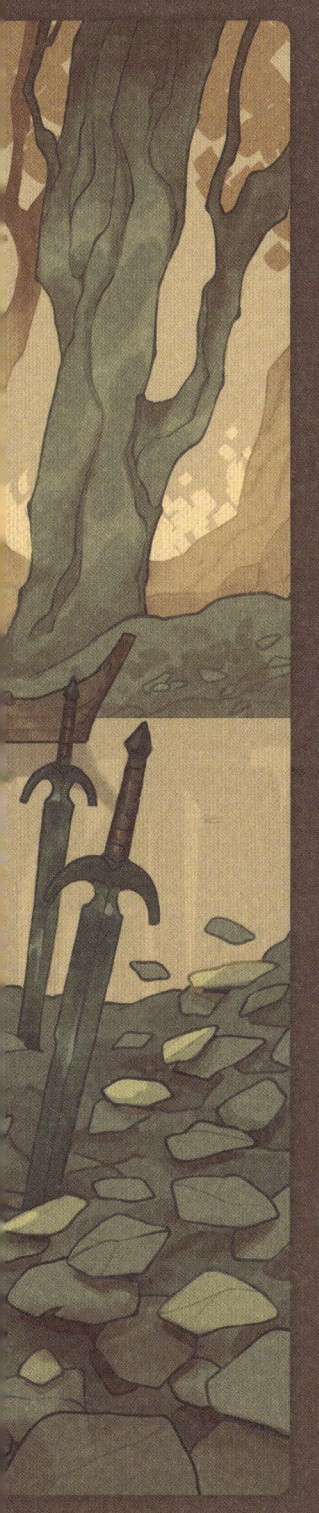

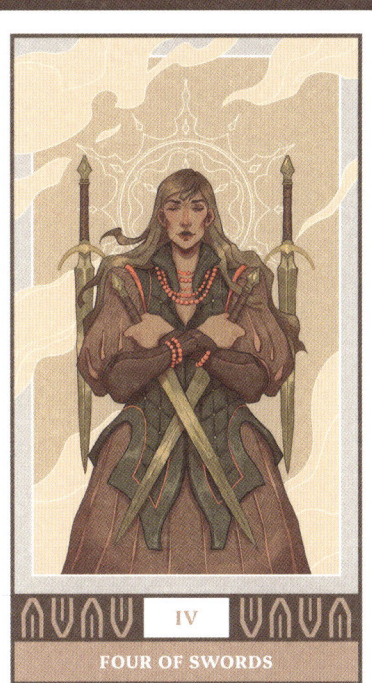

IV

FOUR OF SWORDS

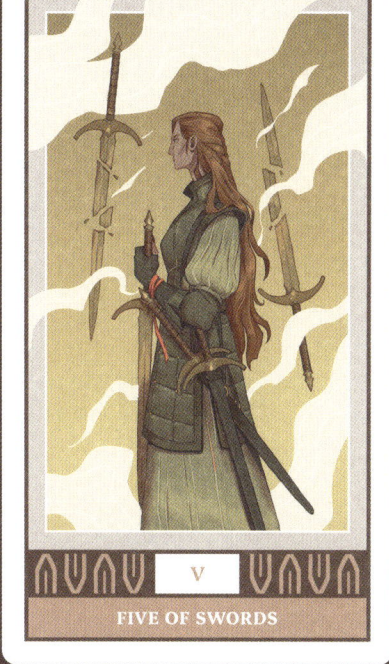

V

FIVE OF SWORDS

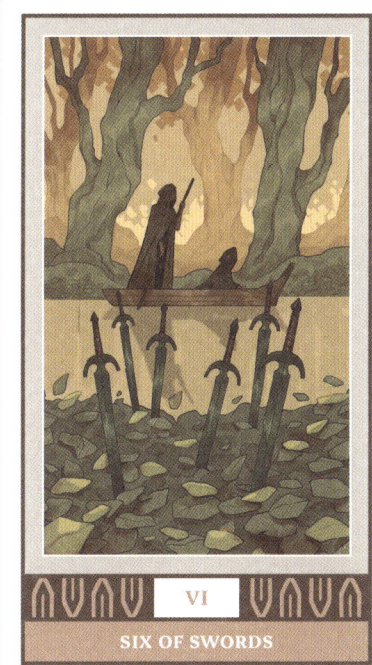

VI

SIX OF SWORDS

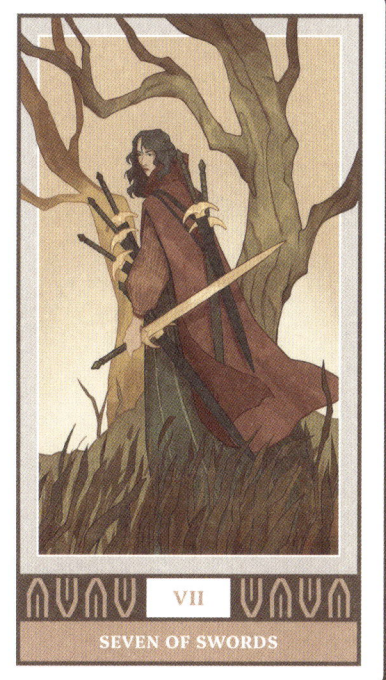

VII

SEVEN OF SWORDS

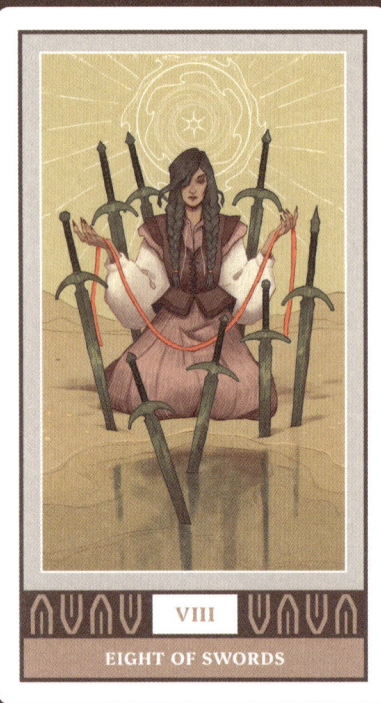

VIII

EIGHT OF SWORDS

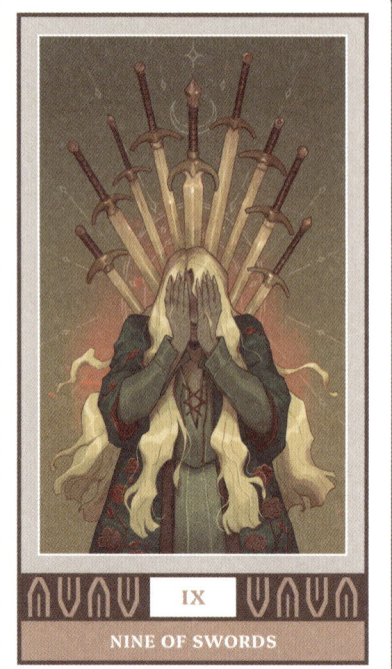

IX

NINE OF SWORDS

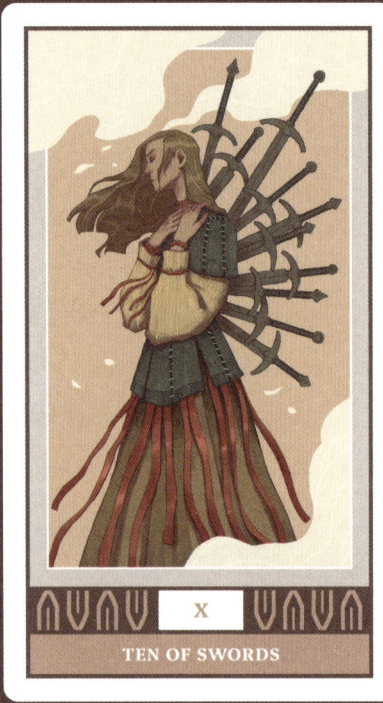

X

TEN OF SWORDS

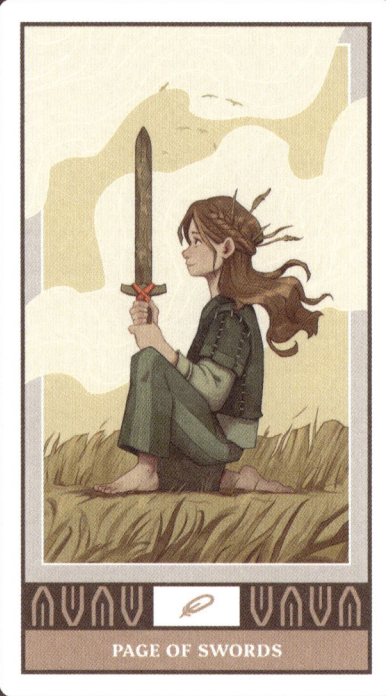

PAGE OF SWORDS

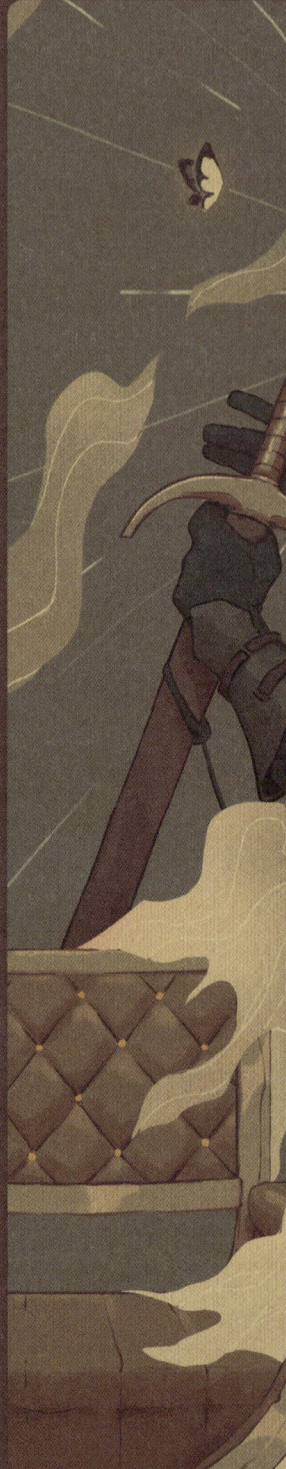

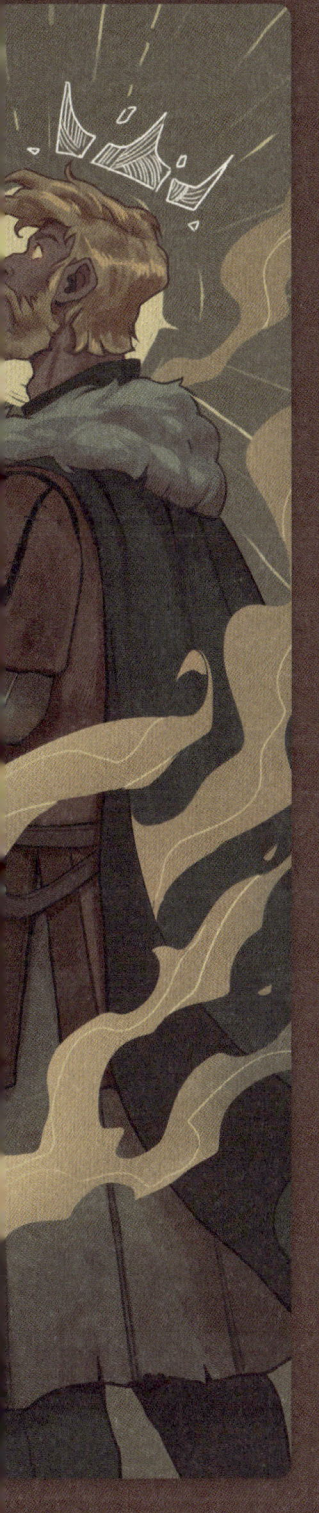

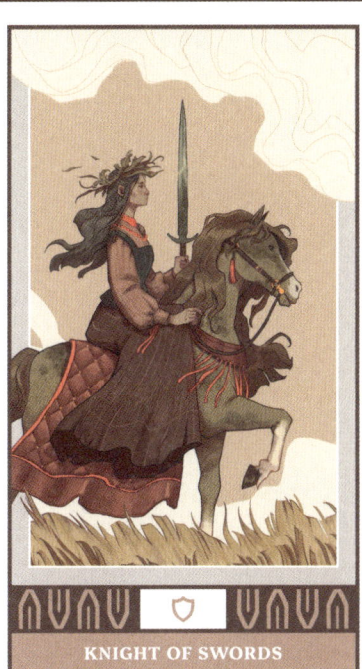

KNIGHT OF SWORDS

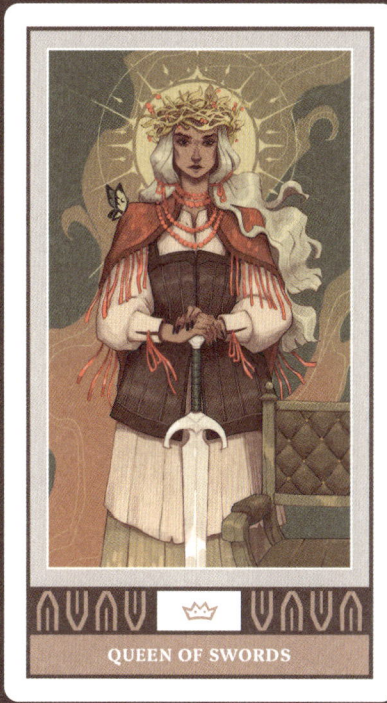

QUEEN OF SWORDS

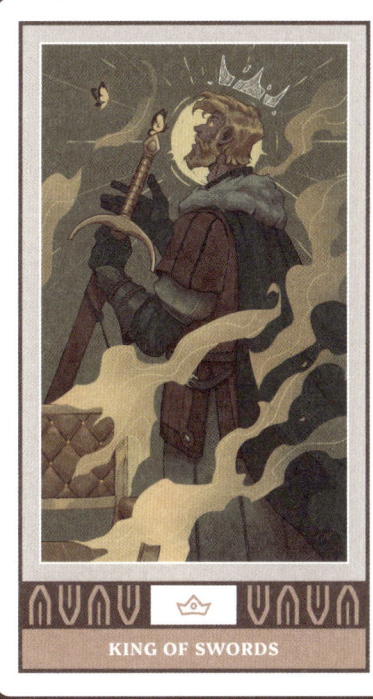

KING OF SWORDS

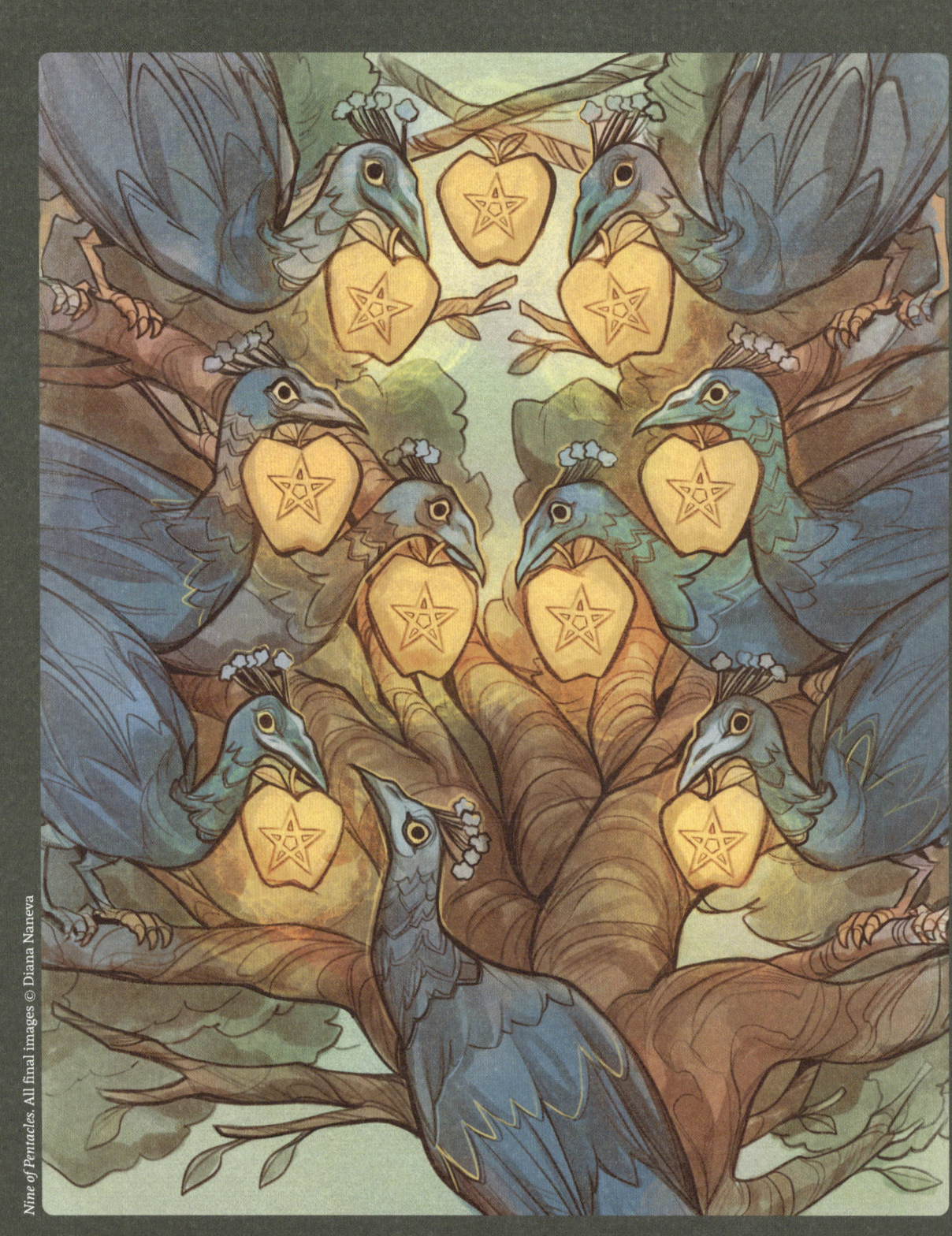

Nine of Pentacles. All final images © Diana Naneva

THE SUIT OF
PENTACLES

INTRODUCTION BY SASHA GRAHAM

Pentacles reflect the world of elemental Earth, which is everything in the material world that can be seen, smelled, felt, touched, tasted, and heard. Pentacles are all things tangible and quantifiable, from people to possessions, to family and friends, to molecules in the body. They reflect earthly things including mountains, valleys, forests, and canyons. Pentacles are resources like land, homes, houses, and cities. Pentacles also represent property and money.

Designing the suit of Pentacles, the artist should consider how the symbol of Pentacles (also called coins, discs, spheres, money, gems, and crystals) will be composed. The Ace of Pentacles is the appearance of the Earth element in the physical world, like a seed or gift. Each subsequent card grows and accumulates more Pentacles until the suit culminates in the Ten of Pentacles.

How will the landscape of Pentacles look? What symbols reflect Earth qualities? Is the landscape a subterranean, cavernous underground world of gnomes or forest animals? Does the suit unfold in a lush garden? What sorts of objects will populate the suit of Earth while exemplifying traditional Pentacle qualities? It helps to imagine how it feels to walk through the world of heavy, earthly things. Are the characters fleshy and physical? Is the vegetation overgrown and lush? Earthly Pentacles are the slowest of all the suits, moving at a snail's pace. Imagine being buried up to your neck in the earth and rock. Consider how dense and heavy earth can be. How long does it take for a mountain range to rise and fall?

The Pentacles court cards are an interconnected ruling family commanding and embodying the energy of Earth. Their cards are often crowded with belongings or lush vegetation, as Earth is the suit of tangible luxury.

DIANA NANEVA

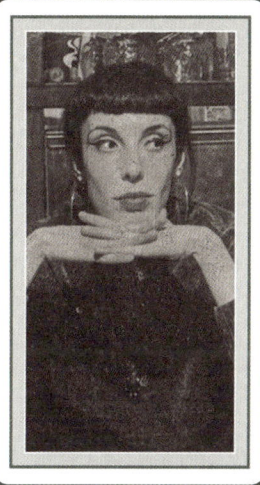

ARTIST'S INSIGHT

In the past few years, I have grown fascinated by the imagery and symbolism of tarot. As a very social person, I like the conversational aspect of tarot reading. I want to approach this suit with a theme that's close to my heart and has symbolism that really reminds me of the Pentacles: the many different Slavic fairy tales involving golden apples. I want to share stories I was told as a child or that I found later in life. My suit will include scenes from Bulgarian, Polish, Ukrainian, Serbian, and Hungarian tales, each being a story of its own or a version of the same tale.

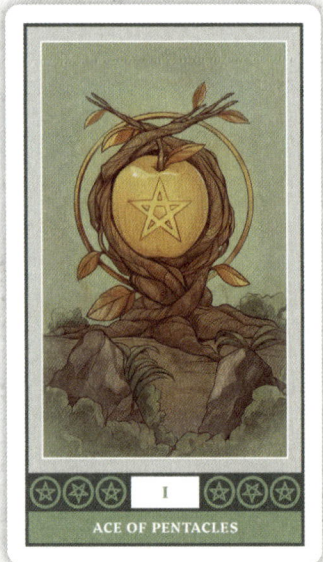

ACE OF PENTACLES

ACE OF PENTACLES

SEED, BIRTH, OPPORTUNITY

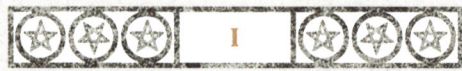

Let's start with the golden apple itself. In the Bulgarian version of the fairy tale *The Three Brothers and the Golden Apple*, a mother and her three sons have a garden with an apple tree. Each year the apple tree grows one golden apple. Despite this giving them the promise of a better life when it comes to wealth, they face many challenges to protecting the tree, such as the apples being stolen by a creature called a hala. The Ace of Pentacles conveys the very start of this story, with its symbolism of opportunity and the manifestation of material security.

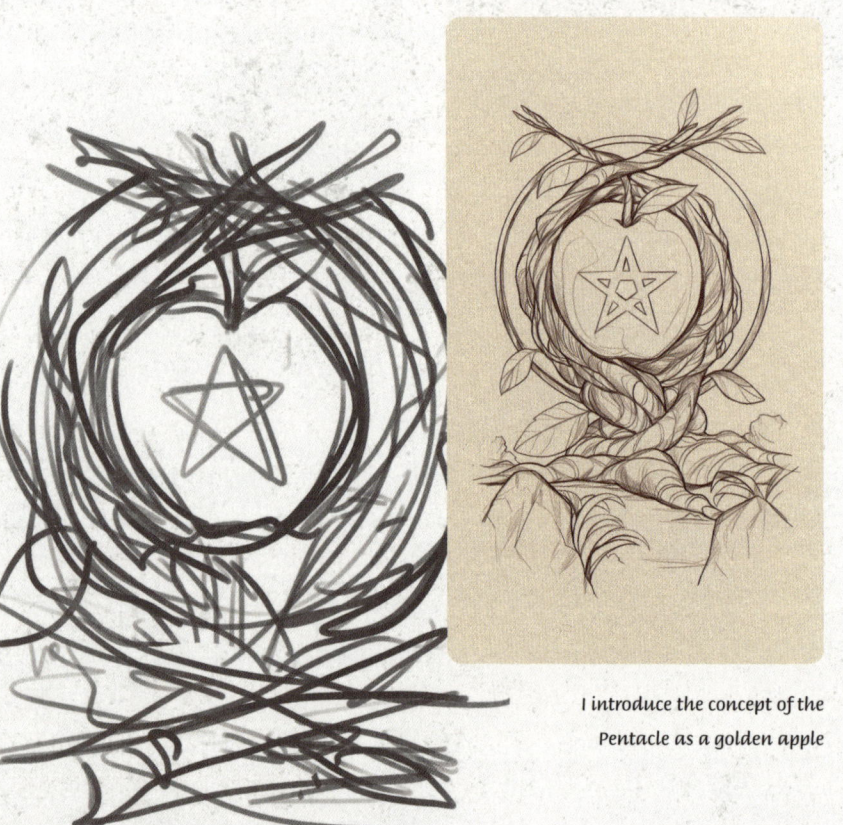

I introduce the concept of the Pentacle as a golden apple

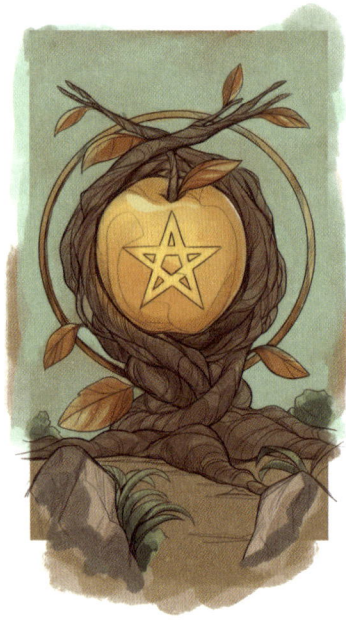

Golden apples are a common motif in many European folk tales

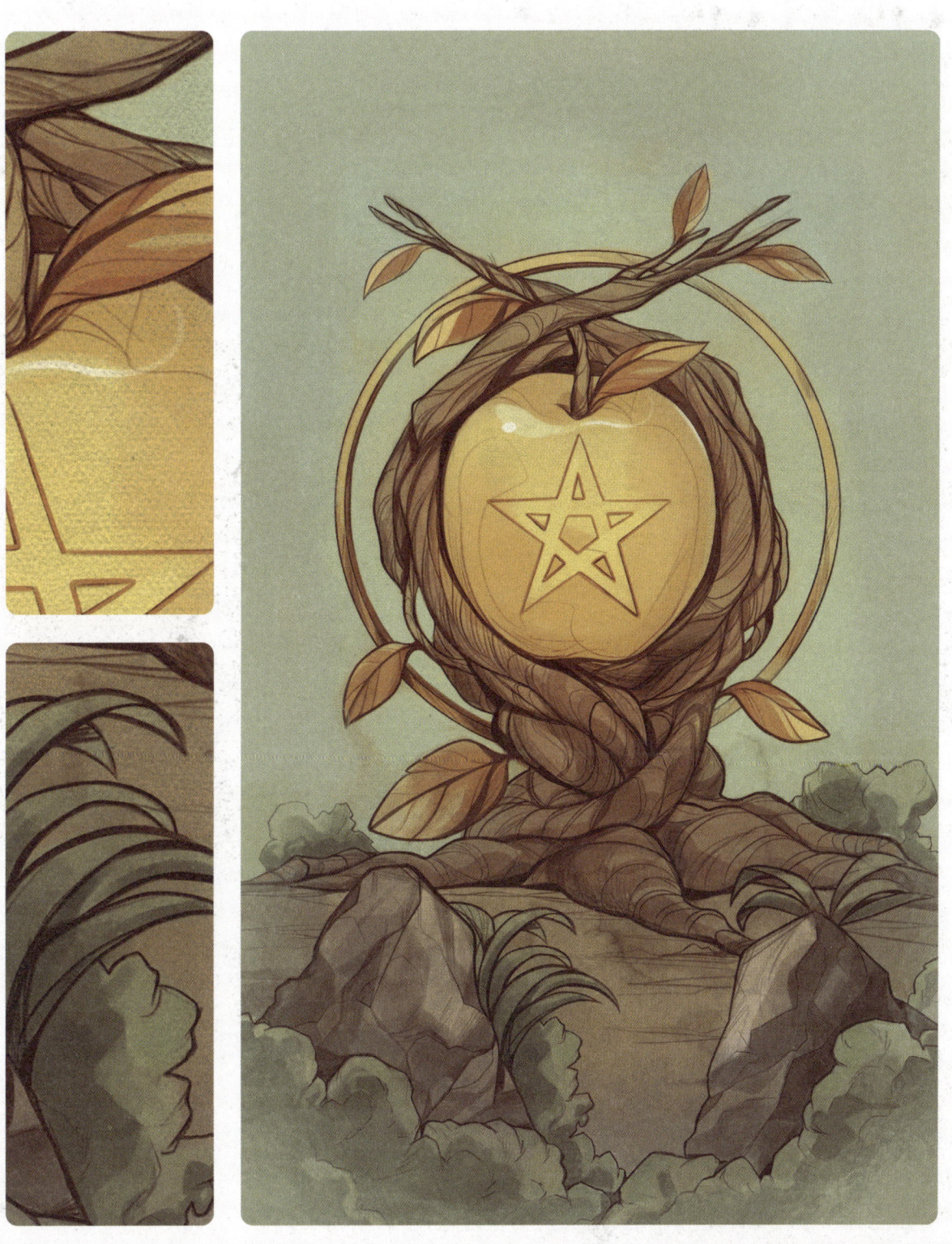

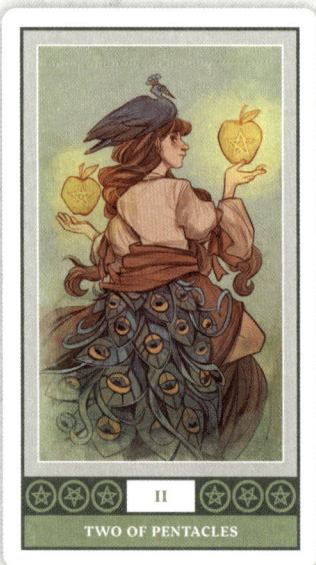

TWO OF PENTACLES

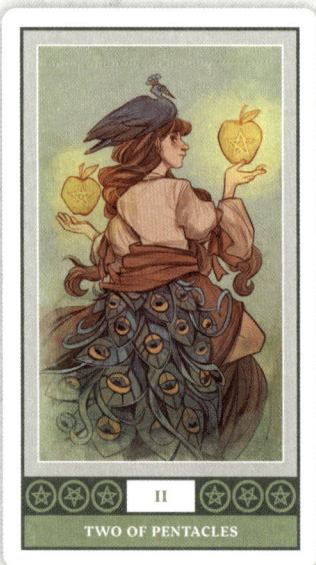
TWO OF PENTACLES

TWO OF PENTACLES

CHOICE, PLAY, FUN

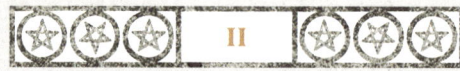

For the Two of Pentacles, I want to show a moment from the Serbian fairy tale *The Nine Peahens and the Golden Apples*, where an emperor's golden apple tree is robbed every night and his sons set themselves to watch it. The older two sleep, but the youngest stays awake. Nine peahens arrive. Eight peahens rifle through the tree, while the ninth comes down beside the youngest brother and becomes a beautiful maiden who talks with him. He begs her to leave one apple, and she leaves two. It is a moment of weighing choices and prioritizing for the character of the peahen maiden.

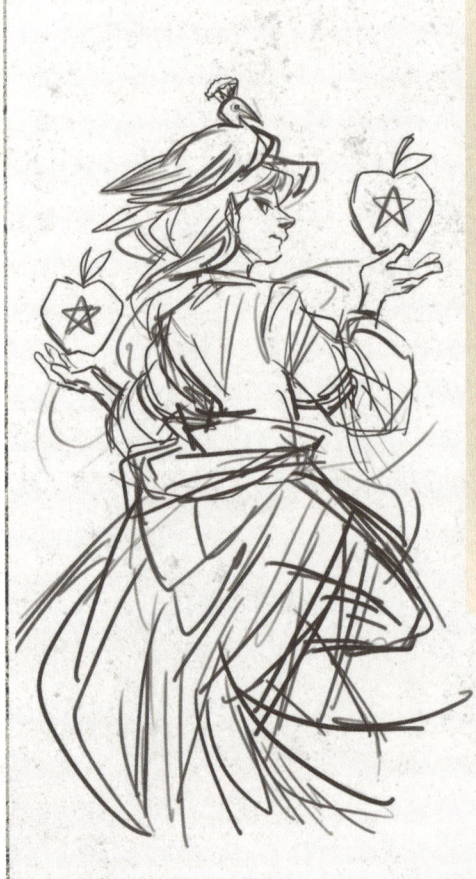

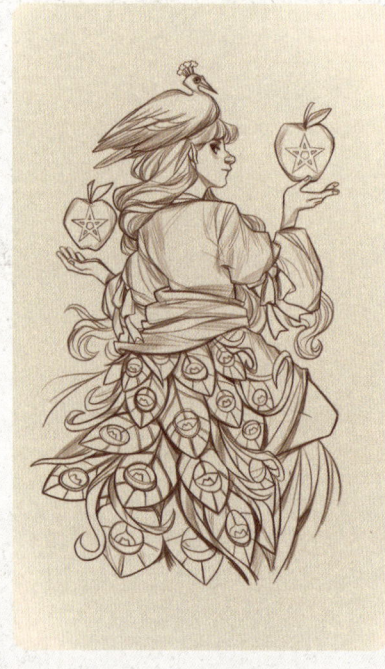

The maiden holds up an apple in each hand, as if considering her options

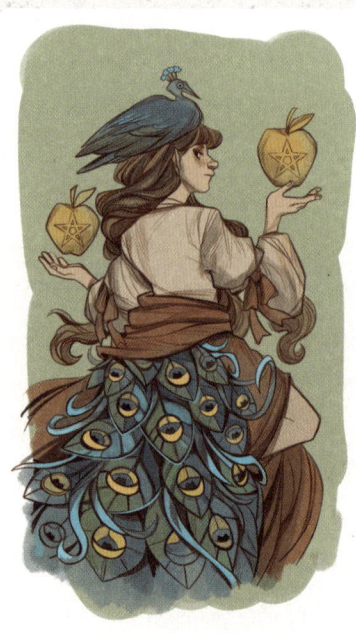

The blue feathers convey the character's origins as a peahen

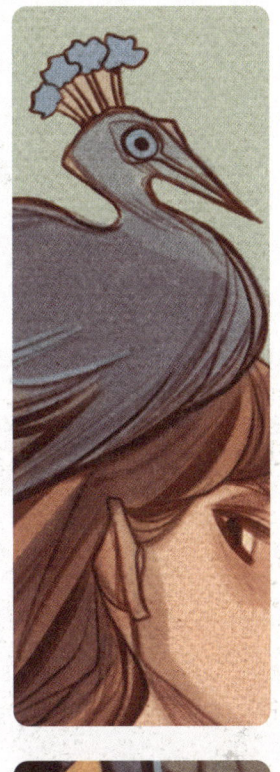
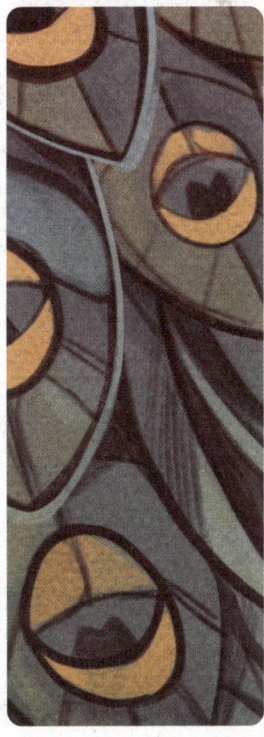

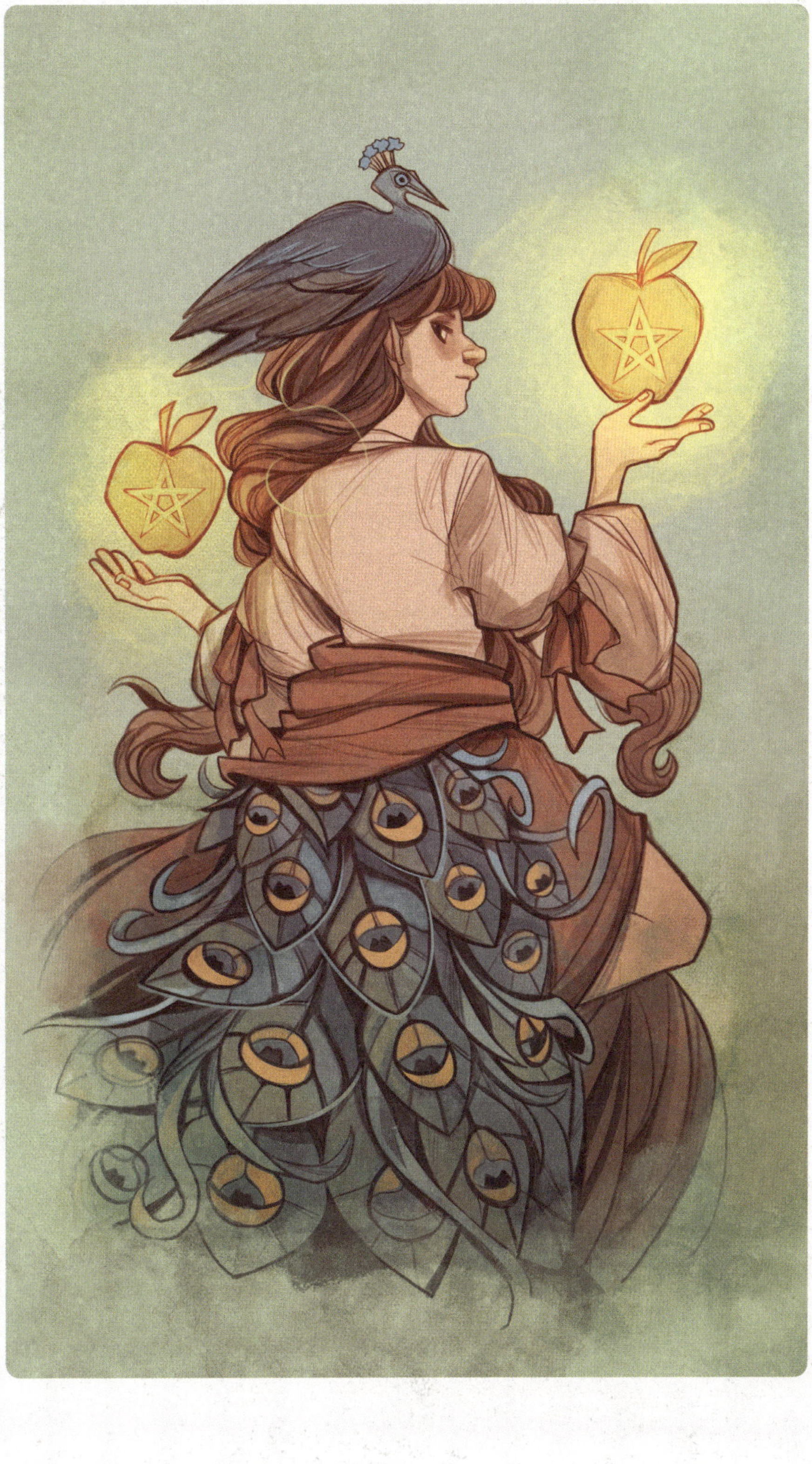

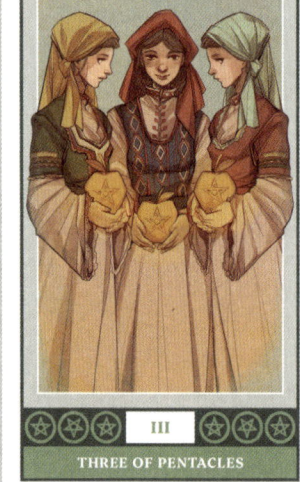

THREE OF PENTACLES

COLLABORATION, CREATIVE PROJECTS, BUILDING

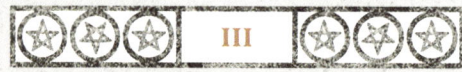

Let's get back to the Bulgarian version once more. The three brothers mentioned in the Ace of Pentacles try to find the hala that's stealing the apples. They reach a deep hole in the ground and lower the youngest brother into it using ropes. When he reaches the bottom, he comes upon a house where he sees three maidens playing with apples. They give him directions and clues to the hala's location. In the original story only two of the girls are playing with two apples, but I show them all holding apples here, in a moment of collaboration that fits the theme.

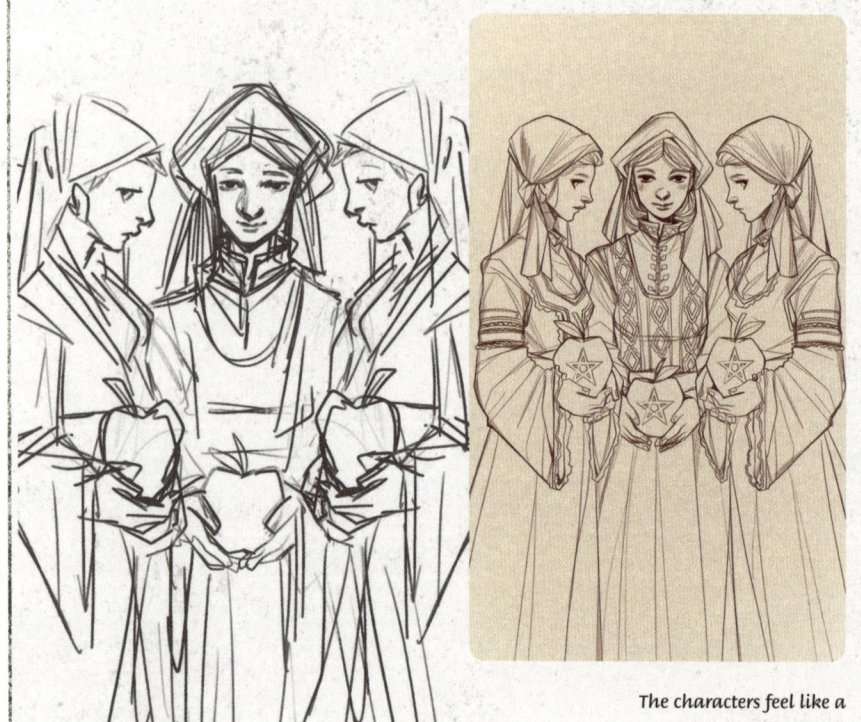

The characters feel like a harmonious unit, which fits the card's themes

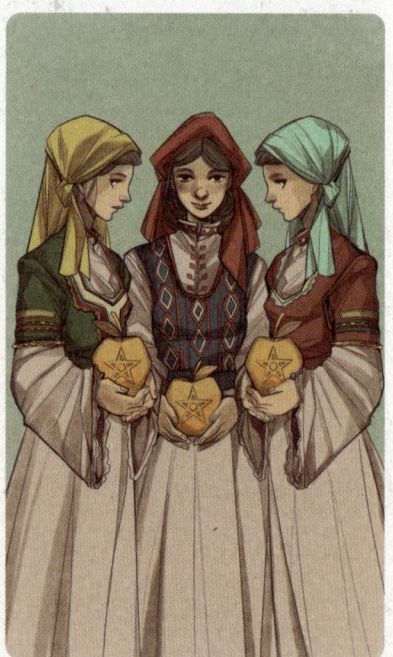

The clues and help from the three maidens are essential to the young brother's success

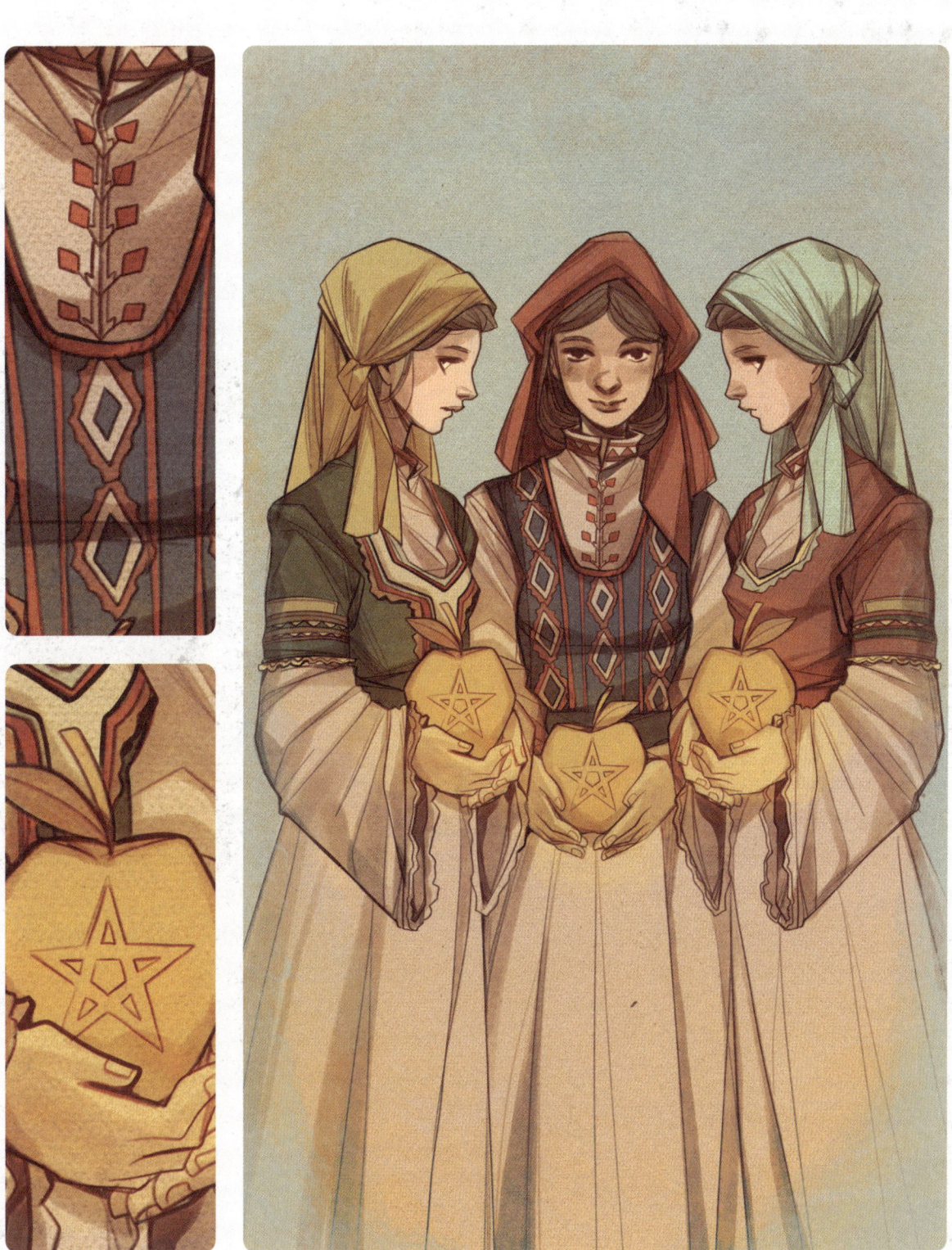

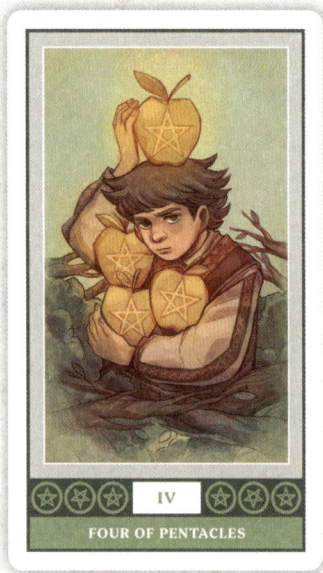

FOUR OF PENTACLES

FOUR OF PENTACLES

FOUNDATION, SECURITY, PARSIMONY

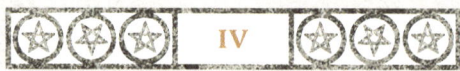

In most versions I am familiar with, the golden apple tree grows in the gardens of noble families such as kings and emperors. Here, however, I refer to both the Ukrainian and Bulgarian variations, where the tree grows in the garden of a rather humble or even poor family's house. In the Ukrainian version, the villain that steals the apples is a hog, not a hala, but they both share a moment of the family members trying to protect their apples and the little that they have. In my Four of Pentacles, a character holds four golden apples guardedly.

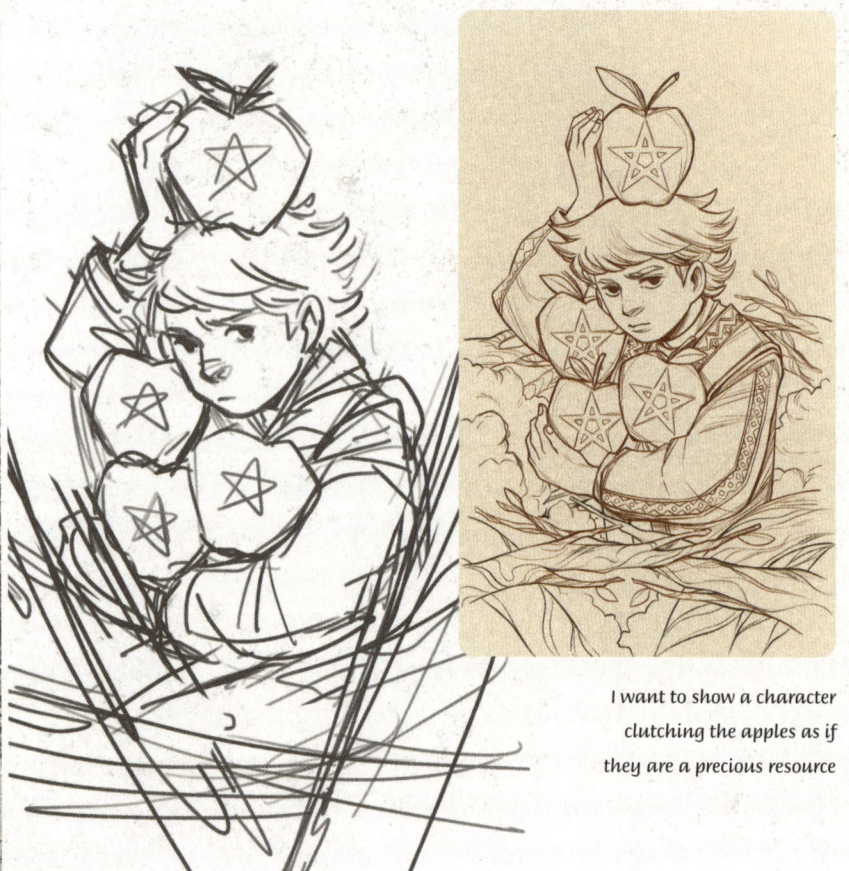

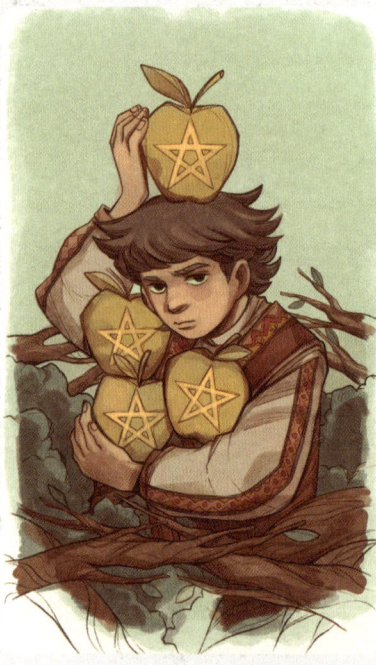

I want to show a character clutching the apples as if they are a precious resource

The boy frowns cautiously at the viewer, showing the card's possessive side

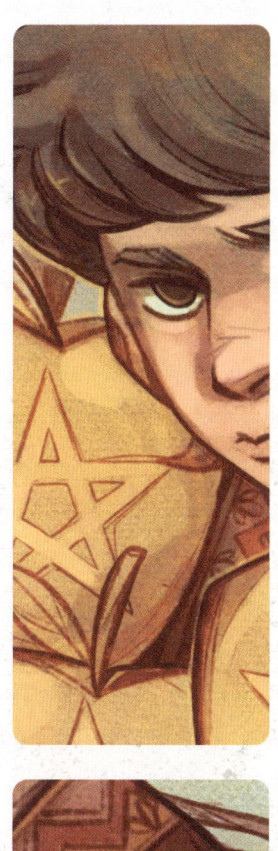

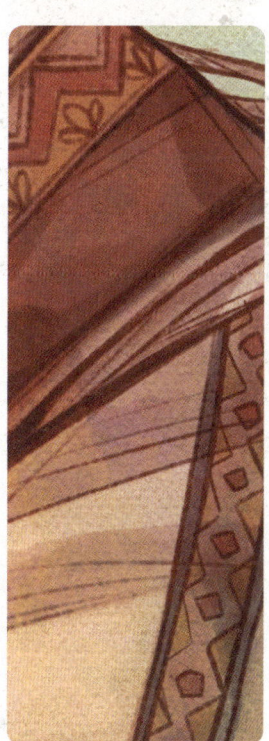

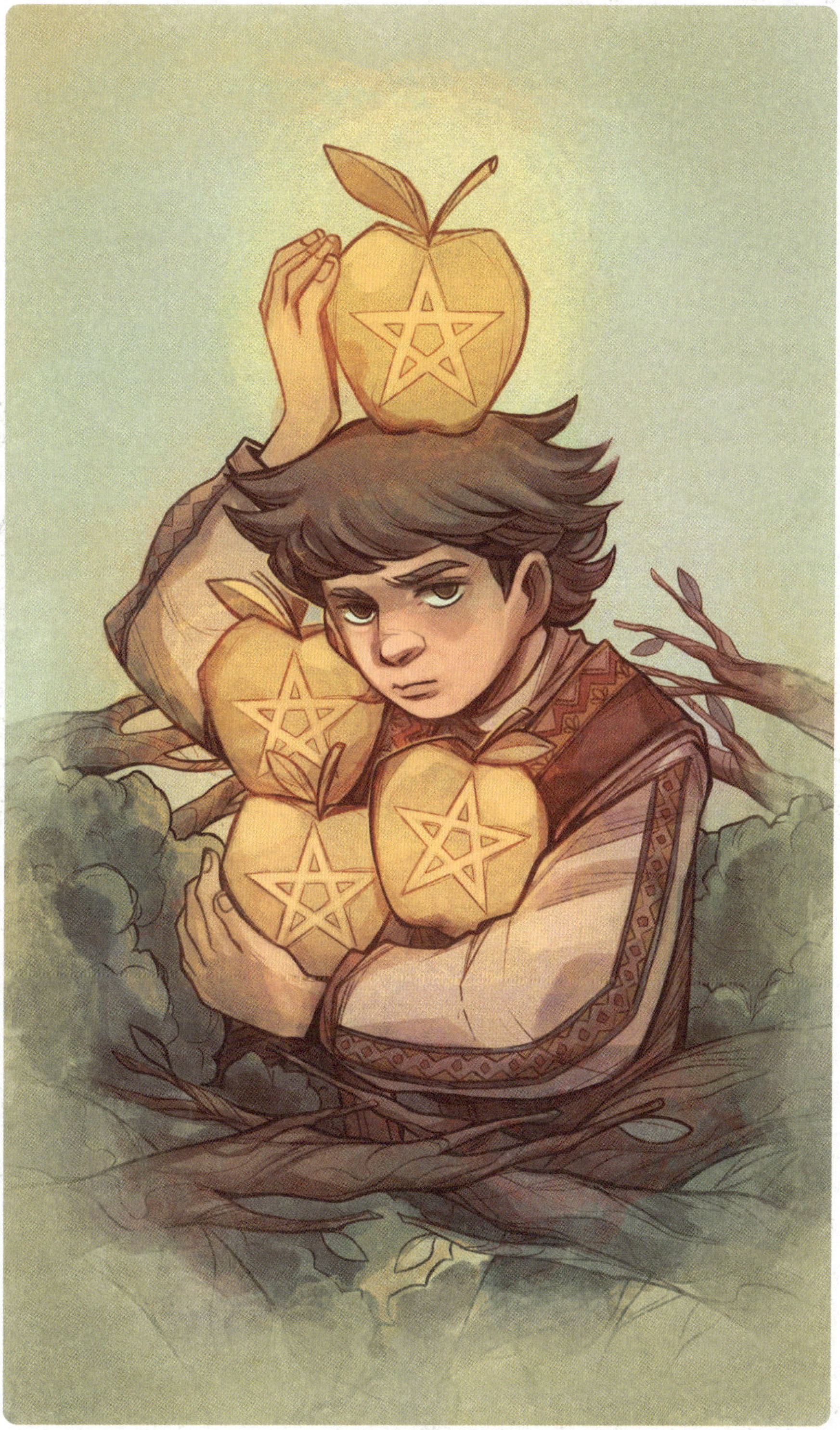

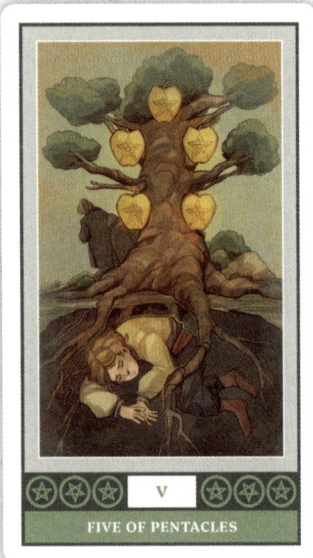

FIVE OF PENTACLES

FIVE OF PENTACLES

HARDSHIP, HIGHS AND LOWS OF RELATIONSHIPS, MISMANAGEMENT

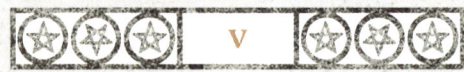

As this card's less-optimistic theme is hard to approach in a traditional way, I look for this feeling of loss, isolation, and poverty in the Ukrainian tale, *The Three Brothers*. In this story, the third brother is known as a 'fool', and his older brothers are condescending towards him. He defeats the hog that stole the apples, but his brothers kill him and bury him under the tree, taking the dead hog to their father and claiming all the glory. Later on, a man cuts a branch from the tree to make a flute. Whenever someone tries to play the flute, it plays of its own accord with the voice of the buried brother, who tells of his unfortunate fate through a song.

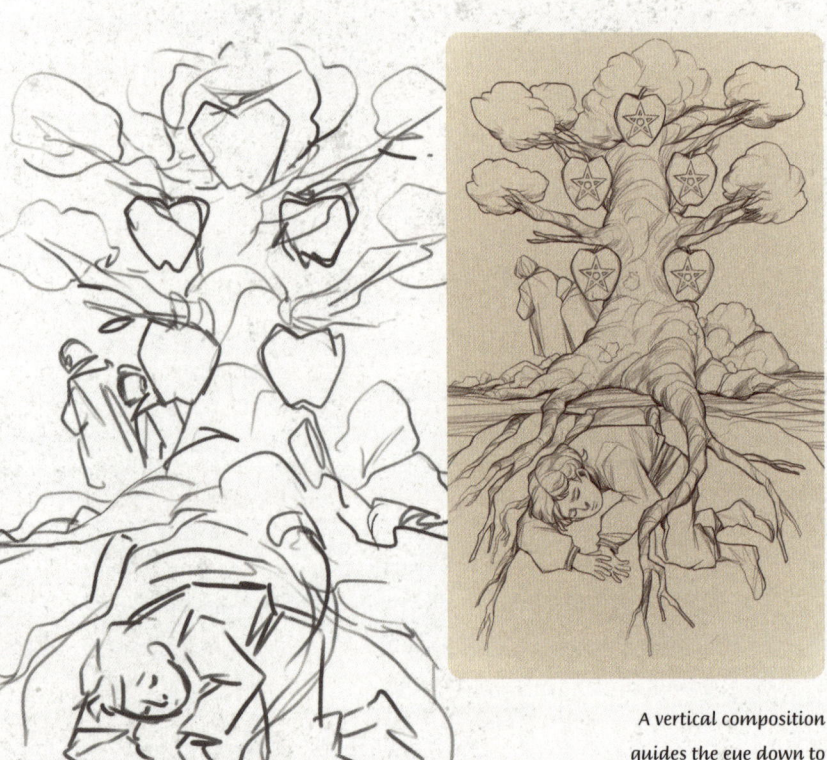

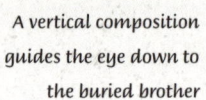

A vertical composition guides the eye down to the buried brother

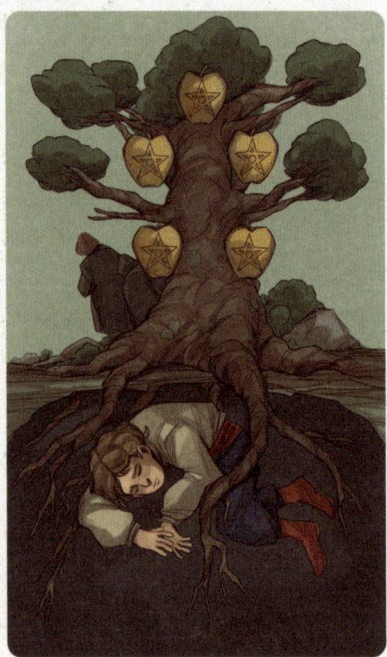

The older brothers are in the background, sneaking away after their terrible deed

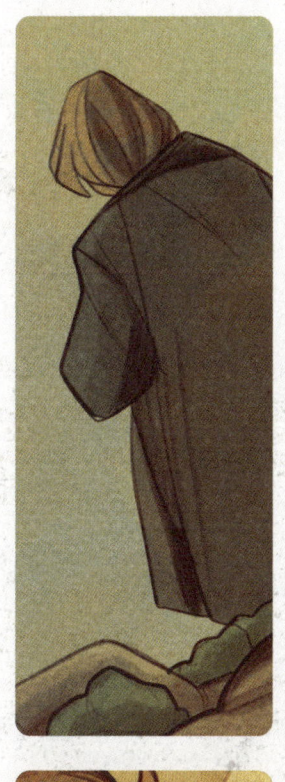

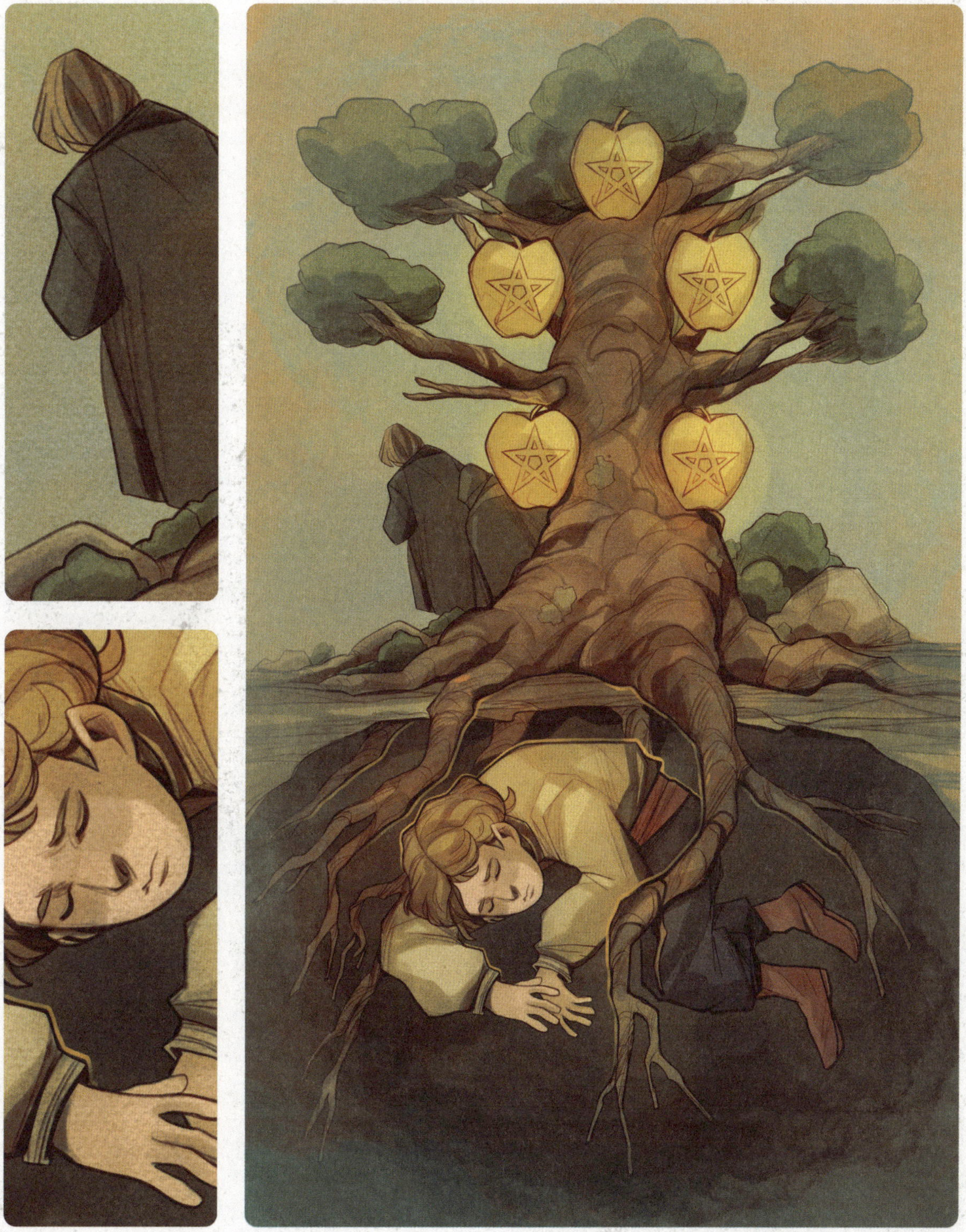

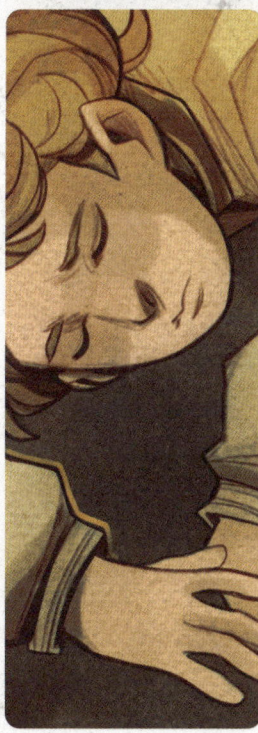

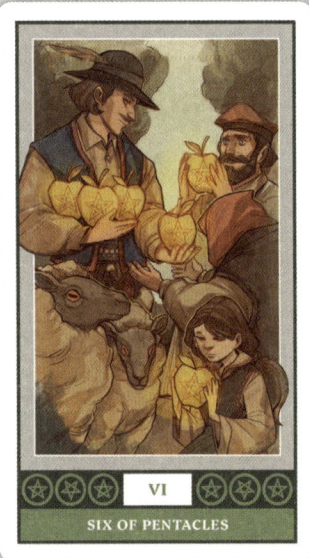

SIX OF PENTACLES

SIX OF PENTACLES

BEAUTY, GIVING, RECEIVING

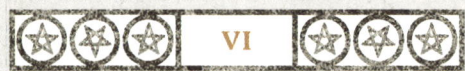

Even though one of the most well-known folk stories from Poland is *The Glass Mountain*, it's by coincidence that I find it's another 'golden apple' story! As the Six of Pentacles symbolizes generosity, sharing, and giving, I choose the moment where a shepherd is giving away golden apples to people from his village. In this story, the golden apples have healing powers, but only if they are given away for free.

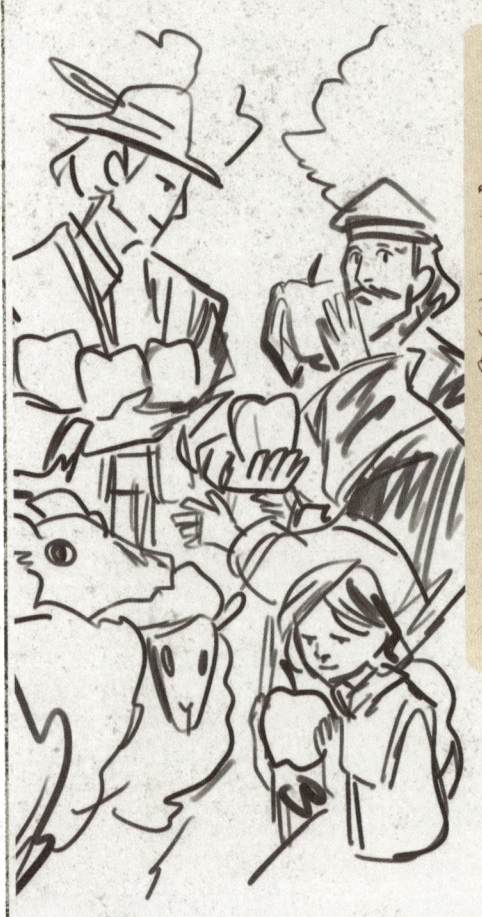

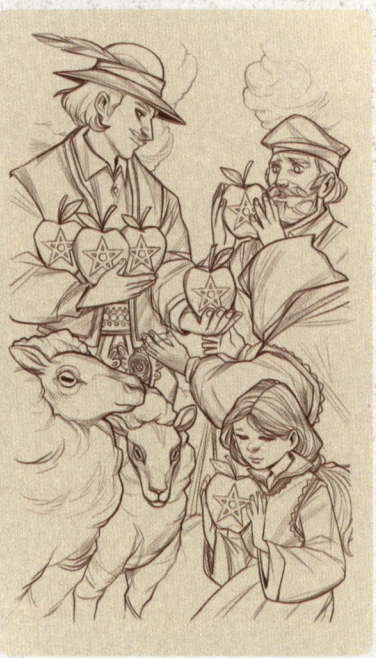

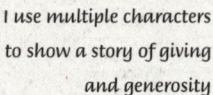

I use multiple characters to show a story of giving and generosity

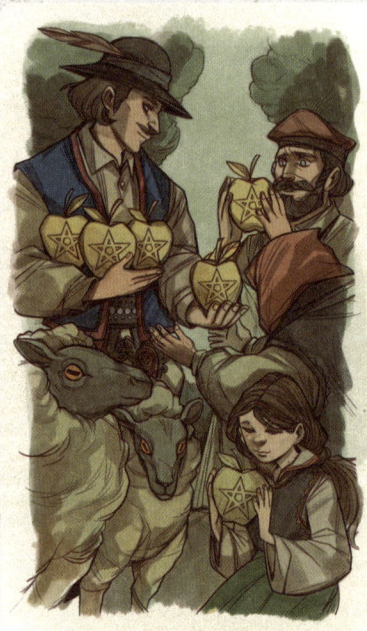

The villagers are pleased and surprised to receive the kind shepherd's gifts

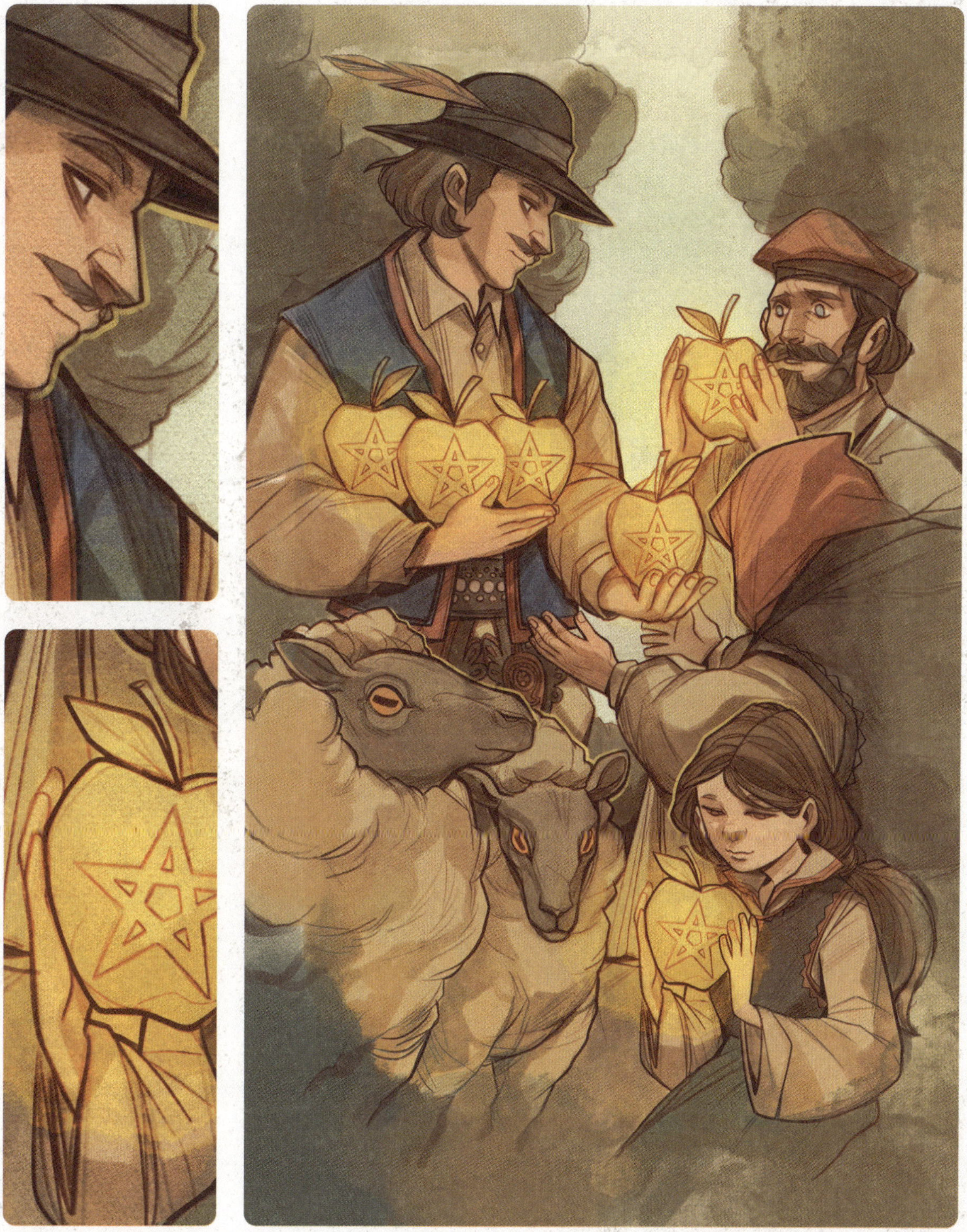

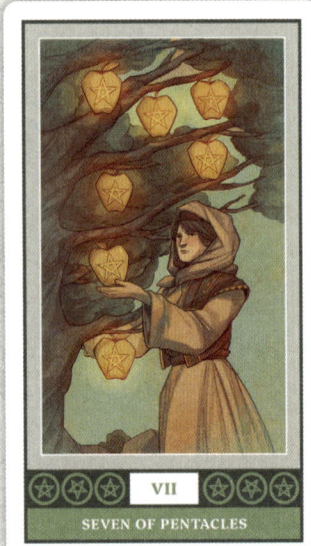

SEVEN OF PENTACLES

SEVEN OF PENTACLES

RESULTS, REASSESSMENT, RECONSIDERING

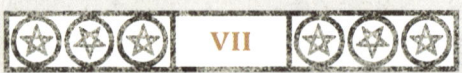

It might not be mentioned in most stories, but a garden with a golden apple tree would need to be taken care of like any other beautiful garden. It's an investment of time, hard work, and attention to detail, just like the main theme of this card. In the Rider–Waite–Smith card (see page 27), there's a little worry in the character's expression – that feeling of wondering if we'll be picking the fruits of our labour, after putting in the hard work. I want to recreate this expression in my own version, which shows the mother from the Bulgarian tale.

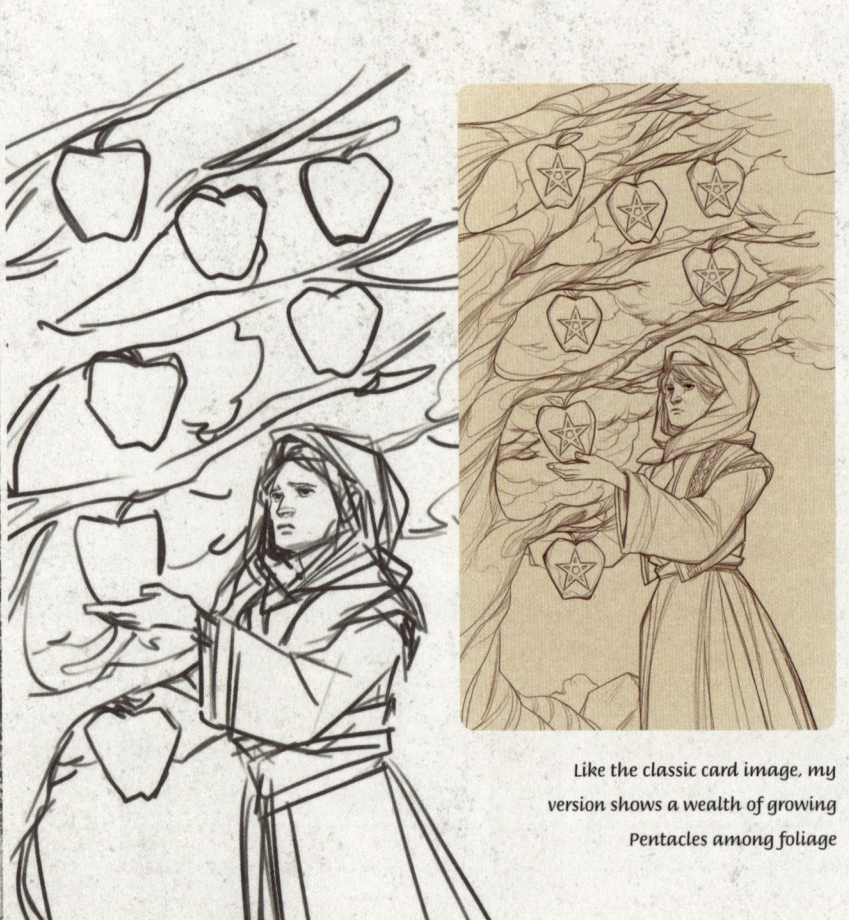

Like the classic card image, my version shows a wealth of growing Pentacles among foliage

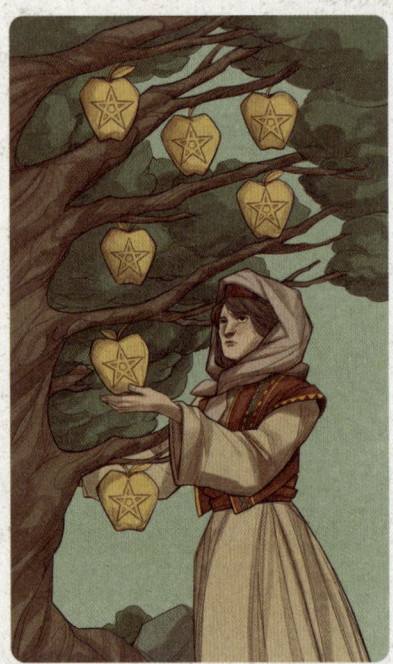

The character looks thoughtful and serious as she considers her crop of apples

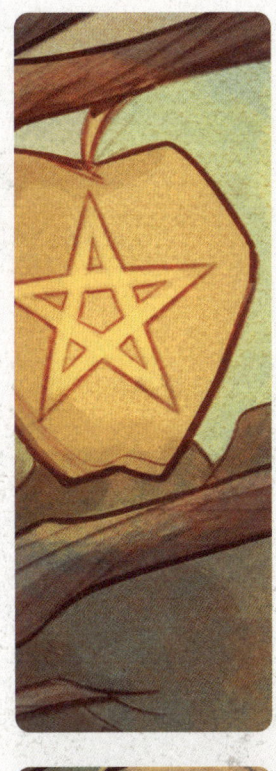

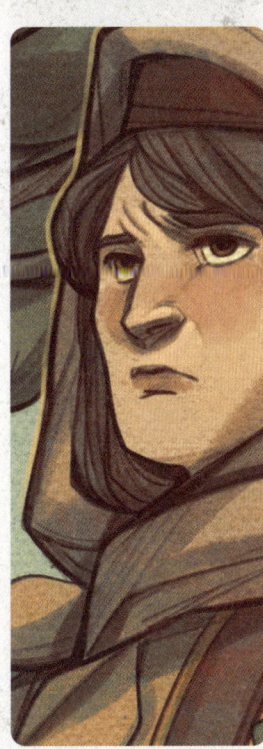

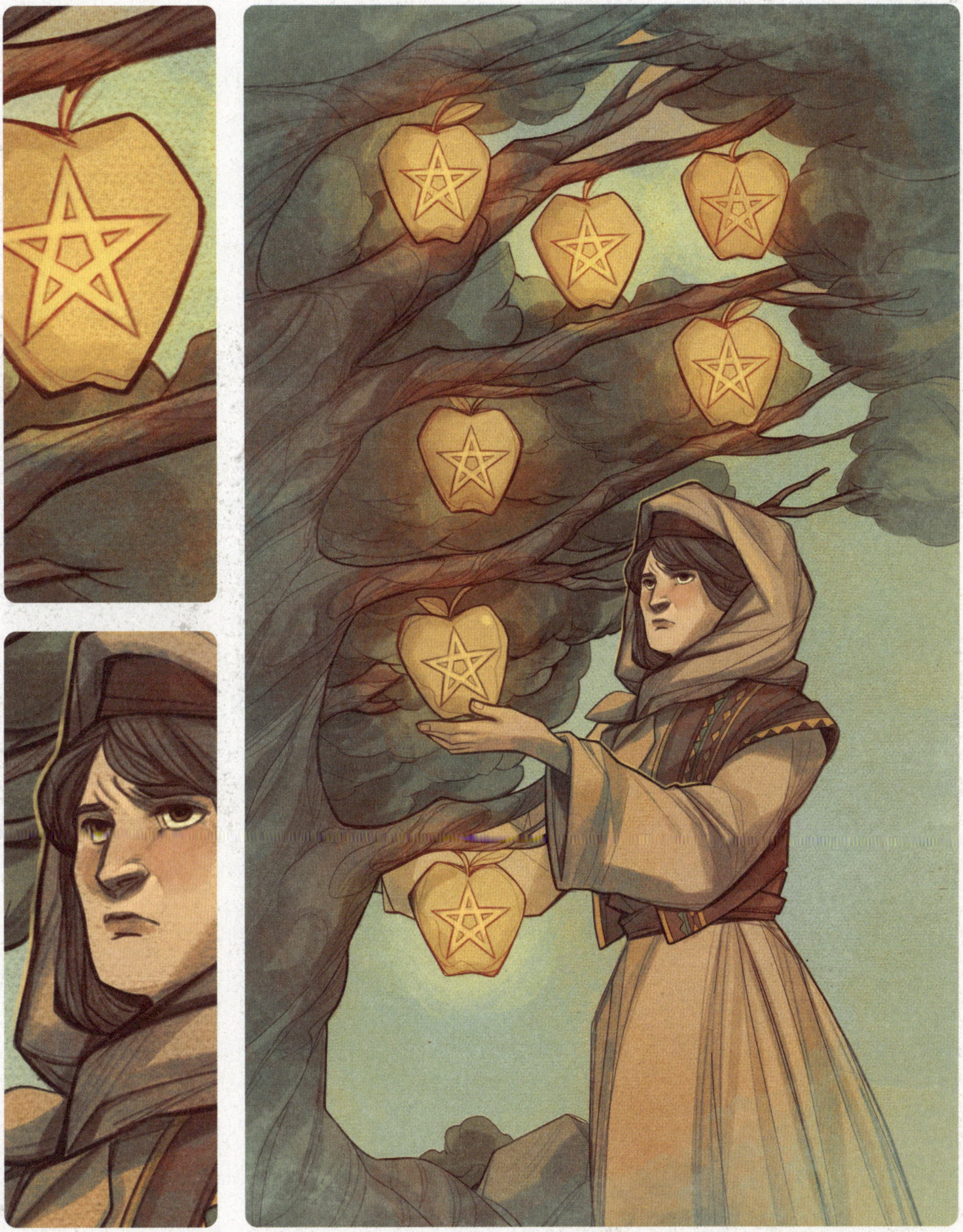

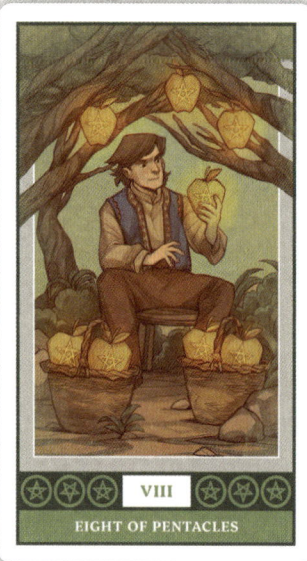

EIGHT OF PENTACLES

VIII

EIGHT OF PENTACLES

EIGHT OF PENTACLES

CRAFTSMANSHIP, DEDICATION, DILIGENCE

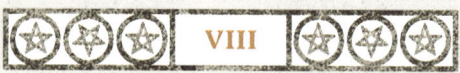

I jump back to the Polish tale about the shepherd. He does not start out as a shepherd in the story, but goes through many jobs and crafts. Despite working hard and being good at all of them, he decides that being a shepherd is what brings him the most joy and fulfilment. I think that is most fitting for the Eight of Pentacles' theme, so I show a scene where he picks his golden apples, preparing for a giveaway at his village.

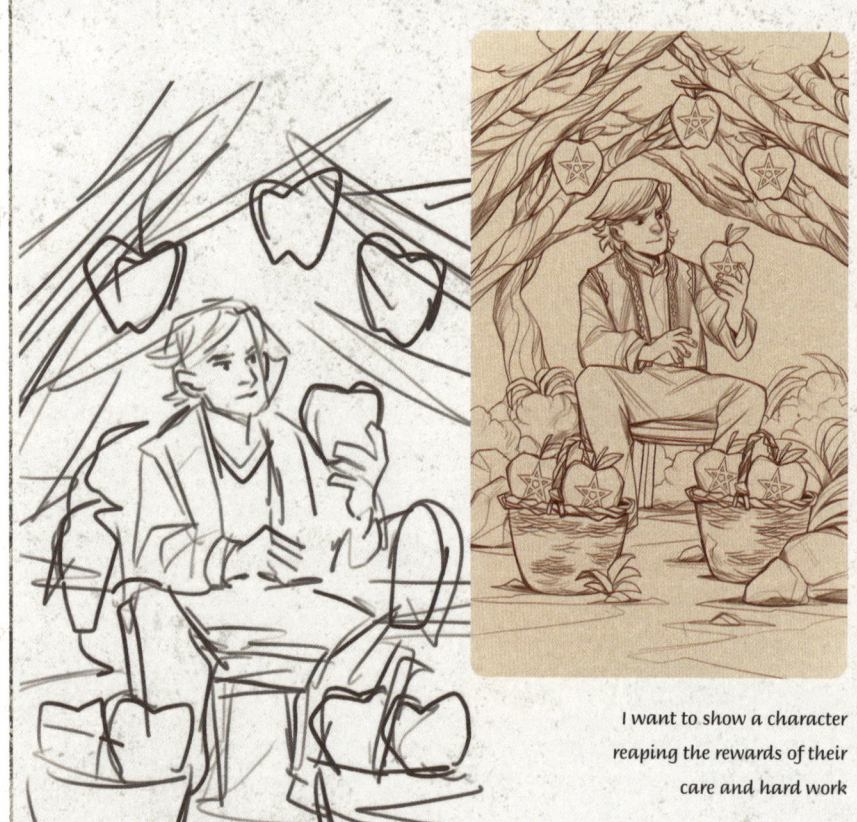

I want to show a character reaping the rewards of their care and hard work

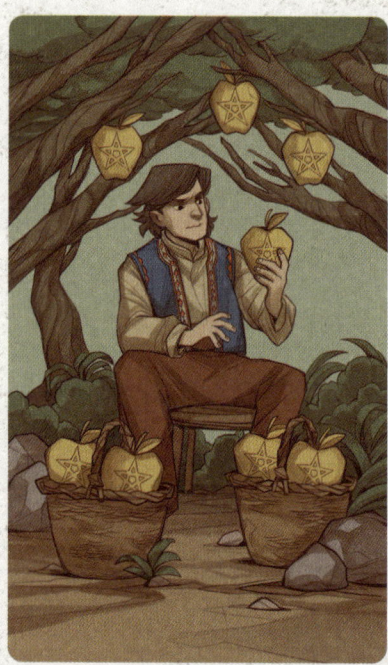

Baskets full of apples show a wealth of resources to share

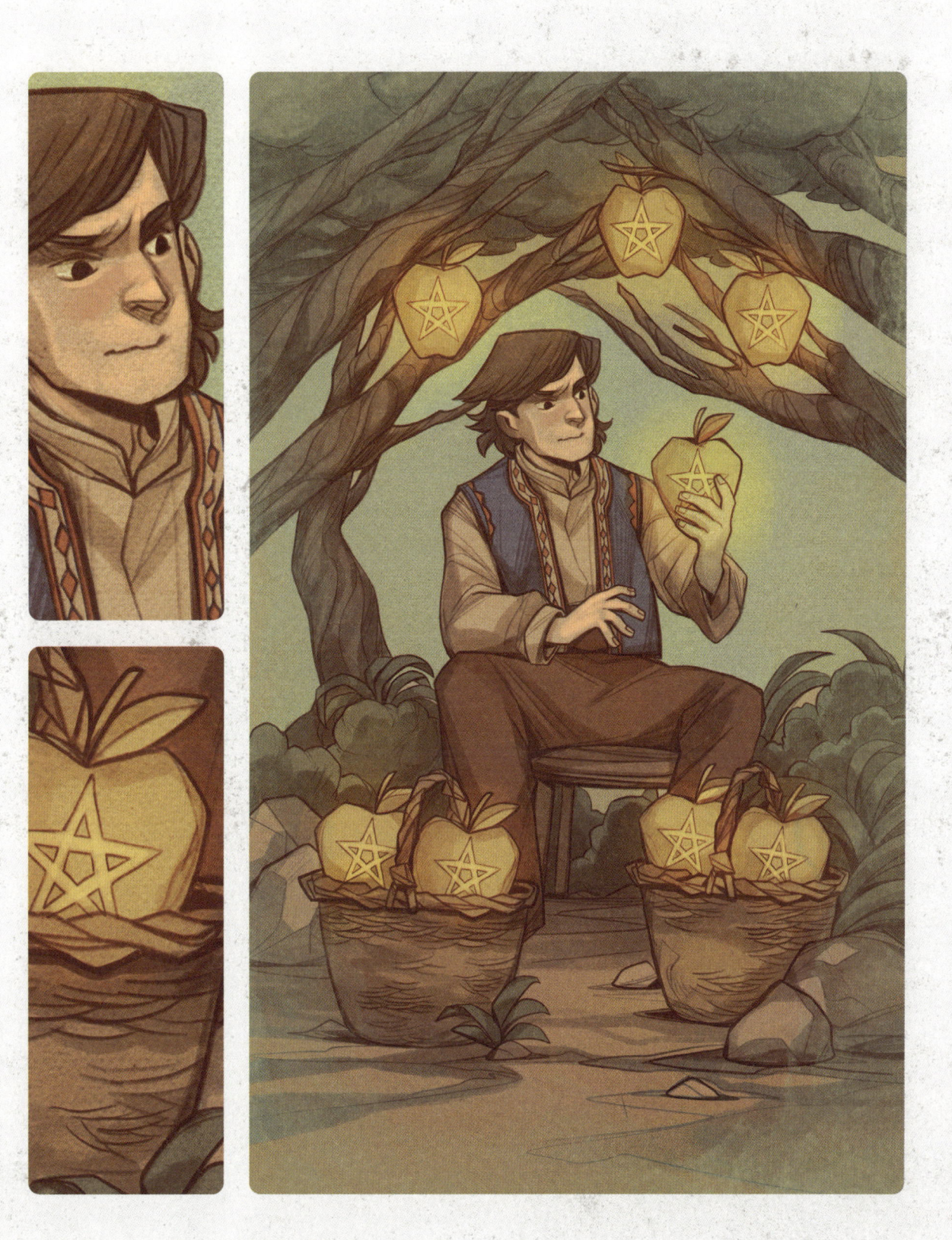

NINE OF PENTACLES

LUXURY, ELOQUENCE, PLEASURE

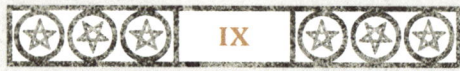

For the Nine of Pentacles, I return to the *Nine Peahens* story that inspired the Two of Pentacles. I want to depict a scene of abundance, where there is a golden apple for each of the nine peahens to take away. Only one bird hasn't picked an apple yet – she will become our future peahen maiden, who comes down from the tree to speak to the youngest brother.

NINE OF PENTACLES

IX

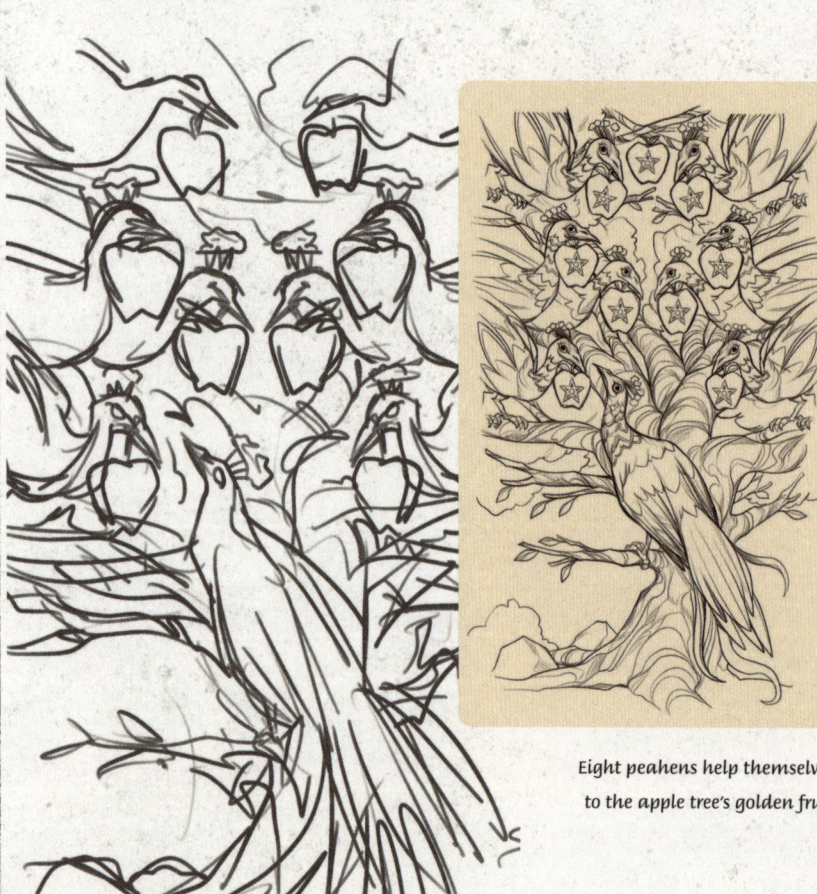

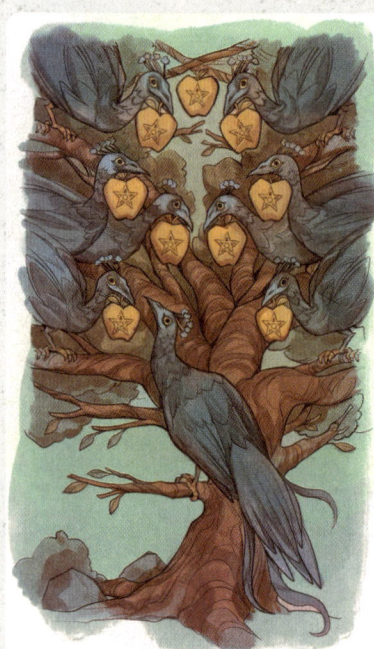

Eight peahens help themselves to the apple tree's golden fruit

Only one peahen doesn't take an apple – both the bird and apple are centred in the composition

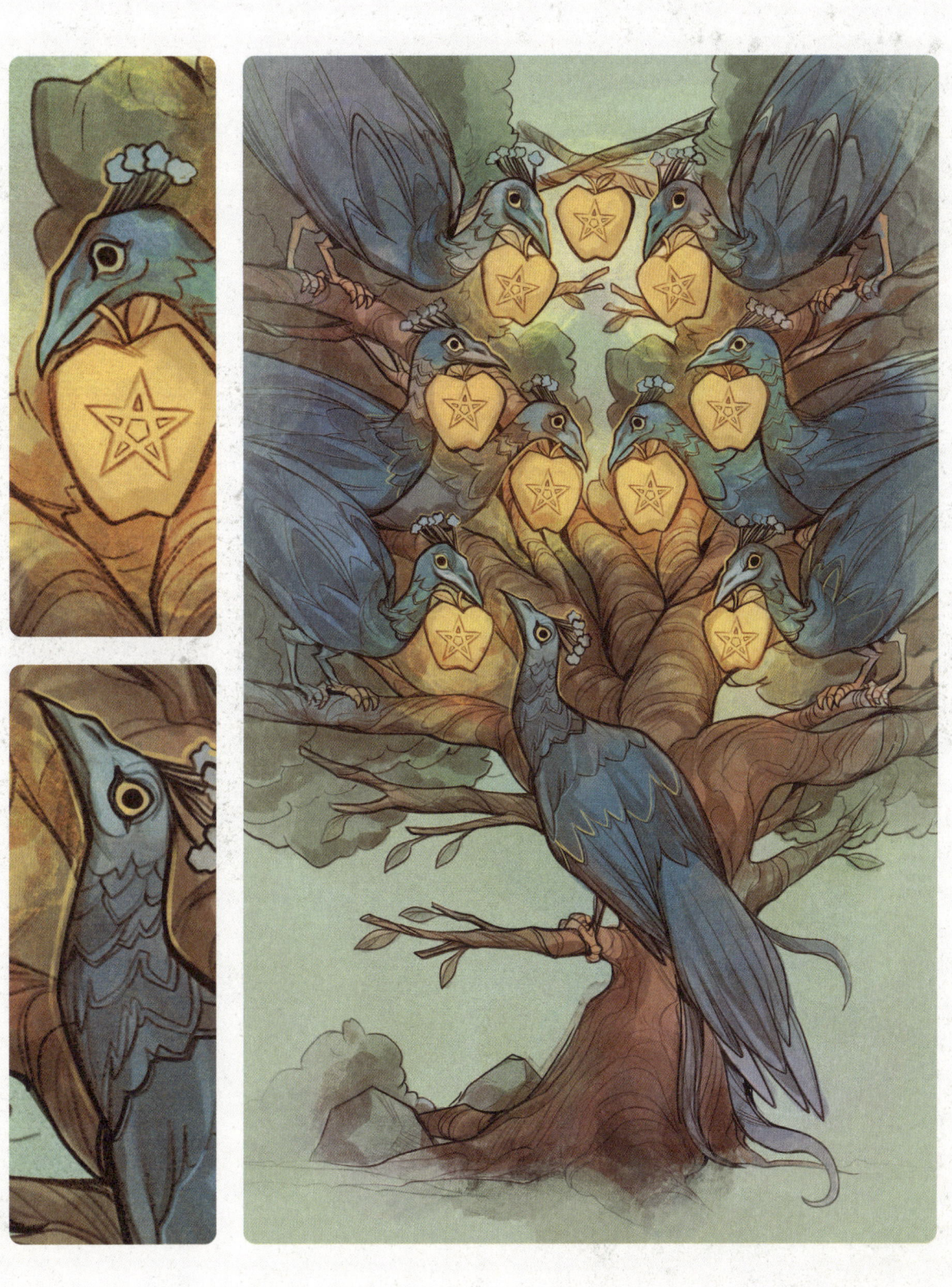

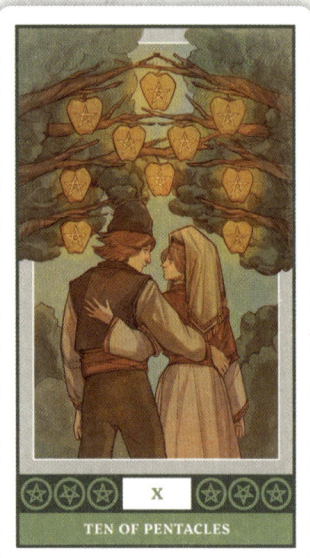

TEN OF PENTACLES

TEN OF PENTACLES

DOMESTIC BLISS, FAMILY TREE, WEALTH

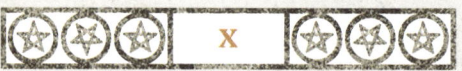

Personally, I am not at all sick of the romance and love-story aspects of most of these tales! A lot of them end with a happy wedding, and with the promise of long life, wealth, and a healthy family. For this card I pick up the end of the Bulgarian version of the tale, where the little brother marries the most beautiful of maidens that he saved from the hala.

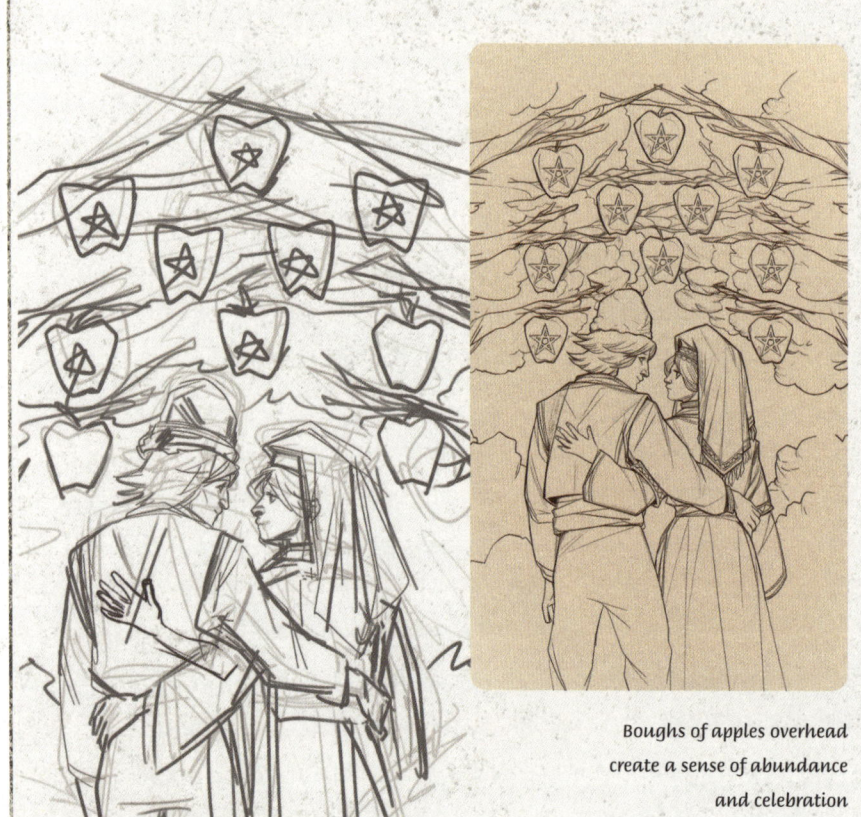

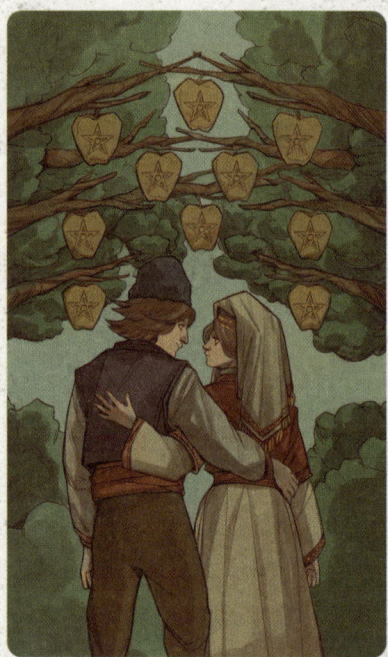

Boughs of apples overhead
create a sense of abundance
and celebration

I want this card to really
evoke that feeling of a
fairy-tale 'happy ending'

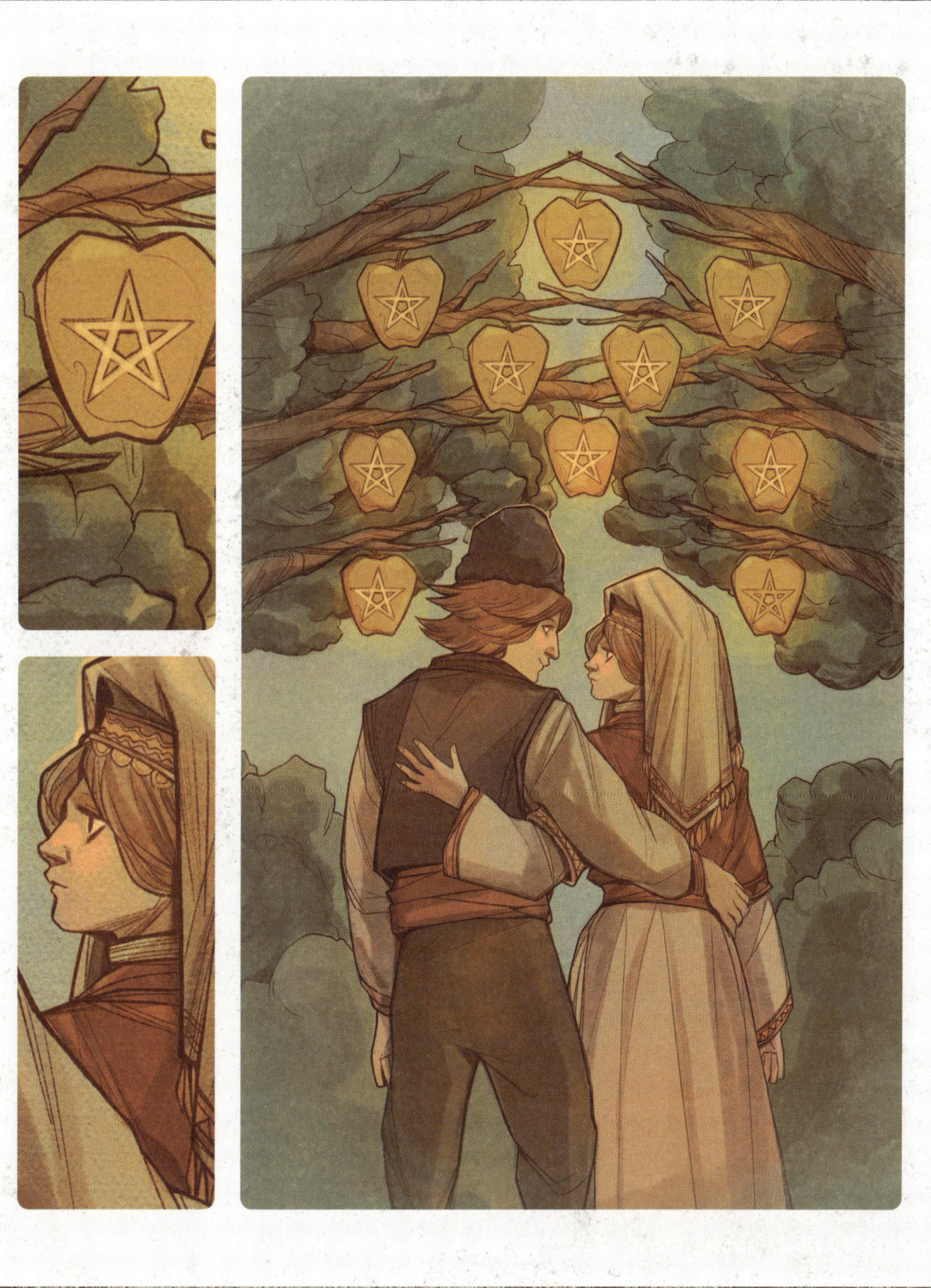

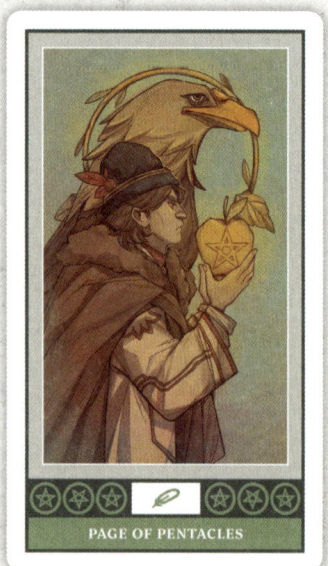

PAGE OF PENTACLES

PAGE OF PENTACLES

PHYSICALITY, LEARNING, PRACTICAL

My pick for the Page of Pentacles is once again the young brother from the Bulgarian version of the tale. He goes on a long journey in the Underworld and is helped back to the surface by a mother eagle, as a gesture of gratitude after he saved her chicks from an evil snake. Just like the Page of Pentacles, the brother shown here has not yet reached his goals, but he has all the motivation and energy to finish his mission.

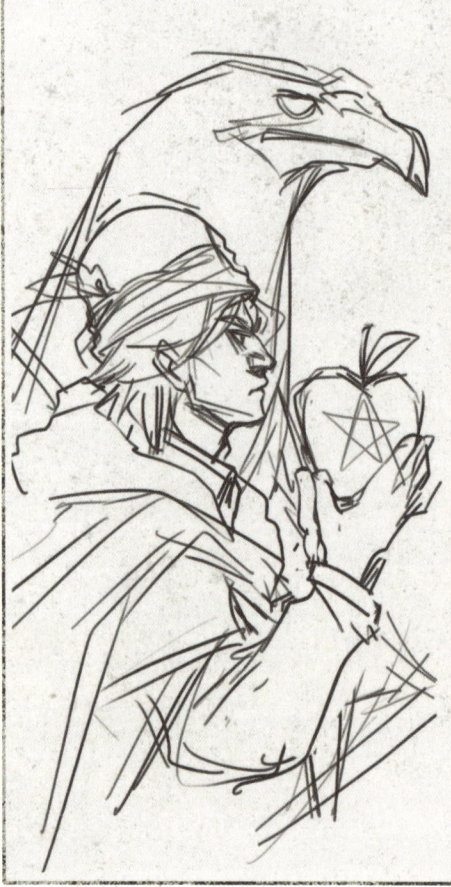

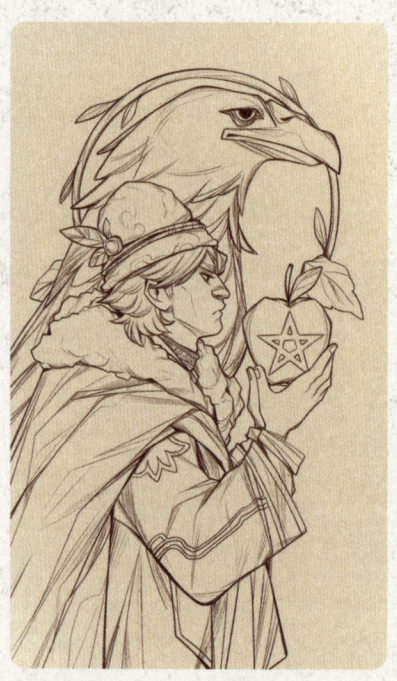

The eagle is a character that the young brother meets and helps on his journey

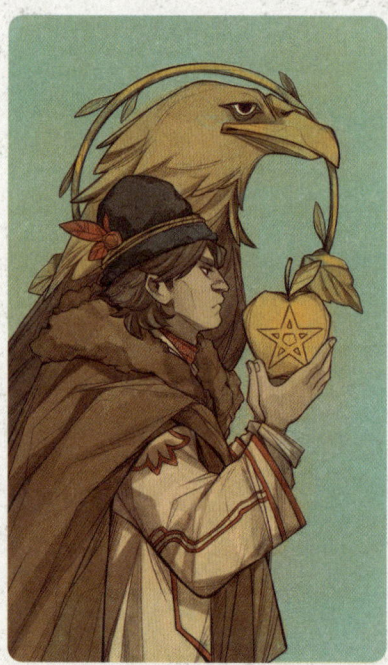

The leafy branch forms a ring – an object that factors into the brother's story later

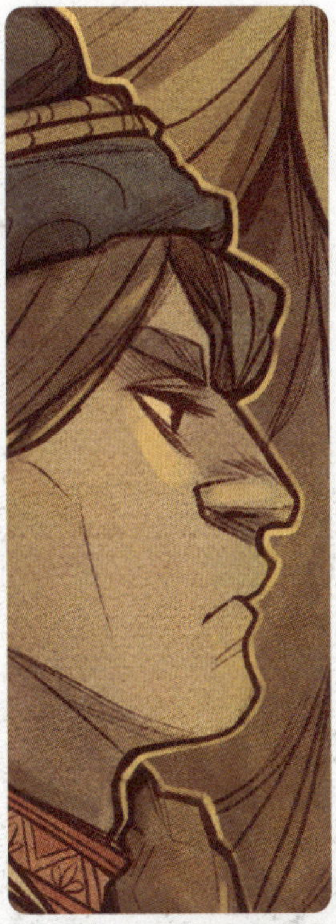

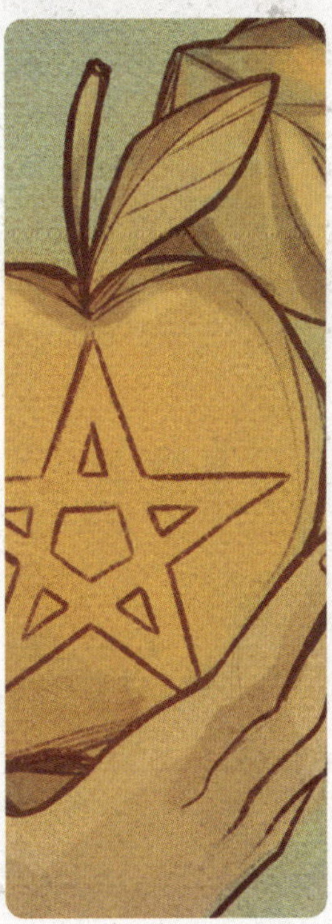

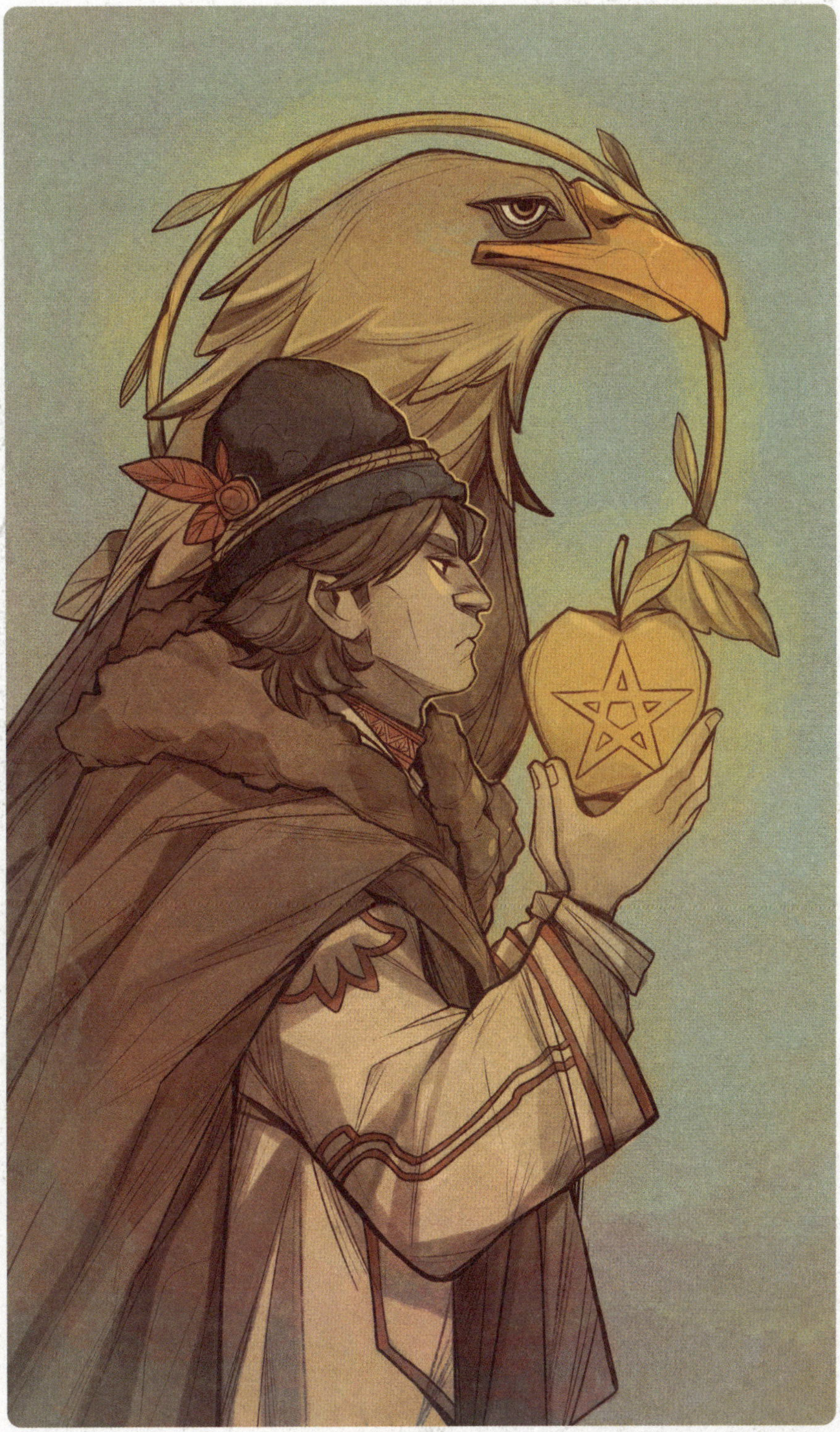

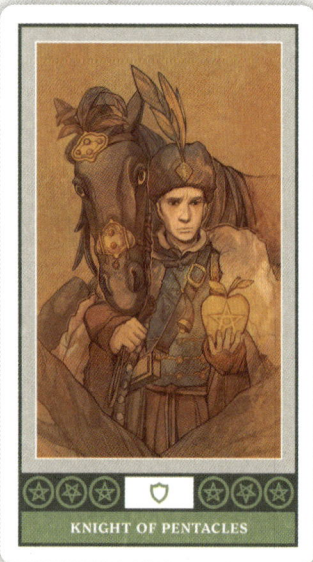

KNIGHT OF PENTACLES

KNIGHT OF PENTACLES

GROUNDED, MESSAGES, SENSUAL

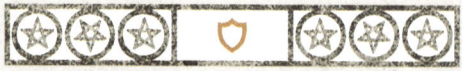

I am familiar with two versions of the Polish tale of *The Glass Mountain*, where the golden apples grant entry to a princess's castle. In one, a boy climbs the mountain but is grabbed by an eagle. He escapes by cutting off its feet and falls into the apple tree, which heals his wounds. He picks a few of the apples and ends the story by marrying the princess. In another version, the one I refer to here, a knight is one of many who attempt to climb the mountain. At the top, he defeats a dragon by throwing an apple at it, and he marries the princess afterwards.

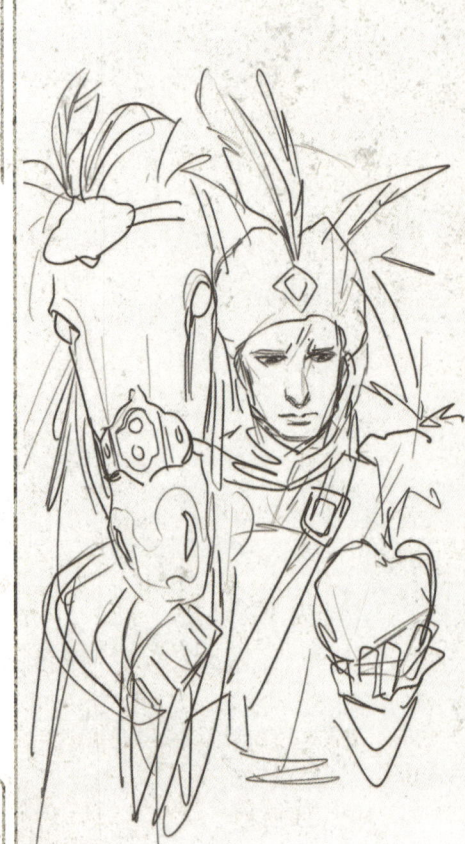

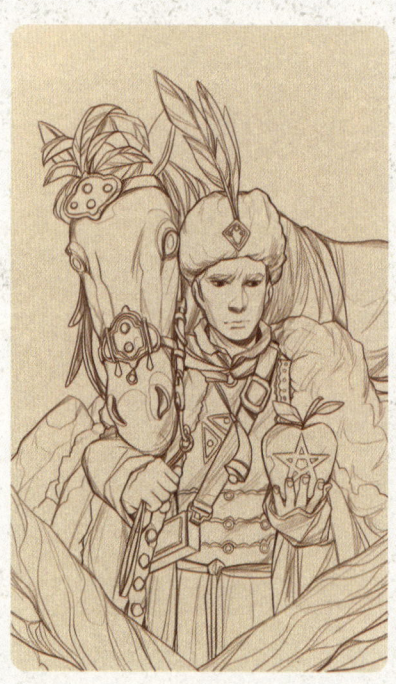

Here a brave knight, or soldier, contemplates an apple he has picked

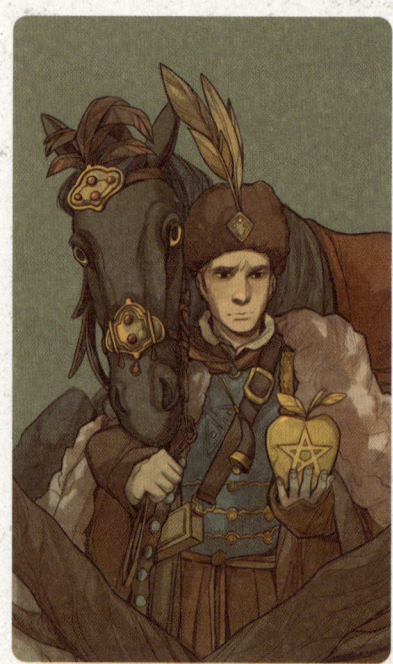

With his horse and heavy cloak, the character appears to be in the middle of his journey

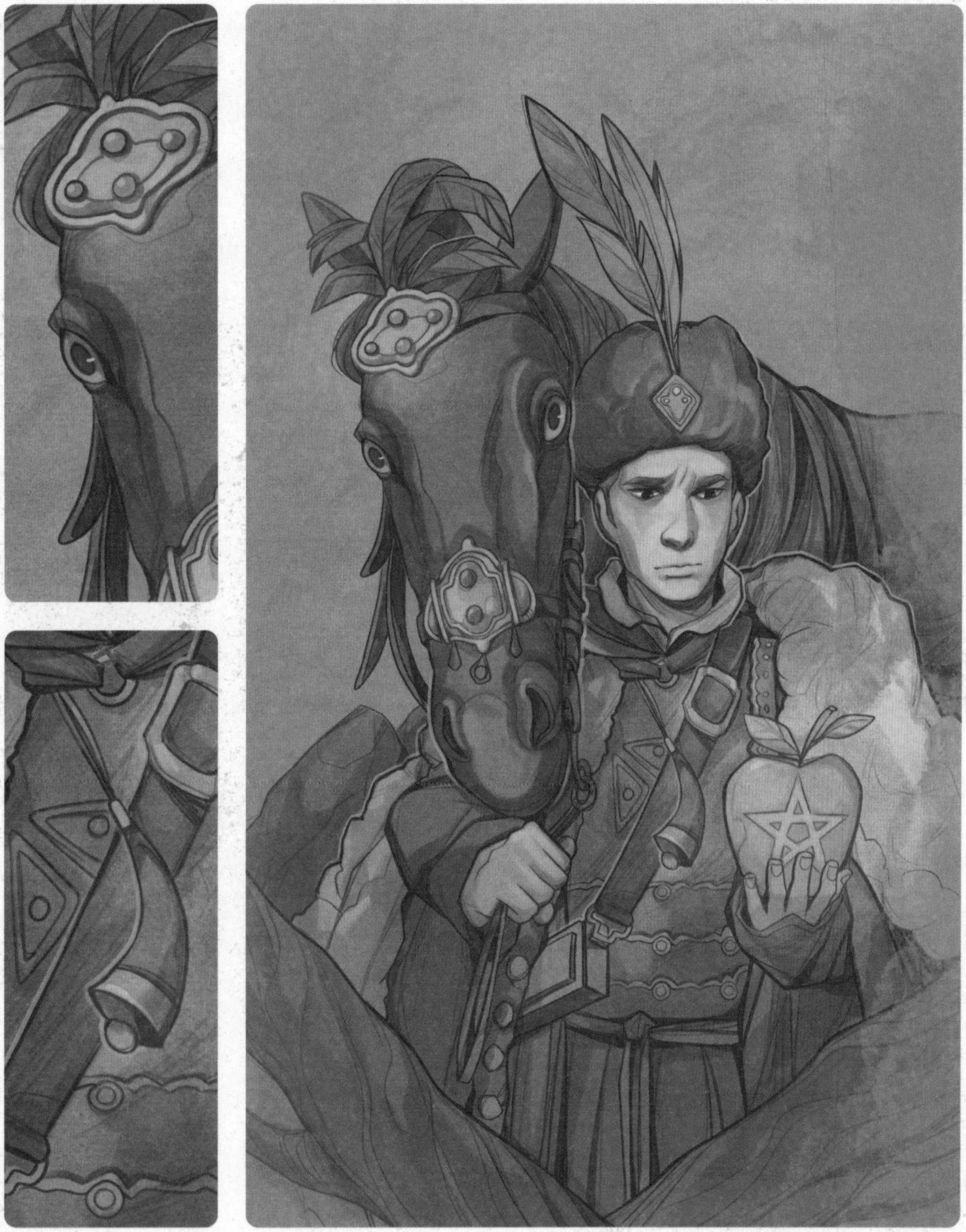

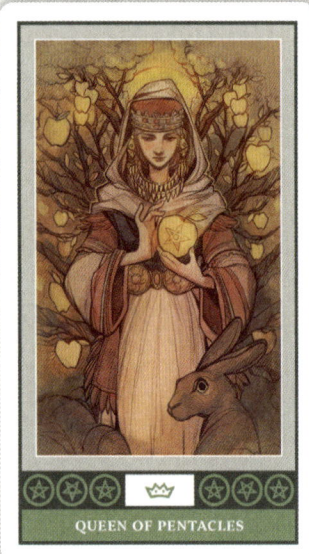

QUEEN OF PENTACLES

CAREGIVER, GROWER, SKILFUL

In the Bulgarian tale, one of the apple-bearing maidens tells the youngest brother that she will marry the man who gives her magical clothes that 'make themselves'. Before they part ways, she gives him a ring, and warns him that his brothers will fight over her when they see her. When he reunites with her after his dangerous journey, she has not chosen an older brother to marry, as they have failed her challenge. He returns her ring, which turns into beautiful clothes, and the two are married. For the Queen of Pentacles, I want to show a character who feels as mysterious, careful, and clever as that maiden.

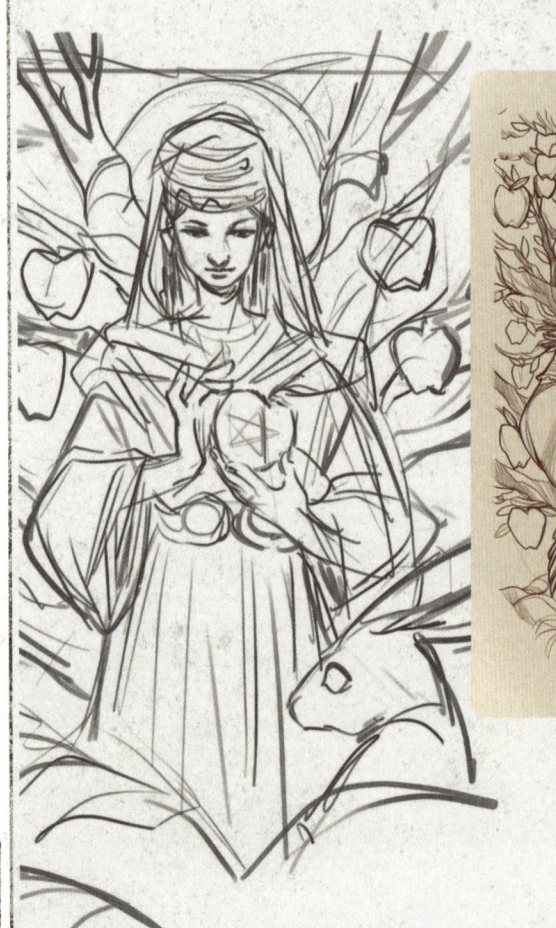

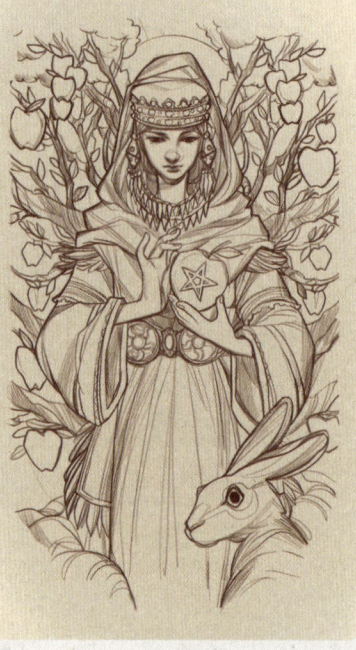

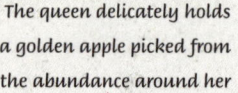

*The queen delicately holds
a golden apple picked from
the abundance around her*

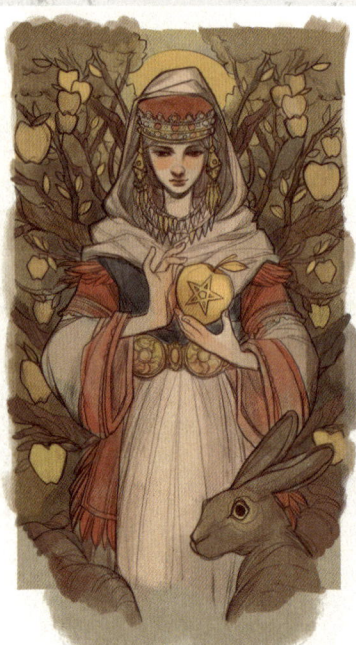

*She is dressed in beautiful
garments and jewellery that
feel ornate and mystical*

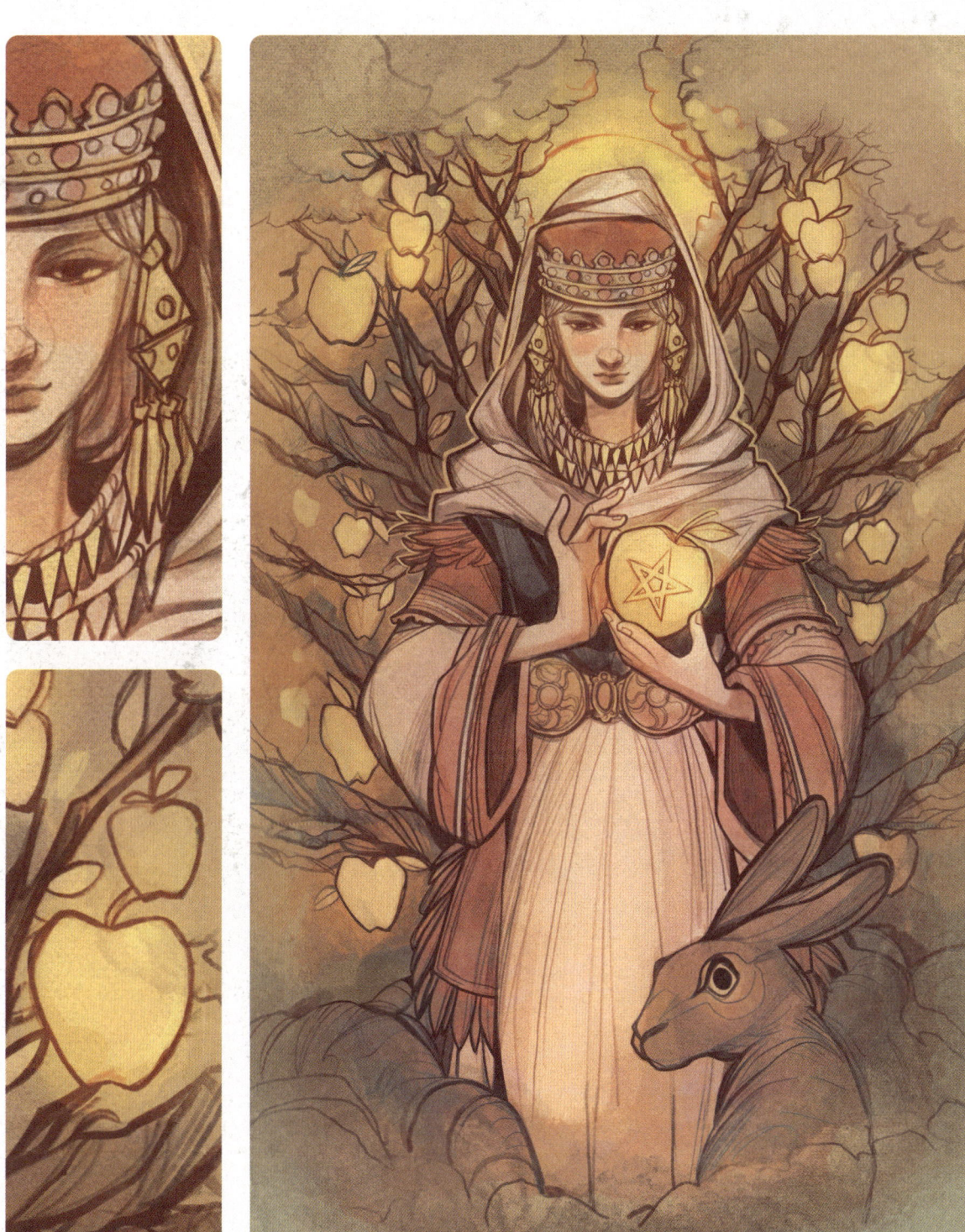

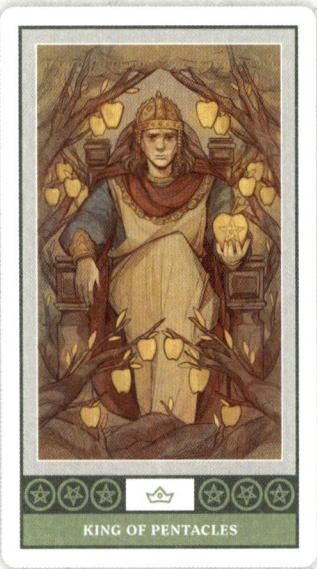

KING OF PENTACLES

PROPERTY, WEALTH, RICHES

As I mentioned in previous descriptions, a lot of these tales include noble people such as kings, emperors, and empresses. In fairy tales, we imagine that any knight or prince, or whoever wins the princess's hand at the end, will eventually become a king. For this card, I want to imagine the little brother from *The Nine Peahens and the Golden Apple* as a king. He is someone who has been through many challenges, but has now earned wealth, leadership, and security.

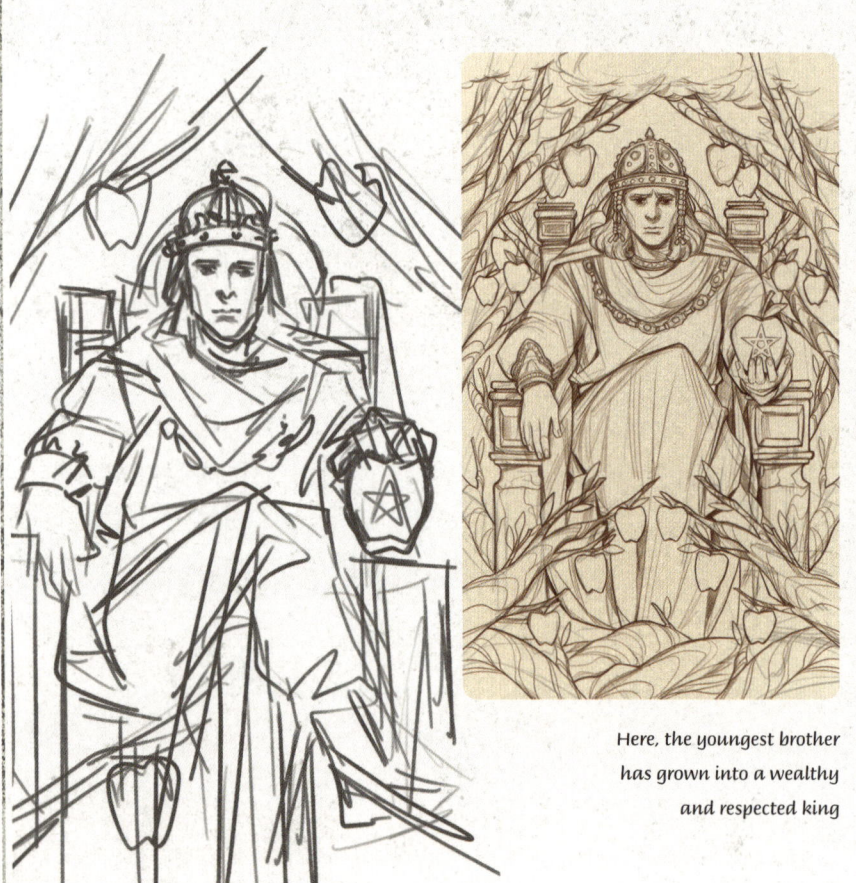

Here, the youngest brother has grown into a wealthy and respected king

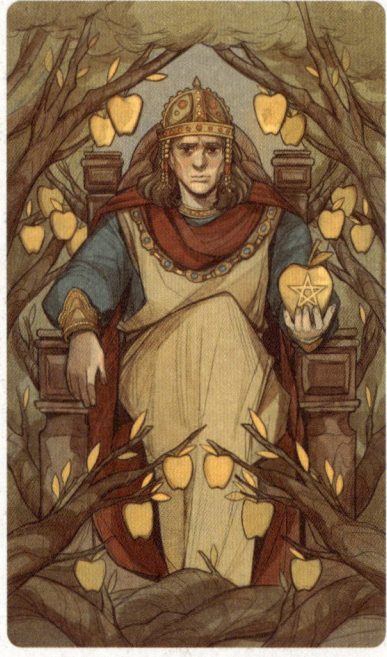

The seated, central composition gives the character gravitas

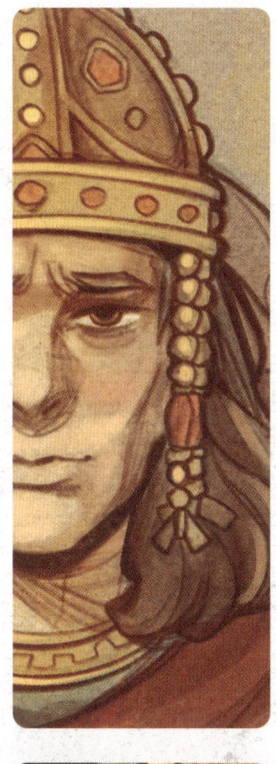

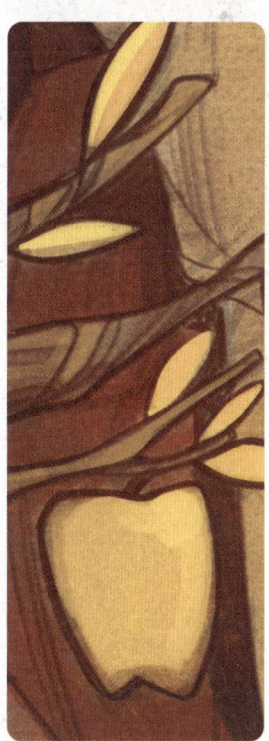

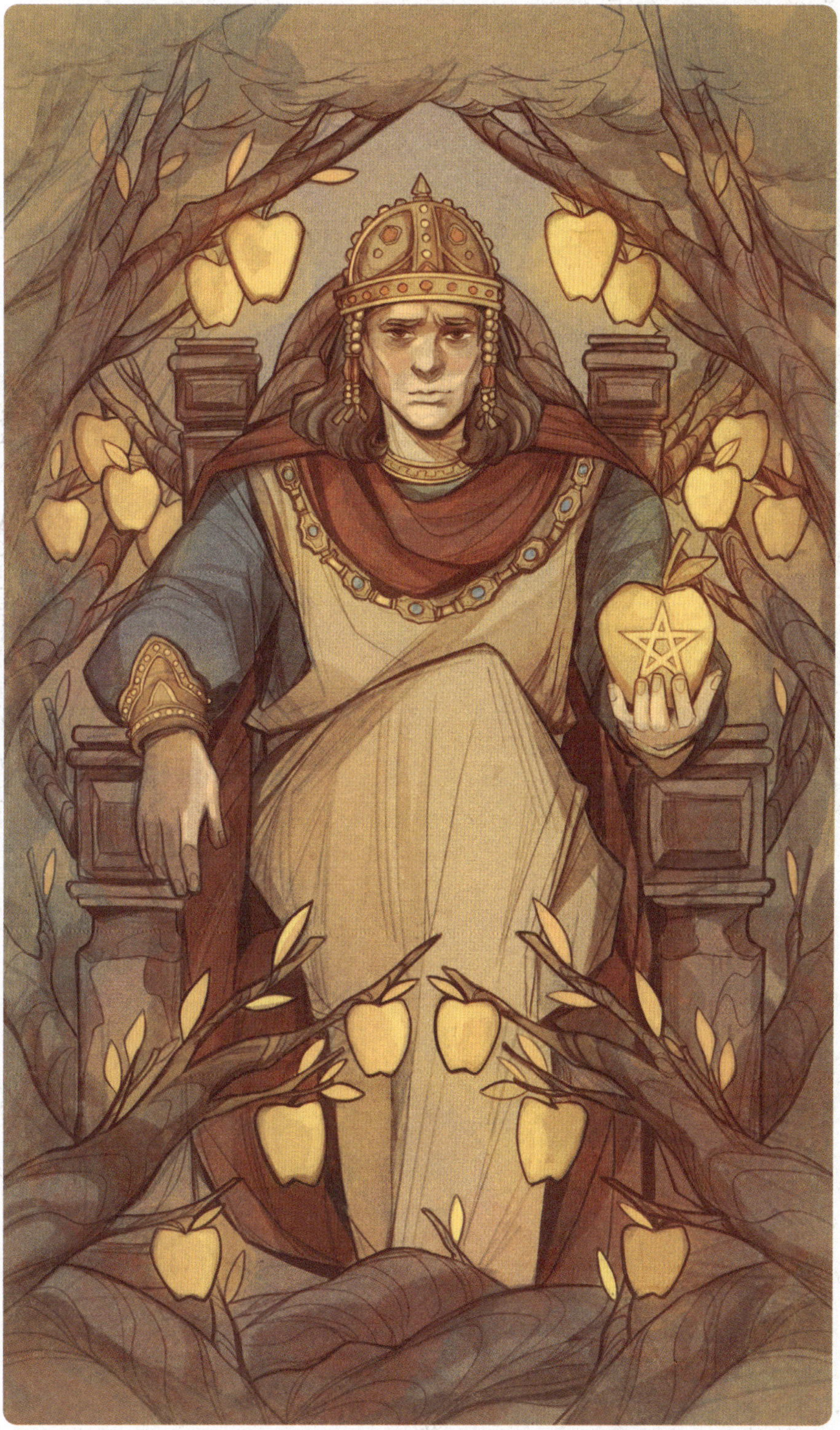

ARTIST'S CONCLUSION

The Pentacles were a challenge for me to interpret, as they symbolize more definite and material things, like labour and wealth, but I found the suit really interesting to work on. As I went through these stories, I realized that I'd actually forgotten how much they have inspired me. It's definitely refreshing to revisit things you liked from childhood and bring them to life using the experience from your creative journey and life as a grown person. What I would love to inspire in people looking at this suit is a spark of interest in the stories related to themselves – in working with elements from their own culture and seeing how they connect.

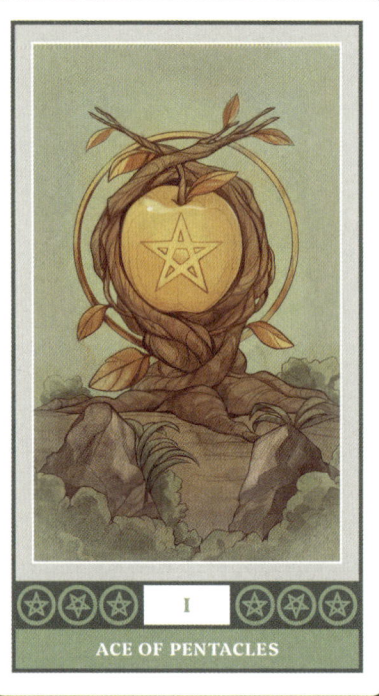

I

ACE OF PENTACLES

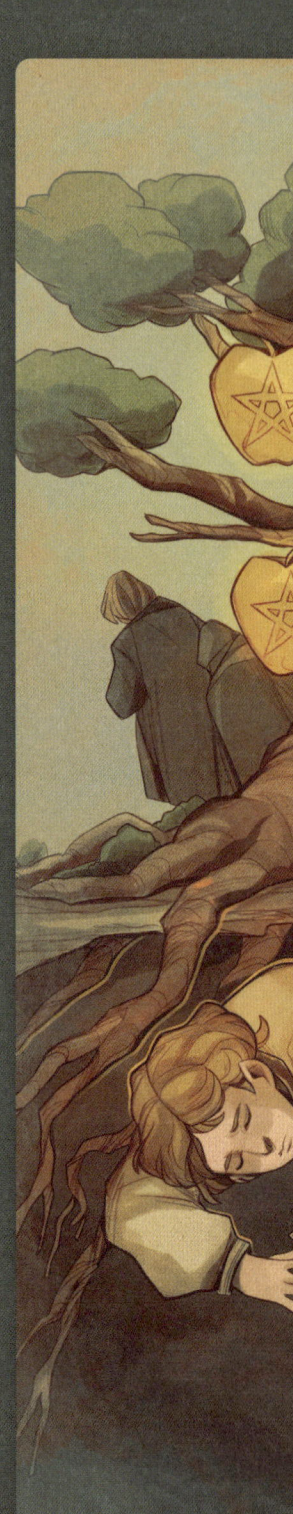

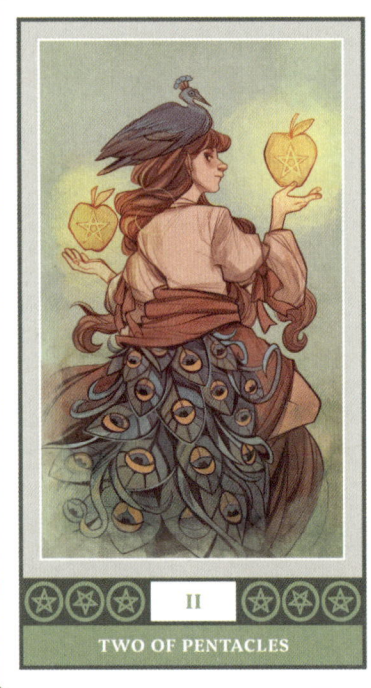

II

TWO OF PENTACLES

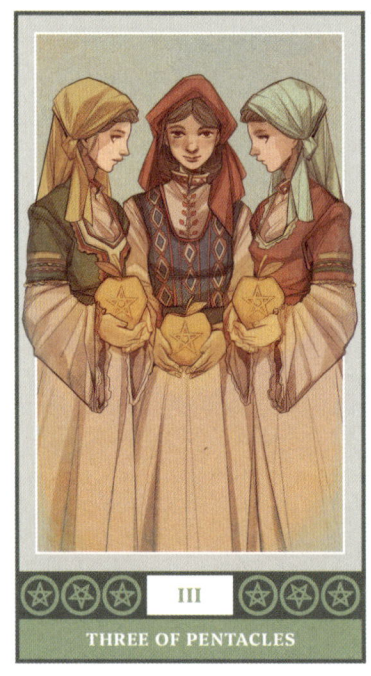

III

THREE OF PENTACLES

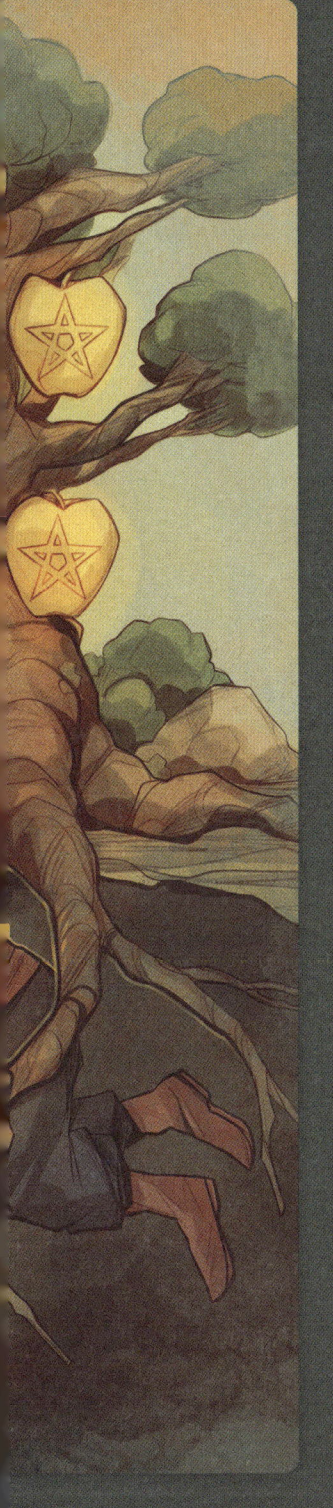

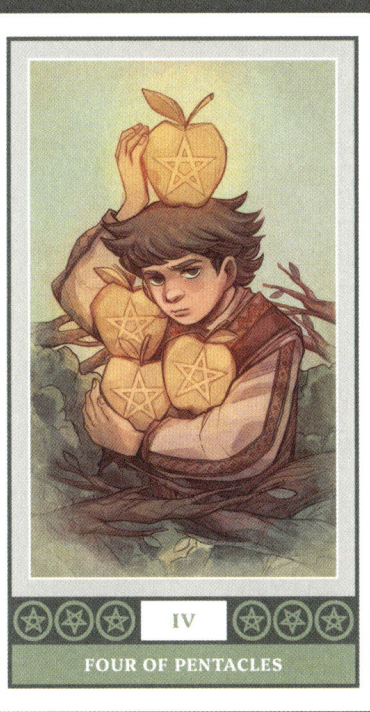

IV

FOUR OF PENTACLES

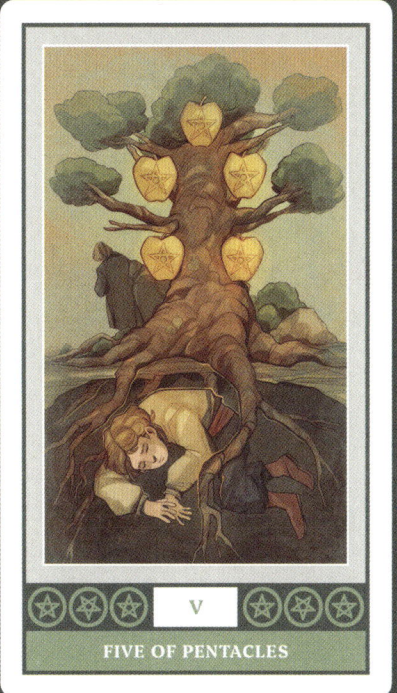

V

FIVE OF PENTACLES

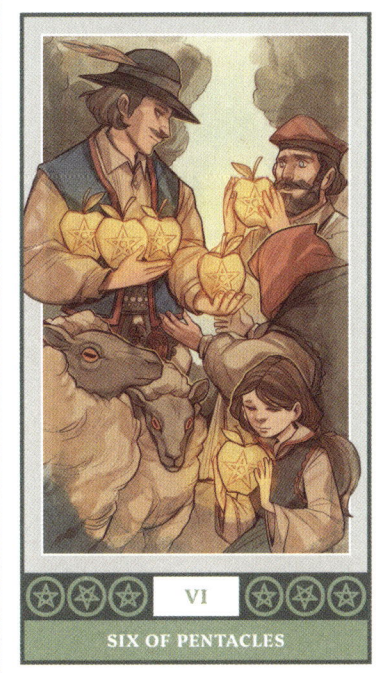

VI

SIX OF PENTACLES

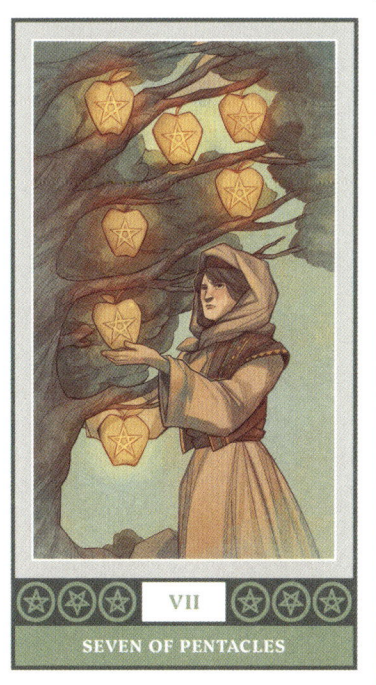

VII

SEVEN OF PENTACLES

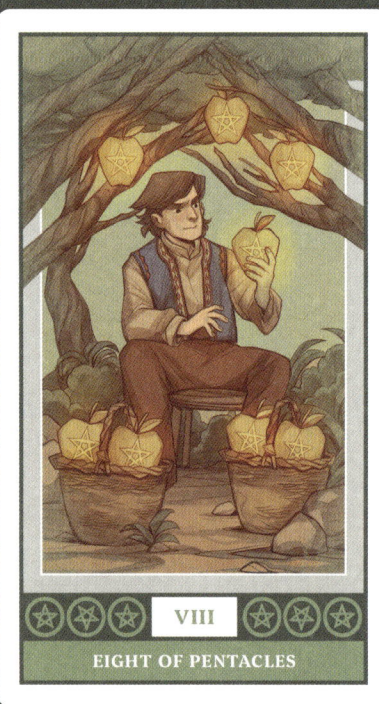

EIGHT OF PENTACLES

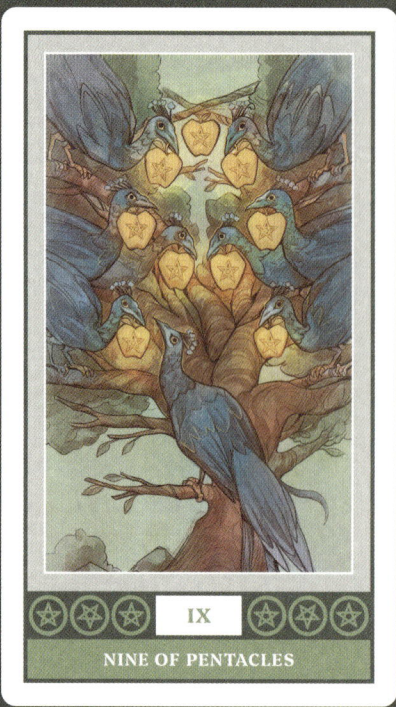

NINE OF PENTACLES

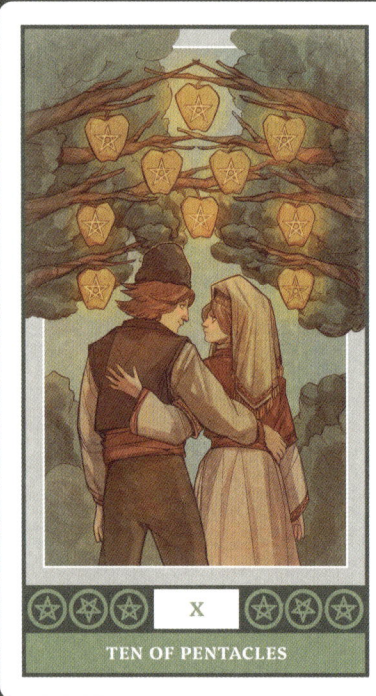

TEN OF PENTACLES

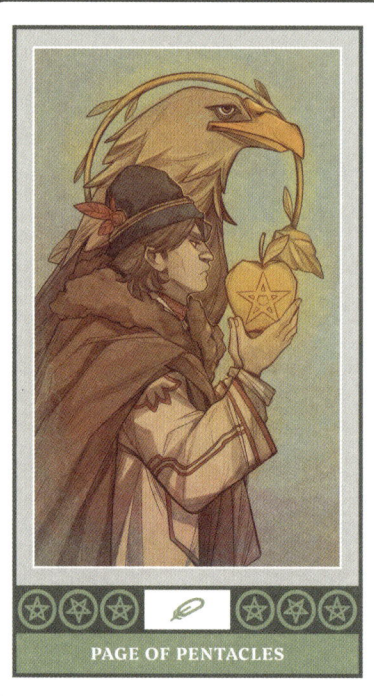

PAGE OF PENTACLES

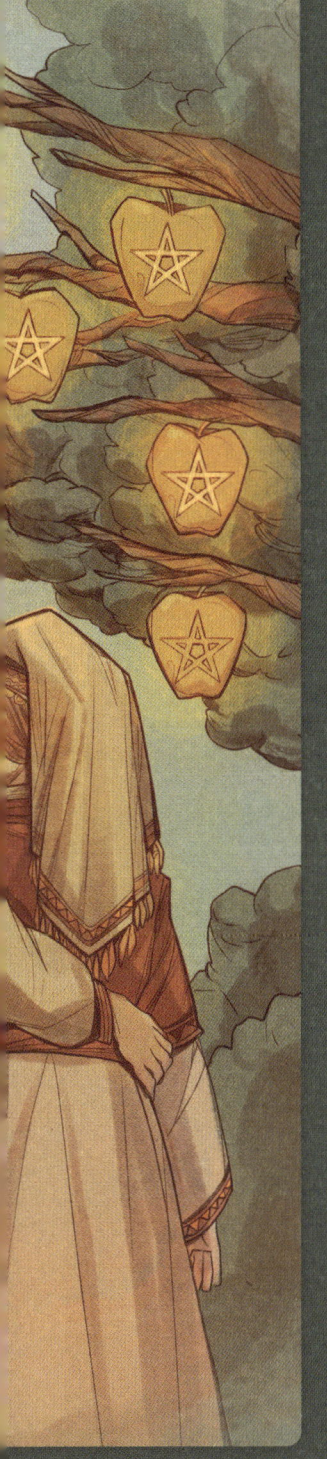

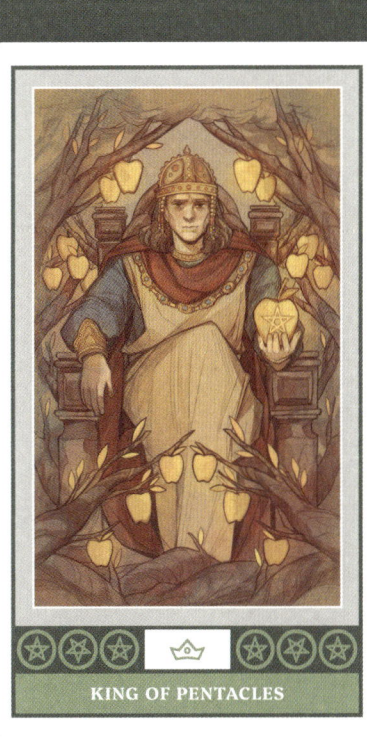

KNIGHT OF PENTACLES

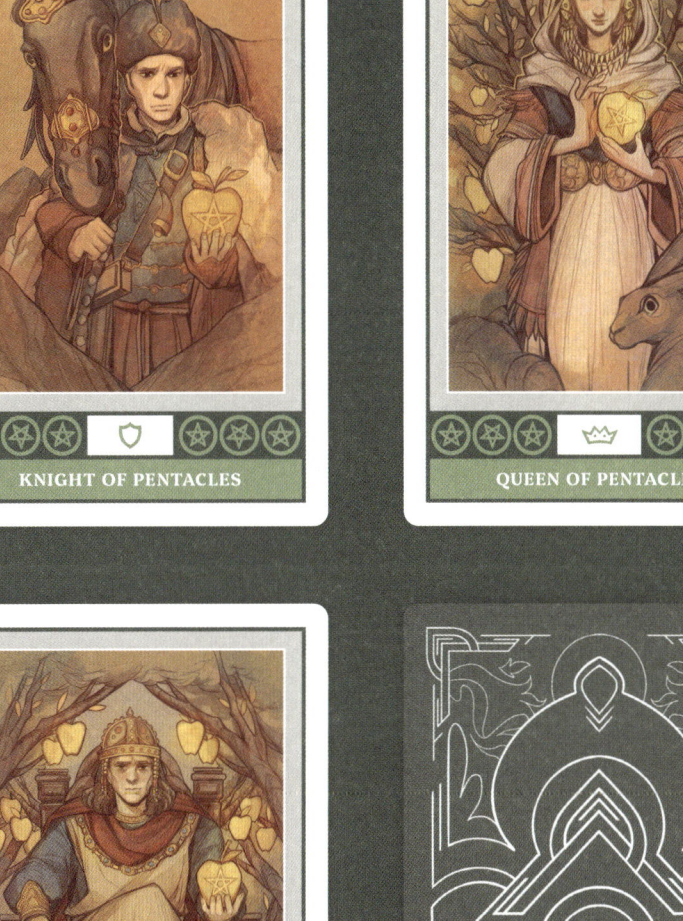

QUEEN OF PENTACLES

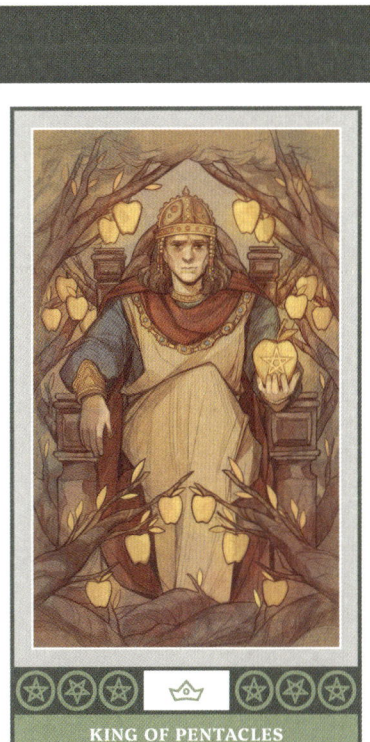

KING OF PENTACLES

THE GUEST
GALLERY

BOTANICA

KEVIN JAY STANTON

What does tarot mean to you? How did you become interested in it?

One of my favourite things in general is the power of symbols throughout human history – just the idea that we have always latched onto objects as something more than they are and made them into something representative. Tarot as an extension of that always interested me, especially after exploring a magic shop in my town and speaking to a reader there. They shared the importance of feeling resonance with a deck, something I have tried to imbue into the meaning of cards in *Botanica*.

What inspired you to design the *Botanica* tarot? What were your goals or aims for this project?

In college, I had made a few cards as a part of a thesis project. After college, I tried again and made exactly one card! I think what held me back from ever getting further was that I was trying to add plants to the iconic Waite–Smith cards instead of focusing on what I really wanted to do, which was just the plants. My goal ultimately was to research the cards, research the plants, and combine them in thoughtful, beautiful ways.

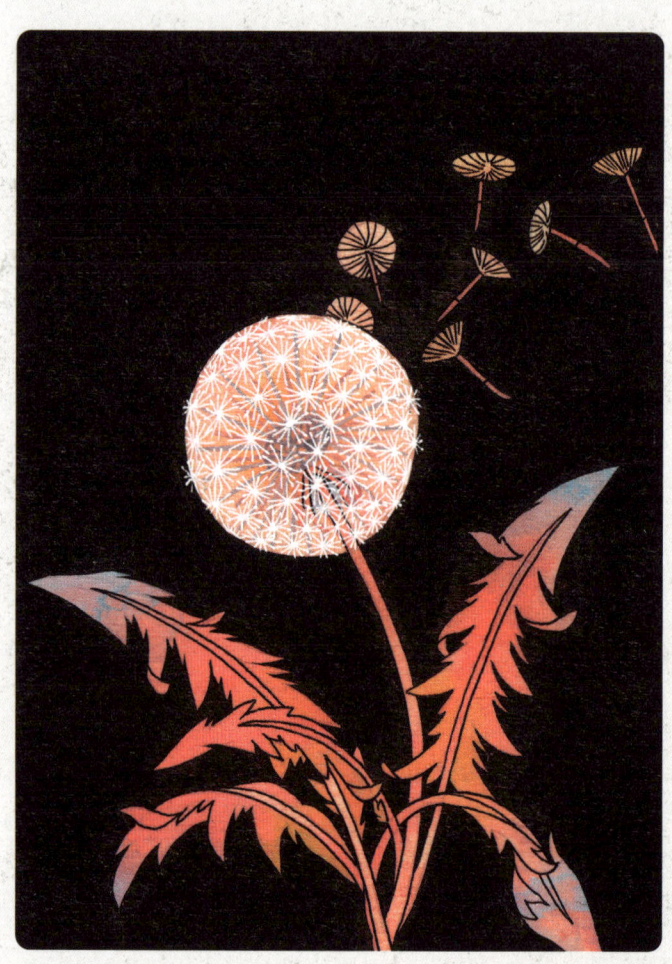

THE FOOL

Combining The Fool with dandelions, because of their air-blown seeds, was such an 'aha!' moment for me. It's a big reason dandelions are the major symbol of *Botanica*, because The Fool wanders through the Majors, and because it was such an important moment in the deck's creation.

266

All images © Kevin Jay Stanton

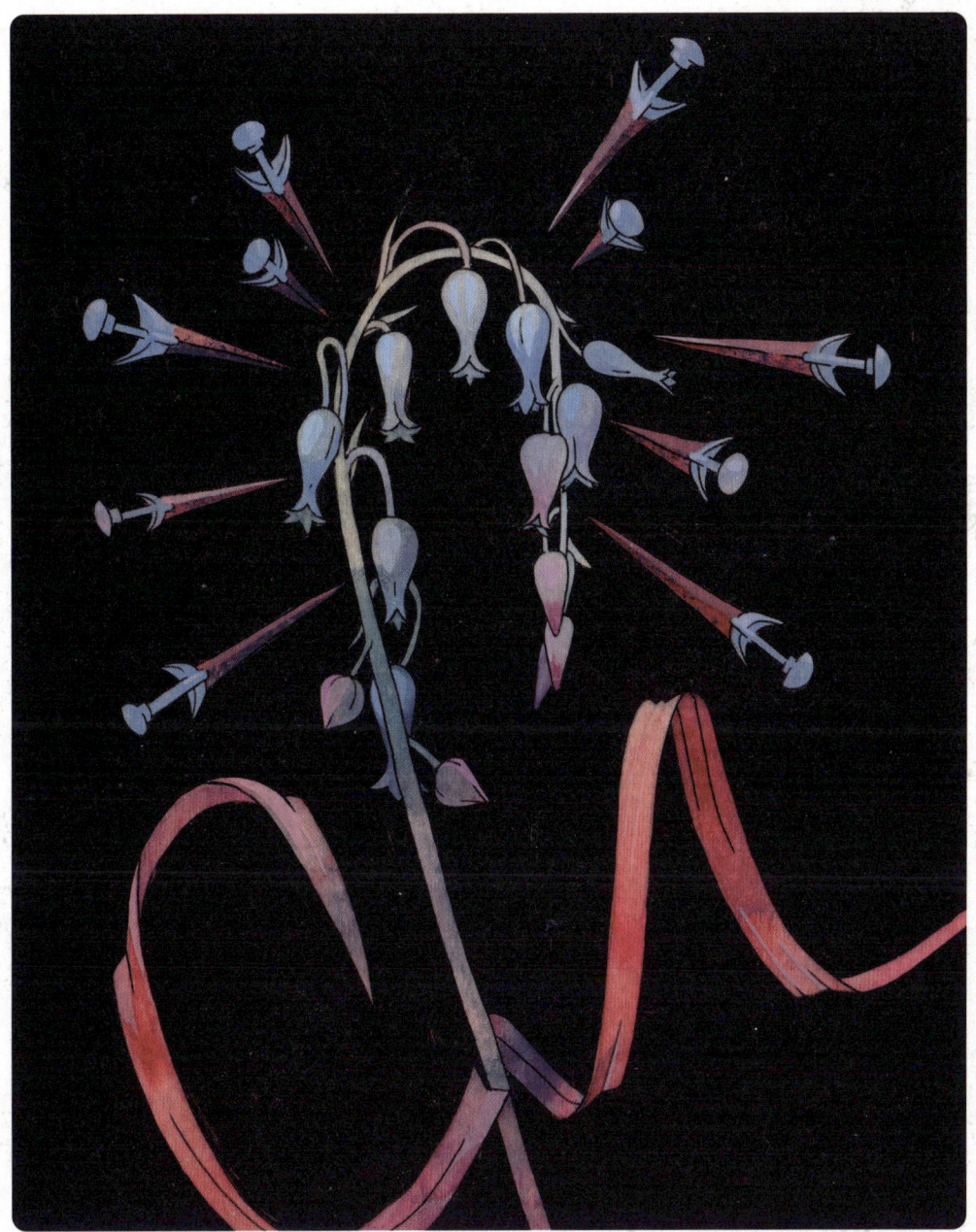

TEN OF SWORDS

The Ten of Swords has a lot of personal meaning for me. I had read that the flowers in the myth of Hyacinthus and Apollo were hyacinths (bluebells) more red than blue. Considering the bloody nature of the story, I tried to incorporate both colours into this painting.

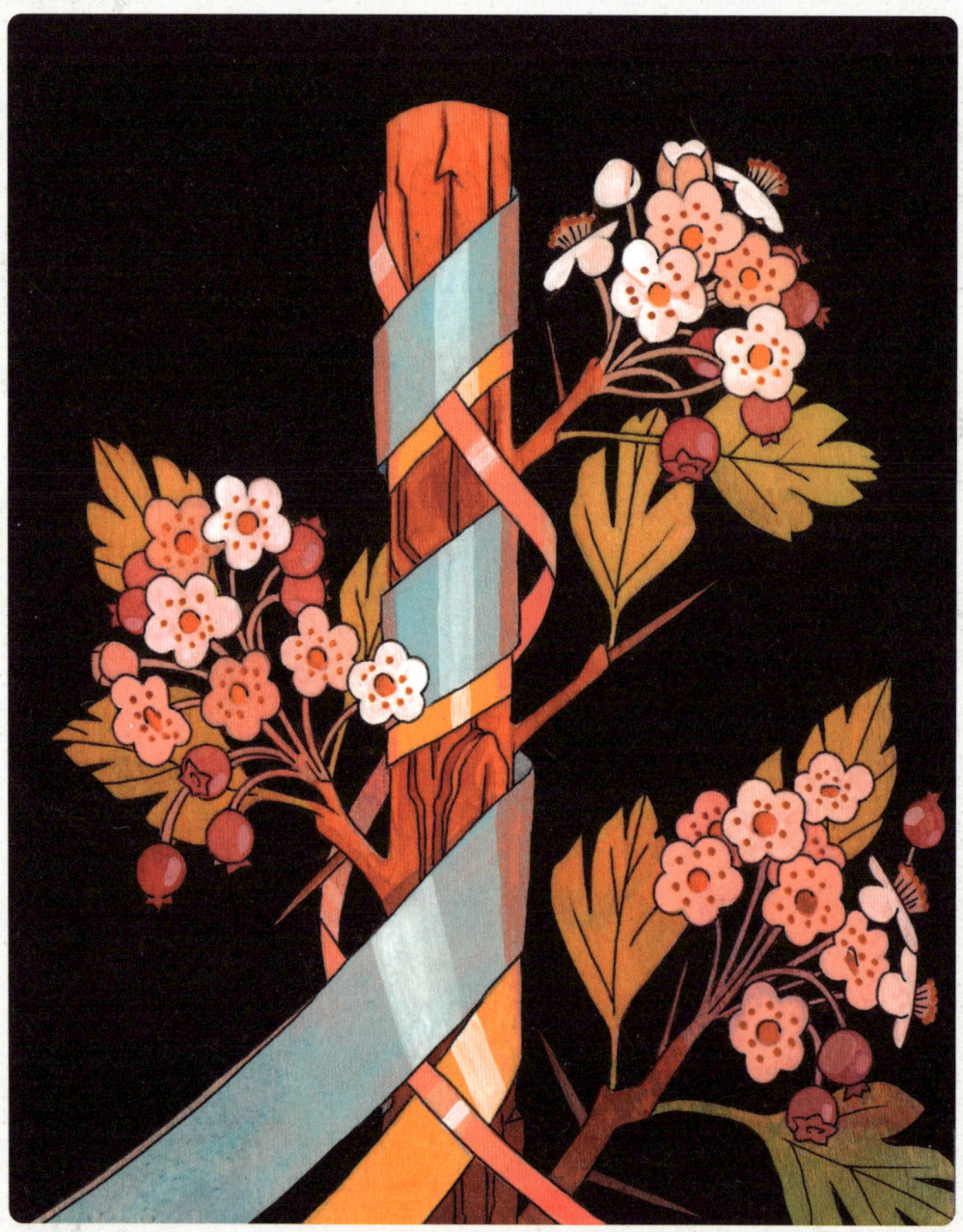

ACE OF WANDS

I love the look of the Ace of Wands so much.
The warm glow on the flowers and the weaving
of the ribbon on the maypole are things I am very
proud to have painted.

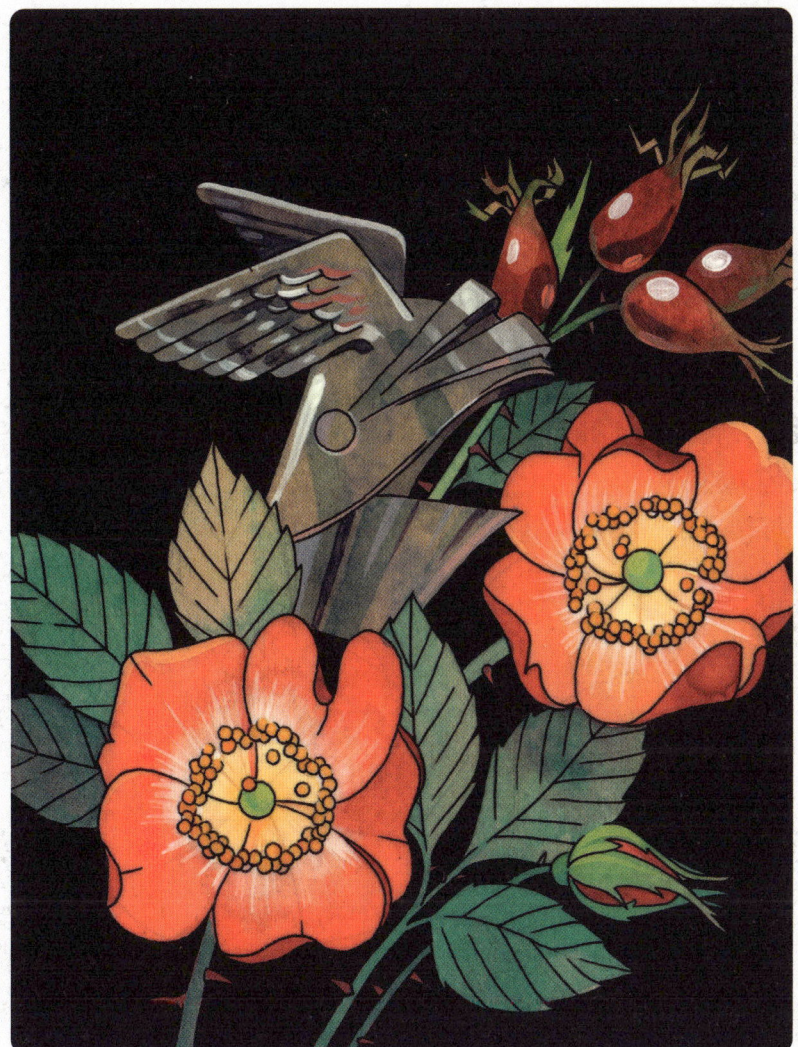

KNIGHT OF CUPS

This is the card I use as a significator. It is the only court card in *Botanica* that retains its original 'crown' from Waite–Smith, because I have been enamoured with the Knight of Cups' winged helmet from the first time I saw it.

How did you decide on a look and feel for the cards?

I had been playing around with paintings of plants on a black background in my sketchbook for a while. I just liked the look of how stark it was, I think, and later realized how inspired I was by a few things I'd had in my childhood, like a book of plant photography where the subjects were against a black background, and the Russian lacquerware my mother collected. I think it really works for *Botanica*, because it makes the symbols the complete focus.

What were the biggest challenges or learning experiences along the way?

First of all, it was a very long project – about five years! I learned so much about the work I wanted to make and how to research for it, too. To date, *Botanica* is still my ultimate passion project, and it was nerve-wracking to put it out, hoping it would resonate with people. It felt too specific, too personal. Hearing from people that their readings feel blunt but gentle is a great point of pride for me, because that came from a time when I really needed a voice like that, too.

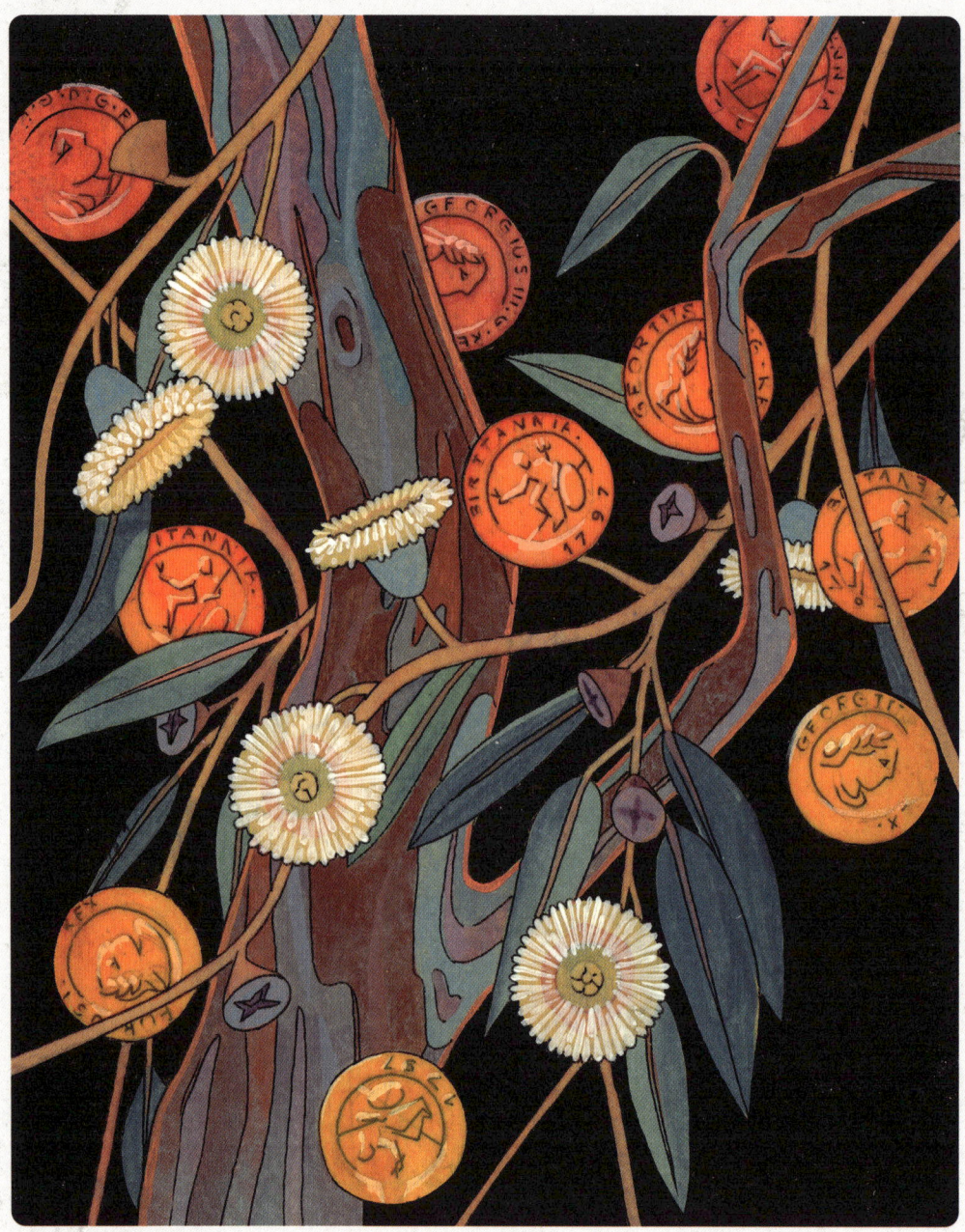

TEN OF COINS

I really struggled with painting the colourful eucalyptus bark balanced against the fiery gradient of the cartwheel pennies. It was one of a few times I thought I would have to repaint a card completely, until I tried to just play around after a break and it started to really work.

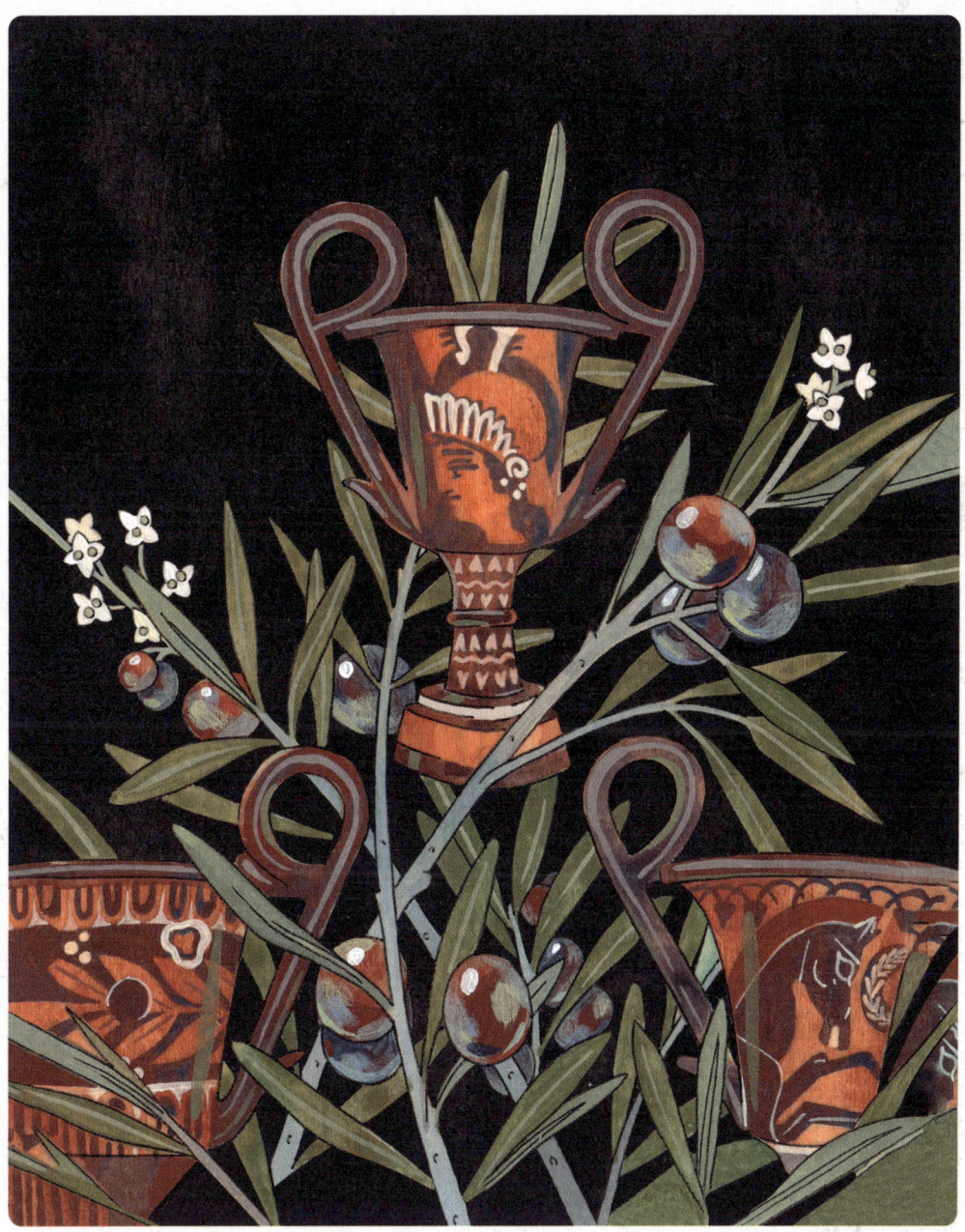

THREE OF CUPS

The Three of Cups is the last painting I did for the deck and is one of the few paintings I kept for myself. It feels strange to me when I look at it, like it's somehow a different style. And in a way, it is, considering how far I came!

TAROT OF FAMOUS WITCHES

RACHEL FORD

What does tarot mean to you? How did you become interested in it?

What I find fascinating about tarot is its depth and versatility; each card is full of symbolism that people can interpret in such a variety of ways. It's interesting how people can draw such different insights from the same card, which can reflect their own experiences and perspectives. No two tarot decks or readings are the same.

I was originally drawn to tarot from an artistic viewpoint, but the more I learned about it, the more I saw it as a tool for self-reflection and growth, and a way to provide guidance and new perspectives. I don't necessarily see it as a way of predicting the future, although that is a perfectly valid way to see the cards; I see it more as a way to gain understanding of the present while using what has happened in the past, and of exploring possibilities to shape your future.

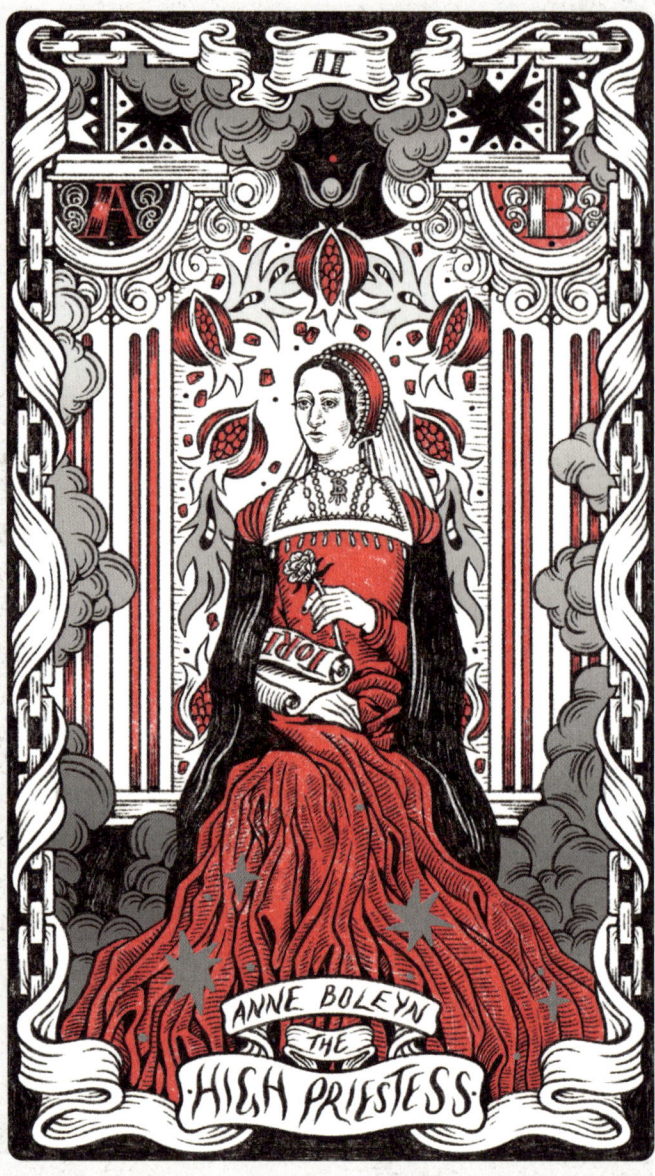

ANNE BOLEYN

The High Priestess is a card of tactical stillness, suggesting a time to retreat and reflect, trusting your gut to guide you through. Following this theme, I chose Anne Boleyn, who was often misrepresented and defamed. Contrary to what people believe of her, she was an active politician, and may have died for her support of humanitarian anti-poverty laws that were radical in her time.

All images © Rachel Ford

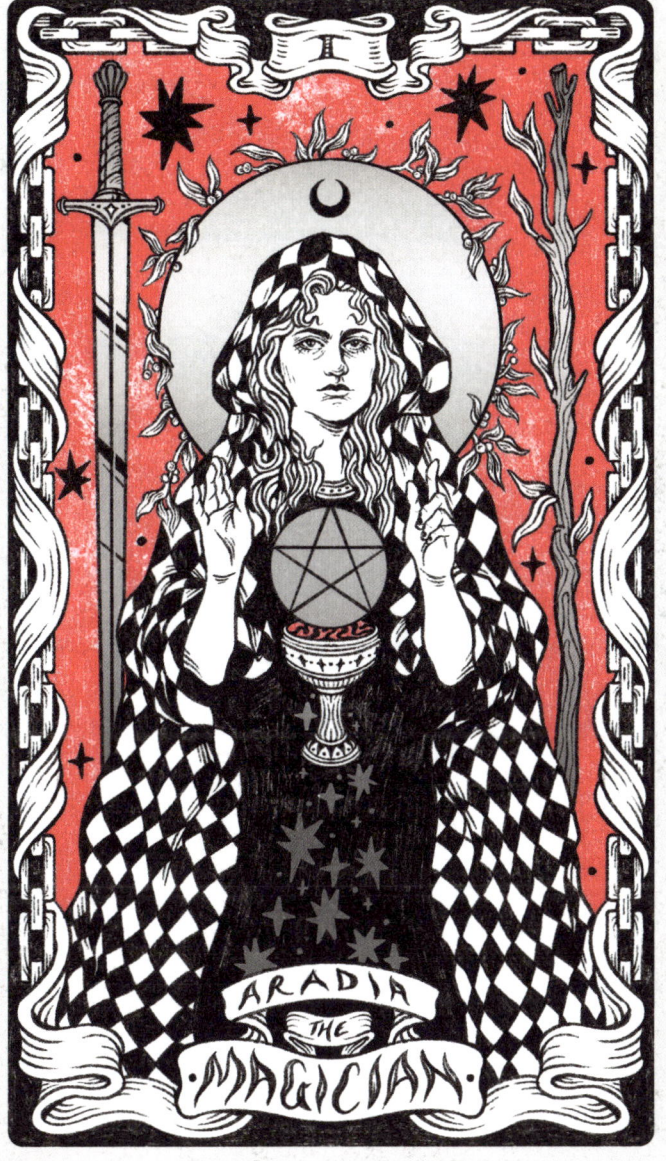

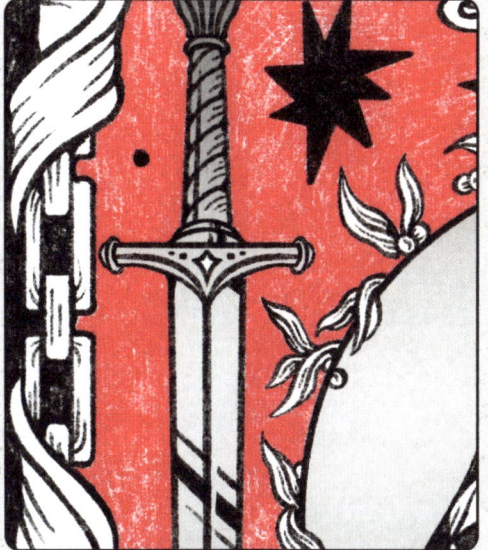

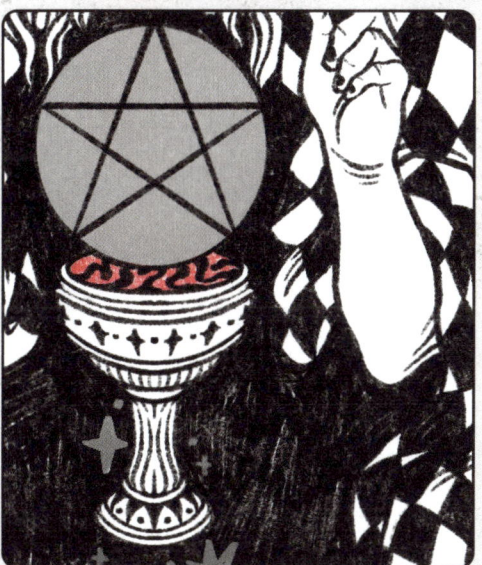

ARADIA

Often described as the first witch, Aradia is a powerful witch who represents new comings and using all the knowledge and skills to tap into one's potential.

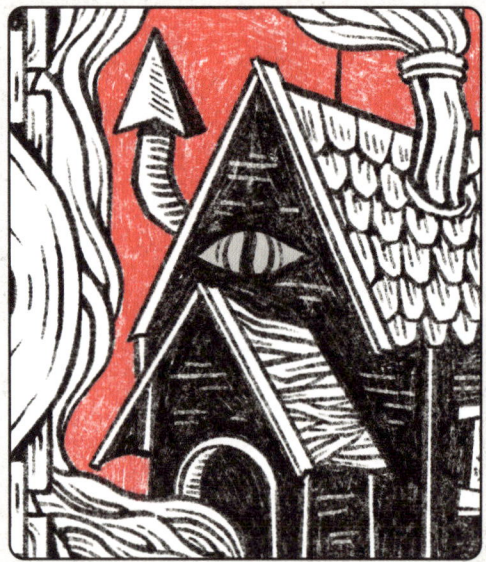

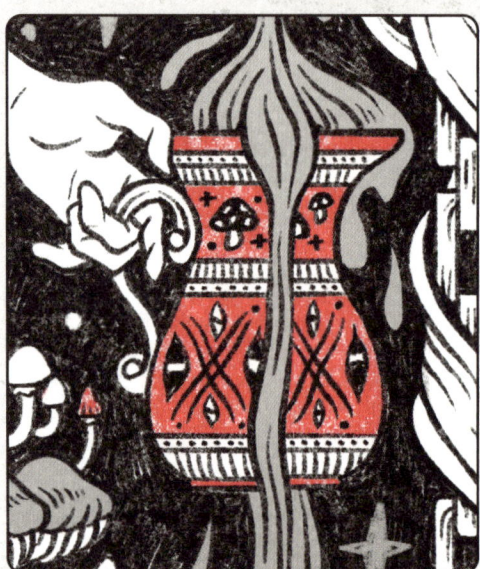

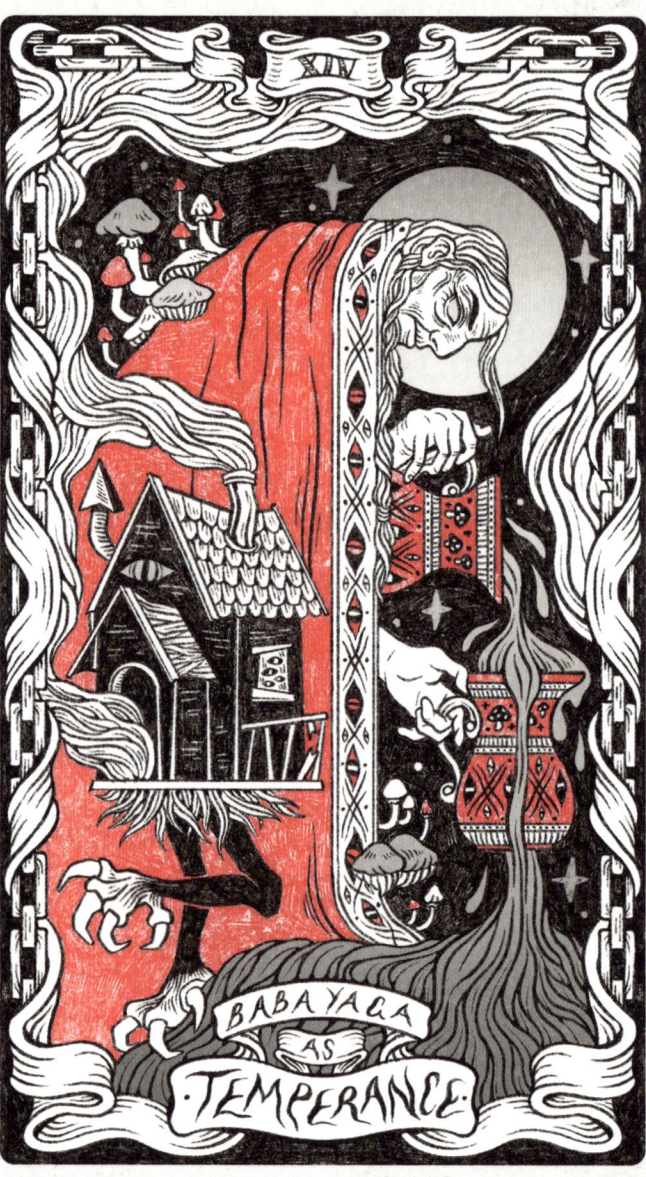

BABA YAGA

Baba Yaga, from Slavic folklore, has opposing sides to her story. She is described either as a guardian protecting the forest or as an evil being who hunts down children who get lost in her woods. She represents Temperance, as the card is all about balance, self-restraint, and control, to avoid disharmony as Baba Yaga's duelling reputation implies.

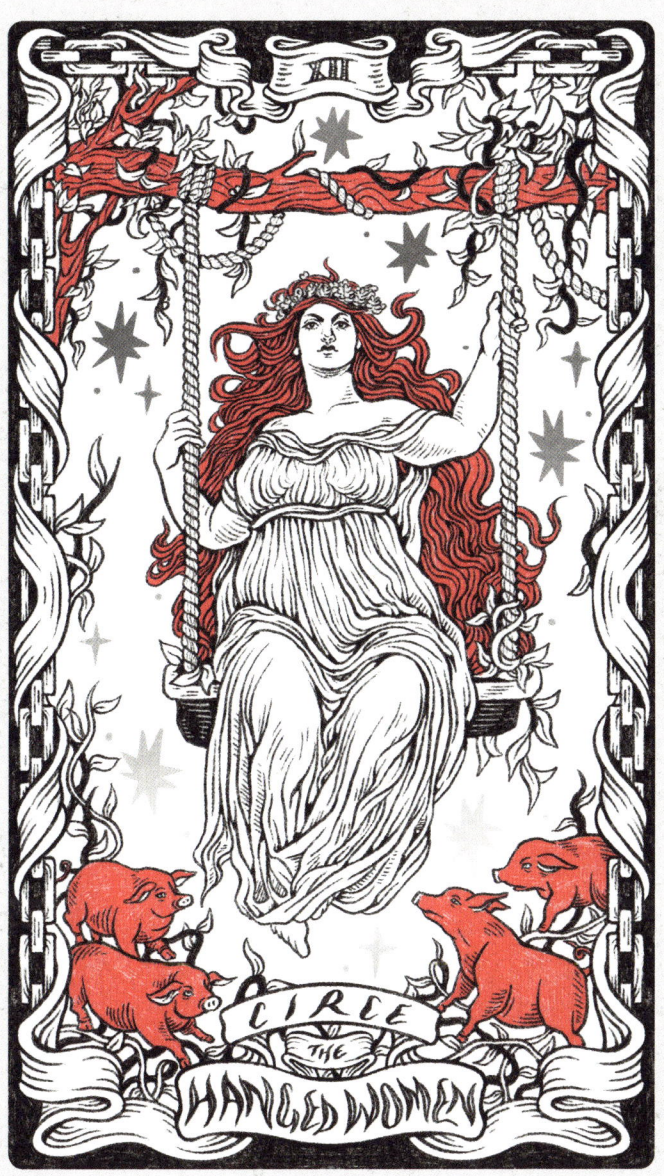

CIRCE

Circe, the enchantress from Greek mythology, embodies the essence of The Hanged Man (or The Hanged Woman). Known for her transformative powers, she forces others to see the world from a new perspective. Like The Hanged Man, Circe represents surrender, the suspension of old beliefs, and the necessity of viewing situations from a different angle to gain wisdom.

What inspired you to design the *Tarot of Famous Witches*? What were your goals or aims for this project?

At university, I created just the Major Arcana, and I always wanted to expand on that. I was inspired to make my own deck because of how compelling it would be to tell the rich stories of witches, whether from history, folklore, or fiction, past or present. I really wanted to tell these witches' stories through the lens of tarot, and show that they are multifaceted beings; this deck's purpose is to transcend what notions society has of witches. It allows people to use their knowledge of the specific witch to educate their reading, and also to learn more about the witch's own history and story through the card they are representing.

How did you decide on a look and feel for the cards?

When designing this deck, I drew inspiration from a range of styles to reflect the varied times and backgrounds of the witches featured, from classic etchings to inked storybook illustrations. I also drew from the symbolic richness of iconic decks like Smith–Waite, Visconti–Sforza, and other more contemporary decks. I aimed to capture the unique essence of each witch. This eclectic mix honours their individual stories and cultural contexts, aiming to create a visually cohesive yet diverse deck that celebrates the mystique and power of these notable figures.

What were the biggest challenges or learning experiences along the way?

One of the biggest challenges in creating the deck was choosing a consistent style that would suit characters and witches with very different aesthetics, from across not only history but various media, too. Deciding which witch best suited each card was tough, as many of their stories could correlate with multiple tarot meanings. Balancing historical accuracy with artistic cohesion was a fun challenge that definitely tested and expanded my knowledge of the cards, and which I hope helped to enrich the deck's depth and authenticity.

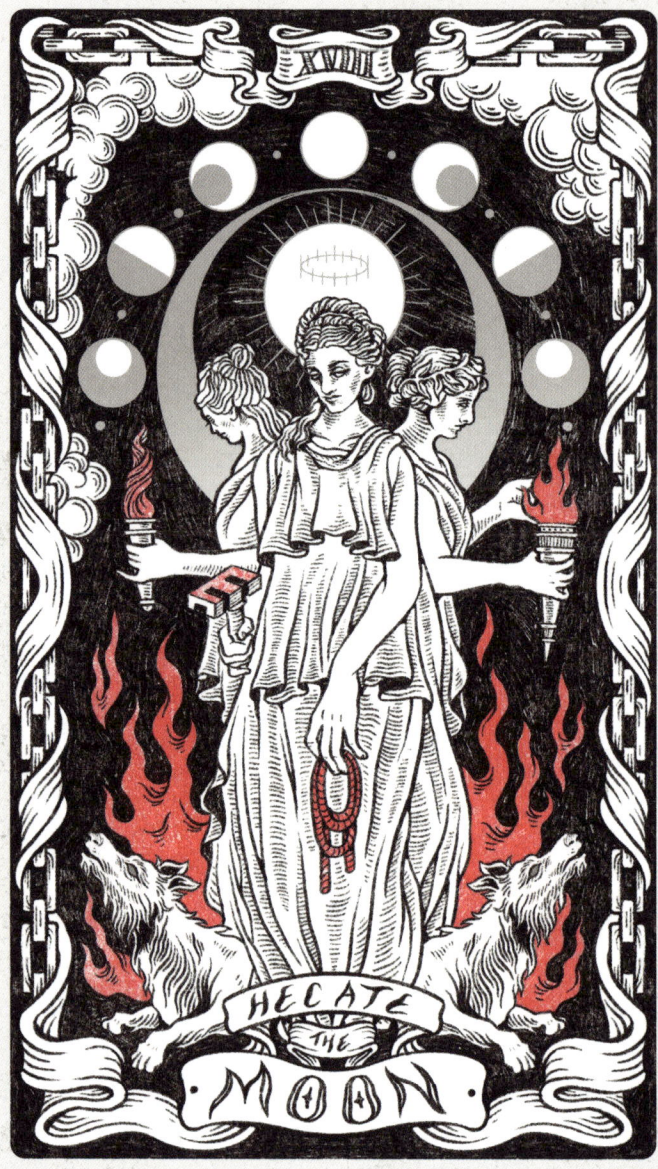

HECATE

Representing The Moon is Hecate, the Greek goddess of magic and crossroads. She embodies intuition, the unconscious, and the mysteries of the night. As a guide through darkness and uncertainty, Hecate encourages trusting one's inner voice and navigating hidden realms with caution and insight.

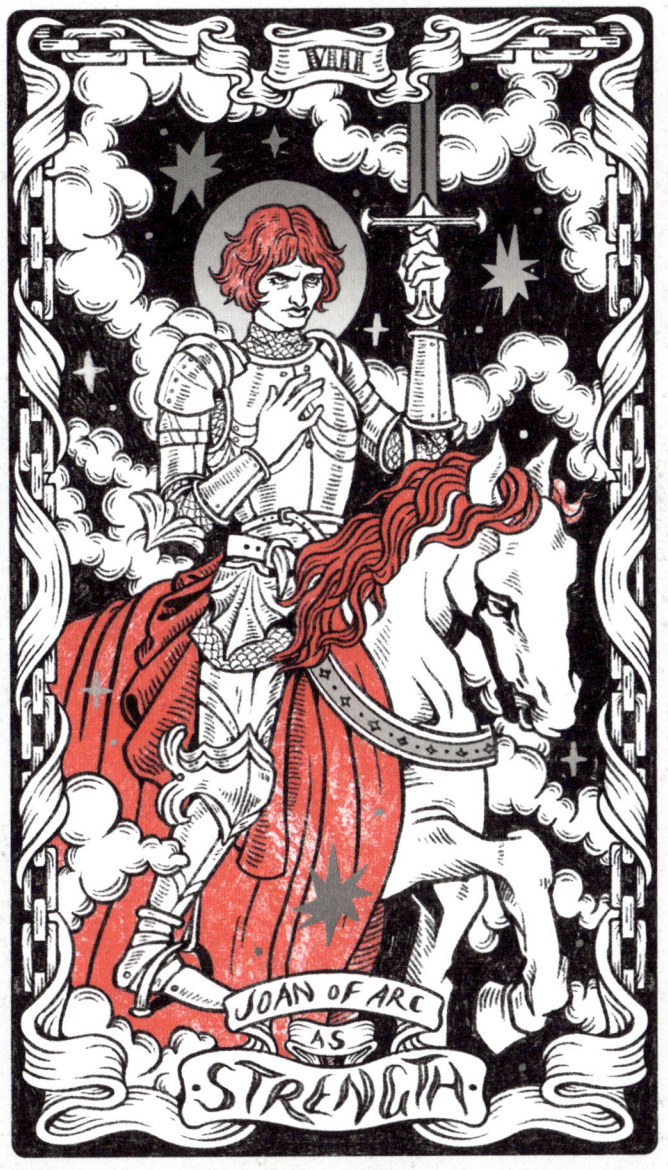

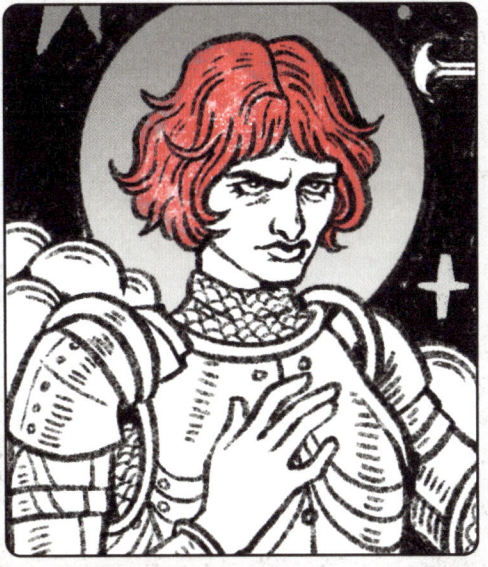

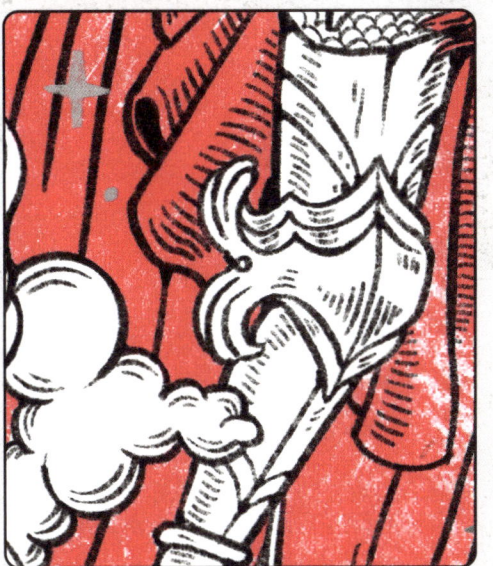

JOAN OF ARC

Joan of Arc as Strength represents a quiet courage in the face of dark times and challenges ahead. The kind of strength needed may not be that of force and action but of tenacity, determination, and patience.

WOODLAND WARDENS

JESSICA ROUX

What does tarot mean to you? How did you become interested in it?

I learned how to read tarot about a decade ago while attending a retreat led by two experienced tarot readers and artists. I fell in love with the artwork first: the colours and bold line work on the Rider–Waite–Smith deck. It was empowering to discover the Strength card, depicting a woman holding a lion's mouth. I loved discovering the little details like the black cat on the Queen of Wands, the pomegranate pattern on The Empress's dress, and the irises on Temperance. I find myself pulling cards whenever I feel lost or conflicted; tarot brings me comfort and clarity in my life.

What inspired you to design *Woodland Wardens*? What were your goals or aims for this project?

I was inspired by the beauty of nature when creating the *Woodland Wardens* oracle deck. Each card depicts one animal paired with one plant, with the meanings behind each card coming from folklore, mythology, history, and the characteristics of the plants and animals themselves. Since flora and fauna are my favourite things to draw, and since I love researching myths and legends, the project was a joy to work on.

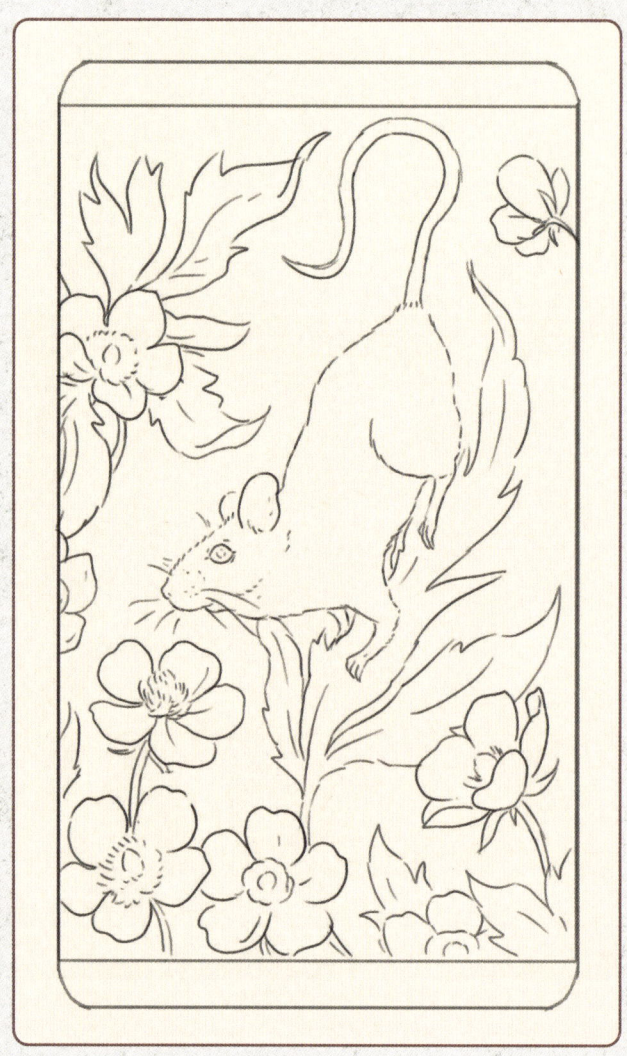

THE MOUSE AND BUTTERCUP (SKETCH)

In the sketch for The Mouse and Buttercup, I loosely outlined the composition but left the details and textures to be created in the final. When I first created the sketches, I hadn't planned on including the meaning of the card below the name, so the borders on the sketches are not exactly how the finals ended up.

All images © 2024 by Jessica Roux, published by Andrews McMeel Publishing.

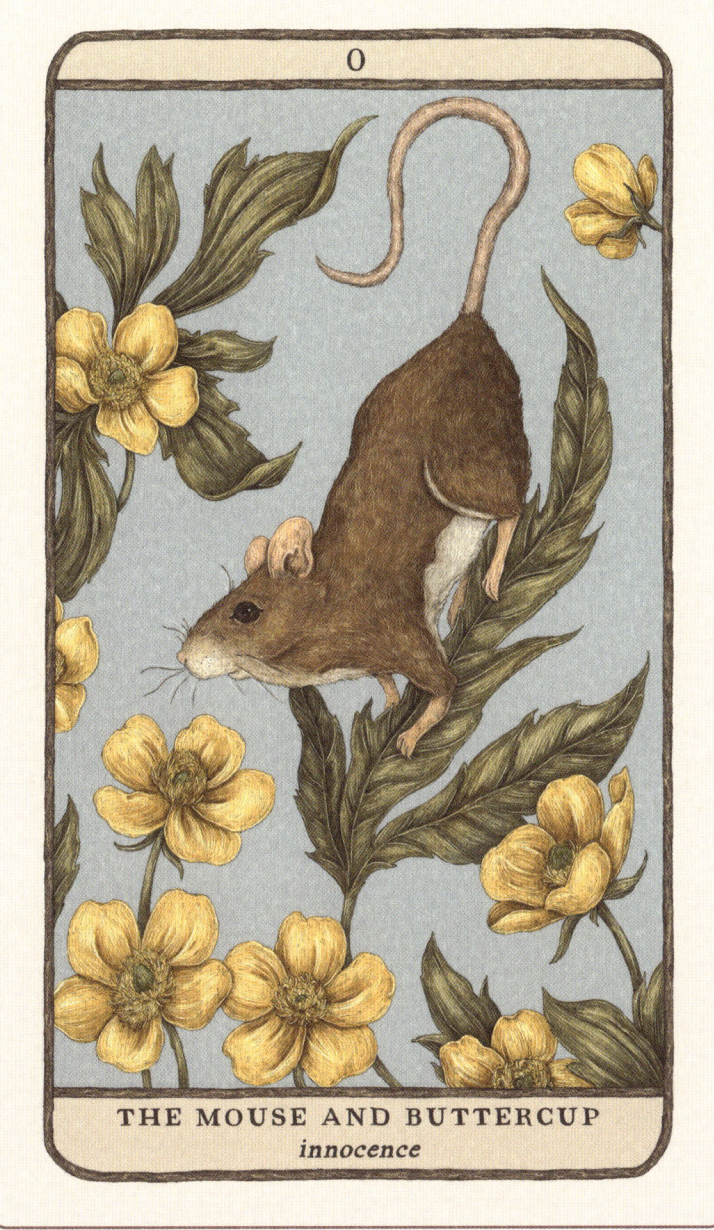

0

THE MOUSE AND BUTTERCUP
innocence

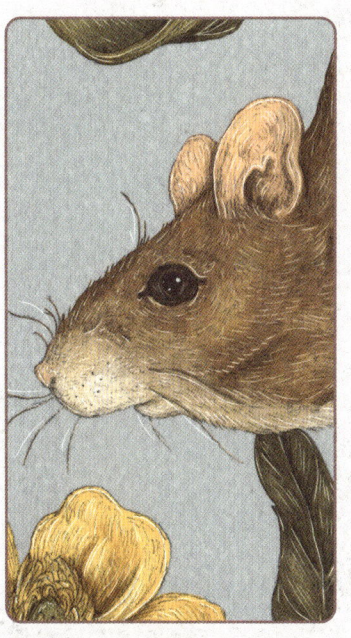

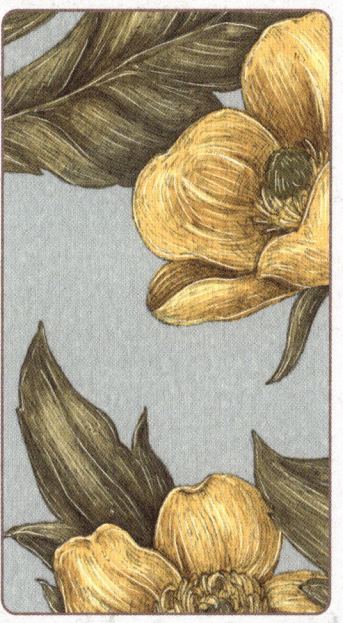

THE MOUSE AND BUTTERCUP

Like The Fool, The Mouse and Buttercup is numbered zero and
marks the beginning of the deck (and the beginning of The Fool's
journey). The card depicts a mouse standing on a leaf, surrounded
by buttercups, and has the meaning of innocence.

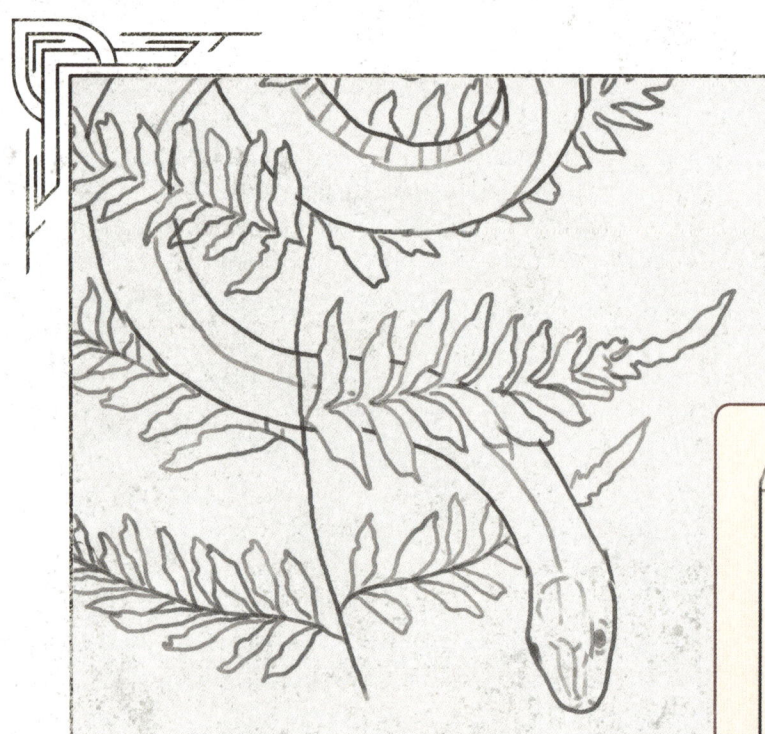

How did you decide on a look and feel for the cards?

Since my work is heavily textured and detailed, I kept the backgrounds to solid, flat colours so that the focus remained on the central figure of the animal and plant. I kept an earthy colour palette throughout for that natural feel. I encapsulated each illustration with a simple wooden frame: a callback to my favourite Rider–Waite–Smith deck, which includes a simple border around each card. The frame treats each illustration like it is an individual portrait in a gallery.

What were the biggest challenges or learning experiences along the way?

I created a list of plant and animal pairings early on, but later found it difficult to stick to that initial plan. The more I researched, the more I found interesting stories and myths that I preferred to my initial list. I went back and edited, adapted, and changed a lot. Flexibility and deviating from a plan can be a challenge for me, but I'm glad I learned to do so on this project.

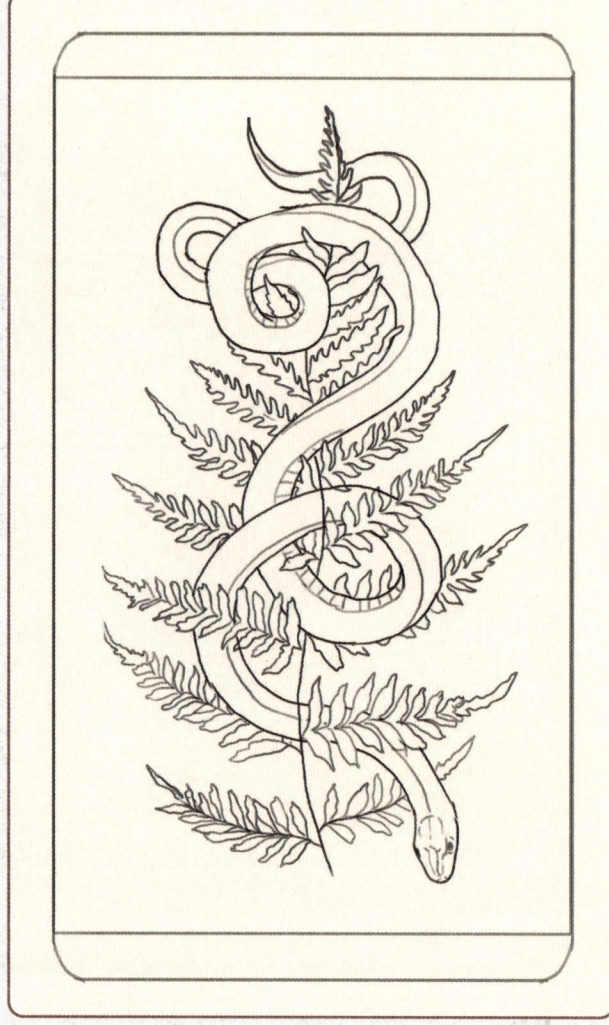

THE SNAKE AND FERN (SKETCH)

The position of the snake's head changed from the sketch to the final, so the final artwork has a bit more flow and fluidity. When sketching snakes, I just doodle squiggly lines until I like what I'm seeing.

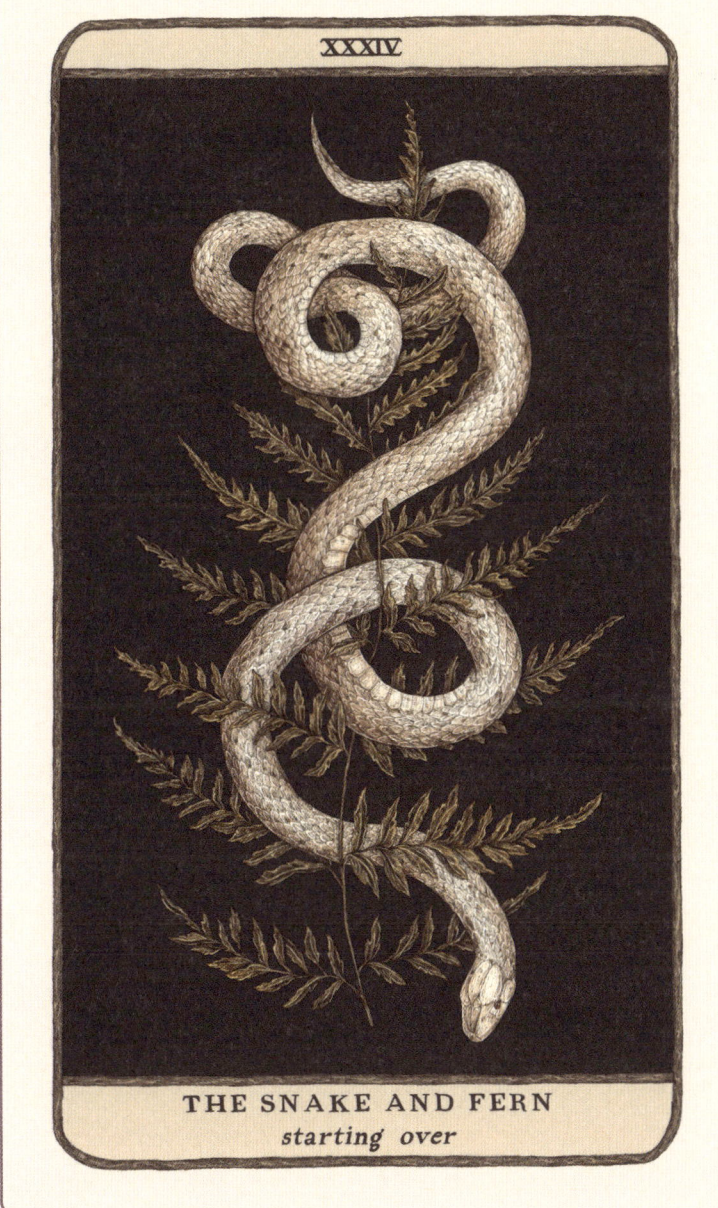

XXXIV

THE SNAKE AND FERN
starting over

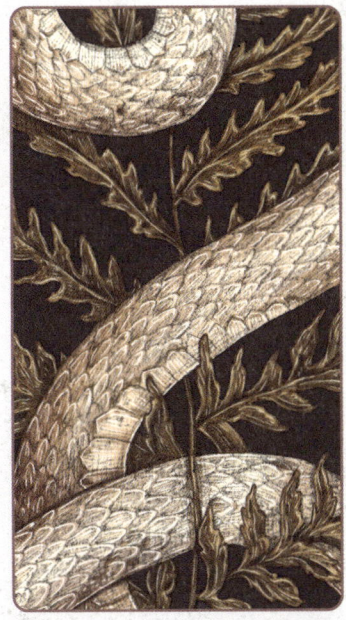

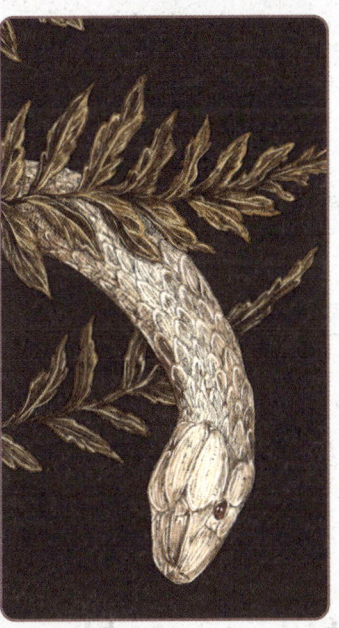

THE SNAKE AND FERN

One of my favourites in the deck, The Snake and Fern depicts an albino snake winding around a single fern. Just as snakes shed their skin, The Snake and Fern is associated with new beginnings and starting over.

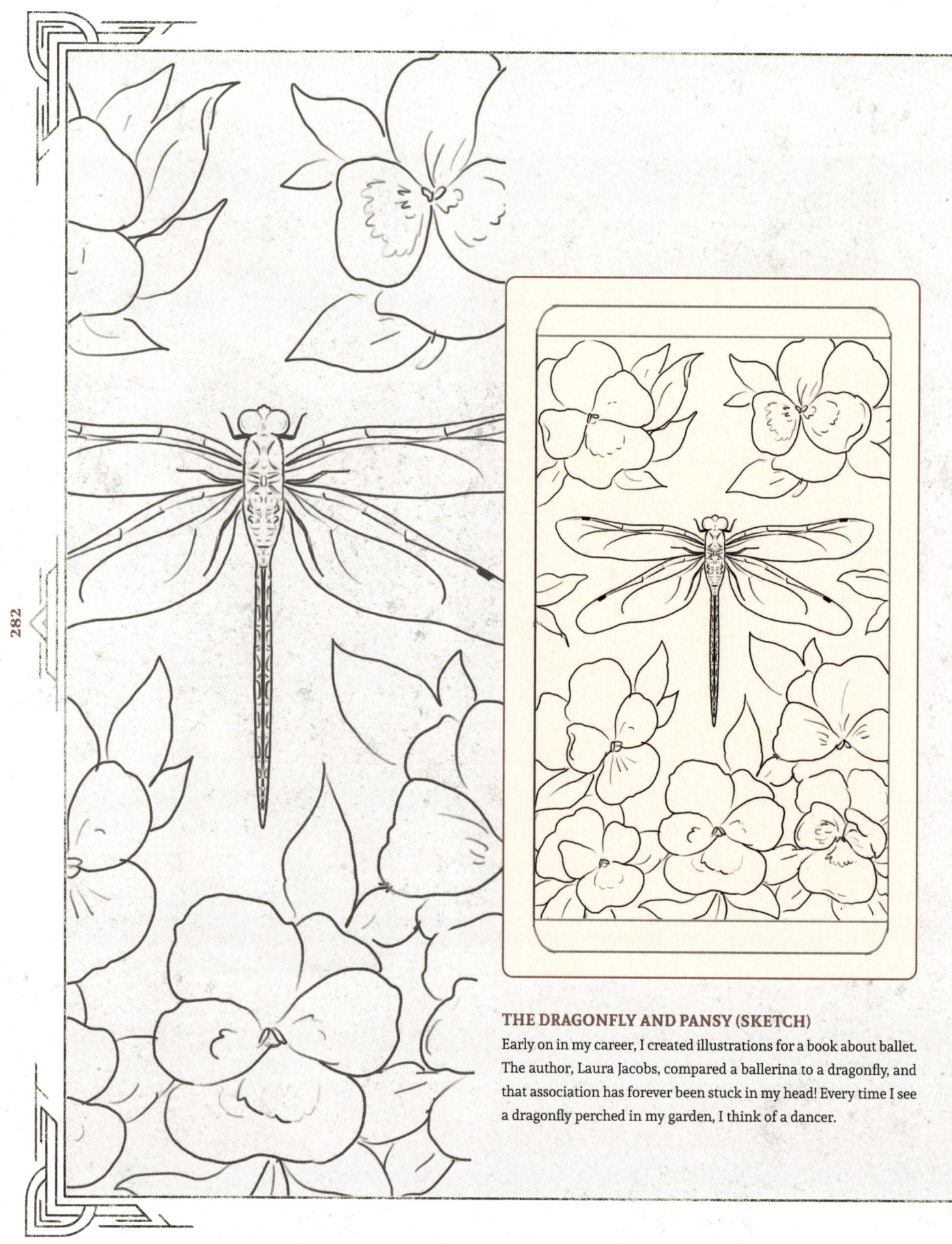

THE DRAGONFLY AND PANSY (SKETCH)

Early on in my career, I created illustrations for a book about ballet. The author, Laura Jacobs, compared a ballerina to a dragonfly, and that association has forever been stuck in my head! Every time I see a dragonfly perched in my garden, I think of a dancer.

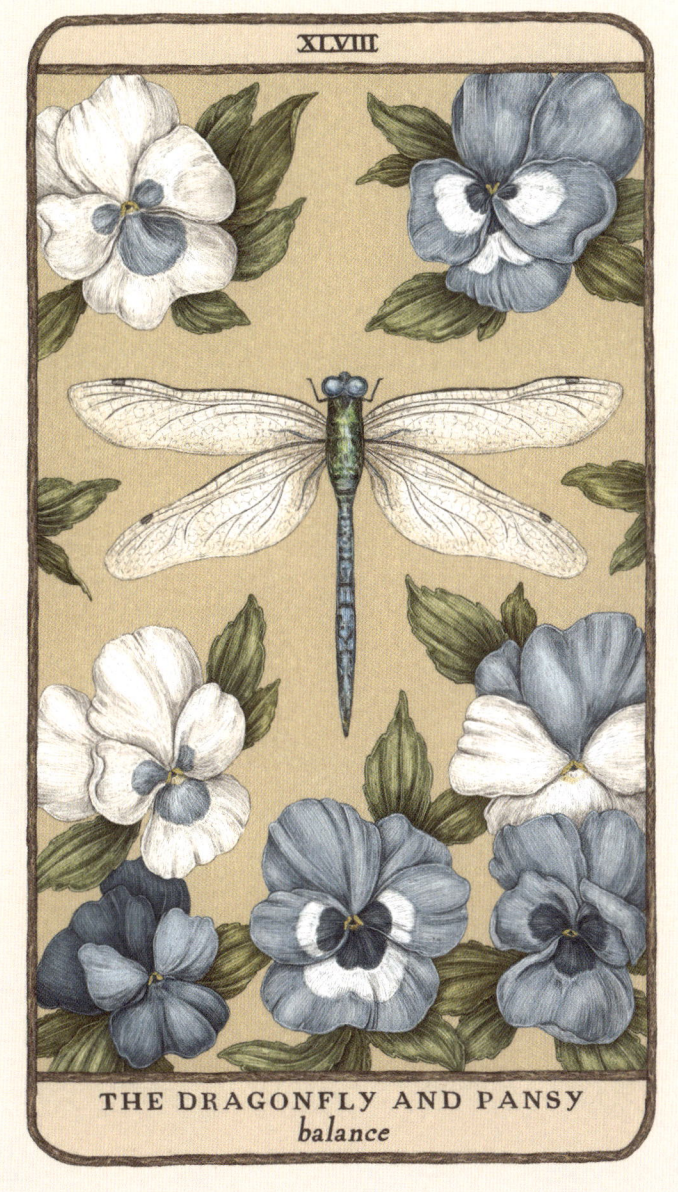

XLVIII

THE DRAGONFLY AND PANSY
balance

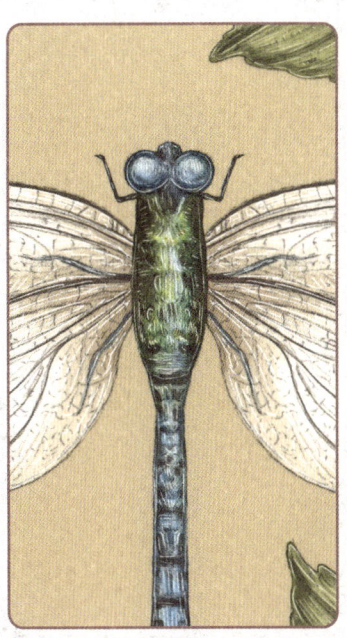

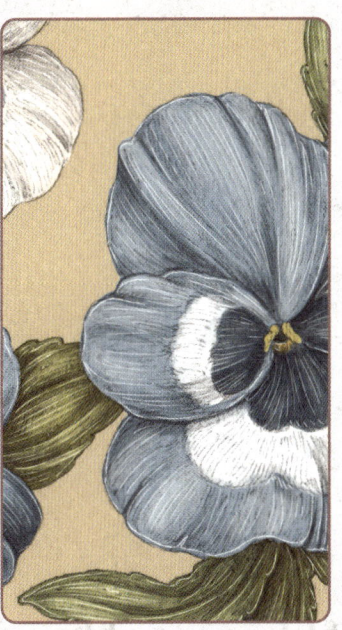

THE DRAGONFLY AND PANSY

The Dragonfly and Pansy is about harmony between thought and action: a perfect balance. While the dragonfly is perfectly symmetrical, the pansies surrounding it are not mirrored in the same way. However, the colour and composition of the flowers create that balance without feeling too exact.

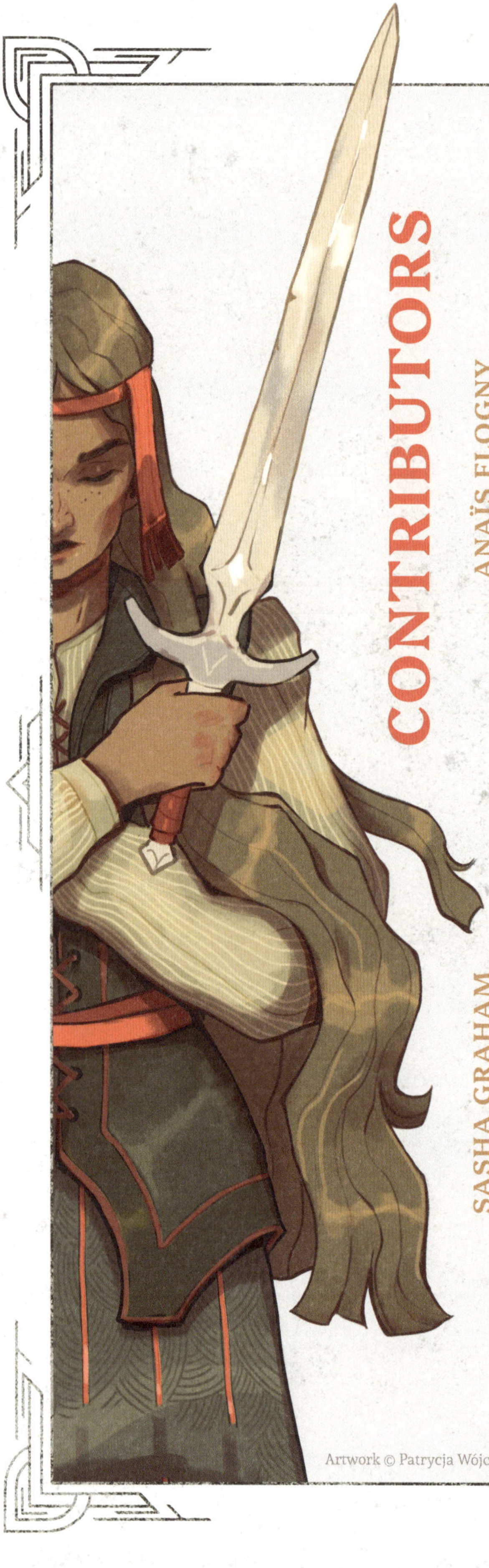

CONTRIBUTORS

ANAÏS FLOGNY
anaisflogny.carrd.co

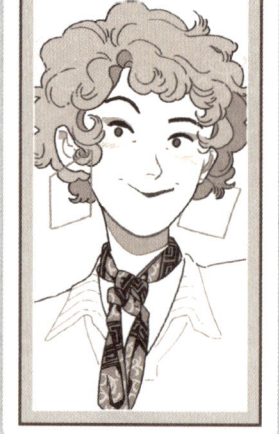

Anaïs is a French illustrator
and comic artist. She loves to
draw hands and is inspired by
medieval and mid-twentieth-
century aesthetics.

RACHEL FORD
rford.uk

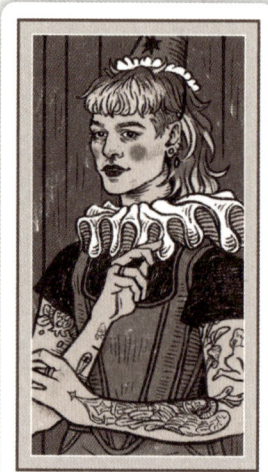

Rachel (they/she) is a sapphic
illustrator based in Birmingham,
England. Their main body of
work focuses on all things
esoteric, cryptic, and mystical.

SASHA GRAHAM
sashagraham.com

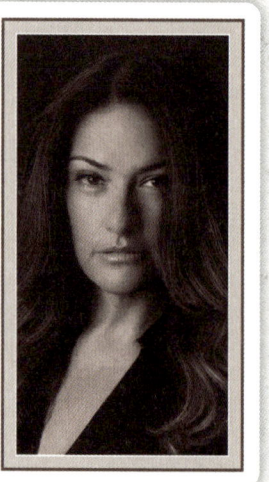

Sasha is a world-renowned
tarot expert, bestselling author,
award-winning tarot-deck
creator, horror actor, and
educator who teaches and
lectures around the globe.

DIANA NANEVA
instagram.com/functionalneighbour

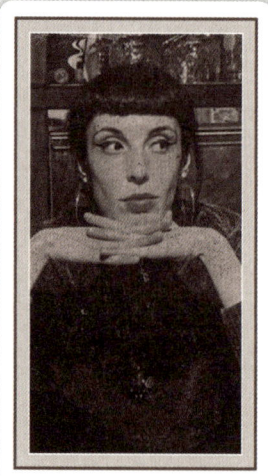

Diana is an illustrator and comic-
book artist from Bulgaria. She has
over ten years' experience with
traditional and digital media, and
is fond of many styles, genres,
and formats of storytelling.

Artwork © Patrycja Wójcik

JESSICA ROUX
jessica-roux.com

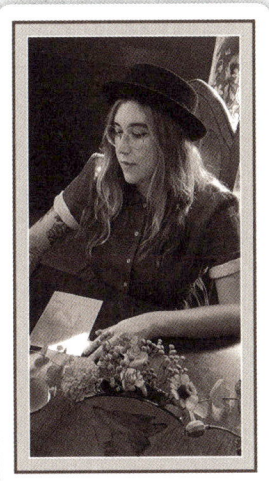

Jessica is a bestselling illustrator, author, and gardener based just outside of Nashville, Tennessee. She renders flora and fauna with intricate detail reminiscent of old-world beauty.

FAITH SCHAFFER
faithschaffer.com

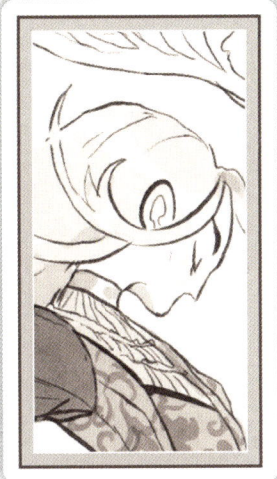

Faith is an artist working in illustration, animation, and comics. She has worked with clients such as Disney Television Animation, Dimension 20, Nickelodeon, and more.

KEVIN JAY STANTON
kevinjaystanton.com

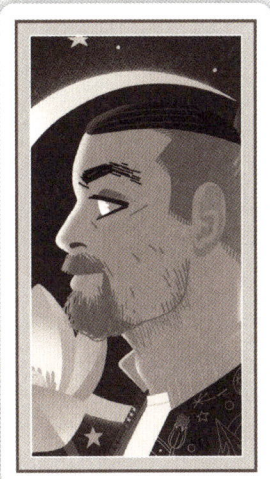

Kevin is an illustrator with a passion for plants and symbolism. He spent his childhood playing video games and reading about fairy tales, mythology, and nature. Nowadays he draws them, too.

NÚRIA TAMARIT
nuriatamarit.com

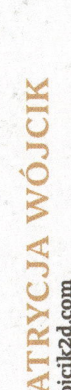

Núria is an illustrator, comic artist, teacher, and eco-feminist based in Valencia, Spain. She works for different media, such as books, graphic novels, and publishing.

PATRYCJA WÓJCIK
wojcik2d.com

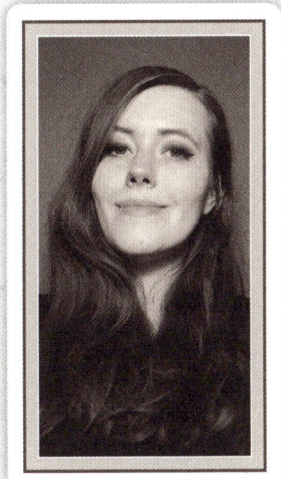

Patrycja is a freelance illustrator and concept artist based in Poland, mainly working in digital media on illustrations and character designs.

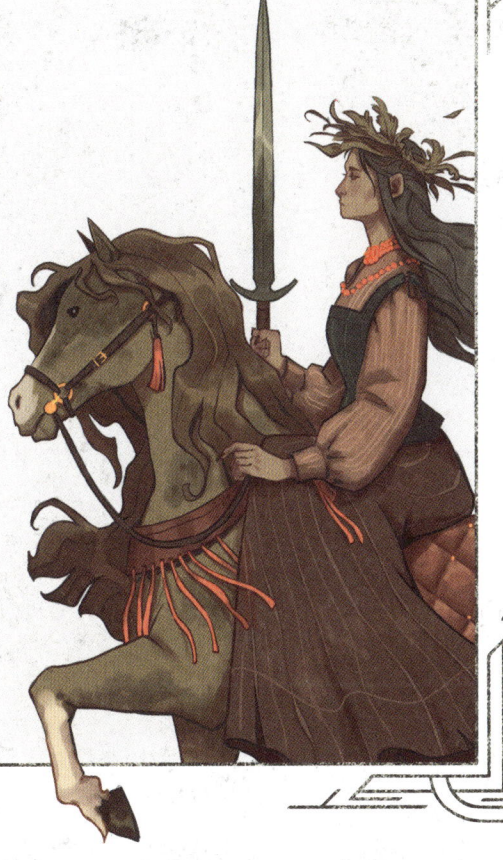

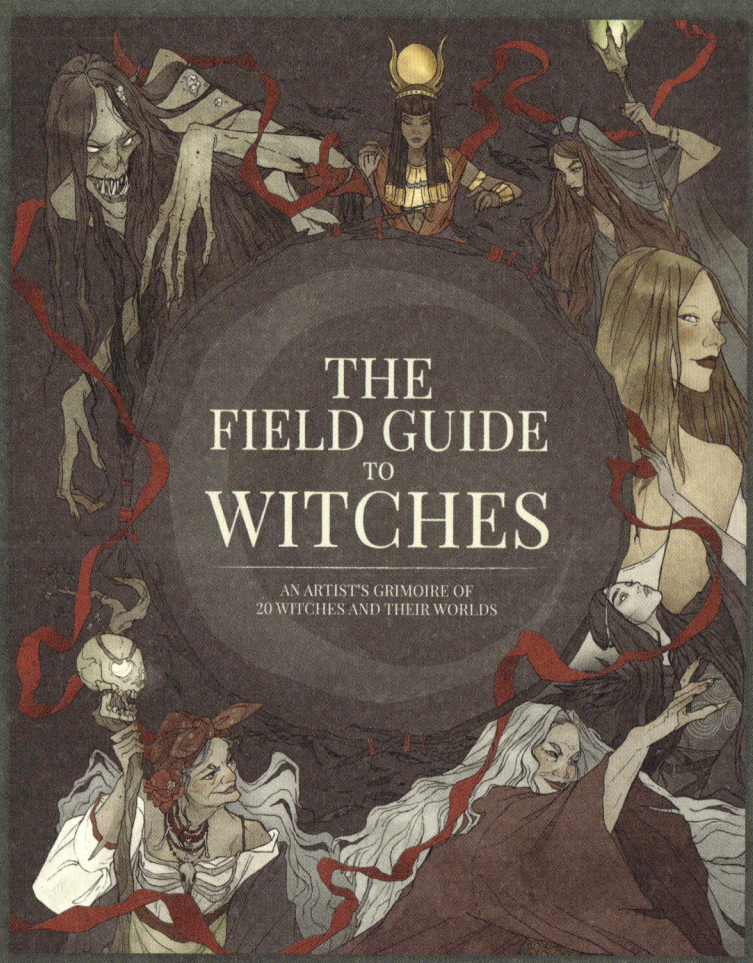

THE
FIELD GUIDE
TO
WITCHES

AN ARTIST'S GRIMOIRE OF
20 WITCHES AND THEIR WORLDS

In this indispensable *Field Guide to Witches*, join twenty talented concept artists and illustrators on a journey through dark forests, ancient mountains, and eerie swamps in search of witches, sorceresses, goddesses, and crones to bring to life. Explore over 300 pages of spellbinding sketches, inspiring illustrations, and invaluable character-design insights, alongside research, rumours, and ruminations from each artist.

AVAILABLE NOW AT
STORE.3DTOTAL.COM

Image © Entei Ryu

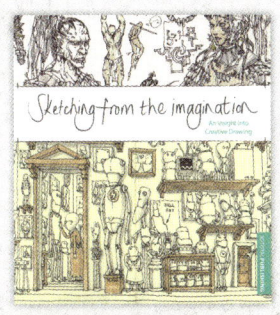
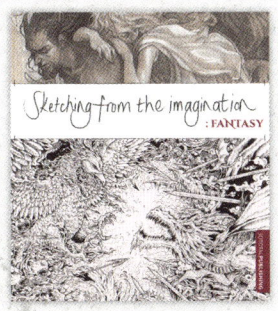
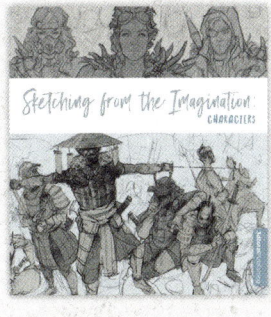
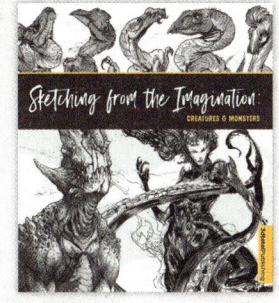

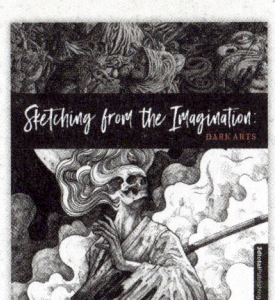
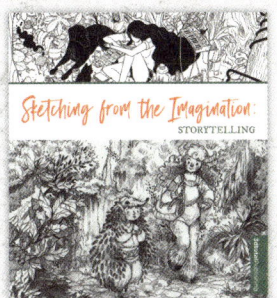
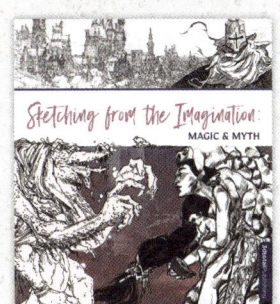
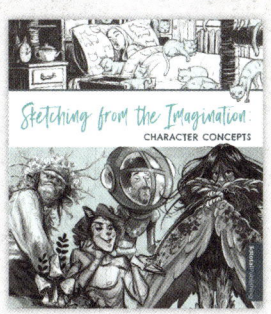

Sketching from the Imagination

In each book of the *Sketching from the Imagination* series, fifty talented traditional and digital artists have been chosen to share their sketchbooks and explain the reasons behind their design decisions. Visually stunning collections packed full of useful tips, these books offer inspiration for everyone.

AVAILABLE NOW AT
STORE.3DTOTAL.COM

Image © Marco Ferraris

3dtotalPublishing

3dtotal Publishing is a trailblazing, creative publisher specializing in inspirational and educational resources for artists.

Our titles feature top industry professionals from around the globe who share their experience in skilfully written step-by-step tutorials and fascinating, detailed guides. Illustrated throughout with stunning artwork, these bestselling publications offer creative insight, expert advice, and essential motivation. Fans of digital art will enjoy our comprehensive volumes covering Adobe Photoshop, Procreate, and Blender, as well as our superb titles based around character design, including *Fundamentals of Character Design* and *Creating Characters for the Entertainment Industry*. The dedicated, high-quality blend of instruction and inspiration also extends to traditional art. Titles covering a range of techniques, genres, and abilities allow your creativity to flourish while building essential skills.

Well-established within the industry, we now offer over 100 titles and counting, many of which have been translated into multiple languages around the world. With something for every artist, we are proud to say that our books offer the 3dtotal package:

LEARN · CREATE · SHARE

Visit us at store.3dtotal.com

3dtotal Publishing is part of 3dtotal.com, a leading website for CG artists founded by Tom Greenway in 1999.

Image © Faith Schaffer